THE
PRINCE
of
WALES

For Rob and Sue —
With best wishes
from the author
Graham Jenkins.
1886.

THE
PRINCE
of
WALES

A Biography

JONATHAN
DIMBLEBY

LITTLE, BROWN AND COMPANY

A *Little, Brown* Book

First published in Great Britain in 1994
by Little, Brown and Company

Copyright © 1994 by Jonathan Dimbleby

Lines from 'To the Queen' from *Collected Poems* by John Betjeman
reproduced by kind permission of John Murray (Publishers) Ltd.

A CIP catalogue record for this book
is available from the British Library.

ISBN 0 316 91016 3

Typeset by M Rules
Printed and bound in Great Britain by
Clays Ltd, St Ives plc

Little, Brown and Company (UK)
Brettenham House
Lancaster Place
London WC2E 7EN

For my mother

Research by
Clare Hargreaves

Contents

Acknowledgements xi

List of Illustrations xiv

Preface xvii

PART I I

PART II 95

PART III 269

PART IV 399

Appendix I 567

Appendix II 576

Notes 580

Bibliography 599

Index 602

ACKNOWLEDGEMENTS

———•———

I am indebted to many people without whom this book would have been impossible to write. To preserve their privacy, a very small number of these have asked that their contribution should remain anonymous. I am glad to be able to make a public debt of gratitude to the following:

Colin Amery, Dr Eric Anderson, Mabel Anderson, Charles Anson, Christian Bailey, Mira Bar-Hillel, Lord Beaverbrook, Peter Beck, Anne Beckwith-Smith, Colonel Blashford-Snell, William Boyd, Lord Brabourne, Lady Butler, James Buxton, Prince Carl of Hesse, Lord Carrington, Lady Elizabeth Cavendish, Lord Charteris of Amisfield, Sir David Checketts, Captain Roy Clare, Dr Jonathan Clark, Michael Colborne, King Constantine, Francis Cornish, Mary Creswell, Keith Critchlow, Philip Crosfield, Elizabeth Crowther-Hunt, Robert Davies, Dr Bridget Dolan, HRH The Duke of Edinburgh, HM Queen Elizabeth the Queen Mother, Lady Amanda Ellingworth, Oliver Everett, the late Lady Ruth Fermoy, Dr Simon Fielding, Harry Fitzgibbons, Commander Robert Fraser, Princess George of Hanover, David Grayson, the Rt. Hon. John Gummer, Rod Hackney, Brian Hanson, Belinda Harley, Lady Harrod, Max Hastings, Sir Edward Heath, Sir William Heseltine, Derek Hill, Oliver Hoare, Patrick Holden, Captain Laurie Hopkins, the Rt. Hon. Douglas Hurd, Lady Susan Hussey, Jimmy James, Robin Janvrin, Baroness Jay, Surgeon-Commander Richard Jolly,

Hywel Jones, Geoffrey Kent, Jorie Kent, Robert Kime, Lord Kindersley, Charles Knevitt, Andrew Knight, Kevin Knott, Clifford Longley, Sir Julian Loyd, Michael Manser, Lord McGregor, Colonel Sir John Miller, Bishop Hugh Montefiore, Countess Mountbatten of Burma, John Napper, Andrew Neil, Charles Palmer-Tomkinson, Patty Palmer-Tomkinson, Michael Peat, John Perrin, Dr Patrick Pietroni, Hugh Raven, Fiona Reynolds, Sir John Riddell, Lady Romsey, Lord Romsey, Guy Salter, Sir Allen Sheppard, the Earl of Snowdon, Nicholas Soames, Bishop Mervyn Stockwood, Colonel H.S. Townend, Emilie van Cutsem, Hugh van Cutsem, Sir Laurens van der Post, Robert Waddell, Marjorie Wallace, Gerald Ward, Sir James Watt, Peter Westmacott, Canon Harry Williams, David Wilson, Bishop Robin Woods, Edward Woods, Admiral Robert Woodard and Sir David Wright.

Some of those named above have allowed me to see memoranda or documents or correspondence; I am especially grateful to them and, in particular, to Lord Brabourne and the trustees of the Broadlands Archives for giving me free access to the correspondence between Prince Charles and Lord Mountbatten; and to Lord and Lady Romsey for providing me with the appropriate facilities at Broadlands.

I owe a special debt of gratitude to Commander Richard Aylard, the Prince's private secretary; to David Hutson, the Prince's Archivist, for locating and providing me with archive material with speed and great goodwill; likewise to Oliver Everett, the Librarian and Assistant Keeper of the Royal Archives, and Julia Melvin, the Archivist, and her colleagues at Windsor Castle. I am also grateful to many members of the Prince's household and staff who have been unfailingly courteous, friendly and helpful in all manner of ways and often at personal inconvenience; similarly to many individuals employed by the Duchy of Cornwall, the Prince's trusts, charities and the organisations with which he is associated; and to Margaret Duerden of Central Television.

Dr Vernon Bogdanor, Julia Cleverdon, Christopher Martin, Stephen O'Brien, Kevin Knott, Countess Mountbatten of Burma, George Pratt, Tom Shebbeare and Richard Sandbrook were kind enough to read parts of the manuscript and to offer astute advice: I am very grateful for their comments. However, as in the case of all those named in these acknowledgements, all errors of fact or faults of interpretation and judgement are my responsibility alone.

My researcher, Clare Hargreaves, who was also the associate producer of the Central TV documentary, *Charles: The Private Man, The Public Role*, conducted many of the initial interviews involving the Prince's charities and organisations, provided me with copious background notes on a wide range of topics and spent many weeks in the Prince's archives at Windsor Castle, selecting original documents which have been crucial to this biography. Over the last two years, she has not only been meticulous and tireless but very supportive, especially on those occasions when the going seemed particularly tough.

Gladys Mooney and Lynette Learoyd transcribed many hours of taped conversation (much of which was only semi-audible above the sound of clinking glasses and cutlery); Marian Gander and Georgie Grindlay not only achieved similar heroics but also kept me on this side of chaos as my secretarial wizards. My heartfelt thanks to them.

My agent, Jacqueline Korn, has been a source of sound advice, being tough and tender in every appropriate respect. At my publishers Little, Brown, Giles O'Bryen, Tim Holman and Helga Houghton displayed enviable talent and great commitment. Their managing director, Philippa Harrison, who commissioned the book, has been judicious as my editor and unfailing as a counsellor and friend: her gentle criticism and constant encouragement were invaluable.

My wife, Bel, who has put up with me for more than a quarter of a century, has had to put up with even more than usual over the last couple of years. She has been understanding, wise and loving throughout. To her, and to our children, Daniel and Kitty, I can only apologise that for much of the time, even when I was with them, I was more absent than present.

LIST OF ILLUSTRATIONS

Section I

1 Princess Elizabeth, King George VI and Queen Mary at the Prince's christening, 1948 (*Topham Picturepoint*)
2 The Prince with his mother, 1949 (*Camera Press*)
3 The Prince with the Queen Mother, 1950 (*Camera Press*)
4 Princess Anne, the Queen, the Prince and the Duke of Edinburgh, 1951 (*Camera Press*)
5 The Prince with King George VI, 1951
6 The Prince with his nurse Helen Lightbody, 1951 (*Popperfoto*)
7 The Prince and Princess Anne, 1951 (*Topham Picturepoint*)
8 The Queen Mother and the Prince at the Coronation, 1953 (*Hulton-Deutsch Collection*)
9 With Lord Mountbatten, Malta, 1954 (*Topham Picturepoint*)
10 With Princess Anne aboard HMY *Britannia*, 1954 (*Popperfoto*)
11 At a meet of the West Norfolk Hunt, 1955 (*Topham Picturepoint*)
12 The Prince arriving at Hill House after the Easter holidays, 1957 (*Hulton-Deutsch Collection*)
13 Returning to Cheam School after church, 1958
14 The Prince with the Duke of Edinburgh and Robert Chew at Gordonstoun, 1962 (*Hulton-Deutsch Collection*)
15 The Prince with his roommate Stuart McGregor, Timbertop, Australia, 1966 (*Hulton-Deutsch Collection*)
16 The Prince at Cambridge, 1968
17 In the language laboratory at University College, Aberystwyth, 1969 (*Popperfoto*)
18 Riding in the grounds of Windsor Castle with Princess Anne, 1968

Section II

19 The Prince and the Queen at his investiture in Caernarvon Castle, 1969
20 With President Nixon and Princess Anne at the White House, Washington, 1970 (*Associated Press*)
21 Learning to navigate, HMS *Norfolk*, 1971
22 Playing deck hockey, HMS *Norfolk*, 1971

23 On safari in Kenya, 1971 (*Anwar Hussein*)

24 With Spike Milligan and Harry Secombe, 1973 (*Hulton-Deutsch Collection*)

25 The Prince facing the press corps in his inflatable diving suit, Canada, 1975 (*Hulton-Deutsch Collection*)

26 Balmoral Castle (*Anwar Hussein*)

27 Sandringham House (*Tim Graham*)

28 Highgrove House (*Tim Graham*)

29 With Lord Mountbatten (*Camera Press*)

30 The Prince and Camilla Parker Bowles at Smith's Lawn, Windsor, 1975 (*Syndication International*)

31 Lord Mountbatten with Amanda Knatchbull (*Camera Press*)

32 On board HMS *Bronington*, 1976 (*Topham Picturepoint*)

33 The Prince gives up his command, Rosyth, 1976 (*Popperfoto*)

34 An official tour, Canada, 1977 (*Anwar Hussein*)

35 Doing the samba, Rio de Janeiro, 1978 (*Anwar Hussein*)

36 The Prince, Lord Mountbatten and Prince Philip, 1978 (*Syndication International*)

37 Lady Susan Hussey (*Tim Graham*)

38 Norton Knatchbull and Penny Eastwood (later Lord and Lady Romsey) with the Prince (*Syndication International*)

39 Hugh and Emilie van Cutsem

40 Patty and Charles Palmer-Tomkinson

Section III

41 The wedding day, 1981 (*Syndication International*)

42 & 43   The nation celebrates (*Rex Features*)

44 The honeymoon: boarding the royal yacht, Gibraltar (*Tim Graham*)

45 The honeymoon: at Balmoral (*Rex Features*)

46 The birth of Prince William, 1982 (*Anwar Hussein*)

47 The family on tour in Auckland, New Zealand, 1983 (*Anwar Hussein*)

48 The Prince and Princess on tour in Sydney, Australia, 1983 (*Anwar Hussein*)

49 At Ayers Rock (*Tim Graham*)

50 Meeting Pope John Paul II, Vatican City, 1985 (*Tim Graham*)

51 With Ronald and Nancy Reagan, the White House, Washington, 1985 (*Camera Press*)

52 Squadron Leader David Checketts (*Tim Graham*)

53 The Hon. Edward Adeane (*Tim Graham*)
54 Sir John Riddell (*Tim Graham*)
55 Lt. Commander Richard Aylard (*Tim Graham*)
56 The Mansion House speech, 1987 (*Topham Picturepoint*)
57 Polo at Windsor Great Park: the prize-giving (*Topham Picturepoint*)
58 The Prince and Princess after a polo match in India, 1992 (*Syndication International*)
59 At the National Cemetery in Seoul, 1992 (*Topham Picturepoint*)

Section IV
60 The Prince windsurfing (*Camera Press*)
61 Playing polo at Cowdray Park (*Topham Picturepoint*)
62 Knight Companion of the Most Noble Order of the Garter (*Topham Picturepoint*)
63 A 'Duchy day' (*Tim Graham*)
64 With Margaret Thatcher at 10 Downing Street, 1986 (*Syndication International*)
65 With John Major at St James's Palace, 1994 (*Rex Features*)
66 'Seeing is believing' (*Nick Garland / Daily Telegraph*)
67 Paints, brushes and paper . . . (*Tim Graham*)
68 Watercolour of Klosters, Switzerland, painted by the Prince (*Copyright © 1993 A.G. Carrick Ltd*)
69 Committee work, 1993 (*Lesley Donald / Central TV*)
70 The Prince's Trusts 25th Anniversary celebration at Penygraig, Wales, 1994 (*Topham Picturepoint*)
71 The shooting incident in Sydney, Australia Day, 1994 (*Popperfoto*)
72 Inspecting the Queen's Lancashire Regiment, Berlin, 1994 (*Topham Picturepoint*)
73 With Prince William, Klosters, 1994 (*Tim Graham*)
74 Fishing with Prince Harry, 1994 (*Lesley Donald / Central TV*)
75 The Prince with his sons, 1994 (*Lesley Donald / Central TV*)

Unacknowledged photographs are taken from private collections. The publishers have attempted to trace copyright owners. Where inadvertent infringement has been made they apologise and will be happy to make due acknowledgement in future editions.

PREFACE

————◆————

This biography originated in a series of conversations with the Prince of Wales which began in the summer of 1992, two years before the 25th anniversary of his investiture. With the monarchy itself under sceptical review, it seemed to me likely that the occasion would trigger an appraisal of the heir to the throne, which would be as unrelenting if not so merciless as the scrutiny of his private life essayed by the tabloid media. I was not unaware of the pitfalls which face the author who is foolhardy enough to write about any living person, nor that, in the case of the heir to the throne, these were likely to conceal craters beneath; yet the moment seemed right to me for a full and, if possible, authoritative portrait of the life and character of the Prince of Wales, setting this against the backdrop of the institution into which he was born forty-five years ago and into the context of Britain's sharply altered status in the world over the intervening years.

It would have been impossible to embark on such a project without a degree of co-operation from the Prince himself; to write a book based on hearsay, gossip and yellowing cuttings would have been to contribute to a familiar genre but, for that reason, self-defeating in purpose and, in any case, unendurable in prospect. The Prince was at first sceptical but, presumably aware that an avalanche of such books was almost inevitable, he agreed to provide me with the kind of assistance which would at least make my purpose feasible. However, I had no expectation that he would offer me the unprecedented and unfettered access to the original and entirely untapped sources on which this biography is based.

Over the last two years, I have been able to comb through his archives at St James's Palace and at Windsor Castle, where an entire floor is filled with scores of thousands of documents and memoranda accumulated over the last four decades. I have also been free to read his journals, diaries and many thousands of the letters which he has written assiduously since childhood. Not only have I drawn heavily from this wealth of original material but I have been free to quote extensively from it. Nor has the Prince discouraged past and present members of the royal household from speaking to me; likewise, at his behest, his friends and some of his relatives have talked about him openly at length, almost all of them for the first time. To protect the privacy of their relationships with the Prince, I have generally refrained from attributing opinions and feelings to particular individuals. However, with their consent, I have identified the names of almost all my sources in the Acknowledgements; in all but a tiny handful of cases, my interviews with them (which total several hundred hours in length) were recorded on tape and will be stored in the Prince's archives for future historians to peruse.

At the outset I volunteered (in a patronising phrase by which I am now embarrassed) that I would treat the Prince 'as someone of substance' but I warned him that my scrutiny would have to be searching. I have not wittingly retreated from that latter purpose: I have neither refrained from candour about the Prince's personality nor from criticism of his attitudes and actions even to the point where he is bound to feel that I have sometimes been uncomprehending and harsh. The Prince asked originally only that I should be 'objective' about him and that I should not use the knowledge that I might acquire in my researches in ways which might hurt other living people. I cannot claim to have succeeded in either endeavour but for different reasons in each case.

I have not only read hundreds of thousands of words which he has written and listened for hundreds of hours to those who have known him intimately but I have watched him at close quarters in Britain and abroad: I have seen him with his friends, with his staff and with the public; I have sat in on his meetings with heads of state, government ministers, business leaders and unemployed teenagers; on several occasions I have been his guest at Highgrove, Sandringham and Balmoral; and, at frequent intervals throughout the two years, I have also had the opportunity to talk to him alone for hours at a time. In this biography I have striven to achieve detachment and balance but I have learned too much about my subject to be either indifferent or dispassionate.

I have also tried to accommodate his sensitivity about the effect of what I might write on other people and, in particular, on his family. My dilemma has been how to reconcile his sentiments not only with my own knowledge but with those aspects of the truth which are fundamental to a proper appraisal of my subject. It is in this biographical territory, of course, where most of the pitfalls lurk, particularly, in this case, when the matter has been complicated by the breakdown of the Prince's marriage to the Princess of Wales.

After their separation (which was announced when this book was already in progress) it became impossible to ignore the circumstances which led up to that sad but very public moment. It had already been widely averred in the tabloid media that the Prince was almost solely responsible for the evidently unhappy state of his marriage; after the separation, this allegation – abetted by the dissemination of speculative untruths – swiftly became the received opinion. Without some knowledge of the facts, the attribution of blame to anyone in such circumstances is inherently repugnant, but in this case it was also damaging in the extreme to the reputation of the heir to the throne, even to the extent that, in some quarters, his suitability to inherit the Crown had become a matter for public debate. A private misery was thus transformed into an issue of national importance. Yet to examine every shard of this fractured relationship would quite properly have been regarded as prurient, as 'dabbling in the stuff of other people's souls'.

I have had to decide how much of what I have learned about the miseries of this marriage should be made public when the couple themselves have already endured so much torment and when their children would have to live with the consequences of what I might write. In seeking to reconcile what has become a matter of public interest with their right to privacy, I have written just enough of what I believe to be the truth about the breakdown of their marriage to establish what a more detailed and intrusive account of the facts as I know them would merely confirm: that no fair-minded and compassionate reader would seek to attribute blame either to the Prince or to the Princess for what went wrong; that both hoped to preserve it from collapse; and, sadly, that perhaps its most remarkable feature is that it survived for as long as it did.

There have been other constraints. I have had extensive access to journals, papers and correspondence affecting both relations between Britain and other nations and those between the Prince of Wales (or, in some instances, Buckingham Palace) and ministers of the Crown. In respect of some of these, I have been persuaded that the verbatim publication of the material might have a deleterious effect either on the conduct of British diplomacy or on the confidential nature of communications between the monarchy and Whitehall or Westminster; in these cases, I have either withheld information or paraphrased the relevant documents or correspondence. However, when it was obvious that only the culture of secrecy which pervades Whitehall was under threat and not the conduct of good governance, I have not complied with requests to delete pertinent material.

In my formal agreement with the Prince of Wales, I undertook 'to take into account any comments made by HRH with respect to factual inaccuracies', while it was agreed that I 'would have the final decision' in my 'sole discretion about the contents of the said work and all interpretations of events therein described'. While I have corrected agreed factual errors, I have not been inhibited from writing what I felt to be the truth about him. By agreeing to co-operate with his biographer on these terms, the Prince committed himself to a course which, for all I know, he might have come to regret. In any case, by allowing an outsider to intrude into his life to that extent and for such a purpose, he took a gamble of trust. I hope I have not violated that trust but I have also had another imperative: to be true to myself and to my readers. At the very least I hope those who read this long and detailed biography will emerge at the other end feeling that they have come to know the heir to the throne as they never could before – and that he is well worth knowing.

I am indebted to the Prince of Wales for his kindness and for the pleasure of his company. I have experienced a wide range of emotions in writing this book; boredom has never been one of them.

J.D.
September 1994

PART I

——◆——

They're changing guard at Buckingham Palace –
Christopher Robin went down with Alice.
They've great big parties inside the grounds.
'I wouldn't be King for a hundred pounds,'
                              Says Alice.

                    A.A. Milne, 'Buckingham Palace'

CHAPTER
ONE

———◆—◆———

J ust before midnight on 14 November 1948, a proclamation was posted on the railings outside Buckingham Palace announcing that Princess Elizabeth had been safely delivered of a son. A little earlier, a policeman on the gate had already whispered the word and the crowd, which numbered more than 3,000, had duly serenaded a tall figure crossing the courtyard with 'For He's a Jolly Good Fellow' in the mistaken belief that he was the Duke of Edinburgh. Now they peered inside each car that crunched across the gravel, and gave the unyielding profile of Queen Mary, the infant's great-grandmother, a cheer of unaffected warmth. The enthusiasm swelled with the crowd so that soon after midnight a police car cruised round the Victoria Monument urging the celebrants through a megaphone 'for a little quietness please'. In Trafalgar Square, the fountains sparkled 'blue for a boy', while editors in Fleet Street shuffled headlines and composed their thoughts for the following day.

The message was cabled abroad at once: across the Empire and the Commonwealth, as in Britain, they raised the Union Jack, hung out the bunting, and rang the church bells. Warships of His Majesty's naval fleet on station across the globe fired a royal birthday salute. Radio stations throughout the United States interrupted scheduled programmes with the announcement, which led every news bulletin and formed the lead story across the front pages of an entranced American press.

On 16 November, Winston Churchill rose from his place in the

House of Commons to congratulate Princess Elizabeth. The leader of the opposition was at his most mellifluous:

> Our ancient Monarchy renders inestimable services to our country and to all the British Empire and Commonwealth of Nations. Above the ebb and flow of party strife, the rise and fall of Ministries and individuals, the changes of public opinion and fortune, the British Monarchy presides ancient, calm and supreme within its functions, over all the treasures that have been saved from the past and all the glories we write in the annals of our country. Our thoughts go out to the mother and father and, in a special way today, to the little Prince, now born into this world of strife and storm.[1]

A few moments earlier, the Prime Minister, Clement Attlee, had spoken more plainly but with no less enthusiasm. Reflecting on the 'deep pleasure' that the birth of a son brings to the life of a family, he spoke of a royal family who by their 'example in private life as well as in their devotion to public duty, have given strength and comfort to many in these times of stress and uncertainty'. He concluded by referring to 'the great responsibilities' that the young Prince might have to carry, adding, 'We shall watch him growing to manhood with lively interest, knowing that in his own home he will receive a training by example rather than mere precept, in that courtesy and in that gracious and tireless devotion to the manifold duties of constitutional monarchy which have won the hearts of our people.'[2]

A second announcement from the Palace imparted the information that the Prince weighed 7lb 6oz. This news was duly reported verbatim on every front page. Even the *Manchester Guardian*, a standard-bearer of nonconformism, felt obliged to remind its readers that the baby's weight was 'regarded by gynaecologists as nearly the ideal for an infant boy', reassuring them that, 'the absence of an evening bulletin on the condition of Princess Elizabeth and her infant son was an indication that everything is going on entirely normally.'[3]

Beyond that, information was sparse. There were no 'sources close to the Palace' willing to inform the nation that while the Princess was in labour her husband, not indifferent but restless, took to the Palace squash court with the Queen Mother's private secretary. Nor was it known beyond the confines of the delivery room (and if it had been, the newspapers would have been too decorous to mention such an intimate detail) that the Princess had been given an anaesthetic to ease the birth pangs.*

The British newspapers were content to echo the mood of popular rejoicing, though the editor of *The Times* – mindful of his role as guardian of the country's principal journal of record – sought to peer through the cosy domestic glow by placing the moment in historical perspective as well:

> The birth of a child to the Heiress-Presumptive is a national and imperial event which can for a moment divert the peoples' thoughts from the acrimonies of domestic argument and the anxieties of the international scene. All can be united in rejoicing as the guns salute and the bells peal. Every newborn child presents to some family the thought and image of the future towards which it moves; this child from the moment of his birth becomes to many peoples the symbol of their common aspirations for an even more splendid realm and Commonwealth than have been handed down to them by the virtue and prowess of their ancestors . . .[4]

Elsewhere, there was much speculation about the name with which the infant would be blessed, a harmless pastime which was arrested a month later when, in the Palace Music Room, Charles Philip Arthur George was baptised by the Archbishop of Canterbury, with water from the River Jordan. In the presence of his parents and eight godparents, whose number included the King and Queen, Prince Charles was thereby admitted into the Church of England, and initiated into the rites of a faith which as future sovereign he would pledge to defend and from which – without jeopardising his claim to the throne – he could never resile. As he would later discover, a christening is but the first bond by which the accident of royal birth fetters a dutiful Prince.

---

* For this information, we are indebted to the late Dermot Morrah, the Arundel Herald of Arms, a title which was first recorded in 1413 and which was specifically revived for Morrah at the Queen's coronation.

  Morrah's 'privileged account' of the early life of Prince Charles, *To Be A King* (Hutchinson, 1968), has been the principal though generally unacknowledged source for most subsequent 'insights' about this period in the Prince's life.

In Buckingham Palace, he occupied the dressing room adjoining the Princess's bedroom on the second floor. There, he was soon put in the care of two nurses supported by a staff of maids and footmen. The Prince slept in the same pink satin and lace cot which had been used by his mother in her infancy, he played with her silver rattle and, in her ancient perambulator, he was taken out across St James's Park and into Green Park, where his presence went generally unnoticed or was politely ignored.

The Queen's sister, Lady Granville, reported that, 'He could not be more angelic looking. He is golden-haired and has the most beautiful complexion, as well as amazingly delicate features for so young a baby.'[5] Princess Elizabeth herself observed that her baby's hands 'are rather large but fine with long fingers – quite unlike mine and certainly unlike his father's. It will be interesting to see what they will become. I still find it difficult to believe I have a baby of my own.'[6]

On the same afternoon that they had performed their loyal duty to the Crown, Winston Churchill and Clement Attlee returned to the parliamentary matter of the moment, the second reading of the government's bill to nationalise the steel industry. Churchill flowed with hyperbole, discerning in this measure a plot by the Labour government, a 'burglar's jemmy to crack the capitalist crib',[7] but, at the forthcoming election, he prophesied, the 'dismal and evil reign' of the Labour government would end in 'obloquy and censure'.[8]

The Churchillian rhetoric owed as much to pique as to his gift for oratory. A little over three years before, the old man had been obliged to sit facing the dispatch box as honourable members on the government benches, seized by the triumphalism of their hour, mumbled their way through 'The Red Flag' (disregarding the Speaker's request for order) to celebrate an election victory which had driven him from office. At that moment it had seemed – and not only to the credulous – that the new masters would indeed wield their 'burglar's jemmy' with relish, and that the entire edifice of the established state might crumble.

By the autumn of 1948, however, a weary caution prevailed in Westminster. Fantasies of revolution may once have spiced the political dreams of the occasional cabinet minister, but these had long since yielded to the mundane and depressing task of keeping Britain afloat in the age of austerity. The ancient institutions by which the governance of

the Empire was still conducted remained intact, threatened less by socialist subversion than by national exhaustion.

The previous year had been dubbed an 'Annus Horrendus' by Hugh
Dalton, then Chancellor of the Exchequer. The freak weather of the
winter of 1947 had paralysed Britain for almost three months. Coal
shortages forced several power stations to shut down, unemployment
leapt to more than two million, and the nation shivered in misery. The
economy was stricken. Food rationing, the leitmotif of Britain's distress,
was no less severe than in wartime: meat, cheese, butter, margarine,
cooking fat, sugar, milk and eggs were all issued in minute quantities in
exchange for coupons. To ease the meat shortage, the Ministry of Food
brought in supplies of whale meat and snoek, running a publicity campaign which included unappetising recipes for snoek sandwich spread,
and snoek pasties.* To stave off a sterling crisis caused by an alarming
'dollar deficit', the government had to cut imports of even basic commodities. Timber imports were squeezed to the point where newspapers
were cut back to four pages, while the basic petrol ration was abolished –
although there was a supplementary allowance for those living more
than two miles from the nearest public transport. Ministers even urged
the public to 'SMOKE YOUR CIGARETTES TO THE BUTTS' (adding 'IT
MIGHT BE GOOD FOR YOUR HEALTH AS WELL').†

Such measures failed to halt the slide in sterling. In September 1948,
to cries of 'national humiliation', the new Chancellor, Sir Stafford
Cripps, was forced to devalue the currency (from $4.80 to $2.80 to the
pound). Surveying the encircling gloom in the year of the Prince's birth,
the London correspondent of the *New York Times* noted drily that
Britain had become 'an impoverished second rate power, morally magnificent but economically bankrupt'.

To make matters worse, the economic crisis was accompanied by a

---

* Snoek was a South Atlantic fish which the public failed to relish. As a result hundreds of tons remained in storage. Later, when rationing was eased, there was a
glut on the market of a suspiciously large quantity of 'select fish food for cats and
kittens'.
† Much of the detail in this chapter about the state of post-war Britain is drawn from
Age of Austerity, edited by Michael Sissons and Philip French (Hodder and
Stoughton, 1963), a book of essays by some of Britain's leading journalists whose
insights remain as vivid today as they seemed thirty years ago.

surge in delinquency, which was referred to as a 'crime wave'. In the decade leading up to 1948 indictable offences had doubled, spurring the Recorder of London to rail against 'this distemper of dishonesty which has swept over the country in the last few years until people have lost sight of the difference between right and wrong'. A bishop intervened in the debate about 'the state of the nation' to avow that Britain was 'drifting', adding mournfully, 'We cannot see the end of it all.' Indeed, although by 1948 the language of 'relative decline' had yet to enter the political lexicon, newspapers and magazines were already asking, 'What's Wrong With Britain?' In the decades ahead, the question would become ever more insistent, nagging at the collective psyche and irritating national sensibilities.

Attlee's government knew at least part of the answer and had to act accordingly, unpalatable though it was. In the year of the Prince's birth, his grandfather still presided over a British Empire of 800 million subjects, and the last Viceroy of India, his great-uncle Lord Mountbatten, had yet to depart those newly independent shores. Britain's strategic reach still circled the globe, and George VI was still the head of an army, navy and air force which between them had almost one and a half million men under arms. It was an exaggeration to say that Britain was bankrupt, but in a nation half ruined by the victory of 1945, something clearly had to give.

In 1947, the government had put the best gloss on the inevitable in a pamphlet called *Cards on the Table*, in which the Foreign Secretary, Ernest Bevin, explained that Britain was now too impoverished to finance so vast a range of commitments. They would have to be scaled down as rapidly as the requirements of national security would permit. He argued, of course, that Britain was still a Great Power but others, namely the United States, would have to shoulder more of the burden. In fact, the retreat had already started – not only from India but from Palestine and Greece as well.

The decision to withdraw British forces from Greece, where since 1944 they had provided a military buffer between a truly bankrupt state and the threat of communist insurgency, had been conveyed to the United States earlier in the year. The President's response – to win over a reluctant Congress and an electorate given to isolationism – was the Truman Doctrine. The President declared that nearly every nation now faced a choice between 'alternative ways of life'. One was based on the consent of the majority, distinguished by free institutions and individual liberty. The other was based on the will of a minority – a minority that 'relies upon terror and oppression, a controlled press and radio, fixed elections, and the suppression of personal freedoms'. He continued, 'I believe that we must assist free peoples to work out their destiny in their own way.'[9]

In those words, the President sketched the contours of a new global role for the United States and defined the terms of what would soon become known as the Cold War. Fired by the optimism of a boundless destiny, the United States was unequivocally assuming leadership of the 'free world', while Britain succumbed to the pessimism of shrivelling greatness.

Decline at home, retreat abroad: in the year of the Prince's birth, these twin themes were already woven into the tapestry of Britain's post-war history. In 1948, however, deference towards the establishment prevailed, and, in so far as people complained at all, they vented their frustrations on a 'monstrous regiment' of civil servants, bureaucrats, busybodies and snoopers – trussing up initiative and enterprise in restrictions and red tape. The popular novelist Angela Thirkell reflected the sense of desolation that chilled the middle classes and conjured up for her readers a thrilling nightmare of socialist tyranny – one of her characters opining sagely that 'if people are wicked to their Royalty, there is a kind of curse on them'[10] – but there was in reality no hint of revolution in the air.[*] Like the Church and the Law, Parliament was still held in respect, while the monarchy commanded a kind of awe born of that remote mystique to which chroniclers had ascribed so much of its institutional vitality.[†]

Notwithstanding this isolation, popular affection for the individual members of the royal family – at least for the King and Queen and their children – was artless and fervent. Nor were they obliged to think of

---

[*] Unless the lone communist MP Willie Gallagher should be counted as a hint. He had greeted the birth of Prince Charles by reminding the House of Commons, 'There are far too many babies in this country being born in sub-lets and in appalling slum conditions.' (*Hansard*, p.212.)

[†] An opinion poll taken in 1956, three years after the coronation of Elizabeth II, confirmed that thirty-four per cent of the population still believed that the sovereign had been chosen by God. (Leonard Harris, *Long to Reign Over Us*, cited by Philip Ziegler, *Crown and People*, p.36.)

themselves as members of a 'family firm'; indeed, the idea that the royal family might have to justify itself in such prosaic and workaday terms had not yet been invented. For at least fifty years, the royal family had been secure in the knowledge that, even when put to the test, loyalty to the Crown had not been found wanting.

While Edward VII grew from young rake to old buffer, so the Crown, which had shivered in the chill of intermittent hostility during Victoria's reign, was passed on untarnished and more secure than ever to George V. His evident decency, combined with his homeliness, perceptibly shifted the role of the monarchy. In addition to its constitutional function, it gradually came to represent – in the person of the sovereign – not so much the embodiment of the age as the values of a generation. In the public mind the distinction between the monarchy and the royal family became so blurred that the King could not fail to notice it. 'I'm beginning to think they must like me for myself,' he remarked, moved by the enthusiasm of the crowds on a visit to the East End during the Silver Jubilee in 1935.[11] By then, he had become a universal 'father figure', the bond between sovereign and subject apparent to even the most sceptical observers. At the end of the celebrations he addressed the nation thus: 'I can only say to you, my very, very dear people, that the Queen and I thank you from the depths of our hearts for all the loyalty – and may I say so? – the love with which this day and always you have surrounded us.' Even those who had never seen him but knew only his voice (not least from the Christmas messages which he had pioneered on the BBC in 1932) spoke of him as a personal friend, demonstrating how potently the intimate and the mystical were enshrined together in his person.

Yet the crisis provoked by the decision of his son Edward VIII to put his love for an American divorcee before his duty to the throne was a sharp reminder of the fragility of the relationship between sovereign and subject. Edward VIII came to the throne enjoying the goodwill of the mass of his subjects, who recognised not only his charm but, apparently, a highly developed social conscience. His distress at the plight of the unemployed in the mining valleys of South Wales soon led him to use the phrase 'Something must be done to find them work',[*] an expression

---

[*] More commonly remembered as 'Something must be done.' (See Frances Donaldson, *Edward VIII* [Weidenfeld and Nicolson, 1974, p.252].)

of raw sentiment that further endeared him to the nation, especially when he went on to say, 'You may be sure that all I can do for you I will.'[12] Three weeks later, Edward VIII abdicated the throne to marry Wallis Simpson. In that liaison he was seen to betray a sacred trust to the Church, to the Crown, and to the people. To put his love for a twice-married American divorcee before his duty was to undermine the collective self-image of the King's subjects. It was shocking and, in the wisdom of the British governing classes, incompatible with the role of the monarch.

It is a measure of how closely the person of the monarch and the institution of the monarchy had become entwined that for a time the institution was exposed, if not actually under threat. The voice of republicanism made itself heard with strident clarity in the House of Commons, and enthusiasm for the new King, Edward's brother George, was notably subdued. The Prime Minister, Stanley Baldwin, was moved to reassure his sovereign: 'If I may say so, you have no need to fear for the future. The whole country is behind you with deep and understanding sympathy.'[13] This was not entirely true, but in his quiet, retiring fashion, George VI, supported by a winsome Queen and two lauded daughters, soon impressed himself favourably on public opinion. He did not exactly cut a dash, but after the alarms of the abdication, the Crown seemed once again to be in the safe hands of a thoroughly decent, if uninspiring, family man. As Philip Ziegler has noted, 'This unexciting prospect appeared entirely acceptable to the British people.'[14]

The restoration of the King in the image of 'family man' – dutiful, traditional, upright – implicit in the case of his father, was made explicit in the reign of George VI, and was magnified by the contribution made by the royal family to the war effort between 1939 and 1945. The King had a limited gift for rhetoric and inspiration (although his voice easily touched the listener), but he was at least seen to share the dangers and care about the suffering. By no means *of* the people, he was most assuredly *with* them and *for* them. As a survivor of the Coventry blitz recorded later, 'We suddenly felt that if the King was there everything was all right and the rest of England was behind us.'[15] It was not that the King had made a quasi-divine visitation but that, in going to the scene of devastation, he represented the 'rest of England', symbolising their empathy as well as offering his own compassion. Though not everyone shared the attitude – some were indifferent, a few were even hostile* – for most people George VI and his family had become emblematic of the trials which they had to endure and the victory which they finally secured. By the end of the war, the consolidation of the familial monarchy had been accomplished.

The marriage of the King's daughter offered a momentary reprieve from the drab austerity of rationed Britain, and the public seized the moment with evident delight. Although she was apparently far from the succession, the newspapers had followed Princess Elizabeth's development from childhood with reverential affection, causing her father on one occasion to write to his mother, Queen Mary, 'It almost frightens me that the people should love her so much. I suppose it is a good thing, and I hope she will be worthy of it, poor little darling.'[16] In 1947, the news that the Princess would marry a young naval officer called Philip Mountbatten was widely welcomed as 'one of those pleasant and happy events which no-one can object to and which the British people invariably love'.[17]

There was some debate about the lavishness of the proposed wedding while Britain was in such straitened circumstances, but on the day of celebration the pleasure principle reasserted itself. Many thousands lined the route to cheer, millions more huddled round the radio at home or in factories. The following day an 'observer' for Mass Observation declared herself astonished – as a socialist – to discover that when she went to buy a paper every copy had been sold. She noted, 'I think the Royal Family is very popular. Were they to disappear, the people would be very upset.'

The Times' editorial panegyric for the birth of Prince Charles echoed its response to the royal wedding, referring to 'the restoration of

---

* A London housewife told Mass Observation, 'It's all very well for them traipsing around saying how their hearts bleed for us and they share our sufferings, and then going home to a roaring fire in one of their six houses.' Until they were superseded by opinion polls, the interviews conducted by Mass Observation, which was founded in 1937, were the principal means of discovering public attitudes in Britain. These interviews, predating the obsession with percentages, offered a deeper insight into the complexity and range of public opinion than the later 'scientific' polling organisations could begin to achieve. The monarchy was an enduring theme to research, and the reports of the 'observers' provide the basis for Philip Ziegler's Crown and People.

traditional pageantry, flashing through the clouds of austerity a ray of light which uplifted the spirits of the nation'. Just as the cheers that accompanied the bride along her processional route had 'testified movingly to the manner in which Princess Elizabeth had already endeared herself to the hearts of the people', so the 'serene joy of motherhood' would serve to surround her with even more 'affectionate pride'. Borne aloft by that thought, the leading article swept on to describe the sovereign as the nation's 'supreme representative', which 'in modern times is a more royal function than any duty of state', affirming that, 'The representative monarchy has made every one of its subjects feel friend and neighbour to the Royal family; and so it is that the simple joy, which the coming of this child has brought to them, is shared by all.'[18]

In these sentiments lay a paradox ensnared by a muddle: a resolute failure to distinguish between the institution of the monarchy and the character of the royal family – a failure which was chain-linked to an insistence that the sovereign should contrive to be both the supreme symbol of the Realm and a model neighbour. In the decades ahead, this well-meaning but self-contradictory injunction was to haunt the monarchy and menace the royal family. Finding no ready means of resolution, neither would emerge unscathed.

For the moment both the muddle and the paradox were not only invisible but benign, embracing the infant Prince throughout his first years. It was an age when even George Bernard Shaw, as radical a socialist as any in Britain, could write:

> [The Constitutional King of England] stand[s] for the future and the past, for the posterity that has no vote and the tradition that never had any . . . For the great abstractions: for conscience and virtue; for the eternal against the expedient; for the evolutionary appetite against the day's gluttony; for intellectual integrity, for humanity.[19]

There could be no doubt that the monarchy was, in the words of Winston Churchill, 'the most secure in the world'.[20]

Across the gulf of more than four decades, the quatrain composed by the Poet Laureate to celebrate the birth seems stilted. Yet, in the winter of 1948, there is every evidence to suppose that John Masefield spoke for the nation:

May destiny, allotting what befalls,
Grant to the newly-born this saving grace,
A Guard more sure than ships and fortress-walls,
The loyal love and service of a race.

CHAPTER
TWO

———•———

When their son was eight months old, Prince Philip and Princess Elizabeth moved out of their quarters in Buckingham Palace to Clarence House, which had been used as offices by the Red Cross in the war but was now restored and redecorated as a home. In the nursery, among the picture books and crayons, the pencils and paints, and the fluffy animals, there was Jumbo, a much favoured blue elephant on wheels who helped the Prince move tenaciously from crawl to walk. Later there were cars, planes, soldiers and tanks.

The day began when the night nursery curtains were opened at 7.00 a.m., Prince Charles was washed and dressed, and then fed breakfast. At 9.00 a.m. he was taken down to the second floor for a thirty-minute session with his mother, before returning to play until 10.30 a.m. when he departed for the morning perambulation, accompanied by one of his two nannies, Helen Lightbody or Mabel Anderson, and the ubiquitous personal protection officer, a plain-clothed constable from the Metropolitan Police. Luncheon (boiled chicken and rice being favoured by the infant) was at 1.00 p.m., followed by a rest, and possibly an outing. Sometimes he would be taken across to Marlborough House to visit his great-grandmother, whom he soon learnt to call 'Gan-Gan'. The revered Queen Mary sat stiffly in her chair with her feet resting on a footstool. Her grandchildren had been forbidden to touch her fabulous collection of jade which was ranged round the room in cabinets, but to her great-grandson she was very accommodating, and his habitual curiosity was freely indulged.

By 4.00 p.m. he was usually back in the nursery, where tea was served. Afterwards his mother would return to the nursery to be with her child while he was bathed and put to bed. When his sister Anne was born in August 1950 she joined her brother in the nursery, and from then on shared his established routine.

Such an upbringing was by no means rare in those days (at least in those households that could afford the appropriate staff). Although Prince Charles was not starved of parental affection,* it was inevitably the nursery staff (interpreting the will of their employers) who taught him to play, who witnessed his first steps, who punished and rewarded him, who helped him put his first thoughts into words. Furthermore, Princess Elizabeth was increasingly preoccupied by her duties as heiress-presumptive to the throne. It was evident to all that her father was ailing, and that she would soon be sovereign in his stead. Not only had she to prepare herself for that role, but she was also obliged to perform those public engagements for which the King no longer had the stamina. As the Duke of Edinburgh was still a serving naval officer in command of his own ship and often away at sea, the little Prince was inevitably separated from his parents more than they might have wished. This, combined with the emotional reserve of both mother and father, did much to ensure that the bonds of affection that grew between young charge and devoted nannies were at least as powerful (and in the case of Mabel Anderson as enduring) as those between the child and his parents.

Soon after the Prince's second birthday, Princess Elizabeth flew to join her husband in Malta, where the Duke had been promoted to take command of a frigate, so that they could spend Christmas together. The children were sent to Sandringham to join their grandparents, who plainly doted on their grandson. 'Charles is too sweet, stumping around the room,' George VI wrote to his daughter. 'We shall love having him at Sandringham. He is the fifth generation to live there and I hope he will get to love the place.'[1] Prince Charles had already been taught to bow as well as to kiss when he entered the presence of the King and

---

* According to Dermot Morrah, the Princess would usually stay for ninety minutes in the evening, 'romping with the children on the nursery floor, bathing them and finally tucking them up in bed'. (Dermot Morrah, *To Be A King*, p.14.)

Queen, but he was nonetheless encouraged to clamber onto the Queen's lap, where, cuddled in her arms, he would listen to her stories with rapt attention. The rapport that was established between grandmother and grandson in these early years grew into a bond of trust and affection which would later develop into the most intimate of the Prince's relationships within the family, and become for him a vital source of praise and encouragement.

On his third birthday, his parents were away again on an official tour of Canada, so the children were once more with their grandparents. There is a photograph of the Prince sitting with his grandfather to mark the occasion. The King had recently endured the latest of three operations in as many years, and it was known in the royal household that his death from cancer could not be long delayed. In the photograph, the drawn face of the sovereign looks down tenderly on the chubby boy, who was to hold that moment as his only personal memory of George VI. By that Christmas, the family had been reunited again, but only briefly. A month later, the gaunt and exhausted figure of the King waved his daughter off on a Commonwealth tour undertaken on his behalf – a commitment that he had been forced to postpone four years earlier. On 6 February, George VI died peacefully in his bed at Sandringham.

Although it had not been unexpected, the death of the King caused an onrush of shock and sorrow. His presence had been remote – a voice on the airwaves, an image in the newsreels – but the sense of loss was peculiarly personal and intimate.* Cutting short her tour of Africa, the new Queen returned to London where her accession was formally proclaimed on 8 February by the Earl Marshal from four places in London: 'The High and Mighty Princess Elizabeth Alexandra Mary is now, by the Death of Our late Sovereign of Happy Memory, become Queen Elizabeth the Second, by the Grace of God Queen of this Realm and all Her other Realms and Territories, Head of the Commonwealth,

---

* Mass Observation recorded a host of examples – a labourer, a shop assistant, a carpenter amongst them – echoing one thought: 'I feel as shocked as though it was someone belonging to me.' In Notting Hill Gate, a drinker who declared that the King was 'only shit and soil now like anyone else' had to be hustled out of the back of the public house for his own safety. (Philip Ziegler, op. cit., p.86.)

Defender of the Faith, to whom her lieges do acknowledge all Faith and constant Obedience . . .'

In accordance with long tradition, the lying-in-state was in Westminster Hall. In the flickering gloom, the coffin of the King, draped in the gold of the Royal Standard, was placed on the catafalque. It was protected at each corner by four Yeomen of the Guard, and near them two Gentlemen at Arms and officers of the Household Brigade, who were also guarding the Imperial Crown in which is set the fabulous ruby that Henry V is said to have worn at the Battle of Agincourt. The only sound in the candlelit Hall was the shuffle of thousands upon thousands of the late King's subjects filing past this mediaeval tableau to pay their homage. The silent queue, which snaked from St Thomas's Hospital, across Westminster Bridge, along the Embankment and towards Westminster Hall, moved forward so slowly that it took many hours in bitter weather for the mourners to reach their destination. Late at night, the BBC wireless commentator, Richard Dimbleby, watched them from his place high above Palace Yard:

> Moving through the darkness of the night is an even darker stream of human beings, coming, almost noiselessly, from under a long, white canopy that crosses the pavement at the great doors of Westminster Hall. They speak very little, these people, but their footsteps sound faintly as they cross the yard and go out through the gates, back into the night from which they came . . . No-one knows from where they came or where they go, but they are the people, and to watch them pass is to see the nation pass.[2]

He did not exaggerate. On the day of the funeral, shops closed, men and women wore black, while only a few were emboldened to defy the mood by ignoring the two-minute silence that brought virtually all movement across Britain to a standstill. And echoing the commentator's widely shared sentiment, one mourner remarked, 'It's a great tribute to him and it's a great tribute to us. Because George VI *is* us. He is us and we are him. He is the British people, all that is best in us, and we all know it.'[3] In the ritual of the sovereign's death, encrusted with ceremony but touched by simplicity, the 'loyal subjects' of the Crown shared – self-consciously – in the pageant of their own history, a reminder of how deeply the monarchy had penetrated the national psyche. Behind the tribal affirmation that 'he is us and we are him' lay the sense of an inner order where concepts of tradition, pride, honour and decency still held sway.

At the death of George VI, his three-year-old grandson automatically took the title of Duke of Cornwall. As the new head of state, the young Queen was now burdened by constitutional responsibility and she was determined to fulfil her duties to the limit. Inevitably, the mother had even less time to spend with her children.

Soon after Easter, with the court still in official mourning, the Queen and her family moved into her official residence at Buckingham Palace. They occupied apartments on the first and second floors on the north side of the quadrangle, while the nursery was immediately above them. Apart from its size – six rooms, including one each for Helen Lightbody and Mabel Anderson, and one which was soon to be reserved as a schoolroom – the nursery floor was unexceptional. Furnished plainly and decorated in chintz, it became the warm heart of what could otherwise be a somewhat overwhelming establishment.

The routine for the royal children changed little, although – at the insistence of their mother – they were no longer required to bow and curtsey on entering the presence of the sovereign. The Queen's decision was widely interpreted within the household as heralding a new age of informality (Dermot Morrah, as Arundel Herald of Arms, discerned that the new reign would be marked by a softening of 'the old ceremony and protocol') but in reality the style of court life changed slightly and slowly.

Prince Charles had been dispatched to Sandringham during the funeral rites for his grandfather as the solemnity was thought to be too distressing for so young a child, and probably beyond his comprehension as well. However, a little over one year later, amid much public speculation, the Queen decided that he should take his place in Westminster Abbey to witness the coronation. Mindful of the fact that he was a fidgety four-year-old, the court decided that he should be allotted no part in the ceremony itself except as a spectator. He would sit beside his grandmother Queen Elizabeth, looking down on the proceedings from the royal box.

Winston Churchill, the Prime Minister, was adamant that the new-fangled medium of television should not be permitted to enter the

Abbey. At first, the Palace concurred and issued an announcement to that effect. But the Queen had not herself been averse to the prospect and, after intense lobbying by the BBC, the Earl Marshal* and the Archbishop of Canterbury†, it was she in person who prevailed upon Number Ten to relent. This was a seismic decision, not merely for television itself, but for the relationship between the royal family and an insatiable medium. In opening the proceedings for the television audience, the BBC announcer, Sylvia Peters, referred to the 'deep significance' of the coronation and, in the same breath, to 'the greatest moment in television history'. The presence of the BBC cameras to witness the intimacies of the holy rite did indeed reveal the power of television to impress on a vast public the splendour and significance of a most solemn constitutional moment. The collusion between the old establishment and the broadcasters was judged, universally and unequivocally, to have been a triumph for the monarchy, for the Church, for Parliament, and for television.

Inside the Abbey, a television camera framed the young Prince at the moment when the Archbishop of Canterbury placed the crown on his mother's head. It was a fleeting glance, but seemed to say, 'You, my child, will be next!' As his mother dedicated the rest of her life to public duty, he heard the incantation, 'Receive the ring of Kingly dignity . . . may you continue steadfastly as the defender of Christ's religion . . . reign with him who is the King of Kings . . .' He tugged frequently at Queen Elizabeth's sleeve but could not later remember what precisely had excited his curiosity. Aside from a vague memory of glorious music and coronets doffed in unison, his only indelible recollection is that beforehand the Palace barber cut his hair too short and plastered it down with 'the most appalling gunge'.[4]

Afterwards, he was brought onto the balcony of Buckingham Palace to join the Queen as she acknowledged the tribute of the vast crowd. He stood there sheltered by his parents, while down below the soldiers marched and wheeled and the people roared approval. This exposure to the force of public emotion formed an elemental part of the process by which he came to appreciate how very different he was from other

---

* The Duke of Norfolk (1885–1972). The Duke assumed the title of Earl Marshal on the death of his father in 1924. By tradition, the Earl Marshal is charged with the organisation of state occasions such as coronations and funerals.
† Geoffrey Fisher (1887–1972), Archbishop of Canterbury 1945–61.

children. In the years ahead, reconciling this discovery with the myth that he was, in the words of the *Sunday Pictorial*, but 'the eldest child of a typical British family'⁵ would prove hard for him and confusing for the nation. The slide from the debatable image of the royal family as 'the symbol of common aspirations' to the notion that it was 'a typical British family' had been precipitous. But the *Sunday Pictorial* was merely stating what had become the conventional wisdom, that this was 'the key to our attitude to royalty today – and of royalty's attitude to us', namely that, 'They are no longer distant, aloof, majestic puppets,' but 'the number one family in a nation of families and a family of nations'. This sentiment was seductive but it was also ludicrous, and dangerously so.

As an adult, discovering that self-deprecation formed a serviceable shield behind which to advance upon the world beyond the royal cocoon, the Prince would claim, 'I am just an ordinary person in an extraordinary position.' The small boy, without that protective veneer and lacking the temperament required to relish his part in the royal scheme, did his best to please by generally doing what he was told. While his little sister (like his mother before her) delighted in discovering that as a member of this particular 'typical' family she could cause the sentries at Buckingham Palace repeatedly to present arms merely by striding back and forth in front of them, the Prince shrank from such boldness. By comparison with his sister, the Prince was timid and passive and easily cowed by the forceful personality of his father. When Prince Philip upbraided his son for a deficiency in behaviour or attitude, he easily drew tears to the child's eyes. According to a close friend, 'Philip was trying to bring up a son who would be able to take over as King in a tough world. Certainly Charles wasn't a cry-baby, but he was terribly sensitive. Prince Philip didn't quite realise how sensitive he was. Another child might not have noticed but Charles used to curl up . . . He just shrank.'⁶* Determined to prepare his son for the rigours that lay ahead,

---

* The press had already got wind of the Duke's resolve if not of his approach: among the sympathetic plethora of speculative articles charting the minutiae of his upbringing, a 'special correspondent' for the *News Chronicle*, who wrote with more apparent authority than his rivals, reported that by his son's first birthday the Duke had already bought him a cricket bat and that he had been heard to say on more than one occasion, 'I want him to be a man's man.' (*News Chronicle*, 12 November 1949.)

the Duke of Edinburgh was to put the relationship between father and son severely to the test. Even at this stage, though the bonds of love were by all accounts strong, they were already strained by impatience on the one side and trepidation on the other.

Shortly before his fifth birthday, one of the rooms on the nursery floor was adapted to become a classroom for Prince Charles. Out went the toys; in came a blackboard, a desk, and a governess. Born in Glasgow but fresh from instructing Prince Michael and Princess Alexandra of Kent, Catherine Peebles – 'Mispy' as she was soon known – had the task of furnishing the heir to the throne with the same basic skills that all primary school children were encouraged to acquire. She was a gentle and shrewd woman, who swiftly discovered that the polite and serious little boy who sat before her was a fragile ego, whose self-confidence was easily shattered. 'He was very responsive to kindness,' she would say later, 'but if you raised your voice to him he would draw back into his shell and for a time you would be able to do nothing with him.'[7] He was diligent and conscientious enough[8] and – in the judgement of Catherine Peebles – had a sense of responsibility beyond his years. Notwithstanding this apparent maturity, he was by no means an apt pupil, finding it hard to concentrate, and displaying no hunger for knowledge. By comparison with the intellectual curiosity that would later distinguish him, he was, if not a dullard, an uninspiring pupil.

The Queen had given instructions that he should not be 'forced'. What little evidence there is suggests that his governess was happy to oblige, overlooking his frailties, encouraging his strengths. He could soon write his own name in capital letters, learnt to read without difficulty, drew with more than usual competence (especially horses and dogs) and enjoyed singing.

For the early months of his nursery education, the Queen and Prince Philip were rarely there to encourage or advise. They had chosen to stay in Sandringham while Prince Charles had his fifth birthday in London, and nine days later they left Britain by sea on official business which would keep them away from their son for six months. Taking the route her father would have followed on the aborted tour of 1948, the royal couple left in November 1953 for a tour of ten Commonwealth countries. Prince Charles traced their route with the aid of a globe in the classroom but did not see his parents until the following April, when they arrived in North Africa.

The announcement that the royal offspring would join their parents in the Mediterranean and stay with them on the royal visit to Malta and Gibraltar was the subject of solemn editorials which applauded the fact that at least some of the Commonwealth peoples would thus have a chance to see the children, welcomed the opportunity given to the pair of them to have a foretaste of what would be required of them in the future, and rejoiced that long separation from their parents (not hitherto the subject of press comment) would thus be attenuated. 'The Queen and her husband', the *Daily Telegraph* intoned, 'have endeared themselves to the British peoples by a devoted family life, and their separation from their children at an age when children specially need their parents has been a real privation.'[9]

On 14 April, Prince Charles and Princess Anne were driven to Portsmouth where they embarked for Malta on board the newly commissioned royal yacht, sailing on her maiden voyage. Seven days later, escorted by a Royal Navy frigate, *Britannia* entered the Grand Harbour at Valetta. The scene imprinted itself vividly on the boy's mind: the aircraft carriers, cruisers, destroyers, frigates and submarines, with white ensigns aflutter but ominous even at anchor; picket boats bustling between them, ferrying men and supplies; and officers, elegant in white and gold, saluting one another under canvas awnings. In the autumn of the Empire, it was still a glorious display. A few days later, the drama was even more dazzling: the entire fleet under the command of Lord Mountbatten steamed past the royal yacht in line astern, engines throbbing and bow waves hissing, while naval ratings, drawn up in their thousands, saluted the Queen, who as head of the armed forces was also their Lord High Admiral.

The Prince's first foreign visit was reported in glowing language by the British newspapers: under the headline 'Royal Children Steal The Show', the *Manchester Guardian*'s special correspondent reported that at the end of one military parade which they attended, 'The Duke of Cornwall took his sister's hand as she pattered down the steps, shepherded her carefully into the car, and turned to wave a little shyly to the photographers and reporters who had formed a polite scrum around the car. "Enchanting, quite enchanting, bless them," said a Maltese government official who had been watching.'[10]

Back in London, the Prince returned again to what passed for normal life. A measure of what that entailed may be gleaned from a letter written early in 1955 by Richard Colville* to the Newspaper Proprietors Association, which represented the owners of what was still a relatively compliant press. Seeking their co-operation in the next stage of Prince Charles's development, the Queen's press secretary wrote:

> I am commanded by the Queen to say that Her Majesty and the Duke of Edinburgh have decided that their son has reached the stage when he should take part in more grown-up educational pursuits with other children.
>
> In consequence, a certain amount of the Duke of Cornwall's instruction will take place outside his home; for example he will visit museums and other places of interest. The Queen trusts, therefore, that His Royal Highness will be able to enjoy this in the same way as other children without the embarrassment of constant publicity . . .
>
> I would be grateful if you will communicate this to your members and seek their co-operation in this matter, informing them at the same time that they are at liberty to publish this letter if they so wish.

The formality and authority in every phrase was finely tuned to the relationship Colville had established with the press: courteous but remote, brooking no dissent. Thus the Prince was free to visit the Science Museum, the Natural History Museum, Madame Tussaud's and the Planetarium without the press in constant attendance.

After almost three years in the nursery schoolroom, the Prince's inside instruction – two hours every weekday morning – had progressed steadily. By the age of seven, he could write neatly and spell competently. He had also started to learn French. Although arithmetic was still beyond his reach, he enjoyed history and geography. Catherine Peebles designed lessons encouraging him to see history through the eyes of children of his own age, not least the history of the Empire and the monarchy, reminders of which in the paintings, sculptures, tapestries, jewellery and antique furniture in Buckingham Palace and Windsor Castle entranced

---

* Sir Richard Colville, press secretary to George VI (1947–52) and to Queen Elizabeth II (1952–68). His sombre demeanour led colleagues to give him the nickname 'Sunshine'.

the imaginative child. He was fascinated in particular by a Van Dyck portrait of his forebear and namesake. The *Three Heads of Charles I* showed the King in both profiles as well as full face, and made such a vivid impression that the Prince was to write later, 'King Charles lived for me in that room in the Castle.'[11]* From Catherine of Aragon's loft in St George's Chapel, where Henry VIII and Queen Victoria also once sat, he watched Sir Winston Churchill process down the aisle as a Knight of the Garter. From the nave it was impossible to see into the loft, and the Prince was thrilled by the darkness inside and by the secret passageway which wound down from the loft to the Deanery below. For him, a child's history of the British Kings and Queens was the story of his own family; it is not surprising that in this subject at least he was an apt pupil.

On 7 November 1956, a week before his eighth birthday, Prince Charles, wearing a velvet-collared topcoat over a new school uniform† and accompanied by Catherine Peebles, was driven to Hill House, a 'pre-preparatory' school in West London.

Hill House had been founded five years earlier by Colonel Henry Townend and his wife, Beatrice Lord. An individual of untroubled vision and clear purpose, the Colonel had resolved to establish a school at which 'half the places . . . would be given to English children and half to non-English children'. The school was based at two sites – one in England, the other in Switzerland, and at each the pupils would 'learn to live with boys and girls of other nationalities, to respect that which is unknown and often very foreign to them, and thus open the door into a world which each day becomes smaller'.[12]

Although his arrival on the first day of the Lent term was supposed to have been accomplished discreetly, the Prince was detected by three Fleet Street photographers. At the end of the day, therefore, with the

---

* The *Three Heads* was sent to Italy for the sculptor Bernini to produce a bust of Charles I. The bust has since been destroyed.

† Two years earlier, in April 1954, in a bizarre example of royal sycophancy, the magazine *Tailor and Cutter* had judged Prince Charles to be the best dressed man of the year, citing not only the aforementioned topcoat as 'a very popular style among older folk' but also – and incongruously – 'his Baby-Bow and Fawn Stalker'.

reluctant assent of the Palace press secretary, Colonel Townend summoned an eager press corps to a briefing at which he listed the guiding principles by which Prince Charles would be taught: 'The most important thing is that a boy should be happy. This is a very happy school. The next thing is the safety of the boy because he is the most precious possession of his parents and at these ages is not old enough to look after himself. The third thing is that boys should be taught to get on well together and to give way if it is in the interests of their form or team.'[13] In return for a brief tour of the classrooms, he enjoined the reporters to refrain from identifying the school while his royal pupil was in attendance – an undertaking which, in those innocent days, they not only gave but subsequently kept as well.

On his first day, the Prince painted a picture which excited much speculative comment in the newspapers, whose reporters had been unable to witness the handiwork for themselves. Obliged to rely on hearsay and their own imaginations, they offered competing descriptions of the Prince's endeavour: depending on which newspaper one read, the painting was variously of 'a seascape with blue and red applied lavishly to depict a ship on a bright blue sea. Pencilled neatly in the top right-hand corner was the name "Charles"'; or 'a ship going under Tower Bridge. A green ship . . . he signed it at the bottom'; or 'the Royal Yacht Britannia approaching Tower Bridge'. As the *Manchester Guardian* observed, 'One thing is clear: on his first day at school the Duke of Cornwall painted a picture.'[14]* The truth may sometimes be many-sided but, as the Prince would later discover, for a royal reporter in search of a story, expediency is invariably the mother of invention.

The decision to send the Prince to what was described as 'an exclusive' private school involved a break, albeit slight, with royal convention. It was widely presumed that the Queen's urge for her son to experience as 'normal' a life as possible reflected her own frustration at the limits imposed on her when she was young. Against that background, the decision in favour of Hill House was a significant initiative; a declaration that the royal family could at least to some extent identify with the

---

* For the record, the painting depicts *Britannia* passing under Tower Bridge and it is signed in the top right-hand corner. According to Colonel Townend, the *Daily Mail* reporter offered the Colonel 'a *lot* of money' for this 'first' painting done by the Prince. The Colonel declined.

subjects of the Crown – even if the subjects in question were likely to be drawn only from the fee-paying classes of the capital city. According to Morrah, it was felt by the Palace that a 'council school would have had far less effective defences to keep at bay those who would inevitably come crowding for a glimpse of the Prince', that the teachers 'would be more likely to be overawed by their responsibility', while his fellow pupils being 'drawn from the humbler strata of society would be more inclined to treat him as a fabulous animal coming from an unknown planet'.[15]*

However, although everyone had been urged to treat the royal pupil as far as possible as an ordinary child, Hill House in reality provided confirmation that no-one would ever treat him as 'normal'. It was not 'normal' for Mrs Townend to be at the door to greet the same pupil every morning when he arrived from the royal home with a royal chauffeur, nor was it 'normal' for the Colonel to see him away every afternoon; it was, however, a duty the Townends imposed on themselves. It was not 'normal' for the boys of Hill House to use the swimming pool at Buckingham Palace, but because it was thought inappropriate for the heir to the throne to use the public baths, Colonel Townend hired two black cabs each week to take the Prince and his classmates to the Palace for that purpose. None of it was 'normal' but it was all inevitable.†

After his first day, the press heeded the Colville injunction and rarely disturbed the Prince's education. Following the school motto from

---

* In addition, a good deal of exculpatory humbug was deployed at the time and later, not least by Morrah himself, to the effect that only by going to a private school could the Prince 'keep an open mind and heart, so as to be ready to sympathise with all sorts of people . . . It is his business to show them . . . what the ordinary human being is capable of becoming.' (Morrah, op. cit., p.47.)

† The newspapers were convinced that their quarry was swimming at the Seymour Baths on the Marylebone Road with the rest of the school, so much so that one photographer became certain that he had '*the photo*' taken through the roof. Colonel Townend felt obliged to disabuse them. Later, he would recall that, 'The press was never a problem. When they got things wrong I never criticised. It was vital to have the press on our side.' The cordial relations between the royal reporters – the term 'rat pack' had yet to be coined – and Colonel Townend was mutually beneficial; the Colonel received favourable publicity while the journalists found themselves with access to the occasional 'inside' story.

Plutarch – 'A boy's mind is not a vessel to be filled, but a fire to be kindled' – the Colonel and his fellow teachers sought to ignite a royal intellect which was as yet dormant. The Prince, however, found it hard to focus for long on the same subject, his attention being readily diverted by faraway thoughts. Nor was it easy to kindle his enthusiasm. The basic laws of mathematics continued to elude him, and he shone only at art and reading. He did discover the underlying principles of elementary anatomy, taught by Mrs Townend, a former theatre sister at Guy's Hospital, who encouraged her pupils in the basics of artificial respiration by lying on her back while they took turns to pummel her chest. No less important to a child who had been so sheltered, he also discovered hitherto unknown aspects of everyday life: he travelled on a London bus to the school games field in the grounds of the Duke of York's Headquarters, a military depot on the King's Road; he was taught to distinguish between the coins of the realm; and as part of the school rota he was required to wash up and sweep the classroom floor.

As a matter of educational principle, the Colonel did not write school reports but occasionally – if asked by a parent – he was willing to draft an informal note of a child's performance. His assessment of Charles at the end of the Lent term of 1957 was characteristically direct: 'Reading – very good indeed. Good expression. Writing – Good. Firm, clear, well formed. Arithmetic – Below form average. Careful but slow – not very keen. Scripture – shows keen interest. Geography – good. History – loves this subject. French – shows promise. Latin – made a fair start. Art – Good, and simply loves drawing and painting. Singing – A sweet voice, especially in lower register. Football – enjoying the game. Gymnastics – Good. Henry Townend, Headmaster.'[16]

At this age, the young Prince was not physically robust. Prone to common colds, influenza and recurring tonsillitis, he was frequently away from school.* These enforced absences from Hill House may have had

---

* In the spring of 1957 the eight-year-old tonsils were removed and preserved in a glass jar. For several months the Prince insisted on taking them with him wherever he went. At Windsor he had conceived an affection for the little chapel which lay between the Grand Corridor and St George's Hall. There, alone, he would stand in the pulpit delivering sermons to an imaginary but rapt congregation. On one occasion he was so taken by his own performance that he swept out into the Grand Corridor – forgetting that he had left his tonsils on the pulpit.

some impact on his modest performance there. Nonetheless, he was handicapped rather more by a lack of self-confidence which was so inhibiting that although he was well endowed with both intelligence and imagination, these qualities were not yet easy to discern behind the carapace of diffidence and reserve with which he habitually protected himself.

CHAPTER
THREE

———— • ————

The royal family have four principal 'homes': their two official
residences at Buckingham Palace and Windsor Castle, and their
two estates at Sandringham House in Norfolk and Balmoral
Castle in Scotland. Prince Charles was soon familiar with all of them.
He had explored the winding passageways of Windsor Castle where the
family spent the weekends, he had joined the shooting parties at
Sandringham (the winter abode) and in the long summers at Balmoral
he had walked among the Caledonian pines, played by the edge of
Loch Muick and wondered at 'The steep frowning glories of dark Loch
na Garr', as Byron had described what would become his favourite
mountain.*

It was Balmoral which was to become his abiding love, for whose fast-
ness he would yearn when he was away, where he would mark individual
trees and get to know every burn, and where in solitude he would lose
himself entirely, entering into that intimacy with nature which the metropolitan mind finds so difficult to understand.

Balmoral became a royal home in 1852, ten years after Queen Victoria
had first become entranced by her 'dear beautiful Highlands'.¹ As the first

---

* The modern spelling is Lochnagar. The name, which means Goat Lake, originally
applied only to the small loch at the foot of the eastern ridge of Lochnagar mountain. It now generally refers to the mountain, which has eleven summits over
3,000 feet.

monarch to establish a footing in Scotland since the Jacobite rebellion of the eighteenth century (in which the House of Stuart rose up against the Hanoverians, from whom she was in direct line of descent), Queen Victoria was blissfully oblivious to the animosities which the Highlanders still harboured for the victors of Culloden. At Balmoral, she and Prince Albert discovered 'a quiet, a retirement, a wildness, a liberty, and a solitude'.[2] A century later, its spirit touched her successors to similar effect.

Once the family had departed the royal train at Ballater Station, offering a smile and a wave to the photographers who waited patiently in place for the annual royal holiday 'snap', they were – within ten minutes – lost in the natural seclusion of their private wilderness. The atmosphere throughout the household would perceptibly yield to another mood. With much of the formality that subdued the official residences discarded, and the public face put aside, the royal caravan would begin to relax, sloughing off the accumulated tensions of Buckingham Palace. The summer routine, though still orderly, was distinctly more casual than could possibly have been entertained in the official residences south of the border.

In the shooting or stalking season, immaculate Land Rovers drew up outside the front of the castle each morning to take the men of the party up to the edge of the moor or the mountain. In the stables, the Queen's horses were again at the ready, coats groomed, saddles and bridles soaped and stirrups polished. The household servants, trained in discretion, appeared only when required, aware that to be seen or heard without a purpose would be to intrude.

If Balmoral was run on a grand scale it was the only scale the young Prince had ever known, the closest approximation to a normal family life that he could conceivably experience. This was the home where he played ping-pong and football in the yard behind the pantry or cycled to the village shop, alone except for the ubiquitous policeman in the background, and where at 1.00 p.m. he was driven with his sister to join his parents and their guests, gathered for a picnic lunch after the morning shoot. By the time he was eight, he was allowed to accompany the shooting party to the hill, walking with the beaters, hearing their conversation and discovering their ways. Swiftly indoctrinated into the culture of a sporting estate, he did not recoil from the sound of gunfire or from the brief death throes of a fallen stag, knowing the relief of a clean kill after the nerve-jangling anticipation of the stalk. Watching a fly cast lightly over a still pool amid the gurgle and whirl of the River Dee, he watched as a salmon, irritated by the disturbance, snapped fatally at the fly. Taught to shoot and fish by his father, he was steeped in these rural traditions and was to grow up to see the hunter and hunted as entwined in a quasi-mystical embrace, in which there was beauty, excitement and innocence.

The indigenous staff – the keepers, gillies and foresters who cared for Balmoral with singular devotion – discovered in the young Prince not only a keen pupil but a kindred spirit. In their company, he learnt the habits of grouse and red deer and of the environment in which they lived. On the hills, he walked along rutted tracks through the heather where bees hummed and butterflies folded their wings on wild flowers. By their sound and their flight he learnt to identify sandpipers and redshank, while falcons stooped in the distance and the occasional eagle circled high above. Lower down, he discovered the vaulted silence of the forest, the majestic austerity of the Caledonian pines – primeval remnants of an age when the lower slopes of the Highlands were covered by trees, before the ravages inflicted by the clearances of the eighteenth century when the pines were felled for timber and floated down the Dee to Aberdeen. Entranced by the secret life of the forest, he saw voles, stoats, weasels, red squirrels and owls. There was no sea, no sand, no buckets and spades or Punch and Judy, but even when the sun was excluded by cloud and it was dank for days, or when the wind moaned and the rain fell in torrents, Balmoral was an idyll which enraptured the child and which he would not willingly exchange for any other place on earth.

At Balmoral, the Prince also saw more of his parents. They would not only find time to play with him, but also to instruct him. Sometimes he rode with his mother, though he was then an uncertain equestrian, timid where his sister was bold. To the relief of his father, Prince Charles did at least demonstrate that he was indifferent to the weather, eager to be out of doors, and anxious to handle a gun.

At the end of the day, when the sportsmen had returned, the family played wild games like 'kick the can' (a form of hide-and-seek) in which everyone would be expected to join, including private secretaries and prime ministers on their annual September pilgrimage to stay privately with the Queen. The only formal event was dinner, when evening dress was *de rigueur* and the meal was accompanied by music played by three Scottish pipers. Dignitaries from the region would attend, and sometimes on Saturday a visiting clergyman came up from Ballater to join them. Every Sunday the royal family joined the congregation at the village church.

On these occasions, the press would also be in attendance for a glimpse of the royal party, although there were no telescopic lenses in evidence, certainly none powerful enough to peer into the seclusion of Balmoral. In any case, deference kept the reporters and photographers at a distance; even when they knew when and where the royal party were going they as yet lacked the temerity to penetrate its privacy.

At this time, Mabel Anderson found herself in sole charge of both children following what the Prince would later remember as a 'to-do' involving his father and Helen Lightbody, although the reason for the contretemps was then beyond the comprehension of the young child. To his relatives and some courtiers, however, the cause was not hard to discern. The contrast in temperament and character between Prince Charles and Princess Anne was already marked. To the adults around them, the little girl seemed noisy, wilful and fearless while her elder brother was sweet-natured but withdrawn, a vulnerable little boy by whose gentleness they were captivated. The complexity of a personality burdened by insecurity and self-doubt but still forceful and resilient had yet to emerge. To the world, glimpsing the children glide past in a royal limousine, the heir apparent often looked solemn or bashful, while his younger sister evidently delighted in the attention of the expectant faces and waving hands that slipped by the window.

The Duke of Edinburgh was unclear how best to stimulate a character so obviously lacking his sister's panache. Without that gentleness of nature and subtlety of mind which might have helped to coax the Prince out of his debilitating reticence, the Duke tempered his own affection with brusqueness, a disposition which served only to make his son withdraw even further from that open communication which would have benefited both of them. From his well-meaning but unimaginative perspective, the Duke detected in Helen Lightbody, the Prince's nurse, an impediment to his son's proper development, an inclination on her part to favour his son over his daughter, indulging the boy's 'softness' while reprimanding Princess Anne for displaying precisely that spirit which he

wished to see in her brother. So sharp was the contrast in the nurse's attitude towards her charges that their father believed that she had virtually
rejected Anne altogether. The upshot was a disagreement between the
implacable father and the doting nurse: Helen Lightbody departed.

Helen Lightbody had certainly lavished affection on the Prince, sharing Mabel Anderson's devotion to their charge. Too often, however, she
allowed herself to become carried away by her own heady responsibilities. Forgetting the parental injunction that he should be treated
normally, she was prone to remind the heir to the throne of his extraordinary and enviable position, confiding that he had very important duties
ahead of him. Her assistant Mabel Anderson was to remain far too discreet and loyal to say so in public, but it was evident that she had different
ideas. The relationship between the two Scottish women had long been
strained, not only by their differing attitudes towards their charge but by
the way in which the senior woman, Helen Lightbody, wielded her
authority. At the Prince's birth, she was in her mid-thirties while Mabel
Anderson was but twenty-two; visitors to the nursery were left in no
doubt that the older woman was very much in charge, and that her own
(not always very clear or consistent) principles held sway. If the younger
woman chafed under such an erratic regime she was at pains to disguise
it; even so, the coolness between them was not hard to detect.

With the departure of Helen Lightbody, Mabel Anderson fully lived
up to Prince Philip's expectations. Although she was devoted to her
employers, she had her own clear sense of how to handle the two very
different children in her care, and she was not easily suborned. Firm,
even strict by the standards of a later generation, and *in extremis* willing
to administer a smacking, she was, by nature, kind and gentle, quick to
comfort and to encourage. Under her regime in the nursery, equerries
and ladies-in-waiting, as well as butlers and footmen – who had not
always found favour with Helen Lightbody – were able to take advantage
of the friendly seclusion of Balmoral from the rigours of Palace duty. For
Prince Charles, who had already discovered that only in the nursery
could he always be assured of a cuddle, Mabel Anderson became 'a
haven of security, the great haven' to whom he invariably turned first for
comfort and support.[3]

With parents who were often away, and were not, in any case, given
to displays of affection even in private, Mabel Anderson came to assume
a vital role in the Prince's life. The adoration of the young child for his

nurse (who was almost the same age as the Queen) led friends and courtiers to conclude that Mabel Anderson had become in effect 'a surrogate mother', while to his father it was clear that she was much the most important influence on him. As he grew towards adolescence, the bond between the child and the nurse would remain no less intense. Even in adulthood,* the heir to the throne would turn as soon to Mabel for comfort and advice as to his parents, whom he did not cease to love and honour, but with whom open and easy communication was to remain difficult. His father, setting a pattern that was to endure, could not bring himself to draw the child out, presuming without any ill-intent that if his son wished to communicate he would do so, and that, as his father, it was not for him to press the issue.

In 1957, at the start of the third week of September, the Prince had to leave Balmoral. Queen Victoria had always been 'quite miserable'⁴ to leave her beloved Highlands; her great-great-great-grandson was inconsolable. It was not so much leaving home he dreaded but his destination: Cheam School in Berkshire, where his parents had decided he should take up his place as a boarder with eighty-five other children aged between eight and fourteen, whose parents were charged ninety guineas a term for the privilege. The decision had been taken some months earlier after his parents had considered a number of alternatives. As the Queen invariably deferred to the Duke in family matters, Cheam – which in any case had a long and respectable lineage – was an inevitable choice.

Founded in the seventeenth century in the City of London 'for the education of the sons of noblemen and gentry', the original school was driven out of the capital by fear of the Great Plague in 1665, to be re-established in Surrey in the village from which the present school takes its name. The social character of Cheam School in those days can be judged by the habit adopted by one headmaster, Arthur Tabor, of referring to the commoners among his pupils as 'my child', sons of peers as

---

* Mabel Anderson not only had charge of Prince Charles and Princess Anne, but later Prince Andrew and Prince Edward as well. On her retirement, she was accommodated in a 'grace and favour' apartment in the grounds of Windsor Castle where, with a flourish of affection that somewhat bemused his relatives, the Prince arranged for it to be decorated and furnished in her taste at his own expense.

'my dear child' and peers as 'my darling child'. Among the names of the landed gentry, generals and governors-general which pepper the school records is that of Lord Randolph Churchill, who in the words of his filial biographer, Winston, 'seems to have been most kindly treated and to have been quite contented'. In the nineteenth century, Cheam had earned the nickname 'The Little House of Lords'. Though a residue of this exclusivity carried over into the twentieth century, the school had gradually widened its intake, and by the time Peter Beck and Mark Wheeler bought Cheam in 1947 – in some trepidation that the Labour government might abolish private education – its reputation for providing 'a good academic education based on Christian values' was well established among the middle classes.

However, the scales were tipped in favour of Cheam by a more visceral attraction. In 1930, a nine-year-old Greek prince, in exile from his birthplace and living in Paris, had been sent across the Channel to become a pupil at Cheam. Although French was not his mother tongue, it had become his first language, and on arrival in Britain his command of English was rudimentary. Cheam not only provided his introduction to British life but helped him rapidly to master the language as well. Prince Philip of Greece (as he then was) was convinced that the school which had served him so well would do likewise for his son. Some years later, as the Duke of Edinburgh, the illustrious old boy was forthright about the character of his old school, and why he had chosen it for his son. 'Children may be indulged at home,' he wrote, 'but school is expected to be a spartan and disciplined experience in the process of developing into self-controlled, considerate and independent adults. The system may have its eccentricities but there can be little doubt that these are far outweighed by its values.'[5]

Like Colonel Townend before him, Beck emphasised that the Duke of Cornwall would be given no special treatment. In fact, in an attempt to ensure that 'normality' would prevail, Beck had already written to all parents to inform them of 'the great honour' that the Queen and Prince Philip had conferred upon Cheam, but continued:

> The purpose of this letter is to assure you that it is the wish of the Queen and Prince Philip that there shall be no alteration in the way the school is run and Prince Charles shall be treated in exactly the same way as other boys . . . It would be a great help if you would

explain this to your boy(s) during the holidays as we shall have no opportunity to speak to the school on the subject.[6]

On the first day of term, the Queen and Prince Philip drove their son in through the front gates and up the drive to the front door, there to be greeted by Beck, his wife Anne, and his colleague, Wheeler. An eye-witness described how, in spite of a request from Wheeler to the press to leave them in peace, especially on the first day of term:

> villagers, reporters, cameramen, in their numbers, assembled about 4pm around the main entrance gateway. But the royal car did not arrive until 6.15 . . . The front drive was full of cars, parents and boys, waiting to see them arrive, and there were faces at every window. Suddenly a hush fell on the whole assembly, police cleared a space and in drove the royal car. Cameras clicked and flashlights appeared every-where.[7]

His parents stayed long enough to see where the Prince was going to sleep and then, after a brief exchange of courtesies, the royal car disap-peared down the drive and the Prince was alone.

In such circumstances, it is not uncommon for a child to feel not merely forlorn but bereft as he unpacks new school clothes on an iron bedstead in a dormitory bare except for seven other identical beds, vision blurred by tears and with only a teddy bear for company; to have that acute physical sensation of emotional distress that is known blandly as homesickness. Prince Charles was badly affected and for several nights he stifled his tears in the pillow. Although he was schooled in the disciplines of his inheritance and familiar with the royal imperatives of public behav-iour – never show undue emotion, always be polite, modest, and do not forget that every gesture is likely to be under the closest scrutiny – he could not entirely conceal his feelings. Soon after the start of term, one of the staff, David Munir (who taught mathematics and had been deputed to watch over the new pupil), went out into the grounds dur-ing a break to find the Duke of Cornwall isolated and in misery while the rest of the school, already forming into coteries from which he had found himself excluded, rampaged carelessly about him.[8] Remembering those days, the Prince would recall that, 'It was not easy to make large numbers of friends . . . I'm not a gregarious person so I've always had a horror of gangs . . . I have always preferred my own company or just a one to one.'[9]

As the other boys were as awkward in overtures towards him as he was incapable of approaching them, it was not an easy induction. He struck one contemporary as 'an ordinary small boy who was above all terribly embarrassed'. But to a member of staff he seemed to be 'a happy and friendly little boy . . . joining in the fun and games and an occasional scrum on the floor'.[10] If the former judgement is flawed by insensitivity, the latter is certainly tinged by wish-fulfilment. Striving to seem as 'normal' as possible, the Prince struggled to be unobtrusive and to cause no unwonted offence. He was indeed friendly, but an emotional and impetuous nature was severely constrained by an outward reserve and formality – behind which he also concealed his painful insecurity.

The school day began at 7.15 a.m. with the clanging of the school bell to rouse the eleven dormitories from sleep. Once washed and dressed, the boys went one by one past matron, to shake hands while she inspected them for cleanliness and tidiness. School prayers followed until, at 8.00 a.m., on their way to breakfast, they filed past one or other of the two headmasters, once more shaking hands on the way. Beck was reported as saying that this daily ritual gives 'some kind of confidence to have to do it properly, to look us in the eye'.[11] This was one lesson in which the Prince needed no practice, as it had been dinned into him already that 'good manners' dictated direct eye contact at all times.

The dining room was decorated in faded ochre and the walls sported three stag's heads, the mask of a fox and a painting of Venice of uncertain provenance. There the boys consumed porridge, eggs and 'an unlimited supply' of bread and butter taken with honey or marmalade, before moving off to the range of dilapidated and strictly utilitarian classrooms in the 'New School' to begin the first of the day's six lessons. The curriculum was dominated by the 'three R's', though music and art were also encouraged. The Prince continued to struggle with mathematics but began to do well at English. He would remember with affection his English teacher, 'who was the most wonderful ex-Indian Army Colonel with a bristling moustache, heavy cavalry twill trousers and a sort of livid, orange, hairy, tweed jacket and a pipe'.[12] He was taught to recite poetry from memory and long passages from Shakespeare – 'which in moments of stress or danger or misery . . . give enormous comfort and encouragement when you are older'.[13] Much of the teaching was by rote: he could declaim a poem by Victor Hugo in French and in geography the Colonel 'drilled into us the names of places and the capital cities, the archipelagos and peninsulas. My goodness it helped.'[14] The headmaster was impressed by his fluency in oral work and on paper, and, unexpectedly, came to the opinion that in English at least he was up to scholarship standard.

There was a school library where G.A. Henty and other period authors were available. The Prince did not avail himself of those facilities but he had become devoted to a boys' comic called *Eagle*, a staple for many of his generation. A subscription had been taken out for him by his great-uncle Lord Mountbatten, the First Sea Lord, who, with character-istic precision, had arranged from his desk at the Ministry of Defence for the publishers, Odhams Ltd, to send the comic to his great-nephew *sine die*, enclosing a white card from him in the Christmas edition to remind him that it was a present. The Prince wrote in gratitude, 'I like *Eagle* very much. It's got such exciting stories.'[15]*

Cheam boasted a 'bank', which provided stationery and sweets (the latter in closely rationed quantities). The recommended pocket money for purchasing these items was twenty-five shillings a term, a sum which was held by the bank and handed out in the form of credits rather than in cash. This did not prevent one newspaper reporting that his parents had been so parsimonious that the Prince had been obliged to sell some personal possessions to finance his contribution to a midnight feast. This concoction was relayed across the Atlantic, where credulous delegates to the Retail Candy Stores Institute of America, then in conference in San Francisco, passed a resolution to the effect 'that we ought to pitch in and help him out of a jam'.[16] Forty-eight tins of 'fine American candy' were duly dispatched to the school whence they were distributed to the local Red Cross.

From the evening of his arrival at Cheam, hardly a day had passed without a press story about the school or its royal pupil. Peter Beck, enduring a crash course in public relations, found himself fielding calls from Fleet Street 'at all hours', usually asking him to react to a story ('from one of our sources') about the Prince's progress or behaviour. As

---

* Each year thereafter, the Prince continued to receive his weekly edition of *Eagle*, until 1963, when at the age of fifteen he had somewhat outgrown Dan Dare *et al*. The magazine folded before it became necessary to remind Mountbatten of this.

it was a school rule that such matters were confidential, a matter for parents and pupils alone, the reporters were given short shrift; in consequence, the tabloid newspapers ran the stories in any case, regardless of the truth and of the unsettling effect on the staff, pupils and parents. By the end of the first term, press attention had become so intrusive that Peter Beck became concerned for the wellbeing of his school. Throughout the term he had been in regular contact with Martin Charteris,* the Queen's assistant private secretary, and Richard Colville, her press secretary, to discuss ways of handling Fleet Street's curiosity, but to no avail. In the Christmas holidays, however, with no sign that the press interest would diminish, the Palace decided to take action.

On this occasion, Colville summoned the editors themselves to Buckingham Palace, where Beck restated the school's request for privacy. He told them that a pall of resentment and unhappiness had started to form over his school and pleaded with them to desist. Colville warned (in the words of the Arundel Herald of Arms) 'that unless this pursuit of petty little paragraphs ceased, the Queen would be forced to take Prince Charles away from school and have him educated privately – for the sake of the other people involved as well as himself'.[17] According to Beck's account, the Fleet Street men were responsive; the deluge of unsolicited inquiries became a dribble and the stories dried up.

It was a school rule that each boy should write a letter home at least once a week, and this occupied the quiet hour after church on Sundays. Prince Charles was as uninspired by the task as any other small boy. They were required to write on more than one side of paper and the Prince was quick to learn that the easiest way to achieve this was to obey the injunction to the letter and then conclude – over the page – by confirming that it had indeed been accomplished.

If most of his letters from Cheam were dutiful, there were also those which had clear purpose. On 12 October 1957, he wrote to the First Sea Lord as follows: 'Do you think I could not have the silly-putty for my birthday but please can I have a bicycle if you can.'[18] Thus enjoined by his great-nephew, Mountbatten took time out from his other duties

---

* Martin Charteris (1913–   ), private secretary to Princess Elizabeth 1950–52; assistant private secretary to the Queen 1952–72; private secretary to the Queen 1972–77.

personally to discover the most appropriate size and make of machine before writing back with a card for his ninth birthday and the reassuring news: 'Your birthday bicycle will be delivered at Xmas. About your birthday present: I don't mind changing the silly-putty for a bicycle, but as a bicycle is much more expensive, it will have to do as a combined birthday and Christmas present from Aunt Edwina and me.'[19]*

Before starting at Cheam the Prince had been given elementary instruction in wrestling and boxing and could protect himself adequately. When a tease turned into a tussle that became an ill-tempered fight he did not back off. As a result of such misdemeanours he was from time to time confined to the classroom; he had to endure the task of pulling couch grass from the cricket pitch; and on two occasions he was beaten after participating once too often in what was still called 'ragging' in the dormitory. After ignoring previous warnings to desist, he not only paid the price but later said, 'I am one of those people for whom corporal punishment actually worked . . . We had two headmasters when I was there, which was odd . . . They took turns at beating us . . . I didn't do it again.'[20]

One Saturday afternoon at the end of the summer term of 1958, a group of boys including Prince Charles was summoned to the headmaster's study. Alerted by a phone call from Charteris at the Palace, Beck told them that they could watch the closing ceremony of the Empire and Commonwealth Games in Cardiff. The children settled in front of the television as the black and white image from Wales flickered onto the screen. The Queen had been due to open the proceedings but was confined to her bed with sinusitis. The Duke of Edinburgh presided in her place, and the boys watched as it was announced to the packed stadium at Cardiff Arms Park that the sovereign would address the crowd and the television audience in a recorded message at the end of the day. The message was clear and simple: 'The British Empire and Commonwealth Games in the capital . . . have made this a memorable year for the principality. I have therefore decided to mark it further by an act which will,

---

* After receiving his Christmas bicycle, the Prince wrote to thank Mountbatten, saying, 'I have had great fun on it and it goes very fast. I love the bell the way it sounds like a telephone. I got some silly-putty from Martin [presumably Charteris] for Christmas but I got a microscope from Papa.' (C to Mountbatten, January 1958, MA.)

I hope, give as much pleasure to all Welshmen as it does to me. I intend to create my son Charles, Prince of Wales, today.' In the stadium the crowd cheered and sang 'God Bless the Prince of Wales'. The Queen added, 'When he is grown up I will present him to you at Caernarvon.'

In the headmaster's study the other boys offered their congratulations, but Beck witnessed the look of acute embarrassment which flashed across the face of the Prince. For him it was not a moment to rejoice but the sealing of the inevitable, that 'awful truth'[21] from which there was no escape. For the purposes of state documents he was now to be described as His Royal Highness Prince Charles Philip Arthur George, Prince of Wales and Earl of Chester, Duke of Cornwall, Duke of Rothesay, Earl of Carrick, Lord of the Isles and Baron of Renfrew, Prince and Great Steward of Scotland. (Later, Knight Companion of the Most Noble Order of the Garter was added.) For an introverted nine-year-old it was quite a drapery.

The newspapers were unanimously enthusiastic about the Queen's decision: the *Manchester Guardian* reported the 'joy' occasioned by the announcement,[22] the *Daily Telegraph* wrote of 'the vivid honour' bestowed on the Prince,[23] and *The Times* recorded 'the spontaneous warmth of feeling in the hearts of Welshmen that after 22 years they are again to be represented by a Prince of their own . . .'[24] A hill farmer in Ruthin to whom the news was imparted the following day paused for a moment and then delivered his verdict. 'Well now,' he said. 'Myself, I think it will be a very good thing for the boy.'[25] In a country where the valleys were still nostalgic for the last Prince of Wales, it was widely felt that the principality needed a Prince once again.

A fortnight later, the Prince made his first visit to Wales, disembarking from the royal yacht which had moored off Anglesey en route for Scotland from Cowes as part of the royal family's annual west coast cruise. With Princess Anne beside him, the Prince was given an 'informal' tour of the island, while their parents went about their official business. On their way back, the children met up with the Queen and the Duke to walk the last twenty-five yards to where the royal barge was waiting at the McKenzie Pier in Holyhead, where, it was reported, 'Cheering crowds broke through police cordons . . . the spectators surged forward bursting through barriers. Police were unable to stem the rush.' When the Prince was almost knocked over by an over-excited dog, he 'patted the dog, laughing and flushed with excitement. His father, laughing heartily, put a reassuring arm round the Prince's shoulders and both waved to the crowd.'[26]

After that brief glimpse into his future, the Prince returned to his usual routine. Aside from his ill-fated captaincy of the First Eleven soccer team (which prompted a censure in the *Cheam School Chronicle*, 'At half, Prince Charles seldom drove himself as hard as his ability and position demanded'), he also played cricket for the First XI and rugger, which he did not greatly enjoy as his fellows seemed to take excessive pleasure in burying him under the scrum; when positions were reversed he was rewarded with shouts of 'Get off, fatty!' He was reported to be rather more lethal with a red water pistol, which he used for shooting 'bears' on the 'outward bound course' for which boys could volunteer.

More rewardingly, he played the Duke of Gloucester in a school play called *The Last Baron*, which had been written by David Munir. The Prince was understudy for the role of the future Richard III, and stepped in when the 'Duke' suddenly left the school. There were sniggers when he intoned a prayer which included the line, 'And soon may I ascend the throne', but the drama critic of the *Cheam School Chronicle* was impressed: 'Prince Charles played the traditional Gloucester with competence and depth: he had a good voice and excellent elocution, and very well conveyed the ambition and bitterness of the twisted hunchback.'

Despite his own inclination he was still inevitably far from being a normal pupil: when he returned to school with a new pencil box, the other children wanted one similar; when he was given a 'doodle-master' (with which to draw complex patterns), the other school lockers swiftly acquired them as well; on the evening that he played the Duke of Gloucester, the headmaster stepped onto the stage after the final curtain to announce that the boy's mother had just given birth to a second son, his brother, Prince Andrew; and when he caught chicken pox, measles, and several bouts of 'flu, or when he fractured a small bone in his ankle after falling downstairs, it was widely assumed that the public 'had a right to know'. When he was taken into hospital for a minor operation, the *Daily Express* was breathless with anxiety, describing how 'Prince Charles was rushed 58 miles from Cheam School to London's Great Ormond Street Hospital early today for an immediate appendicitis operation. And later surgeons reported: It was successful.'[27]

By 1962, after five years at Cheam School, the Prince of Wales had been appointed head boy. He had yet to demonstrate any unusual talent academically, on the sports field or as a potential leader, but there were qualities of character that impressed the staff. He was gentle, unusually thoughtful of others, exceptionally modest, and courteous beyond his years – a precocity which sprang as much from his royal upbringing as from his nature: 'We were made to do things you didn't want to do, which we were told were "jolly good for you",' he would recall approvingly. 'We were made to make polite conversation, to put people at their ease. Not just to sit there because it didn't suit you.'[28]* If he was not the stuff of which schoolboy heroes are made, he had a rare combination of innocence and maturity, which suggested that even if his appointment as head boy had sprung in part from deference it did not fly in the face of common sense.

The Prince himself had no more affection for Cheam by the end of his five years than he had had at the beginning; his heart was always elsewhere. Evidently writing with the approval of the Queen, the Arundel Herald of Arms recorded that his mother 'knew that his first few years at Cheam had been a misery to him',[29] and according to a member of the household who spent much time with him in his last year at Cheam, the Prince 'loathed' his time there.[30] In his notes for an essay on 'The Advantages of Boarding Schools', the child could muster but one bleak thought: 'Preparing you for the outside world. Away from your homes for so long.'[31]

---

* The importance of 'being polite' had been drummed into him so effectively that as an adult he would come to regard 'courtesy' as a cardinal virtue, akin to chivalry. The prevalence of boorish or even ineptly off-hand behaviour would shock and dismay him. Always impeccably well mannered himself, he would expect others to behave similarly towards him. The absence of such grace (particularly in politicians or civil servants) would drive him to private fury; nor would the offence be swiftly forgotten.

CHAPTER
FOUR

———•———

T he Prince's early love of the outdoors was developing into a passion. 'It was an awful pity we didn't catch that big salmon that
was under the bridge,' the nine-year-old wrote to his great-
uncle after going to stay for the weekend at Broadlands, the Mountbatten
family home, in the early summer of 1958. 'It was so enormous and it
was such fun watching it take the bait under the water. I have never seen
that before in my life.'¹ In the same year, he shot his first grouse, and the
following New Year he went on the annual coot shoot with his father at
Hickling on the Norfolk Broads, where they were driven to take shelter
for two nights at the Pleasure Boat Inn, marooned there by a heavy
flood.

A sense of his feeling for these pursuits can be discerned in some notes
he made for a Cheam essay called 'Evening Flight':

Bird Watchers leaving. Duck out at sea as there wasn't hardly any
wind at all in morning. Sitting in hide you could see the marshes all
round. Solitary places of their own. The mournful cry of the Oyster
Catcher and Feet in water . . . Duck coming in in trickles. Banging
from other pools. Swishing of wings. Gets rather dark. Hear plops and
splashes as they land around you without being seen. V. difficult to see.
Only hear them beat their wings. Got 4 duck altogether . . . Pity there
weren't more that evening. Might have got more.²

45

In 1960, when he was eleven, he again wrote to Lord Mountbatten: 'I have been having great fun shooting lately. Yesterday I got 23 pheasants and today I got ten and a partridge, a moorhen and a hare.'[3] He was already a promising shot, with a keen eye and steady hand.

By this time, he had already attended his first fox hunt. The news that he might attend a meet of the West Norfolk Hunt provoked the first controversy to surround the Prince of Wales. Clinton Gray-Fisher, the chairman of the National Society for the Abolition of Cruel Sports, wrote to the Queen to protest. The letter was couched in the courteous terms that prevailed in those days:

> This news, we venture to suggest, will dismay a great number of your Majesty's subjects since, as your Majesty is no doubt aware, there is continually increasing evidence of public resentment against cruelty in the hunting field . . .
>
> May we respectfully suggest that the mere presence of Prince Charles at the hunt implies approval of this so-called 'sport', and he could find sufficient opportunity for his enjoyment of riding, for exercise, and for his love of animals, by attending drag-hunts and point-to-point meetings rather than in patronising events wherein cruelty so manifestly enters?[4]

This protest prompted a thundering rebuke from an editorial in *The Times* under the headline 'Leave The Prince Out of It'. The child's enthusiasm for field sports (or 'blood' sports as they were termed by opponents) was not surprising. Life at Balmoral and Sandringham revolved around horses, guns and fishing rods, and it would have been strange if he had turned his back on an inheritance established by his great-great-great-grandmother at Balmoral and her son, his great-great-grandfather, at Sandringham. Edward VII was an enthusiastic shot, though less gifted than his son, George V, who was famous on the moors for shooting fast-flying grouse with two guns, his loader fully stretched to keep pace, and who could shoot a stag on the move like none other. Then and later, house parties on both estates were effectively self-selecting, being drawn from the ranks of the nobility and the landed aristocracy, and among them, only the keenest shots.

When the Prince was at Sandringham, he became part of a routine no less established and organised than at school, though on a very much grander scale. For novitiates it was a daunting experience. Sandringham House had been bought by Queen Victoria for her son Edward ('Bertie') when he was still Prince of Wales, in 1862. Under his self-indulgent beneficence, Sandringham not only provided a more than adequate pheasant shoot but also the most lavish and glittering house parties as well. His son George V had less extravagant tastes but wrote of 'Dear old Sandringham, the place I love better than anywhere else in the world'. George VI was similarly enamoured, writing to his mother Queen Mary, 'I have always been so happy here and I love the place.' On the day of his death, he had spent the afternoon at his favourite pastime, out on the estate with his dogs and a gun.

By the late 1950s, the scale had been somewhat modified but (by the standards of a later generation) the style was still elaborate. After break-fast, taken in the dining room by the men and in their bedrooms by the ladies, the shooting party, now including the Prince of Wales, gathered in the saloon, the largest room in the house which doubled as the main entrance hall and the principal reception room. Suitably dressed in thick jackets, plus fours, brightly coloured woollen socks and stout walking boots, the men departed in Land Rovers for the first drive. The Queen repaired to her study to 'go through' her boxes with her private secretary, or went out on horseback while the other wives remained in their bed-rooms or took a turn in the garden until later in the morning when they were summoned to the saloon to await the arrival of the Queen. Then they departed in another fleet of Land Rovers to join their spouses for a picnic lunch.

The meal was frequently taken in the private room of a public house in one of the six villages which form part of the 20,000-acre estate, the table being prepared by royal footmen dressed in their livery of battle-dress blue. The food – substantial quantities of soup and meat – was served from ancient silver boxes which were kept in insulated bags to preserve the heat. The conversation tended to the jocular and mainly concerned the morning's tally and the prospects for the afternoon in front of them. As soon as the meal was over, the entire party went on to the next drive, the women standing in small groups or beside their spouses to watch and admire. It was usually cold, and sometimes – with a Siberian wind slicing across the flat Norfolk farmland – perish-ingly so.

With the light fading, and a tally of more than three hundred birds on a good day,* the royal party returned to Sandringham where baths were drawn for the men and the women changed into silk cocktail gowns for tea, a ritual from which the children were excluded. The Queen sat at one end of the table and one of her ladies-in-waiting at the other. A silver urn, supported on hinges and warmed by the flames of methylated spirits, provided boiling water which a lady-in-waiting poured into a Georgian silver teapot filled with tea from a silver caddy.

Afterwards, the Queen took her guests through to the saloon where Prince Charles and Princess Anne, who had been given tea in the nursery, were usually watching children's television, the Prince dressed formally in shorts, silk shirt and a tie, the Princess in a party frock. The television was turned off and the games started. Ostensibly for the children's sake, they played hide and seek or tag, with the Duke, the Queen, the Queen Mother, Princess Margaret, the Duke of Gloucester and even Princess Marina casting off all inhibition and chasing one another as well as the Prince and Princess round the saloon, along the corridors, into the drawing room, up the stairs and along the landing, tripping up guests, shrieking and squealing the while.

After this revelry, the children said their goodnights before returning to the nursery floor and thence to bed. The adults went up to their rooms to change into dinner jackets or long dresses before going downstairs again for a drink before dinner. Afterwards they retired to the saloon to play canasta or racing demon (but rarely the word games in which, according to the mythology, they were supposed to delight) or, frequently, to the ballroom to watch a popular film, following which plates of sandwiches were available for those for whom dinner had not sufficed.

Despite the intense pleasure that the entire family derived from the sporting life at Sandringham and Balmoral, the Prince was frequently subdued and withdrawn, serious to the point of solemnity. To friends and relatives it was also clear that the Duke of Edinburgh found this demeanour irksome, a reaction which seemed only to exacerbate his

---

* The tallies varied greatly as the estate relied on wild pheasants, the numbers of which were determined by the weather conditions in the breeding season. The amount shot each season was matched strictly to the need to preserve a surplus to maintain the stock.

son's tendency to retreat from the family fray. Princess Anne, who was now the dominant sibling, seemed very obviously her father's favourite. Openly indulging her often brash and obstreperous behaviour, he was quick to rebuke his son, in public no less than in private, for inconsequential errors. Indeed, he often seemed intent not merely on correcting the Prince but even mocking him as well, so that he seemed to be foolish and tongue-tied in front of friends as well as family. To their distress and embarrassment, the small boy was frequently brought to tears by the banter to which he was subjected and to which he could find no retort. On occasion, even his closest friends found the Duke's behaviour inexplicably harsh. One remembers that after a paternal reprimand at lunch, 'the tears welled into his eyes with a whole table full of people staying there . . . And I thought how could you do that?'[5] Another, who both liked and admired the Duke 'enormously', observed the 'belittling' of the Prince and drew the conclusion that the father thought the son was 'a bit of a wimp . . . and Charles realised what his father thought, and it hurt him deeply'.[6] A close relation, who is today on intimate terms with both men, would recall 'the rough way' the father addressed the son: 'very bullying . . . which had the effect of driving Charles more and more back into his shell'.[7] According to one otherwise devoted retainer, 'Prince Philip did rather jump down his throat. Charles was frightened of him.'[8] As an adult, the Prince was to remember these moments but would balance them against other aspects of his father's character: the patience with which he taught his son to make models, the readings from Longfellow's *Hiawatha*, and the visits to meet 'characters' like the actor James Robertson Justice and the dinghy sailor Uffa Fox, all of which were to leave the abiding impression that even if his childhood had difficulties, his father was at least trying to do his best and that even if there were moments of misery at home, there was also much happiness.

Observing friends were also frustrated by the failure of the child's mother to intervene by protective word or gesture. She was not indifferent so much as detached, deciding that in domestic matters she would submit entirely to the father's will. It was the more perplexing because they otherwise had every reason to believe that both parents had a deep if inarticulate love for their son, and that this love was reciprocated. They had seen them all together shooting or fishing or out on horseback; they had watched the games they played, and they knew that both parents could be found in the nursery seeing their children to bed and reading them to sleep. So witnessing this behaviour, loyal friends drew the conclusion that Prince Philip hectored his son because it was the only means he knew to achieve his supreme objective – to mould a prince for kingship.

Others sought further explanation in Prince Philip's own background. If he was overly severe or unduly irascible, they would say, those moods were to be seen in the context of the insecurity and resentment occasioned by the savage predicaments he had been obliged to face in his past life. Debonair and incisive though he indubitably was, he had been the victim of exile and a broken marriage. His father, Prince Andrew of Greece, had been made the scapegoat for a military disaster in the Turkish war of 1920–22 and, in the year after Prince Philip's birth, was charged with treason by the 'Revolutionary Committee' which had temporarily seized power. Facing the prospect of the firing squad, he was only spared by the intervention of George V, who sent a Royal Navy gunboat to rescue him on terms agreed with the Greek insurrectionists. The military 'pardon' was couched in brutal language: accusing him of abandoning his post in the face of the enemy, it condemned him 'to perpetual banishment'.[9] The exiled Prince took his family to France, where they set up home in a small villa in St Cloud on the outskirts of Paris. While Prince Philip was still a child, his father, burdened by angry gloom, removed himself to a small flat in Monaco where his life ebbed quietly away until he died in 1944. Subsequently, his mother became ill and was obliged to retire to a sanatorium in Switzerland, only re-emerging to become a nun and to found her own religious order. A proud family that could trace its roots back to Queen Victoria was thus reduced, if not to penury, at least to severely straitened circumstances. The youngest of five children, Prince Philip was cared for by his sisters until at the age of nine he was sent to Cheam. Thereafter, he was parcelled from one relative to another until he was old enough to join the Navy. Though the family had endured acute distress with stoicism, it was widely presumed that behind a carefree but disciplined façade, there lurked in Prince Philip of Greece a young spirit in turmoil.

In 1940, after Cheam, Gordonstoun and the Royal Naval College at Dartmouth, Prince Philip, retaining his Greek nationality, joined the Royal Navy as a midshipman. Soon afterwards, he applied for naturalisation, approval for which coincided with the decision of the King, six years later, to accede to the marriage between the Greek prince and his daughter, Elizabeth. In the process of becoming an English commoner –

when it was agreed that he should take his mother's name, Mountbatten – he was required to surrender his own Greek titles. Moreover, as a member of the Greek Orthodox Church, he was required – at the insistence of the Archbishop of Canterbury – to 'have his position regularised' by being 'received formally into the Church of England'.[10] For a proud and independent man, these were assuredly not easy decisions to accept. The closest he came to a public admission of frustration at this process is to be found in the breezy words of his official biographer: 'political, constitutional, and ceremonial fuss can defeat the liveliest imagination. You pick a wife, and half the world, as of right, joins in.'[11] To make matters worse, when he re-emerged after his marriage as His Royal Highness the Duke of Edinburgh, the court treated him with an insouciance that bordered on disdain.[*] His friends also recall his further humiliation after his wife's accession in 1952 when Sir Winston Churchill and Sir Alan Lascelles,[†] the Queen's private secretary, decided between them, apparently in fulfilment of the wishes of George VI, that the Queen and her offspring should adopt the family name of Windsor. Her consort argued his patrimony should at least be acknowledged by linking his new identity formally to that of his spouse, so that their children would belong to the House of Windsor and the House of Edinburgh, but the Prime Minister was opposed and the Queen was then too young and inexperienced to demur when her private secretary endorsed the government view. It was a petty slight perhaps, but one that was bound to rankle.[‡] When the title of 'Prince' was restored to him, ten years after his marriage, his original nationality was symbolically erased altogether; as HRH Prince Philip, Duke of Edinburgh, he had been thoroughly grafted onto a branch of the British royal tree.

---

[*] More than forty years later, a guest at Balmoral in those days would remember being 'appalled' in particular by the offensive and patronising tone adopted by the King's private secretary, Sir Alan ('Tommy') Lascelles, towards his employer's son-in-law. (Confidential conversation.)

[†] Previously private secretary to King George VI, Lascelles became private secretary to the Queen on her accession to the throne. He was replaced in 1953 by Michael Adeane.

[‡] Prince Philip was particularly dismayed by the decision to incorporate Mountbatten into the family name as Mountbatten-Windsor in preference to his own wishes. His eldest son was to develop a distaste for the 'Windsor' title, which he was to regard as a pointless artifice.

In the meantime, he had also been obliged to struggle to establish himself as the Queen's consort. The court had shown little urge to release 'Philip the Greek' (as he became derided by xenophobes) from the shackles which would have doomed him to a modest place in the British hierarchy, entitled merely to follow a few paces behind his wife while she fulfilled her duties as sovereign. That he refused to accept this designated obscurity, forcing his way through the constraints of precedent and protocol to emerge as a significant public figure in his own right, was a mark of unusual tenacity. In matters of state, his wife was constitutionally obliged to heed the advice of her government ministers but she was strongly influenced by her private secretary, while her husband was excluded from her counsels and denied access to the secret government papers which occupied so many hours of her time. In creating a role for himself commensurate with his energy and talent, he was neither equable nor sensitive. He had to struggle against the weight of established opinion, and – at least in the judgement of his closest relatives – the prejudice of the British establishment against a foreign upstart from a minor royal house. If, in triumphing against these odds, he acquired a reputation for being prickly and boorish, it was perhaps not surprising; if he could be overbearing and impatient, it was perhaps inevitable; and if, as Prince Philip approached his fifth decade, the Prince of Wales had to pay the price of his father's tribulations, that too was perhaps understandable – even if it was painful at the time and, in the long term, injurious to the relationship between two strong but very different personalities.

The contrast in temperament between father and son, combined with the Queen's own absorption in her duties, meant that the Prince came to depend increasingly for intimacy both on his grandmother and on individual members of the household, among whom Mabel Anderson continued to be a source of comfort. A restraining influence on Princess Anne,* she encouraged Prince Charles to overcome his inhibitions. With Mabel Anderson he could talk unashamedly about his feelings and frustrations. She told him about her upbringing in Scotland, her family and her relations, providing him with his first anecdotal evidence of a world

---

* The Princess could be so exasperating that on one occasion at Sandringham, it is said, when she complained of feeling ill, Mabel Anderson packed her to bed, took her temperature and confirmed that the little girl should remain there, although the thermometer revealed that any fever was in the mind and not the body.

beyond the household and Cheam School. Though she was unimpeachably loyal to her employers, he knew that he could explain his confusion and resentment in the certain knowledge that she would keep those things to herself. For Prince Charles, and to a lesser extent for Princess Anne as well, Mabel Anderson remained a fount of warmth, common sense and stability.

From his grandmother, Queen Elizabeth, he learnt about the history of his own family. After breakfast he often went to her room in Sandringham, where she talked about her own childhood and upbringing. She told him about his grandfather, who had been forced to become King because of his brother's abdication – for which selfishness, knowing the strain that burdens of sovereignty would impose on her husband, Queen Elizabeth could never forgive her brother-in-law, Edward VIII. The young Prince was fascinated by her account of court life before the war, and by the history of the costumes, jewellery and paintings by which they were surrounded. She also encouraged his enthusiasm for music and painting, telling him about her early travels through Europe, which filled him with a yearning to see Italy for himself.[*] As a young child he had been taken to a children's concert at the Royal Festival Hall but neither of his parents were music lovers; it was Queen Elizabeth who took him to see the Bolshoi Ballet at Covent Garden when he was seven, a memory which remained with him, and from which he dates his own abiding passion for music.[†]

Lord Mountbatten was not yet the confidant he was to become. Distinguished in war and peace, the former Viceroy of India was now First Sea Lord, and very sure of his own opinions and importance. He was one of the few people to refer to the Queen as 'Lilibet', and he rarely

---

[*] His mother's commitment to the Commonwealth, his father's indifference, and his own ties to Sandringham and Balmoral meant that this ambition would not be fulfilled for another quarter of a century.

[†] Music was to become a constant solace. Today he carries a CD player with him wherever he goes at home and abroad. He listens to Mozart (or Haydn, Schubert, Beethoven or Wagner) in the bedroom, the bathroom, the drawing room and the study, when he is resting and when he is working. His father would find the habit impossible to understand and – as fathers will – never fails to say so. When one senior member of the household once told Prince Philip that great music invariably moved her to tears, his revealing response was to explain that it was for this reason that he never went to a concert: 'I don't want to be too moved by it.'

refrained from reminding others how close their relationship was. The royal family and the household were much in awe of him, except, that is, for Queen Elizabeth the Queen Mother, who retained a degree of scepticism about her dashing relative. His presence dominated family gatherings and, although the relationship between them was cool, he shared with Prince Philip a tendency to make Prince Charles the object of banter, and even ridicule, while he doted on Princess Anne. This did not prevent the great-nephew from admiring him to the point of hero-worship. The First Sea Lord also chose good presents. On Christmas Day 1961, the thirteen-year-old boy wrote in gratitude, 'I've heard of these DYMO label makers but I never possibly believed that anyone would give me one. I sit playing with it all day. It is fascinating . . . quite the most wonderful present I have had . . .' His father's present – an electric toothbrush – did not find such favour: 'It's like using an electric drill in one's mouth.'[12]

If shooting was the key to Sandringham, horses dominated the weekends at Windsor. The Prince was still a cautious rider, who accompanied his parents when the family rode out of the castle without great enthusiasm. In 1962, at the instigation of his father, an array of cross-country fences was constructed in the home farm, not for the Prince, who was not yet ready for such endeavours, but for Princess Anne, who was a good pupil and quite without fear. However, the new crown equerry, Lieutenant-Colonel John Miller,* who soon became an influential figure in the household, encouraged the Prince to overcome his timidity until, when his father gave him an old polo pony a few years later, he had started to ride with panache if not style.

Princess Anne, who spent many hours in the Royal Mews, was by now so absorbed by horses that she rapidly acquired the language by which equestrian enthusiasts communicate with each other and with their animals. Like her parents she did not tire of discussing the most arcane details of conformation, training, and horsemanship. For all three

---

* Lieutenant-Colonel Sir John Miller (1919–   ) was crown equerry from 1961 to 1987. With direct access to the Queen, he was not a man to cross. His colleagues remember that, as a passionate hunting man, he not only encouraged the Prince's own enthusiasm for 'the sport of kings' but vigorously defended him against senior members of the household who thought that it was bad for the royal image.

of them, often moderated by Lieutenant-Colonel Miller, the topic provided an inexhaustible source of ideas and argument. When, as often
happened, Prince Charles revealed himself to be ignorant of the finer
points of equine debate, unsure perhaps of the precise location of the fet-
lock or the exact purpose of the martingale, he was mockingly taken to
task. Sometimes in these matters – as in others – he would be put to the
test at mealtimes, an inquisition that he found so unnerving that he frequently failed the course, to the general amusement of the rest of the
gathering.

There were good times as well, and many of them. Although he was
acutely sensitive to a slight or a rebuke, the Prince also knew how to
enjoy family gatherings. With the marriage of Princess Margaret to
Antony Armstrong-Jones (who became The Earl of Snowdon the following year),* he acquired a relative by marriage who clearly thought
his enthusiasms were admirable, who took him seriously and forbore to
mock him. 'Tony', as he was always called, listened with care and
offered his own opinions and insights about art and music. They also
shared a sense of mischief which invariably lightened the atmosphere.
The Queen was immensely fond of her brother-in-law, who was witty,
entertaining, and a reliable source of jokes and laughter. Egged on by
Lord Snowdon, the Queen and her son, who shared a similar sense of
the ridiculous, would reveal a bond between them that the mother's
brisk and cool demeanour usually disguised.

At Windsor, the Prince was very much happier exploring the wonders
to be discovered in the state rooms, and especially in the library. For official visits, which always included a tour of the state rooms, it was
customary to lay out in the library a selection of treasures designed
specifically to appeal to the head of state concerned, an opportunity
which the Prince rarely missed. One damp spring afternoon, he took
himself to the library and started to rummage through the shelves with
the librarian who was delighted by his enthusiasm. Among a set of
ancient royal diaries and an intriguing assortment of books and paintings,
the Prince discovered a collection of drawings by Leonardo which held
him spellbound. At the end of the afternoon he returned to the private

---

* The Earl of Snowdon (born Antony Armstrong-Jones in 1930) married Princess
  Margaret in 1960, but the marriage, which produced a son and daughter, was dis-
  solved in 1978. He is now, as he was then, a photographer of distinction.

apartments to share his find, with such excitement that at least one member of the household who witnessed the moment never forgot it.[13] The rest of the family seemed somewhat bemused and, as so often, he felt squashed and guilty; as if by choosing the library rather than the horses he had in some indefinable way let his family down.

CHAPTER FIVE

———— ◆ ————

There was no lack of advice as to where to send Charles after Cheam. In the *Evening Standard*, the playwright and barrister John Mortimer ruminated mildly over the rival merits of his old school, Harrow, and a hypothetical grammar school. At the former, where loneliness would be complicated by 'a series of regulations evolved by Kafka', he would find compensation in the right to attend the Eton–Harrow match, 'a few stations down the Bakerloo line'; at the latter, however, he could decide for himself whether to have his jacket buttoned or unbuttoned and he would not be forbidden from meeting 'the girls from the polytechnic on the corner after the biology class'.[1]

Three years later, in the *Evening News*, the journalist Ivor Herbert made the case for his old school, Eton: '95% of the people who went there enjoyed pretty well every minute . . . and reckoned that the odd few who weren't happy there were invariably sad, uncertain creatures who were probably doomed to mope in paradise . . . It would be nice to think that any boy due for the long confinements of the throne could be as happy as we were from 13 to 18 before duty clobbers him up.'[2]

As it happened, despite the widespread assumption that the Prince would attend Eton, the die had already been cast in favour of Gordonstoun, his father's old school on the north-east coast of Scotland. As an adult, the Prince of Wales would insist that the decision to send him to Gordonstoun, which at the time he regarded as 'a prison sentence', was in fact beneficial, instilling in him the self-discipline and a

57

sense of responsibility without which he might have 'drifted'.[3] The point is arguable. What is beyond doubt is that the new boy who arrived at the start of the summer term in April 1962 was on the threshold of the most miserable few years he had yet to encounter.

The decision in favour of Gordonstoun, as with Cheam, had been carefully made and for many of the same reasons. Though the virtues of other schools were canvassed, the final decision was made by Prince Philip in his omnipotent role as paterfamilias. He believed that if his son was likely to dislike Gordonstoun, he would detest Eton, which was preferred by his grandmother but ruled out as being too close to Windsor and to Fleet Street. On the face of it, however, Gordonstoun was a strange choice. Attempting to explain the matter for his American readers, the journalist Peregrine Worsthorne wrote:

> What is unique about Eton is not the way it teaches Latin or maths but the fact that virtually all its pupils come either from the upper class or upper middle class . . . Thus the significance of the decision not to send Prince Charles there, and not to have him educated by private tutors, but to send him instead to Gordonstoun is . . . that he will be the first monarch to be educated in an institution which is fundamentally classless.[4]

Though it is true that the pupils at Gordonstoun were distinguished not by uniformity but diversity – of background, culture and nationality – they did have attributes in common. With the fees at Gordonstoun being higher than at Eton, their parents had to have the appropriate financial means, although those who could not afford the full amount were, in some cases, subsidised by those who could. They were also likely either to be resistant to the traditions of the old public schools or to believe that their offspring were ill suited to them. These factors could not of themselves secure a classless community but, as Worsthorne reflected, 'there is clearly a strong case for his not growing up exclusively in the company of an upper class which has long ceased to fulfil its proper function', particularly when social change was bound to accelerate as Britain adjusted from an Imperial to a European role.

To what extent these considerations influenced the decision has not been recorded except by the Arundel Herald of Arms (Dermot Morrah), who noted approvingly that Gordonstoun had a bias 'towards the future'.

There was an undoubted attraction for the father: as Philip of Greece, he had been happy and successful there a quarter of a century before and he was now the most distinguished old boy. What had been so good for him, he thought, could hardly hurt his son, and as the heir to the throne was of 'a shy and reticent disposition', he would surely benefit from 'something that would draw him out and develop a little more self-assertiveness in him'.[5] However well meaning the sentiment, it is hard to think of any prospect more calculated to have the opposite effect than the educational eccentricity which had been established on the shores of the Moray Firth in 1934 by a refugee from Nazi Germany, Dr Kurt Hahn.

Gordonstoun was modelled on a school which had been founded in 1919 at Salem in southern Germany by the last Chancellor of the Hohenzollern Empire, Prince Max of Baden. His injunction to the teaching staff and in particular to Kurt Hahn, his choice as headmaster, was inspired by the humiliating collapse of Germany at the end of the First World War: 'Build up the imagination of the boy of decision and the will-power of the dreamer so that in future wise men will have the nerve to lead and men of action will have the vision to imagine the con-sequences of their decisions.' In 1933, the rising level of hysteria in Germany had driven Hahn, as a Jew and an active opponent of Nazism, to go into exile. The following year he bought the lease of the 300-acre Gordonstoun estate just outside the town of Elgin, opening its forbid-ding doors to his first pupils later that year. Among them was Prince Philip of Greece, who had been his pupil at Salem.

Kurt Hahn derived his educational principles from Plato's master-piece of political and moral philosophy, *The Republic*, in which he averred that, 'There will be no end to the troubles of states, or . . . of humanity itself, till philosophers become kings in this world, or till those we now call kings and rulers truly become philosophers, and political power and philosophy thus come into the same hands.'[6] According to Plato, the only means to this end was education – education as an intellectual, moral and physical training not only of the mind but the character as well. Adapting this rubric to the confines of a fee-paying establishment, Hahn believed that it would be possible to construct an egalitarian society free of inter-nal hierarchies, except those of merit and character, wherein the common weal would be served by self-reliance and self-discipline.

By the time Prince Philip came to his decision, these guiding princi-ples had been entrusted to Robert Chew, who had taught at Salem and had risen to become headmaster at Gordonstoun on Hahn's retirement. Chew was a remote and austere character who adhered to the founder's beliefs with the conviction of a true disciple. Awkward, even gauche, in his dealings with staff and pupils, he shared Hahn's vision of a school at which the accident of financial privilege should not inhibit a commitment to social equality.

In 1934, his mentor had established a Training Plan through which his pupils would be 'bound by trust' to the Platonic ideal. To the inside of every locker there was pinned a chart, 'ruled into columns, each column a day of the week, each line marked on the left with such phrases as Teeth Brushed, Rope Climbed, Skipping, Press-Ups, Cold Shower . . . a plus or minus sign to be marked opposite each phrase'.[7] Each boy was entrusted to fill his own chart every evening. A failure to accomplish the relevant tasks was not a matter for punishment but for self-discipline: 'To fill in the chart each evening forced a boy to face facts and to face the truth. There is little point in lying if one is only lying to oneself. The Training Plan helped each boy to become self-reliant.'[8] Hahn also introduced a penalty system – which was voluntary – to reinforce the Training Plan, the principal punishment involving a solitary walk (the distance determined by the nature of the offence) before breakfast. By 1962, this elaborate structure of self-supervision was still an essential feature of the school, only modified by the recognition that self-supervision is likely to be more effective when it is itself supervised.*

The Prince's incarceration at Gordonstoun had been preceded by the familiar statement from the Queen's press secretary, enjoining the press to leave him alone: 'Her Majesty and His Royal Highness fully understand the very natural interest in the Prince of Wales's education, but they feel that he will only be able to derive full benefit from his days at school if

---

* For this account of Gordonstoun I have drawn on letters written by Prince Charles from Gordonstoun and his memories; the recollections of his friends, including Norton Knatchbull (the son of Lord Brabourne and Lady Patricia Brabourne, and grandson of Lord Mountbatten), later Lord Romsey, who was a contemporary at the school; and the reminiscences of the journalist Ross Benson and the novelist William Boyd, who were also contemporaries. Some believe that Boyd's coruscating essay, *School Ties* (Penguin, 1985), is far-fetched. However, Robert Waddell, who taught both Boyd and the Prince of Wales, confirms that Boyd's impressions mirror his own.

he is not made the centre of special attention.' On the day itself, he was delivered by Prince Philip and met by Chew, the headmaster, Captain Iain Tennant, the chairman of the board of governors (whose nearby family estate was later to offer respite from the school), the warden, and the 'guardian' (Hahn's idiosyncratic title, derived again from Plato, for the head boy). He was allocated to Windmill Lodge, one of the seven 'houses' scattered through the grounds, and his ordeal began.

Like the others, Windmill Lodge was a wooden 'prefab', acquired from the RAF as temporary accommodation but never replaced. At night he slept in a dormitory of fourteen; by day there was neither the space nor the time for privacy. In what he described as 'retrospective revulsion', the novelist William Boyd has written of 'the concrete and tile washrooms and lavatories, the pale-green dormitories with their crude wooden beds',[9] while the journalist Ross Benson would recall that the windows were 'kept open throughout the night, which meant that those closest to them were likely to wake up with blankets rain-soaked or, in winter, covered with a light sprinkling of snow'.[10] Every boy in the school was required to wear short trousers, and each day before breakfast to run through the grounds and then refresh himself under a cold shower.* However, these physical privations, by no means uncommon in the public schools of that era, were as nothing by comparison with the mental cruelty to which the Prince found himself subjected.

Despite Chew's best endeavours, 'God's purpose' at Gordonstoun had somewhere gone awry. In Boyd's account, 'We were members not so much of different houses as of different tribes . . . My house, at least when I first joined it, was very hard.' The casual brutality that erupted once his housemaster had retired for the night revealed a corruption which would have appalled the school's founding father: a gang of thugs roamed the house beating up smaller boys, extorting food and money, pilfering, and creating an atmosphere of 'genuine terror'. To deliver a message from one house to another was to cross a no-man's land into enemy territory, where the victim might expect at best humiliation by ridicule, or, quite possibly, violent physical assault.[11] Benson has written that it was the custom to greet new boys 'by taking a pair of pliers to

---

* The Prince later recalled that the boys were required to take two hot showers, each followed by a cold shower every day. He has adopted this practice, so that nowadays he always follows a daily hot bath with a cold shower.

their arms and twisting until the flesh tore open. In all houses boys were regularly trussed up in one of the wicker laundry baskets and left under the cold shower, sometimes for hours.'[12] In the face of those prospective terrors, to sweep the floors or empty the dustbins were the least of the indignities imposed by Gordonstoun's rites of passage.

In this environment, Prince Charles had to face a set of torments that were more precisely tailored to his particular predicament. His house-master Mr Whitby was an intimidating disciplinarian whose capricious temper provoked a sense of dread among the boys under his charge, including the heir to the throne, whose miseries he never began to appreciate.* He had warned the boys of Windmill Lodge that anyone caught bullying the heir to the throne would hazard immediate expul-sion. Despite – or because of – this injunction he was, according to a fellow new boy, picked upon at once, 'maliciously, cruelly, and without respite'.[13]

Each day, the boys of Windmill Lodge had to walk down to the main Gordonstoun building, a quarter of a mile away, for breakfast and then back to their house again after supper. For most boys it was a time to stroll and chatter in small and amiable groups; for Prince Charles it was a twice daily penance as, apparently cold-shouldered by his fellows, he was left to walk alone. It would have been hard enough in any case for a prince, let alone a shy and insecure prince, to befriend his peers, but to break through the barrier which the boys at Gordonstoun had immedi-ately erected around him was virtually impossible. Even to open a conversation with the heir to the throne was to court humiliation, to face the charge of 'sucking up' and to hear the collective 'slurping' noises that denoted a toady and a sycophant. Those boys who might have been compatible were in any case the least likely to thrust their attentions upon the Prince; those who did reach out could not for long withstand the accompanying taunts and jibes, while those who persisted were either too thick-skinned to care or were indeed flatterers on the make, and were thus – in either case – undesirable companions. As one of his contemporaries wrote at the time, 'How can you treat a boy as just an ordinary chap when his mother's portrait is on the coins you spend in

---

* Whitby was not only a man of erratic temper but had quaint views about educa-tion, boasting to a colleague that, as a history teacher, he had not found it necessary to open a book 'in ten years'.

the school shop, on the stamps you use to mail your letters home, when a detective trails him wherever he goes?'[14] The solitary teenager was lonely and unhappy.

A different version of the same punishment was meted out in full measure on the rugger pitch, where in the inter-house league matches it became a matter of honour for thugs to crush the Prince at every opportunity. He was not a gifted athlete so when he did get hold of the ball he was easily felled. This gave ample opportunity for the opposing forwards to lay into him with boots and fists, the better to boast afterwards, as William Boyd would remember overhearing, 'We did him over. We just punched the future King of England.'[15] The Prince bore this thuggery with stoicism, apparently nurturing no enmity, though it reinforced his abhorrence of gangs.

His letters from Gordonstoun became a form of solace, a confessional, where he could pour out his distress and confusion. Innocent and artless, they reveal in bleak monochrome the despair by which the adolescent boy was consumed and which he was far too proud – and too disciplined – to allow his fellow pupils at Windmill Lodge to witness. 'I hate coming back here and leaving everyone at home . . .' he wrote in the middle of his third term.

> Papa rushed me so much on Monday when I had to go, that I hardly had time to say goodbye to Mabel and June* properly. He kept hurrying me up all the time . . . I've been in bed for the last week suffering from a cold or 'flu, I'm not sure, but I came out on Thursday morning worst luck! It was much nicer in bed. I hardly get any sleep at the House because I snore and get hit on the head the whole time. It's absolute hell.[16]

Despite the removal of his tonsils as a small boy, he continued to have trouble with his sinuses. The infections which had worried Mabel Anderson when he was at Hill House and Cheam continued to afflict him, and at Gordonstoun he was given no quarter. In the same letter, clearly pining for home, he wrote longingly of his parents' return from an official tour to Australia, of being comforted by a telephone conversation with 'granny', and of his urge to be back with 'Mabel, June and

---

* June Waller, Mabel Anderson's assistant.

Andrew'.* 'It's a pity I can't have lessons at home again with Miss P.† Oh dear! It's Monday tomorrow. However one Monday more means one less, there are only six and a half weeks now. I hope it goes quickly . . . I don't like it much here. I simply dread going to bed as I get hit all night long . . . I can't stand being hit on the head by a pillow now.'[17]

Later the same year, he wrote in similar vein, 'It's absolute hell here most of the time and I wish I could come home,' adding the postscript, 'Please tell Mabel to send me some more Vosene as I broke the bottle the first time I used it. Tell her I'm very sorry but it slipped off the pipes in the shower room and smashed. Very silly of me.'[18]

His troubles were the worse because he had no confidant. Aside from Norton Knatchbull, who was in another year and thus a world away, and his cousins Prince Welf of Hanover and Prince Alexander of Yugoslavia, there was no-one from the families of friends and relations with whom he had been brought up and who understood each other's ways. The price of his entry into a 'classless' school was that he was suddenly cut off not only from his own family but also from the only class which he had ever known, where there was precisely that intimacy of shared values and customs which Eton possessed and Gordonstoun denied.

If there was a refuge, it was the art room. There, under the tutelage of Robert Waddell, a sympathetic teacher who was himself a scion of the upper classes,‡ he took up pottery. He soon demonstrated both dexterity and flair; if he was shy, gauche, diffident and insecure, he could work here safe in the solitude of private endeavour. As his competence – and self-confidence – grew, he began to join Waddell at the weekend to help fire the pots which he had moulded during the week. The teacher swiftly discerned that the pupil was not only lonely but miserable as well. Seeking to help, he tried to discover what was wrong; eventually, after much prompting, the truth emerged. Perhaps fearing that his tormentors would only redouble their efforts, the unhappy boy was insistent that no other member of staff should be told of the bullying; his secret should remain with Waddell and his pottery.

Waddell was in a quandary. He had no urge to violate the trust which had been placed in him but he was also distressed by what he had been

---

* Prince Andrew, who was now nearly three, and on whom his elder brother doted.
† Catherine Peebles, his tutor.
‡ Robert Waddell (1935–   ), art master at Gordonstoun 1959–89.

told. He was dismayed that the Prince's housemaster had not apparently detected any sign of trouble, but knowing the man's intemperate nature, resolved instead to pursue the issue directly with one of the Prince's persecutors, his 'dormitory leader'. Without telling the Prince, and affecting to have no knowledge of the bullying, he asked the boy to keep a special eye on the Prince, and to help him if he seemed at all miserable. This appeal to the better part of the Gordonstoun character may have had some brief impact but, if so, it did not last for very long.

Perhaps because his son had downplayed the extent of his unhappiness, the Duke of Edinburgh's reaction was to write bracing letters of admonition to the Prince in which he disguised whatever feelings he had for his predicament, urging his son instead – doubtless with the best intentions – to be strong and resourceful. This did not help.* Noticing that the Prince was withdrawn and, it seemed to him, secretive, he did not believe that it was his place to draw him out or, as he was prone to put the matter, 'to quiz' him about his life at school.

After two years at Gordonstoun, his fellow pupils had yet to show mercy:

> It's such hell here especially at night. I don't get any sleep practically at all nowadays . . . The people in my dormitory are foul. Goodness they are horrid, I don't know how anyone could be so foul. They throw slippers all night long or hit me with pillows or rush across the room and hit me as hard as they can, then beetle back again as fast as they can, waking up everyone else in the dormitory at the same time. Last night was hell, literal hell . . . I still wish I could come home. It's such a HOLE this place![19]

There was more as well. He was also mocked relentlessly about his ears, which were larger than average and somewhat protruding. It is hard to exaggerate the anguish which this minor irregularity caused him; in

---

* Although the Prince was to refer publicly to his father's attitude only once, it was a telling intervention. Asked if his father was a 'tough disciplinarian' and whether he'd ever been told 'to sit down and shut up', he answered, 'The whole time, yes,' adding, with either the benefit of hindsight or filial loyalty, 'Yes, I think he has had quite a strong influence on me, particularly in my younger days . . .' (BBC television interview with Cliff Michelmore, 26 June 1969.)

his baleful imagination, he would be made to suffer not only at Gordonstoun but – as indeed the cartoonists would confirm – for the rest of his life.* Mortified and perplexed by such pitiless and to him unfathomable barbarity, he had no defences save a stubborn refusal to complain either to the perpetrators themselves or to his housemaster. He wrote, 'People in this House are unbelievable. They have hardly any manners worth mentioning and have the foulest natures of any people I know. I don't know why people are like that.'[20]

It was a revealing reaction. The importance of 'manners' had been drilled into the Prince from his earliest days; he had been chastised for failing to say thank you, for 'pulling a face' at a Palace servant, or for dropping a piece of litter from the car window. He already knew that, as heir to the throne, he had a cardinal duty always to display 'good manners' at all times and under any provocation. As a result he was invariably polite; the only pupil, in Waddell's experience, to come up at the end of a class to thank him for a lesson, dutifully but without any trace of priggishness. He was also kind. Even as a small boy he had touched family friends with his guileless concern for others. At Balmoral, one of them noticed that in selecting a team for a game of tag he always chose first those who were least likely to secure victory for his side but most likely to be left until last. On another occasion he similarly impressed his grandmother's lady-in-waiting, Ruth Fermoy.† She had been deputed to accompany the Prince and his sister to a party some miles from Sandringham House. It had been snowing and afterwards the royal party slithered home along frozen roads until they reached the edge of the estate, when they noticed that every yard of tarmac had been thoroughly gritted. Ruth Fermoy expressed her relief but the thirteen-year-old boy retorted, 'But think of the poor workmen who've

---

* Lord Mountbatten had frequently urged the Queen and the Duke of Edinburgh to arrange for their son's ears to be 'fixed', but to no effect. Perhaps to drive the point home, Mountbatten once even told Prince Charles, 'You can't possibly be King with ears like that.' The teenager was stung by the uncharacteristically crass remark but did not press his parents to remedy a problem which was later to cause him much distress.

† Ruth, Lady Fermoy (1908–93), lady-in-waiting to Queen Elizabeth the Queen Mother from 1960; maternal grandmother of Lady Diana Spencer, later the Princess of Wales.

been out in the cold doing it.'[21] To such a gentle nature, it was beyond belief that anyone could behave with the cruel abandon of his Gordonstoun peers.

According to Adam Arnold-Brown, Prince Philip's contemporary at Gordonstoun, the pupils in those days were self-consciously upright in thought and word. Even as an eighteen-year-old, the meaning of 'two much used and much advertised four-letter words', as Arnold-Brown put it, was still unknown to him. 'The tone of the school was manly and clean . . . at Gordonstoun we were forbidden to smoke; dirty talk and actions were taboo; we had school bounds and school rules.'[22] Thirty years on, the rules were still in place but evidently to be honoured only in the breach. The bounds were ignored entirely. Smoking was *de rigueur*, likewise drinking, not least in the public houses of Elgin; 'joy-riding' in 'borrowed' cars was not exceptional and pilfering from the local shops was commonplace.

Kurt Hahn had been acutely concerned about the awakening of sexual proclivities among the pubescent teenagers under his charge. Through the regime at Gordonstoun, he sought to kindle instead 'non-poisonous passions which act as guardians during the dangerous years'. Apparently it had worked. 'There is little doubt,' Arnold-Brown declared, 'that creative activity during and after adolescence can by-pass that energy-sapping, distracting, all-powerful interest in sex which can fill the vacant mind'.[23] By the 'swinging sixties' these guardians had lost their force. There was an illicit trade in pornographic magazines, and sexual banter 'of the vilest and coarsest sort' was evidently endemic, accompanied, in the case of the 'local' girls, by 'a male lust at its most dog-like and contemptuous';[24] even sexual intercourse (between sixth formers and consenting kitchen maids) was not unknown.

There is no evidence that Prince Charles entertained any of these juvenile vices, though he had once puffed at a surreptitious cigarette in the bushes at Cheam, and may not have entirely kicked the habit. Otherwise, his letters suggest that he was dismayed by a coarseness which he had never before experienced but from which his senses recoiled: 'The language people use is horrid. I think it is probably because they're too lazy to use anything else.'[25]

It was not all misery. One of the strengths of Hahn's doctrine was the commitment to a belief that every individual has some talent which, if nurtured, might develop into a useful skill as well as boosting the self-esteem of an otherwise undistinguished adolescent. The unusually wide range of extra-curricular activities at Gordonstoun was devised for that purpose, which was why Prince Charles could spend so much time in the art room. He also took to the sea. Taught to swim at the pool in Buckingham Palace by his father, he was by now a powerful swimmer and, acquiring a life-saving certificate at the public baths in Elgin, he took his place in the school's surf-rescue unit. He was proficient in a canoe, skilled enough to paddle from Hopeman Beach to Findhorn Bay, twelve miles in a direct line, but almost double the distance allowing for wind and tide. In deteriorating weather the venture took an entire day, which was exhausting but exhilarating. He also joined the Coastguard Service and took his turn at the look-out point on the cliffs.

In his second year, he became a member of the crew of the *Pinta*, one of Gordonstoun's two ketches. On his first expedition in June 1963, he sailed into Stornoway Harbour on the Isle of Lewis. He and four other boys were given shore leave, to have supper and then see a film. His private detective, Donald Green, was with them.

As they walked towards the Crown Hotel, they attracted a small crowd. By the time they were in the lounge, the onlookers had gathered round the window. Cameras began to flash. Hopelessly self-conscious and embarrassed by the attention, the Prince retreated, 'desperately trying to look for somewhere else to go'. Followed by Donald Green, he walked straight into the public bar. 'I thought "My God! What do I do?" I looked round and everybody was looking at me. And I thought, "I must have a drink – that's what you are supposed to do in a bar." I went and sat down at the bar and the barman said, "What do you want to drink?" I thought that you had to have alcohol in a bar, so I said, "Cherry brandy." '[26] At that moment, a journalist walked in and the 'cherry brandy' incident became headline news.

Fifteen months earlier, when Colville requested a little privacy for the royal schoolboy, the newspapers had readily assented, the *Daily Mail* editorialising: 'The Queen and Prince Philip have made it known publicly that they want the heir to the throne to get a perfectly normal upbringing, unmarred by the disturbing effects of too much publicity. We agree. It is not only the wish of his parents but also of the whole nation . . . it would be the summit of stupidity if this bold and sensible policy were undermined by sensation-mongering or oppressive public curiosity.'[27]

However, the cherry brandy incident ('Charles is Ticked Off Over a Quick One' was the headline in the *Daily Mirror*[28]) was far too good a story to be spiked by a scruple. The response of the Palace, after a hurried conversation between Colville and the Prince's detective, was to issue a denial that the Prince had bought a drink or touched a drop. Two days later, when the truth refused to lie down, the *Daily Telegraph* proclaimed, 'Palace Withdraws Its Denial On Prince: He Did Buy Cherry Brandy'.[29] Blaming 'the Metropolitan Police officer with the Prince of Wales' for misleading him, Colville said, 'It is therefore regretted that the original story was denied and that newspapers were subsequently given incorrect information in answer to their inquiries.'[30]

With hindsight, the slavish attention devoted to such a trivial episode seems even more ludicrous than it was at the time. However, it was a salutary experience for the school, for the Prince, for the Palace and, not least, for the media. Once he had been detected by 'that dreadful woman', as he would later refer to the journalist, the Prince and his detective fled the bar to be hustled into a Land Rover for the journey across Scotland back to Gordonstoun, the Prince lying on the floor, covered by sacks to protect him from a posse of photographers who gave chase. Back at the school, he was sent to see his headmaster, who was unforgiving. 'I don't think [he] quite believed me. I wished he had beaten me . . . slightly sore backside for a day or two . . . but instead I was demoted.'[31] This lingering punishment – the revocation of his Junior Training Plan – caused him distress, but it was the retribution exacted against Donald Green, who was removed from royal duty by the Metropolitan Police, which the Prince would never forget. 'I have never been able to forgive them for doing that because he defended me in the most marvellous way and he was the most wonderful, loyal splendid man . . . I thought it was atrocious what they did.' Humiliated by the press, horrified by the sacking, and wounded by the headmaster, the Prince was profoundly shaken: 'I thought it was the end of the world.'[32]

It was not the first time he had been in the eye of public criticism. In itself, facing a phalanx of outraged teetotallers was little worse than having to endure a tirade from the League Against Cruel Sports, which had recently condemned him for shooting a stag, or from the minister of the Free Church of Scotland who attacked him for 'invading the Lord's Day' by skiing in the Cairngorms on the Sabbath. The latest incident, however, haunted him, fuelling his suspicion of the press. For its part, the press had been confirmed in its suspicion that the word of the Palace was not necessarily to be trusted, and in any case might usefully be ignored. The slide from deference to cynicism in the attitude of the media towards the monarchy and from suspicion to enmity in the attitude of the Prince towards the media was too gradual to locate precisely, but the cherry brandy incident was symptomatic.

Where the British media feared to tread, the foreign press went in with hobnailed boots. In those days, the British law relating to the theft of private documents still had some force. When a book of essays written by Prince Charles 'went missing' from Gordonstoun, soon to be discovered being hawked around Fleet Street, the national press treated them as stolen goods and refused to trade. Six weeks after the theft, a Scotland Yard detective traced the school book to the offices of a small publishing house in St Helens, Lancashire, where it was recovered, though not before a photocopy had found its way to the German magazine *Der Stern*, which duly published the essays in translation. Of course their provenance made these adolescent *pensées* somewhat more interesting than they would otherwise have been, but not very much so. A careful perusal revealed that he was able to précis the work of an academic historian on the 'corrupting effects of power'; that, if marooned on a desert island, he would hope to have with him a tent, a knife, and a portable radio; that he was not enamoured of a political system which encouraged the electorate to vote for the party rather than the candidate; and – most revealingly, given his recent experiences – that he believed strongly in the need for a free press to criticise and expose the abuses of government.

With no other recourse, the Queen's press secretary issued a statement declaring that it was 'highly regrettable that the private essay of a schoolboy should have been published at all in this way', an expression of dismay still enough to arrest any temptation that British editors might have had to test the Palace and the law by translating *Der Stern*'s disclosures for the benefit of their own readers. The American media was not similarly inhibited: fastening on a claim made by *Der Stern* that the Prince had sold his essays for thirty shillings because he was short of cash, a team of investigative journalists from *Time* magazine traced a number of the financial transactions apparently involved in the sale of the document to *Der Stern*, which had allegedly bought the first serial rights for £10,000. *Time* further embellished the story by alleging that the Prince had once sold his autograph to another boy when he was still at Cheam. Colville countered with a furious if impotent rebuke:

> There is no truth whatever in the story that Prince Charles sold his autograph at any time. There is also no truth whatever that he sold his composition book to a classmate. In the first place he is intelligent and old enough to realise how embarrassing this would turn out to be, and second he is only too conscious of the interest of the press in anything to do with himself and his family. The suggestion that his parents keep him so short of money that he has to find other means to raise it is also a complete invention.[33]

Except for the matter of the 'rights' of the media in relation to stolen goods – which would become ever more contentious – the ethical issues involved in the case of the missing essays were trivial by the standards of a later generation of tabloid editors. In 1964, however, it was not so hard to appreciate that the sixteen-year-old boy was cruelly embarrassed by the publication of his essays, and mortified by the suggestion that he could so easily forget himself as to barter with the accidental privilege of his birth.

At Gordonstoun, there was precious little of the spiritual peace the Prince sought. He was dismayed at the pagan atmosphere of his surroundings. 'There's hardly any religion . . . and you should see where we have to have church. It's a sort of hall which is used for films and assemblies and plays, sometimes for football or gymnastics if the weather is too foul for going outside during break. And then one is expected to worship in there. It's hopeless, there's no atmosphere of the mysterious that a church gives one . . .'[34] Brought up to honour the Established Church of which his mother was the Supreme Governor, he was already very much more serious about the Christian faith than most boys of his age. He was in preparation for confirmation under the guidance of the Dean of Windsor, Robin Woods,* assisted by the school chaplain, Philip

---

* Rt. Revd Robin Woods (1914–   ), Dean of Windsor and domestic chaplain to the Queen 1962–70; Bishop of Worcester 1970–81; Assistant Bishop, Diocese of Gloucester since 1982.

Crosfield,* who gave him private instruction in his rooms at the school. In the school holidays, the Dean would see him in his study to counsel him in the doctrine of the faith which, as heir apparent, he might one day be called upon to defend. In the spirit of the age, that doctrine was under fire not from without but from within the Church itself, where self-doubt and dissent had become the new orthodoxy. Two years before, Dr John Robinson had published *Honest to God*, in which he directly challenged some fundamental Christian precepts. In the fashionable spirit of relativism he suggested, in a chapter entitled 'The New Morality', that, 'Nothing can of itself always be labelled as wrong.' At the instigation of its vicar, Hugh Montefiore, the pews of St Mary's, Cambridge, were packed to hear Christian dissenters assert their secular credentials. At Gordonstoun itself, Prince Charles listened to a radical avowal of Christianity delivered by Mervyn Stockwood,† the Bishop of Southwark, who arrived 'wearing a purple tie instead of a dog collar and saying he was a working priest'.[35] There was no shortage of alternative ideas to stimulate the seeker after truth.

The Queen's own Christian commitment was unambiguously in the tradition of her Anglican inheritance, though her husband was less free of doubt. Prince Charles had neither the certainty of his mother nor the scepticism of his father. Though he was later to find inspiration in other religions, he was at this stage still exploring his own, curious to learn about the authority of the Bible and the origin of the gospels. He pursued these inquiries with a diligence and awareness which was to lead more than one thoughtful clergyman to discern in him an unusual, questing spirituality.

Prince Charles's confirmation itself took place in the privacy of the royal chapel at Windsor, when he was sixteen. The service was conducted by the Archbishop of Canterbury, assisted by the Dean of Windsor. Throughout, Prince Philip read quietly from a book which, in the minds of those conducting the service, was neither the Bible nor the Book of Common Prayer; which was disconcerting to both churchmen, who interpreted his behaviour as hubris.

*

---

* Philip Crosfield, chaplain at Gordonstoun School 1960–68; Vice-Provost at St Mary's Cathedral, Edinburgh 1968–70; Provost 1970–90.
† Rt Revd Mervyn Stockwood (1913–   ), vicar of the University Church, Cambridge 1955–59; Bishop of Southwark 1959–80.

As well as in pottery, the Prince found further consolation at Gordons-toun in music. The great houses in which the Prince lived as a child were usually silent. Apart from his grandmother, who had a pretty voice and could sing her way faultlessly through reams of songs that were popular in the first three decades of the century, the family betrayed little affection for classical music, though his parents were happy to encourage the Prince's enthusiasm. At Cheam he had played the piano without distinction. At Gordonstoun he attempted the trumpet. By his own account, this was even less successful. Demonstrating a gift for mimicry which he had picked up from the *Goon Show* (by which he was then infatuated), the Prince recalled his contribution to the school orchestra:

> I can hear the music teacher now. We would all be playing away and making a hell of a din, and suddenly she couldn't stand it any longer, and she would put down her violin and we would all stop and she would shout – she had a heavy German accent and somehow that made her sound more agonised – 'Ach! Zoze trumpets! Ach! Zoze trumpets! Stawp zoze trumpets!' So I gave up my trumpet.[36]

In fact, as his letters show, he played the trumpet with enough competence to perform in a public recital at Edinburgh when he was fifteen, and then in the following year in the *Messiah*. He also sang in the choir at Elgin Town Hall: 'It was a wonderful thing . . . and I'm so glad I did it. There were about 150 to 200 people in the chorus and four soloists from London who were very good. It [the *Messiah*] lasts for 2½ hours and it was unbelievably hot; I, as usual, came out looking like a beetroot. People remarked upon my condition volubly.'[37]

It was, however, the cello which really excited his commitment. Ruth Fermoy (who had herself been distinguished as a professional pianist) would recall an impromptu performance he gave at her house near Sandringham: 'He could have been a very good cellist because he's such a sensitive musician and he made a lovely sound. At the end he said, "I'm hopeless".'[38] Such self-deprecation did not spring from false modesty, but reflected a deep – and, to his friends, frustrating – feeling of inadequacy. The Prince would openly admit that he was chronically burdened by 'low self-esteem' – a condition which was eased neither by his experiences at Gordonstoun nor by the failure of his family to offer him the encouragement and praise he needed. Nevertheless, within two years he was playing in weekly concerts at the school and was soon proficient enough to play in public.

The art room and the concert hall were a refuge, but only a temporary one. Otherwise, shipwrecked by loneliness, the Prince yearned for news from home, and when members of the family were to visit him he counted the days as a marooned sailor waiting for rescue: 'I'm longing for when Mummy has the baby* and I can go down to London I hope. She said she was going to write to Mr Chew so I ought to be able to go.'[39] Soon after the birth of Prince Edward, he wrote to one of his confidantes at the Palace, the Queen's lady-in-waiting, Susan Hussey,† who had just given birth to her second child, 'I do hope your baby is very well. Does she have all sorts of things now? It's so wonderful having babies in the house again isn't it?! The only trouble is they grow up so quickly . . . It was great fun when Alexandra and Angus‡ came three weeks ago . . . Mummy and Papa came up that weekend too and it was wonderful to see them after six weeks or so.'[40]

In 1964, the atmosphere in the staff room at Gordonstoun was sharpened by the arrival of a talented and ambitious young graduate who had already secured an English doctorate. At his interview with the headmaster, Eric Anderson§ was charged with resuscitating the tradition of the school play, which had been asphyxiated by a pall of lethargy that clung about the school for more than two years. Before that, it had been a tradition to perform a Shakespeare play in the Round Square, an elegant stone and cobbled stable block which had been converted into classrooms and provided a natural outdoor 'theatre in the round'.

Anderson pinned a list to the school notice board, tendering for actors to perform in *Henry V*. Prince Charles applied and, along with many others, went for audition. That evening Anderson returned home in some consternation: there was no doubt, he told his wife Poppy, that of all those he had auditioned, 'the best reader, and I suspect possibly the best actor, is the Prince of Wales'. Partly out of self-confessed

---

* Prince Edward, born 10 March 1964.

† Lady Susan Hussey, lady-in-waiting to the Queen since 1960. Married to Marmaduke 'Dukie' Hussey, Chairman of Board of Governors of BBC 1986– .

‡ Princess Alexandra of Kent and Angus Ogilvy, who had married in 1963.

§ Eric Anderson (1936–   ), Gordonstoun master, 1964–66; headmaster Eton, 1980–1994.

cowardice – fearful that he might be thought 'keen to be noticed by royalty' – and partly because if the heir to the throne failed at the part of
Henry v it would damage his frail self-confidence, he cast the Prince as
Exeter instead. It was the custom for the good people of Morayshire to
attend these Shakespeare evenings, complete with tartan rugs and hip
flasks, appropriate accoutrements for an event they treated with due
seriousness. On this occasion, after what was widely regarded as a successful production, the gentry departed aglow with approval, making but
one persistent criticism: 'Pity your best actor was playing Exeter.'[41]

In early October of that year, Anderson, who had now begun to take
a more than passing interest in his royal student, discovered from Eric
Varley, the Prince's new detective, that in the following spring his charge
was to leave Gordonstoun for a 'sabbatical' term at a school in Australia.
Thus forewarned, Anderson persuaded the headmaster that in 1965 he
should mount a winter Shakespeare play and he asked Prince Charles if
he would play the lead. A few weeks later, the Prince wrote:

> We're doing *Macbeth* this term for the school play. Mr Anderson, the
> producer, only decided to do it after about two weeks of term, so
> we've had five weeks of rehearsal. I was asked to play Macbeth and of
> course I said 'yes'. I wasn't going to miss a chance like that. Tomorrow
> is the first performance – Thursday – and Mummy and Papa are com-
> ing to see the third one on Saturday night . . . I shall see them on
> Saturday and Sunday which is marvellous. I do hope they'll enjoy
> it . . . I've had a large number of lines to learn, but it's great fun and it
> will be VERY sad when it's all over as it will be all too quickly I'm
> afraid. The costumes are quite good and I have a splendid beard,
> moustache and bushy eyebrows, the remains of which I've been trying
> to pick out of my eyebrows and temples since lunch . . . I shall be
> quaking in my boots before I go on stage tomorrow at 8 o'clock.[42]

The play was performed indoors, in the dreaded school hall which so
lacked 'the atmosphere of the mysterious'. According to Anderson, the
Prince's performance was remarkable in insight and maturity: 'Of course,
I produced it and one has rose-tinted spectacles . . . but the play only
really works if Macbeth is a sensitive soul who is behaving in a way that
is really uncharacteristic of him because of other forces . . .'[43] The naked
sensitivity and humanity of the Prince's performance convinced not

only the producer but staff and pupils as well: 'He spoke the words beautifully. And there was something very regal about him . . . He put a cloak around his shoulders and it immediately swished most beautifully behind him as he walked.'[44] Like others who are by nature reticent and introverted, he could – on a public stage – entirely lose himself, if not in the skin of another individual, then at least in the dramatic illusions of performance.

After the weekend of the final performance, in November, he was back in the classroom, trying to succeed where he had failed so often before. 'I've got to take maths again and I shall go mad if I don't pass this time,' he wrote.[45] In all other subjects – at least set against the standards prevailing at Gordonstoun – he had no need to suffer any sense of intellectual inferiority. Nevertheless, he had always quailed at the prospect of the examination room: 'I'm jolly glad we haven't any exams this term,' he had written in 1963. 'I hate exams. I always get very nervous about them.'[46] In the summer term of 1964, he had worked hard enough at his GCE 'O' levels to pass in Latin, French, History, English language, and English literature. He wrote afterwards, 'It's such a relief not to have any more exams and tomorrow morning I'm off to Balmoral for a fishing trip until Friday which ought to be great fun and I can't wait for it . . . It will be wonderful to see everyone and to see Edward again. Mummy says he's great fun and laughs and turns over . . .'[47]

Australia was now an imminent prospect:

I'm rather looking forward to it, though one doesn't know what to expect . . . It is an awful long way away and I shall hate leaving everyone for so long, especially Edward and Mabel. I hope he isn't too big when I get back. The term begins on 1st February which gives me slightly longer holidays, although I expect I shall be going several days earlier. I also hope to see something of Australia before I come back.[48]

It was the first time in his life that he had voiced any optimism – however cautiously – about the unknown.

CHAPTER
SIX

————————

Thursday December 2nd [1965]

Dear Charles,

I thought you would like to know how the plans for Australia are progressing and how very pleased I and my family are to be going with you. I think we will have lots of fun and am doing my utmost to ensure that we do . . .

You are probably, and quite naturally, apprehensive about going to Australia and if I can be of any help with any doubts or fears you might have please let me know. I give you my word that they will go no further than me . . .

I couldn't be more delighted to be going with you and sincerely hope you will feel free to ask me any questions and for any advice or help, which, unless you wish otherwise, will remain purely between us.

Yours sincerely,

David.[1]

Squadron Leader David Checketts* was then equerry to the Duke of Edinburgh, who had selected him to accompany his son to Australia in the unofficial role of private secretary and adviser. The decision that Prince Charles would benefit from the experience of Australia had been taken by Prince Philip in consultation with Sir Robert Menzies, the Prime Minister of Australia, who was a fierce anglophile and monarchist, and who relished the prospect of the heir to the Australian Crown having a taste of Commonwealth education. The two men had debated the matter while the Australian leader had stayed as a guest of the Queen at Balmoral in the autumn of 1965. Sir Robert recommended the Geelong Church of England Grammar School in Victoria. Arrangements were made for Thomas Garnett, the headmaster, to come to England, where Prince Philip spoke to him at great length about his son.

It is clear that the Duke had finally divined that Prince Charles had not responded to the spirit of Gordonstoun. 'The contrast between their son's naturally introspective temperament and the determinedly outward-looking ideals promulgated by Kurt Hahn,' Morrah wrote, '. . . was driving him still further in upon himself.'[2] In temperament and outlook, the contrast between the father and son was indeed vivid. From the intimate perspective of a Palace courtier, the Duke was in those days 'an impatient man of action', the Prince 'a romantic dreamer'.[3] To his father's disappointment, his son had failed to show any interest in scientific subjects. Instead of excelling at team sports, the Prince preferred to wander in the grandeur of the Morayshire countryside, contemplative among the rocks and pools, utterly absorbed by the natural world.

Garnett recommended that Prince Charles should be sent to Timbertop, an outback offshoot of the main school, 100 miles to the north-east of Melbourne in the foothills of the Great Dividing Range, where all Geelong boys spent some part of their schooling. According to the school prospectus, the purpose of Timbertop was to 'develop initiative and self-reliance'. When this prospect was presented to the Prince he did not demur, but his compliance was cautious. He was anxious not to find himself in an Australian version of Gordonstoun, and worried too about

---

* Sir David Checketts (1930–   ), flying training, Rhodesia 1948–50; 14 Squadron, Germany 1950–54; instructor, Fighter Weapons School 1954–57; Air ADC to C-in-C Malta 1958–59; equerry to Duke of Edinburgh 1961–66, to Prince of Wales 1967–70; private secretary to Prince of Wales 1970–79.

the social isolation that he might face in such a remote area. Checketts moved to reassure him, explaining that Timbertop had:

> achieved the untrue aura of being a sort of cross between Gordonstoun and Atlantic College* with the accent on physical education. In fact during the week you will receive as good, if not better, tuition, in your particular subjects for 'A' levels with boys of your own age, and only at the weekends are you expected to take part in camping expeditions in the 'bush' . . . I shall stay with you at Timbertop until both you and I are certain that you have settled in.[4]

As ever, the Queen and Prince Philip were determined that the Prince be treated as 'normally' as possible. To this end they insisted that his time in Australia should be treated as a private visit and not as an official tour. This royal wish raised matters of diplomacy and protocol of a kind with which the Prince would become ever more intimately acquainted. In this case, the issue was what, if any, formal duties were to be required of him in Australia before his admission to Timbertop. In a sharp exchange of letters between Buckingham Palace and Government House in Canberra, the latter insisted that the Prince should not enrol at Timbertop before an official meeting with the governor and the premier of the state of Victoria in Melbourne. 'He is the Heir to the Throne, he is 17 and what is more natural and proper than for him to do this before he becomes a school boy so to speak in Victoria.'[5]

The implied rebuke – that the people of Australia would, not unnaturally, be dismayed and offended if he failed to follow the suggested protocol – was discussed in London but rejected. Even so, it took an emphatic reminder from the Palace that the Queen and the Duke of Edinburgh were adamant about the question before Canberra finally yielded.

Behind the divisive complexities of royal protocol there lurked a no less awkward matter. The Palace was only too aware that, smarting from his experiences at Gordonstoun, the Prince's attitude to Australia would be, in the words of the Queen's assistant press secretary, 'very largely

---

* The international school founded in 1962. Its establishment led to the formation of the United World Colleges movement, of which Mountbatten became president in 1968, succeeded by the Prince of Wales in 1978.

determined by the success, or otherwise, of our joint attempts to get press and public to recognise the essential distinction between official and private, and not to make him an object of such unremitting attention as will render his life intolerable.'[6] Unless Government House was able to win over the Australian press and thereby (it was hoped) the public as well, an 'interesting experiment' would fail. Yet the officials in Canberra were already aware that Australian curiosity about the heir to *their* throne would be intense.

To reconcile the protection of the Prince with a widespread and legitimate public interest required a fine balance of judgement. Any attempt to exclude the press altogether would be not only ineffective but certain to offend a prickly corps of journalists, a potent consideration at a time when some sentiment in favour of a republic was already stirring below the surface.* It was resolved therefore to allow the media a number of 'photo opportunities' (though that troublesome phrase had yet to be coined) during the Prince's first week, in the hope that he would be left alone for the rest of his stay. Checketts wrote to the Prince accordingly: 'Inevitably, the first few days will be full of attention by the Press and the Public. In fact certain facilities are being made for them to cover as much in the first week as they should need throughout the whole stay. Bear with this and you have a great chance of then being left alone to thoroughly enjoy all that Australia has to offer.'[7]

In Australia, no fewer than 320 representatives of the media were waiting to cover his arrival. No other member of the royal family had ever been required to face such a barrage at such a tender age. His grandparents' generation had been brought up at a time when international communications depended on the telegram and the envelope; his mother had been shielded from intrusive scrutiny even when, at the age of ten, she unexpectedly became the heiress presumptive. Prince Charles was not only in direct line of succession from birth, he was also a child of the revolution in mass communications through which, by the

---

* Senior officials in the Australian government were already sensitive to the 'faintly anti-monarchical, anti-British policy' of the Murdoch press in Australia. On 21 November 1965, the *Sunday Citizen* had reported that, 'A powerful new voice has been added to the growing body of Australian opinion which favours loosening the traditional ties with Britain. It comes from the *Australian*, the country's first national newspaper.'

mid-sixties, the old deference had started to disappear. In Canberra, wilting officials in Government House were caught between exhilaration and frustration, one of them writing drily, 'People keep telling me that this visit of Prince Charles is unofficial and private. All I can say is that I would far rather organise a full scale highly official visit by a couple of Kings and Queens!'[8]

When the plane touched down in Australia on a sullen and humid morning, the Prince disembarked in trepidation to greet the welcoming party, which included the Governor-General and the Prime Minister. 'I was getting nervous by the time I got off the plane at Sydney, having been kept on the plane for five or ten minutes watching the goings on outside and people being lined up at the foot of the steps. However I did nothing as foolish as to fall down the steps and land on my face at the bottom,' he wrote to his great-uncle. 'I'm dreading the day when I do that!'[9] Unaware of the contretemps between London and Canberra which had preceded his arrival, the greeting accorded him 'appeared to be almost like a State Visit. No doubt it's good practice.'[10]

The party then flew in the Governor-General's Viscount to Canberra, where it was raining. 'Touchingly', there were 'some sodden brave people who had come to wave. On the way to Government House there were also several people by the car who waved and all seemed to be happy and kind.'[11] Apart from his trip to Malta as a five-year-old and a brief skiing holiday in Switzerland, this was his first overseas visit; the discovery that people would come out into the rain to greet him was disconcerting but heart-warming. Still awkward in public and reserved in private, the Prince of Wales was on the verge of discovering that despite his low self-esteem he mattered to other people and, even more important, they might like him as well.

Checketts' characterisation of Timbertop somewhat glossed over the reality: in fact, it had been established precisely according to Hahnian principles, and as a 'colony in the wilds' the regime was designed to be tougher than that of its Scottish forebear. Its founder, Dr Darling, the former headmaster of Geelong Grammar School, had been greatly impressed by Gordonstoun, and Timbertop was his attempt to graft the Germanic principles adapted from the Platonic ideal onto the Australian outback. He used to refer to the year that his adolescent pupils spent at Timbertop as 'the spotty year', an appropriate moment for fourteen- and fifteen-year-olds to discover the delights and responsibilities of 'self-reliance'. At Timbertop, they fended for themselves, preparing their own food, cutting trees from the forest for heating and undertaking arduous expeditions into the hills which surrounded the school. What little academic work they did was lightly supervised by a skeleton staff of masters from Geelong.

As befitted his age, the Prince had joined the small group of older boys who were put in charge of the nine 'huts' which between them accommodated about 140 'spotty year' juniors. The Prince, in the role of a quasi-NCO, had charge of three of these compounds, a total of forty-five boys. 'To begin with,' he wrote to Mountbatten, 'it was all a bit bewildering and until one gets to know masters and boys things all always seem to be a bit difficult. I'm not good at going to any school at the beginning of term and this was no exception!'[12] He was allocated to a 'flat', which he shared with another boy of his own age, Stuart McGregor, who had been carefully selected by the headmaster to keep him company. McGregor was evidently a clever choice because for the first time the Prince was able to set up an immediate, if superficial, rapport with a fellow pupil. They shared a kitchen, a bathroom, a bedroom and a study: 'I was amazed by the rooms we have here,' he wrote. He was cautiously relieved that some of the other boys were 'really quite nice', though 'of course, there are always those who make life difficult and get into groups. At the moment a large majority are overawed but it won't last for long.' He found that the masters were friendly and, in particular, that the chaplain, like Stuart McGregor, was 'good to talk to'. In addition, there was 'a beautiful chapel', which was made of wood 'in the shape of a very steep roof going right down to the ground with a window behind the altar reaching also to the ground with a lovely view over the treetops and hills'.[13]

For the first week, Checketts was still at hand to help oversee the pre-arranged photo opportunities and to secure a gentle immersion, reassuring the staff that when the Queen said that her son should be treated as any other pupil she did indeed mean it. By the time he and the media had departed, the Prince was already discovering – for the first time – that school could be enjoyed. For the first time, he was not stricken by homesickness. Though he thought about his parents, he did not pine for home as he had throughout his first four years at Gordonstoun. At Timbertop even his complaints, which at Gordonstoun had been bitter with pain, were laced with a modicum of self-confidence and perhaps insulated by a sense of his new responsibilities:

> Yesterday we all staggered up Mount Timbertop behind the school. It was very steep and very hot and very thick in places. Coming down was even worse and I think I had blisters on both my big toes. On Friday we also did a cross-country run which nearly killed me. We have to do two a week and then an expedition each weekend for four weeks, and then it's not compulsory . . . In a short time I shall have to go and chop logs and see that no-one cuts off their toes or someone else's head![14]

The following month, he wrote to Mountbatten:

> we have to do two cross-country's a week and this week has been doubly ghastly due to the heat . . . One certainly drinks a lot any-way! . . . So far I've been on three weekend expeditions, which get longer and longer and more and more blistering. After the last one my feet had monumental blisters all over them. I must have looked a pretty hopeless sight hobbling down the road to school clutching a large stick to support me.[15]

Six weeks later, he walked seventy miles through the hills in three days. By day, he broiled under the sun; by night he shivered in a damp sleeping bag. 'It was absolutely freezing and after shivering compulsively all night I woke up to find ice on the tent which was like cardboard.' On the final day he walked for thirty miles and, 'having stopped at the top of the last hill to wait for the others, I could hardly move at all as my joints had all stiffened up. I don't think I've ever been so glad to get back to school! There's one good thing about an expedition and that is it makes you appreciate all the small things like a bath or shower and a lovely bed and clean clothes.'[16]

The other boys were studying – intermittently – for Australian exam-inations; the Prince was working – no less intermittently – for 'A' levels in French and History. Unsupervised except by an occasional visit by a master from Geelong, who had been detailed to act as his supervisor, he was trusted, in conformity with the commitment to self-reliance, to tutor himself. It was not always easy, especially when the temperature hovered in the nineties Fahrenheit: 'I'm not used to it so I find myself sweating quite a bit. It's very difficult sometimes to force oneself to work on a hot afternoon and I can never concentrate. I always seem to drowse.'[17]* Even when he was fully awake he found it more congenial to remove himself to a nearby stream to fish for trout – 'So far I have caught one trout big enough to keep . . . I use a dry fly most of the time which seems to be very effective in the small pool'[18] – than to complete an essay.

After his first month, he was allowed to leave the school at the weekend to stay with the Checketts family who had set up residence on a small farm in the village of Coldstream just outside the market town of Lillydale, some 120 miles away. With David and Leila Checketts and their three children he could wander freely in the streets of Lillydale, fish in nearby rivers or build barbecues in the garden. There he established a relationship with the Squadron Leader which was to flourish for more than a decade. Checketts was a bluff, direct and quietly extrovert individual who was sensitive to the very different character of the adolescent he served. On his first afternoon at Devon Farm, the Prince and Checketts were experimenting with a boomerang; on his first throw, Prince Charles hit himself over the head, slipped and fell into a cow pat, at which – to Checketts' delight – he collapsed in howling laughter. Naturally reticent, the Prince had already discovered in himself an outlet, through mimicry, for his unusually well-developed sense of the absurd. At ease in the Checketts household, and stimulated by an offhand remark or a remembered incident (usually involving pompous or deferential grandees), he would assume the role of a Goon, mimicking Spike Milligan or Harry Secombe with well-honed precision. 'Sometimes we were reduced to dribbling hysterics,' Checketts remembered. 'We were literally helpless with laughter.'[19] The Prince of Wales would later discover that the mere hint of a joke from his lips was prone to convulse most listeners with sycophantic delight; the Squadron Leader was by no means a sycophant (indeed as their relationship grew they were to have

---

* He eventually overcame this propensity. As an adult, whenever possible, he would choose to work in the hottest sun, lying in bathing trunks, surrounded by official documents and correspondence, to prepare speeches or write letters. To the dismay of his personal physicians he refused to wear a hat or to apply 'sunblock', saying, 'Don't worry, I'm protected by my Greek blood.'

frequent, and occasionally fierce, disagreements), and at Devon Farm the laughter was genuine. Perhaps because of the distance from Britain, Prince Charles came to regard the Checketts household as his home and Checketts as a surrogate elder brother, and there formed an uncompli- cated bond of affection between the worldly-wise equerry and the perceptive but naive seventeen-year-old. Checketts was touched by the tenderness with which Prince Charles treated his young children, play- ing with them in the garden, reading with them, laughing with them and wiping away their tears. On one occasion, the mother and father were woken in the night by their son Simon, who had a severe attack of croup. They rushed to his bedroom to find Prince Charles already there, sitting the child upright, comforting him and patting his back. It was a small incident but one that stayed with Checketts as a reminder, during later bouts of mutual frustration, that the Prince was unusually gentle and kind. The Prince also spent time in the kitchen discovering from Leila Checketts how to make bread-and-butter pudding (a recipe which he later claimed as his own), and with both of them he sat in his pyjamas and dressing gown watching a Channel 9 mini-series starring Gregory Peck.

His Australian programme had presupposed that he would spend two terms at Timbertop but his parents, mindful of his diffidence, had decided that he should decide for himself whether to stay the course or return to Britain after one term. In fact, he had already made up his mind within six weeks of being in Australia. A key consideration in his decision to stay on was the prospect of joining the school trip to Papua New Guinea, led by his history tutor Michael Persse. The Prince wrote in excited anticipation:

> When we get to New Guinea we have a long launch trip round the coast and arrive at a place called Dogura* where there is a cathedral which the Papuans have built. I believe it's huge and rather lovely. I don't think it has any pews so you sit cross-legged or stand on the con- crete floor. I'll probably get piles or something ghastly like that! . . . Apparently there are huge mosquitos up there and some of them carry

---

* The head-station of the Anglican Mission on Goodenough Bay near the eastern tip of Papua.

malaria so I shall have to smother myself in mosquito repellant and nets. I'm already taking malaria pills but no doubt I'll come back all yellow and shrivelled up with skin like parchment![20]

For several days in the village of Wadua, which adjoined the Anglican mission at Dogura, the drums had been beating in anticipation of the royal visit. On the night before the school party was due to arrive, one of the missionaries, who had been chosen to join the welcoming party, recorded that 'the drums went on right through the night'.

As the launch carrying the school party approached Wadua, the Prince and his companions could see a great crowd lined up on the beach, Papuans and Australians, some in clerical garb, some in school uniforms, others in grass skirts and feathered headdresses, one of his companions wrote. 'There was an absolute silence as the boat drew to the wharf. As the boat came in we drew away from the Prince so that the people could see him. He was dressed in a yellow open-necked shirt and khaki bombay shorts. Then suddenly the crowd saw and recognised the Prince and there was a mighty shout of "Egaulau" (the Wedau word for greeting).'[21] It was the Prince's first experience of such a ritual but, in the complete absence of journalists, he seemed much more relaxed, much less on show, able more freely to explore, to look and to listen.

The cathedral did not disappoint him. The boy who had been dismayed by the absence of 'mystery' in the chapel services at Gordonstoun was much taken by the relish with which the communicants worshipped at Dogura: 'Everyone was so eager to take part in the services, and the singing was almost deafening. One felt it might almost be the original Church. Where Christianity is new, it must be much easier to enter into the whole spirit of it wholeheartedly, and it is rather wonderful to go somewhere where this strikes you.'[22] According to the Dean of Windsor, as retold by Morrah, the experience of worship at Dogura marked 'the most formative period of his spiritual development'. If so, it was the evidence of transcendent faith among 'primitive' peoples rather than, as Morrah suggests, 'the Church of England really at work in its missions' which moved the Prince.[23] He was as much intrigued by 'several cases of faith-healing at Dogura amongst a people who had their roots in spirit life and in the power of the witch doctor – which perhaps make it more natural for them to believe so sincerely . . .'[24] as by the sight of so many converts taking the Anglican communion. The experience of Dogura suggests that, as the Defender of the Faith 'apparent', his religious curiosity was already ranging beyond the confines of the tradition into which he had been born.

He was intrigued by the folk art of the Papuan people and disturbed that the younger generation were allowing traditions – which were, he wrote, 'an essential part of a nation's life' – to wither. 'I can't help feeling that less and less interest is being taken by the younger Papuans in the customs and skills of their parents and grandparents because they feel they have to live up to European standards and that these things belong to the past and have no relevance to the present or future . . .'[25] The embryo anthropologist was content merely to observe in detail the rites and rhythms of a Papuan welcome. He feasted, he danced, he threw spears, he walked freely through the community, and – in a way that would have seemed inconceivable six months earlier – he shared openly in a popular festival, betraying none of that self-consciousness which hitherto had blighted his public appearances.

His four days at the Dogura mission left a powerful impression on at least one of the Anglican sisters, who wrote, without thought of publication and with no need to flatter:

We loved his natural goodness, his thoughtfulness for others, and he was so very interested in many things; and he has a wonderful smile which resembles that of his mother . . . In any company he is outstanding. It was grand to see him walking around Dogura – walking alone with no gaping crowds waiting for him . . . I do not suppose there are many opportunities for such times in his life. One of the ordinands, when taking prayers before lessons the other morning, gave thanks for the Prince's visit and then went on to give thanks for the one who had come amongst them as if in a cage and how before their eyes he had become free.[26]

If great efforts were made to give the impression that his Australian interlude had been spontaneous, the truth was otherwise. Even before he left London, the Palace and Checketts had drawn up a provisional itinerary for him covering the first few months at Timbertop. It had included – among other engagements – dates for film shows, sheep-shearing, bird-watching, polo matches, an art gallery, water-skiing, chopping wood for war widows, gold panning, mustering cattle, the expedition to Papua New Guinea, prospecting for precious stones, lunching at Government House and finally departing Australia for Mexico City – more than fifty engagements in addition to his weekly routine at Timbertop. Although almost all of these were private occasions, it was inconceivable that any of them should be left to chance or to whim. Even the vacation on which he and Checketts now set out had been meticulously planned and organised in advance. When the Prince was presented with the proposed itinerary he was – not surprisingly – enthusiastic. 'We can go to the barrier reef for the day and go deep sea fishing and water skiing on other days,' he wrote. 'I think it should be great fun. I'm also going to a cattle station in Queensland for a few days where I think I should be able to go out on horseback and round up semi-wild cattle probably . . . I may even get some surfing in somewhere if I'm lucky, which will be wonderful.'[27] Such unrestrained enthusiasm, even for what would be for others of his age an enviable opportunity, was quite new, and telling evidence that at last he was feeling at least some of that self-confidence which his father had been so determined to instil.

Despite every precaution, the press was again in attendance: 'the usual business of binoculars on the house, telephoto lenses and chase cars, and although we managed to evade them on the first morning they had caught up with us in a few hours' as Checketts described the intrusion. Summoning the media to a parley, he explained that if they insisted on following every move the Prince made, it would ruin the holiday. 'To my absolute amazement they all agreed that, if they were allowed an occasional photograph, they would leave Charles entirely alone. They stuck to this . . .'[28]

The Prince returned to Timbertop for the two months of the winter term, where instead of teaching fly-fishing he acted as a ski instructor. Then, at the end of July, he made his farewells and returned to London at the end of his first officially unofficial trip overseas. Checketts has since been quoted as saying, 'I went out with a boy and came back with a man.'[28] The words oversimplify and exaggerate but there was an important kernel of truth in the observation. Those around the royal family who were close to the Prince remember that he looked more mature and that the chubby clumsiness seemed to have left him; he was leaner, more alert, more active, less easily cowed. When he ventured an opinion, he was still diffident, but more as though he was weighing the balance of argument rather than doubting his right to address it. He was more disciplined, more apt to think for himself. Part of this change was in the nature of adolescence, but some element of it lay in the opportunity he had been given in Australia to find himself – free of Gordonstoun, away from his parents, away from the British press, away from the suffocating certainties of royal life.

In a statement which he had drafted but was read out to the media on his behalf by Checketts – the Prince had yet to speak for himself in public – he thanked the Australian people for 'a marvellous and worthwhile experience' and for their 'kindness'. He promised to return as soon as possible, saying, 'I am very sad to be leaving.'[29] There is no doubt that he spoke from the heart.

The return to Gordonstoun after Australia in the autumn of 1966 was filled with the usual foreboding. As a small boy he had imagined himself running away, escaping to the mountain of Lochnagar that loomed over the Balmoral estate and hiding in a secret cavern. On the day of departure, members of the household would glimpse him sitting on the lawn at Balmoral, clasping his labrador for comfort. Even as he approached his eighteenth birthday, he found it impossible to shake off the despair, knowing that once back at Gordonstoun he would return to that isolation imposed on him by birth and character.

But this term, after the misery of the first few days, he adjusted more easily to the Gordonstoun regime than he had found possible before the Australian experience. Working his way up through the arcane system of preferment established by Kurt Hahn, he had been a 'colour bearer' (prefect) and a 'helper' (head of house). Now, to his mother's evident surprise,* Robert Chew appointed him head boy – or 'guardian' to use the Platonic ascription. His precise qualifications for the task were not divulged and the decision provoked a predictably cynical response. Indeed, even in a system so self-consciously egalitarian, it would have seemed invidious for a future King of England (the first heir to the throne to be thus exposed) to be considered lacking in the right stuff for the task of leadership. Yet the headmaster's decision, however it was influenced, was justifiable. The Prince was not in the heroic mould still favoured by public school romantics, and he lacked the physical grace or

---

* Morrah's authorised account suggests that the Queen was uncertain whether Prince Charles had the qualifications to become a 'helper'.

the sporting prowess in which leadership potential was so often, wrongly, discerned; nevertheless, he had now acquired a range of experience that his peers lacked. He had demonstrated self-reliance; he was modestly competent in a number of skills and he excelled at one or two. Moreover he was kind and sympathetic. As the principal intermediary between staff and pupils at Gordonstoun, he was well equipped to humanise the prevailing culture and to moderate some of its barbarities, if not by fiat then at least by example: 'I don't know that I'm doing my job very well as it is a rather vaguely defined one,' he wrote to Mountbatten, 'but I hope I shall get into the hang of it though as term goes on . . . I've come to the conclusion that I'm not very good at organising people.'[30]

He had already been put to the test in the previous term as 'helper' at Windmill Lodge. Someone had come to him to report a rumour that two members of the house had been responsible for a spate of local burglaries. 'They had been out at some unearthly hours in the morning at various stages in the term and had broken into cigarette machines and had shop-lifted and so on. To cap it all they had to go and burgle a village shop of a large quantity of cigarettes, which consequently left the old lady in charge of it in a state of shock . . .'[31] The Prince summoned one of the suspected offenders to an interview which took place in the presence of his accuser. At first, the suspect:

blindly swore he hadn't done anything. He kept on contradicting himself and if I'd been doing it alone I'm afraid I'd probably have believed what he said because, apart from the fact that I find it very difficult to believe that anyone would lie to such an extent, the only evidence I had was articles from his locker and various tools which he carefully told good stories about.

Innocently credulous, the Prince was not disabused until 'new thefts kept appearing and the whole thing was like an idiotic farce'. Despite the lies and contradictions he wanted to save both miscreants and tried to 'talk some sense' into them, but 'I don't think it even went in one ear'. Despite this, he interceded on their behalf with the headmaster, pleading that although their offences were grave, the boys themselves were not beyond redemption. But Chew was adamant and both boys were expelled, to the distress of Prince Charles who judged the decision to be an abdication of responsibility. 'I'm sorry to bore you with these stupid stories,' he wrote to his great-uncle, 'but I thought you might like to know. I've certainly learnt something from this incident.'[32]

As school guardian, the Prince was for the first time spared the worst indignities of communal living, with his own study-bedroom in the Round Square adjoining the flat occupied by his art teacher, Robert Waddell. The two of them spent long hours in each other's company. Waddell was an aesthete, cultivated and bookish. Without any such stimulation at home, the Prince was still on the cultural nursery slopes. Except for set texts, his appetite for literature had yet to graduate far beyond John Buchan and Sherlock Holmes, while his knowledge of painting and sculpture was limited to the pleasure he took in looking at the priceless works of art in the official residences at Buckingham Palace and Windsor. He had yet to set foot in Europe (except to ski in Switzerland) and the great works of European art, the palaces, cathedrals, sculptures and paintings, were virtually unknown to him. Now, with Waddell's quiet encouragement, he began to explore this new world, and to look behind the surface pleasure of art towards its inner meaning.

His dexterity with the potter's wheel had also developed. According to Waddell, 'He really did some seriously good stuff. A lot was of professional standard . . . you'd be glad to buy it in a shop.' He specialised in creating zany mugs in the shape of animals complete with legs, horns, tails and eyes. Sometimes a horn was crumpled, a tail was twisted or an eye would squint ghoulishly. The end result – deliberately – 'was straight out of a Giles cartoon or Thelwell. It sounds juvenile but they were actually very clever and quite hard to do.'[33] Whether they appreciated them or not, various members of his family received these grotesqueries as Christmas presents for several years in a row.

The sense of the absurd which inspired these creative flippancies appealed to his art master as much as it had convulsed Checketts. The two men were very different in character but each succumbed – without fawning – to the *farceur* buried just beneath the surface of a solemn Prince. The 'full blossoming of this wonderful wit and mimicry' led to bouts of goonery between teacher and pupil, which left each of them 'on the floor, absolutely rolling with tears streaming down your cheeks . . . Thank God for it.'[34]

Waddell belonged to that social milieu which gave him access to every grand house in the region. At weekends, he and the Prince would sometimes find themselves together in the same house for Sunday lunch.

On one occasion, the Prince was persuaded to take his cello and, with Waddell playing the piano, they performed before the other guests, including the hostess's mother, a woman of over ninety who snored gently in the corner. They had not rehearsed and both had a sense of lurking disaster. Nevertheless, they started off *con brio*, Waddell recalls:

> The noise was beyond belief. Terrifying. And then suddenly Prince Charles stopped. I stopped. And we looked at each other. He said 'I'm there.' I said 'I'm here.' We were playing from two different pages, two totally different pieces of music. The labrador and the poodles looked stunned. The old lady was snoring louder than the cello. The other guests were trying to look as if it was wonderful. We had hysterics.[35]

His enthusiasm for music was greater than ever. In February 1967, he was to take part in a recital at St Giles Cathedral in Edinburgh:

> I shall play the cello in about two things, including I hope the Sixth Movement from Handel's Water Music which is such bliss to play on a cello, 'tho rather fast. I'm also supposed to play the trumpet and sing, so I shall have to be carried home! All the same I adore it and wouldn't miss it for anything. At least it's something which gives me great enjoyment and also relaxation, which I feel is really quite important. It's a misery having to sit down at a desk all day and you can't even play it!![36]

At the start of his final term − 'it was pretty good hell coming back here again, especially as it was snowing when I arrived and is still revolting weather. I'm still trying to forget about home . . .' − he comforted himself with the prospect of singing in the Bach *B Minor Mass*, 'which is incredibly difficult in places. It requires immense concentration as it goes so fast but I expect it will be yet another wonderful experience to sing in a large and semi-professional choir.'[37]

There was another recompense as well. As guardian, the Prince was at liberty to forgo lunch in the school hall. Waddell's bachelor flat at Gordonstoun had no kitchen, so he secreted a portable electric stove in a cupboard in his sitting room, where together he and Prince Charles prepared omelettes and ate strawberries and cream to the accompaniment of Vivaldi or Mozart, interspersed with recordings of the Goons. The Prince's own study was often filled with wild azaleas and sweet peas that he had picked himself.

To his art master, who had watched the Prince from his very first day at Gordonstoun, he was still very different from the other boys of his generation. Not only were his aesthetic antennae more alert than theirs but, despite the gaucherie and self-doubt, he preferred always to converse as an adult, talking about music and painting, history and archaeology, with a curiosity born of imagination and commitment. Where they were rowdy in adolescent groups, rough in behaviour, and crude in language, he was invariably gentle and courteous, always a little apart. It was as if his youth had passed him by on the other side: then he was still a child and now he was almost an adult.

Such maturity did not absolve him from the anxious business of taking his 'A' levels in July 1967. As soon as they were over, he reflected on the pressure they had put on him: 'It's amazing how tired one can get just through revising and sitting exams . . . I tend to get into a feverish sort of panic before and sometimes during an examination, but I can't always think or write straight and say what I wanted to say. I thought I was going steadily berserk the other day because I had the feeling that I was writing on a mirror and my pen was being held from the other side of the paper! It was a most curious sensation.'[38]

He was the first heir to the throne to expose himself to so open a test of academic ability, and his reward was a B in history, and a C in French; in addition he took a special paper in history in which, according to the secretary of the Oxford and Cambridge Schools Examination Board, he 'shone'. The Board secretary declared publicly that the Prince's performance 'was extraordinary, especially when you consider he was digging about in Australia and that kind of thing. He has so many things to do, he must have worked like a demon.' The special paper was designed to identify 'high-flyers' in respect of 'judgement, initiative, and historical acumen. If a boy has done well in this paper . . . it is a very good guide to university.'[39] Even allowing for a touch of hyberbole it was a significant achievement to be among the top six per cent of 4,000 candidates in that paper.

Before the end of his final term at Gordonstoun, the school guardian had one last responsibility: 'There is a dance here in a fortnight's time which fills me with horror as I have to arrange most of it. The idea is so awful as thirty girls are being transported from an Aberdeen school to provide material for dancing. I shall do my best not to dance or become involved but will no doubt be required to search every nook and cranny for enterprising dancers.'[40] As it was, this annual ritual passed off without trouble: 'They were pretty hardy lasses with an equally hardy bespectacled mistress in charge of them. I danced with quite a lot of them and in the end there was only one left without a partner – and so was I, so all was well for the last five minutes. Fortunately nothing ghastly happened and I wasn't head-hunted!'[41]

As the date of his release approached, the Prince could hardly bear the waiting. Enduring that claustrophobia which eventually afflicts even those who have relished their school years, he longed to be free of the atmosphere, of the people, and of the place. Late in July, on the last weekend of term, his parents arrived to make their formal farewells. 'I expect that day will be pretty average misery with over a thousand people and all sorts of press tottering about . . .' the Prince reflected morosely, but after that endurance test, another party for the staff, and yet another 'for all the local people who have been most kind to me while I've been up here',[42] he was finally able to depart for Balmoral. After six years, Prince Charles left Gordonstoun for the last time without even a twinge of regret.

PART II

———◆———

For, though I speak it to you, I think the king is but a
man, as I am: the violet smells to him as it doth to me;
the element shows to him as it doth to me; all his senses
have but human conditions: his ceremonies laid by, in his
nakedness he appears but a man . . .

William Shakespeare, *Henry V*, IV.i

CHAPTER
SEVEN

———— •— ————

By 1967, the world beyond the isolated confines of Gordonstoun was in the throes of a social upheaval of seismic proportions from which, perforce, the Prince had been entirely insulated. The New Elizabethan age, that phrase with which romancers had crowned the accession of the Prince's mother, had failed to materialise. Britain had groped obediently through the fifties in search of a role that fitted the lingering aspirations of the first generation of post-war leaders. Unable to reconcile himself to Britain's shrunken status, Sir Anthony Eden, who had inherited Sir Winston Churchill's mantle but was endowed with more vanity than wisdom, led the nation into the débâcle of Suez, a humiliation which finally put paid to Britain's imperial pretensions, destroyed the political consensus, split his own party, and – its only virtue – accelerated an internal review of Britain's place in the world which at last began to reflect the realities of dwindling power. Domestically, the economic imperatives of relative decline came to shape the character and the language of political discourse. By the sixties, repeated promises that sustained economic recovery would not only put the nation back together again but would also restore the country to its rightful place at the top of the economic league of developed nations no longer carried conviction. Indeed, the evidence to the contrary was remorseless. The pervasive symbol of this debilitating truth was the state of the pound, whose chronic ill-health was now monitored with all the attention that a cardiac specialist might lavish on a distinguished but ailing patient. Failing to secure the confidence of international investors, Britain slipped into that baleful economic cycle which was characterised by the phrase 'stop-go'.

Whether this demoralising condition was the consequence of a necessary war, or of the terminal decay of imperial power (or both), or whether it was to be located in the rust of a social structure so antiquated that a pervasive stand-off between management and workers was known as 'industrial relations', it bore within it the seeds of a collective sense of cynicism and alienation.

Ground between memories of the past and aspirations for the future, Britain in the sixties looked back nostalgically and forward with anxiety. There had been an Empire, now there was the 'special relationship', and ahead there was only Europe – a fall from grace no less traumatic for the fact that the leading economic power therein was the very state that had been the cause of the Second World War, while the most influential political power had only been liberated from collaborative occupation because Britain had 'stood alone'. Yet Germany and France seemed already to belong to the future, while Britain trembled on the brink, in a state of flux and uncertainty. By the opening of the decade, Harold Macmillan, who had discerned the 'winds of change' that not only blew across Africa but gusted through Britain as well, had already hastened to dismantle the old Empire's lingering presence in that continent. Yet when he tried to shuffle a dubious nation into its European destiny, he was rebuffed from entry into the European Economic Community by General de Gaulle, whose veto postponed the inevitable by almost a decade. In that limbo, Britain made the most of an umbilical link with the United States which rested less on mutual affection (however genuine) than on Washington's military commitment to a strategic role in Western Europe countering that of the Soviet Union in the East. Despite the posturing, the experience of post-imperialism – more advice than consent – was far from agreeable. The prevailing sense of Britain's dilemma was captured with exquisite precision by the playwright Alan Bennett in Forty Years On: 'To Let. A valuable site at the crossroads of the world. At present on offer to European clients. Outlying portions of the estate already disposed of to sitting tenants. Of some historic and period interest. Some alterations and improvements necessary.'[1]

On the eve of the decade, Macmillan had told the voters that 'most of our people have never had it so good'. He spoke no less than the truth (the majority *did* have more disposable income than ever before) but the phrase was to haunt him because he missed the more important point that, true or false, it jarred with the national mood. By the time of Macmillan's departure and certainly after it when, following Sir Alec Douglas-Home's brief interregnum, a Labour government under Harold Wilson held power, any expression of complacency from above was resented by those below.

The institutions which still incubated the mores and customs of the old order came under intense bombardment, not only from without but more especially from within. 'Custom and ceremony' – where the new iconoclasts believed outmoded principles of conduct and belief to be embalmed – fell into disrepute; tradition and order, the twin pillars of established authority, were scorned. The deference once owed to Parliament, the Church and the Law yielded to an attitude of suspicion and cynicism. Even the monarchy was not exempt.

The death of the old order took symbolic form in the funeral of Sir Winston Churchill. On a cold January morning in 1965, the representatives of more than a hundred nations arrived in London to pay their homage: monarchs and presidents, generals and politicians, old men in mourning not only for the greatest among them but for the age to which they had also belonged. Afterwards, as if summoned to the Last Post of the British Empire, they stood in silence on the steps of St Paul's while the funeral cortege rumbled out of sight. The nation grieved as well. More than 300,000 people filed by his coffin at the lying in state, twenty million watched the pageant of death on television, and, so rapidly had the technology of the new order developed, a further 350 million people were able to witness the obsequies 'live' by satellite.

In the 'global village', television was not only the conduit for shared memories but for the new fashions and values which swept Western Europe and North America. In culture and politics, television relayed the message back and forth that a new generation had arrived which owed little to the past and was contemptuous of the present. 'Liberation' was the word: in matters of taste, dress, attitude and behaviour. The new medium had the power not only to reflect the anarchic simplicities of the new order but to invest them with transcendent authority. For the sixties generation the 'Theatre of the Absurd' and the 'Theatre of Cruelty' were not simply experiments by avant-garde dramatists but reflections of the world as witnessed on television – in Vietnam or Biafra or

Czechoslovakia or South Africa. Disillusioned by images of present wars and the promise of future conflict, despairing of a world in which babies starved and nuclear weapons proliferated, where impersonal technologies were deified and utilitarian certainties held sway, the 'baby-boom' generation had come of age and did not care for it at all. Better off and better educated they may have been, but they were in revolt against the future their parents had bequeathed them. Across the western world, linked by the ubiquitous medium of television, at rock festivals and on the streets, 'flower-power' hedonists inspired by the melancholia of Bob Dylan vied with pedlars of Marxist elixirs who chanted the battle hymn of safe revolt, 'Ho, Ho, Ho Chi Minh, we shall fight, and we shall win.'

Students across the western world became inflamed by a passion for revolution. Nineteen sixty-eight was the year of the Tet offensive, the Soviet invasion of Czechoslovakia, the murder of Robert Kennedy, and a Democratic Convention memorable for violence and tear-gas. In revolt against the carnage of the Vietnam War, students in the United States fought the police and the National Guard. Shaken by demonstrations and strikes, France was on the verge of that insurrection which became known as 'les événements'. In Britain itself, scores of thousands of students converged on Grosvenor Square chanting anti-American slogans, and calling for the overthrow of capitalism. University buildings were occupied in a show of revolt against 'the system'; in public meetings and private seminars across the country young people vowed that the revolution was at hand and that the working class was about to inherit the earth. In all this fervour there was much froth, delusion and vanity but, even so, the mood of defiance shaped and sharpened the political dialectic of an entire generation.

Of course, they did not lack apostles in the generation that preceded them. Indeed, the 'permissive society' was not made by them but for them – by a host of writers, artists, lawyers and university professors who still nurtured the iconoclasm which had been suppressed in their own generation. In the arts, in music and drama, new sounds and new forms sprang into being, while official censorship of books and the theatre was ridiculed towards oblivion. The unofficial guardians of beauty and good taste were trampled in the rush to be overt and explicit – or merely different. The new arbiters had no taboos and little restraint.

Despite the iconoclasm, the sparse evidence of the opinion polls indicated that the proportion of the British people favouring a republic in

1970 was – at 10 per cent – the same as it had been in 1960;[2] yet neither the institution of the monarchy nor the royal family was any longer immune from critical or sometimes hostile commentary. Though the tabloid floodgates had yet to open, a trickle of grievance was permitted to percolate into circulation. Oddly, the first to venture on this course, even before the opening of the decade, was a young peer of the realm, called Lord Altrincham, who owned and edited an obscure monthly magazine called the *National and English Review*. Writing as a self-declared monarchist, Altrincham caused an outrage by describing the Queen's speaking style as 'a pain in the neck' while 'the personality conveyed by the utterances which are put into her mouth is that of a priggish schoolgirl, captain of the hockey team, a prefect and a recent candidate for Confirmation'.[3] Well aware that his remarks 'may have struck some readers as intolerably disrespectful', even he could not have expected the torrent of outrage provoked by this act of lese-majesty. Condemned by *The Times*, denounced by the Archbishop of Canterbury, and struck in the face by an elderly man in Kingsway,* Altrincham was unrepentant, believing that the furore over a few phrases had obscured his overall purpose, which was to warn against complacency. 'Many influential people, of varying political opinions, are able to combine a high regard for the Royal Family with a fundamental scepticism as to the viability of the institution,' he wrote, adding, 'When she has lost the bloom of youth the Queen's reputation will depend, far more than it does now, upon her personality. It will not then be enough for her to go through the motions . . . As yet there is little sign that such a personality is emerging.' Arguing that it was not enough to have 'dignity, a sense of duty, and (so far as one can judge) goodness of heart', he urged the reform of her court which had 'lamentably failed to move with the times'. This 'tight little enclave' of the British upper crust needed a leavening of other classes and nationalities, gradually making the institution 'more catholic and more representative' and thus ensuring the 'sturdy, not servile, loyalty' of her subjects.[4]

---

* In sentencing Altrincham's attacker for a breach of the Queen's peace, the Chief Metropolitan Magistrate, Sir Laurence Dunne, stated, 'I suppose ninety-five per cent of the population of this country were disgusted and offended by what was written . . .' He was wrong. Although initial reaction was universally hostile, a 'nation-wide poll of public opinion' in the *Daily Mail* revealed that 35 per cent of respondents agreed with the sentiments expressed by Altrincham.

It was quite true that the court was drawn exclusively from the upper classes, and particularly from those of a landowning or military background. Although there were exceptions, the image, as Altrincham correctly observed, was 'tweedy'. Shrewd and broad-minded they might have been, but 'of the people' they were not. As inhabitants of the closed world of Buckingham Palace, they were more inclined to venture forth to White's and the Guards Club, and, at weekends, to the grander retreats of rural England than to visit the pub or watch a football match. Following Altrincham's intervention, the presentation parties at Buckingham Palace, when the Queen welcomed the annual crop of debutantes to tea in the royal gardens, were dropped from the season's fatuities, but little else appeared to change. The 'tweedy' advisers remained and the stately progress of the royal year was not apparently impeded by the sounds of crumbling masonry in the world beyond their gilded cage.

In broadcasting at least, a sense of decorum still prevailed. Although Altrincham's commentary ricocheted around the world, the BBC did not see fit to question him about it and when another journalist of somewhat greater renown entered the fray, the BBC promptly banned him from the airwaves – principally for savaging the Corporation's own coverage of the monarchy. Fastidious of intellect and waspish in style, Malcolm Muggeridge described the BBC as 'that serene temple of contemporary orthodoxy' and complained that when dealing with the royal family 'the voices of its announcers and commentators become hushed and reverent. The whole atmosphere suddenly changes, as when, at a church social, in the midst of festivities, a word of prayer is offered.'[5] Muggeridge, like Altrincham, had a point of substance to make. The royal family, he detected, had begun to constitute 'a kind of royal soap opera', and he commented presciently on 'the difficulty of striking a balance between a soap opera and dignity, of keeping the Monarchy both popular and respected'.[6]

While the prevailing coverage in the media was still adulatory, Altrincham and Muggeridge could be dismissed as eccentrics, but the more thoughtful members of the royal household were already aware that the warnings should not be ignored. Although the dilemma posed was easier to state than to resolve, it would have to be addressed if the monarchy was to flourish amid the turmoil of the forces unleashed by the sixties revolution. The task was not merely to reconcile 'mystery' with 'popularity', to remain remote and yet cosy, it was also to define the function of the monarchy (and the role of the royal family within it) and to clarify its purpose in a democracy of 'meritocrats' and egalitarians. This would require flair as well as intelligence; originality as well as a sense of history; curiosity about the nature of the tribe, its rituals and its icons, as well as an appreciation of the constitution; a knowledge of the media that went beyond the 'photocall'; and a recognition that the immanence of the institution could not be sustained merely by the rules of precedence and the traditional rites of passage, though both of these still mattered.

It was not at all clear that the court at Buckingham Palace was blessed with such qualities.

On 22 December 1965, the Queen had arranged a dinner party at Buckingham Palace. The guests included the Prime Minister, Harold Wilson; the Archbishop of Canterbury, Michael Ramsey; the Chief of the Defence Staff, Lord Mountbatten; the Dean of Windsor, Robin Woods; and Sir Charles Wilson, then Principal and Vice-Chancellor of Glasgow University and Chairman of the Committee of Vice-Chancellors. After dinner, at her request, they formed an *ad hoc* committee under the chairmanship of the Duke of Edinburgh to discuss the further education of the Prince of Wales. According to the Arundel Herald of Arms, the Queen listened but did not intervene in their discussion.[7] By convention – endorsed by both the Duke of Edinburgh and Mountbatten – the Prince of Wales would have to enter one or more of the armed services. The issue was whether he should also go to university, and if so which should have precedence, military service or higher education. He would not be the first Prince of Wales to attend university. In dilettante fashion Edward VII had been to three universities; Edward VIII had been to Oxford; and, when there was no expectation that he would later be King, the Prince's grandfather, George VI, had attended Cambridge. According to one of the participants, the Prime Minister spoke strongly in favour of Oxford, the Archbishop argued for Cambridge and – with the dogmatism for which he was renowned – Mountbatten urged that he should be sent directly to the Royal Naval College, Dartmouth.

The committee eventually concluded that the Prince should first attend a university and afterwards enter one or more of the services.

However, the rival graduates of the competing universities could not agree on which should be chosen. The Prince – almost en route for Australia – was informed of their conclusions and, without giving the matter great thought, acquiesced in the broad contours of a future others were devising on his behalf.

It was not until the autumn of 1966, some nine months later, that a decision was finally made in favour of Cambridge. From the Prince's point of view, Cambridge had the advantage of being not far from Sandringham; beyond that, he had no firm view on the matter except that under no circumstances did he wish to attend one of the 'redbrick universities'. The decisive influence was almost certainly that of Robin Woods, the Dean of Windsor, on whom the Prince as well as the Queen and Prince Philip – neither of whom had any experience of university – placed great reliance.

Once the decision had been taken, the Queen dispatched the Dean to sound out six colleges: King's, Magdalene, Selwyn, Corpus Christi, Churchill and Trinity. After visiting all of them, Woods swiftly concluded that his *alma mater*, Trinity, had advantages that the others could not possibly match: it was much larger than the others and in its Master, the former Conservative minister Lord Butler,* the college was blessed with an *homme d'affaires* who would be in an unrivalled position to ensure that the heir to the throne made the best possible use of his time at Cambridge. The heads of all six colleges had been sworn to secrecy but – with his customary guile – Butler lobbied with discreet fervour in favour of Trinity, pressing his suit with, among others, Mountbatten, the royal family's *éminence grise*.

It had not been easy to square the Prime Minister. Harold Wilson did not easily yield the case for Oxford, where he had been such a distinguished student almost thirty years earlier. In the end, Woods was required by the Queen's private secretary to draw up a carefully argued document in favour of Cambridge which was then sent to 10 Downing Street. At this confirmation of the Queen's will, the Prime Minister gave Cambridge his blessing, prompting Mountbatten to write to his great-nephew

---

* Richard Austen Butler (1902–82), Conservative Chancellor of the Exchequer 1951–55; Home Secretary 1957–62; Foreign Secretary 1963–64; Master of Trinity College, Cambridge 1965–78. 'Rab', as he was popularly known, was described by admirers as 'the greatest PM we never had'.

welcoming 'the glad news that it has definitely been agreed now by all concerned that you will go to Trinity . . . I know that you hoped this was going to come about . . . I feel that I must write and congratulate you.'[8]

The decision posed a host of dilemmas for Trinity, no less than the Palace. What should the Prince study? Where should he live? How should his detective be housed? Should he have a car at his disposal? What clubs should he join? Who should be responsible for his welfare? Where should he eat? Each question led to another and then to another until the college and the Palace were immersed in an intricate and elaborate process of consultation which lasted for nine months. Nothing was left to chance. On 4 January, accompanied by the Duke of Edinburgh and the Dean of Windsor, Prince Charles visited the college for the first time. While the Dean kept his father occupied with a tour of the area, the Prince was taken to meet the Dean of Chapel, the Revd Harry Williams,* and Dr Robert Robson, a history fellow, both of whom were to exert much influence over his undergraduate life. He also discussed the academic possibilities with Dr Denis Marrian, the senior tutor. The following day, Dr Marrian wrote to Checketts proposing the establishment of a small committee, including the Master, to consider the best course of study for the royal student and, in particular, whether he should take an established degree course or undertake a range of studies fitting his peculiar needs, which would also excuse him from taking a final degree with the attendant – and possibly adverse – publicity that would ensue.

After intense discussion between the Duke of Edinburgh, Woods, Butler, and the relevant scholars at Cambridge, it was resolved – somewhat vaguely – that the Prince should undertake a course tailored to the particular needs of his role as heir to the throne that would take in anthropology and archaeology but would also include history, economics, constitutional law and a modern language. In late February 1967, the Dean went to Gordonstoun to put this proposal to the Prince, who made it very clear that it was not at all to his taste and that he knew precisely the course of study he wished to pursue. Almost three months earlier he had written, 'I'm very pleased that I'm going as there's so much more I'd like to learn about and pursue further, especially in the field of archaeology.'[9] By February, the Prince was even more determined. The

---

* Harry Williams (1919–), chaplain and tutor of Westcott House, Cambridge 1948–51; fellow of Trinity College, Cambridge 1951–69; Dean of Chapel 1958–69.

Dean accommodated him accordingly. 'I think it is a very good thing that he has such a defined interest in Archaeology and Anthropology,' he wrote to Butler. 'I found him reading *African Genesis** and he makes a really academic pursuit of these matters, and enjoys having conversation about them.' The Dean added that the Prince had also insisted that he wished to take a full one-year Tripos, 'qualifying for a part-degree entirely on his own abilities'.[10] Thus the matter was settled.

Denis Marrian, the senior tutor, was anxious that the Prince should make the most of his time at Trinity, and not spend too much of it poring over his books alone in his rooms. 'As I said to him yesterday . . . it seems to me to be vitally important that he has plenty of time available to make friends with his contemporaries and to spend time doing what every other undergraduate does. It seemed clear from my short talk with him that he will want to go to concerts and possibly play some music and visit art galleries as well as take some exercise . . .'[11] Checketts, who had been kept informed of these deliberations, and knew his charge, commented, 'Whatever else happens, he must finish University with some sort of qualification, other than having thoroughly enjoyed himself.'[12]

In a vain attempt at anonymity, Prince Charles arrived at Trinity College at the start of the autumn term in a Mini Minor. From that perspective, his view of the welcoming party at the gates of the college was somewhat distorted:

> All that could be seen were serried ranks of variously trousered legs, from which I had to distinguish those of the Master and the Senior Tutor . . . Perhaps the most vivid and memorable moment of arrival was when several burly, bowler-hatted gentlemen proceeded to drag shut those magnificent wooden gates to prevent the crowd from following in – it was like a scene from the French Revolution.[13]

As usual, the Palace had prepared a detailed plan to accommodate the needs of the media. William Heseltine,† the Queen's assistant press

---

* The influential anthropological study be Robert Ardrey.

† Sir William Heseltine (1930–   ), born Freemantle, W. Australia. Assistant information officer to the Queen 1960–61; assistant press officer to the Queen 1965–67; press secretary 1968–72; assistant private secretary to the Queen 1972–77; deputy private secretary 1977–86; private secretary 1986–90.

secretary, proposed five photo opportunities in various parts of the college and an informal meeting with the representatives of the national press based in Cambridge, who 'seemed a reasonable group of people, very anxious not to make a nuisance of themselves'.[14] The Prince agreed to the cameras but at fewer locations, writing, 'I am reasonably prepared for half an hour of hell',[15] but he baulked at Heseltine's latter suggestion: 'This does appear somewhat risky,' he insisted, 'and is perhaps best forgotten about.'[16] He also refused to wear the college gown that the Palace had urged on him for one of the photographs.

Behind this suspicion of the media, another factor was at play. Hitherto, the Prince had invariably followed the guidance of his advisers. Now, he began to demonstrate a reluctance to submit automatically to the 'advice' tendered by officials on the assumption of his compliance: long accustomed to assume his consent, the Palace was disconcerted by the evidence that its charge had a mind of his own. Adjusting to the implications of this was not easy for either the Prince or the officials. As he struggled to assert his own identity against their received wisdom, he could appear truculent and testy but at least at Cambridge he was able to mature in an atmosphere that was quite free of the proprietorial certainties of the Queen's court.

To satisfy the needs of the media, it was arranged that the Dean of Windsor's elder son, Robert Woods, who was already a student at Trinity, should escort him around the college for the benefit of the cameras. Together, they moved from location to location accompanied by a respectful 'pool' of four reporters, three television crews, and six photographers who watched him receive the keys to the college, admire a view, visit a reading room, and pose beneath a stained-glass window in the Hall, which contained the coats of arms of some of his forebears. This task accomplished, he retired to his rooms in the corner of New Court.

The Palace was sensitive to any suggestion that the Prince would be given special privileges, a concern that Butler shared and for which he was not slow to take some credit. Recalling that some of the Prince's forebears had 'lived out of town in mansions with their own staffs, and the college tutors came to them', the ever-communicative Master of Trinity insisted that, 'We were absolutely determined that Prince Charles was going to live in college and share as far as possible in the everyday life of the ordinary undergraduate.'[17] A room was provided for the Prince's detective, and the college suggested this be prepared 'a few months before Prince Charles sets up residence . . . otherwise we anticipate tiresome inquiries, indicating that the heir to the throne is occupying double accommodation which is preventing other students entering the College.'[18] In August, the Queen had taken the unusual decision to view his prospective quarters for herself. Following her visit – which went entirely undetected – the college redecorated the walls of his sitting room, provided a socket for a shaver in the bathroom (which had been installed in the Prince's staircase despite earlier protestations from the Palace), and an electrical point for a Belling stove (which was to be supplied by the Prince himself). Although a standard set of college furniture was made available, it was agreed that the Palace would provide a new carpet, curtains, and an eiderdown.

It was unusual for a Trinity 'fresher' to have the privilege of a set of rooms to himself. In addition, he was provided with his own telephone and a security cabinet for his mail, while his detective was to look after his laundry – a precaution against the theft of his underclothes by trophy hunters.

Unlike other students, he was not entirely free to follow every youthful whim: he was carefully watched and invariably accompanied – albeit with practised discretion – by his detective. Nor was he able to be carefree about joining college societies. Without the Prince's knowledge, his tutor drew up a list of 'sensitive' organisations that were effectively proscribed, including – among others – Amnesty International, the Buddhist Society, the Fabian Society, The Heretics, the Marxist Society, and the Society for Anglo-Chinese Understanding, the Conservative Association and the Labour Club. To become a member of any one of these societies would risk courting opprobrium or trespassing inadvertently into political activism.

At first, he moved with exceptional caution, finding his way into a new world with diffidence. He took breakfast by himself, and then, like other undergraduates, walked to the archaeology and anthropology lecture theatres. By contrast with Gordonstoun, he was not alone on these occasions. Edward Woods, the Dean of Windsor's second son, who was in the same year to read for the same Tripos, had also been spirited into rooms across the courtyard, which he shared with his cousin James Buxton; these two formed a nucleus of undergraduates that gradually developed into a circle of intimates around the Prince, accompanying

ıckingham Palace, December 1948: Princess Elizabeth, King George VI and ıeen Mary at the christening of the Prince

The Prince with his mother, 1949

The Prince with the Queen Mother,
October 1950

Princess Anne, the Queen, the Prince and the Duke of Edinburgh at Clarence House in the summer of 1951

The Prince with King George VI Buckingham Palace, 1951

The Prince with his nurse Helen Lightbody in St James's Park, 1951

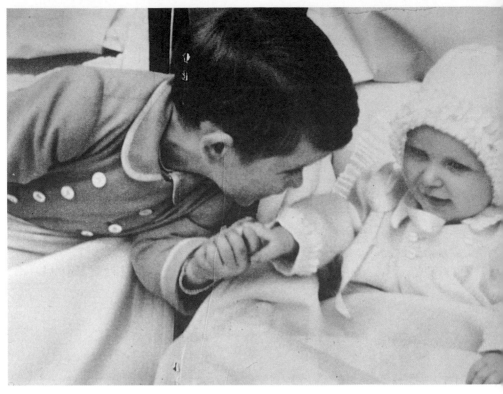

The Prince and Princess Anne, 1951

The Queen Mother explains the
Coronation ceremony to the Prince,
Westminster Abbey, June 1953

With Lord Mountbatten, Malta, April 1954

aboard HMY *Britannia* with Princess Anne, in the care of two yachtsmen, Gibraltar, May 1954

t a meet of the West Norfolk Hunt, June 1955

The Prince arriving at Hill House
after the Easter holidays, May 1957

Returning to Cheam School
after church, July 1958

The Prince with the Duke of Edinburgh and headmaster Robert Chew at the start of his first term at Gordonstoun, May 1962

The Prince with his roommate Stuart McGregor, Timbertop, Australia, February 1966

The Prince at Cambridge, 1968

In the language laboratory during a Welsh lesson at University College, Aberystwyth, April 1969

Riding in the grounds of Windsor Castle with Princess Anne, 1968

him to lectures and to lunch in the Hall, sharing dinner with him in their rooms, going to cinemas and concerts.

The Prince's choice of friends did not entirely find favour with Lord Butler, who later told the journalist Ann Leslie that 'rather regrettably' his 'cronies tended to be conventional huntin' and shootin' Army types from public schools'.[19] Butler's proprietorial attitude towards him irritated the Prince. Later, when he read the Master's indiscretions to Leslie, he commented, 'Most of what Rab Butler says is preposterous and a reflection of some curious desire to be seen as my constitutional and philosophical tutor without whom I would still be a semi-moron.'[20] Long after he had left Cambridge, any reference to the Master of Trinity as his 'mentor', 'guru' or '*éminence grise*' was guaranteed to infuriate him.

Underlying his irritation at the Master's presumption was a deeper resentment which sprang from his very first dinner party at the Master's lodge. Anxious to make the evening a success, Mollie Butler had invited her husband's research assistant, Lucia Santa Cruz, the daughter of the Chilean ambassador and his wife, who were old friends of the Butlers. In an affectionate memoir of her husband, Mollie Butler wrote that Lucia was 'a most charming and accomplished girl' whom she was confident would find favour with Prince Charles. Her judgement was astute and the two students soon formed a friendship that was to last several years, and which was close enough for Mollie Butler to comment that it was a 'happy example of someone on whom he could safely cut his teeth, if I may put it thus'.[21] She was reminiscing some eighteen years later, but her husband was rather less discreet, intimating even at the time and with less equivocation that – among his many other contributions to the Prince's education – he had facilitated a liaison in the course of which the young South American had instructed an innocent Prince in the consummation of physical love. Whatever the truth, the Prince could not abide either the general presumption or the particular breach of trust.

In his strictures about the Prince's limited circle of friends, Butler failed to appreciate that the royal undergraduate found it exceptionally difficult to reach out beyond the safety of his own circle. Chronically self-conscious, he found communal gatherings in the absence of 'his cronies' acutely embarrassing: there would always be a space around him caused by a peculiar reluctance to engage the Prince of Wales in conversation, to stand by him in a queue, or take the empty seat at his side. If he wanted to communicate across that void between the monarchy and its subjects, he had always to make the first move, but to make contact with his fellow undergraduates required an effort of will that he could not yet achieve. The Prince was only too aware of this failure and – characteristically – blamed himself: 'I've been ruminating that I am a "single" person that prefers to be alone and is happy just with hills or trees as companions so that when I come here and try to go around with people it is a pretence and the awful thing is that I feel they can feel it. However, I must try to improve myself.'[22]

His demeanour and appearance were not calculated to encourage mateyness. According to one of his circle, 'He was unbelievably straitlaced. He was always dressed in corduroys and rather well-polished, rather heavy shoes and heavy jackets. He was very much reserved and never let down his guard.'[23] Another found that there was 'a sort of maturity about him, a different stamp on him . . . much more sensitive, much more sensible, much more cultured and cultivated than the average person'.[24] If this too kept others at a distance, there were one or two who lacked inhibition, who had the chutzpah needed to work their way into his company.

Such encounters were generally unproductive, but in one case led to an unlikely friendship. Hywel Jones was a scholarship boy from Wales, an amateur rock musician, and a promising economist. Early in the first week, the two undergraduates met on the staircase below Prince Charles's rooms. Over a mug of coffee they shared the confidence that, from their very different perspectives, they had both found the idea of university an exciting but daunting prospect. The Prince asked about the Welshman's background in the valleys, and they began to talk about politics. Jones was a socialist, the first with whom the heir to the throne had yet had any significant contact. According to the Prince, they used to talk about all manner of issues until 'very late into the night'. In Jones's memory they discussed, among other subjects, Britain's economic decline, the competing ideologies of the political parties, and the Vietnam war. On one occasion the Prince came into Jones's room and noticed on his mantelpiece membership cards for both the Conservative Association and the Labour Club, as well as the Marxist Society (or 'the mad leftists' as Jones called them). The Prince was bemused: 'Why all of them?' he asked. Jones explained that this was the only way to attend all their meetings.[25] Well aware that he had to avoid any suggestion of political bias but anxious to share in the debate, the Prince, according to

Jones, decided to seek out Butler for advice. Were he to follow the example set by Jones, would any potential allegations of bias cancel one another out, he wondered? After some thought, the Master gave his verdict that the risk was too great to chance. The Prince was compliant.

Although he was intrigued by Jones, the relationship was not as close as the latter allowed himself to believe. Even within his own circle, to which Jones did not belong, the camaraderie was neither intense nor enduring. With the exception of James Buxton, with whom the Prince shared an empathy of outlook and spirit, he was united to the rest of the group more by a commonality of background and upbringing than by any stronger bonds of affection; even the ties of childhood with Edward Woods failed to blossom into a deeper friendship. They played occasional games of squash or tennis (though the Prince had little aptitude or enthusiasm for either) and they dined together, but even these were neither intimate nor memorable occasions. They drank and (with the exception of the Prince) smoked, and there was casual discourse, especially about their common interests in hunting and shooting, but they rarely strayed beyond that comfortable territory. To varying degrees, all of them were inhibited both by the introspection of the Prince in their midst, and by their lack of curiosity about the world beyond the familiar confines of their own exclusive society.

At weekends during the season, it became the Prince's habit to invite his friends to shoot with him at Sandringham. It was often a last-minute invitation on Friday: 'I'm going to shoot tomorrow. Would you like to join me?' When they arrived, the day was immaculately organised, with an ample supply of beaters and keepers for the handful of 'guns' that the Prince had invited. At Sandringham, 'you really had the crème de la crème of wild birds. They are beautifully driven. Everything is perfect. Serious shooting,' one of the group recalled.[26] The Prince was keener on the sport than ever. Hardly a weekend passed without a shoot on one of the large estates which delighted to satisfy this great enthusiasm.

According to Hugh van Cutsem, a landowner and sportsman who had become a close friend, the Prince was already a fine shot, with the timing, grace and co-ordination which – for the committed – can transform a slaughter into a sport. His own delight in his prowess shines through many of the letters that he wrote in this period. 'I can't tell you to what extent I enjoyed it, especially as all those pheasants flew so well and were so exciting. Thank you very much,' he wrote to van Cutsem after one outing.[27] In a later letter, he confessed, 'Any excuse to escape from Cambridge and plod across ploughed fields instead of stagnating in lecture rooms is enormously welcome.'[28] He also enjoyed waiting in the wind and the rain of a late afternoon to down wood pigeons flying in to roost: 'What happened yesterday was very nearly the stuff of which dreams are made and as I've never got over 25 in an evening flight my day was completely made . . .'[29]

The hearty fellow who strides through the pages of those and similar letters was in such contrast to the troubled and sensitive spirit who roamed about so much of his adolescent correspondence that it was tempting to think that the Prince had slithered out of the skin of boyhood to adopt a quite different identity as a young man. In reality, these were but two facets of the same character, caught in different moods and framed from a different perspective. Had his passion been for cricket or rugby or even golf, this appearance of contradiction might have aroused no comment. It was the fact that his passions involved death – death for the bird, for the fox, for the stag and for the fish – which brought the apparent contradiction so sharply into focus. For many people, unused to country pursuits, it was not easy to understand, especially when their judgement was clouded by a vague resentment against the 'landed gentry' of whose hospitality the Prince so readily availed himself. A decade later, the Prince would himself recoil from the easy carnage of the organised shoot. Even so, he was always able to reconcile his love for the natural world, and the quest for spiritual redemption which would increasingly preoccupy him, with his enthusiasm for the field sports in which he continued to participate despite the adverse judgement of lobbyists, who became especially vociferous when he took up hunting.

Indeed, the revolutionary spirit which informed so many of his contemporaries seemed largely to pass him by. He was shocked by the murder of Martin Luther King and bemused by the reaction to Enoch Powell's 'Rivers of Blood' speech which, he wrote, had 'dockers suddenly marching on Westminster and booing such unlikely figures as Ian Mikardo* while cheering Sir Gerald Nabarro.† I fear the whole problem is going to get far worse in the near future.'[30] Accompanied by Buxton,

---

* Ian Mikardo (1908–   ), Labour MP 1945–87; member of Labour's National Executive 1950–59 and 1960–78.
† Gerald Nabarro (1913–73), Conservative MP for South Worcs 1966–73.

the Prince also witnessed at first hand the student demonstration in Cambridge that was known as the 'Garden House Riot'.* But perhaps the closest he came to experiencing the iconoclasm which agitated the era was at the Sunday evening lectures in the church of St Mary's in Cambridge. Inheriting a tradition from his predecessor Mervyn Stockwood, Hugh Montefiore,† the vicar, regularly filled the church with voices of provocation and dissent. In the spirit of ecumenicism, Montefiore's *galère* included Calvinists and Jesuits, politicians and artists, among them Enoch Powell, W.H. Auden and Duke Ellington. One of the most remarkable sets of lectures was delivered by the Revd Harry Williams, who was widely renowned not only as a mesmeric preacher but for the unorthodox brilliance of his theological inquiry, illuminated by his immersion in the writings of Freud and Jung and his growing fascination with the 'inner self'. A quasi-existential approach to faith led him to argue for the view that to say 'I believe' is tantamount to saying 'I am', using the insights of psychoanalysis and anthropology to explore the wellsprings of faith and to offer a radical interpretation of Christian doctrine. This shocked traditionalist and fundamentalist alike. As Dean of Chapel at Trinity, Williams built on the rapport he and the Prince had established at their first meeting and the Prince was a frequent guest at the Dean's table, where conversation was infused by the spirit of radical inquiry.

Williams had been impressed by the Prince's modesty but also by his acuity: in response to a question about the Archbishop of Canterbury, he replied, 'I thought he was a very deep man but I couldn't get very far down.'[31] On more than one occasion the Prince served at Holy Communion and read the lesson. Afterwards, they would retire to the Dean's rooms for breakfast and talk. Williams was touched and impressed by the 'spiritual potential' which he saw in the Prince:

> I always thought he was a deep person, that he wasn't taken in by the surfaces of life. He had an interest in the deeper things of life, in the source of life, an openness of mind, a readiness to evaluate ideas, not

---

* A group of students disrupted a Greek tourism promotion held at the Garden House Hotel, in protest at the regime of the colonels in Greece.

† Rt Revd Hugh Montefiore (1920–), Vicar of Great St Mary's, Cambridge 1963–70; Bishop of Birmingham 1978–87.

taking things off the peg but thinking them out for himself . . . It may sound absurd but I always thought he had the makings of a saint when he was young: he had the grace, the humility and the desire to help other people.[32]

Despite all the diversions of undergraduate life, the college had presumed that the Prince would have no difficulty in passing Part One of the 'Arch and Anth' Tripos. He was determined to succeed. He knew that critics would always assail him, that disparaging remarks about his intellect hovered around him, and he was insecure enough to mind about it. Assiduous about attendance at lectures and seminars, he produced essays on time, went on the appropriate excavations, and read until late into the night. By dint of this effort he secured an upper second class in the Part One examinations at the end of his first year. He was particularly delighted by the fact that his achievement was applauded in the national press, a significant boost to his intellectual self-esteem. 'I am so pleased that the papers have given the exam results a fair deal,' he wrote to Checketts. 'I have achieved my desire anyway, and shown them, in some small way at least, that I am not totally ignorant or incompetent! The tables will now be turned and I will be envisaged as a princely swot!'[33]

At the age of eighteen, Prince Charles had taken his place as a Counsellor of State, one of the four members of the royal family nearest to the succession authorised to act for the sovereign when she is absent abroad. In the event of her death, he would also become empowered to exercise the full rights of the Crown; were the Queen to become disabled to the extent that she could not carry out her duties, he would become Regent. Presumably through an oversight, someone at the Palace omitted to tell the Prince of these privileges and responsibilities: 'The first thing I heard about being a Counsellor of State was from the 6 pm news! However, I assumed there was nothing for me to do and didn't rush to pack my bags.'[34] The following year, on 31 October 1967, he attended the State Opening of Parliament for the first time and in December he undertook his first foreign visit on the Queen's behalf, to attend the funeral of Harold Holt,* the Australian Prime Minister.

---

* Harold Holt (1908–67), Prime Minister of Australia 1966–67.

Among the heads of state there, he met a grim Asian trio in the persons of President Marcos of the Philippines, President Van Thiem of South Vietnam, and President Park of South Korea, as well as the President of the United States, Lyndon Johnson, who seemed bowed by the burdens of office: 'I don't think I've ever seen a man look so exhausted but he spoke in a somewhat languid manner about the hours he works and how little sleep he has . . .'[35]*

Prince Charles was encouraged by his reception. 'The Australians seem relieved and very grateful that we'd come out,' he wrote to Mountbatten. 'I think it is so important to show them that we care about them, because they are some of the finest people . . . They were incredibly friendly and a large crowd was waiting at the airport. I only hope that politicians realise how loyal they are and don't leave them in the lurch . . .'[36] His sense of a mission well accomplished was touchingly personal: 'I am so glad to be able to do something like that for mummy,' he wrote to Patricia Brabourne, his godmother. 'The Australians seemed very pleased that someone from the family had come out to show we still care.'[37] He was accompanied on the journey by the Prime Minister, Harold Wilson, and the leader of the Conservative Party, Edward Heath. It was only on the way back that the two politicians spoke to each other. 'I don't know how sincere these politicians are in their statements,' the Prince observed, 'but Mr Wilson made all sorts, mostly about himself.'[38]

The following June, the Prince was invested as a Knight of the Garter at Windsor, and in July he attended his first garden party at Buckingham Palace. He also went on an official visit to Malta where, at the St Anton Palace, he attended a garden party for 400 people, who were 'sweating profusely and occasionally stepping backwards into goldfish ponds with little accompanying "cris de cœur"'.[39] He evidently impressed himself on the gathering, including one guest who wrote to Mountbatten, 'This is a young man who reminds me very much of you; he's immensely inter-ested in humanity and the details of human suffering . . . Anyone can have brains but a warm heart is rare among the young today.'[40]

But the main purpose of his visit was to play in the centenary match of the All Malta Polo Club, of which Lord Mountbatten was president. The Prince had become as besotted with polo as he was with shooting,

---

* Three months later, Johnson stunned the world by announcing he would not run for the Presidency in 1968.

and was quite ready to divert to any destination in search of a match and good enough as a player to win a half Blue at Cambridge. From Malta, after winning the Prince Louis Cup, he wrote to his great-uncle ('From a very dust-begrimed Great-Nephew, who is eternally grateful to you for arranging the games . . . and extremely proud to have won your cup . . .') to describe the Old Palace at Valetta, where his mother had once stayed: 'I cannot tell you how sad it is to see what must have been such a beautiful house in so dreadful a state. You may have seen it, but it looks like a Hitchcock Horror film house . . .'[41] On his last evening he went to dinner at a restaurant 'in the middle of the most beautiful and complete mediaeval walled town where the streets are very narrow and the houses crowd together above you. It is dead quiet, and many of the houses are late Roman in design and quite beautiful.'[42]

After the summer vacation, he left Scotland ('I cannot tell you how I miss Balmoral and the hills and the air – I feel very empty and incomplete without it all'[43]) to start his second year at Cambridge. Discarding archaeology and anthropology, he had decided to read history for his Part Two Tripos: 'I am beginning to re-establish myself and sort out what kind of programme history will entail. It appears there are hundreds of lectures, all clashing with each other, all in different places at once and all packed solid with hairy unwashed student bodies! At the moment I'm wrestling with George III's problems, faced with a boggling choice of six books and no apparent prospect of completing the essay by Friday . . .'[44]

After some thought, he also applied to join the Dryden Society, Trinity's drama group: 'I took my fate in my hands the other day and decided at last to be brave enough and go for an audition.'[45] His application for an audition caused consternation among the Dryden *habitués*. Should they agree to his request (and run the risk of rejecting the heir to the throne) or should they return his application with a note explaining that every available part was already taken? They decided on the braver course. 'It was utterly terrifying,'[46] the Prince wrote afterwards. But he delighted the two producers who ran his audition. 'I shouldn't think I'd ever laughed so much. Talk about natural,' one of them, Christian Bailey, said later. 'We were rolling round on the floor he was so funny.'[47]

He was offered the part of a padre in a revue – 'So far I've not tried my hand at contemporary drama but there's always a first time'[48] – and accepted with trepidation. The news that the Prince was to perform publicly on stage soon leaked. The telephone lines to the college were swamped not only by the national and international press but by actors and actresses of renown as well as by dons and their families who had never before found occasion to patronise such events. Prince Charles played the part as a gentle parody of Michael Ramsey, the Archbishop of Canterbury (although Hugh Montefiore assumed that it was *his* performances at St Mary's which were the inspiration). Later, he rekindled the part in Joe Orton's *Erpingham Camp*, a black comedy about a holiday camp taken over as a fascist training centre.

Cameras had been banned from the performance, but *Paris Match*, whose photographer had taken up residence in Cambridge, acquired some 'exclusive' photographs of the Prince in performance complete with a custard-pie over his face, which became a four-page feature under the headline '*Une tarte à crème en fait la vedette*'. Although the photographs found their way round the European magazine circuit, no British newspaper broke the embargo.

The following year, in an attempt to prevent a similar breach, the Queen's assistant press secretary arranged with the Dryden Society for a formal press show in advance of the first night. Among other luminaries, correspondents of *The Times* (Philip Howard) and the *Daily Telegraph* (Sean Day-Lewis) duly arrived to pronounce on his performance in a series of skits, entitled 'Quiet Flows the Don'. In addition to performing as 'an expert on Bong Dynasty Chinese bidets called Louis Quatorze Bloggs', in a send-up of the BBC Television programme *Going for a Song*, he also acted a monologue as a weather forecaster, which he had written himself. After delivering lines like, 'By morning promiscuity will be widespread, but it will lift, and may give way to some hill snog . . . Virility will at first be poor . . . A manic depression over Ireland . . . A warm front followed by a cold back', the Prince fluffed a phrase, a stumble which was widely reported the next day but which Philip Howard generously ascribed to the fact that the audience was 'a grim, poker-faced posse of press'. Summing up this front-page occasion, *The Times* concluded that it was 'all good, clean, intimate undergraduate fun, rather unfairly exposed to the insatiable voyeurism of the world's press.'[49]

CHAPTER

EIGHT

A fter only four terms at Trinity, the Prince's new life at Cambridge was interrupted by a term at the University College of Wales at Aberystwyth. Just before his departure, he recorded his first radio interview,* in which he was asked about the hostility that he was bound to face from Welsh extremists in the principality:

> It would be unnatural, I think, if one didn't feel any apprehension about it. One always wonders what's going to happen . . . As long as I don't get covered too much in egg and tomato I'll be all right. But I don't blame people demonstrating like that. They've never seen me before. They don't know what I'm like. I've hardly been to Wales, and you can't really expect people to be over-zealous about the fact of having a so-called English Prince to come amongst them . . .[1]

The decision to send him for one term to a Welsh university had been made two years earlier in response to representations from the government, in the person of George Thomas, Secretary of State for

---

* The interview had been set up with Jack de Manio of the *Today* programme by David Checketts, who was a close friend of the BBC interviewer and also a member of the public relations company Neilson McCarthy, where de Manio had a seat on the board.

Wales.* That this was principally a political, rather than a cultural or educational, decision there can be little doubt. Thomas believed that it would 'further strengthen the bonds that bind the Principality to the Royal Family' and he had hoped to persuade the Palace that the Prince should use his time in Wales to attend some 'public occasions'[2]; he was also anxious in due course to brief him on what the Palace delicately phrased 'some current problems of Welsh significance'.[3] Although the Queen rejected the first proposal, she authorised the briefing. By 1969, the 'current problems' in Wales had become a source of deepening anxiety to the government in the run up to the formal investiture of the Prince of Wales, which had been set for 1 July 1969, and for which the term at Aberystwyth had been judged a fitting prelude.

In the upheaval of the sixties, the old assumptions of British politics had started to fracture as the disaffected of all parties looked beyond their traditional loyalties for salvation. In this atmosphere, the dormant seeds of nationalism suddenly germinated. Witnessing this challenge to the established order, the two main political parties were dismayed. The leader of the Conservatives, Edward Heath,[†] jibed that the nationalists offered 'flower politics for flower people' while a Labour minister, Merlyn Rees,[‡] declared that 'Welsh Nationalism shows many of the traits of fascism'.[4] A nostalgic sentiment in favour of 'home rule' had long been part of the cultural tradition in the Celtic fringes, but it had not previously caused quite such a *frisson* of alarm at Westminster. The threat to the established political structure of the United Kingdom was demonstrated only too clearly by the victory of the Welsh Nationalist, Gwynfor Evans, at the Carmarthen by-election in July and of the Scottish Nationalist, Mrs Winifred Ewing, at Hamilton in November 1967. If this run of separatist fervour should become a rout, then not

---

* George Thomas (1909–   ), now Viscount Tonypandy. Formerly Labour MP for Cardiff; chairman of the Welsh Labour Party 1950–51; Minister of State in the Welsh Office 1966–67; Secretary of State for Wales 1968-70; Speaker of the House of Commons 1976–83.

† Sir Edward Heath (1916–   ), Leader of Opposition 1965–70; Prime Minister 1970–74; Leader of Opposition 1974–75.

‡ Lord Rees (1920–   ), Labour MP South Leeds 1963–83 and for Morley and Leeds South from 1983; Minister of State at Home Office 1968–70; Home Secretary 1976–79.

only would the survival of the United Kingdom as a unitary state be at risk, but – a more immediate anxiety – the government's majority at Westminster, built as it was on the socialist tradition in the Celtic heartlands, would soon be in peril as well.

If narrow considerations of party advantage were not a fit subject for discourse between a government minister and the heir to the throne, the constitutional issue most certainly was. Of even greater concern was the growing security problem, fuelled by the separatist rhetoric that flowed eloquently and unceasingly from the nationalist leaders. The Free Wales Army had long been a minor irritant to the police and security services, using clandestine radio transmitters to call on the Welsh people to rise up against their English oppressors, performing quasi-military manoeuvres on wet hillsides, and stealing the occasional stick of gelignite with which they threatened to blow up the institutions of their 'colonial' masters. This small gang of amateur desperados had been regarded none too seriously, until in 1968 an RAF warrant officer was severely injured by a bomb planted by Welsh extremists. Soon afterwards, a bomb destroyed the Temple of Peace in Cardiff and another was found in the lost luggage department of the main railway station. It was only by chance that no-one was maimed or killed. No-one claimed responsibility for these acts of terrorism and when the Prince of Wales himself was identified anonymously as a target, the security services were obliged to treat the threat with the utmost seriousness.

In the week of his arrival at the university, a stick of gelignite encased in a metal tube exploded in the street outside the police headquarters in Cardiff, shattering surrounding windows. In accordance with a plan which had been prepared eight months before, more than a hundred police were drafted into the area around the university campus, causing *The Times* to report that 'a crack army bomb disposal unit has moved into Aberystwyth to spearhead the most elaborate security operation Wales has ever known . . .'[5] The *Daily Telegraph* noted that the police had removed a set of round black candles with the word 'BOMB' stencilled on them from the local crafts centre, 'on the grounds that they are not funny'.[6]

The Prince had already been given his first taste of hostility. As he told de Manio, following a visit to the university to view his new rooms, 'I asked one chap who was holding a placard what it meant because it was in Welsh and I'm afraid to admit I haven't learnt it properly yet. So I asked him and he just in fact hurled abuse at me . . . "Go home Charlie" or something like that. So after I'd asked him more questions I gave up. There was no point.'[7] A few weeks later at the Welsh History Society dinner at Aberystwyth, seven guests had refused to stand for the loyal toast, and one lecturer was quoted as saying, 'We wouldn't have minded if he was coming for a full three years. But we don't like him popping over for a quick academic wash and brush up before Caernarvon.'[8] The president of the Geltaidd Society, Yvonne Davies, wrote to inform him that the society had decided 'to oppose the political action of sending Charles Windsor as Prince of Wales to the University College of Wales and to the Welsh Nation. The society also supports the protest which was made in Aberystwyth on Monday January 20th, and the bravery of the four students on hunger strike.'[9]

Thus forewarned, the Prince arrived at Pantycelyn Hall, where he was to share accommodation with 250 other students, expecting a demonstration. It was to his immense relief, therefore, that the crowd of some 500 people waiting for him was effusive in welcome. 'Teenage girls shouted out "Cariad bach" and women called out "Bless him!"' the *Daily Mail* reported.[10] The following day, accompanied by a horde of plain-clothes officers, he went into the town to buy clothes hangers and picture hooks for his room, the *Guardian* reporting that, 'Behind him he left a series of swivelling heads and quivering shopkeepers, one of whom declared: "I went all to pieces when he came in."'[11] The Prince was touched by the welcome, writing to a friend at Cambridge a few days after his arrival, 'So far no demonstrations have occurred and in fact the welcome has been incredibly warm and reassuring. Everywhere I go I am recognised and people run up to wish me luck or bid me welcome. On the other hand the crackle of walkie-talkies still fills the air . . .'[12] The only sour note was struck by the president of the Students Union who predicted that the Prince would have a lonely nine weeks in Aberystwyth, explaining that, 'No-one can make any real friends in nine weeks and we just don't have the more aristocratic type of person here.'[13] Callow though the sentiment was, it proved to be an accurate forecast. 'The difference of this place from Cambridge is very marked,' the Prince wrote to his friend. 'The whole atmosphere is different . . . I miss Cambridge immensely and realise just how lucky we are to be there.'[14] Although he put a brave face on it, he was sensitive to the alien atmosphere and retreated into the privacy of his 'cell'[15] (which he tried to make more civilised with prints and paintings) or left Aberystwyth to explore the hinterland of rural Wales. Towards the end of term he was asked about his sense of isolation at the Welsh university. 'You see the trouble is that one has to remember that I'm in a slightly different position from several other people . . .' he faltered in explanation. 'I think out of certain necessity I have perhaps been more lonely, if they like it. I mean I haven't made a lot of friends, if that's what they mean . . . essentially it is, I suppose, compared with other people's lives, more lonely, and in this sense I suppose I've had a lonely time.'[16]

The pain in those words was the more evident as they formed part of the first television interview that he had ever given which, he had written, in expectation of his encounter with his inquisitors, Cliff Michelmore for the BBC and Brian Connell for ITV, 'should be pretty average hell'. Had he been a politician or a diplomat, he would have found the phrase to disguise the truth without quite telling a lie. But then as later Prince Charles was quite unable to deploy the characteristic wiles of public life. To a degree that dispassionate observers would never comprehend, he found it impossible to feign his feelings. To the anguish of those who loved him and the frustration of those who advised him, it was virtually impossible for him to hide either his emotions or his beliefs; rather than dissemble, he would either withdraw into silence or torture himself towards the truth – occasionally mangling syntax along the way. This propensity endeared him greatly to those who had some understanding of his nature, but in an unforgiving age it was to cause him untold trouble in the decades ahead.

The surge of nationalism in Wales had found non-violent expression in renewed demands that Welsh should become the official language of the principality, or at least have equal status with the 'colonial' language, English (which was, in fact, the only language that most Welsh people could even understand, let alone speak). But in politics there is no necessary connection between the logic of an argument and its potency. Thus civil servants, educationalists and local authorities throughout the principality were hastening to adopt a policy of bilingualism, not only in schools and colleges but for official communications as well. It was a Gadarene commitment from which the Prince of Wales could not possibly escape. Following the advice of the Welsh Office and the university authorities, Prince Philip noted that his son 'will have to harden his heart'[17] and apply himself accordingly, and the Prince did not contest the issue. At Aberystwyth he was put under the tutelage of Edward Millward, who happened to be not only a member of the Welsh Nationalist Party, but the prospective candidate for Montgomeryshire. Millward explained that, 'It's quite possible for a serious student to get a good grounding in Welsh in eight weeks. Enough to get the pronunciation and to make a speech.' He also declared that it was most important for the Prince to understand the history of Welsh nationalism, insisting that 'at my lectures he is just plain Mr'.[18] It was not a promising opening but the crash course in Welsh fulfilled its purpose for both of them. The tutor was encouraged to discuss the origins and significance of nationalism and the Prince listened carefully. 'I'm sure speaking to these people sympathetically is the best thing one can do,' he wrote to a Cambridge friend. 'So many people in the Government seem to dismiss them as bogeymen and I feel that is fatal.'[19]

By the end of his endurance test at Aberystwyth the message had been fully absorbed. 'If I've learnt anything during the last eight weeks,' he said, 'it's been about Wales in particular and its problems and what these people feel about Wales . . . they feel so strongly about Wales as a nation, and it means something to them, and they are depressed by what might happen to it if they don't try and preserve the language and the culture, which is very unique and special to Wales, and if something is unique and special, I see it as well worth preserving.'[20] The thought was simple enough but it was a good deal more sensitive than the bombast of Edward Heath about 'flower politics'. It was also said with an innocence and sincerity for which no public relations specialist could have trained him. As a result, the public expression of such sentiments had a marked impact on public opinion in Wales, just as the government had hoped.

At the end of the term he went to the Urdd National Eisteddfod* where, before an audience of some 6,000 people gathered in a vast marquee, he had to conclude the competition by making his first public speech of any significance. In so far as his nerves allowed him to concentrate on the proceedings at all, he was not overly impressed: the speeches were too long and the singing lacked panache. By comparison the clog dancing seemed positively exciting. In response to a challenge from the organisers, he had agreed to deliver his speech in Welsh. However, this genuflection did not prevent nationalist militants from

---

* The Annual Welsh youth festival for poetry, drama and music.

threatening to infiltrate the Eisteddfod to disrupt his appearance. In a letter to one of his Cambridge friends, however, he made light of his
prospective ordeal, writing, 'It should be highly exciting and if I make a
linguistic blunder I expect they will hurl the bardic harps and druidic
oaths at me.'[21] True to their word, as he rose to speak, the demonstrators
rose in unison from their places in the amphitheatre to protest, 'screaming and heckling'.[22] According to his equerry, the Prince 'just stood
there and looked at them without any reaction – and before long the
natural sympathy of the other people in the marquee started turning on
these demonstrators'.[23] Using their handbags as weapons and seizing the
placards, elderly women set about driving the militants from the marquee. Soon there was pandemonium and the police moved in to help
eject them. 'It was extraordinarily warming to have so many people
applauding and cheering and as a result many of my nerves were dissi-
pated by the time I was allowed to get anywhere near the microphone,'
the Prince recorded in his diary.[24] Outside, the protesters climbed onto
the marquee and banged on it as noisily as possible but failed to deter the
Prince from delivering his speech, which was greeted at the end by a
standing ovation: his pronunciation was passable, he appeared at least to
have some command of the language, and more to the point he had
shown himself to be undaunted. 'It was an interesting experience,' he
noted, 'and what people don't seem to realise is that it was the first
proper and prepared public speech I have made, and then it was in
Welsh. Nothing like being original!'[25]

For the government, the purpose of the term at Aberystwyth had
been to reaffirm the indivisibility of the United Kingdom and to dampen
the militant flames of nationalism; for the Palace it was a preparation for
the investiture, a chance for the heir to the throne to endear himself to
reasonable opinion and to disarm the unreasonable; for the Prince himself it had been a test against which his highly developed sense of
obligation did not for a moment rebel. As the investiture would demonstrate, the mission had been accomplished to very much better effect
than might have been expected.

The radio and television interviews Prince Charles had given did not
happen by chance but were the product of a carefully wrought plan
masterminded by the Queen's new press secretary, William Heseltine.
Richard Colville, from whom Heseltine had taken over, had operated on

the assumption that all news about the royal family was bad news unless
it had previously appeared in the Court Circular;* he strove to protect
the privacy of the royal family and to the best of his cautious ability he
was prepared to accommodate the media when 'royal progress' was officially underway. By the prevailing standards Heseltine was a brash
outsider. Though schooled in decorum, he was an Australian by birth
and, by contrast with Colville, he was at ease in the company of journalists and respected their trade. As press secretary, he had direct access to
the Queen and every other principal in the royal family, a right which he
did not hesitate to exploit in his search to modernise relations between
the monarchy and its subjects. It was under his influence that the royal
family began to emerge from behind the barricades of their remote and
mysterious world.

For a policy which was to have such a profound impact, it evolved
almost casually, and evidently without that careful historical and constitutional heart-searching which might have been expected. No-one
consulted Dicey† or pored over Bagehot.‡ For Heseltine, who was not a
theorist, the issue was simple and immediate: times were changing. The
convulsions of the sixties had created a wave of new expectations which
the media – and especially television – were hastening to satisfy, and from
which the monarchy could not be exempt. Already, by 1969, the public
had begun to weary of the formal state occasions which had engendered
such excitement a decade earlier. The vast set-piece 'outside broadcasts'
which had brought the coronation to the people were slipping out of
vogue: it was not enough to watch the Trooping the Colour or the State
Opening of Parliament or the arrival of foreign dignitaries by gilded
coach at Buckingham Palace, wondering at the precision and order of a
meticulous ceremony. Pageantry had not lost its appeal entirely, but the

---

* The daily bulletin of official engagements undertaken by members of the royal
family.
† A.V. Dicey (1835–1922), jurist whose work *Lectures Introductory of the Study of the
Law of the Constitution* (1855) has itself become a reference work for constitution-
alists.
‡ Walter Bagehot (1826–77), the Victorian journalist, economist and political ana-
lyst. The *obiter dicta* about the monarchy contained in his famous work *The English
Constitution* (1867) have survived to become clichés, repeated by generations of
successors to demonstrate their academic credentials.

public appetite, anxious for the shock of the new, was jaded. Challenged by the requirement not simply to reflect the form but also to examine the content, television had started to probe beneath the surface. Public officials were under scrutiny, required to answer for their actions; politicians, even distinguished statesmen, had to subject themselves to interrogation by television interviewers who arrogated to themselves the right to insist upon an answer before the court of public opinion. The mismatch between that searching and sceptical attitude and the sepulchral formality with which the monarchy was portrayed was glaring: if the public's 'right to know' was inviolate, why should the institution of the monarchy be exempt?

These notions were not discussed with such insouciance in Buckingham Palace, but the atmosphere within which they had been nurtured encouraged Heseltine to break out of the constraints imposed by Colville. If it was a slippery slope, it was, so far as Heseltine could see, the only route available; otherwise the monarchy would either fade into unwonted obscurity, or find itself under growing assault by the disaffected, reviled for being aloof and indifferent. The endeavour to reshape the relationship between the royal family and the people in a fashion befitting the electronic age rested on three implicit assumptions: that the public would remain curious about the workaday official duties of the sovereign and her family; that the media would not intrude into their private lives; and therefore that those private lives – at least so far as the public was aware – would continue to represent the 'family values' which successive generations of the monarchy had so effectively cultivated. All three assumptions were ill founded.

In the course on which Heseltine was set to embark, the Prince of Wales had a pivotal role – indeed he was, in effect, the guinea pig for the experiment – and in Checketts the Queen's press secretary had a forceful acolyte.

The investiture was not only the presentation of the Prince of Wales to his 'constituency' but his emergence as a public figure with official duties and responsibilities. For this reason it seemed imperative to both Checketts and Heseltine to quash an image of the heir apparent which they both knew to be false but which, in the absence of any public evidence to the contrary, had started to cling to him like poison ivy. Though it was not stated in such crude terms – even in the tabloid press – there lurked the suspicion in the media that the Prince was ineffectual, that he lacked the resilience and character for the part that he was called upon to play; in short, as one of the courtiers of that time expressed it, that he was something of a 'wimp'. Until the 1969 broadcasts, the public had never heard the Prince utter a word and they had only seen him in fleeting glimpses as a motorcade swept by or in official photographs which, while he was still in adolescence, were not calculated to inspire great confidence. In the absence of alternative evidence, it is by such ephemera that an image is moulded and, cast in gossip and speculation, sets hard as received wisdom. No outsider could know that there was spirit, and even a touch of arrogance, in the heir apparent.[*] In the television age, where it was already clear that image and reality would not be easy to distinguish, it seemed important to prevent Prince Charles from being miscast. As the very first such campaign of its kind, the emergence of the heir to the throne was a triumph of public relations.

As ever, the Prince was cautious and mistrustful, not at all certain that Heseltine's plans were wise: 'I am myself convinced that everyone will be sick to death with seeing, hearing and reading about me in such over-concentrated doses,' he wrote, 'but the press office think otherwise.'[29] As Checketts had presumed, the radio interview with Jack de Manio demonstrated that even if the Prince was shy and introverted, he was also intelligent, alert and possessed of a self-deprecating sense of humour that made for effective broadcasting. So effective was his performance that large portions of the interview were carried verbatim in the following day's newspapers, which reported on it in glowing terms. Heseltine, confident that in the Prince he had 'marvellous material to work on', that 'here was a young man who was both sensitive and witty and with a tremendous sense of the history of the institution of which he was part . . .'[30] felt able to go on the offensive on behalf of his charge, sanctioning a television interview for which the BBC had been pressing (to

---

[*] The files of that period provide several examples. For instance, in a letter to his equerry from the registrar at Aberystwyth which ended with the hope, 'I look forward to an uneventful term,' the Prince scribbled in the margin 'How boring!';[26] on another seeking his approval for an unofficial portrait for a commemorative stamp, he wrote, 'I do not approve of this monstrosity';[27] on a memorandum from the university noting that while at Aberystwyth 'His Royal Highness . . . would comply with the College rules and regulations,' he added the postscript, 'Like hell!'[28]

similarly beneficial effect), and then compiling a list of 'media' excursions for him. Aware that the investiture itself would emphasise tradition and history, the Palace press office resolved to secure some 'judicious publicity' around the ceremony so that the Prince would have 'the right sort of opportunity to show himself off as a strongly contemporary figure'.[31] With the reminder that 'if newspapers are not provided with material, they will manufacture it',[32] Heseltine proposed that the editors of national newspapers be invited to a cocktail party at Buckingham Palace attended by the Prince and his parents; that the Prince give a dinner party for the younger journalists who had already been invited by Heseltine to join a 'rota' party covering the Prince's public engagements; that a Welsh newspaper and the Press Association be allowed to interview the Prince; that Rank and Pathé be invited to take some 'informal footage' of him; and, most remarkably of all, that a television documentary be made about the life of the royal family for transmission on the eve of the investiture. Aside from the dinner party, the proposals were accepted with uncharacteristic enthusiasm by the Prince. This unprecedented blitz by Heseltine heralded the start of an entirely different relationship between the media and the royal family – and one from which there could be no easy retreat.

The date of the investiture had been set for 1 July 1969 at Caernarvon Castle. The planning for what was envisaged from the beginning as a 'television event' had begun over two years before in the spring of 1967. That autumn, an Investiture Committee was established which was chaired by the Duke of Norfolk, the Earl Marshal, and included the Earl of Snowdon, rejoicing in the mediaeval title of Constable of Caernarvon Castle. It was with great relish that Snowdon, a photographer of renown and endowed with creative vigour, accepted the role as the unofficial producer of a spectacular artifice, the inventor of a pageant, which had to be rich in historical resonance and contemporary purpose, that would not seem absurd except to the most unyielding cynic, and which would touch and entertain not only the 3,500 invited guests, but an audience in Britain and around the world of perhaps 500 million people.

Not everyone was excited by this prospect. In the *Daily Mirror* the columnist Cassandra, echoing a wider sentiment, expressed some sympathy for the predicament in which this 'stunt' would place the Prince: 'He is to be turned into a puppet, publicly in front of all our eyes and ears. He is dressed up in daft clothes. He is presumably trained to speak a few glib words in the Welsh form of Gaelic.' Condemning the decision which had taken him from his studies at Cambridge – 'which cannot be for the good of his education; and I doubt if it is for the good of his soul' – he concluded, 'I find myself extremely sorry for Charles, principal boy in the pantomime at Caernarvon next July that should never have been ballyhooed at all; a young man who is already the plaything of outmoded politicians and is to be next July the puppet of an antique Duke.'[33]

The only available precedent for the prospective ceremony was the investiture of the last Prince of Wales (later Edward VIII) in 1911, which was itself a confection.* The occasion had been marked by a deal of pomp and circumstance but available memory of the event was that it had been dreadfully overblown and somewhat chaotic. It was not an encouraging precedent: George Thomas, as Secretary of State, was particularly concerned not to repeat what had been widely regarded in Wales as 'a militaristic, pompous and essentially alien ceremony'.[34]

There were sharp divisions on the Council of the Welsh League of Youth, an ostensibly non-political body, about whether to attend the investiture. As the largest and most effective youth organisation in the country, a boycott by the Welsh League would have been a severe embarrassment to the government and to the Palace. Only after persuasive argument by the founder of the movement, Sir Ifan ab Owen Edwards, to the effect that Prince Charles's commitment to Wales had been unambiguously demonstrated by his decision to spend a term at Aberystwyth, did the Council – by a whisker majority – decide against boycotting the event. This decision led some of the League's officials to threaten resignation. Sir Ifan was fearful of 'a hard core of opposition to the investiture' which could no longer be ignored. To soften this opposition he urged that the Prince should make a speech in favour of 'the policy of bi-lingualism' which, he argued, would 'do more to help the

---

* Prince Charles was the twenty-first Prince of Wales, descending from a line which started with the future Edward II, who was invested as Prince of Wales in 1301. In mediaeval days, the ceremony was performed by the sovereign in the Palace of Westminster but the custom fell into disuse with the investiture of the future Charles I in 1616. In the intervening 295 years, eight Princes of Wales acquired their rights and duties without recourse to a public investiture.

investiture and to stop the present wave of direct action than the seemingly rather feeble attempts of our police'.[35]

The threat of direct action – and worse – had already been made explicit by the Free Wales Army, one of whose leaders told the BBC in the summer of 1968, when the date of the investiture was announced, that his fellow terrorists had already organised 'a lot of trouble . . . The rusty chains of England have bound our country too long and now we have to set the country on the path to freedom.'[36] Though such threats contained more bombast than substance and came from extremists who were already under surveillance by the police, they alarmed politicians, who stepped up their denunciations accordingly. The Welsh Secretary, for instance, referred to them as 'fanatics' and 'a lunatic fringe'.[37]

The growing anxiety prompted a spate of letters to the Palace, to politicians, and to other prominent figures, urging that the investiture be called off. A fan of the Welsh comedian Harry Secombe wrote to him begging him to exert his influence 'to put an end to this farcical Investiture as we are terrified the Prince will lose his life or be badly injured; the majority of the Welsh people are against it and the Prince is just a pawn – an innocent victim being led like a lamb to the slaughter . . . Please, please get it stopped.'[38] Secombe passed this missive to the Palace where it joined a pile of similar correspondence. Describing himself as 'a little disturbed, as all Welshmen must be', Secombe, who was renowned as the Goon with a girth, offered to interpose himself between the Prince and the public, 'which should be quite good protection, although I have recently lost nearly three stone'.[39]

Three weeks before the investiture, after a ceremony in Cardiff to inaugurate the Royal Regiment of Wales,* the Prince, as its first Colonel-in-Chief, made a speech in what *The Times* described as 'faultless Welsh' calling for tolerance, patience and understanding, declaring, 'A greater interest in the language and ideals of Welsh culture is being taken by an increasing number of people.' *The Times* wrote:

> But at the same time tensions tend to build up between Welsh speakers and the many non-Welsh speakers who feel themselves, quite rightly, as much a part of Wales as any other Welshman . . . It would

---

* Formed by the amalgamation of the South Wales Borderers and the Welch Regiment in June 1969.

be more than tragic if these tensions were allowed to build up to too great a degree outside as well as inside Wales. Tolerance and patience are needed: and the simple effort to understand the other person's point of view and his idealism, and not condemn it outright.[40]

The theme of the speech was approved by the Welsh Office and drafted for the Prince by the Palace, but the tone and phrasing were quintessentially his own. Others might have shared the sentiment but no-one else – with the exception perhaps of the sovereign herself – could have made the same impression; even from the lips of George Thomas, who was a gifted orator, the words would have been discounted as a political gambit, rich in passion but lacking in sincerity. As it was, in a speech which was above party politics but of real political – and constitutional – substance, the Prince 'won hearts and crowned a brilliant day in the capital' which ended with the crowd breaking into a cheer as, in 'clear and flowing Welsh',[41] he accepted the Freedom of the City of Cardiff on behalf of the new regiment.

Sensitive not only to the Welsh language issue but also to concerns about any militaristic flavour given to the investiture, the Palace and the Welsh Office wrestled with the problem of how to incorporate the armed forces into the pageant in a non-militaristic fashion. Even before the surge of nationalist feeling had become manifest, the Investiture Committee agreed that a mere 3,000 troops – as opposed to the 12,000 in 1911 – would be deployed on ceremonial duty to line the route and act as escorts and guards of honour. To stay within the limits of an over-all budget for the event (set by the Chancellor of the Exchequer at £200,000), a Light Air Defence Regiment was to fire the Royal Salute rather than King's Troop, Royal Horse Artillery, which normally had that privilege. Recognising that he could not 'go back' on these decisions, Thomas was still anxious to reduce the 'military content' of the investiture, suggesting that 'military personnel' should not be too prominent within the confines of the castle, where the ceremony was to take place.[42]

Heeding the government's concern (which in any case conformed with his own view), Snowdon choreographed the pageant to exclude even a symbolic reminder of the fact that until the final subjugation of the Welsh by King Edward I, 687 years earlier, Wales had been an independent nation. Under the genial patronage of the Duke of Norfolk, who told him, 'You know about art, you get on with it,' Snowdon set about devising a simple fantasia in which romance and modernism would be entwined in a theatrical embrace, drawing on tradition but looking to the future. Within a budget of £50,000 he devised a simple set in the middle of the grass courtyard: three raised thrones (for the Prince and his parents) made of Welsh slate and brutal in shape, that would be protected from the rain by a clear perspex canopy, with Prince of Wales feathers embossed on its surface, and supported on steel pikestaffs – 'just like Henry V would have done it, if he'd had perspex'.[43] The guests were to be seated around this dais on collapsible chairs in red wood, starkly sixties in design, which for £12 a piece could be taken away afterwards as memorabilia, thus defraying the cost of the proceedings which was a subject of close parliamentary scrutiny.*

So much had attitudes changed since the coronation that the entire event was conceived by Snowdon to ensure that the television cameras could observe every moment of it from all angles without obstruction, while themselves being virtually invisible. Thus did the monarchy move to satisfy the demands of a medium whose very presence had begun to define the significance of a public occasion.

Unlike the Duke of Norfolk, who had adapted to the new age with alacrity, the Garter King of Arms, Sir Anthony Wagner, belonged to that traditional school which regarded television as an intruder, and to pander to its demands as demeaning; his relationship with Snowdon and his team was therefore bracing in the extreme. As Constable of the Castle, Snowdon was free to design his own uniform (which was dark green and, in keeping with the non-military imperatives of the hour, entirely lacking in buttons or decorations) but he did not have the power to insist that the royal family should wear the flowing robes that would suitably dress his set. The Garter King of Arms also vetoed Snowdon's design of the investiture crown as a simple band; Wagner insisted on a traditional design, 'too large and too gaudy'[44] for Snowdon's taste. Sir Anthony was not the only observer to regard the Snowdon set as overly stark and 'modern', but it was without doubt far more sensitive to the public mood and to critical fashion than the vulgar excesses of the 1911 extravaganza.

As preparations for the investiture were finalised, viewers of BBC television were treated to the first-ever glimpse behind the royal tableau

---

* At auction in 1993, one of these period pieces sold for £500.

to witness the Queen and her family 'off duty'. The documentary *Royal Family* was conceived by William Heseltine, working closely with John Brabourne,* as a means of using television to show the public a little of the life the Prince would eventually be expected to lead as the future sovereign and of the preparations that were being made for him to fulfil that role. Working under the overall control of a committee chaired by Prince Philip, the BBC producer Richard Cawston was given unprecedented access to the family and to the household. The film showed Prince Philip barbecuing sausages, the Queen washing up, and Prince Edward and Andrew having a snowball fight at Sandringham. Later, those critics who blamed the Palace for allowing the monarchy to be turned into a 'soap opera' would cite *Royal Family* as the first step down a disastrous slope which led directly to the nadir of *It's A Royal Knockout.*† At the time of *Royal Family*, however, such soothsayers were not yet in evidence: the film received universal accolades for revealing that the monarchy was represented by three-dimensional personalities, among whom the Prince was revealed to have the most self-deprecating manner but the sharpest sense of humour.

On the eve of the investiture, accompanied by his parents, his grandmother, and a clutch of courtiers, the Prince boarded the royal train to Wales. Under the direction of the Duke of Norfolk in a mood of some levity, the mother and son had rehearsed their parts as for a pantomime, reminding themselves of every detail to ensure that the chaotic proceedings of 1911 were not repeated. Now, with the event upon them, they were all exceedingly nervous that the pageant should be flawless and that they would successfully negotiate that fine line between high drama and low farce. The tension was heightened by the security threat which, according to the South Wales Constabulary, posed 'a major problem'. Bombs had already gone off in North Wales and others were threatened for Caernarvon on the day itself. There was also 'acute anxiety about

---

* Lord Brabourne (1924–   ), Director Thames Television since 1978; chairman 1990–92. Married to Lady Patricia Brabourne (later, on her father's death, Countess Mountbatten of Burma).

† A television entertainment 'hosted' in June 1987 by Prince Edward in which Princess Anne and the Duke and Duchess of York ignored the pleas of the Prince of Wales (who had prevailed on his wife not to take part) and others and made fools of themselves in the most vulgar 'show' then available on the BBC.

emotions engendered by the trial of Free Wales Army members in the Guildhall at Swansea . . .'[45] Although 250 extra policemen, both uni-formed and plain-clothed, were drafted in from other parts of the principality to man barriers and roadblocks and to search every building, bridge and likely place for planting explosive devices, the Palace and the security services were on edge. The atmosphere on the train was relieved by much ribaldry, joshing and horseplay. The BBC producer Antony Craxton had arranged for a television set to be rigged on the train so that the passengers could watch a re-run of the 1911 investiture which was being shown on the BBC. There was great mirth when the Prince entered the compartment in the middle of this ancient recording to be told by his grandmother that because of the security situation it had been decided to go ahead with the ceremony using a stand-in. So far, she explained, the investiture was proving a great success. It was not a night for sound sleep.

On the day of the investiture the Prince woke 'very early at 6.0 am out of anticipation and gnawing feeling in tummy before a special event'. Eight hours later, he was driven in an open carriage through the streets of Caernarvon to the cheers of a vast crowd and the 'crump' of incen-diary devices exploding far enough away to cause no threat but not so far as to be ignored. 'Surprisingly,' he noted, 'no missiles were seen to be thrown at the carriage although some idiot threw a banana skin in front of the Household Cavalry.' He entered the castle to the strains of 'God Bless the Prince of Wales', which 'was sung rather feebly by what was termed the "upper crust" section of the guest list, although the choir at the far end sung lustily and very well indeed'. He was conducted to the dais where he knelt before the Queen to be invested with the symbols of his office. 'For me,' he noted afterwards, 'by far the most moving and meaningful moment came when I put my hands between Mummy's and swore to be her liege man of life and limb and to live and die against all manner of folks – such magnificent mediaeval, appropriate words, even if they were never adhered to in those old days.'[46]

At the end of the ceremony, like his predecessor in 1911, he was for-mally 'presented' by the Queen to the people assembled outside the castle precincts at the Queen Eleanor's Gate (which, he noted, 'looked straight down on the local conveniences and a lot of police and TV vans'), at the Eagle Gate, and finally to the people assembled in the lower ward, which he found 'very moving', although the sound of the 'magnificent fanfares' was drowned out by the enthusiasm of the crowd. After parading once again through the streets of Caernarvon, to a 'warming reception', he left for dinner in the royal yacht at Holyhead, exhausted.[47]

The following day, he set off on a whistle-stop tour through the principality to the acclaim of those who had witnessed a ceremony that just escaped pastiche and contrived to be simple but grand and, for monarchists at least, a dignified and touching occasion. In North Wales he was given 'an incredible reception' at Newtown, where some schoolchildren became so excited that he could not hear the national anthem above the sound of their cheers. It was the same in Cardigan and Fishguard. In Pembrokeshire his route was lined by people all the way, and in Carmarthen he drove round in an open car, 'utterly amazed' by the reaction. The children 'seemed to go wild and broke ranks to run along behind the car'.[48] After two days on the road, the enthusiasm was unabated. 'Passed through many towns and villages crammed with happy-looking people,' he wrote. 'Roads became fuller and fuller and slower and slower. I now became extremely weary and I was boiled in the glass Rolls.' However, his sense of irony did not desert him: 'Declared Swansea to be a city, which was received favourably,' he noted.[49]

The following day he was driven through the mining communities of South Wales, the route once again 'lined with people all the way'. The sun was so hot that 'in the back of that goldfish-bowl car' the heat was almost unendurable. But 'the genuine cheerfulness and enthusiasm of the people gave me great encouragement to keep going'. Here the towns were 'touchingly and lovingly decorated with flags and flowers and pictures – even the streets I did not go down were decorated – which made the grim streets look unnaturally colourful and bearable'.[50] At every stop there were dignitaries to greet – Lords Lieutenant, mayors, town clerks, police chiefs and politicians – as well as representatives from the Scouts, Guides, Rangers, Boys' Brigade and the British Legion. In Ebbw Vale, however, the welcome was noticeable for the absence of the local MP, Michael Foot, which the Prince interpreted as a snub from a politician who had been described to him as 'extremely left-wing' but whom he had been keen to meet. In Pontypool, however, he was entertained by the sight of Leo Abse, the flamboyant Labour backbencher, who was dressed eccentrically and seemed to the Prince to be modelling himself on Benjamin Disraeli.

At the end of an exhilarating and exhausting week, he returned late to Windsor Castle, hoping to share his experiences with his family. However, both his father and his sister had already gone to bed, while his mother was at Buckingham Palace recovering from a cold. Devoid of company, he went to his room and wrote up his diary instead:

> Last week has been an incredible one in my life and it now seems very odd not to have to wave to hundreds of people. The air seems so silent now, since the cheering and clapping has ceased abruptly and the handshaking has stopped too. I now seem to have a great deal to live up to and I hope I can be of assistance to Wales in constructive ways. To know that somebody is interested in them is the very least I can do at the moment.[51]

If his intimate family took his success for granted, others were effusive. Among the flood of congratulatory letters which flowed into the Prince's office, one stood out.

> My Dear Charles,
>
> Confidential reports on Naval officers are summarised by numbers . . . pretty poor 2 or 3, very good 7 or 8. Once in a way an officer achieves 9 – your father did it . . . your performance since you went with Fleet coverage to Wales rates you at 9 in my opinion . . . I'm sure you'll keep your head. Realise how fickle public support can be – it has to be earned over again every year. Your Uncle David had such popularity that he thought he could flout the Government and the Church and make a twice-divorced woman Queen. His popularity disappeared overnight. I am sure yours never will provided you keep your feet firmly on the ground. Well done, and keep it up,
>
> Your affectionate and admiring Uncle.[52]

In reply the Prince wrote:

> I, myself, cannot believe that I have really had an effect on people, particularly young ones, but several people have been writing recently saying very flattering things. The immediate problem is to remain sane and sensible and I try hard to do that. As long as I do not take

myself too seriously I should not be too badly off. I thoroughly appreciate all you say in your letter and realise the fickleness of the public.
The trouble is, they may expect too much of me, but I shall certainly
do my best even if they do.[53]

The intense and sustained correspondence between Mountbatten and
the Prince initiated by this exchange reflected a deepening affection
through which the influence of the older man on the younger man
would be greater than that of anyone else in the formative decade ahead.

CHAPTER NINE

After an absence of seven months, it seemed strange returning to Cambridge for the final year. 'The contrast with Aberystwyth is so great that one might be living in another world, except that so many of the students are of the same long-haired, bare-footed and perspiring variety that could be found in the forest of Aberystwyth!' he commented.[1] His tendency to grumble (unchecked by friends who lacked the temerity to mock him for it) was exacerbated by an aversion to communal life. After 'the pure bliss of Balmoral' where he had spent the long summer, it was 'pure hell' to be confined in a town, even one as beautiful as Cambridge. Only in private correspondence, and then only to his dearest friends, did he feel free to express his feelings openly:

> I miss the mountains deeply and that noisy silence of Deeside. Nothing has the same meaning and soul-refreshing quality that Balmoral can provide although I can comfort myself with the thought that I would never appreciate it if I was there all the time. At the moment, in Cambridge, I feel as though I am in a zoo. There are people wandering about everywhere staring at everything that moves and if it happens to be me they seem to gaze and point even more. After the solitude of the past two months it is a shock and I tend to remain in my room.[2]

For his final year, he had been provided with a larger set of rooms in

Trinity which had dark panelled walls and looked over Great Court, where 'instead of dust carts to wake me up I have a chiming clock on one side and noisy traffic on the other!' In his mercurial fashion, the student who pined for solitude also resolved to 'give endless dinner parties in a crazy way!' in surroundings so congenial that he could hardly wait to show them off to his friends. At weekends he continued to flee Cambridge 'to pursue other people's pheasants' and even during the week he was often away to listen to music, attend a film gala, open a building or make a speech. In November, sharing the stage with Mountbatten, and in the presence of the Prime Minister, he addressed an audience of 5,000 Indians at a meeting in London to celebrate the centenary of the birth of Mahatma Gandhi. Written in longhand, his speech proffered an insight not only into the virtues of passive resistance but also into his own self-deprecating character:

I myself have discovered in a small way that it is perseverance that counts, even if you are frustrated 10 or 20 times over . . .The consequent sense of achievement is overwhelming . . .The only trouble about this is that it requires effort, willpower and discipline. Some would have us believe that these are out of date concepts but as long as man has an ounce of humanity left, they will survive.[3]

'Willpower and discipline' were virtues that had been dinned into the Prince from infancy, but his attitude to extra-curricular activities, like shooting and polo, revealed that he had not entirely succumbed: 'The variety and alternative they provide from poring over dull books here is exactly what I need if I'm not to become depressed.'[4]

After the success of the investiture, Harold Wilson had urged that the heir to the throne should build on his achievement by undertaking a number of engagements on behalf of the Queen. In fact, the Prince's official diary was already starting to fill up as he was introduced to yet more public duties. In July, a fortnight after the investiture, he was with the Queen to welcome the President of Finland, Urho Kekkonen, at Victoria Station. The Prince's initiation into the rites of a state visit began when the head of state failed to recognise him: 'He looked straight through me and had to be steered to my outstretched hand by Mummy,' the Prince wrote.[5] On a very hot day they set off in a carriage procession to Buckingham Palace, which, the Prince noted, 'looked magnificent and the clanking and clinking of the Household Cavalry never fails to stir my blood . . . John Lennon of the Beatles, for some unaccountable reason, was espied looking out of his window above Horse Guards Parade.'[6]

His first state banquet seemed no less magnificent as he walked into the dining room past the Yeomen of the Bodyguard and the Gentlemen at Arms, escorting his grandmother. The Queen made her customary speech which, her son noted, was 'quite good', though he felt sure that it 'would be marvellous if she could write it herself'. After dinner he spoke to the Prime Minister, Harold Wilson, sundry high commissioners and ambassadors, and finally went to bed with 'feet v. sore from new pumps worn with breeches and the garter', observing wryly that his long black stockings were 'boiling to wear and come up to one's thighs – a crazy outfit really, but the only way (as yet) to wear the true garter'.[7]

Later in the month, he attended a formal lunch for the ruler of Abu Dhabi, Sheikh Zaid bin Sultan bin Zaid Al Nahayyan, who sat beside the Queen. At the end of a taciturn meal the sheikh informed his hostess that he did not normally talk to women. 'Mummy was of course delighted to receive this piece of information after struggling unsuccessfully to get a word out of him!' the Prince noted.[8] Formal occasions of this kind now became a routine part of his life, a duty to be fulfilled without much pleasure but without complaint.

In October, he once again attended the State Opening of Parliament, which in 1969 coincided with the disruption caused by a tube strike. There was talk of cancelling the royal procession from Buckingham Palace to Westminster but, after consulting the Prime Minister, the Queen decided otherwise. The Prince wrote:

> It would have been sad and unnecessary to have cancelled the State drive, because quite a large number of people were watching . . . I walked beside Mummy from the Robing Room, through the silent, eye-filled gallery, between the line of splendid old Gentlemen at Arms and then into the crowded, somewhat expectant chamber. Familiar faces all around. The Archbishop* craning forward with eyebrows

---

* Archbishop of Canterbury, Michael Ramsey.

twitching furiously, Uncle Dickie looking rather bored, the Law Lords like a scene from Gilbert and Sullivan and the Lord Chancellor* with uncontrollable palpitations of nervousness.[9]

The following February, the Prince was formally introduced into the House of Lords, where a misunderstanding about the protocol surrounding the introduction led to the exclusion of his father from the proceedings. In a note to Prince Charles's private secretary, the Duke of Norfolk had explained that Prince Philip could only be one of his son's 'supporters' if he had himself taken the Oath of Allegiance in that parliament. Through a failure of communication, which frequently afflicted the Palace network, the Duke of Edinburgh was not told about this requirement or, indeed, asked to take part in the ceremony at all. When he discovered this oversight, four weeks before the event, the Duke first questioned the ruling, then decided that he could not in any case take part as he was due to leave the country the same day. In explaining this to his son, he made it quite clear that he was not able to change his plans at such short notice even if such an apparently pointed departure was noticed by the public (which, in the event, it was not).

The Prince recorded the event in his diary:

> Quite awe-inspiring to process slowly into the Chamber and make the obeisances and take the oath to the accompanying pregnant silence and occasional baronial cough or ducal splutter. However I was determined not to be overawed and didn't feel too nervous. I took my seat on the right of the throne, placed the cocked hat on my head and sat there blinking for a few excruciating seconds and then rose to shake the Lord Chancellor's hand to the accompaniment of a low roar of 'hear! hear!'[10]

After listening to a few speeches, he began to enjoy himself and to consider the prospects. 'It has a relaxed atmosphere and an air of great dignity and civility. It really is like a large club,' he wrote. 'One day I intend to make a speech if I find something reasonable and non-controversial to

---

* Lord Gardiner (1900–90), Lord High Chancellor 1964–70; Chancellor of the Open University 1973–78.

interest myself in sufficiently. In some ways I think I ought to take my membership fairly seriously.'[11]*

Three weeks later and only three months before his finals, he flew to Australia, Hong Kong, New Zealand and Japan for official visits which together lasted four weeks. He flew via New York and Los Angeles, and his fastidious sketch of the scene at Los Angeles revealed a glimpse of that sense of the absurd which was to become so marked in the increasingly copious letters and journals which recorded his evolving attitudes, feelings and judgements:

> A bevy of microphones, pushy photographers and reporters, a host of bulging-bodied cops with itching fingers, the Mayor of L.A.'s Chief of Protocol who presented me with the City's Keys with much back-slapping, hand-clutching and endless speechifying to the photographers; the Governor of California's (Ronald Reagan) representative who 'very formally' insisted on reciting the Governor's telegram of welcome . . .'[12]

He was irritated by one official who was 'pretty insufferable, rather pompous, and drank too many gin and tonics. He talked too much and wouldn't let me get a word in edgeways . . .'

As the leading player, invariably at the centre of the stage and yet somehow apart from the action, observing himself being observed, he was already a compulsive correspondent, snatching time on cars, trains and planes to record his impressions of the world into which he had been thrust. Flying from Los Angeles to Sydney, he described the view from the plane:

> It has been quite superb as the South Sea sun rises out of the Eastern sky in an ever-expanding arc of blood red, then pink with a trace of purple, and finally the whole sky filled with a glorious golden trickling light, which lights up the wispy tropical clouds like rough icing on a

---

* The Prince did eventually find a subject which he deemed 'reasonable' and 'non-controversial' enough to make the theme of his maiden speech in the House of Lords on 13 June 1974: the use of leisure. It touched on the issue of community service by young people, a subject of which he would never tire.

huge natural wedding cake. It is moments like these which bring loving tears to one's eyes and inexplicably cause one to 'worship'
something far greater and more mysterious than oneself or someone
else.[13]

As a self-confessed late-developer, brought up in a household where
the love of literature was not conspicuous, his reading had been correspondingly limited. Now, at the age of twenty, he had belatedly
discovered the wonder of great writing. 'I have been reading Anna
Karenina,' he wrote from 35,000 feet above the South Seas, 'and never
realised to what extent words could move me. I've been experiencing the
same sensations from this that I have from beautiful and stirring pieces of
music. I'm sure it does the soul immense good.'[14]

Arriving in Australia, he felt 'in an extraordinary way' that it was like
being back 'in a long lost and loved home . . . The people were so welcoming and it was a real joy to see the place again.'[15] In New Zealand, he
joined the Queen and Prince Philip, who had arrived for the State
Opening of Parliament. After the speech from the throne he talked to a
range of foreign representatives, saying 'all the things I ought not to have
said to the Czechoslovak Ambassador, who appropriately, was standing
next to the Russian'. He was not impressed by the 'anti-Vietnam and
anti-everything demonstrators' outside, who were 'hemmed in by the
bobbing helmets of hundreds of police'.[16]

In Hong Kong, he was much taken by 'one of the last old-style
colonies', noting, 'My greatest regret is that I spend my time travelling
non-stop from one place to another and so never get enough time to
break the journeys and stay in a place for longer than just one hour.'[17]
The frustration at his circumscribed existence was to become a refrain of
almost every official visit; yet, as his harassed officials would observe, he
loathed to have any gap in his diary, feeling guilty about time wasted and
bored by longueurs.

The purpose of his visit to Japan was to attend the international trade
fair Expo '70. After arriving at Tokyo airport, he was driven to the
British embassy at great speed: 'There were police everywhere along the
route and there was much siren-blowing and loud-hailing.'[18] This was a
facet of official visits which he came to abhor. At the Emperor's new
palace as the guest of honour at a court banquet he was conducted along
'literally miles of ochre coloured corridors forming a square around a

huge courtyard covered in cobble stones'. Unimpressed by the 'sad' mix of traditional Japanese and Western culture, he noted that:

> the whole place is built on the bungalow principle . . . Every corner bore a servant who bowed low and long in true Japanese style. After what seemed an interminable distance and what for most people would have been an exercise in how to be made to feel smaller and smaller until one reached the divine presence, two huge doors were slid open by boot-faced gentlemen in dinner jackets and the Emperor appeared at the top of the stairs.[19]

The Emperor spoke no English, but the Prince noted in his journal that he thought the Empress and her daughter, Princess Hitachi, charming. At pains to cross the cultural barrier between East and West, the Prince found himself in what would become a routine predicament. His first reaction was to talk 'from start to finish' but he was subsequently told that 'apparently no Japanese really talks at meals anyway, so I must have appeared incredibly rude'. He was also informed that Japanese culture values intuition over the intellect, an attitude for which he was later to have some sympathy. 'Conversation', he wrote in his diary, 'is limited to the exchange of platitudes and endless "polite phrases". Thus you refer to someone's wife as "your beautiful, divine lady" and to your own as "my dilapidated spouse". To your hostess you say "You have feasted me like a God" and to you she says "I have fed you the most abominable filth etc etc." '

After dinner, he asked the Emperor a stream of questions about Japanese life. In response, speaking through an interpreter, Hirohito was formal in the traditional Japanese style, asking for instance, 'Would you convey to her Majesty our earnest desire to maintain solicitous relations between our two countries.'[20] For the Prince, the evening was a prototype for many future occasions when, as the official representative of the Queen, he had to fulfil the inescapable duties of international relations, surviving the encounters by applying the disciplines of anthropology to political leadership, and recording his impressions afterwards in his diary and journals. He accepted formality and treated diplomatic niceties with the irreverence of a true believer.

At a return dinner in the British embassy, he was serenaded by an unusual version of 'God Bless the Prince of Wales' played by two musicians on bamboo recorders. Even on such splendid occasions, his sense of the absurd would cause him numerous moments of acute diplomatic danger. On this occasion, his composure returned only after a fine performance of Bach and then 'Greensleeves' by the Nippon Ensemble.

At Expo '70, followed by a posse of photographers and reporters, he toured no fewer than twenty-three pavilions, at each of which he put on the required display of intense curiosity. Remembering details of each one, he made notes on the variety of national aspirations they displayed. However, after ten hours of official enthusiasm he was 'desperate . . . I longed to blow up every glistening chrome and plastic symbol of a nation's materialism and conceit.'[21]

He was much happier the next morning when he was guided round a temple garden outside Kyoto. Its 'gracefully curving stone bridges, drooping dwarf pines, willow trees and pink puffs of cherry blossom' were 'beautiful', 'marvellous' and 'superb'. He also enjoyed lunch in a country restaurant where he sat on the floor served by *geisha* girls who were 'charming', and one of whom massaged his sore back.[22] There were more motorcades ('the usual escort of police cars and furiously wailing motor cyclists, who always seem to enjoy themselves to distraction in causing chaos . . .'[23]), more banquets, more tours, more receptions, and more hands to shake: the common round of a royal tour. He managed to hide his ambivalence, and the British embassy enthused, 'The whole of Japan was tremendously gratified by the visit.' It cited a senior government official who had declared that, 'Prince Charles had been the most successful and well-publicised visitor to Japan in Expo year.'[24]

A fortnight later, back in London, the Prince attended his first Privy Council. It was held at Clarence House and Queen Elizabeth the Queen Mother deputised for the Queen. Although the business was 'routine and dull', the Prince noted, 'I was amazed how much has to go through the Council. Most bills from Parliament require an order in Council and very little can happen without the Queen in Council.'* Realising how deeply the monarchy is embedded in the constitutional structure of Britain, he wrote of the Privy Council, 'I daresay many politicians would like to do away with this particular institution and establish something

---

* The Prince's knowledge was shaky. In fact only a minority of bills require an order in Council.

more rational and modern but it is one of the very last remaining links between Crown and Parliament and does help to remind ministers that there is one final authority that is not themselves.'[25]

At the end of May, his crash course in royal diplomacy and the function of the monarchy was interrupted when the 'dreaded' moment of his history finals arrived. 'Although I had been hating the idea of these monstrous tests of scholastic knowledge', he wrote in his diary, 'I was very relieved when they finally began and some of the tension could subside.'[26] He even mustered the will to reply to a 'good luck' telegram urging him 'to beat the examiners' with the words, 'Your message has worked wonders. Several battered examiners in hospital.'[27] Lord Butler, the Master of Trinity, who had opposed the decision to interrupt the Prince's Cambridge studies by sending him to Aberystwyth, judged that in his final year he had been required to undertake far too many royal engagements. These, he thought, had handicapped the academic potential of a student who, he was reported as saying, was 'really very clever'.[28]

Despite his lack of revision, the general paper turned out to be 'quite reasonable'. But, according to his own account, the Prince felt he had made a 'complete mess' of the paper on political thought: 'Partly due to an element of panic over a question on Locke when I could not remember what his theory of natural law was. My mind went a despairing blank aided, I may say, by an excited, noisy football demonstration outside the exam room.' As if that were not enough, a carnival float went past no fewer than three times during the three-hour paper, making 'the most ghastly noise imaginable – whistles, hooters, rattles, megaphones', while on the steps of the University Church some evangelicals began a meeting which 'continued in a fairly loud-mouthed way for most of the rest of the exam'.[29] He was tempted to complain but decided against such a public statement of outrage.

He was duly awarded a lower second class degree, which, given the disruptions of Aberystwyth, the investiture and his royal duties, was hailed by the college as a fine achievement. Not only was he the first heir to the throne to secure a degree but, according to his tutor, Denis Marrian, the result was 'extremely good from both the country's and his own point of view' – an assessment widely echoed in the media, which was generous in praise. At the end of July, Checketts wrote to Marrian on the Prince's behalf, 'It will almost certainly appear as one of the periods of greatest freedom he will ever enjoy, and I am sure His Royal Highness is already aware of the profound effect it has had on his attitude to life, his fellow human beings and himself.'[30]*

After the May Ball at Trinity, he left Cambridge for a celebratory week at Windsor for Royal Ascot, and 'four days of glorious weather, marvellous company, delicious food, good polo', only occasionally interrupted by an obligatory visit to the races, which held little appeal for him. He spent much time in the castle, which was at its best in Ascot Week when 'full of flowers which sent wafts of delicious smells creeping down the corridors', while all the state rooms were in use 'as they should be' for the paintings and treasures to be admired by the guests.[32]

For most of the country, the Thursday of Ascot Week 1970 was more significant as the day of the General Election. That night, the royal family watched the election results programme on the BBC until the early hours, by which time it was clear that a sensational result was in the offing. At Balmoral the previous summer, Harold Wilson had confided his ambition to emulate Lord Liverpool by winning three elections in a row. By Friday morning he was on his way out of Downing Street after his defeat at the hands of the Conservative leader Edward Heath. That evening, to the Prince's 'intense astonishment', the new Prime Minister honoured an invitation to appear at a seventieth birthday party for Queen Elizabeth, Lord Mountbatten, Princess Alice and the Duke of Beaufort, attended by 800 guests. The state rooms at Windsor, he recorded, 'looked magnificent and groaned under the gigantic floral arrangements which drew gasps of wonder . . .' As many of the guests were also rejoicing at the defeat of the Labour government, the atmosphere was 'lighthearted and heady. Beaming, jolly faces peered from behind bubbling champagne glasses and people hobbled up to each other to express their amazement in the day's events.' Heath 'looked shattered' but happy, 'bemused by all the attention and congratulations'. As the

---

* The disappointment was that the Prince was unable to receive his honours degree in person. A jail sentence imposed on the students found guilty of criminal damage to the Garden House Hotel, and the deportation of the student activist, Rudi Dutschke, had so inflamed radical opinion at the university that the Vice-Chancellor felt compelled to advise that the presence of the Prince of Wales at the ceremony could provoke hostile demonstrations. (File note by Checketts, 29 September 1970.[31])

Prince noted, 'It could have so easily been the other way round and he would probably have been out of the leadership fairly rapidly.'[33]

Soon afterwards, the Prince resumed his apprenticeship in royal diplomacy with an official visit to Canada and the United States. The crowds in Ottawa were subdued (in marked contrast to the enthusiasm he had encountered in Australia). In Washington, however, he was elated by his reception at the White House, where (with Princess Anne) he stayed as guest of the President, Richard Nixon. A few weeks earlier, the arrangements for his trip had provoked a diplomatic *frisson* when a journalist on the *Washington Evening Star* had reported that Buckingham Palace had delayed approval of the programme suggested by the White House, the inference being that the Prince and the Princess were unhappy with what was proposed. As it happened, the Prince had indeed been unenthusiastic about visiting Camp David and the prospect of a 'cook-out' there, prepared by the US Navy for the royal visitors and a group of selected 'young people', but he had not in any way resisted the idea. The British embassy, only too aware of the 'extreme sensitivity' of America's First Family, had moved swiftly to reassure the President but did not entirely succeed.[34]

The Washington visit began with the customary welcome on the White House lawn, with a photo opportunity at which the President genially 'manhandled' the royal pair for the benefit of the photographers. Two days later, after a hectic round of sight-seeing, the Prince, at his own request, was ushered into the Oval Office for an audience with Nixon. 'The conversation started falteringly and we began to talk about polo and baseball in that dreadful pre-conversation chit-chat', he noted in his diary.[35] Anxious for insight, the Prince steered the conversation towards Russia and China, at which the President explained his familiar preference for the latter, speaking with feeling about the threat to the West from 'aggressive Russian communism dedicated to assisting revolution anywhere in the world'.[36] Yet when the Prince sounded him out on the possibility of a visit by the Queen to the USSR, he responded with enthusiasm, urging only that any such visit should not be confined merely to Moscow, 'where he said the party is extremely strong'.[37] Expecting the audience to last half an hour, the Prince was amazed and gratified when the President so warmed to his theme that he seemed to forget the time.

It was an impressive *tour d'horizon* which included a discourse by Nixon about 'the need to give people a car, a fridge, a T.V. and a house', the 'success' of his Cambodia strategy, his frustration about America's lonely role in South-East Asia, his fears about communism in India, and his anxieties about the Middle East. The President went on to counsel the Prince about his own role in the world, urging that the heir to the British throne should be a 'presence' while not avoiding controversy altogether. 'I pointed out one must not become controversial too often otherwise people don't take you seriously,' the Prince noted in his diary. 'To be just a presence would be fatal. I know lots of Americans think one's main job is to go around saying meaningless niceties, but a presence alone can be swept away so easily, I feel.' After ninety minutes, although Nixon 'seemed happy to go on', the Prince felt obliged to bring the conversation to an end 'because I was sure the President had people to see'.[38]

The Prince had not only enjoyed his first encounter with an American president, but also relished the opportunity to play his diplomatic part, taking it upon himself to detail the contents of the conversation in a longhand letter to the Foreign Secretary. The President had spoken with admiration of the 'special relationship', prompting the Prince to tell Sir Alec Douglas-Home,* 'The President was extremely hospitable and overflowing with kind remarks. He said that the special relationship between this country and the U.S. was a result of a common language, heritage and traditions. He did genuinely seem very pro-British and anxious to be friendly . . .'[39]

Unwittingly, the Prince had alighted on what had become a most sensitive matter for the Foreign Office, which, under Heath's new administration, was pressing assiduously for entry into the EEC. Due to make a speech a few months later at the annual dinner of the Pilgrims of Great Britain, the Prince decided to use the occasion to echo Nixon's amiable sentiments. However, when word of this reached the government, the Foreign Office intervened to excise any mention of the 'special relationship' from the draft. According to a memorandum from the Prince's secretary, the Foreign Office view was that 'whereas there

---

* Lord Home of the Hirsel, (1903–   ), Leader of the House of Lords 1959–60; Secretary of State for Foreign Affairs 1960–63; Prime Minister 1963–64; Secretary of State for Foreign Affairs 1970–74.

once was such a relationship, there no longer is'. Any such references would not only be 'inaccurate' but would also 'annoy all the Europeans'. The Foreign Office thus advised 'strongly' against the inclusion of any such remarks by the Prince.[40] Not to be thwarted entirely, the Prince obliged by replacing the offending phrase with the words 'the close relationship', but then spoke effusively of the historical bonds of culture and language by which the two countries were united.[41]* The issue was the first but very far from the last potential *casus belli* between the Prince and the mandarins.

Two days after his return from Washington, the Prince was in Scotland at Holyrood House for a particularly ill-humoured gathering of Commonwealth heads of state. Commenting on the 'posturing' of some African states, he was naively perplexed that so 'minor a question' as the British decision to resume the sale of arms to South Africa should have provoked countries like Tanzania, Zambia, India and Ceylon to such ire. However, as an earnest student of international affairs, he did not discount the view of the Commonwealth Secretary-General that in its determination not to be blackmailed, the new British government was perhaps 'insensitive to the real psychological effect that any dealings Great Britain has with South Africa will have on many black Africans'. He concluded in his diary, 'It seems the whole thing must be handled with extreme care and delicacy. It would be worse than catastrophic to destroy the Commonwealth over something like this.'[42]†

In the autumn of 1970, after his usual summer break in Scotland, the Prince left Balmoral 'with <u>extreme</u> reluctance' to make an official visit to Fiji where he was to represent the Queen at the island's independence celebrations. For the first time he was provided with his own aircraft,

---

* Despite the Foreign Office's best endeavours, the phrase would not lie down but would be persistently resurrected by prime ministers clinging on to a vision of Britain that denied its diminished status as a middle-ranking European power.
† The Wilson government had imposed a 'voluntary' arms embargo, whereby companies were recommended not to sell arms, but were not banned by law. In 1970 the Heath government allowed the sale of Wasp helicopters to South Africa to meet previous defence agreements. In 1977 the United Nations Security Council passed Resolution 919 imposing a mandatory arms embargo on all UN member states. It was lifted on 25 May 1994 after the South African elections brought Nelson Mandela to power.

which lost an engine four hours out from London. Forced to wait at Bahrain for the back-up VC10 he sat in the VIP lounge, 'hot, sticky, growing rapidly more grumpy and sleepy'.[43] However, the warmth of the welcome he was given in Fiji soon dispersed his gloom. 'My part in the proceedings', he noted, 'was to take limitless Royal salutes, read Mummy's message and hand the constitutional instruments to the P.M.' He was greatly taken by the spirit of the people. 'What was so interesting about this independence was that there were no incidents or demonstrations or anything. Simply peaceful, happy and dignified good behaviour,' he wrote. 'Personally I found the Fijians some of the most attractive and charming people I have ever met. They have the most perfect and touching manners and the greatest dignity and good humour I have ever seen. It is banana skin humour which makes them so marvellous for me, at any rate. Their smiles erase all cobwebs of depression and sourness . . .'[44]

Though he wrote that 'one very much hopes' the Fijians would still 'get on well' with the Indian community on the island, he was irritated by the dour reaction of the latter to his visit. One commissioner was so offensively two-faced that the Prince was soon 'sick to death with his presence', a feeling that he managed to keep to himself. Off duty, however, there were compensations in abundance. With his friend and newly appointed equerry, Nicholas Soames,* he went snorkelling over a coral shelf:

The world under water is beyond belief, I am finding it less frightening now, though the man with us said they usually saw every sort of shark . . . This of course added to my brimming confidence . . . In the end only one shark was spotted in the surf but I never saw it. I was too busy watching platoons and regiments of yellow and black striped fish march and counter-march as if they were suspended effortlessly on Horseguards Parade . . .[45]

He tried to harpoon a fish. It was not a success:

---

* Nicholas Soames (1948–), son of Lord Soames, equerry to Prince of Wales 1970–72; Conservative MP for Crawley since 1983; parliamentary Secretary, Ministry of Agriculture, Fisheries and Food, 1992–94; Minister of State for the Armed Forces since 1994.

I succeeded only in knocking in my collar bone by holding the gun too close to my shoulder. Nicholas and I both swallowed gallons of the Pacific and rose spluttering and gasping to the surface only to find a huge, wind-blown wave bearing down on one's frail form and once again filling every open orifice with stinging salt. Nicholas from underwater presents a novel sight . . !⁴⁶

The once timid adolescent was still an introverted young man, but he had learnt to school himself in the physical and psychological virtues. Lacking the prowess of a natural athlete, he had nevertheless started to lose the forlorn clumsiness which had so frustrated his father, treating any physical challenge as a test not of talent but of character. As a result, he had not only learnt to master his fears, but was, to the point of reckless-ness, ready to test himself to the limit on polo ponies, in the hunting field, on skis, and on surfboards; soon he was to fly jet planes and jump by para-chute. The evolution may have been harsh but, as his father had willed it, he was now a very much tougher and more resilient individual than he had once promised to become. By the end of his first year of public duty, he was also an assured performer on the diplomatic stage. Although he regarded the routine obsequies as irksome, much preferring the informal meetings and private conversations which offered more substantial fare, he had become a more than adequate deputy for his mother.

In November, representing the Queen at the funeral of General de Gaulle, he flew to Paris with prime ministers from three decades – Edward Heath, Harold Wilson, Sir Harold Macmillan and Lord Avon. With Heath, he discussed the effect on the Commonwealth of Britain's prospective membership of the Common Market and was advised (wrongly as it transpired) that the economic impact on Commonwealth countries like New Zealand and Australia would be negligible. When the Prince pressed him about the value of a multi-racial Commonwealth, the Prime Minister only grudgingly concurred, saying that 'there was one thing he could not stand and that was being told what to do by var-ious African countries'.⁴⁷

Lord Avon recounted why he had resigned as Foreign Secretary from Neville Chamberlain's government in protest at the policy of appease-ment towards Mussolini; how he and Macmillan had joined forces with Churchill – becoming known as 'the Glamour Boys' – to argue for rearmament against Hitler; and how 'he had sat opposite Hitler at a dinner sometime before the war, and during the course of the meal he discovered they had been opposite each other in the trenches in the first war. A Frenchman, upon discovering this information, wailed to Lord Avon, "*Monsieur! Pourquoi n'avez-vous pas tiré le fusil?*" ' Later, at dinner in the British embassy, the architect of the Suez campaign offered an apologia for that fiasco, according to which a 'mental blockage' in the United States about colonialism combined with the meanness of the British Treasury turned triumph into disaster. Apparently, Lord Avon still believed that 'we could in fact have gone on to complete the situation but it was far too big a risk to take at the time'.[48]

After dinner, he sat beside Sir Harold Macmillan, who was at once consumed by a fit of sneezing which lasted almost ten minutes:

Tears poured out of the corners of his bloodhound eyes and he apologised for his hay fever. Eventually peace o'ercame him and he settled down to tell me in his inimitable and ponderous way how he had enjoyed working for Mummy as P.M. He said she was a very astute woman and made their interviews very enjoyable. Apparently he always wrote a letter a few days before saying what points there were for discussion and this helped enormously when it came to the weekly meeting.

He proceeded to inform the Prince about the rights and responsibilities of the monarchy: 'With suitable flourish and statesmanlike emphasis he patted my knee and slowly said "My boy, the Sovereign has the right to be informed (long pause), to protest (longer, more meaningful pause), and to warn (voice rising to a climactic crescendo)." ' This paraphrase of Walter Bagehot's dictum, delivered as if it were an original insight, greatly entertained the heir to the throne; he also noted in his diary that the British ambassador, Christopher Soames,* thought that the great showman's 'elderly hobbling about' was put on entirely for effect.[49]

The following day in Notre Dame cathedral, the Prince took his place among the crown princes of Europe, immediately behind the Emperor of Ethiopia, Haile Selassie, and the Shah of Iran. From that

---

* Lord Soames (1920–87), Secretary of State for War 1958–60; Minister of Agriculture 1960–64; ambassador to France 1968–72; Governor of Southern Rhodesia 1979–80; Leader of the House of Lords 1979–81.

vantage point, he watched the arrival of heads of state from all over the world:

> Endless African delegations swept down the aisle, rustling like a pile of stationery. Then President Podgorny [of the Soviet Union] appeared surrounded by large numbers of flat-footed henchmen, whose trouser bottoms were about 4 inches above their shoes and hair close-cropped under ill-fitting hats. Eventually Pompidou and Madame swept past me and settled themselves in separate seats in front.[50]

After a 'moving, simple' service, he stood in the 'milling herd' of dignitaries, 'jammed between Makarios and Mrs Gandhi', waiting for his car until Christopher Soames used his great bulk to force a passage through to the waiting Rolls and thence to lunch.[51]

It was the last formal engagement of a year in which the Prince had learnt much. Perhaps the most important lesson was that his future would be frustratingly circumscribed unless he chose to make more of his role than precedent strictly required – or observers expected.

CHAPTER
TEN

———— ◆ ————

The decision about the next stage in the Prince's life had first been mooted at the Buckingham Palace dinner in December 1965, where it was agreed that he should attend university before entering any of the armed services. As ever, Mountbatten was a powerful influence. Such was his authority that he was rarely excluded from any significant council of state within the family. This was despite, not because of, the attitude of some of its members. For though his charm was formidable, Queen Elizabeth the Queen Mother was unconvinced and Prince Philip was at pains to distance himself from his overbearing didacticism. Where the future of Prince Charles was concerned, Mountbatten was never short of advice, arguing with such eloquence and persistence that he was not easily gainsaid. In any discussion about the rival merits of the competing services Mountbatten was always in there, making the case for the Navy and urging that his great-nephew had no need to dabble in the other services as well. In the autumn of 1966, when the Prince was still at Gordonstoun, he had pressed the point directly with the impressionable eighteen-year-old. Even if – as others had argued – it was appropriate for him 'to do some time' in all three services, he wrote, 'I would like to repeat . . . I am quite certain that you must have a "mother service" that you really belong to and where you can have a reasonable career. Your father, Grandfather, and both your Great Grandfathers had a distinguished career in the Royal Navy. If you follow in their footsteps this would be very popular . . .' He added with the guile of a patient persuader, 'However, there is no hurry about any decision and perhaps we can have a gossip about this when you are staying at Broadlands . . .'[1] Now he had retired as Chief of Defence Staff, he had even more time to devote to the future of his beloved great-nephew.

As it happened, the Duke of Edinburgh was equally enthusiastic about the Navy. His own prospects as an outstanding naval officer had been abruptly arrested by his marriage to the future Queen in 1947; twenty years later he applied himself with tenacity to his son's military 'career', discussing the options with military commanders, naval officers and in particular with the First Sea Lord, Admiral Sir Varyl Begg. In a series of handwritten notes to his son, Prince Philip reported on these meetings in detail and proffered his own advice. Eventually, after a formal meeting with both his parents, the Prince agreed to enter the Navy for three years, after which he could decide whether to stay or move on to other ventures. However, on advice from the Admiral, who warned that he could only give the Prince his own command after three and a half years of service, and that 'to make anything of it' he would need a captaincy lasting no less than eighteen months, it was agreed in principle that a five-year stint would be desirable. However, the Duke of Edinburgh did not altogether welcome Mountbatten's close involvement, suggesting that while the Prince should consult 'Uncle Dickie', his great-uncle should on no account be allowed to intervene directly with his former naval subordinates, which, Prince Philip judged, would produce 'a dreadful muddle'.[2]

The memoranda show Prince Philip to have been attentive and concerned but remote, as if conducting the affairs of a business rather than guiding and nurturing a son. The tone and language was factual and abrupt, doubtless in consequence of the fact that the relationship between father and son was by now largely conducted in this form. As their respective activities took them in different directions, they seldom saw each other except at the traditional house parties at Balmoral, Sandringham and Windsor, when neither would find the occasion to broach issues of substance or share intimacies. In Buckingham Palace, though their apartments were but a short walk apart, they lived separate lives. The gap of communication between them also reflected the Prince's efforts to become 'his own man', while a reluctance to face the paternal rebuke that seemed always to hover in the atmosphere between them had by now become habitual. The affection between father and son, deep though it might have been, was rarely in evidence; in a family where the concept of duty was a daily assumption, criticism sprang much more easily to the lips than praise, which was often lacking. Though he was too proud to admit it, the Prince still craved the affection and appreciation that his father – and his mother – seemed unable or unwilling to proffer. Therefore, in self-protection, he retreated more and more into formality with his parents, which their closest mutual friends could do nothing to dissolve. Business between them was thus conducted with dispatch but detachment. Nonetheless, he had grown to admire his father and especially his ability 'to get to the heart of the matter and to analyse things in a practical way'.[3] Being so different in character, the Prince had learned to recognise that his father was bound to be frustrated by his 'incurable romanticism'; and he was grateful, too, for advice, which was 'all the more valuable because it came from a perspective so different from my own' – even if the manner in which it was given was often somewhat brusque.

In February 1970, after securing the official blessing for the decision from the Prime Minister, Buckingham Palace announced that the Prince of Wales would enter the Royal Navy in the autumn of the following year. It added that before enrolling at the Royal Naval College, Dartmouth, he would do a four-month attachment with the Royal Air Force at Cranwell, with the purpose of qualifying as a jet pilot. In his second year at Cambridge, Prince Charles had chosen to take up flying, receiving instruction from RAF, Personnel and Training Command. Still hoping to enlist the heir apparent into their ranks, the Command had been eager to know whether the university undergraduate would want to progress from a Chipmunk to a Provost jet. As a Squadron Leader, his equerry favoured the notion, but the Prince had remonstrated, 'The thing to do would be to see how I get on and then decide . . . Remember also that I have yet to see whether I am in fact capable of flying an aeroplane and we better wait and see!'[4] As it was, the Prince soon showed himself to be capable enough as a pilot for the Captain of the Queen's Flight to enthuse about 'the wonderful progress he has made' to the Duke of Edinburgh. Thereafter, in his meticulous fashion, Prince Philip had established that a course at Cranwell would be appropriate, and the Prince had readily assented.

*

The Prince of Wales flew into Cranwell on 8 March 1971, at the controls of a twin-engined Basset of the Queen's Flight. As ever, concerns about protocol, security and the press were paramount. It was agreed between the Palace and the RAF that senior officers and those of equal rank would refer to their royal colleague as 'Prince Charles', while junior ranks would call him 'Sir'. Off duty, he would be accorded the normal privileges of a member of the royal family: everyone would either bow or curtsey when first meeting him, addressing him as 'Your Royal Highness' and afterwards as 'Sir' or 'Prince Charles'. Two press facilities were arranged – one before his arrival for a briefing about Cranwell, and the other on the day itself – in the hope that thereafter he would recapture the relative obscurity of Cambridge.

The usual security precautions were complicated by the need to designate the two aircraft assigned to the Prince as 'Royal Aircraft', which had to be kept in a hangar apart from the other planes behind a security barrier and guarded at all times by RAF police. A team of authorised technicians was appointed to carry out routine maintenance behind closed doors and in the presence of the security staff. By long-established precedent the safety of the royal family in the air was presumed to be the responsibility of ministers answerable to Parliament. It had thus become a matter of course to consult the Prime Minister on matters of principle, while arrangements for the Queen's Flight were the responsibility of the Secretary of State for Defence. Within the guidelines established by this precedent, the Prince was permitted to undertake any flights from Cranwell which formed part of the normal course. However, before allowing him to fly in any exercise which 'may involve risks not normally included in the course',[5] the Commandant had both to inform the Queen of the proposal and to ask the Secretary of State for authorisation. To his chagrin, these safety precautions would more than once prevent the Prince from taking part in operations that were undertaken by other young officers with similar experience.

Despite his characteristic misgivings about a new institution, the Prince enjoyed Cranwell from the start:

> I can't tell you how strange it seems to be a serving officer all of a sudden. I am now just beginning to get used to the fact that I have a uniform on and I ought to be calling senior officers 'Sir'. The latter I find most difficult because I haven't called anyone 'Sir' for a long time

and I've got so used to meeting senior officers over the past two or three years that the element of fear subsided. They seem more nervous of me than I do of them – but I dare say the element of fear and subservience will soon return to me via the agency of a well-placed boot![6]

He was in the company of a more homogeneous group than he had encountered at Cambridge; individuals whose military approach and style he trusted and understood, and who were of a stamp with which he had been familiar from childhood: 'The people themselves are really very friendly and the chap who lives on my corridor is charming and likes the Goons – immediate compatibility! . . . I have a splendid fussing batman who does very well and uses the Royal "we" all the time, i.e. "What suit shall we put on this evening, Sir?"'[7] To Mountbatten he wrote about course lectures on the fuel and electrical systems of the jet engine, aero-dynamics, the mechanics of flight and the laws of motion: 'To my amazement I find I am beginning to understand some of it and I am convinced that the secret is continuity all day and every day. They certainly keep one busy here and I am up early and in bed fairly early as well. The food is pretty revolting, and at unearthly times, but the atmosphere is very like that of a University.'[8]

After two weeks of ground training he was in the air at the controls of a Jet Provost. He found navigation hard to master but nevertheless was soon permitted to fly solo. His diary entry on 31 March 1971 noted, 'The day when I went solo for the first time in the J.P. Did it after 8 hours instead of the normal 10. An exciting feeling to be let loose in my own jet. Convinced I flew it far better without Dick Johns* in it to criticise my every move . . . I did one circuit and managed to bring off a very passable landing . . . The feeling of power, smooth, unworried power, is incredible.'[9] He was also allowed to practise solo aerobatics, flying at 25,000 feet. 'I can't tell you how rewarding it is when one begins to feel increasingly more professional at some skill,' he wrote to Hugh van Cutsem, reporting that, 'Recently I went on a cross-country solo flight and managed – just – to find my way back here again.' He was 'amazed' how much he had enjoyed the experience.[10]

On one occasion, he was allowed to fly in the back seat of a Phantom

---

* Squadron Leader Richard Johns, later Air Marshal, was the Prince's instructor from September 1970 to August 1971.

of 43 Squadron: 'We climbed into the cockpit of the Phantom – on scramble readiness – and when the 2 minute warning was given both engines were started at once and we taxied straight out onto the runway from a shed and took straight off. After a re-heat take-off we climbed to 35,000 feet in 2 minutes at a virtually vertical angle. An attack was then made on a Canberra flying at 48,000 feet and I worked furiously to operate the radar properly.' Later, after refuelling in flight, they flew low over his beloved Scottish home: 'Bad weather meant . . . dropping down through a hole in the cloud over Ballater. We flew twice over Balmoral at 400 feet, scattering deafened tourists and causing 7 locals to ring up the police in protest. We then roared off at 420 knots past Lochnagar and over Loch Muick . . . The whole visit was an unforgettable experience.'[11]

Towards the end of July, he made his first parachute jump with three fellow officers from Cranwell. Wearing the parachute harness made him feel like a 'retired tortoise', while his stomach harboured 'flocks of butterflies' which 'indulged in the biggest population explosion since Adam and Eve'. When they reached the dropping zone over Studland Bay, he watched two of his colleagues 'vanish sideways in the slipstream', which almost 'finished' him:

> As I had been clever enough to say I wanted to jump and the press had said I was going to jump I was going to.
>
> It was a curious sensation standing in the doorway and just waiting. I was certainly nervous, but I was longing to experience the sensation of launching myself out of the door . . . I kept having morbid reflections on wrapping myself round the tailplane or hitting my head on the side of the aircraft, or even dropping out of the harness before I reached the water.

When his turn finally came, the Prince jumped almost before the green light. There was a 'tumbling, unreal sensation' but as he came out of the slipstream and the parachute opened, he found himself upside down, his feet entangled in the rigging lines: 'I thought how stupid of them not to warn me of this, but I was extraordinarily calm and in command of the situation and quickly removed my feet . . . There was only a short time to admire the view and enjoy the sensation before my feet touched the water and I was trying to get free of the harness.' His predicament, which would have been alarming if the lines themselves had become entangled, was apparently extremely rare, leading him to note, 'I can only imagine I have hollow legs.' Afterwards, keenly aware that he had demonstrated a reserve of courage that even the most sceptical critic would respect, he felt 'exhilarated and happy beyond belief'.[12] Even twenty-five years later, recalling his 'icy' calm in the moment of crisis, he could not resist a note of defiance: 'I've done it . . . And nobody can take that away from me.'[13] Later, when he was appointed Colonel-in-Chief of the Parachute Regiment in 1977, he insisted on joining its parachute training course. He explained later, 'I felt I should lead from the front or at least be able to do some of the things that one expects others to do for the country . . . I didn't think I could look them in the eye or indeed ever dream of wearing that beret with the Parachute Regiment badge unless I'd done the course . . . So they all put their hands up in horror – or rather the RAF did – but somehow it was organised and I did it.'[14]

After almost five months with the RAF, the Prince was awarded his wings and, feeling 'very sad', left his new friends: 'So many people kept saying how much they had enjoyed having me and how they were going to miss my presence that I was practically reduced to shamefully sentimental tears.' On his last evening, he was called upon to make a speech at a guest night in the officers' mess, a celebration where ritual dictates formality of dress and excess of alcohol. In this ambience he was delighted when they laughed at his jokes, and even more so when they gave him a standing ovation at the end: 'I became rapidly intoxicated . . . Twice I fell over my legs which kept on getting in the way of my feet . . . Finally I rocked on my heels backwards into a large Squadron Leader who was busily engaged in operating a vast tankard of beer. There was a saturated scream as his face disappeared inside the tankard to reappear seconds later with a moustache covered in foam.'[15]

After posing for an official photo – 'complete with steely expression and far-away look in cold blue eyes'[16] as he self-mockingly described the ensuing memento – the Prince hastened to Balmoral for the summer. In September, he returned briefly to Cranwell for the passing-out parade, where he was required to stand on parade for over an hour, most of the time at attention: 'I now know what the poor guardsmen have to go through. I was in agony, my back ached, my knees felt like lead balloons and my feet swelled until I felt my toes were going to pop out of the front of them. However, I avoided fainting and managed to have my wings pinned on my chest without mishap. A marvellous moment.'[17]

The prospect of joining the Navy was daunting. 'Please remember one unfortunate sub-species of naval life, Sub Lieutenant, the Prince of Wales, who will be wedded to his ships for at least five years as part of Great Britain's NATO contribution,' he wrote to a friend. 'I am beginning to pale at the thought of what Dartmouth is going to do to me. Whatever it is it's going to be far worse than the most excruciating tortures they could ever dream up at Cranwell!'[18]

The foreboding and trepidation with which Acting Sub Lieutenant Prince Charles embarked on the naval career which had been mapped out for him by his father and the Admiralty was not swiftly dispelled. Founded early in the century to train the naval officers of a great empire, Dartmouth was an institution in rapid transition. The rules and procedures of the college reflected the kind of discipline that was considered appropriate for officer cadets entering the Navy straight from school. Like several of his peers, however, Prince Charles was a university graduate, and like them he found the constraints irksome: 'It was exactly like being locked up at school again and we weren't allowed out, except on rare weekends. It really was quite a business . . . endless rushing about, drill . . . It really was quite a shock to the system.'[19] One of his contemporaries at Dartmouth, who later served with him aboard ship, noticed how almost every graduate found the experience 'irritating and incomprehensible at once'[20]: it was demeaning to be treated as an adolescent but the education in seamanship and naval technology was demanding and intense.

It had been decided to place the Prince on the 'fast-stream' intensive course which ran for six weeks rather than for a full twelve-week term. In this time, he would be instructed in the 'traditions, customs, and discipline'[21] of the Navy, the structure of the service, navigation, and the art of leadership. A week after his arrival, he wrote with mixed feelings:

I have hardly had a moment to breathe since I arrived. We get up at six am most days and have to suffer the early morning indignities of being bawled at by a Whale island GI* with a voice like a horse. It's either

---

* Gunnery Instructor. In the Royal Navy, the gunnery branch is responsible for drill.

that or torture by Morse Code . . . I've joined the college sub aqua club and have passed my diving tests. I'm going to dive outside the harbour tomorrow . . . I'm also trying to go surfing as and when I can get away at weekends because I have an Australian board and am desperately trying to achieve the standing position . . .

Everywhere I look my eye catches some familiar face peering down at me from a portrait on the wall. Papa wrote and said I could console myself with the thought that I was serving 'Mum and Country'! I hope I can and it fills me with pride to think I might be able to be of some service. No doubt six weeks here is quite enough though. I am doing a twelve week course in six and I doubt if I could keep this pressure up for more than six weeks.[22]

Though he could not hope to rival the achievements of his great-uncle or – in a mere six weeks – his father (who had emerged from three years at Dartmouth as the winner of the 'King's Dirk'* as the best in his class), the Prince was resolute in his ambition 'to be of some service'. He did not think of himself as a 'natural' seaman, but he had the judgement of a steady pilot and soon showed himself capable of handling the small craft with which the cadets were entrusted, 'driving Picket boats and kitchen-rudder Jolly boats into pontoons, generally terrorising the seafaring populace of Dartmouth'.[23] However, he found even the rudiments of military technology – to which the future of the service and the career prospects of high-flyers were already in thrall – baffling. In contrast to his father, and even more so to Mountbatten, the science of navigation eluded him as well; in the confines of an overheated classroom, the details of astro-navigation were prone to lull him towards unconsciousness, a process which his fellow students noted with assiduous attention.

At first, his brother officers found his presence intimidating, but when he shared with them his sense of incompetence they warmed to the self-deprecation with which he habitually protected himself. 'If we'd seen him as another officer under training,' one of his contemporaries recalled, 'we'd have thought, "What a nice man. What's he going to do for a living?" . . . He had a sort of endearing vagueness. And yet there was a quality . . . a mystique perhaps . . . whether that's an innate quality or

---

* A small sword awarded to a midshipman when he gains a commission as a Sub Lieutenant. Today, the award is known as the 'Queen's Sword'.

whether it's part of the royal training . . . that's what set him apart from all the others.' They envied his aplomb, the 'wonderfully mature, measured, purposeful way' in which he could talk to a senior officer without breaching protocol and etiquette, and they were touched by his modesty.[24]

In the months before his incarceration in what, in anticipation, he described as that 'nautical penitentiary', there had been some doubt about which ship he would be posted to when he left. As often when anxiety pricked his confidence, he could be irritable to the point of petulance. 'What is wrong with everyone?' he wrote furiously to his private secretary, David Checketts. 'When I asked the CDS* the other evening at Windsor what ship I was going to, he said Antrim – you say Norfolk. Which is it?'[25] It did not apparently cross his mind that the career details of even a royal Sub Lieutenant might not have been uppermost in the mind of the Chief of Defence Staff. Though he was usually gentle and solicitous, he was also inclined to indulge a streak of selfishness, which the deference of those about him did little to stem.

In August, with confirmation that he would join HMS *Norfolk* in the Mediterranean six weeks after entering Dartmouth, he wrote a note to his secretary, Edward Smith, about the date on which he would fly to Gibraltar, where he was to join the ship. 'Originally the plan was to join Norfolk on 8th November. They now want me to be there on Sat. 6th. Is that correct? It makes planning one's life more complicated and incredibly annoying.'[26] On this occasion, the source of his frustration was the prospect of forgoing a treasured evening with his great-uncle at Broadlands, followed by a day's shooting on the estate. In a characteristic intervention, Mountbatten had spoken to the Vice-Chief of Naval Staff to discover his great-nephew's itinerary and had concluded with kindly intent that the Prince could squeeze in a day with the pheasants – which would have been his only such outing of the season – before joining *Norfolk*. After his last visit to Broadlands the year before, the Prince had written, 'Nothing, literally nothing, is adequate enough to thank you for that "day of days". You are the most astonishing Great Uncle ever . . . The pheasants were carefully drilled to ensure the most exciting, indescribable, memorable, exhausting, record-breaking, finger-burning,

---

* Chief of Defence Staff. At that time this was Admiral of the Fleet Sir Peter Hill-Norton, who was CDS 1971–73.

shattering, thoroughly well organised day. Thank you Uncle Dickie, more than ever I can say for letting me come – I shall never forget it.'[27]

Confined to a pre-ordained path planned months, even years in advance by others, the Prince had come to crave the independence which was usually denied him; his moments of liberty, when he could decide for himself where to go, whom to see, and what to do, therefore acquired intense, almost obsessive significance. In others of a similar age, his intemperate response to even a minor disruption of his own plans would have been disproportionate; but aware that he was not quite as others were, his staff bore his bouts of ill humour with weary patience. Nor was the Prince then to know that, in consultation with the Foreign Office, the change of date which had so frustrated him had been made to ensure that the heir to the throne should spend only the minimum of time on the Rock, in order to spare the feelings of the Spanish authorities, whose long-standing claim to the British colony was a continuing source of friction with the government at Westminster.*

On Friday 5 November, after passing his exams at Dartmouth, Sub Lieutenant Prince Charles flew from Brize Norton in an RAF Britannia to Gibraltar to join the destroyer HMS *Norfolk*. 'The flight out was excruciatingly uncomfortable – being a trooping aircraft there was no room for your legs and there was no escape from a pall of cigarette smoke which always drifted towards me,' he noted in the first entry in a naval journal in which he was to record his impressions of life at sea every day for the next five years.† In *Norfolk*, he met his Captain, who,

---

* Spain lays claim to Gibraltar, ceded to Britain by the Treaty of Utrecht (1713) which concluded the War of the Spanish Succession. Britain argues that transferred sovereignty over Gibraltar in perpetuity. In 1963 the Franco government in Spain began a campaign, through the United Nations, to force Britain to cede Gibraltar. Spain imposed restrictions on Gibraltar, culminating in the closure of the frontier in 1969, the withdrawal of the Spanish labour force, and the severing of transport and communication links with Spain.

† Every newly appointed midshipman in the Royal Navy was required to keep a daily journal of his first six months at sea, the purpose being to train junior officers to record accurately and clearly the salient facts about the organisation and operation of a warship at sea; for this reason an 'IMPORTANT NOTE' on the cover of every journal states that, 'This is a SECRET document during Hostilities. Commanding Officers are to make adequate provision for its security.' In his

to the delight of the new Sub Lieutenant, was blessed with the surname Cook; 'I was to be treated like any other Sub Lieutenant, but there were obviously differences and I suspect no one was sure how I would behave or how pompous I would be.'[28]

In fact, the presence of the Prince of Wales in *Norfolk* was to impose a set of additional responsibilities on his fellow officers, and especially on the Captain. A long and detailed naval memorandum made clear that concern about his personal safety was paramount. The threat posed by the IRA and (at the time) by the Angry Brigade* was persistent, while the risk that a disenchanted or deranged seaman might run amok or wreak vengeance on the heir to the throne was not to be taken lightly. Yielding to the wishes of the Duke of Edinburgh and the Queen, the security services agreed to lift the permanent protection by his protection officers, Sergeants Paul Officer and John Maclean, when he was at sea – though one or other of them would be with him ashore and, occasionally, on short sea passages from one port to another. To cover their absence, the ship's company was instructed by the Captain on the need to be extra vigilant on his behalf. For diplomatic as well as security reasons, the ship's programme had to be cleared with the Foreign Office, while the Ministry of Defence had to be informed of any change of plan. Noting that, 'Prince Charles keeps himself very fit . . . he is a fresh air fiend and spends as much time in the open air as possible,' the office memorandum records that when he was engaged in 'slightly dangerous sports' like diving and water-skiing his fellow officers would form a discreet presence. A doctor was always on hand in case of emergency.[29]

---

* A small extremist group which planted a number of small incendiary devices around Britain at this period. In January 1971, the group claimed responsibility for bombing the Hertfordshire home of Robert Carr, Secretary of State for Employment. It also claimed responsibility for machine-gunning the Spanish embassy in London, and for planting bombs near a BBC van during the Miss World contest.

---

journal, the Prince defied convention by sustaining a daily entry for much longer than required and – even more defiantly – by ignoring statistical ephemera and eschewing nautical jargon. Written in longhand, the 60,000 words of reflections, observations, impressions and reactions to the new world about him constitute a document of limited naval value but of inestimable worth to the biographer.

There were also special arrangements for handling his monthly pay cheque and for protecting his personal belongings, including his clothes (to guard against souvenir hunters), his memoranda and his correspondence. A line of communications was established between HMS *Norfolk*, relevant government departments, the Admiralty and the Palace (in the person of Checketts) so that each could liaise with the other with speed and efficiency. No detail was left to chance: Queen's Regulation (Royal Navy) 1354, for example, stated that the Queen's health was to be drunk seated 'except when HM the Queen or when other members of the Royal Family' were present.[30] Aboard HMS *Norfolk* it was considered *de rigueur* to seek the royal Sub Lieutenant's permission to remain seated for the loyal toast.

The day after his arrival, greatly looking forward to 'my first day at sea in one of Her Majesty's finest warships', he was to have watched the guided missile destroyer in gunnery practice. However, a shell jammed in a gun barrel and the exercise had to be called off. As the Prince noted, 'Not everything in the Navy, as I was to discover, happens like clockwork, and certainly not on time.'[31] The *Norfolk* set sail for Toulon to join a NATO exercise, where 'our ship looked by far the best and most glamorous one in the long line of vessels. No one else I felt could possibly know how to operate at sea as well as we could!'[32] At Cranwell, the Prince had compressed a year's course into five months, and at Dartmouth three months into six weeks. In *Norfolk*, he was expected to gain a Bridge Watchkeeping Certificate in nine months,* and he felt the pressure: 'I believe in being well occupied and busy . . . but I expect more is learnt and accumulated by midshipmen who have longer to explore and investigate . . . However I did obtain my Wings reasonably fairly . . . as I passed the exams at Dartmouth, but I lacked that touch of professionalism which only comes after longer periods.'[33]

After a day of preparation in the harbour at Toulon, he joined a party of officers ashore for dinner, where they consumed a delicious meal and quantities of Barsac, Champagne and Armagnac. They staggered into the street and headed towards the 'red light area' where, in his account:

---

* A Bridge Watchkeeping Certificate, which authorises the holder to take charge of a ship under all circumstances and in any conditions, is a vital milestone in an officer's career, essential to promotion. This normally takes between six and twelve months to gain.

We went into one bar where a group of our sailors tried, successfully, to force beer down my throat. I had already attempted to drink pastiche [*sic*] but gave up abruptly . . . We then moved on to another bar even more crowded with our sailors and Dutch matelots . . . A young lady of little attraction grabbed me by the wrist and drew me to the counter muttering 'Rum and Coke?' with a heavily disguised French accent. I meekly accepted while the bar reverberated to the sound of inebriated voices singing 'There'll always be an England' accompanied by a Dutch sailor playing the accordion!

At this point I began to think I was a marked man. Not one, but TWO naval patrols appeared outside the bar. Newspaper headlines flashed through my sub-conscious – 'Sailor Prince arrested in sleazy French Bar – Admiralty Probe'. It all contributed to my general education though.'[34]

Once the NATO exercise was underway, Prince Charles had little to do except observe his superiors about their business. He was not overly impressed by the coordination between the Allies, which he judged to be half-hearted. On one occasion, he was allowed to manoeuvre *Norfolk* alongside a French tanker for refuelling, a task he managed to accomplish without recourse to the ship's Battenberg* which had been invented by his great-great-uncle† expressly for that purpose but which the Prince regarded as a 'hideous device'.

On their way back to Toulon, on passage through the Bonifacio Straits, the wind rose and the ships were soon pounding through steep seas:

All the time we were coming down in speed, a knot a time, as the ship rose and shuddered out of a trough, only to fall back into one with a great thump that sent reverberations the length of the ship. Huge clouds of spray and great curtains of water came flying over the bows and thundered all over the fo'c'sle – occasionally over the bridge windows too. It was a magnificent sight to watch . . . When I went back to my cabin, though, and climbed into my bunk, the movement of the

---

* A device used to calculate the course and speed required for one ship to take up a particular position relative to another.
† Prince Louis of Battenberg, Mountbatten's father.

ship was so violent in the rolling plane that I honestly felt on occasions that the ship was never going to right herself . . .[35]

His early attempts at navigation were not blessed with success. Instructed to plot a course from Toulon to Plymouth, a thousand miles away, he pored over books and charts, measuring heights and distances, and noting currents and tides. 'Chaos reigned in the charthouse,' he noted, and worse, 'No sooner had I completed my artistic handiwork than the navigator appeared and proceeded to rub everything out . . . In the end the ship sailed in the direction of my revised lines and by some curious accident Plymouth hove into sight at approximately the right time in the morning. My relief was ill-concealed . . !'[36]

The self-doubt which had always plagued him surfaced in a letter to Mountbatten about the debilitating effect of his inexperience:

I've been made to work extremely hard ever since I set foot in this mighty vessel. I stumble around the ship, falling down hatches and striking my head against bulkheads in an effort to find my way about. There are so many departments to learn about that the task seems more than any brain can cope with . . . I have been what you call 'thrown in at the deep end' in the most obvious manner . . . I'm afraid I tend to suffer from bouts of hopeless depression because I feel I'm never going to cope . . . One is surrounded in a ship this size by such scores of hideously professional officers and ratings that I find I appear even more useless than usual. I'm hoping that suddenly all sorts of things will slip into place and I will see the light.[37]

Despite the burden of these anxieties – all the heavier for fear that his failings were subject to more than usually close scrutiny – he was learning to suppress the symptoms in public. Although he did not attempt to disguise his misgivings from fellow officers, he did not complain about his lot but tried instead to conceal his dejection behind his habitual façade of self-deprecation. However, his diffidence did not prevent him from the expression of strong opinion, buttressed by the certainty that as heir to the throne he had inherited a responsibility to record his views – at least in his journals – for the benefit of posterity. His commitment to the Royal Navy was coloured by a romantic vision of Britain's maritime tradition. Loyal to the image of a Sceptr'd Isle protected from invasion by a maritime force of matchless worth, he regarded the relentless contraction of the Senior Service as alarmingly short-sighted. During a joint exercise involving the RAF and the Navy off the coast of Scotland, he was scathing about the cumbersome network of communications between the two services: 'The real difficulty, I feel, lies in the limited war which could take place a very long way from the U.K. The RAF has certainly proved it possible to fly out to the Far East in a short time, but what is to guarantee the unchallenged passage of strike aircraft through several countries' airspaces?'[38]

The young officer was strongly opposed to the decision to scrap the Royal Navy's last aircraft carriers, HMS *Eagle* and HMS *Ark Royal*, a decision which originated in the Labour Party's defence review in 1967.[*] 'The decision to scrap the carriers may have been a political one and, indeed, a necessary financial economy. But it is still an unfortunate move. Without carriers the Americans would have been in an even worse plight, long ago, in Vietnam. However, a new system has to be made to work by the services and I think the RAF and R.N. are sufficiently flexible and professional to achieve this.' In the column beside this observation his Commanding Officer noted cryptically, 'They will have to be.'[39]

As part of a missile and gunnery course, the technicalities of which left him 'bewildered', he attended a lecture on 'The Threat': 'Before six minutes were up I felt like handing in my resignation and joining the Other Side! The overall threat posed by the Warsaw Pact countries and the Russian navy is horrifying . . .'[40] Thoroughly alerted to the Soviet threat, he went on to learn how to escape from a submarine holed by a missile or depth charge: wearing nose clips and goggles, he was secured in a chamber which was then submerged to a depth of 100 feet in a water tank – 'anyone with claustrophobic tendencies would have passed out there and then'. Wearing an escape suit incorporating a life jacket, he was ejected from the chamber and 'came up like a cork and practically flew out over the side of the tank'.[41] A crash course in submarine warfare evoked memories of stalking in Scotland:

> but the main difference is that one is being stalked oneself. This is not a pleasant sensation particularly as . . . the stalker tends to have an

---

[*] Following withdrawal from the East of Suez, it was decided that the RAF could undertake the tasks previously fulfilled by the aircraft carriers by using fixed wing aircraft from land bases.

advantage over the stalked. A submarine can virtually do as she pleases; loitering sufficiently far away from a main body or single ship to avoid being picked up on sonar, much as a lion patiently waits for a herd of zebra to feed its way towards her. Then the weakest is singled out and run down.[42]

His sense of the absurd, as ever only just below the surface, made him a wry observer of even the best laid plans. During a three-week attachment to the frigate HMS *Hermione*, while *Norfolk* was in dry dock, he went to the exercise area south of the Isle of Wight to watch the testing of the new Seacat missile system: 'Nothing ever happened to plan on any of the days. It was either because of the weather or due to the aircraft targets being unserviceable or grounded by fog . . . However, the trials teams left with some notes in their little books or in their bulging brains.'[43]

Although his technical skills were modest, he began to acquire a reputation for caring for the 'other ranks'. In small ways, his journal confirms the impression. On exercise in a storm, the ship lurched violently through the night keeping him awake, but the Prince noted:

It was nothing compared to the purgatory suffered by the P.O.'s* in the forward mess. They literally get flung out of their bunks when the ship lashes about, and it says a great deal for the quality and character of the British N.C.O.* that they suffer this gladly and retain their irrepressible sense of humour. On my part I find it hard to retain a sense of humour when returning to my cabin and discovering everything rattling about on the floor . . .[44]

Discovering a world where the language and manners belonged to a class and background with which he was already acquainted from a life spent in a world of foremen, chauffeurs and grooms, he warmed to the men of the lower deck, believing them sincerely (if without originality) to be the 'salt of the earth'.[45]

After that exercise, he was transferred briefly to the nuclear submarine, HMS *Churchill*. Before Dartmouth, the Prince had resisted pressure to join the submarine fleet for a sustained bout of training; his experience

---

* PO, Petty Officer; NCO, Non-Commissioned Officer.

in *Churchill* served only to confirm his reluctance: 'I had been warned that nuclear submarines were far more spacious than conventionals but the mind boggles at the thought of how small a conventional must be when you see the size of the wardroom and bunkspaces in a nuclear.'[46] He was given the top bunk in the First Lieutenant's cabin. Thinking he was alone, he was astonished by 'a grunting and rustling noise somewhere below me and a small officer (I suppose it was!) crawled out sleepily from the bottom bunk like a dormouse emerging from hibernation and disappeared. When I woke up at breakfast time there was somebody else of unknown description hidden by a curtain.'[47]

On a tour of the vessel, he was told that some visitors had asked 'unhelpfully' how many hospitals could be bought for the £30 million cost of a nuclear submarine, a question which provoked in him an outburst of indignation:

> What they fail to realise is that these nuclears, and the Polaris boats in particular, provide the greatest assurance for peace that the world has, I believe, ever known. Without such a powerful deterrent (even one Polaris sub. is enough) we could not have the security to build 10 hospitals, let alone 50 for an equivalent sum of money. It is misguided enthusiasm which leads to this unrealistic attitude.[48]

At one point in the exercise, when *Churchill* was stalking the frigate, he was allowed to 'fly' the submarine, strapped into an aircraft seat and steering on the basis of a complex range of data fed into a panel in front of him. It is easier to steer a submarine at speed but at only six knots, he complained, 'I succeeded in porpoising Churchill through the bleak waters of the Clyde . . . It was very difficult to find the straight and level attitude . . . After hearing from everyone how brilliantly my father drove the thing a few months ago (at 20 knots and fairly deep) I was beginning to lose my sense of humour!'[49] Asked persistently whether he was enjoying himself on *Churchill* and when he intended to join the submarine service, 'I tried to give non-committal answers.'[50] His humour was not improved when a wave soaked him as he transferred from the hull of the submarine to *Hermione*'s Jolly boat:

> I leapt with a howl of rage into the boat which by now had dropped into a trough, so I floundered about in the bottom . . . As if this was

not enough, we roared off at extreme speed straight into the sea, which of course entered the boat, and then spent a very long time manoeuvring into a position to be hoisted inboard to Hermione. Despite lines to bow and stern we sat immobile 50 yards from the ship's side and no amount of encouragement on my part would persuade the coxwain or the line-holders on board to do anything constructive![51]

On a four-week 'work-up' in March 1972, he was taught how to lead a riot squad. Instructed in the rules of engagement by a Marine Colour Sergeant who had been on three tours of duty in Northern Ireland, the Prince noted that:

the sort of riot or disturbance that a naval riot squad would be called upon to disperse would be very different from the virtual war that is being waged in Ulster. The Navy is far more likely to have to cope with a violent situation in the Caribbean for instance. To this end it was impressed upon us that we should look business-like and deadly as we came clumping round the corner of the street and confronted the crowd with an awe-inspiring body of hard-faced men. To begin with we looked more like an outing from the local Sunday School . . .[52]

In a letter to his great-uncle, he commented:

If we had to confront a proper riot I think I would have been almost more frightened of being shot at by one of the sailors than one of the rioters. The former seem to have no idea whatsoever of how to handle a rifle safely. The rioters played with sinister realism . . . They hurled (very inaccurately) large and solid potatoes, bags of flour, clods of earth and bits of galley gash but gave up rather rapidly when we 'shot' the ring-leader.[53]

Ever alert to the ridiculous, and not afraid of self-mockery, he reported how a simulated CS gas canister in the form of a smoke flare 'went off up my sleeve in my haste to hurl it towards the "mob" and to my amazement it flew out of my hand at right angles to the threat and landed in a bush beside the riot squad.'[54] At night, he was dispatched to take charge of the 'guards' protecting their camp against infiltrators: 'A figure appeared creeping along the hill and we succeeded in arresting and searching the suspect and taking him to the interrogation centre from which issued a series of bloodcurdling screams and furious bellows.'[55]

These wargames aside, the 'work-up' was not at all to the Prince's taste. The entire crew rose early and went to bed late while for three weeks the staff 'threw almost everything' at them. Practising the drill for 'man overboard', he was in charge of lowering a lifeboat. He mistimed an order and 'there was a nasty falling noise, a heavy splash and an expensive wooden splintering noise as the forward thwart was torn out of its socket . . .' These drills were, for the Prince, the worst part of this training which ended with 'a hot, miserable day entirely devoted to action stations . . .' In a footnote entered later to his journal, his Commanding Officer, Captain J.D.W. Cook, reprimanded him: 'You paint a fairly black picture of the work-up. It did in fact do us all a power of good, and Norfolk is a better tuned weapon as a result.'[56]

His irritation was evidently sharpened by another entry in which the Prince wrote with an openness that must have bewildered his superiors, 'A week of astro-navigation practice has been planned, so I resigned myself to the sheer mental torture of working out star sights again – a long and tedious process on my part . . .' His Commanding Officer responded tartly, 'A reappraisal on completion of your last para, please.'[57] In fact the astro-navigation course was surprisingly successful. Five days after his bleak self-appraisal the Prince discovered that:

> as the week went on I progressively gained confidence and began slowly to appreciate something of the principle of what I was doing. By the end of the week in fact the last starsights I took, I was deter-mined to succeed by myself in producing a proper 4-point fix on the plotting sheet. To my intense joy and amazement everything worked and the Navigator was suitably impressed. I actually went to bed before midnight in a haze of starlit glory![58]

Throughout the spring and early summer, Norfolk sailed the Channel and the Mediterranean, returning briefly again towards Gibraltar where seven months earlier the Prince had embarked in cloak-and-dagger style. Contemplating 'the familiar, secure shape' of Gibraltar in the morning haze, he wrote a succinct and pertinent appraisal of Britain's dilemma over the Rock, noting that, for the Spanish people, the possession of

Gibraltar by Britain was bound to arouse similar feelings as an occupation of The Lizard by Spain would arouse in the British people. However, he made it clear he was aware that, although the Treaty of Utrecht had been signed more than two and a half centuries ago, it still reflected the powerful feelings of the people of Gibraltar and was likely to remain in force for as long as such loyalty to Britain persisted.

HMS *Norfolk* had been assigned to screen the 87,000-ton American aircraft carrier, USS *John F. Kennedy*, as part of a NATO exercise. Comparing himself to a 'small child who has been taken to London airport for the first time',[59] the Prince was spellbound by the waves of Phantoms, Corsairs, Skyraiders and Trackers, which took off from their decks to soar overhead, circling round and then landing again in rapid succession. The experience rekindled his frustration at the decision to phase out the carrier HMS *Eagle*: 'I appreciate the problems of finance and the cost of running her, but surely there would be sense in retaining her until an adequate alternative has been found for a strike capability for the fleet.' Reading this, the Commander commented in the margin, 'You are right about Eagle but there is also a manpower bill to be paid and this also influenced the decision not to extend her along with the Ark Royal,' adding the mildly patronising, 'An excellent journal which is fun to read.' The Number 2 was less generous, complaining, 'There are still too many non-nautical terms appearing.'[60] Despite this, the unorthodox and — by the prevailing standards — eccentric account of his nine months in *Norfolk* evidently impressed the Admiralty Board in Whitehall. In his final entry, the royal Sub Lieutenant described the ship's progress up Portsmouth harbour 'past a dejected sad-looking HMS *Eagle*' and concluded, 'As we partook of a glass of champagne on the bridge I was rather pleased to have taken part in Captain Cook's last voyage.' Without equivocation, writing on behalf of the Admiralty, Sir Roderick Macdonald, president of the Fleet Board, observed, 'The best journal this Board has seen.'[61]

CHAPTER
ELEVEN

———— •◆• ————

By the time Prince Charles reached his twenty-third birthday, Mountbatten had become his closest confidant and the greatest single influence on his life. Calling him 'grandpapa' in private, in correspondence the great-nephew had started to refer to his great-uncle as 'honorary grandfather'. Mountbatten responded in kind, calling Prince Charles 'honorary grandson'. Based ashore at Portsmouth for several weeks in the autumn of 1971, the Prince declined to billet in the officers' mess at HMS *Dryad* but – at Mountbatten's invitation – commuted daily between the naval base and Broadlands, which he thought of as 'the best and most welcoming of homes'.[1] The bond of affection between the 'juvenile foolish offspring' and the' 'elderly wise uncle'[2] (as the Prince described them both) was reinforced by unbounded admiration on the one side and paternal care and pride on the other. Greatly moved by the trust placed in him, Mountbatten, who had now entered his eighth decade, never tired of the Prince's company. 'I miss you a lot,' he wrote when the Prince had departed after one long visit, 'for there is no one whose company I enjoy more, as I expect you realise.'[3]

As a meticulous planner who immersed himself in the minutiae of every venture on which he embarked, Mountbatten's urge to mould his surrogate grandson into his own image of a prince meant that no detail was too trivial to ignore, though in admonition he was never harsh or disparaging. 'You do write and speak amusingly and well,' he wrote in March 1971, 'so well in fact that I am going to strain our friendship by

pointing out a mistake which many people make in grammar . . . I hope
you won't mind an Old Great Uncle taking advantage of his seventy
years to point this out.'⁴ In this gentle way, he cited several examples of
the way in which the Prince had used the nominative case when he
should have used the dative ('I' for 'me'). Responsive to criticism
couched so genially, the Prince wrote back, 'I quite see what you
mean . . . and consequently curl up in literary excruciation! Thank you
for pointing it out to me – that way I shall <u>never</u> do it again.'⁵

As their mutual affection deepened, the Prince began to consult
Mountbatten on issues of state and family matters as well. Since in those
days the Queen rarely found occasion to confide in her son either about
her own role as sovereign or that of the royal family, and as his own
curiosity was at best intermittent, it was Mountbatten's egocentric but
illuminating memories which in these years did most to shape the
Prince's understanding of the ways of Whitehall and the constitutional
realities of the relationship between the monarchy and the state.
Mountbatten was uniquely placed as an 'insider', who had wielded
power and responsibility (notably as the last Viceroy of India and later as
the Chief of Defence Staff), to instruct the Prince with authority and
intimacy about the governance of Britain and help him interpret the
duties and opportunities he faced. Didactic but not pompous, he communicated his *aperçus* in anecdotes, which were invariably self-serving but
so tuned as to hold the most wayward listener. For hour after hour,
Prince Charles was entranced by these insights and the morals that
Mountbatten drew from them. Although some of those who worked for
him were to draw the conclusion that the Prince lacked the diligence to
pursue issues which did not immediately engage his imagination, he was
blessed with a strong memory for names, dates and places. Mountbatten's
tutelage was, fortuitously, well tailored to his pupil's aptitude; the Prince
rarely forgot anything that his great-uncle told him, and he was invariably disposed to believe him.

It was from Mountbatten that he learnt the details of the bitter conflicts surrounding Edward VIII's abdication in 1936, and from whom he
was to derive a conciliatory attitude towards his estranged great-uncle
David.* Mountbatten had been angling for some time to secure an invi-

---

* As Prince of Wales, before his accession to the throne as Edward VIII in 1936, he
  had been Mountbatten's close friend and companion.

tation for the Duke of Windsor to return to Britain with the Duchess to effect a reconciliation, if only of a formal kind, with the rest of the royal family. Prince Charles was susceptible to the discreet pressure that Mountbatten applied:

> I, personally, feel it would be wonderful if Uncle David and his wife could come over and spend a weekend. Now that he is getting old he must long to come back and it would seem pointless to continue the feud . . . Apart from anything else it would be fun to see what she was like . . . it is worthwhile getting to know the better side of her. I dare say it is much easier for me to speak like this because I knew nothing of what it was like before . . .[6]

To achieve this outcome, the Prince raised the possibility with his grandmother, Queen Elizabeth, but it was immediately apparent to him how difficult she would find it to be reconciled with the man whom she held responsible for consigning her husband to an early grave. Later the same year, however, the Prince made a private visit to France, where the British ambassador, Sir Christopher Soames, arranged for him to see the Duke of Windsor. It was a remarkable encounter which he recorded in his diary thus:

> I drove up with no small degree of anticipation as to what I would find in the Bois de Boulogne and upon entering the house I found foot-men and pages wearing identical scarlet and black uniforms to the ones ours wear at home. It was rather pathetic seeing that. The eye then wandered to a table in the hall on which lay a red box with 'The King' on it . . . The whole house reeked of some particularly strong joss sticks and from out of the walls came the muffled sound of scratchy piped music. The Duchess appeared from among a host of the most dreadful American guests I have ever seen. The look of incredulity on their faces was a study and most of them were thoroughly tight. One man shook hands with me twice, muttered something incomprehen-sible in French with a strong American accent and promptly collapsed into the arms of a strategically placed black footman . . .
>
> To my relief I managed to escape into a small sitting room where I was able to have a word with Uncle David by himself. He seemed in very good form, although rather bent and using a stick. One eye was

closed most of the time, as a result of his cataract operation, but apart from that he was in very talkative form and used wide, expansive gestures the whole time, while clutching an enormous cigar . . .

We got onto the subject of his relationship with his father and he said he had had a very difficult time with him and that Gan-Gan* was a hard woman and he had been brought up extremely strictly. Hence his feeling against older people and traditions of all sorts.†

While we were talking the Duchess kept flitting to and fro like a strange bat. She looks incredible for her age and obviously has her face lifted every day. Consequently she can't really speak except by clenching her teeth all the time and not moving any facial muscles. She struck me as a hard woman – totally unsympathetic and somewhat superficial. Very little warmth of the true kind; only that brilliant hostess type of charm but without feeling. All that she talked about was whether she would wear a hat at the Arc de Triomphe the next day.

Uncle David then talked about how difficult my family had made it for him for the past 33 years . . . I asked him frankly if he would like to return to England for the last years of his life, and he hesitated to ask Wallis if he should give me 'the works'. It sounded as though he would have liked to return, but he felt no one would recognise him. I assured him that would not be the case. On the other hand most of his contemporary friends are dead and there may be very little point in his coming back.

The whole thing seemed so tragic – the existence, the people and the atmosphere – that I was relieved to escape it after 45 minutes and drive round Paris by night.[7]

Eight months later, the Duke of Windsor was dead. On 2 June 1972, Prince Charles flew back from Malta, where he had been entertained in the uncongenial company of the Prime Minister Dom Mintoff, to attend the funeral. On the night of his arrival, he had dinner at Buckingham Palace with the Queen and the Duchess of Windsor, who was there for the first time since the abdication. As at their previous meeting, the Duchess 'prattled away' throughout the meal, provoking the Prince to

---

* The Prince's nickname for his great-grandmother, Queen Mary.
† The Duke of Windsor relates these difficulties in his memoirs, *A King's Story* (Remnant Society, 1953).

wonder 'what sort of strain she was suffering under – whether all the social chatter was part of a brilliant facade or whether she was really like that all the time and didn't really notice Uncle David's departure'. After dinner, they were joined by other members of the royal family to watch Mountbatten paying tribute to the Duke on television. It was, wrote the Prince, 'very moving and beautifully done'.[8]

The following day, he was at the Trooping the Colour, where he was powerfully affected by the 'mysterious' sound of the pipes and drums of the Scots Guards playing a lament in memory of the Duke of Windsor. After dinner that evening, he accompanied his great-uncle to St George's Chapel, Windsor, where they met the Duchess again in front of her husband's coffin at the lying-in-state. 'I shall never forget the scene,' the Prince wrote:

> The Chapel was silent, almost dark except for the huge candles round the catafalque, which cast a flickering peaceful glow on the great pillars and on the statuesque figures of the Guards Officers who stood vigil round the coffin. With great bearskinned heads bowed they stood absolutely motionless and silent . . .
>
> The Duchess did not seem to be well. Apparently there had been several crises that evening and it was only through the agency of her doctor that she came at all. Thank God she did. It would have been disastrous if she hadn't, I believe. Uncle Dickie supported her all the time and at one point she moved away from us and stood alone, a frail, tiny, black figure, gazing at the coffin and finally bowing briefly . . . As we stood she kept saying 'he gave up so much for so little' – pointing at herself with a strange grin.
>
> After she had gone back to B.P. [Buckingham Palace] Uncle Dickie and I waited until the Welsh Guards Bearer Party had removed the coffin to the Albert Memorial Chapel . . . The whole evening was full of grandeur, simplicity, beauty and mystery and I shall never forget it. I only wish I had known Uncle David better.[9]

Two days later, the royal family prepared to attend the funeral. 'No one could really be said to be in a funeral mood – except perhaps Granny,' the Prince wrote. 'Uncle David had become so remote that none of us really knew him.' Inside St George's Chapel, walking alone, he followed the coffin down the side aisle and round into the nave. He was once again touched by the grief of the moment: 'Somehow I felt deeply moved by the whole experience and felt that it was right that we were honouring Uncle David like this . . .' The service, he wrote, was 'simple, dignified to perfection, colourful and wonderfully British'. When the state trumpeters of the Household Cavalry blew the Last Post, the Prince trembled 'and my eyes filled with tears'.[10]

Within a few weeks, however, he was dry-eyed in correspondence with Mountbatten, who was conducting labyrinthine negotiations with the Duchess over the fate of the Duke's estate, which had all been left to her. As the royal family's 'shop steward' (as his biographer, Philip Ziegler, later described him[11]), Mountbatten had conceived the idea that a foundation should be established in the name of the Prince of Wales to distribute the income from the estate among British charities. Unfortunately, the Duchess had decided to entrust her affairs exclusively to a French lawyer, Maître Suzanne Blum, who was frostily unreceptive to Mountbatten's scheme. Only after Mountbatten brought to bear all his powers of persuasion did the Duchess finally agree at least to discuss the idea; but he failed to make headway and was eventually rebuffed in terms which, in the words of Ziegler, 'even he recognised must be final'.[12] Insisting that 'everything has been taken care of according to David's and my wishes', she rebuked Mountbatten for making her 'terribly depressed' when he visited her 'by your reminding me of David's death and my own, and I should be grateful if you would not mention this any more'.[13] The matter was closed.

As the Prince's counsellor, Mountbatten played an increasingly influential role. After one typical conversation, the Prince wrote in gratitude, 'You really are becoming exactly like Queen Victoria in her old age and nobody will know what to do when you aren't there to help and advise.'[14] Only with Mountbatten could the Prince talk 'man to man' about affairs of the heart and the romantic entanglements to which he now found himself drawn. Inexperienced in the fumbling liaisons that are formed by most young men in puberty or soon after, and shielded in adolescence from close contact with the opposite sex by the rituals of his family life, his discovery of romantic passion had been belated. By contrast, his great-uncle combined a traditional view of women with a worldly attitude to sex. Believing that every young man should 'sow his wild oats'[15] generously but with discretion, he unambiguously encouraged his 'honorary grandson' accordingly. Broadlands offered an environment in which the Prince could at least spend a little time in the company of an unattached young woman shielded from the prurience of reporters speculating about the honour of his intentions. In his role as surrogate grandfather, Mountbatten was quick to appreciate that in no other way could the heir to the throne make more than nodding acquaintance with the opposite sex, let alone dally in private like any other adult of his age. Over these years, therefore, he took it upon himself to welcome at Broadlands a number of potential *inamoratas* – whose names were never trawled through the gossip columns – taking care, by one means and another, that they were given the opportunity to be alone with the Prince. Without this collusion by Mountbatten and one or two other friends it is doubtful whether the Prince of Wales could ever have given expression to the commonplace passions of a healthy young man.

Among the young women whom he serenaded after leaving Cambridge, one – and one alone – had an immediate and indelible effect on him. She was introduced to him by Lucia Santa Cruz, with whom he had retained an affectionate relationship after leaving Cambridge. More than a year later, Lucia Santa Cruz reported with innocent enthusiasm that she had found 'just the girl' for the Prince, and arranged the occasion at which he first met Camilla Shand.

Camilla Shand was pretty, bubbly, and she smiled with her eyes as well as her mouth. Unlike some others he had met, she lacked coquetry and did not preen herself. She laughed easily and at the same sillinesses that brought him to tears of laughter. Theirs was not a sophisticated humour, neither dry nor arch, and it lacked that edge of malice required by a jaded palate. Like him, she was convulsed by the Goons, by silly accents and daft looks, while his taste for the absurd was complemented by her down-to-earth irreverence. Not caring for fashion or style, she was at home in the country with horses and hunting and familiar with the established hierarchies and simple traditions that still distinguished an unglamorous squirearchy from the urban *arrivistes* who had started to spend their way into ersatz ruralism. She was affectionate, she was un-assuming, and – with all the intensity of first love – he lost his heart to her almost at once.

As yet, the media speculation about when and whom he might marry, which would later help bend him into submission before the popular will, was not even a whisper in the wind; after all, he was only twenty-three and he had only just embarked on a demanding career. As portrayed in the press, he was a fresh-faced sailor of 'Action Man' potential, an adventurer who was resolute in his search of what the world might offer to a dashing young man, the most eligible bachelor on earth. So far as the tabloid pundits were concerned, he was having the time of his life – and good luck to him; they knew nothing of his quickening emotional turmoil. He was already aware that to accept his hand in marriage would be to enter a contract as much with an institution as an individual and to accept obligations that would go far beyond the conjugal bonds imposed either by the Law or by the Church. His consort would be the future Queen, the object of insatiable curiosity, and the creature of public whim. With that self-doubt and sensitivity which made him so beguiling to women, he had already confided to one or two of his intimates that he could not conceive that anyone he might hope to marry would want to marry him. In Camilla Shand, however, he dared to hope that he had stumbled across a resolution of that conundrum. In the late autumn of 1972, he saw her frequently and the more he was with her the more confident he became. In London or at Broadlands, he was at ease in her company and felt that she could be a friend and companion to love and to cherish. To his delight, it seemed to him that these feelings were reciprocated.

Their delight in each other's company was bounded by the knowledge that in the New Year the Prince was due to leave for the Caribbean in the frigate HMS *Minerva*, a commitment from which he could not conceivably escape but which would separate them for at least eight months. Later there would be speculation that before his departure, the Prince was close to asking her to marry him. In fact, although he was powerfully attracted to his new girlfriend, he was still too young and too uncertain of his feelings to contemplate such a huge step while both of them were far too reserved with each other even to mention the subject. Barely at the threshold of what was to become the most intimate friendship of his life, the Prince faced the prospect of departure without seeking any reassurance that their relationship would endure the separation. If he hoped that her feelings for him might survive his absence, he was far too reticent to say so.

Prince Charles joined *Minerva* three weeks before Christmas. A few days later, when Camilla Shand was staying the weekend at Broadlands, the Prince invited her and Mountbatten to join him for a tour of inspection and lunch. She returned the following weekend, 'the last time I shall see her for eight months', as he wrote sadly to Mountbatten.[16]

Six months earlier, an astute naval Captain at HMS *Mercury** had observed that Acting Sub Lieutenant the Prince of Wales was 'reaching saturation point after an interminable succession of training courses of one sort or another'. Urging that the Ministry of Defence undertake an urgent review of his training programme, he commented, 'He needs to get his teeth into a responsible and worthwhile job as soon as possible.'[17] Otherwise, the officer noted, he would be destined to spend his entire life in the Navy on one or another training programme, to no-one's obvious benefit (except, the writer forbore to say, to satisfy the competing demands of every branch of the Navy to have him aboard).

The Prince's limited technical prowess, and especially his failure to grasp the essence of navigation, had become a source of concern at higher levels of the Navy. Although he had passed the navigation exams at Dartmouth, officials were concerned at the Prince's self-confessed 'inability to add or generally to cope well with figures'.[18] For the Naval Secretary at the Ministry of Defence, writing soon after the Prince had joined *Norfolk*, this called into question the suitability of the programme which had been mapped out for the Prince to prepare him for command: 'The thought of Court Martialling the heir to the throne for a navigational error is good nightmare material.'[19] As a result of this shortcoming, the Prince had failed to acquire his Bridge Watchkeeping Certificate by the end of his time in *Norfolk*, which had been the ambitious target set for him. To the Captain of HMS *Mercury*, it seemed clear that his training schedule should be adapted accordingly, to help him secure this basic qualification – without which no command would in any case be possible. Evidently sensitive to the Prince's lack of confidence in his own ability to master the technological complexities of a modern navy, the Captain advocated that the Acting Sub Lieutenant be given 'some respite' from the wide range of formal training courses which loomed ahead of him and should return to sea 'as soon as possible' to concentrate on the practicalities of navigation and watchkeeping.

---

* HMS *Mercury*, the Communications School in Petersfield, Hampshire.

This wisdom went unheeded, and throughout the autumn until he joined *Minerva*, the Prince was whisked from one intensive course to another. His aversion to this force-feeding was palpable: according to one fellow officer, who later became a trusted colleague, 'He had to have "one to one" tuition, which was potentially embarrassing . . . He'd ask a question which would indicate that he hadn't a natural flair but he applied himself diligently.' Those around him assumed – correctly – that he had come to rely heavily on the knowledge and experience of Mountbatten to help him cross the theoretical minefields through which he sought to steer. After a frustrating day of navigation, 'He'd go home in the evening looking very grumpy. The following day he'd come back having grasped a concept. Mountbatten's great strength was that he was very good at detail . . . certainly up to sorting out navigation for a Sub Lieutenant.'[20] However, as he set sail for the West Indies, the Acting Sub Lieutenant was still far from confident that he would make the grade as a naval officer, despite the private assessment of senior officers that he 'clearly' had 'considerable potential'[21] and that he was 'a remarkable young man' into the bargain.[22]

As he related it in his journal, the voyage in *Minerva* was somewhat less rigorous than the Prince might have feared at the outset. After crossing the Atlantic 'in a raging gale' – 'when I went up on watch at 2000 the sea was breaking in huge fountains and explosions over the top of the bridge'[23] – the ship spent the following seven months in the Caribbean. Cast uncomfortably in his twin roles as a very junior naval officer and heir to the throne, he attended between forty and fifty cocktail parties either ashore or on board, 'ploughing our way through an alcoholic haze'.[24] He was warmly welcomed almost everywhere, which surprised and touched him, 'considering their past history and the general trend today of trying to find a truly West Indian culture and lifestyle'. Despite this sensitivity, he was not responsive to the sermon delivered to him by the governor of one island colony who was 'what I would call a "God-botherer". His actions are entirely governed by the bible, his conversation is biblical, and his attitude is "testamentary". He gave me a long lecture about how the white man's treatment [of the black islanders under British rule] . . . had been a result of evil spirits entering their minds and causing them to reject God.'[25]

Nor was he enamoured of very many of the politicians he met. One

premier was 'a very self-important man . . . I gave up the unequal struggle of trying to carry on a normal, civilised conversation'; another was
'aloof and self-important'; and the Interior Minister of another island was
'a sinister piece of work'. In a revealing passage in his journal he dispar-
aged the smoothness and self-assurance of politicians generally,
contrasting their complacency with 'others, possibly infinitely more suitable for public service and leadership' who are 'plagued by elements of
self-doubt and doubt as to their abilities and dedication. I cannot help
feeling that people with some elements of doubt and uncertainty are
often far more honest, self-effacing characters who appear at least human
to the majority of citizens . . .'[26]

It was an essential paradox of his maturing character that while he
remained plagued by self-doubt and diffidence, his commentaries about
the people and places he visited had started to acquire a mordant and
opinionated edge, the product of precise observation and a critical eye,
an intelligence in which intuition usually played a greater part than reason. His judgements too became increasingly unequivocal and pointed:
'I cannot envisage a useful future for the Caribbean unless the individual
islands are prepared to give up a considerable amount of their
Sovereignty and form a wider Association of States,' he wrote to the
Foreign Secretary, in the first of scores of similar missives which would
thump royally onto many ministerial desks in the decades ahead, '. . . But
always the politicians, and particularly the premiers frustrate the
process . . . So much of the politics of the Caribbean is akin to local politics in England because, presumably, they are dealing with the same basic
issues – sewage, roads, housing and education – which seems to engen-
der so much pettiness and self-importance.'[27]

The Queen's insistence that the Prince of Wales should be treated
merely as any other junior officer of his rank had been faithfully transmitted by the Foreign and Commonwealth Office to Her Majesty's
representatives in those places which the Prince of Wales was likely to
visit while serving in the Navy. In particular, it was stressed that 'any
entertainment offered by or to him should be consistent with that appropriate to a member of the wardroom mess of his rank . . . While there
will be nothing to stop Governors who do not normally give receptions
for ships from doing so for HMS *Minerva* . . . it would be inappropriate
for them to move to some more formal function if the intention to honour HRH were made overt.'[28] This well-intentioned inhibition had

already caused some dismay, especially among those local dignitaries for whom the imminent arrival of the Prince of Wales was the highlight of their Commonwealth or colonial year.

Early in the tour, after receiving a warm welcome in Monserrat, the Prince had himself come to the conclusion that, 'the Foreign and Commonwealth Directive as to how I should be treated ashore was not flexible enough and was tending to confuse Her Majesty's representatives particularly when the locals were themselves having difficulty appreciating the rules. I felt, and the Captain of Minerva agreed, that countries administered by us directly and displaying genuine interest should not be thwarted altogether in "getting a glimpse".'[29] When this message was relayed by his equerry to the Palace, the Queen agreed to relax the instructions to allow the Sub Lieutenant to be – occasionally – a Prince as well. This pleased the crowds and the heir apparent, who, despite his habitual reticence, was not at all indifferent to any enthusiasm of the populace for the British monarchy. Even so, the Palace stressed that it was important to prevent 'the whole business getting out of hand'.[30]

In early April it very nearly did. Even as modified, the Foreign Office guidelines almost provoked a diplomatic incident and caused a furious row between the Captain of *Minerva*, John Garnier, and the British High Commissioner of Jamaica. The first such incident, it neatly exposed the irreconcilable demands made on a Sub Lieutenant who is also heir to the throne. After almost two months at sea, the Prince had intimated that he would relish a game of polo during the stopover in Jamaica, and *Minerva* signalled the High Commissioner accordingly. Four days later, after a game had been arranged with some of the island's best players, the Jamaicans proposed that, while ashore for the polo, the 'heir to the throne of Jamaica' should pay a short visit to the acting Governor-General.[31] The High Commissioner relayed the invitation to the Captain of HMS *Minerva*, which by this time had just arrived in Kingston. The Captain telephoned to say that regretfully he could not agree to this meeting as it conflicted with the instructions given to him by the Ministry of Defence. He suggested that the Governor-General might meet the Prince informally at the polo match instead. The High Commissioner hurried down to the quayside to explain the acute embarrassment that would be caused to Her Majesty's Government by what would be interpreted in Jamaica as a gratuitous snub. With time running out and the Jamaican cars already on their way to pick up the

Prince for his polo, the issue was resolved by the skilful application of diplomatic balm. It was agreed that the Governor-General would invite the senior naval officer of the West Indies to call on him, accompanied by a Sub Lieutenant from *Minerva*, who just happened to be the heir to the throne. As this complied with the Foreign Office ruling, Garnier relented. Honour was duly satisfied, and the Prince had his polo as well.

Two weeks later, in the port of Cartagena in Colombia for a joint Anglo-Colombian naval exercise code-named Colombritex, there were similar difficulties. As a member of the ship's company, the Prince had volunteered to carry the colour at a wreath-laying ceremony in the Plaza de Bolivar: 'I have always wanted to do this,' he wrote home to the van Cutsems, 'but the damned pole is so heavy and the ensign so enormous that it acts exactly like a spinnaker and I know I shall vanish down the main street close-hauled on the starboard tack and be wrapped around a lamp-post in the suburbs of Cartagena.'[32] The Colombian authorities had other concerns. Plagued by urban guerillas, they had insisted that the Prince's attendance at the ceremony should not be announced. However, evidently because he was overheard talking about it at a reception, a large crowd turned up which 'had no difficulty in identifying Prince Charles',[33] who, according to his own account, could concentrate only on the 'exquisite agony' of holding the colour six inches off the ground during the two national anthems, both of which were played, it seemed to him, twice over: 'I found myself leaning backwards at an angle of 45 degrees and shaking all over, while beads of perspiration formed on the forehead and cascaded down to my boots.'[34] Happily, the crowds failed to notice his distress but greeted him with warmth and enthusiasm. In effect, despite the Foreign Office, the naval visit had become a royal tour in all but name. According to the British ambassador, the monarchy had a 'special fascination' for the Colombians and it had all along been an uphill task to persuade the authorities to fall in with the Queen's wish that her son should be treated like any other officer. They protested vehemently that 'it would be discourteous on their part to do so', that protocol demanded an official welcome, and that in any case his visit provided an ideal opportunity to demonstrate the 'high regard they have for Britain, and in particular for the Monarchy'.[35] In Cartagena, the ambassador was able – just – to hold the line. However, when Prince Charles responded favourably to the prospect of a polo game in the capital, the Colombian authorities could take no more. Were the Prince to go to

Bogota, they insisted, he would be treated as a Prince and that, it was intimated, would be that. The polo was cancelled.*

After a similar greeting in the Venezuelan port of Maracaibo, he was at pains to convey to *Minerva*'s crew his own sense of the value of such occasions. 'I have been trying to impress on the sailors,' he wrote to Douglas-Home, 'what an effect these sorts of visits can have and that they can achieve positive results, improving Britain's prestige abroad, and once they begin to realise this they feel that all the spit and polish and ceremonial may have been worthwhile. It is therefore very important that people are told of the useful things they have done abroad.'[36]

The longer he was at sea, the more he was afflicted by the familiar curse of homesickness. His consolation was the prospect of seeing his great-uncle in April on the tiny Caribbean island of Eleuthera where Mountbatten's daughter Patricia – the Prince's godmother – and her husband, John Brabourne, owned a house. At the instigation of Mountbatten, and with the encouragement of the Brabournes, he intended to stay on Eleuthera for a long weekend, flying there from Bermuda. However, the plan was scuppered by the assassination of the Governor, Sir Richard Sharples, on 10 March, which led the security services to insist that the Prince of Wales should on no account be allowed to land on the island. As every other route to Eleuthera was complicated either by logistical or security considerations, his superiors urged him to cancel the trip. For once the Prince refused. 'I'm afraid I'm taking a leaf out of your book (to a certain extent!) and am putting my foot down and not taking "no" for an answer,' he wrote to Mountbatten. 'I shall use every method at my disposal (including bribery!) to get to Eleuthera and I am determined I shall succeed.'[37] His tenacity was eventually rewarded and on 13 April he came ashore in Antigua to fly directly in a hired HS 125 to Eleuthera, where 'Uncle Dickie' and the Brabournes were waiting to greet him.

---

* The decision averted another diplomatic incident. It was almost certain that the Colombian President would have offered the Prince the use of his own aircraft for the flight from Cartagena to Bogota, but the safety record of the Colombian air-force would have obliged the Captain of the Queen's Flight to advise against the flight – not a judgement the ambassador relished having to transmit to the presidential Palace.

The next seven days surpassed even his wildest imaginings. The house itself, which was simple in style and modest in size, stood on the edge of a deserted beach overlooking the sea. Every day the Prince went off early in the morning to walk along the sand and to swim. After breakfast he went sailing or sunbathed. There were outings by boat and family picnics. Recovering his childhood enthusiasm for art, he set up an easel and painted the surrounding views of the sea, the beach, the palm trees, all set against the intense blue of the sky. The family shared the preparation of meals with the cook, and the Prince showed off his prowess at making scrambled eggs and bread-and-butter pudding. In the evening, they talked and read before going early to bed; the Prince slept in what had been the maid's room at the back of the house, listening to the hiss of the surf and the moan of the wind which blew in steadily from across the ocean making the palm leaves crackle through the night.

'I've never experienced life more closely resembling paradise on earth,' he wrote to a friend in England. 'The weather was glorious, the sea warm, the sand fine like powder, we were never out of swimming trunks all day.'[38] As the days merged one into another the Prince found himself taking more than usual notice of the Brabournes' daughter Amanda, who at the age of fifteen was blossoming from a gawky child into a young woman. 'I must say,' he wrote self-consciously to his great-uncle, her grandfather, 'Amanda really has grown into a very good-looking girl – most disturbing.'[39]

At the end of his week's leave, the Prince flew out of Eleuthera to join HMS *Fox*, a coastal survey vessel to which he had been temporarily transferred. He wrote to the Brabournes:

> In a cloud of . . . deeply despondent homesickness I am back on board this tedious ship. You probably won't believe it . . . but when I climbed into the aircraft this afternoon and saw you all standing there on the tarmac a terrible lump came rushing up into my throat and the old tears began to trickle out of the corner of the eye. That same ghastly feeling of empty desperation and apparent hopelessness invaded my tummy and I spent a long time gazing rigidly out of the window . . . It was so utterly similar to going back to school that it frightened me . . .
>
> How can I ever convey the pure joy it was for me? Every single moment was savoured to the utmost. Every drop of water, every

gamma ray of sunlight, each particle of sand, every glutinous drop of oil was . . . stored away in the luckiest of brain cells. From now until September I can organise a free film show in the mind to fill me with contented happiness when I am feeling low and desperate.[40]

To Mountbatten he wrote, 'I felt completely at home . . . Thank you . . . most brilliant and kindest of Great Uncles/Grandpas (Hon) for giving me what was the time of my life.'[41]

Back in Antigua, he was able to delight in English Harbour, with its sailing yachts, Nelson's dockyard and row of eighteenth-century storage rooms. By contrast to the town itself, which seemed 'sinister and unfriendly' while the 'locals had a slovenly air about them and looked at you in a hostile fashion',[42] the atmosphere in the harbour 'was one of complete peace and tranquillity – typically English. So much so that I felt I was in some small Devon or Cornwall harbour . . .'[43] But thoughts of England brought other memories flooding back to test his resilience once again. He had just learnt that the new love of his life, Camilla Shand, had decided to accept an offer of marriage from Andrew Parker Bowles, who had been a suitor before she met the Prince. Whatever the reason, it seemed particularly cruel to him that after 'such a blissful, peaceful and mutually happy relationship' fate had decreed it should last a mere six months. With 'no one' to go back to in England, he wrote forlornly, 'I suppose the feeling of emptiness will pass eventually.'[44] He brooded alone in his cabin, but concealed his feelings from those about him.

In early May, he had a letter from Prince Philip informing him that his sister Princess Anne was to marry an army captain called Mark Phillips. The news filled him with 'a spasm of shock and amazement'[45] at what he was convinced was a ghastly mismatch. His resentment was intensified by an overwhelming sense of loss and insecurity: Anne, who had become an essential part of his life, to confide in and fool with, now belonged to someone else who had first call on her affection. His misery at that prospect provoked an onrush of nostalgia so intense as to induce a state of near panic. Though the relationship with both his parents was not uncomplicated, his image of the family had been framed within the romantic certainty that at least it would always be there, a rock against adversity. Now, suddenly, the family unit seemed on the point of disintegration, with a newcomer barging into their private domain. The surge of raw feeling, self-absorbed as it may have been, reduced him to tears of impotence and regret, the more severe because he was lonely and so far from home. In a forlorn attempt to raise his spirits, he noted wanly, 'I can see I shall have to find myself a wife pretty rapidly, otherwise I shall get left behind and feel very miserable!'[46] It was several days before he could contemplate his sister's betrothal without despair.

Yet he soon recovered his equilibrium. By the time of the public announcement on 30 May, he was already protective of his prospective brother-in-law, who was notoriously inept in public – except when he was on horseback. 'I suspect he has no idea whether he is coming or going at the moment and even Olympic Gold Medals etc. are not enough to prepare a person for the interest, fascination (plus boorishness) shown by the press,' he wrote, commenting with asperity on a press interview which Captain Phillips had been forced to endure. 'That people should ask such damn stupid questions is beyond imagination and must have floored Mark. At least he had a tank to lean against!'* When he heard that church bells had pealed in celebration of the engagement, he wrote of being 'deeply moved, in a hopelessly romantic way . . . and the thought of church bells ringing in that beautiful countryside and people feeling happy about something for a change sent tingles of pleasure and pride up and down my nautical spine – "shiver my timbers" they call it in the Navy!'[47]

If the Prince's response to his sister's marriage was emotional, Mountbatten's had been dynastic. According to Mountbatten's account, the decision to bestow the name Mountbatten on Prince Philip before his marriage had been taken by the Labour Home Secretary, James Chuter Ede,[48] a choice of name which had given more pleasure to Mountbatten than to Prince Philip, who suspected the work of Mountbatten behind the scenes. Five years later, when it was announced at the Queen's accession that the royal house would henceforth adopt the name of Windsor, Prince Philip (who had already been thwarted in his own choice of the House of Windsor and Edinburgh) did not at all mind that his descendants would not carry the surname that the court had foisted on him. Mountbatten was crestfallen but refused to give up. In 1960, a little before the birth of Prince Andrew, another Order in

---

* Captain Phillips was at the time serving with the Army of the Rhine in West Germany.

Council announced that in future the Queen's descendants would – after all – bear the name Mountbatten-Windsor. Once again the decision bore Mountbatten's imprint.

Pointing out that Princess Anne's marriage certificate would be 'the first opportunity to settle the Mountbatten-Windsor name for good', Mountbatten asked the Prince to intervene to ensure that 'her surname is entered as Mountbatten-Windsor . . . I hope you can fix this.'[49] The Prince replied, promising to do his best, and, true to his word, wrote to Lord ('Chips') Maclean, the Lord Chamberlain, asking him to remind the Queen about 'the names on the marriage certificate which should be "Mountbatten-Windsor". The Queen already knows about this and has asked to be reminded about it in good time,' he added.[50] The marriage certificate duly bore the appropriate signature and Mountbatten was able to relax somewhat.*

Throughout the rest of May, June and July, *Minerva* cruised the Caribbean from one island to another, sometimes on exercise but more usually dispensing Royal Navy goodwill at receptions and cocktail parties. He was entranced by the premier of St Kitts, who drove a yellow Rolls-Royce and wore pinstriped trousers, a crumpled morning coat, a wing collar, a carnation, and a top hat, 'which, thanks to his brilliantly designed car he could wear while driving'. The royal party arrived at an unveiling ceremony precisely on time:

> I walked purposefully along the edge of the stand to my seat while two people scrambled backwards in front of me bent double, unravelling a great length of red carpet for me to walk on. I tried to slow down, but kept on overtaking the unravellers until the inevitable happened and the end wasn't straight. It finished up over the feet and knees of the Governor and his wife who spent the rest of the morning trying to free their 80 year old legs from underneath a very heavy red carpet.[51]

---

* But not entirely. Three years later, after hearing that Prince Andrew, then sixteen, was confused about the matter, Mountbatten wrote to Prince Charles asking him to make it quite clear that when the time came he should sign the marriage register as 'Mountbatten-Windsor' and not 'Windsor' alone. (Mountbatten to C, 6 December 1976, MA.)

In Barbados, he went parascending, and crash-landed on the first attempt. On the second:

> I rose smoothly into the air and cruised happily along at about 25 feet until a gust of wind caught me and I shot up and down, hit the water, lost one ski, flew violently up into the air again, stalled, regained height again and then did a death-defying dive into the sea at some vast, uncontrollable speed, striking my nose forcibly against an aluminium spar conveniently situated to do just that . . . Blood poured out and I decided enough was enough.[52]

On several stopovers, he was able to indulge his growing passion for polo, at which his commitment still outstripped his talent. At Nassau, the ponies and players had been flown in specially for the match, but it proved to be 'a ghastly game' and the ponies 'abysmal'. He confided furiously to his journal:

> I lost my temper completely when first the horse ran away with me and galloped twice through the pony lines, cutting an artery in its shoulder, and second the commentator, Tom Oxley, became so incredibly facetious and unnecessary in his wet little remarks that I was forced, in a rage, to stump up to the top of the commentary box and ask him to stop making pathetic remarks. The whole game was an unmitigated disaster.[53]

His sense of duty was put severely to the test by a garden party for 2,500 people in the stifling tropical heat, and by the 'mediaeval torture' of an inter-denominational service, where the head of the Baptist Church in Nassau worked himself into 'an evangelical frenzy' that drove the congregation to ecstasies of fervour: 'At the end of his fantastic tirade there was practically a standing ovation and the Rev. Cooper tottered back to his seat shaking all over and pouring with perspiration!'[54]

In his role as the Queen's representative, the Prince of Wales was in Nassau for the independence celebrations, for which he prepared with a painstaking attention to detail which owed much to the influence of Mountbatten. In a stream of reminders to his private secretary, annotated on the draft programme, he variously gave instructions about the car in which his detectives should travel ('in the front of my car – and NOT in the car ahead or behind'); the attendance 'at all functions' of his doctor, who, he said, should travel in 'Car 2 (Austin Princess) of the motorcade where he could 'sit on the Dickie seat like I am made to do in the Rolls'); about crowd control at a polo ground ('the only time you need to worry about that . . . is when the cup is presented'); about the potential 'fiasco' of the state ball for which he drew up his own timetable ('a. arrive, b. National Anthems, c. Move to a table – meet one or two people, d. Dance once or twice, e. Leave quietly after ½ to ¾ of an hour . . .'); about the photographs to be taken at Government House ('excessive to say the least'); and about the need to play not the National Anthem but 'God Bless the Prince of Wales' at the end of a reception ('I am not standing to attention for the latter since it is not a national anthem and if it is played as I leave I can simply turn and wave [or something!] . . . thereby signifying that the reception has come to an end').[55] Such meticulous attention to detail was soon to be a hallmark of his approach to such events; but he had already discovered that only by attention to such minutiae could he face the ordeal with confidence. Even so, he was anxious. 'I cannot abide this business of trying to prepare an engagement while so far away from yourself and the office,' he complained to Checketts. 'It is not a good idea and I am not keen to repeat the performance.'[56]

In the event, the hiccups were few. He delivered five speeches (which he had written himself when off watch), laid foundation stones, visited schools and hospitals, and presided at the flag-raising ceremony itself. Taking the salute, he winced as he watched *Minerva*'s guard of honour shuffle past, out of step and out of time with the band; and when the Union Jack was lowered he watched with irritation as the Minister of Finance went 'berserk', jumping up and down and shouting 'Hooray!' at the top of his voice, which made him look 'extraordinarily stupid and damn rude'. That night he attended the Prime Minister's garden party and three state balls. At the first, he danced with a beautiful and very pregnant actress, who was wearing her best 'lace tablecloth', in the middle of which she had cut a hole to place the 'dress' over her head; at the second, he danced 'as I have never danced before – purely to show everyone that I was just as good, if not better, than they were!'; and at the third, he 'had the misfortune to fall into the clutches of a pear-shaped lady who was suffering from the adverse effects of alcohol. She clasped me to her ample bosom and enquired after my general "well-being" at Government House.'[57]

From the Bahamas, *Minerva* sailed via the Cayman Islands, Jamaica (again), Venezuela, St Vincent and Mustique, where the Prince was shown round Princess Margaret's Caribbean retreat by the island's owner, Colin Tennant. A balmy day was ruined later when he arrived back at *Minerva* an hour late for a dinner engagement, because the trawler on which he had taken a lift could only manage six knots, not ten as promised. After offering profuse apologies, the Prince was outraged to be summoned to the Captain's cabin to be upbraided for his discourtesy. 'Now there is one thing I do not consider myself to be,' he scribbled in his journal, 'and that is discourteous. I was hurt and angry that I should be accused of that, particularly as I had arranged for everyone involved to be informed by radio telephone as soon as I knew we were going to be late.'[58] Quick to take offence, the Prince rarely forgot a slight though he was usually – as on this occasion – quick to forgive. In this case, the episode served only to reinforce his feeling that he had served for long enough in one ship.

Despite the efforts of his fellow officers, the agonies of navigation had continued to haunt him throughout the voyage. 'I am writing this at 0730 in the morning, having been up at 0500 in order to take star sights', he had written in April to the van Cutsems. 'There is a sinister plot in the higher strata of the navy to make me the navigator of the ship fairly soon but I consider myself manifestly unsuitable for such a task.'[59]

Affected by this failure more than he showed, he was increasingly prey to bouts of mild depression, which were not relieved by being at sea with the same group of men in a confined space for weeks at a time. He thought wistfully of England. In Ascot week, he imagined the familiar scene at the Windsor house party and at the course itself:

I could smell the roses in the garden, hear the fountain and the sound of countless horses hooves on the gravel, imagine the flower-decked green corridor and lunch being laid out in the big dining room. Worst of all I could plainly see, touch and smell the strawberries and cream at tea-time at the race course – and THE ICE CREAM! I really hate missing an English summer. It is always special; every year it comes round again, but each time it is new and original . . .[60]

By August, en route for Britain, *Minerva* was in the American base at Portsmouth, New Hampshire, where the Prince was overwhelmed by the hospitality of the local population and by 'the Georgian dolls house' quality of the early-nineteenth-century town. At a reception in the Old Town, the Mayor 'propelled me through the company assembled on the lawn. I was unable to escape his vice-like grip . . . dashing about shaking hands, with the Mayor muttering confidentially into my ear "just great" and that I was "a beautiful mover"!'[61] The Prince longed to be home but their departure was postponed by engine trouble; twice they tried to leave and twice they had to turn back. On the second occasion, the Prince recorded, 'I was nearly in tears and tried hard to remain cheerful. Many of the single sailors said they'd far rather stay out longer than go home. I swallowed hard and bit my lip!'[62] At last, however, they were under way: 'I breathed a great sigh of relief and fresh visions of Balmoral rose before me, no longer clouded with miserable uncertainty, but bathed in glorious light and full of excitement and happiness.'[63] They sailed into the middle of an Atlantic depression through mountainous seas in a force 10 gale, but as they neared the coast of 'dear old England', suddenly 'Drake's own country appeared blue and hazy under dark scudding clouds and shafts of August sunshine'[64] and his spirits soared. On the last day of August, he left *Minerva* in a 'gloomy, grimy' Chatham dockyard to escape to 'the best place on earth – Balmoral'.[65] The extent to which he had acquired the moral resolve to conceal his bouts of self-doubt, depression and misery from his shipmates aboard *Minerva* may be gleaned from Captain Garnier's final report on his progress:

> An honest, loyal and outstandingly cheerful officer whose quick wit and charm have enabled him to integrate most successfully in the ship. He has taken an active part in all the ship's activities and, while there is room for improvement professionally, he has become less critical of his own abilities and has gained in self-confidence as he has become aware of his increasing competence.
>
> He has an exceptional facility with all grades of society, and on board his division has responded most favourably to his sympathetic handling of their affairs and to his natural concern for their problems and welfare.[66]

The Prince was even more pleased by a note which was later added to his West Indian Journal: 'In 60 years experience of Junior Officers' Journals I cannot remember reading any whose accounts were so vivid, humorous and penetrating. I don't suggest this is the World's Best Journal – all I can testify, I have not seen a better one.' It was signed: Mountbatten of Burma.

CHAPTER
TWELVE

———— ◆ ————

On 20 June 1973, David Checketts, the First Sea Lord and his staff met to review Prince Charles's progress and the options now facing him. The First Sea Lord, Admiral Sir Michael Pollock, reported back on a conversation he had had with the Duke of Edinburgh, who had intimated that Prince Charles was frustrated with the career which had been planned for him. He wanted to fulfil more of his responsibilities as Prince of Wales, and he longed to pursue his enthusiasm for flying. According to the minutes of the meeting, Checketts intervened to say that, 'Prince Charles lacked confidence in his own progress, particularly in navigation, and was uncertain of his ultimate ability to command a minesweeper. He felt that the programme to which he was committed was in a way restrictive and exerted undue pressure on him.'[1] The private secretary went on to stress that the Prince wanted to achieve recognisable success but that he was not committed to a naval career; that although he still hoped to take command, he did not want 'his whole life' to be 'a relentless progress to achieve this objective'.[2] He urged, therefore, that the Prince's naval programme should be taken step by step. Afterwards, Checketts reported back to the Prince that the First Sea Lord had been 'extremely understanding and fully sympathised' with his 'unique problem of dual identity' and, unlike his predecessor, he had made it clear that he wanted the royal Sub Lieutenant to enjoy his years in the Navy. For this reason, his programme would remain flexible and his 'terminal date' could be decided when it was felt that there was 'no further benefit by remaining in the Navy'.[3] The Navy had at last come to the conclusion that his career in the force should be tailored to his aptitude, which was unexceptional, rather than to their aspirations, which had been boundless.

Thus, many months after the Prince had first semaphored his distress, he was relieved of the responsibilities of navigator and set off for Singapore to join HMS *Jupiter* as a seaman officer instead.

According to one of his fellow officers, who was to become a good friend, the wardroom in *Jupiter* was 'harum-scarum', the conversations were 'pretty revolting', and some of the jokes were 'really earthy, very basic'. Try as he might, the Prince could not altogether hide his unease, while to the rest of the mess he initially seemed 'diffident, unsure and wary . . . very vulnerable'.[4] As if to remind him that he was but one of them, his mess decided to defy protocol and refer to him simply as Wales, an insouciance which the Prince bore without reproach. He soon began to acclimatise to the heartiness of his new environment, even joining in wardroom japes with something like abandon. 'This evening for instance,' he wrote to Mountbatten two weeks after joining *Jupiter*, 'we had a series of the most punishing tug-o'-war battles I've ever had in my life; the ward room team which I pulled got into the finals, though we were all on our last legs and fingers at the end. Sailors were dropping like ninepins all over the place! I then played a game of volleyball on the flight deck, organised a messdeck quiz, had dinner and now I'm due to go on watch for the Middle. It is all non-stop stuff.'[5]

In the course of the next four months, *Jupiter* steamed in leisurely style from Singapore to New Zealand, Suva, Tonga, Western Samoa, Honolulu, San Francisco, Acapulco, Panama, San Juan and Bermuda. Although his journal was now for the edification only of his friends, he used it not only as a record of incidents and personal feelings but to record his political and diplomatic insights as well, exercising a self-discipline in putting pen to paper that few twenty-five-year-olds would have mustered in such circumstances. He was angered by the 'short-sighted and rather pointless piece of pre-election promising' which had led to the Australian decision to pull out of ANZUK* at a point when

---

* The defence force formed by Australia, New Zealand and the United Kingdom to provide external security for Malaysia.

military commanders were seized by fear of communist terrorism and infiltration in Malaysia. 'Together with an Australian withdrawal,' the Prince observed, 'the Malaysians are rapidly ensuring for themselves that a communist threat is once again no empty jest.' Facing the regime's discrimination against them, it seemed that 'communism could well be the only way for the Chinese to obtain what they consider to be their fair share of the cake. The domino theory, to my mind, is no make-believe. Look at Aden.'[6]* The views were by no means original, but reflected the conventional military and diplomatic opinion of the time. Their significance lay less in what he wrote than in that he wrote it at all: that he was already driven by the need to record for posterity (as he then intended) his impressions and observations, delivering his opinions not with the indignation of youth but the sagacity of age. As if to vanquish the demon of self-doubt, he found himself again and again trying to repress the ambiguities and uncertainties which assailed him; this superficial certitude was to become intrinsic to his public persona, leading some critics to conclude that in matters of public policy the Prince was an opinionated *parvenu*.

The purpose of *Jupiter*'s tour of duty – subtitled in the Prince's journal as 'The Incredible Pacific Voyage, 1974' – was to spread the Royal Navy's goodwill and 'show the flag' in the Commonwealth and other friendly nations. Despite an apparently onerous list of responsibilities as signals officer, assistant intelligence officer, flight deck officer, officer of the watch and entertainments officer, the Prince was not so burdened by nautical duties that he was unable to indulge in the diverse pleasures of the Pacific with more abandon than he had previously allowed himself. The experience of this voyage from Australia ('every time I come back to this country I find I feel more deeply about it and about the people . . . it has engraved itself upon a part of my soul – rather like Balmoral is written deeply on my heart'[7]) to the United States allowed him to combine his dual role as junior naval officer and Prince of Wales with more confidence and aplomb than had been possible under the restrictive guidelines that his mother had originally deemed appropriate. The round was by now familiar: joint exercises at sea; receptions, garden

---

* Aden, the former British protectorate which in 1967 gained independence under a quasi-Marxist dictatorship after a long war of subversion against the British. It now forms part of the People's Democratic Republic of Yemen.

parties, barbecues, dinners and dances on land; and, in his case, parachuting – all of which left plenty of time and opportunity for mild flirtations with pretty girls.

In his first attempts to initiate a passing romance as a naval officer he had been prone – by his own account – to encourage 'over-excited French girls' by declaring '*Je vous aime*' when intending to express a less extravagant emotion.[8] When he was with HMS *Norfolk*, curiosity had led him to follow his brother officers into Toulon's red light zone. With fellow officers from HMS *Minerva*, he had acquainted himself with the inside of a Colombian brothel, where – as an observer – he noted the lurid green lights and equally lurid *mesdames*; one of these painted ladies had momentarily placed a hand on his thigh, which had added 'yet another of life's essential experiences to my collection. Not literally, I hasten to add.'[9] However, he was far from immune to the attractions of a romantic encounter. He succumbed to a commanding officer's daughter in the West Indies, and in Venezuela was much taken by the wife of a polo player. 'Never in my life', he wrote of this encounter, 'have I had such dances as I had with this beautiful lady. She is unbelievable is all I can say and I danced with every conceivable part of her. I fell madly in love with her and danced wildly and passionately, finally doing a Russian dance at one stage which cleared the floor because I was wearing my mess boots . . .'[10]

His self-confidence began to bloom. In a letter home he wrote artlessly but with evident pride of his effort to overcome the self-consciousness which had always plagued him: 'You may find when I get back that the Navy and six months out here have made me considerably more extrovert than I was. I am continually amazed at my audacity nowadays.'[11] In respect to the opposite sex, his temerity was of a kind which a sailor – or indeed a travelling salesman – would regard as routine; in his case it bore the hallmarks of an innocent but untutored upbringing in a boys' public school: 'I tried to tickle a belly-dancer last night at a hotel where we were having dinner! She came up to me and wobbled everything at me and so I ran my fingers up her tummy (rather hot and sticky!) and she hit me on the head with her castanets! I think she rather liked it . . .!'[12] By the time he joined HMS *Jupiter*, he was discovering how to deploy his charm – 'the old eye-flashing technique'[13] as he called it – with somewhat greater sophistication and to greater effect than he had previously imagined possible. In the islands of the South

Pacific, the presence of the Prince of Wales acted as a magnet for every unattached woman (and not a few erring wives as well) in every port of call – to the chagrin of his fellow officers, who vied with each other in gallantry and more. As they ruefully observed, the Prince was always the centre of attraction, if not necessarily to his advantage: in Tonga, he was persuaded to attend a party at the Yacht Club, where he danced with:

> gigantic lady after gigantic lady, around all of whom I was incapable of putting my arms! The third amazon finally finished me. She announced in halting English that she had been wanting to dance with me since she was 12 and now she had finally 'got me'. Apart from the fact that she was like dancing with several tractor inner tubes mounted on top of each other and vibrating slowly in different directions, she began to feel me all over with a wild look in her eye . . . It wasn't so much her eye that I minded, but what she was going to do with her teeth! I thereupon left the steaming, sweating Yacht Club and headed back for the ship, past bushes which kept saying 'Psst! Hello sailor,' and appeared to be occupied (as it later transpired) by off-duty policemen.[14]

In Acapulco, he and a group of officers, including the Captain, went to a discotheque:

> While the Captain and I sat pensively in a corner fingering a gin and tonic the others immediately set off like dogs into every dark recess of the club and soon appeared on the dance floor armed with some lady who had been whisked off her feet! Not being accustomed to the art of 'picking up' a girl in a discotheque I could bear the suspense no longer and finally plucked up the courage to go across and ask a lonely looking girl if she would come to join us at our table. 'No thanks,' replied this paragon of beauty and virtue in a terrifying American accent – and so I shrank back to our table, and immediately sank into a gin and tonic-induced reverie.[15]

There were, however, more rewarding encounters. In Samoa, he met a beautiful girl 'with superb black hair down to her waist and with a devastating smile' with whom he stole half an hour that 'must have shattered all the illusions she had had about me through excessive reading of

Woman's Weekly.[16] In San Diego, he was smitten by what one of his colleagues described as 'a tall blonde lovely in a shimmering green dress' who had mesmerised them all at a cocktail party on board; arranging to meet her again, he went to the wrong address, and had to be redirected to the right apartment where he duly serenaded her over a lingering drink. At a cocktail party in Hawaii he met 'two spectacular blonde ladies', whom he invited out to dinner: 'They were incredibly keen and purred that they would give me an evening I would never forget . . .!' Invited back to the small apartment belonging to one of them he was eventually:

> left alone with these two blonde bombshells wondering what on earth was going to happen – I must be very naive! However, after a long time it transpired that all these girls wanted to do was 'to get the Prince loaded' as they put it. In other words they wanted me to smoke the rarest, most expensive form of marijuana, which comes from Thailand. They showed me this large cigarette thing in a plastic bag, which is known as an 'Elephant', but I refused to try it and said I did not like smoking for one and secondly had no need of artificial stimulation . . . Both my policemen and the two locals were outside in the car and so as soon as I could I made a retreat; rather reluctantly because they were great fun.[17]

Despite the relative daring of these encounters, the Prince remained an unworldly suitor – a tentative explorer blessed with an inconvenient conscience, whose sense of propriety invariably intervened to challenge his basic instincts. His accounts of such episodes are so gauche as to suggest that he was still somewhat of an innocent abroad. The impression is confirmed by the whirl of correspondence during this period that flew between him and Mountbatten, who, in such matters, was more knowing.

In February 1974, on the anniversary of his first Eleutheran holiday, he received a letter from Mountbatten, whom he had seen briefly in New Zealand when *Jupiter* had docked at Christchurch. It was a long epistle, the subject of which was his granddaughter, Amanda Knatchbull. Twelve months before, Mountbatten had apparently discerned 'how deeply' (as he put it) the teenage girl had fallen for the Prince when they were together on the island. In his abiding affection for them both, and touched by a romantic vision of the future, he allowed himself to believe that one day his granddaughter and his great-nephew should be betrothed, to the benefit of all the individuals involved and, most certainly, to that of the institution of the monarchy as well.

Mountbatten's counsel – which he was frequently to repeat – was unequivocal: 'I believe, in a case like yours, that a man should sow his wild oats and have as many affairs as he can before settling down. But for a wife he should choose a suitable and a sweet-charactered girl before she meets anyone else she might fall for.'[18] From the perspective of a later generation, Mountbatten's advice on matters of the heart may seem trapped in the values and traditions of another age. Had the Prince been endowed with greater self-assurance or more independence of spirit, had he been able to discuss such intimate matters openly with his mother or father, or indeed any other mature adviser, then it is conceivable that he might have weighed the old man's words a little more carefully. As it was, they seemed to be models of acuity and wisdom, with the result that Mountbatten's worldliness would leave an indelible imprint on Prince Charles's introverted and impressionable nature.

Far from regarding his counsel as in any way intrusive, the Prince opened his heart in reply. 'Perhaps being away and being able to think about life and about the future (and her) has brought ideas of marriage in to a more serious aspect,' he wrote. As Mountbatten had declared, Amanda was indeed 'incredibly affectionate and loyal . . . with a glorious sense of fun and humour – and she's a country girl as well which is even more important'. Although he 'couldn't possibly get married yet', the Prince wrote, the more he thought about the prospect 'the more ideal' it began to appear . . . I am sure that she must know that I am very fond of her simply by reading the letters I write to her.'[19]

The quasi-constitutional imperative for the heir to the throne to find a wife by whom to continue the line of descent already preyed on the Prince's mind; although he was still only twenty-five years old, he felt a burden of responsibility that weighed the more heavily as, one after another, he saw his friends settle down to marriage. 'Everyone is becoming engaged left, right, and centre . . . I am now becoming convinced that I shall soon be left floundering helplessly on a shelf somewhere, having missed everyone!'[20] he had written to the van Cutsems, congratulating them on the birth of their first child. His peculiar problem was to find someone who could not only be a wife and mother but a Princess of Wales as well.

His affection for Amanda, the sense that she would intuitively under-stand the role required of her, and the feeling that the project would be nurtured and shielded by no less a guardian than his great-uncle gave the thought of marriage into the Mountbatten lineage a reassuring allure. How Amanda Knatchbull herself might regard the prospect was another matter, and one to which neither Mountbatten nor the Prince had yet given much thought. For the next five years, however, the older man used every wile to steer his great-nephew and his granddaughter towards wedlock. The endeavour was prompted by a real love for both of them, as well as by the enticing prospect that the House of Windsor and the House of Mountbatten might be entwined for ever on the throne of Britain.

A reputation for kindliness and compassion had followed the Prince from *Minerva* to *Jupiter*. As a Divisional Officer responsible for the wel-fare of some fifteen ratings, his unobtrusive manner soon impressed itself upon his colleagues. He was quite capable of administering a rebuke or punishment, although the nature that had hoped to spare the Gordonstoun thief from retribution was invariably to the fore. He lis-tened to their problems – marital and financial woes especially – with a sensitivity and attention that in the bluff traditions of the Royal Navy was not often forthcoming. When one of his seamen was knocked down and killed by a car while hitchhiking back from Surfer's Paradise outside Brisbane, the Prince recorded in his journal:

> I was absolutely shattered. Having a division induces an extraordinary feeling of responsibility, I find, and the worst part was not being able to do anything to help. The communications department was shattered by the news and all was very quiet and subdued. Altogether a horrible thing to happen and made worse by the fact that [he] was soon to be engaged when he got home.[21]

There is a naval tradition that when a seaman is killed his kit is auc-tioned among his peers, the proceeds going to the next of kin. In this case the auction was held in the ratings' dining hall. Although the man had been a popular shipmate, the bidding was lacklustre as there was no widow to support. Then came his 'pussers' suitcase – naval issue made of green cardboard – and a voice from the back called £400. In anyone else, it might have seemed a vulgar gesture, an embarrassment, but in the Prince of Wales it was at once interpreted as an attempt to raise the bidding – and it worked. Socks which had been sold for fifty pence began to sell for twenty pounds, so that once all his effects were sold, the auction had raised £1,500.*

Mountbatten wrote to the Prince about his success. As ever eschewing false modesty, Mountbatten attributed it to 'Royalty', adding, 'I don't mind betting that when you have done as long at sea you will be a greater legend than your old Great Uncle seems to have been – and for the same reasons.'[22] By his own account, the Prince modelled himself closely on Mountbatten, but his modesty was unfeigned. 'I know what you mean about "Royalty" – and it certainly helps to be "known" in the Navy – but in your case there was definitely a great deal extra which transcended any minor considerations of royalty. I shall only be remembered as having been in the Navy from 1971 – whereas you are a legend through indisputedly significant and glorious deeds,' he replied.[23]

Towards the end of the 'Incredible Pacific Voyage', *Jupiter* sailed for San Diego. Yet again, the Prince was bemused by the fascination he exerted on Americans, and by their lack of inhibition. His journal relates one conversation with an American:

> 'O.K. You're a Prince, right?'
> 'Yes, quite right,' I replied.
> 'Say, does that mean you become a King one day, is that the deal?'
> 'Well, I . . . eh . . . suppose so,' I stuttered.[24]

At a cocktail party in *Jupiter*, 'a vast horde of Captains and Admirals came on board accompanied by their overpowering wives who came rushing up to me . . .' At another, as soon as he walked into the 'hot and sticky room', everybody 'seemed to be swept like water towards a plug' to where he was standing. There then followed '20 minutes of intense hand-shaking and elbow-clutching and moustache-twitching until I shot out from within the ring of people and again found the room practically deserted . . .'[25] Despite the 'agony' of some of these parties, the Prince wrote, 'I strongly believe it is absolutely true that they are the Navy's best

---

* The Prince neither spoke nor wrote of this; the incident is recalled by the officer who had acted as auctioneer. (Confidential conversation.)

peacetime weapon and a surprising amount can be achieved as a result of a successful reception. Most of what is achieved is invisible, but in terms of prestige gained, political contacts made and atmosphere engendered, it is invaluable.'[26] The latter thought was to become one of his recurring themes in frustrated explanation of his own, often 'invisible', role as standard-bearer for Britain abroad. On more than one occasion the royal Sub Lieutenant had cause to be underwhelmed by Britain's permanent representatives abroad, especially in America, where it was particularly important to impress. 'I only wish', he wrote, 'we were represented by higher calibre people in places like San Diego, Los Angeles, Hawaii etc. . . . it can't do much for our image abroad.'[27]

On 16 March, he stayed with Walter Annenberg* and his wife at their palatial retreat in Palm Springs. There he had dinner with Ronald Reagan, the Governor of California, and his wife Nancy, and next day played golf on the Annenbergs' 1,000-acre private golf course – an emerald-green swathe in the desert, complete with trees which had been planted fully grown.

The Prince was not a golfer either by inclination or talent:

> My first shot went off at right angles to the fairway and vanished down a hill. My second hit a tree and rattled about within the branches before ricocheting out at right angles to the direction of my drive. At length I made the first hole in 11 shots! At the next hole my spectacular drive again veered cleanly off to starboard and disappeared with a 'plop' into a nearby lake! As we advanced across the Battle area I left great divots all over the virgin turf, so that it looked exactly as though a game of polo had been played all over it![28]

In fact he had hoped to play polo instead of golf on that day but was prevented by an anonymous phone call warning that he was to be assassinated at the polo ground: as it was St Patrick's Day, he was advised to stay away, which he did with great reluctance. His only consolation on the golf course was that Annenberg and Reagan played almost as badly

---

* Annenberg was US ambassador to Britain (1969–75), renowned for the 'elements of refurbishment' undertaken at his behest at the US ambassador's residence in Regent's Park. Annenberg became honorary president of Operation Raleigh, of which the Prince was patron.

as he did, while, fittingly in this fantasy land, Bob Hope emerged out of the haze to intercept them in another golf buggy. 'I was in swimming trunks and he took one look at me and said, "With a physique like that the future of England is certainly assured." I wonder if he is being sarcastic?' the Prince noted in his journal.[29] That evening, Frank Sinatra came over for a drink, 'looking like Tonto in *The Lone Ranger*, as he was dressed in pale yellow leather and boots'. At dinner, the Prince listened to the future President Reagan condemning former President Kennedy for pusillanimity over the failed CIA Bay of Pigs invasion of Cuba, an assessment at odds with a previous conversation the Prince had had with Harold Macmillan, who had praised the courage and foresight of the American President. He concluded, therefore, that the aspiring Republican Governor was biased. Although encounters of this kind were his for the asking, the Prince did not take them for granted. Always curious and asking questions, he was surprised but delighted on those infrequent occasions when his views were canvassed as well. At the age of twenty-five, he had yet to feel any conviction that he might have an insight from which others could benefit. Even at a private dinner table he was still invariably a listener – modest, attentive, and rarely venturing opinions of his own; he kept them to himself or confined them to his journals and correspondence. This reticence paid off: blessed with a powerful memory, he retained the arguments, mulled them over, fitted them into his own emerging framework of reference and began slowly to shape a personal vision – as yet unencumbered by the urge or need to impart it to a wider audience.

Two days later, he was in Hollywood at the Universal Film Studios, where he met Charlton Heston and Ava Gardner ('who has rather gone to seed now'). However, the anticipated thrill was to meet Barbra Streisand, 'my only pin-up'. At the Prince's request, the Hollywood producer Hal Wallis had arranged for him to meet the star of *Funny Girl* on the set of her sequel *Funny Lady*, at Columbia Studios. Accompanied by fifty reporters and photographers, he walked onto the set for his rendezvous, where 'she appeared to be rather nervous and kept asking me endless questions in a rather tight-lipped fashion'. After this enforced photo opportunity, the two of them went to a corner of the set and 'gossiped for about 15 minutes'. In the course of this *tête-à-tête*, the Prince discovered that the actress had no intention of doing live shows in future because 'she only liked acting in front of people she knew' and that she wanted to spend more time with her children, which prompted him to ask her, 'why, therefore, she went on acting at all?' – at which point Miss Streisand returned to the set to continue with the rehearsal. 'People look at me in amazement when I say that she is devastatingly attractive and with a great deal of sex appeal (all based on one film!)' he confided to his journal, 'but I still contend she has great sex appeal after meeting her.' But he did concede that 'the attractiveness has waned a little'.[30]

On his last day in California, he was summoned from a luncheon in San Diego by alarming news from London. According to *Jupiter*'s First Lieutenant, Princess Anne and her husband Mark had just been attacked in the Mall: 'All he told me was that a report had just come through saying that shots had been fired at the car . . . I was dumbfounded.' Within the hour he was on the phone to his sister:

> Her story was exactly like a nightmare and she told me about it as if it were a perfectly normal occurrence. Her bravery and superb obstinacy were unbelievable – imagine refusing continually a kidnapper's demands for her to get out of the car and climb into his with all the time a pair of pistols being waved at her? Imagine seeing four people shot in cold blood in front of you and still refusing to get out; to struggle to prevent the man pulling you out of the car while Mark held on to your other arm until, after what must have seemed an eternity, the police arrived in sufficient numbers to overpower the man? My admiration for such an incredible sister knows no bounds![31]

'The worst part', he wrote some weeks later, 'was being 8,000 miles away in California and desperate to be back home with Anne, and just to be there . . .'[32]*

It was July before *Jupiter* was back in British waters, and she was now

---

* Both Princess Anne and Captain Mark Phillips were unhurt. Princess Anne's bodyguard, the chauffeur, a policeman patrolling the Mall and a passing taxi passenger who tried to tackle the gunman were seriously wounded. The attacker slewed his car across the path of the Princess's limousine and planned to demand a £1 million ransom, but was foiled as he tried to drag her from the car when the bodyguard drew a pistol. After the gunman fired, he fled into St James's Park before being arrested by police reinforcements. The Princess's bodyguard, Jim Beaton, was subsequently awarded the George Cross.

placed on twelve hours' notice to sail for Cyprus with a naval task force, following a signal from the Mediterranean about a sudden crisis between Greece and Turkey over the island. The Prince was at Balmoral for the weekend when he heard the news of the Turkish invasion, and at once presumed – correctly – that he would be recalled to his ship. 'I was rather keen to be sent to Cyprus,' he wrote. 'I had a yearning for some sort of action – some sort of constructive, useful naval operation where perhaps a medal could be won and I could supplement the one I have (for supreme gallantry at the Coronation!) with a proper one.'[33] Along with the rest of the ship's complement he hurried to Rosyth where the ship was being stored, only to be told that *Jupiter* would not be required to sail for Cyprus after all. In his journal he echoed the intense disappointment of the rest of the crew at the apparent dithering by the Ministry of Defence.* 'Men are not machines and just because people are in armed services, and therefore expected to do as they are told, it is not as simple as that,' he wrote. 'People are quite prepared to take sensible orders, but patience and willingness wear thin when things are constantly changed, cancelled and then re-instituted. What an extraordinarily good thing it is for me to experience all this at the grass roots level so that I can at least appreciate the things that people have to endure.' In what would become a much-repeated refrain when successive governments announced plans and policies of which he disapproved, he added, 'The trouble is that only a very few of the present government have ever served in the armed forces or in an organisation where other people's decisions directly affect your life and family.'[34]

Instead of Cyprus, *Jupiter* joined a NATO exercise in Scapa Flow, an operation which aroused the Prince's romantic sentiment for the great days of the Imperial Navy:

> When I stepped up on to the upper deck it was a most spectacular sight which greeted me. A great line of grey ships stretched out ahead, all creaming along at 20 knots on a glorious Orkney morning, with

---

* Aside from the devastation of Cyprus itself, the threat posed to Britain was twofold: first, that the two British sovereign base areas at Dhekelia (including access to the port of Famagusta) and at Episkopi (including access to the RAF airfield at Akrotiri) would be caught up in the battle; second, that the conflict over Cyprus would develop into full-scale hostilities between two NATO allies, Greece and Turkey. It soon emerged that neither of these threats was likely to materialise.

the islands looking their green and yellow best and the sea positively sparkling. It sent an enormous shiver of excitement down my spine (rather like the Trooping does as well) and conjured up all sorts of images of the old Home Fleet steaming into Scapa led by the battle-ships, battle cruisers, aircraft carriers and followed by the cruisers and squadrons of destroyers . . .

Once they had anchored (which was accomplished with rather less precision than the Home Fleet used to achieve), he took a walk along the cliffs. Accompanied as ever by policemen but putting his companions out of his mind, he wondered at the natural beauty around him: 'I had for-gotten how beautiful the Orkneys were and it was an unexpected and glorious surprise to see them again. The colours were unbelievable – greens, yellows, browns, and staggering blues where the sea came in in great sweeping arms . . .'[35]

Moved by the solitude of landscape yet excited by warships at speed, the heir to the throne was not an uncomplicated personality. Opinionated but reticent, insecure but wilful, gentle but impassioned, reflective but impulsive: the paradoxes of a volatile character were abundant and intriguing to that handful of friends and colleagues who were close enough to see beyond the image which the Navy and the Palace were determined to cultivate.

So far the press coverage of the Prince's naval career had been inter-mittent but sympathetic. When HMS *Jupiter* went to the rescue of a Malaysian tug stranded on a coral reef in the Java Sea, the *Daily Mirror* reported – under the headline 'Charles in Rescue Drama' – that the Prince and his comrades had 'braved gales, sharks, and even 2nd World War mines to rescue the vessel and its crew'. The *Daily Express* went fur-ther, recording that his 'expert advice' had helped save the day.[36]* Yet

---

* Only the *Morning Star* and the Labour MP Willie Hamilton were in dissent, the former reporting that Britain's 'imperialist Navy showed its true colours' when the crew of the 2,000 tons of 'neocolonialist aggression' sold rice and beer to the stranded crew 'at exorbitant prices' before 'they set off at high speed with a fat profit', while the latter confined himself to the assertion that the Prince 'should go down the pits' instead. (Palace press office verbatim extracts, 'As Others See Us', undated, RA/POW.)

when tabloid photographs of the Prince 'relaxing in Fiji' appeared in the *Mail*, *Mirror* and *Sun*, the Queen's press secretary was dismayed. Despite the coverage of the 'recovery operation by *Jupiter*' he averred that only a 'photo session of the Prince at <u>work</u>' could offset the 'rapidly growing impression among the public that Prince Charles' life is mostly play and little work'. The Prince should be persuaded by his private secretary, Checketts, to contrive a media event 'showing him to be an integral part of the ship's company and to be thoroughly earning his keep'.[37] Accordingly, it was 'engineered'[38] for the Prince of Wales to appear at a press briefing given by *Jupiter*'s Captain in Honolulu. This attempt to manipulate the tabloid media to the Prince's advantage had no discernible effect, either on the coverage or on public opinion, which at this point was in any case far less critical than the press secretary had allowed himself to believe. However, the 'photo-opportunity' was a diminishing asset for the monarchy, while the Prince's ambivalence towards the media did not help: he was fully aware that the press could not be ignored, but was reluctant to perform for the benefit of a camera, except on his own terms, and was contemptuous of the 'stupid questions'[38] that assailed him from the serried ranks of royal reporters assembled for a contrived event. The result was always mutual frustration, except on those rare occasions when he behaved spontaneously, driven by the impulse of the moment.

One such occasion took place on an official trip to Canada, more than a year after the 'relaxing in Fiji' episode, when he flew to the edge of the Arctic to go diving in Resolute Bay. Wearing an inflatable diving suit, he swam under the ice, absorbing the extraordinary marine environment about him:

> There were fascinating ice crystal formations and icicles suspended under the ice and inside the layers of these wafer-thin crystal structures were large, white shrimp-like creatures. Because of the cold every living creature under the Arctic tends to move slowly and therefore once they have expended their energy in short bursts they are exhausted and you can pick up small fish and tentripods etc. in your hand. There were beautiful jelly-fish like creatures, completely transparent, which acted like prisms reflecting all the colours of the rainbow inside themselves . . .

*

Because he could not 'trim' his suit, he kept banging his head on the ice, but 'I had long enough to revel in the experience . . . I even tried to walk upside down on the under surface of the ice, but could not make my top half hang downwards.'

Eventually he rose to the surface, exhausted but so exhilarated that, for once, he did not grumble at the presence of the media:

> I couldn't resist the temptation to fool about and inflate my suit with air so that I looked like some animated form of dirigible balloon. I then stepped outside . . . wearing a funny old hat . . . and faced an amazed press corps which couldn't believe their eyes. I then had great pleasure in demonstrating the deflating characteristics of the suit which so astonished the press with mirth that they all downed their cameras and burst into spontaneous applause.[39]

A few days later, after he ate a piece of raw seal meat for their delectation, the press corps – 'to my amazement' – presented him with a diploma honouring his epicurean fortitude, but 'they also gave me a magnificent Narwhale's Nar (or tusk) about 6 feet long. One of these tusks is immensely valuable so they must have been completely mad in giving me this present – but apparently they were determined to do it and I was much touched by such a gesture.' The mutual goodwill, the product of shared discomfort over ten days in close proximity, was not to last. Indeed, the Prince could not forbear to add the note, 'I shall have to make the most of it as it is bound to be the last time!'[40]

In the autumn of 1974, the Prince of Wales finally was allowed to fulfil his desire to join the Fleet Air Arm. At Yeovilton in Somerset he joined a helicopter conversion course before being assigned to 845 Naval Air Squadron as a pilot on board the commando carrier, HMS *Hermes*. From March until June 1975, he enjoyed what he described at the end of four months as 'the happiest and most rewarding' days of his naval career.[41]

Within a few days of joining the ship he was at the controls of one of the two helicopters that had been assigned to him, both of which had been painted with bright 'dayglow' red markings on nose and tail to distinguish the royal machines from the rest. As a result, he noted, 'whatever I do I am immediately noticeable and everybody insists on reminding me

of what they think I have been doing wrong!'[42] The Prince's early enthusiasm for flying had been blighted by the Ministry of Defence, which had
found it impossible to reconcile the instruction to treat him as a normal
officer with the requirement to safeguard the life of the heir to the
throne. In October 1971, after consultation with the Captain of the
Queen's Flight, who was the final arbiter in the matter, the Ministry
informed the Commander-in-Chief of 'certain restrictions' that had to
be placed on his flying activities. In particular, he was banned from the
Wasp helicopter because of its poor safety record (at Dartmouth he had
pleaded to fly in the College Wasp, but to no avail); for the same reason
he was not allowed to fly single-engined helicopters over the sea, while
flying in fixed-wing aircraft was to be 'strictly circumscribed and is not
normally to be permitted'.[43] The Prince found these restrictions irksome
and embarrassing. Why was it, he wondered, that an aircraft too dangerous for him to fly was safe enough for his friends? To minimise the
risk to his life, the two royal helicopters on *Hermes* were maintained to
the uniquely exacting standards of the Queen's Flight. As soon as the
Marines discovered this, the Prince, who had no illusions about the
cause, found himself the most sought-after pilot in the squadron.

As it happened, he was a more than competent pilot. His colleagues
were to remember in particular one Sunday when he was deputed with
one other pilot to restock *Hermes* with beer from a supply ship lying off
the port beam. The two helicopters worked as a pair, picking up the full
crates from the supply ship, circling round to drop them off on *Hermes*,
moving forward to pick up the empties, in a steady circular pattern. It
soon became clear to the group of off-duty officers watching from the
flight deck that the Prince was outperforming his fellow pilot, moving
more smoothly and faster as he adjusted his height, speed, angle and
power with such finesse that the machine seemed to execute the
manoeuvre with hardly any change of speed, hovering only for a
moment to hook up each load, and sweeping away so steadily that the
crates swayed only slightly as they flew between the two ships. 'What we
were seeing was "pole-handling" of the highest order,' one of them
recalled. 'He was doing it instinctively, it was terrific stuff.' That evening,
however, the Prince came into the wardroom 'with a thunderous look
on his face'. After ordering a drink he explained to his fellow officers
that he had been summoned to the Commander's cabin to be given a
reprimand for 'showing-off' instead of executing each component of the

manoeuvre separately. At which the other young pilots cheered him immensely by saying simply, 'Join the Club.'[44]

At the end of a further NATO exercise – the organisation of which the Prince again thought less than impressive – he flew to Eleuthera for a second, 'blissful' week at the Brabournes' house on Windermere Island, followed by ten days criss-crossing Canada as an official guest of the government in Ottawa. He then returned to the ship for a final round of intensive training, at the end of which he wrote:

> I had more fun flying than I had ever had before. The flying was extremely concentrated, but there was masses of variety and interest; troop drills, rocket firing, cross-country manoeuvres (day and night), low-level transits, simulated fighter-evasion sorties, parachute dropping flights and commando exercises with the Marines. There were no interruptions from any other source and as a result I ended up as 'Hog of the Month' with about 53 hours' flying in May![45]

By the time he left *Hermes* after logging more than 500 hours at the controls of a Wessex 5 double-engined helicopter, he had established a reputation for being a good pilot and a congenial fellow officer.

His apparently carefree attitude to personal danger – headline-writers now persistently referred to him as 'Action Man' – was the cause of frequent concern to those responsible for his welfare. In the late autumn of 1975, he was staying at Broadlands with Mountbatten when it was proposed that he should take a flight in a hot-air balloon from the grounds of the estate. The Prince agreed with alacrity, though on account of the weather the first royal balloon flight was aborted before take-off. When Checketts heard of the plan a few days later, he wrote to Mountbatten expressing his horror at what was but the 'most recent example' of the dangers courted by the Prince. 'Your influence on the Prince of Wales is enormous, and he has an immense admiration and respect for your wise advice,' he wrote with well-tuned flattery. 'I would therefore be everlastingly grateful for your valuable help in avoiding or restraining some of the more adventurous endeavours of this remarkable young man, who is far too important for the United Kingdom and the Commonwealth to hazard unnecessarily.'[46] Checketts was relieved when Mountbatten's reply was not only gracious but apparently contrite as well. 'On reflection I agree with everything you have written and the fact that I had an amusing ascent the week before in perfect weather was really no excuse for not thinking about the risks,' he conceded, even going on to warn Checketts that the Prince was planning to try again at Sandringham.[47]

There is no evidence, however, that Mountbatten made any effort to curb the Prince's taste for excitement and adventure. Although, in the words of Checketts, the Prince seemed to have 'a total lack of concern for his own safety', Mountbatten was well aware how precarious was the self-confidence which such apparent recklessness concealed. Much of the old man's time was spent encouraging the Prince to recognise his own potential and to have faith in himself; it is inconceivable that he would have thought the private secretary's prescription conducive to that endeavour. In the final weeks of 1975, Mountbatten spent long hours reassuring the Prince that his next posting would be very far from the catastrophe which, in his darker moments, the royal Lieutenant imagined.

On 9 February 1976, the Prince of Wales took command of the coastal minehunter HMS *Bronington* at Rosyth. 'The great and terrifying day had arrived at last,' he wrote:

> The whole prospect weighed heavily upon me as I drove across the Forth Bridge. There seemed so many things to worry about, particularly as I am not the sort of person who is endowed with supreme self-confidence. Starting off somewhere new is always an effort, not to mention meeting new people and wondering what the officers were going to be like. My head was positively brimming with advice and helpful suggestions from Uncle Dickie and a whole host of naval officers and I could bear the suspense no longer. Above all else was the sensation I simply had to make a success of this particular aspect of my life because so much seemed to be expected of me . . .[48]

The anxiety that perpetually hovered about him was sharpened by the sense of the public humiliation to which he would be exposed if he were to fail. 'No doubt many people were willing everything to go well,' he noted, 'but the press will give no quarter if anything goes wrong.'[49]

The Navy had taken every precaution against calamity by ensuring that he was served with the best available junior officers. In particular, his First Lieutenant, Roy Clare, had already been marked out as a high-flyer, while the navigating officer, James Rapp, was widely regarded as the best of his generation. In the early days of his new command, the Prince was incessantly on the move, armed with a notebook to which he would refer before checking with his fellow officers that this or that task had been properly accomplished. His questions sometimes betrayed the influence of Mountbatten and on occasion, therefore, they had tactfully to inform their commanding officer that over the years naval practice had moved on. They were soon impressed, however, by his air of modest authority.

'It really does seem quite extraordinary to be sitting here as Captain of this ship!' the Prince wrote to Mountbatten two weeks after taking command. 'You really were absolutely right (as usual) – you do feel frightfully grand and not a little confused. Fortunately a considerable proportion of the confusion has worn off since last week and I am now enjoying the whole experience of "being in command".'[50] In his journal, he recorded, 'There is nothing like being ultimately responsible for everything and therefore being kept in the picture all the time, making it easier to make decisions than one imagined.'[51] A few days later, the Duke of Edinburgh arrived to make a tour of inspection. As always when facing paternal judgement, the Prince anticipated the visit with qualms:

> I was feeling quite nervous, seeing everything from the other side for a change and standing on the fo'c'sle surrounded by clicking cameramen. Papa shook hands with me when he stepped on board, which caused a certain amount of confusion and merriment on my part. I then attempted to introduce him to the officers, but as I forgot their names instantly it was nearly a dismal failure![52]

However there were no further mishaps: the Duke of Edinburgh toured the ship, took tea and departed for Holyrood House.

For the next nine months, HMS *Bronington* patrolled the waters of Britain, from the lochs of Scotland, down through the Irish Sea, into the English Channel and on to the North Sea, her Captain learning all the time. In retrospect, he would say, with a touch of self-deprecating hyperbole, 'I spent most of the time petrified that I was going to run aground or we'd have a collision or some major horror like that because I knew that all these people from the media were just waiting like sharks for the

kill.'[53] At the time, he wrote to Mountbatten, 'I've come to the conclusion that my best way of operating in the environment I have in the ship
is to listen to all the available advice and ultimately decide in my own
mind if it is sensible or not . . . I find that with ultimate responsibility for
a ship one tends to be more cautious . . .'[54]

HMS *Bronington*'s modest part in the Royal Navy's scheme was routine
to the point of tedium, sweeping back and forth along a carefully plotted
course, surveying below the surface of the sea with sonar detection
devices for any evidence of underwater mines. Despite his responsibilities,
the Prince was soon bored: 'A large part of our operations at the moment
is excruciatingly dull. I spent 12 hours non-stop on the bridge the other
night while we were mine-hunting and felt like dying quietly then and
there.' Anxiety, however, was always at hand to ward off complacency:
'I've already aged ten years since I took over the ship and keep waking up
at night (at sea and on shore) convinced we are dragging the anchor or
something ghastly has gone wrong. I actually found myself shouting out
the name of the OOW [Officer of the Watch] the other night as I woke
up thinking something appalling was about to happen!'[55]

The routine to which *Bronington* was committed was interrupted by
two incidents, both of which were very nearly as 'appalling' as the
Prince's nightmare. In the middle of March, the minesweeper put in to
Stranraer to pick up a party of ten naval cadets. At the end of a frustrating day at sea in worsening weather, during which most of the cadets
succumbed to seasickness, *Bronington* returned to Loch Ryan to put the
visitors ashore at a decrepit jetty on the edge of a deep but narrow channel. With the wind almost at gale force it was a hazardous operation,
hovering head to wind while the cadets were offloaded in an inflatable
dinghy, known by its trademark as a Gemini. The hazard became a
drama when the Gemini's outboard engine broke down at the jetty as
Bronington was driven remorselessly up the channel by the wind. When
the Gemini eventually returned, the little craft came alongside *Bronington*
in what had become a rough tideway. As soon as the two Gemini crewmen had made fast, the Prince gave the order to steam slowly forward
towards the relative safety of open water, heading into a short, steep sea.
At the same moment one of the two crewmen moved to make an adjust-
ment at the bows of the Gemini just as the inflatable dipped into a wave.
The dinghy was immediately swamped and capsized, flinging both sailors
into the freezing water of the loch. A second Gemini was lowered into

the water but its engine failed as well. By the time they had it started, the two men in the water were at the point of exhaustion. Although they had lifejackets, they were wearing none of the protective clothing needed for survival in those temperatures. When they were at last hauled aboard, they were both very cold indeed; a little longer in the water and they would certainly have perished. As it was, they recovered swiftly and the incident was over. Had either man been lost, there would have been a full inquiry, and – given the facts of the case – the Prince would almost certainly have faced the censure of the Admiralty. Knowing this, both Lieutenants Clare and Rapp, guilt-stricken for failing an inexperienced commanding officer, resolved that they would share the blame between them in the forlorn hope that the Prince would be exonerated. Mercifully for them all, there were no injuries and no damage, and thus no inquiry; 'the sharks' which so troubled the Prince were kept at bay.

Four months later, *Bronington* was minehunting off Holyhead, a routine exercise which involved anchoring at carefully plotted positions on the chart and then using the ship's detectors to search laboriously among the rocks on the sea bed beneath. Towards the end of one long day, they lowered the anchor for perhaps the twentieth time without noticing that they had chosen a spot on the chart that was bisected by a fine magenta line, marking an underwater cable. When the order was given to weigh anchor, they discovered that it was stuck fast to the bottom of the sea – or rather, as they soon realised, to a main GPO telecommunications cable linking the British mainland to the Irish coast. After a hurried conference between the senior officers, the Prince agreed that two divers should be sent down to investigate. While they were underwater, the line which attached them to the ship parted, and, with darkness falling, they drifted away into the gloom in the four-knot current – tidal conditions which the Prince reported as dreadful even at slack water. A Gemini was lowered and, mercifully, both men were recovered. But, as the Prince noted, 'the conditions were so bloody that we very nearly lost two divers'.[56] Twenty-four hours later, after repeated but fruitless attempts to extricate his vessel from her embarrassing predicament, the Prince gave the order to slip the anchor, thinking to himself, as he later explained, 'I've got to live with the GPO for the rest of my life. What happens if I break the damn thing? I've had enough of this.'[57] Under the circumstances it was a prudent decision but when the appropriate forms explaining the circumstances fell on the relevant Whitehall desk, the Prince received a stern rebuke from his superiors in the Ministry of Defence. In losing his anchor – whatever the circumstances – he was, they judged, at fault.

Long afterwards, he would report how, while his crew was struggling to disentangle the anchor from the cable, he was assailed by the ludicrous image of every telegraph pole and phone box in County Donegal being dragged slowly but inexorably by an invisible but irresistible force towards the coast and thence into the Irish Sea.[58] At the time, however, he sent a terse note to his private secretary: 'For your information – and that of the press office, if necessary – I have just had to slip my starboard anchor, having spent 24 miserable hours trying to free it from an underwater telephone cable . . . If the press happen to find out, it is something that can occasionally happen and I got rid of the anchor to avoid damage to telephone cable.'[59] Happily for him and for his ship, not a word of either mishap reached the ears of an ever attentive Fleet Street.

In the absence of bad news or contrary evidence, the newspaper image of the Prince of Wales as 'Action Man' had impressed itself on the public mind. After five years in the Navy, the shy and withdrawn child had been transformed into a naval hero: 'Fearless, full-of-fun Charlie', in the words of one tabloid, 'The get-up-and-go Prince Charles', in the words of another, and 'Charles, scourge of the seas' in a third. The creation of this one-dimensional paragon was not so much a conscious distortion as the product of ignorance and conjecture; however, it fitted precisely the tabloid notion of how a Prince should be. The caricature was not at all malicious – indeed, it was quite flattering – but it was utterly superficial. From the perspective of Fleet Street, however, such niceties had a low priority. In a contracting and competitive marketplace, the tabloids were being influenced, if not yet driven, by the need to maintain sales and increase profits. In this environment, truth and falsehood were no longer the iron opposites by which editors decided whether to print or not to print; the competition was starting to make such decisions for them. For those who chose to court public attention, the signs were ominous enough; for the royal family, which had no choice in the matter, they were alarming. For the Prince of Wales, who saw no means of redress, his tabloid image gave him no pleasure but served merely to confirm his deepening mistrust of journalists; whether their intentions were benign or malevolent, they were, from his perspective, usually wrong, and on those rare occasions when they were right, it was merely a matter of chance. Despite these misgivings, the Prince had as yet little conception of how merciless the press might become. As 'Action Man' at sea, he was still sheltered from the whirlwind.

After an exercise in the Baltic in September, when *Bronington* was sometimes shadowed by East German patrol boats, the minesweeper headed back across the North Sea for the Firth of Forth. The weather was deteriorating and by the time they were 200 miles from the Danish coast the gale was so severe that they were forced to 'heave to' in confused and breaking seas. It was the first rough weather for eight weeks, and the Prince suffered a severe bout of seasickness, sitting on the bridge, as his fellow officers would recall, looking most unregal with a bucket between his legs. '<u>Never</u> in my life', he wrote, 'have I felt so ill or been so appallingly sick as I was that day and night. I found myself feeling quite happy at the prospect of the ship quietly turning over and sinking – I was well beyond the point of caring and couldn't have been more grateful for the fact that Roy Clare doesn't feel seasick (or so he says!) and therefore was perfectly capable of taking decisions.'[60] However, when Lieutenant Clare advised that they could put on speed once more, the Prince protested from the depths of his misery that the motion was horrible enough as it was and that he was not going to make it worse by going any faster. It was only when the first lieutenant persisted that the Captain yielded, and thereby allowed the ship to reach its destination in time for the weekend leave for which his shipmates pined.

According to Clare, the Prince seemed to regard the human frailty of seasickness almost as a failure of character. The junior officer was intrigued by the self-criticism by which his Captain seemed so frequently to torment himself, especially as he commanded the ship with an authority which seemed effortless: 'He looked the part. He was different. He was special. And the ship's company was very proud that they were his ship's company . . .' In a small ship with a crew of only thirty-three men, when every personality is magnified by proximity, it is impossible to dissemble with impunity; arrogance or insincerity – especially in a commanding officer – are swiftly exposed. The Prince's modesty was pervasive and endearing: 'Many of us loved him as our CO. He was a very good CO. The ship's company were genuinely fond of him . . . I don't think any of them ever saw him rattled or irritated. He never shouted at them . . .'[61]

In December 1976, in the Navy's final report on the Prince of Wales, Commander Elliott, the senior officer of his squadron, confirmed this impression. 'In spite of enormous outside pressure Prince Charles has attained an excellent level of professional competence as a Commanding Officer,' he wrote. 'He has a natural flair and ability for shiphandling and consequently his manoeuvres have been a pleasure to witness.'[62]

The Commander also paid tribute to his subordinate's qualities: 'Prince Charles has shown a deep understanding for his sailors and their families and their problems and as a result the morale of his ship has been of an extremely high order.'[63] As Captain, the Prince had responsibility for the wellbeing of the ship's company, a role in which sympathy and compassion had notably prevailed – to the consternation of the ship's coxswain who was a disciplinarian in the traditional mould. One seaman who was repeatedly late back from shore-leave offered such an implausible excuse that the coxswain suggested that an exemplary penalty would be in order. The miscreant was summoned before the Captain, in whose presence he explained that, after the last offence, he had bought a second alarm clock to ensure that he awoke in time. Unfortunately, his wife had bought a budgerigar which, that very night, had escaped from its cage and had perched on each clock, suppressing both alarms in the process. This defence was offered with such panache that the Prince was hardly able to retain his composure. Moving swiftly to judgement, he acknowledged the validity of the mitigating circumstances and dismissed the case without further comment. However, he could contain himself for only a moment longer and, even before the reprieved seaman had left the wardroom, his Commanding Officer surrendered to a bout of uncontrollable mirth. Even the coxswain allowed himself a smile. By such incidents the Prince imprinted his character on the ship; in his generation there were sharper officers, cleverer navigators, and finer sailors, but, as a Captain, he was – by common consent – 'a natural'.[64]

On the day he left the Navy, the officers and crew of *Bronington* slung a black lavatory seat around his neck and carried him ashore in a wheelchair. As the crews of other ships at Rosyth joined in the cheering, the wheelchair was trundled along the quay while the Prince waved farewell to the insulation of a military club by which he had been so protectively and respectfully embraced. The manner of his departure, an affectionate (if, to the uninitiated, quite ridiculous) rite of passage, reflected the trust that bound together not only the individuals but the institutions which they served. Their shared values – which without embarrassment evoked traditional concepts such as loyalty and duty – bound them the more closely together because they sensed how rapidly they were under erosion in the world beyond the bounds of ships and palaces. It was to this world that the Prince of Wales now returned to find a role for himself on the public stage.

CHAPTER
THIRTEEN

———

Prince Charles's decision to leave the Navy, where he had not reached the peak of his potential, was motivated both by the sense of duty which always nagged him and by an appetite to move away from the unfulfilling confines of service life. He had gained in experience and confidence in the Navy and, now approaching the age of thirty, he wanted to put this to good purpose. 'Perhaps I'm wrong or have an over-inflated sense of my own importance,' he wrote a little before that decision, 'but I feel I could be more useful at home than miles away.'[1]

The sentiment was admirable but it begged the question which would always dog him: how could the Prince of Wales be both useful and fulfilled? Always in the spotlight, invariably under police protection, on call for royal duty at home and abroad, and chained to a destiny which required him to be available at any time to succeed as sovereign and head of state, the constitutional 'baggage' by which he was encumbered severely limited the options available to him.

It would not have been hard to fill the official diary with public engagements – to drift from one reception to another, dispensing good-will, encouragement and compassion, earning the respect and affection by which the monarchy still thrived – but that was far from enough to satisfy his restless spirit. With his customary candour, he referred to his dilemma in a speech at Cambridge University: 'My great problem in life is that I do not really know what my role in life is. At the moment I do not have one. But somehow I must find one.'[2]

Aware of the predicament that was going to face the Prince, his private secretary David Checketts had searched through the files in search of guidance about the role of the heir to the throne. He drew a blank; if any wisdom had been accumulated through the ages it had not been recorded for the benefit of posterity. This constitutional vacuum was not an oversight but documentary evidence of the peculiar position that the heir apparent occupies; there is no formal 'role' except to wait.

One apparent way of solving the Prince's dilemma which appealed to Checketts was the Governor-Generalship of Australia. It would be a 'proper job' and appropriate experience – a prospect which he had first mooted a decade earlier after the Prince's return from Timbertop in 1966. In a memo to Michael Adeane,[*] the Queen's private secretary, Checketts outlined the advantages and the pitfalls of such an appointment, noting that the Prince would need a wife before embarking on such an enterprise, because as a bachelor in Government House, he would face all manner of social difficulties. Who would act as his 'hostess' on formal occasions? Who would organise his domestic life? And how would his reputation be protected from a galaxy of young Australian women eager for betrothal into the House of Windsor?

However, in the absence of a better alternative, the Checketts proposal hovered in the background as an ever-available and, to the Prince, attractive option. Then, in 1975, a minor political crisis in Australia erupted into a constitutional melodrama. Following the failure of the Prime Minister, Gough Whitlam, to secure the passage of his budget through Parliament (in the face of blocking tactics adopted by a coalition of opposition parties), Sir John Kerr, the Governor-General, exercised the royal prerogative by dismissing the Prime Minister – by whom, incidentally, he had originally been nominated for the post. In Australia, Sir John's action was widely regarded as precipitous, and the smouldering resentment it engendered had the side-effect of eliminating Prince Charles as a candidate for his post. Though he would sometimes still toy with the notion, the Prince knew quite well that for the heir to the throne to inherit the Governor-Generalship in the wake of Sir John would have been seen as a calculated provocation. Even if, with his obvious affection for Australia, he had been

---

[*] Michael Adeane (1910–84), equerry and assistant private secretary to George VI 1937–52; to the Queen 1952–53; private secretary to the Queen 1953–72.

able to anaesthetise the wound to the national pride of a former colony, his appointment would have been fraught with constitutional peril. What, for instance, if circumstances arose in which as Governor-General the Prince of Wales was called upon to consider similar action? Or if he were manoeuvred into some other, unforeseeable drama? In any case, his very presence would have been a focus for a divisive debate about the future of the monarchy. Moreover, despite his charm and tact, he had not yet acquired the diplomatic experience needed for such a sensitive task of mediation. A decade later, when the idea surfaced again in different circumstances (only to be dismissed for similar reasons), there was at least a dilemma. On this occasion it had already perished by the time the media had started to promote it.

This background did not inhibit the Foreign Secretary, Lord Carrington,* and Lord Soames, who at the end of the seventies approached the Palace with the suggestion that the Prince of Wales might become British Ambassador to France (a post which Soames had himself occupied between 1968 and 1972). In their blithe enthusiasm, the two statesmen had evidently failed to consider the constitutional implications of parachuting the Prince into the heart of a diplomatic combat zone where Britain and France were at loggerheads over the future of the European Economic Community. With his customary grace, Lord Carrington later acknowledged that the idea of inviting the Prince of Wales to become the official representative of Margaret Thatcher's administration was indeed 'crazy'.[3] At the time, he thought that it would be a 'proper job' for which the Prince was admirably suited; that it would provide him with the disciplined environment which, by all accounts, he needed; and that the French, being inveterately snobbish, would be immensely flattered by his presence. The idea did not for a moment find favour with the Prince or the Palace.

During the latter half of the seventies, the question of whether the Prince of Wales should have a 'proper job' had become a matter of desultory chatter in the establishment and of serious discussion within the Palace and between the Palace and 10 Downing Street, which was then

---

* Lord Carrington (1919–), Leader of the House of Lords 1963–64; Defence Secretary 1970–74; Secretary of State for Foreign Affairs 1979–82; Secretary-General, NATO 1984–88.

occupied by James Callaghan,* the Labour Prime Minister. A flurry of letters and memoranda reflected their general awareness of the dilemma facing the Prince. In December 1977, Checketts wrote a note to the Queen's private secretary, Sir Philip Moore, defending the Prince against those who seemed to think that only by taking up a 'proper job' could the Prince make appropriate use of his time. 'I find it most revealing that the question "What is Prince Charles going to do now that he has left the Navy?" is still being raised, when even a brief investigation of the problem would reveal that the true question is "How is Prince Charles going to be able to do all there is for him to do?" '[4] he wrote. To support this contention, Checketts supplied the Queen's private secretary with a list of the Prince's current involvements, which included the Duchy of Cornwall, the Prince's Trust, the Prince of Wales Environment Committee for Wales, the United World Colleges,† the Joint Jubilee Trusts, the Chancellorship of the University of Wales, his role as Colonel-in-Chief of five regiments, and his patronage of the British Sub Aqua Club and the Royal Anthropological Institute. For good measure, his private secretary loyally appended a list of the Prince's formal engagements and foreign tours.

In any case, according to Checketts, the difficulties involved in selecting an appropriate 'proper job' were immense:

> bearing in mind that whichever Government department, industrial or commercial concern is selected to absorb the Prince of Wales into its work force will immediately enjoy a privileged status . . . Several other factors become immediately obvious. Among them being the realisation of the difficulty of integrating 'The Prince of Wales' into any working unit, without experiencing all the inevitable human attitudes a Royal presence inevitably engenders, and yet allowing His Royal Highness the normal opportunities and privileges . . .[5]

---

* Lord Callaghan of Cardiff (1912–   ), Chancellor of Exchequer 1964–67; Home Secretary 1967–70; Secretary of State for Foreign Affairs 1974–76; Prime Minister 1976–79.

† The United World Colleges, founded on principles similar to those espoused by Kurt Hahn at Gordonstoun, was a movement to establish a network of international schools at which future leaders of diverse nationalities, chosen by merit and financed by scholarships, should study together. The Prince had followed Mountbatten as president.

As Checketts recognised, the central question was whether the apparent advantages of taking a 'proper job' were not outweighed by the obvious disadvantages:

> It is my firm belief that his Royal Highness has a far more important role to play by continuing to expand his activities as Prince of Wales, in the interests of service to society as a whole and not to one particular segment of it. The effect of limiting his Royal Highness to a specific profession would do nothing but frustrate the growing awareness of this remarkable young man in his responsibility to the people of the United Kingdom and the Commonwealth . . .[6]

Armed with that forceful defence, and after a long conversation with the Prince of Wales, the Queen's new private secretary wrote to the Prime Minister's private secretary to confirm what his predecessor, Sir Martin Charteris, had already indicated in an earlier letter – that in the interests of the country and the Commonwealth the Prince did not intend to withdraw from public life to undertake full-time or part-time employment. Commenting that the Prince was already making a considerable contribution to the country both at home and abroad, Moore added that the heir to the throne was anxious to acquire more first-hand knowledge in depth of the working of the country. To this end, he reported, the Prince intended to set aside a number of days each year for further education in the fields of government, industry, commerce and agriculture.

Moore suggested that the Prime Minister might himself identify a programme of instruction in government, a proposal which James Callaghan initiated by arranging for the Prince to spend time at NEDO (the National Economic Development Office), an official forum for government, the CBI and the TUC to discuss the state of the economy in the context of investment, employment and pay.* Despite the Prime Minister's goodwill, the prospective programme failed to excite the enthusiasm of the Prince to the degree that either Moore or Callaghan might have hoped. It was widely believed that Callaghan was disappointed by the Prince's failure to immerse himself more thoroughly in the ways of Whitehall but, in any case, the embryo programme was buried in the fall of the Labour government only eighteen months after the idea was first broached.

The Prince's curiosity in the details of governance was not easy to kindle, but his anxiety to have an overall understanding of public affairs was not feigned. On an official trip to Belgium in November 1978, he was scheduled to visit the European Commission. The draft programme proposed 'opening remarks by Mr Jenkins,* possibly with reply from HRH'. In the margin, the Prince wrote tartly, 'This is ridiculous. I'm trying to <u>find out</u> things not <u>tell</u> them anything.'[7]

The Palace remained sensitive about the 'proper job' issue. In February 1978, an item in the *Daily Mail* written by the gossip columnist Nigel Dempster, which began, 'Situation sought: Prince, 29, degree, ex-Army, Navy, RAF, seeks employment. Will go anywhere, try anything once', failed to amuse.[8] A few days after that, the Queen's press secretary, Ronald Allison, wrote to her private secretary, after lunching with the London editor of a regional newspaper, to note that the journalist had almost immediately raised the subject of the Prince of Wales, asking what the Prince was going to do with his life and in the same breath expressing the hope that the heir to the throne would not simply confine himself to the 'royal round'. This conversation prompted Allison to remind the Queen's private secretary that the public had expectations of the Prince that were not being fulfilled: there had been hopes that he would involve himself in enterprising but un-royal activities but, instead, people were left with the impression that he spent a great deal of time hunting, shooting and skiing.

Allison sent a copy of his memo to the Prince's private secretary and earned himself an immediate rebuke:

> As His Royal Highness's relations with the public and general popularity have never been higher, and this is borne out at every public appearance and by the vast amount of correspondence received daily, I do not believe it is the public which hold such expectations, as much as the media . . .
>
> Perhaps what should be considered is some means of revealing to

---

* Roy Jenkins, later Lord Jenkins of Hillhead (1920–   ), Home Secretary 1965–67, 1974–76; Chancellor of the Exchequer 1967–70; Deputy Leader of Labour Party 1970–72; President of European Commission 1977–81; First Leader, Social Democratic Party 1982–83; Leader of Social and Liberal Democratic Party in 1988; Chancellor, University of Oxford since 1987.

the media more of the immense amount of important work carried out by the Prince of Wales when not in the public eye, and which seems to be totally unnoticed.[9]

The Prince was himself frustrated by the limitations of royal duty. 'I want to consider ways in which I can escape from the ceaseless round of official engagements and meet people in less artificial circumstances,' he noted in November 1978. 'In other words, I want to look at the possibility of spending, say, 1. three days in one factory to find out what happens; 2. three days, perhaps, in a trawler (instead of one rapid visit); 3. three or four days on a farm. I would also like to consider 4. more visits to immigrant areas in order to help these people to feel that they are not ignored or neglected and that we are concerned about them as individuals.'[10]

Not all of these ideas materialised, but the Prince's concern about the 'immigrant areas', forshadowing many of his own initiatives, was regarded as a sensitive issue for him to alight on. In a note to the Queen's private secretary, one of the Prince's team, Oliver Everett, wrote, 'On the immigrant areas, I know you have views. HRH is meeting the three senior members of the Commission for Racial Equality on 20th November. And David [Checketts] has discussed with Robert Armstrong* so we would move cautiously and only with advice on this one.'[11]

Alert to the constraints of his position but searching for a role, the Prince was reluctant to accept what he detected among some courtiers as a resistance to his growing concern about the most deprived and disadvantaged communities. Whether they feared that he would become too identified with an emerging political cause or whether they thought that the balance of his alignment should lie more with success than with failure, their reluctance to encourage his eagerness to become more closely involved in the problems of the inner cities became a growing source of irritation to him. Once an idea had caught his imagination, it was not easy to divert him from pursuing it with all the passion with which he had been liberally endowed. Painfully aware that at one level his only role was 'to wait', he was very unwilling indeed to drift on the tide of events.

*

---

* Lord Armstrong of Ilminster, (1927–), principal private secretary to the Prime Minister 1970–75; secretary to the Cabinet 1979–87.

That there could be many years to wait was brought into sharp focus by the Queen's Silver Jubilee on 7 June 1977, when his mother, only fifty-one years old, celebrated twenty-five years on the throne. On the eve of the celebrations the Mall had steadily filled with people, armed with sleeping bags, deck chairs and Union Jacks. As they had done twenty-four years before at the coronation, British royalists (among them West Indians and Asians) and foreign tourists (with Americans in the ascendant) mingled genially along the route of the Silver Jubilee procession which would leave Buckingham Palace the following morning. There was no discernible difference in the mood of the crowd from that of 1953. The dustcarts were cheered, the policemen chuckled. One group sang 'Two, four, six, eight, who do we appreciate?' before yelling in unison, 'Lizzie!' – although traditional favourites like 'Rule Britannia' and 'Land of Hope and Glory' predominated. In among the comic hats and patriotic socks were banners and badges with the inscriptions 'Liz Rules, OK' and 'Cool Rule, Liz'. It had been predicted by some that the crowd would be largely composed of pensioners, middle-class matrons and a sprinkling of reluctant children; in reality, the young – of all classes – were in the majority.

On the following day, which was blessed by fine weather, much of the nation revelled in a spontaneous carnival in city streets, town squares and village greens. There were tea parties and picnics, fancy dress parades and beauty contests, tombolas and raffles, barn dances and whist drives, barbecues and bingo, tugs-of-war and cricket matches. For a day, at least, the elusive spirit of community rose momentarily to embrace a union of every class, as rich mingled with poor and old with young. In the capital, from the Mall to the City, there was hardly space to stand as the golden coach, exhumed from the Royal Mews for the occasion, trundled through a cheering crowd bearing the Queen and Prince Philip on their way to the solemnities at St Paul's Cathedral. The Prince of Wales rode on horseback behind his parents and the crowd delighted in the proximity. 'He looked right at me! Did you see that, man? He did. He looked right at me!' one said, and, as the procession came to a halt for a moment, others joined in:

'Good old Charlie.'

'Look over here, Charlie.'

'Hey, Charles!'

'Come on, give us a smile!'

'Charlie, come on, over here!'

'You're doing well, son.'

As if in response to these summons, the Prince seemed to turn towards the group. Interpreting this evidence from Mass Observation, Philip Ziegler observed, 'The nod from the Commendatore's statue could hardly have caused a greater sensation. The Prince of Wales and the crowd had suddenly been transformed into "Charlie and Me".'[12]

It was, of course, an illusion of the moment. The procession passed by, the crowd dispersed and before long the Silver Jubilee was but a fading glow in the popular memory. For the Prince of Wales, however, it was of more than passing significance. Just over a year earlier, in May 1976, he had written to the Poet Laureate, John Betjeman, from a 'creaking, tossing ship in the middle of the English Channel' in his capacity as chairman of the King George Jubilee Trust, which was to administer a charitable appeal to coincide with the Queen's Silver Jubilee. 'I am determined that it should be as much of a success as possible . . .' he wrote. 'It would be marvellous if you could find the time to construct one of your masterpieces of scansion for the Queen's Jubilee . . . I would be enormously grateful, personally, if you felt able to conjure up your muse! . . . I am sure you will agree that a Silver Jubilee is something to be remembered with suitable splendour.'[13]

Betjeman duly obliged, though his letter enclosing the poem was inadvertently put on a 'B' pile, so that the Prince did not see it until several days after it had arrived at Buckingham Palace. When he finally read it, he was aghast, though he noted with uncharacteristic understatement that 'this poem is not exactly what I was expecting'.[14]

> In days of disillusion,
> However low we've been,
> To fire us and inspire us
> God gave to us our Queen.
>
> She acceded, young and dutiful
> To her much-loved father's throne;
> Serene and kind and beautiful,
> She holds us as her own.
>
> Now, twenty-five years later,
> So sure her reign has been
> That great events are greater
> With the presence of the Queen.

That look of dedication
In her trusting eyes of blue
Make accession, Coronation,
Both mysterious and true.

For our Monarch and Her People
United and yet free
Let bells from every steeple
Ring out the Jubilee.[15]

Doubtless conceived 'in humble duty', Betjeman's five stanzas were lacklustre to the point of pastiche, without that verve which had rightly earned him a reputation as a great contemporary poet. The Prince was so dismayed that he contemplated asking the Poet Laureate to try again, but since the Queen had already given her approval to a modified version of the same poem to be put to music by Malcolm Williamson, the Master of the Queen's Musick, he decided reluctantly not to press the matter. The Prince's reaction to the Betjeman poem revealed a trait of character which had emerged belatedly – an assertion of conviction which those around him would increasingly have to reckon with. The acquiescence, which in virtually all matters save his private life, they had for so long taken for granted would no longer be so easily forthcoming. Neglectful of explanatory detail and impatient of lengthy exegesis, he was disconcertingly swift to judgement, but often in the process reached directly to the heart of a matter. Once he had declared himself, he was not easily moved. In the case of the Queen's Silver Jubilee, his motives sprang less from filial piety than an aspiration which he had conceived almost five years earlier.

In December 1972, the Conservative government had introduced a long-awaited penal reform, known as Community Service by Offenders. Its purpose was to provide the courts with an alternative to prison for a range of minor crimes in cases where the offender had no previous convictions. A modest proposal, it caused a predictable rash of hostile comment. Among others, George Pratt, the Deputy Chief Probation Officer for Inner London, who had been a member of the Home Office Working Party which had prepared the legislation and had conducted the pilot Community Service Scheme in London, came under ferocious scrutiny by the media for being unduly 'soft' on crime.

In the midst of this media barrage, Pratt answered a call from Buckingham Palace: it was Checketts, the Prince's private secretary, who told him that the Prince, who had already begun to worry privately about the effects of alienation on young people, had been following the debate and wanted to know if he could help in any way. A few days later, in the Chinese Drawing Room at the Palace, Pratt met 'this young, enthusiastic and idealistic person' who said that he wanted to help those who had lacked his own advantages.[16] He spoke with fervour about the ideas of Kurt Hahn and (clearly forgetful of his own adversities there) with spirit about Gordonstoun's bracing environment from which he had come to believe he had, in large measure, benefited. He suggested, among other things, that communities throughout Britain might borrow from the example of his old school by establishing a network of part-time volunteer services, like the fire brigade, to divert young people from vandalism and other mischief. Touched by his sincerity, Pratt felt obliged to point out that in the communities with which he was familiar such a scheme would produce as many young arsonists as firefighters, each group collaborating with the other to create their own brand of inner-city adventure.

A little the wiser but no less passionate, the Prince was encouraged by Pratt to host a further meeting at which a group of specialists, including representatives of the Church, the social services and the police, could discuss in more detail how the royal purpose might be achieved. Aware of the historical pitfalls, the Prince himself was in no doubt that his great-uncle's assertion that 'Something must be done' had to be replaced by the question 'What can I do?' The challenge was to find an appro priate answer.

In 1935, the former Prince of Wales (later Edward VIII) had founded the King George's Jubilee Trust to celebrate his father's Silver Jubilee. He had been dismayed by the lack of playing fields and other facilities for boys leaving school – as they then did – at the age of fourteen. To inau gurate the Trust, the Prince of Wales had made an appeal to the nation on the radio which by the autumn of that year had raised more than £1 million to address 'the urgency of the problem of youth'. In the inter vening years, the Trust had prospered steadily but without inspiration, dispersing modest grants to sundry appropriate causes – including the Junior Red Cross, the Girl Guides, the Outward Bound Trust, the YMCA and Voluntary Service Overseas. Forty years on, however, in a new age of 'street-wise' charities, it had acquired a distinctly arthritic veneer, with a governing council still dominated by Lords Lieutenant and peers of the realm, supportive of good works but lacking both initiative and the fund-raising energy to offset the effects of inflation. The projects which they supported, valuable though they were, also failed to penetrate the decaying inner cities which incubated the alienation that worried Prince Charles. The implacable rise in the rate of juvenile crime also indicated that the 'problem of youth' had become even more pressing.

Only marginally aware of the diminishing role played by his predecessor's Trust (he did not become its chairman until 1974), Prince Charles was adamant that any initiative endorsed by him should be focused directly on deprived communities; that it should be designed to release the talent which, he argued, lay imprisoned within even the most recalcitrant individuals (or 'characters' as he would persist in calling them); and, strongly influenced by what he had discovered from his time in the Navy about the ability of young ratings (and army NCOs whom he had met) to command respect regardless of background, that it should stimulate a sense of adventure and public service.

After prolonged and sometimes heated debate, the Prince proposed that Pratt and his team should establish a number of pilot schemes to test their ideas in the field. With the help of an informal network of voluntary helpers and with the minimum of 'red tape', the embryo charity would make individual grants of up to £300 (or £500 for groups) to help young people escape from what was fashionably known as 'the cycle of deprivation'. Sensitive to the charge of 'do-gooding' and convinced that the association of his name with any such venture would deter those whom he most wanted to reach, the Prince resolved to stay in the background until the scheme had established itself.

The Palace 'old guard' were no less mindful of the pitfalls than the Prince himself, and very much more cautious. In the summer of 1974, with the first three pilot schemes already underway, the Queen's private secretary, Martin Charteris, intervened to warn of a potential 'conflict of interest' between the Prince's scheme, the existing King George's Jubilee Trust, and the prospective Trust to commemorate the Queen's Silver Jubilee – a conflict that was likely to involve the Prince himself as he was almost certainly going to be asked by his mother to become chairman of both Jubilee Trusts. 'I think the message', Charteris wrote to the Prince's private secretary, 'is go steady on the Trust Prince Charles has in mind until the dust settles.'[17]

he Prince does homage to the Queen during his investiture in Caernarvon Castle, July 1969

ith President Richard Nixon and Princess Anne at the White House, Washington, July 1970

The Prince learning to navigate on board
HMS *Norfolk*, 1971

Playing deck hockey, HMS *Norfolk*, 1971

On safari in Kenya, 1971

...rry Secombe and Spike Milligan with the Prince, London, 1973

...couldn't resist the temptation to fool about and inflate my suit with air so that I looked like ...ne animated form of dirigible balloon. I then stepped outside ... and faced an amazed ...ss corps which couldn't believe their eyes.' Canada, 1975

Balmoral Castle, Scotland

Sandringham House

Highgrove House

Lord Mountbatten with the Prince

The Prince and Camilla Parker Bowles
t Smith's Lawn, Windsor, 1975

Lord Mountbatten with his granddaughter
Amanda Knatchbull

On board HMS *Bronington*,
November 1976

The Prince gives up his command,
Rosyth, 1976

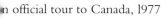
n official tour to Canada, 1977

Doing the samba, Rio de Janeiro, 1978

he Prince, Lord Mountbatten and Prince Philip, 1978

Lady Susan Hussey, lady-in-waiting
to the Queen

Norton Knatchbull and Penny Eastwood,
later Lord and Lady Romsey, with the Princ

Hugh and Emilie van Cutsem

Patty and Charles Palmer-Tomkinson

Although the judgement was sound enough, the 'message' was couched in terms that could not have been better calculated to irritate the Prince. Although Charteris was clever, wise and warm-hearted, even he was unable to divest himself entirely of the prevailing attitude among the Queen's senior advisers – most of whom had been at court since the Prince's childhood – that the heir to the throne was still too young to be taken entirely seriously and that although he should be humoured, it would not be wise to let him off the Palace leash too soon.

Though the Prince disguised his growing resentment – except from his intimates – he was quick to detect any apparent slight from the Queen's officials and began resolutely to distance himself from them. Determined to establish his own identity as a loyal but independent member of the royal family, he had no intention of allowing an apparent 'conflict of interest' to arrest the growth of the very first initiative that he had established on his own account. His private secretary was instructed to inform Charteris that while he took note of the concerns, the Prince was by no means certain that 'his own ideas could be successfully absorbed' into the Jubilee Trusts.[18]

Early in 1975, with promising results from experimental schemes in London, Chester and Cornwall (where early awards included the cash to buy a fishing rod for a teenager whose parents were too poor to buy it themselves),* Pratt, as chairman of the Advisory Group, drafted a 'strictly confidential' document. He outlined the need for the new scheme to support young people, aged between fifteen and twenty-five, who 'may seem aimless or lacking in purpose', who might feel 'alienated or rejected' and 'unwilling or unable to make constructive use of the traditional and well-established educational and recreational routes to economic and personal autonomy'. Stripped of its sociological language, the message was plain: a growing number of young people were destined for the scrap heap almost before reaching adulthood, and neither the state nor the existing voluntary bodies could reach them. By making small grants to 'independent, spontaneous groups' in the target age band, the proposed trust would help them set up 'self-help schemes' through which they could 'devise and carry through their own ideas and ambitions' so that 'their restless energy and talents may be canalised into

---

* A year later, in a gesture of appreciation, the youth sent the Prince a box of 'flies' for salmon-fishing which he had made himself.

constructive activities'.[19] By the standards of conventional opinion, however, the venture was not only radical but risky as well – a rapid way of
squandering other people's hard-earned money on soggy-minded phil-
anthropy, and of making a fool of its founder overnight.

By 1975, the Prince himself was aware of the potential 'conflict of
interest' between his own scheme and the King George's Jubilee Trust. In
any case, he was concerned to avoid an 'excessive duplication of effort' of
the work of the wide range of other charities that were moving into the
same territory.[20] His partial solution was 'eventually' to use the King
George's Jubilee Trust as a means of 'putting all this into action'.[21] As
chairman, the Prince hoped to be able to transfer some of its resources to
realise the ambitions of his own embryo scheme. In October of that year,
his private secretary wrote diplomatically to the secretary of the King
George's Jubilee Trust, Major Sir Michael Hawkins, explaining that, 'His
Royal Highness sincerely hopes that the Jubilee Trust will become the
"parent" or "landlord" of the scheme.'[22] Hawkins replied with caution,
barely disguising his own misgivings: 'There will be many objections
because of the lack of safeguards; because of the lack of faith in the ability of young people to be masters of their own fates.' However, he added
with the tact of a courtier, 'We do not share these reservations . . .
Fortunately charitable money can be used for experiments, and it is generally realised that experiments are not always successful.'[23] If Hawkins
harboured the thought that his chairman's innovative scheme was somewhat harebrained, it did not behove him to say so.

By the end of December, the Charity Commissioners had before
them the draft deeds for the Prince's Trust, complete with a logo incorporating its founder's new personal cypher, a 'C' with a crown. By
January 1976, the Prince was reiterating to sceptical supporters that,
'The whole point of the exercise is to find challenge and adventure,
combined with an element of service, for young people – not going into
people's homes for coffee . . . If we don't insist upon challenge and
adventure, to a certain extent, we become like all other voluntary groups
and I shall give up at once!'[24] His insistence on 'challenge and adventure'
sprang from the conviction that, in essence, he was not so very different
from the dispossessed; that under other circumstances he too might have
'gone under'; and therefore, that if they were given even a fraction of the
opportunities he had enjoyed, they too could overcome the odds. His
faith in this vision was obdurate. At the inaugural meeting of the

Trustees, he emphasised yet again the crucial value of 'challenge, adventure, and service', reminding potential backsliders, 'I established this for a special purpose and to fulfil a need we all agreed was there.'[25] In a personality that was otherwise so diffident, this implacability was a revelation; a sharp reminder that in the Prince of Wales indecisiveness and single-mindedness sat side by side. In some matters he would acquiesce at once, in others he would prevaricate, and in others he was immovable. Wise courtiers moved therefore with caution, probing gently and manoeuvring with delicacy to achieve their purposes. Others who were less sensitive to the complexity of his nature soon found themselves excluded from his counsels, without influence, on the outside looking in.

By April 1976, although the Queen had given her approval to the Prince's Trust, the rumblings about 'a clash of interests' had not abated. In June, the Duke of Edinburgh, noting pointedly that the Prince's Trust and the Queen's Silver Jubilee Trust seemed to have 'a rather similar purpose',[26] asked his son's private secretary for clarification. Checketts did his best but was hard put to define the distinctions, concluding, 'If you find this explanation as inadequate as I sense it might be, I would be very pleased to try and explain both Funds to you personally.'[27] In truth, the terms of reference of all three trusts were so flexible that, given the will, the objectives of all of them could easily have been incorporated under the umbrella of one organisation – as the Prince himself had already realised.

The most significant – and pressing – difference between the three trusts for which the Prince was now responsible was that while the King George's Jubilee Trust was already substantially endowed and the Queen's Silver Jubilee Trust was soon to raise in excess of £14 million, his own trust had virtually no money at all. By September 1976, his lawyer, Matthew Farrer, was so concerned that he wrote to the Prince's private secretary warning that unless funds were swiftly forthcoming, the Prince's Trust would suffer a severe reverse and that, in the process, the Prince himself would come under adverse scrutiny.[28] Hamstrung by his commitment to the Queen's Silver Jubilee Trust, the Prince was unable to appeal publicly for his own organisation. A few haphazard approaches to private individuals had yet to produce a benefactor willing to finance such an uncertain venture.

The inevitable recriminations within the Prince's Trust itself caused by looming insolvency were arrested by the timely arrival of a cheque for £4,000 from the proceeds of an interview given to American television by the Prince about George III. Soon afterwards, the actor Terry-Thomas contributed £105, the proceeds from an abortive attempt to cross the English Channel on water skis. Then a letter arrived from Harry Secombe enclosing a cheque for £2,000 which, he wrote, came from 'selling my mother-in-law to an Arab, and for doing a special charity concert'.[29] Even with the receipts from rock concerts and film premieres attended by the Prince, it was clear that if the new trust was to prosper, a more regular and substantial source of revenue was required than was available from such generous but sporadic initiatives. The need to integrate the overlapping efforts of the three trusts – the Prince's original objective – was imperative.

By May 1978, after much cajoling by the Prince in person, the first step had been accomplished – the amalgamation, administratively, of the King George's Jubilee Trust and the Queen's Silver Jubilee Trust, which were thenceforth referred to jointly as the Royal Jubilee Trusts. However, the Administrative Council for the trusts ordained that organisations only were entitled to apply to the Jubilee trusts for funds, thus excluding those individuals and informal groups which the Prince was determined to reach and for whom his trust had been set up. Realising this, and irritated by the bureaucratic niceties which seemed to thwart his ambition, the Prince warned that the two bodies would 'have to come to a sensible arrangement' otherwise, he threatened in exasperation, 'I shall give up [the] Jubilee Trusts and concentrate on the Prince's Trust.'[30] This intemperate response did little to hasten the outcome he sought; nor did his chronic failure to focus on financial or administrative detail help either. Those who came into his presence nervously armed with a long list of such items to resolve rarely got through the agenda before the Prince began to look surreptitiously at his watch. This disconcerting habit would generally have the desired effect, but only at the price of postponing crucial decisions. Meanwhile, the entrenched attitudes of many of the trustees and officials within the Royal Jubilee Trusts ensured that the struggle to establish the Prince's Trust as the 'lead' agency of the three could not be achieved by dictat; it would require a dogged and meticulous campaign for which the intuitive and potentially inspirational character of the Prince was conspicuously ill suited. Desultory negotiations continued until almost the end of the decade, interspersed by flashes of princely ingenuity about the issues which ought to have been consuming the energies of the negotiators.

However progressive its purpose, the Prince's Trust could not advance very far without the resources needed to put its aspirations into practice. The appointment of a fundraiser (who, like other members of staff, was prepared to work for nothing – either from a commitment to the cause, or from the *frisson* which came from close proximity to the Prince, or sometimes because of the advantages presumed to accrue from such an exalted contact) kept the Trust afloat in the early years. However, a combination of suspicion from Buckingham Palace, bureaucratic infighting and the patchy interest of the Prince himself delayed the emergence of what, under his inspiration, was eventually to become a multi-million-pound organisation – the biggest independent charity of its kind in the country.

In his urge to find fulfilling work for his restless young master, Checketts alighted on the Duchy of Cornwall, from which, at the age of eighteen, the Prince had started to draw an income and which was his only source of wealth. Urging the Prince to establish himself in the role of executive chairman of the Duchy, Checketts argued that, in running his own organisation, he could acquire an understanding of management and administration that would otherwise be denied him.

The Duchy had been created 640 years earlier by King Edward III for his son the Black Prince.* Since then, it had enjoyed mixed fortunes. According to the temper of the age, land had been bought and sold or seized and stolen. In some eras the Duchy prospered, in others it fell into neglect, but it survived every depredation. By the nineteenth century, the Duchy was administered on behalf of the Prince of Wales by a council, its independence guaranteed by statute.†

Under the direction of Prince Albert, who managed it on behalf of his wayward son Prince Edward (later Edward VII), the ramshackle structure of the Duchy had been radically overhauled. Tenancy agreements were redefined, land was improved, buildings were repaired and, for the first time, in the spirit of Victorian paternalism, the estates flourished to the

---

* The historian A.L. Rowse traces its origins back even further to Saxon times.
† When the Crown lands were made over to the state in 1760 in return for the Civil List, the Duchy lands were – anomalously – excluded.

advantage of landlord and tenant. Before Prince Albert took control, the Duchy's net revenue was just over £25,000 a year. Twenty-five years later, despite the financial drain of his commitment to beautifying the natural landscape, the excess of revenue over expenditure had almost doubled to over £46,000 a year. Prince Albert also arranged for the Treasury to oversee the affairs of the Duchy, a disposition that was to rankle with Prince Charles more than a century later. Despite the ravages of the agricultural depression of the early twentieth century and the slump of the thirties, it was – in spirit at least – Prince Albert's legacy which Prince Charles inherited in 1969.

Much diminished in scale from the days of the Black Prince but with the revenues from 128,000 acres – scattered over nine counties – it was still one of the great English estates, and for the Prince of Wales an exclusive source of personal income. At the Queen's accession, the Treasury had agreed that she should take one ninth of the Duchy surplus to provide for the heir apparent, which, when he was eighteen, gave him an income of £21,000 a year; the rest was held by the Treasury and offset against the cost of the Civil List. When he reached the age of twenty-one, the entire income of the Duchy – £248,000 – was made over to him, though by arrangement with the Treasury he elected to forgo 50 per cent in lieu of income tax, which at that time was in excess of 90 per cent at the top rate.

Until well into the twentieth century, the Duchy had paid the same tax as any other landowner, including super-tax. In 1913, however, the Treasury was persuaded that the Duchy should no longer be subject to these constraints. In 1921, citing the 'higher cost of repairs and similar outgoings' and the 'greatly increased' expenditure to which he was committed by virtue of his public responsibilities now that he had 'come of age', the Prince of Wales (the future Edward VIII) pleaded successfully that his income from the Duchy should be exempt from tax. The arrangement between the Prince and the Inland Revenue was concealed from public scrutiny, to the extent that the tax on Duchy rents (which was deducted by the tenants themselves) was still taken at source but returned subsequently to the Prince. In return for this arrangement, Edward made 'a voluntary contribution' to the government, which between 1921 and 1935 amounted to 22.4 per cent of his income. It was this arrangement which was in place on Prince Charles's twenty-first birthday, when he volunteered to more than double his predecessor's contribution to the Exchequer.[31]

In 1969, with 70,000 acres of farmland in nine counties, including 240 farms (ranging from a 10-acre holding on the Isles of Scilly to 900 acres in Dorset), 50,000 acres of forest and moorland on Dartmoor, 3,000 acres of woodland, 1,500 dwellings in London and elsewhere, 230 miles of foreshore, and 14,000 acres of fundus (river-bed), the Duchy employed around 200 people. There was much to be done. The management of the Duchy had been allowed to lag behind the times, failing to invest adequately in the post-war revolution in mechanised and subsidised agriculture which elsewhere had led to higher profits and spiralling rents. On the Duchy estates, rents had fallen behind the market and, to offset rising costs, the Prince's Council had authorised the sale of farms and other assets. Instead of expanding, the Duchy was contracting. To reverse that trend, the Duchy needed a judicious mixture of investment and sales, improving the value of the tenancies but selling suitable urban land and buildings to take advantage of the boom in property prices. The task for the next decade was to manage the assets of the Duchy so as to provide a large enough investment fund both to provide an income for the Prince of Wales (qua Duke of Cornwall) and to secure the capital base for his successors; to run an efficient business, but, mindful of the peculiar status of the Duchy, to do so in a way that would enhance the reputation of its principal beneficiary. It was in this challenge that Checketts hoped Prince Charles might find the inspiration that would give greater purpose to his life. At that stage though, despite his awe for the memory of Prince Albert, the Prince showed little inclination to seize the moment and do for the Duchy in the twentieth century what the Prince Consort had done in the nineteenth. For the time being, he seemed content to chair the Prince's Council, but otherwise to leave its affairs in the hands of others.

Unable to find a suitable challenge for his ill-focused energy, the Prince had more time on his hands than he either wished or cared to admit. To his friends he seemed troubled by anxiety and discontent, which he sometimes allowed to affect his behaviour towards his staff. Easily provoked by minor irritations, he became uncharacteristically impatient and peremptory. Whereas a decade earlier his comments about the official programmes put before him had been innocent and dutiful, by the late seventies his response to yet another 'Away Day' could seem reluctant and jaundiced – as if recoiling from the relentless mundanities that stretched ahead of him. A decade before, he might have complained at a particularly unappealing engagement by commenting, 'Have I got to spend 4 hours at this thing?'[32] By 1978 he was – on occasion – brusquely dismissive. In the margins of a letter asking him to attend a celebrity golf tournament to which he had donated a Challenge Cup (in the hope of securing funds for the Prince's Trust), he scribbled, 'I am sorry but I only agreed to [donate] this idiotic trophy on the clear understanding that I would not have to present it or go anywhere near a golf match.'[33] Usually thoughtful and humorous memoranda were peppered with irritable asides. 'How many times do I have to say that I am coming back to Rothesay not Rosyth on Mon. 12th? Please get it right,'[34] he admonished on the corner of a memorandum from his office detailing elaborate attempts to dovetail his public and private engagements, but making that single mistake. A poorly drafted memo or letter, or a typist's error – which invariably annoyed him – sometimes goaded him further. 'I am fed up with these mistakes which are thoroughly inexcusable and are purely the result of inadequate checking,' he scribbled to one careless secretary. 'If it happens again I shall totally lose my patience and will do something more drastic about it.'[35] He never carried out such threats and no-one thought he really meant them. To his uncomplaining lieutenants, such outbursts of rage – which were as swift to subside as to explode – simply highlighted the mood of disaffection which, in private and only in private, seemed so often to hang about him.

It was his closest aides like Checketts and, more especially, Michael Colborne who bore the brunt of his temper. Colborne had joined his office in 1975, leaving a career as a Petty Officer in the Navy (where he had served with the Prince in HMS *Norfolk*) to work for him as his personal secretary. In this role he not only organised the Prince's private life but became a discreet and loyal confidant as well. Over the next few years a bond of affection grew up between them, but even Colborne's devotion was occasionally put severely to the test. For no apparent reason the Prince would suddenly give way to an alarming display of uncontrolled anger, his face suffused with intense emotion. The proximate cause was invariably a minor lapse, but the disproportion of the response was so great that Colborne was not so much demoralised as perplexed. After one particularly fierce outburst, Mountbatten took him to one side to explain that he should understand that, in his lonely eminence, the Prince had no-one else on whom to vent his feelings; that – paradoxically – it was evidence of his regard, not a mark of animosity,

and that the outburst had assuredly been provoked by some other dis-
connected irritation. Colborne was mollified, knowing that, since he had
not himself raised the matter, the Prince must have been contrite enough
to mention his outburst to Mountbatten, even though he had not quite
been able to bring himself to apologise directly.

As they watched the heir to the throne casting about himself in search
of a future, a number of senior courtiers were tempted to disparage his
lack of direction and resolve. Others were critical but sympathetic. In the
words of one of the latter, 'it was a great pity for somebody who was
shaping up to take over this particular role [that he] should be victim to
so many misgivings and doubts and anxieties about it . . .'[36] Only his closest friends, glimpsing beneath the agitated surface to the turmoil of
spirit below, realised that, in his role as Prince of Wales, he had reached
a new point of departure only to confront a limitless void in front of him.
So far his life had been programmed, if not packaged, by others: every
major decision – about school, university, the armed forces – had been
taken for him by his father or by Mountbatten or by committees of 'the
great and the good', all of whom went through the forms of consultation
but took his compliance for granted. Now, approaching his fourth
decade, he was on his own, starting again from the beginning, trapped in
a role that had an outer form but no inner meaning, in which custom
and ceremony – the rush from one engagement to another – concealed
a vacuum from which he recoiled almost in despair.

CHAPTER

FOURTEEN

———◆———

In the latter half of the seventies, the Prince embarked on a private voyage of spiritual inquiry which guided him to the further shores of faith and belief and led him far away from the certainties of the culture into which he had been born. An intuitive aversion to the laws of scientific materialism drew him towards a study of mysticism, where he began to find explanations for the self and the human soul which were, for his uncertain spirit, a revelation and a reassurance from which he was to derive lasting inspiration. Confirming his own instincts and intuitions, a world of 'inner reality' took shape for him which gave coherence to his feelings and attitudes. His pursuit of self-discovery through the alternative dogmas of other religions put his own commitment to the Church of England severely to the test. Though he would never sever the bonds, he stretched them to the limit, concluding only latterly that 'one should not move too far from one's culture'. This venture was a stepping stone along a route which led him eventually to declare in public, and with full knowledge of the implications, that, as sovereign, he would hope to be 'Defender of Faith' rather than 'Defender of *the* Faith'.[1]

Living under the shadow of his mother's consecration at her coronation as 'the defender of Christ's religion', the Prince's faith had at first seemed to be as conventional as the apostles of the Established Church would expect from the heir apparent. At Gordonstoun he had sought comfort in what he had then described as the 'mystery' of the Church. In preparation for confirmation he was diligent and receptive, far more so than many would-be communicants of his age. According to the school chaplain, the Revd Philip Crosfield, he showed no inclination to challenge the certainties of the Apostolic Creed. Crosfield detected that as a young teenager the Prince was 'very lost and very lonely'. He also noticed how readily he responded in class to lessons about nature and 'the universal world'.[2] Other than in his unfashionable regard for the natural world, he was by no means an iconoclast.

It was at Cambridge, where the Dean of Chapel, Harry Williams, had noticed his 'spiritual potential', that the Prince was first drawn to test the orthodox perimeters of the Anglican Faith. In a flurry of correspondence with Mervyn Stockwood, the Bishop of Southwark, whom he had first encountered at Gordonstoun, he began a tentative inquiry into the field of what its practitioners referred to as 'psychical research' or 'parapsychology' – and which its adversaries ridiculed as 'dabbling in the occult'. Stockwood was one of several prominent Christians who had refused to dismiss the validity of 'psychic happenings'. Intrigued by the quasi-academic research into these apparently inexplicable phenomena, Stockwood had accumulated a sample of the relevant literature and a number of case histories. These included that of a Mrs Brown who had been the subject of a BBC documentary because of her remarkable ability to 'compose' works by Beethoven, Brahms, Debussy and others, without – apparently – the benefit of musical training. In response to the Prince's inquiry, he sent these to the Palace.

As a student of parapsychology, the Bishop had come to believe that 'psychical' powers were a development of 'immense and unsuspected' capabilities of the mind, as demonstrated in primitive form by the skill of the hypnotist. Thus the miracles of Jesus were not – as conventionally interpreted – supernatural phenomena but natural episodes, a demonstration of the Saviour's oneness with all Nature. In support of this, he cited St Paul: 'The whole creation is on tiptoe to see the wonderful sight of the sons of God coming into their own . . . And the hope is that in the end the whole of created life will be rescued from the tyranny of change and decay, and have its share in that magnificent liberty which can only belong to the children of God.'(Romans 8: 18–21.)

The world of the parapsychologist has its roots in natural magic, in astrology and alchemy, in the occult beliefs which predate the rituals of western religion and which had a great flowering in the Renaissance, but were swept away by the apparent certainties of material science which followed the Hellenic revival. The parapsychologist is also intrigued by mysticism – by a 'supernatural' magic through which religious scholars believed it was possible to divine the will of God, to make prophecies and even to summon angels. It was from this source that the spiritualists of the nineteenth century derived their 'authority' to facilitate the apparent communication between earthly mortals and those who had 'gone over' into the afterlife.

The Prince was ill disposed towards the determinist implications of scientific naturalism, the all-embracing 'laws' of nature revealed and given philosophical weight by the scholars of the Enlightenment. Feeling himself to be part of the natural world and in awe of its mysteries, he was, self-confessedly, a romantic. If he was sometimes afflicted by nostalgia for the pre-industrial age, he was, more significantly, conscious that modern science had effectively disposed of metaphysics – and more especially of the human soul and the immanence of a divinity, both beyond and within the human psyche, in which, tentatively, he had come to believe.

Although the Prince did not pursue his preliminary inquiries in any detail, he did not surrender a predisposition in favour of parapsychology, a propensity to believe in the supernatural world of the spirits. A few years later, when he read that a number of British universities had been reluctant to accept a bequest from Arthur Koestler to establish a Chair of Parapsychology, he wrote to the Vice-Chancellor of the University of Wales in his role as Chancellor, urging him to consider the bequest: 'I am strongly of the opinion that such a chair would be of the greatest importance in advancing man's knowledge of a field that is given scant attention and yet is of immense significance in terms of the "invisible" aspects of our existence in this universe.' Pointing out that unless the offer was accepted within a year of Koestler's death it would go elsewhere, he continued, 'I believe it would be an absolute tragedy to allow an opportunity of this kind to go by default and I would like to think that the University of Wales was open-minded and far-sighted enough to take up such an offer where other, more "old-fashioned" universities fear to tread.'[3]*

*

---

* As a result of the Prince's intervention, the University of Wales pursued the issue but the Chair was eventually established at the University of Edinburgh, where it is held by Dr John Beloff, whose *Parapsychology, A Concise History* (Athlone, 1993) has been the main source for the author's summary above.

In the mid-seventies, the Prince also fell under the spell of Laurens van der Post, the South African-born writer, explorer and mystic. The two of them had first come into contact when Prince Charles was in his early twenties, although van der Post had known Queen Elizabeth the Queen Mother through a connection to her mother's family, the Bowes-Lyons. Early on, van der Post had formed the view that, for the Prince, there was 'a missing dimension' in the extrovert and outward-bound atmosphere created around him by the Duke of Edinburgh. The impression was confirmed by the Prince's immediate look of recognition when van der Post once remarked, only half seriously, 'I think one should be outward-bound the inward way.'[4] By 1975, they had formed a close rapport, as a result of which van der Post felt free to counsel him about spiritual matters, urging him to explore the 'old world of the spirit' and 'the inward way' towards truth and understanding. The Prince had already been captivated by the legends which van der Post had woven around the ancient myths of the bushmen of the Kalahari Desert (celebrated in his book *The Lost World of the Kalahari*, and television series of the same name). Derided as a charlatan by incredulous rationalists, van der Post was a mesmeric storyteller, conjuring images and ideas in a language so rich and vivid that only the most sceptical of his listeners failed to succumb. So far from being a sceptic, the Prince was entranced by the magic in van der Post's cosmology.

In *The Lost World of the Kalahari*, van der Post described the immersion of the bushman in the natural world, which was never merely one of hunter and hunted. 'On the contrary,' he wrote, 'he knew the animal and vegetable life, the rocks and stones of Africa as they have never been known since . . . He and they all participated so deeply of one another's being that the experience could almost be called mystical.'[5] Others might scoff but that was how the Prince had already experienced Balmoral: van der Post was expressing his own sensations. When van der Post, in another book, *The Heart of the Hunter*, wrote, 'We suffer from a hubris of the mind. We have abolished superstition of the heart only to install a superstition of the intellect in its place,'[6] the Prince felt what van der Post meant. When the writer continued, 'We behave as if there were some magic in mere thought, and we use thinking for purposes for which it was never designed. As a result we are no longer sufficiently aware of what we cannot know intellectually, what we must know in other ways, of the living experience before and beyond our transitory knowledge,'[7] the Prince did not pause to question the coherence of the author's cascade, but embraced the mystical meaning where others saw only a vapour trail.

Late in 1975, van der Post conceived the notion of retracing his steps into the interior of the Kalahari desert with the Prince as his companion and a camera at their side to record the adventure for the benefit of BBC television and its viewers. Believing himself to be the last man alive capable of passing on the 'meaning' of that vast wildness, he proposed to undertake a journey lasting seven weeks early in 1977. When the Prince responded positively, he followed up with a long letter to his prospective companion in which he wrote rhapsodically about the role of the Prince in transforming the monarchy into 'a dynamic and as yet unimagined role to suit the future shape of a fundamentally reappraised and renewed modern society', a reappraisal that would be 'so widespread and go so deep that it will involve a prolonged fight for all that is good and creative in the human imagination'. An aspect of this battle, he went on, would be 'to restore the human being to a lost natural aspect of his own spirit; to restore his reverence for life and his love of nature, and to draw closer to the original blueprint and plan of life . . .'[8] Hence the need for the Prince to witness the Kalahari for himself – and to transmit his experience via the medium of television to his future subjects. Someone of a more cynical cast of mind than the Prince might have concluded from the grandiloquent generalities and the high-flown prose that van der Post was a flatterer and a self-publicist. The Prince had no such suspicions, recognising that in his esoteric fashion van der Post was entirely sincere. When the Prince read van der Post's description of the game parks which had been established in the days of the British Empire as 'temples and cathedrals where the wayward spirit of modern man comes into contact again with the original inspiration and model of creation and that the trees, animals and insects are the priests and schoolmasters of this world', his heart sang. When he read how 'by merely taking the most sophisticated people into the bush and wilds of Africa, we have produced the most startling re-educative and therapeutic effects upon their divided personalities',[9] his intuition at once responded 'Amen'.

The Prince was enthused by van der Post's scheme; the Foreign Office, after a year's deliberation, took a contrary view. Against the background of the negotiations over Rhodesia then taking place in Geneva, in the light of the threat to Prince Charles personally as a result of guerilla action, and of the potential for political embarrassment, the

Foreign Secretary, Anthony Crosland* reached the conclusion that his 'firm advice' to the Prince was 'against going to Botswana next year'.[10] As if to sidestep van der Post's repeated protestations that the Kalahari was 600 miles from the warfront, the Foreign Office also confirmed that the main ground for the Foreign Secretary's decision was less the security of the heir to the throne than the political implications of the proposed visit: even if Botswana were not sucked into the worsening conflict in Rhodesia, the death toll there would rise sharply. For the Prince of Wales 'to take what amounts to a holiday in Southern Africa' at a time when events in the region were 'reaching a climax' would be to open up the British government to the accusation of 'taking the aspirations and suffering of the African people too lightly', while exposing the royal family to criticism in the process.[11]

At this juncture even van der Post acknowledged that the expedition would have to be abandoned at least for the time being. Instead, a trip to Kenya was hurriedly arranged, and after a number of last-minute changes of destination brought about by yet more anxieties about security, the Prince and van der Post were delivered to the relative isolation of the Aberdare Mountains, where they spent five days of long walks and intense conversation. During the day they explored the natural world around them; in the evening they explored the 'inner world', in the belief, as van der Post explained, that the 'outer depends on the inner' and that the Prince, as future King, should be equally sensitive to the welfare and integrity of both.

Van der Post was an insistent advocate, rapturous in admiration and devotion to the Prince, repeatedly assuring him of the great work that lay before him as an inspirational symbol of what a benighted nation might still become. Behind the occasional dollop of unction and hyperbole was a tenderness for the Prince that was reciprocated in full measure. It was in the Aberdare Mountains, at the instigation of van der Post, that the Prince began systematically to record his dreams for the older man to interpret. Van der Post had been a friend and disciple of Carl Jung, and his influence permeated the vision which van der Post explored with the

---

* Anthony Crosland (1918–77), Secretary of State for Education and Science 1965–67; president of Board of Trade 1967–69; Secretary of State for Local Government 1969–70; for the Environment 1974–76; for Foreign and Commonwealth Affairs 1976–77.

Prince. Jung was fascinated by the occult, by the mysteries of religion, and by the search for value and meaning beyond the range of what was explicable in natural science. In the words of one of his most illuminating interpreters, Anthony Storr, he was concerned principally with the 'processes of growth and development of personality seen as taking place within the charmed circle of the individual psyche'.[12]

Through van der Post and then the writings of Jung himself, the Prince explored the belief that dreams bring to the surface 'the archaic knowledge' that a child carries into the world with him, and which is inherited from his ancestors. He discovered the idea of the 'collective unconscious', that pool of ideas and images which humanity inherits from other minds remote in time and culture.[13] Contemplating the notion of the 'Wise Old Man', an archetypal figure representing that 'superior insight' which Jung discovered within himself, the Prince was encouraged by van der Post to believe that this 'guru' was, in his case, represented by the Old Man of Lochnagar – the mythical figure created by the Prince who inhabited the mountains at Balmoral and who was the subject of the children's book which he had written for his younger brothers when he was twenty. Defining himself, in Jungian terms, as an 'introvert', the Prince was susceptible to the psychoanalyst's influential theory that the supreme purpose of life was the integration of the self, a journey towards self-discovery away from 'the senselessness and aimlessness' that, in Jung's clinical experience, afflicted so many creative individuals. In Jungian theory, this integration could only be achieved by realising what Storr has described as 'a consciousness detached from the world', an objective to which the Prince was at first intermittently attracted and then, much later, drawn with a compulsion so strong that neither public scepticism nor mockery could divert him.

In the late seventies, van der Post became infatuated by the idea that the Prince should withdraw from the world for a period, cancelling his public engagements, to contemplate the inner life of the soul. Despite the lure of the proposition, the Prince did not hesitate to resist van der Post's blandishments, his sense of duty overriding his impulse. Nevertheless, his search for 'an inner world of truth' did not abate. For van der Post, the greatness of Jung lay in his concern, as he wrote to the Prince, to 'restore western man to his soul and recover his religious meaning'.[14] Encouraged by his mentor, the Prince found himself increasingly at odds with those churchmen and theologians who seemed to him to have hijacked religious experience and imprisoned it in a doctrinal straitjacket for clerical disputation.

Searching beyond the confines of Christianity, the Prince began to explore the ancient religions of the East, which, he sensed, retained the mystical elements of faith for which he hungered. He read about Buddhism and Hinduism and became familiar with the doctrine of reincarnation, the process by which the soul passes through a sequence of bodies from the most primitive life form until the human stage of existence, after which its human transmigration is determined by the moral and spiritual life which each individual chooses to lead. It came to exercise a powerful influence over him, so powerful that he was not prepared to relinquish it, encouraged in his susceptibility by the knowledge that there are eminent if unconventional theologians who see no incompatibility between reincarnation and Christianity.

In this spiritual quest, he was introduced, in 1979, to a book called *The Path of the Masters*,[15] a comprehensive guide to the spiritual wisdom of the Eastern gurus: 'saints' who are held to be incarnations of the Supreme Being, expressions of God on Earth – all love, all wisdom and all power, who manifest the Truth in their lives and through whom, by diligence, it is possible for the disciple to reach the highest goal of life, 'the supreme union' with God.

The book had been given to him by a young Indian woman who telephoned Buckingham Palace relentlessly until he finally accepted her call. She told him that her mission as a Buddhist was to convert him to an understanding of the role of the Masters. Instead of extricating himself, the Prince was so intrigued that he arranged a meeting. At once, the two began a relationship that on both an emotional and a spiritual level swiftly became so intense as to send a *frisson* of alarm through the household. Evidently fearing that her hold over the Prince had become so powerful as to jeopardise his sense of perspective, his new private secretary, Edward Adeane,* confided to more than one of his close friends that, 'it's got to be stopped'.[16] Soon afterwards, the relationship did indeed cease, but not before the Prince had been persuaded by her

---

* Edward Adeane (1939–   ); private secretary to Prince of Wales 1979–85. He was the son of Sir Michael Adeane, formerly the Queen's private secretary.

arguments in favour of vegetarianism and against the killing of animals to change his own habits accordingly.

The Prince was not only bedazzled by the messenger but by the message, by the insights that he gleaned from *The Path of the Masters*. He was particularly taken by the assertion that religious experience should be seen as an individual sensation, free of creed and dogma but compatible with all faiths. In a surge of excitement, he told his closest friends about the dramatic effect which these revelations had had on him. Mountbatten responded warmly, telling him that 'the great thing is to have some inspiration to cling to'.[17] Others were more sceptical, fearing that by turning in on himself he was in danger of turning away from the world and from his duty. In the first draft of a considered response, another, a devout Anglican, admonished, 'You particularly have the enormous privilege of being loved and respected and admired by thousands maybe millions of people – the very last thing you could possibly contemplate under any religious theory is to neglect these people, to let them down or to shatter their hopes . . .'[18] The letter was never sent but the writer made the same points face to face in an animated and sustained debate with the Prince. As they both recognised, there was more at stake than the private faith of a public man.

It would be some years before the Prince felt able to air his views in public, but, early in 1981, in accepting an honorary fellowship from William and Mary College, Williamsburg, he spoke of the relationship between the individual and the environment in economic, social and spiritual terms. It was a large and unconventional canvas. Though he made no direct reference to his exploration of the human spirit, his words were infused with the values which had started to coalesce within him and which were to become the hallmark of his public pronouncements.

'It is perhaps not surprising,' he would declare, 'that Great Britain, which produced the industrial revolution, should have been the first to question the consequences of industrialisation and to begin to feel that the price it demands of the human being and the sacrifice of the quality of his own personal life must be too high for the material benefits it has conferred.' Referring with approval to the concept of a 'nation of individuals' (which, from an opposite point of departure, was already the emerging theme of what was yet be to be known as Thatcherism), he argued that its validity centred 'on the basic assumption that both the individual and the nation served a meaning greater and more abiding than a purely personal and national one . . . Human beings seem to be able to endure anything – except a loss of meaning.' Contrasting the material wealth of the West with the poverty of India (where he had made an official visit five months earlier), he spoke of the 'individual security' which the Indians derived from their culture and religion but which seemed to have been lost in the West, where the human being was but a statistic in a vast and impersonal collective enterprise. 'We need, I think,' he said, 'to rediscover the importance of the small and vulnerable as opposed to the materially vast and physically great. We have to learn that the modern way of growing great is through growing small again so that men can operate in small units where everyone is recognisable as an individual.'

A few weeks later, he would permit another hint of his innermost feelings to surface into the public domain in a speech to celebrate the centenary of the Salvation Army. Criticising the doctrinal disputes which divided Christendom, he urged that 'what we should be worried about now is whether people are going to become atheists; whether they are going to be given an idea of what is right or wrong; whether they are going to be given an awareness of the things of the Spirit and of the meaning and infinite beauty of Nature. These are the things that mat- ter . . .' If the threads did not entirely connect, the attitude was clear enough.

The Prince's early essays into an alternative approach to the prevailing values of his own culture received scant attention, but his spiritual yearn- ing was to be the wellspring of the secular role which he was on the brink of establishing, and which would provide the essential coherence that his public life had lacked. The statements that he was soon to deliver in public on a range of apparently unrelated issues derived their convic- tion and unity from an inner alliance of his own intuition with a faith in the immanence of a non-denominational human spirit. Driven by this resolve, he would seize on topics that seemed peripheral as if they were fundamental, and debate issues that seemed fundamental in ways that were apparently peripheral. Within the range of his talent and the con- fines of his constitutional position, he was in the throes of discovering that he enjoyed a unique privilege: the right to explore great matters in unfashionable ways and yet to be heard. He lacked a plan of campaign, but what he was soon to say about alternative medicine, architecture and the environment sprang from a spiritual feeling for the mystical in mankind; and his themes were given focus by a growing anxiety about the disintegration of communal identity in Britain – a condition he was prone to attribute to the fruits of scientific materialism. At this pivotal stage in his life, as he struggled to reconcile the turbulence of his private emotions with the exigencies of his public role, the potential of this unifying idea was barely visible even to those who loved him most.

To the outside world, the Prince was still regarded as Buckingham Palace's 'Action Man' in residence. When he was not at the controls of a plane he was on the back of a horse, either in the hunting field or on the polo ground; when he was not stalking at Balmoral he was shooting at Sandringham; when he was not skiing he was behind the wheel of an Aston Martin in London speeding from dinner party to nightclub accompanied by one or another of the glamorous young women for whom he was 'the world's most eligible' bachelor: as a debonair Prince about town he was widely portrayed as the luckiest man on earth.

There was some truth in the image. He relished the hunt and was bold across country. With Sir John Miller, the Queen's equerry, at his side, he criss-crossed southern England in search of the best packs in the land. The initiative had originally come from the Prince, writing to the Duke of Beaufort asking if he could join his famous West Country hounds for a day. The Queen was consulted, and although her private secretary, Michael Adeane, had once warned Miller that the royal family should adopt a low profile to avoid 'the antis' running amok on the Sandringham estate, she declared that Prince Charles was old enough to make up his own mind on the issue. Mindful of the growing popular antipathy towards 'blood sports', Michael Adeane's successors wished to cool his ardour for foxhunting, but they evidently failed to summon the courage to confront him directly. In any case the Prince was unrepentant. For him, hunting was an 'exciting', 'challenging' and 'dangerous' sport, an 'extraordinary thrill'. Irritated by urban critics who failed to appreciate either the 'romance' of the hunt or that country people could both 'love wild life and kill foxes', he resented the moral posturing of sentimental agitators who, he was inclined to think, loved neither very much but hated the hunters a good deal. Recognising, however, that it was impolitic to ignore entirely the groundswell of opposition, he would later insist that the great virtue of fox-hunting for him was that it gave him a chance to meet people 'from all walks of life' in the privacy of their own homes, listening to their concerns well away from the intrusion of the media or the formality of an official visit.[19] While it is true, as Miller would testify, that after a day following hounds the local people often gathered in a nearby farmhouse to 'sit down and talk on level terms'[20] with the heir to the throne, it stretches credibility to suppose he would have forgone his pleasure if such accidental benefits had not been available.

In midsummer, he was preoccupied by an equally 'mischievous' passion: polo. His obsession with the exclusive pastime rivalled his passion for the chase. Excited accounts of triumphs and disasters, of ponies good and bad, goals scored and missed (more often missed) bubble through his correspondence with his friends and his family. Eager to emulate his father's dash, he was an intrepid player, if a rough horseman, not afraid to gallop, and reckless with his own safety. Very little was allowed to interfere with afternoons at Cowdray Park or Windsor, although his hard-pressed office managed to fit some public engagements around his sporting commitments. The officials at Buckingham Palace did not universally approve. One or two of the bolder ones had the temerity to remonstrate with him, though no more than hinting at an unspoken rebuke to the effect that, in the words of one of them, 'If you can't set aside a couple of games of polo in order to do something really rather important in Canada or Ottawa or something, then there's something wrong with your priorities, young man.'[21]

The criticism was not entirely fair. Either he played polo in the season or not at all, for unless he were available throughout the tournament period no serious team could afford to have him as a member; and (as he was quick to remind them) at any other time of the year he was almost always available – albeit reluctantly – for even the most tiresome of royal duties. The Duke of Edinburgh, the only occupant of the Palace who could still bend the Prince to his will with a single memo, approved of his son's attitude, enjoining him to win the Queen's Cup at Windsor, 'for the honour of the family'.[22]

In the winter he went skiing, an enthusiasm he acquired in 1977 when he joined Charlie and Patty Palmer-Tomkinson at their chalet in the Swiss resort of Klosters, after befriending them at a dinner given by the Duke and Duchess of Gloucester. The Prince arrived with a bevy of local policemen and officials from the British embassy, dressed in formal suits and black leather shoes. As the Prince teetered down the icy path to the chalet he slipped, almost fell over and, grasping vainly at the front door, finally slid into the chalet at high speed, laughing helplessly at the absurdity of such an arrival. Within an hour he was on the slopes with Charlie Palmer-Tomkinson and, being a resolute pupil, was soon off-piste, skiing in the powder snow in the bewitching solitude of the mountains. Far away from the photographers who had trailed him to Klosters, he fell over and over, again and again. According to the Palmer-Tomkinsons, he seemed always to be laughing. When the snow got in his hair, in his ears, behind his goggles and all over his battered body he simply got up, shook himself down, and raced off again. 'Sometimes he couldn't ski for laughing . . . he was always wrapped around one tree or another,' Patty Palmer-Tomkinson recalled. 'He used to come down the next morning bent double. It was really exquisite agony. He liked being physically absolutely spent and I used to worry that he wanted to exhaust himself so much. He wanted to take it to such an extreme . . .'[23]

After that holiday, the Prince went back to Klosters for a week every winter for the next four years. Under the guidance of Charlie Palmer-Tomkinson, who was the ablest amateur skier in Klosters, he improved so much that he was able to ski away from the crowd in the exhilarating loneliness of the highest peaks. Although not elegant, he was accomplished and fast; so fearless that he seemed to court danger, pushing himself to the edge of, even beyond, his limits. To the Palmer-Tomkinsons it sometimes seemed not merely that he was testing himself but declaring war on the fates, daring them to do their worst. They resisted the temptation to detect a hint of desperation in 'the loneliest human being' they had ever met.

In London, his devil-may-care image was tinged with expectation. The gossip columns were filled with photographs of young women whose mere presence in his company evoked in editors a spasm of speculative anticipation. As he approached thirty, which he had once unwisely intimated was an appropriate age for marriage, they detected a future Queen in almost every casual date. Among others, the faces of Davina Sheffield, Sabrina Guinness, Lady Jane Wellesley, Anna Wallace, Lady Cecily Kerr and Lady Sarah Spencer were paraded – like bartered brides-to-be – before the populace for its delectation. When he was caught out with one of them in public, he managed to affect indifference to this tabloid solicitude, smiling for the cameras like a modest Lothario, somewhat surprised by his accidental prowess. In private, he grew more and more dismayed, until sometimes he was close to the point of panic. What for others was harmless entertainment, for him was an excruciating embarrassment. In a speech to members of the Parliamentary Press Gallery in favour of a free and 'self-disciplined' press he made a wry reference to his predicament: 'I have read so many reports recently telling everyone whom I am going to marry that when last year the Duke of Wellington's daughter* was staying at Sandringham a crowd of 10,000 people turned up when we went to church,' he said. 'Such was the obvious conviction that what they had read was true that I almost felt I had better espouse myself at once so as not to disappoint so many people . . .'[24]

For all but the steeliest of his partners, the pressure could not be endured for long. To be serenaded by a member of the royal family was flattering at first, but daunting: the phone call from Buckingham Palace, the instruction to arrive at Windsor for lunch, the presentation to the Queen, the visit to Ascot or Cowdray Park or Broadlands, and the weekend party (with the knowing glances from other guests). One of those whose name was 'linked romantically' to him in the late seventies arrived at Aberdeen Airport on her way to stay at Balmoral to find herself besieged by reporters and photographers. 'Leave me alone,' she implored, trying to shield her face and thereby providing precisely the front-page picture they desired. At Balmoral the following day, she sensed the rebuke in the atmosphere: not only had she failed to avoid the publicity, she had – so the looks seemed to say – courted the attention, exploiting the liaison with the Prince to her own advantage.[25]

If the prurience of the tabloid media was unnerving – typified by a trawl through earlier relationships so that a single romance began to seem like promiscuity – the reaction from within the household was worse: instead of reassurance and comfort, frostiness and even anger prevailed. The household was unprepared for the media's unwelcome interest in the Prince's girlfriends and ill equipped to deal with it. With a first duty towards the institution, senior members of the staff, taking their cue from the family, were suspicious of those whom they would refer to quaintly as 'fortune-hunters'. Although they did their modest best to protect others who were self-evidently modest and discreet, they were less helpful to those whom they suspected of leading life in the fast

---

* Lady Jane Wellesley.

lane. To have dallied with a pop star or an actor or to have appeared in a gossip column was interpreted as evidence of a flightiness that starchier members of the household could not abide; in these circumstances it was made very clear to the 'culprit' that the royal family was not amused. On at least one occasion Prince Philip intervened directly to inform a victim of the tabloid treatment that in the interests of his son she should make herself scarce. Although the royal family did not discuss such matters, he once rebuked his twenty-six year old son by letter after he had allegedly 'paraded' one of his girlfriends too openly. 'I only wish other people who say these things would do it to one's face,' the Prince complained to Mountbatten, but added in contrition, 'I suppose one only learns from one's mistakes.'[26]

These circumstances were hardly conducive to the flowering of genuine affection. His closest friends began to worry about the rate with which young women came in and out of his life, too often – it seemed to them – picked up and discarded on a whim. Flattered by the attention of so many sparkling women, he did not refrain from following Mountbatten's advice about sowing wild oats, but he seemed to derive precious little joy from these encounters. With more 'suitable' candidates frightened away, he dallied too often with more brazen companions, affecting a cynicism about these relationships which seemed quite out of character. Those who knew him well presumed, generously but correctly, that he was not only in search of a role but of himself as well.

His most loyal friends – not the flatterers – worried less about his unconventional enthusiasms than the lack of direction and focus in his life which they seemed to expose. More than one of them, reflecting on the contrast between the intensity of his 'inner' quest and the imprecision of his outward purpose, began to fear that by following his own devices he was at risk of re-tracing the footsteps of the Duke of Windsor. Detecting in the Prince a streak of selfishness that alarmed him, Mountbatten had not hesitated, in 1978, to warn him against 'beginning on the downward slope which wrecked your Uncle David's life and led to his disgraceful abdication and his futile life ever after'.[27] It was a devastating parallel and the Prince responded with shock and incredulity. A year later, when the two of them were on holiday with the Brabournes on Eleuthera, Mountbatten was again driven to a similar rebuke, admonishing the Prince for showing 'no signs that you were pulling yourself together'.[28]

It was not that the Prince was failing in his public duties, which he dispatched with charm and aplomb, but that too often he failed to put the interests of others before his own. Even before the holiday began, for example, Mountbatten had been dismayed at the cavalier way in which the Prince had treated the invitation from the Brabournes to stay with them on Eleuthera – accepting one set of dates and then, to their great inconvenience, seeking to change them in order to fit in a couple of polo games in Palm Springs. Although the Brabournes had not mentioned it, Mountbatten had written to remonstrate, 'I would urge you to stick to your later dates and either make the Americans change their dates or be generous and helpful and give up your 2 days polo.'[29] The Prince had heeded the advice, but almost as soon as he arrived on Eleuthera he yet again incurred Mountbatten's dismay with 'a glaring example' of the behaviour which his great-uncle had warned against the previous year.

After only a couple of days in the sun, walking and water-skiing, by his own account the Prince had become 'a complete cripple', covered in blisters and sores. He was also suffering the effects of an ear infection which had made him almost deaf. To make matters even worse, his cousin Amanda had stayed behind in England to revise for her finals. In her absence, he had 'immersed' himself 'in reading, painting and writing letters'[30] but he was soon disgruntled enough to consider cutting short his holiday to fly back home. Mountbatten was appalled at the prospect of this discourtesy and said so. It was, he wrote afterwards, 'unkind and thoughtless' and so 'typical of how your Uncle David started'; indeed, the Prince's attitude had kept him awake at night 'worrying whether you would continue on your Uncle David's sad course or take a fall'.[31] The Prince had flared up in anger at the reminder of this comparison but, acknowledging his error, he changed his mind and stayed. In relief, Mountbatten wrote, 'What impressed me most was your desire to be generous, kind-hearted, and to think of others before your own interests.'[32]

Immediately after the episode, in a letter to a close friend, the Prince confided, 'my conscience got the better of me', adding with rueful candour, 'I must say I am becoming rather worried by all this talk about being self-centred and getting worse every year. I'm told that marriage is the only cure for me – and maybe it is!'[33]

Thoughts of marriage had come to preoccupy the Prince with ever greater intensity, as a matter both of the heart and of duty. After a six-week visit to Australia and Canada in the spring of 1979, he had come to the conclusion that 'the media will simply not take me seriously until I do get married and apparently become responsible. At the moment I'm convinced that they see me as "marriage" or "bird" fodder.'[34] In Canada, where he visited Pearson College as president of the International Council of the United World Colleges, he had turned on 'the wireless' at breakfast to hear the announcer say, 'You know we have a visitor here in Victoria. It's Prince Charles – the world's most eligible bachelor!' As he wrote from Eleuthera, in what would become an ever more familiar refrain, 'It's a bit depressing sometimes when I try to get on with things.'[35]

It was particularly galling because he had inherited the mantle of president of the United World Colleges from Mountbatten and had approached the responsibility with a similar enthusiasm and energy. So strong was his own vision for the future of the UWC that, on the eve of his appointment, he had even written to Mountbatten urging him to retire gracefully:

> I hate having to say this, but I believe in being absolutely honest with you but when I take over as President I may easily wish to do things in my own particular way, in a way which could conflict with your ideas so please don't be surprised if, like the other evening at Broadlands, I disagree with your approach or appear to be awkward or argumentative. I'm only taking a leaf out of your book after all![36]

In his earnestness, he found it impossible to understand why the media should be more intrigued by the women in his life than by the future of the UWC and his role in it.

It had been the same in Australia, where the speculation had been so intrusive that David Checketts, his private secretary, had been compelled to oppose his plan to spend a private weekend in the company of two former girlfriends. He argued vigorously that if the press were to discover the assignation, the serious purpose of an important official visit would be destroyed in a flurry of prurient gossip which could only damage his own reputation and that of the monarchy. At first, the Prince had insisted on his right to a private life. It was only when Checketts made the ultimate threat that he would refer the issue to Buckingham Palace for the Queen to resolve that the Prince finally yielded. The predicament was demoralising: because the media cared more about his love life than his public duty, he was apparently required to forgo the former while they persisted in ignoring the latter.

The possibility of marriage to Amanda Knatchbull, which Mountbatten had mooted in 1974, came to the fore again four years later during preparations for a visit to India by the Prince planned for early 1980. Mountbatten had engineered for himself an invitation from the Indian President to accompany the Prince on the proposed tour. At the same time, he had suggested that his granddaughter Amanda Knatchbull should accompany the two of them on the trip. Unknown to the public, the mutual affection between Amanda Knatchbull and the Prince of Wales had ripened to the point where Mountbatten, at least, had convinced himself that the outcome would be the betrothal of the two young people he loved most in the world.

Five years earlier, in 1974, following his correspondence with Mountbatten on the subject, the Prince had tentatively raised the question of marriage to Amanda with her mother (and his godmother) Patricia Brabourne. She was sympathetic, but counselled against raising the issue with her daughter, who had yet to celebrate her seventeenth birthday. The Prince, who was himself in no hurry, wrote to Mountbatten accordingly, urging his honorary grandfather not to press the issue. Stressing that too much pressure would be counter-productive, he went on to express an anxiety which troubled him more and more. 'I've been trying . . . to put myself into her shoes in an effort to imagine what it would be like to be asked what I might ask – and I must say, (even to me) it does seem an immense sacrifice and a great loss of freedom.'[37] The more he contemplated the burdens that marriage to the heir to the throne would impose, the more incredible it seemed that anyone should willingly submit themselves to such a test, although it seemed possible that his second cousin might at least be willing to face the burden of that prospect.

Amanda had grown fond of Prince Charles, warming to his energy and enthusiasm, his sense of the ridiculous, and his kindness. She admired his immense seriousness, his understanding of the natural world, the fact that he had read *Small is Beautiful*, the seminal work on the environment by Fritz Schumacher, and that he could quote from Laurens van der Post. She was also touched by his love for her family, and especially for her grandfather. As the two men strode together along the shore at Eleuthera or in the park at Broadlands, deep in conversation, arms clasped behind backs, or (in Prince Charles's case) left hand in pocket, they seemed alike and lovable. She did not mind that the old man doted more on the Prince than on her or his other grandchildren. She had noted how pleased Charles had been when her mother, treating him like her other children, called him 'darling'. It was clear to her that he not only held his own parents in awe but loved them as well, even though he seemed perplexed and wounded at their failure to demonstrate reciprocal emotion. Despite his vigour, there was about him an air of sadness and vulnerability that aroused a great tenderness in her.

Between 1974 and 1979 they saw each other with increasing frequency – in London, on Eleuthera, at Broadlands, Windsor and Balmoral – free from the tabloid gossip which usually afflicted even the semblance of a princely entanglement. As cousins, the offspring of two Houses – the Windsors and the Mountbattens – which were already united, their friendship was not a matter of conjecture or innuendo. Thus when Mountbatten suggested that Amanda should join them on the visit to India, the Prince agreed, assuming that it would raise no eyebrows and eager to please the seventy-nine-year-old Mountbatten, who had made it clear that this was to be his Indian swansong. Thus encouraged, Mountbatten put the matter directly to the Queen and Prince Philip. To his dismay, the Duke at once expressed his opposition, warning that, as the last Viceroy of India, his presence in the royal party would so overshadow the Prince of Wales as to undermine the purpose of the visit. The Queen was ambivalent, but, as Mountbatten reported back to the Prince, she was obliged to recognise that the press would be bound to highlight the presence of his granddaughter, 'even if we claimed she had come to keep her grandfather company'.[38]

Mountbatten then consulted his son-in-law John Brabourne, who was, he informed the Prince, 'typically understanding and sympathetic' but made it very clear that he shared the views of both Prince Philip and the Queen. Somewhat to Mountbatten's surprise he said he thought that the Prince and his daughter were 'moving slowly towards ultimate marriage' but stressed that this prospect would be vitiated if the press were to 'get in the way and spoil it'. Posing the rhetorical question, 'What do you think the Press will do to Amanda if she comes out in Charles's party?', her father gave his own answer: 'The Press will hound them both and Amanda, who has providentially escaped Press notice so far, will become target No. 1 and her life would be made intolerable. If as a result the prospects of eventual marriage are spoilt her inner self will become scarred and you', he said, indicating his father-in-law, 'will be to blame.'[39] Shocked by this, Mountbatten then spoke to his daughter, Patricia, who endorsed her husband's opinion, confirming that if Amanda were to join the Prince's entourage even with her grandfather, 'action would be needed either to announce an engagement immediately before Charles and she were ready for this or a denial would have to be issued in circumstances which Amanda would find very wounding'.[40]

There could have been no better illustration of the power of the media over the lives of the royal family than this inter-family council of state. As Mountbatten wrote touchingly to the Prince, 'From a purely selfish point of view I must confess that I will be very, very sad to have to forego the great happiness of being with two young people I love so much and showing them the country which means so much to me. But if the price of my selfishness were to spoil the future happiness of you both then that would be a price I would not even contemplate.'[41]

Mountbatten knew that Amanda and the Prince were not in the throes of a passionate affair but were bound to one another by ties of mutual affection for which the term 'love', that embraces so many emotions, was not inappropriate but misleading. Nonetheless, the Prince was later emboldened to raise the question of marriage directly. Amanda Knatchbull had already anticipated – only too well – the responsibilities that would be expected of her as consort to the heir apparent: the loss of independence, far greater than matrimony usually invites; the surrender of self to a system, far more absolute than the transient entry into any other institution; and the exposure to publicity, an intrusion more pervasive than attends any other public figure except at the zenith of a chosen career. Lacking that intensity of emotion which might have made such sacrifices worthwhile, the prospect was too daunting. Her refusal, which was considered and gentle but immediate, did not surprise the Prince. Amanda Knatchbull was strong-minded, independent and not without her own ambitions; her response served only to confirm his own belief that to marry into the House of Windsor was a sacrifice that no-one should be expected to make.

Throughout the seventies, as Prince Charles had striven to establish his spiritual self and his public role, Mountbatten has been his linchpin, trusted above all others. It was Mountbatten's faith in his potential which had preserved his fragile sense of identity. While so many others either stayed aloof or fawned on him, only Mountbatten provided the combination of compassion and criticism that no other friend or relation was able to offer. Troubled though he was by the conflict between his sense of duty and his low self-esteem, the Prince was resolute at least in one thing: he would avoid the perils which Mountbatten had so powerfully invoked with his warnings about the self-centredness of Uncle David and he would strive mightily never to disappoint him.

'I have no idea what we shall do without you if you finally decide to depart,' he wrote after one of their numerous discussions. 'It doesn't bear thinking about, but I only hope I shall have learnt something from you to carry it on in some way or other.'[42] In August 1979, the Prince wrote to Mountbatten from the royal yacht, reporting that Amanda (who had joined him on board) had described to him the beauty of Mountbatten's summer retreat at Classiebawn Castle in the village of Mullaghmore, on the west coast of Ireland. 'I do wish I could come and see it,' he wrote, '. . . I know I would be captivated by it.' He concluded, 'I do hope you are having a rest in Ireland and aren't working unnecessarily hard.'[43]

A few days later, a group of IRA terrorists detonated a bomb on board the Mountbattens' fishing boat, *Shadow V*, in which the family had just left the harbour at Classiebawn. Mountbatten, his fourteen-year-old grandson Nicholas and the young Irish boatman, Paul Maxwell, were killed instantly. His daughter, Patricia Brabourne, his son-in-law, John, and Timothy (Nicholas's twin brother) were severely injured. John Brabourne's mother, Doreen, Lady Brabourne, survived the night but died the next morning. The Prince of Wales was in Iceland when he heard the news. That evening, in the full flood of his grief, he wrote in his journal as follows:

> When I was told some very bad news was about to be recounted to me my heart literally 'sank' and I felt quite sick in the pit of my tummy. All sorts of hideous possibilities raced through my mind before the awful truth emerged . . . I still can't believe what has taken place and continue, vainly, to imagine that he will somehow revive and prove to everyone that he has yet again survived . . A mixture of desperate emotions swept over me – agony, disbelief, a kind of wretched numbness, closely followed by fierce and violent determination to see that something was done about the IRA . . .

All these thoughts raced through my confused mind as I walked back along the river to the house in order to telephone Mummy to find out what exactly had happened and hoping that it was a nightmare . . . I had always dreaded the day when he would die, but somehow I had always thought it would be several more years – at least until he felt 'ready' and no longer felt there was anything to go on living for. Life has to go on, I suppose, but this afternoon I must confess I wanted it to stop. I felt supremely useless and powerless . . .

I have lost someone infinitely special in my life; someone who showed enormous affection, who told me unpleasant things I didn't particularly want to hear, who gave praise where it was due as well as criticism; someone to whom I knew I could confide anything and from whom I would receive the wisest of counsel and advice. In some extraordinary way he combined grand-father, great uncle, father, brother and friend and I shall always be eternally grateful that I was lucky enough to have known him for as long as I did. Life will never be the same now that he has gone and I fear it will take me a very long time to forgive those people who today achieved something that two world wars and thousands of Germans and Japanese failed to achieve. I only hope I can live up to the expectations he had of me and be able to do something to honour the name of Mountbatten.[44]

PART III

As in a children's story, all princes are in extremes. Delightful in the sunshine above the wall into which chance lifts the flower for a season, they can but plead somewhat more touchingly than others their everyday weakness in the storm.

Walter Pater, 'Shakespeare's English Kings',
Appreciations

CHAPTER
FIFTEEN

———•———

The decade of the eighties opened with the nation in the depths of economic recession and gripped by social unrest. The Conservative government led by Margaret Thatcher had been in power for a year and was engaged in a radical assault on the threadbare fabric of the political consensus by which Britain had been ruled for forty years. After a decade in which administrations led by Harold Wilson, Edward Heath and James Callaghan had failed to halt the nation's relative decline, a mood of apathy, if not despair, clung about the institutions of the state and numbed those individuals who were the principal victims of that lassitude, the poor and the unemployed.

In 1970, Edward Heath had promised to displace the ailing consensus with a radical programme of economic and social reform, which was to include a sharp reappraisal of the welfare state, an unambiguous commitment to the market economy, and a fundamental reform of industrial relations. Dubbing him 'Selsdon Man' (after the name of the Selsdon Park Hotel in Croydon, where the party leadership had endorsed this approach), Harold Wilson castigated Heath for seeking to reward the aggressive and the strong at the expense of the downtrodden and weak. As it was, the new government's blueprint – prefiguring much of Thatcherism – was soon shredded by the effects of recession, rising unemployment and subsequently, as the government sought to reflate a stagnant economy, by the ravages of inflation (which by 1973 had reached an annual rate of almost 9 per cent). All of this was compounded

271

by the oil crisis caused by the outbreak of war between Israel and the Arabs in October 1973. Against the background of this deep malaise, the Heath government's attempt to reform industrial relations, which was thought to be a precondition for a sustained recovery, led to industrial unrest of a scale and bitterness unknown since the thirties. When the government tried to curb wages by introducing a pay policy (against which 'Selsdon Man' had resolutely set his face), the trades unions rebelled and the miners went on strike, causing such a severe energy shortage that British industry was reduced to working a three-day week. In exasperation, Heath called an election in February 1974, asking the voters 'Who rules Britain? The Government or the Unions?' The electorate responded wearily by voting the Conservatives out of office.

The return of a minority Labour government (converted into a majority by a second election eight months later) did little, if anything, to restore public morale. Despite a 'social contract' with the unions and austerity budgets, the economy was still stricken by low growth and high inflation, low productivity and shrinking markets. By the time Harold Wilson handed over to James Callaghan in 1976, Britain was commonly regarded as the 'sick man of Europe', trapped in a spiral of decline, in retreat from global influence and still unable to define for itself a new destiny. It seemed apposite that in 1979 a Labour government was brought down by its own supporters, following the 'Winter of Discontent' during which public sector workers went on strike against a last-gasp pay policy, leaving ambulances unattended and even, on one occasion, a corpse unburied.

The massive swing to the Conservatives in May 1979 sprang less from hope than despair, as if the collective will was for anything other than a repetition of the last decade. As the new government initiated the measures from which 'Selsdon Man' had retreated a decade earlier, there was no sign of a mass conversion to the uncertain ideology of a cabinet which was itself sharply divided about the merits either of Margaret Thatcher's instincts or of her zeal. Disaffection was widespread, and in some parts of Britain had become endemic. Beyond the factional confines of the Conservative Party, where rivals debated the relative values of the 'individual' and 'society', the social fabric of stricken communities was beginning to disintegrate, most alarmingly in the decaying heart of the inner cities.

With unemployment edging towards three million, the percentage of those without work in the inner cities was three or four times the national average. In some streets almost every young male was out of work, the ethnic minorities, specifically blacks and Asians, being most affected. Discrimination against blacks in jobs, housing and education fuelled a deepening resentment which exploded on the streets of Bristol, London and Liverpool, and, on a smaller scale, in many other cities, during the spring and summer of 1981. The anarchic violence of these 'race riots' – a maelstrom of arson, looting and pitched battles with the police that the British television audience had previously seen only via satellite from the United States – horrified the public.

The Prince of Wales was no less alarmed but much less surprised. Four years earlier, in June 1977, he had caused some controversy by intervening in an angry dispute between a group of protesters and the police outside the Moonshot Club in the London Borough of Deptford. To find out the cause of the conflict, he had walked over to the police barricades and spoken to the demonstrators who told him that they were there to protest against police harassment of the black community in the area. Eight days later, under the auspices of the Prince's Trust, the Prince held a meeting at Buckingham Palace at which both sides to the dispute made their case. The Prince promised that his Trust would do what little it could to help.

The following year, in November, increasingly perturbed by the growing hostility between the Metropolitan Police and the black community, he instigated a meeting between the administrator of the Prince's Trust, George Pratt, and the Commissioner of the Metropolitan Police, Sir David McNee. Clearly sensitive to the Prince's anxieties, the Commissioner confirmed that a major factor in the conflict was the disparity between the policy of the Metropolitan Police and the attitude of police officers 'on the beat'. At the prompting of the Prince, the Trust resolved specifically to work closely with the police and at least one of the organised ethnic groups in each region in which it had started to establish itself. Later that year, the Prince's Trust brought together nineteen chief constables for a private seminar to work out a strategy to arrest the deterioration in community relations. The Prince, who had just returned from a visit to the North-East, wrote on his copy of the minutes from that meeting, 'Having met with minority groups in Bradford (a good record in racial terms) the other day it is clear that police relations with West Indian youths is a priority area. I believe the Prince's

Trust and Jubilee Trust should strive to tackle the racial minority problem to dampen down a potentially disastrous situation.'[1]

By 1981, the combination of economic gloom and the breakdown of
law and order had induced a growing sense that Britain was becoming a
nastier and more dangerous country in which to live. The old structures
of society seemed to have fractured, to be replaced only by individual
rapacity and selfishness.

Against that depressing backdrop of insecurity and helplessness, the news
that the Prince of Wales was to marry seemed to offer a balm and a symbol, the possibility of escape from present troubles, and a glimpse of the
values and traditions to which most of the nation still clung. Reflecting
this, the Archbishop of Canterbury, Robert Runcie, told a news conference: 'I think it could be a healing element.'[2]

The announcement itself came, after months of speculation, on 24
February 1981: the Prince, at the age of thirty-two, was to marry Lady
Diana Spencer, the nineteen-year-old daughter of Earl Spencer and
Frances Shand Kydd. The news prompted a universal surge of delight. In
freezing weather, a large crowd gathered outside Buckingham Palace
where the band of the Coldstream Guards played 'Congratulations', a
pop song which had won the Eurovision song contest. Diana Spencer's
father and stepmother, Raine Spencer, were there, each liberal with
'quotes' for the attendant reporters. According to her father, Diana
Spencer 'had come through' the media pressure 'with flying colours . . .
She is obviously a remarkable girl . . . She never breaks down because
Diana does not break down at all.'[3] Her stepmother, noting that she was
neither highly-strung nor prone to depression, affirmed that the bride-
to-be 'was terribly anxious to do the right thing, not to say too much or
do the wrong thing'.[4] At Westminster, Margaret Thatcher congratulated the couple during Prime Minister's Question Time. A debate on
marriage at the General Synod was interrupted to report the good news.
The managing editor of *Debrett's* revealed that the Prince's fiancée would
bring Stuart blood back into the royal family as she was descended five
times from Charles II ('four times on the wrong side of the blanket, and
one on the right side').[5] The Prince said that he was 'positively delighted
and frankly amazed that Diana is prepared to take me on', and his fiancée
declared, 'I am absolutely delighted; thrilled; blissfully happy.'[6]

Only the Labour MP William Hamilton, the leading and almost the only voice of republicanism at Westminster, offered dissent. Declaring that the timing of the announcement was a deliberate distraction from the latest unemployment figures, he rasped, 'The winter of discontent is now being replaced by the winter of phony romance with the active connivance of the government.'[7] Inevitably, this act of apostasy served only to confirm to Hamilton's colleagues that the betrothal of the Prince of Wales must indeed be a cause for rejoicing.

In welcoming their 'private happiness', the *Daily Telegraph* celebrated the affirmation of the monarchy which the engagement symbolised:

> For a nation more than ever starved of symbols of hope and goodness in public life, the Royal example, far from fading, becomes more important . . . The best private feelings inspire the greatest public acts. In its monarchy, the British nation has at its pinnacle an institution that commands such feelings and a family that embodies them. With so many commoners who hate, it matters more than ever that a Prince who loves should one day sit upon the throne of England.[8]

If this royal encomium placed a heavy burden of responsibility on the prospective marriage, *The Times* went even further. Playing its customary part as the high priest of secular opinion, the newspaper reflected the attitude of the rest of the media, but in more elevated language. In an editorial on the constitutional significance of the royal engagement, the leader writer sought to identify two aspects of the monarchy, the 'practical' and the 'sentimental'. 'There is,' he asserted, 'the business of state and Commonwealth to be done and there is the place the Monarchy occupies in the hearts of the people in the United Kingdom and of the contracting numbers of others in the Commonwealth for whom it is a real focus of allegiance.' Thus the betrothal of the Prince of Wales had its 'practical' aspect in reinforcing the succession 'by potentially extending the direct line' and its 'sentimental' aspect in the 'confirmation of a Royal Romance . . . It is fitting that the Prince of Wales should enter married life when one considers the extent to which the monarchy is now regarded as an exemplar of family life.'[9]

According to this interpretation, the betrothal of the heir to the throne was not only a source of public delight but a 'function' of the institution into which he had been born. With this blithe pronouncement, *The Times* finally − if unwittingly − consigned to oblivion what had once been a precise and crucial distinction between the role of the monarchy and the behaviour of the royal family. The process which had started in the reign of George V had reached the point where the 'practical and sentimental' aspects of the monarchy were apparently inseparable.

In the intoxication of the hour, no-one cautioned against the implications of the convergence wrought by *The Times*, to observe that if the proper function of the monarchy really was to exemplify family values as well as to act as a symbol of the state, a failure at the former would have as much potential to undermine the monarchy as a corruption of the latter. In constitutional terms it was as if to assert that the function of Parliament was indistinguishable from the performance of its elected members, the frailties of the latter implying the ruination of the former. As applied to the monarchy, the proposition was, or should have been, a self-evident nonsense. Instead, the prospect of a royal wedding allowed a dangerous confusion to seep even deeper into the national consciousness to become the conventional wisdom.

The Prince of Wales had approached his betrothal with trepidation. His stated amazement that Diana Spencer would consent to marry him was not just a disingenuous formality or a self-conscious response to the need to speak in public of what was intensely private. He had long been aware of the burdens which marriage to the Prince of Wales would impose. Twelve years earlier, he had told the television interviewer, Brian Connell, that, 'You have got to choose somebody very carefully I think who could fulfil this particular role . . . it has got to be somebody pretty special.'[10] Five years later, he told another interlocutor, Kenneth Harris, that in his case, 'A woman not only marries a man; she marries into a way of life into which she's got a contribution to make. She's got to have some knowledge of it, some sense of it, or she wouldn't have a clue about whether she's going to like it. And if she didn't have a clue, it would be risky for her, wouldn't it?'[11]

He told another interviewer, 'My marriage has to be for ever.'[12] His attitude sprang not only from personal faith but from his inherited sense of constitutional necessity, in the full awareness that his choice of spouse was uniquely circumscribed by convention and law. Under the 1701 Act of Settlement, he was forbidden to marry a Catholic; under the 1772 Royal Marriages Act, he needed the formal consent of the sovereign and both houses of parliament; and, as the future Supreme Governor of the

Church of England, it was inconceivable that he should contemplate marrying a divorcee or a woman with what was euphemistically referred to as 'a past'.

Reconciling himself to the emotional implications of these external constraints, he shared his peculiar predicament with the public, expressing his fear that:

> whatever I say is not going to be understood by the vast majority of people . . . A lot of people get the wrong idea of what love is all about . . . It's basically a very strong friendship. As often as not you have shared interests and ideas in common and also have a great deal of affection. And I think where you are very lucky is when you find the person attractive in the physical and the mental sense . . . To me marriage, which may be for fifty years, seems to be one of the biggest and most responsible steps to be taken in one's life . . .

In a remarkably sober appraisal, he added, 'Marriage is something you ought to work at. I may easily be proved wrong but I intend to work at it when I get married.'[13]

The Prince was mindful of how his immediate predecessors, Prince Albert Edward (later Edward VII) and his great-uncle David (later Edward VIII) had both failed to reconcile the demands of the role with the affections of the heart. Discussing his own dilemma in private, the Prince used to call in evidence the marriage of his grandfather George VI and his grandmother Queen Elizabeth, a relationship which grew into love but which derived its initial strength from sharing duties and raising children.

The Prince's attitude towards marriage was also complicated by his feelings for Camilla Parker Bowles, who had once again started to play an important part in his life. Her husband, Andrew Parker Bowles, had been a regular guest at Balmoral, Sandringham and Windsor, a friend of Prince Charles and the rest of the royal family. After his marriage to Camilla, the invitations were extended to his wife as well. Her warmth, her lack of ambition or guile, her good humour and her gentleness endeared her to the household. The Prince had come to regard her as his best friend, in whom, more than any other, he could totally confide. She was, as he would later explain, his 'touchstone' and his 'sounding board'.[14] They were not often alone together but they talked frequently and at length on the telephone, and in the process their feelings for each other grew in strength and intensity to the point where their deep friend-ship could properly be described as 'love'. Whatever the precise character of this intimacy, some of those closest to them began to suppose that they were having a clandestine affair, which they feared would become known and cause a public scandal. Their private consternation was shared by one or two members of his own family, to the point where he was warned that an illicit liaison would be damaging to his own standing and to the institution of which he was so crucial a member. However, his friendship with Camilla Parker Bowles had become a vital source of comfort to him and the Prince was not willing or – at this time – able to loosen, let alone sever, so precious a bond merely because of the anxiety of those about him.

In an earlier age, the Prince would have been able to contemplate marriage with rather more insouciance than he was now able to muster. Members of royal families across Europe had long been accustomed to enter a 'marriage of convenience' or an 'arranged' marriage in which each partner would appreciate above all their dynastic responsibilities. So long as they both acted with discretion, the outside world would have respected the privacy of any arrangements they might have made to compensate for any absence of 'true' love. By the last quarter of the twentieth century, however, what had been convention had come to be regarded as hypocrisy. Moreover, the collusion between the guardians of the constitution and the purveyors of news and comment had collapsed. Though the fetters on the monarchy were still in place, a significant pro-portion of the media had long since yielded to prurience in the name of the 'public interest'. Ground between these millstones, the Prince had not for a moment been under any illusion that he could both build a happy marriage and at the same time exercise a royal droit du seigneur somehow adapted for the twentieth century – nor, as a child of his times, had he any wish so to do.

The evidence is overwhelming that it was his natural disposition to create within marriage precisely that exemplar of family life which the media had ordained to be his constitutional duty. As a child, he had doted on his sister. His letters from Gordonstoun had been peppered with fond references to her and then to his baby brothers, Andrew and Edward. In the holidays he used to spend hours playing with them in the nursery. At the age of twenty he had written *The Old Man of Lochnagar* for their bedside reading. Despite the awkward relationship with his parents, he anticipated family gatherings with artless excitement. When friends and relations gave birth he wrote in delight to congratulate them. For example, to one: 'I do hope your baby is very well. Does she have all sorts of things now? It's so wonderful having babies in the house again isn't it?!'[15] And to another, while he was confined to his bunk on board HMS *Minerva*: 'For some time I entirely forgot that I was meant to be feeling sick and had a headache, and leapt about in my bunk with joy and squeaks feeling incredibly happy for you both . . . By the time you receive this I expect you will be out of hospital and beginning to wonder how on earth you're going to cope with a small screaming thing that requires feeding every four hours!'[16]

In public, he had spoken about the marital home as 'a secure family unit in which to bring up children, to give them a happy, secure upbringing – that is what marriage is all about. Essentially one must be good friends, and love I'm sure will grow out of friendship and become deeper and deeper.'[17] It was this very urge for a happy family life that made him so hesitant about embarking on the enterprise. Yet by the turn of the decade, the need to reconcile that search with his duty to perpetuate the House of Windsor had become – at least in his own mind – an overriding imperative.

Prince Charles first met Diana Spencer at her family home, Althorp Park, in 1977, where he had been invited by Sarah, her eldest sister who was then his current girlfriend. His first impression of the younger sister was that she was, as his friends put it, 'jolly' and 'bouncy', an unaffected teenager who was relaxed, irreverent and friendly. Two years later, after a few more equally casual encounters and without any apparent surge in feeling, he began to think seriously of her as a potential bride.

He was later to recall being greatly touched by a conversation that Diana Spencer had with him in July 1980, when they were sitting together on a hay bale at a barbecue in the grounds of a country house near Petworth in Sussex. He mentioned the murder of Mountbatten, prompting her to say how sad he had appeared at the funeral in Westminster Abbey, and how she had sensed his loneliness and his need for someone to care for him. A few weeks later, he surprised one of his closest confidantes during Cowes week by intimating to her that he had met the girl he intended to marry. She responded drily that if that were the case, he should keep the matter to himself.[18] Not heeding the advice, he spoke of Diana Spencer's easy and open manner, of her warmth, of her enthusiasm for rural life, and of her background through which she knew a little of his family and certainly enough, he presumed, to have few fears of marrying into it.

The impression was widely shared. The Queen's assistant private secretary, Robert Fellowes,* and his wife Lady Jane, Diana's elder sister, occasionally joined the royal family for the weekend at one of the cottages on the Balmoral estate. A friend of the Prince remembers Diana Spencer at Balmoral when the Queen was away. There was a picnic for which the kitchens had prepared a royal hamper, prompting the teenager to exclaim with delight at the exquisitely prepared meal, which came complete with table napkins, silver cutlery and a menu card. Without affectation, she had joked, 'Oh! this is the life for me. Where is the footman?' She wore jeans all the time and gave the impression to the Prince's family and friends that she was one of nature's 'tomboys'.

In the autumn of 1980, the Prince invited Diana Spencer to join a house party at Balmoral. Again she reinforced the initial impression that she had made on his friends. She was so obviously happy and he seemed so attracted to her that his friends warmed to a prospective love match. Patty Palmer-Tomkinson, who was staying there with her husband Charlie, was particularly taken by her:

> We went stalking together, we got hot, we got tired, she fell into a bog, she got covered in mud, laughed her head off, got puce in the face, hair glued to her forehead because it was pouring with rain . . . she was a sort of wonderful English schoolgirl who was game for anything, naturally young but sweet and clearly determined and enthusiastic about him, very much wanted him.[19]

There were the usual picnics, and the Prince taught her to fish on the River Dee. In the evening at dinner, the Prince's brothers competed with him to sit at Diana Spencer's side and he appeared to be flattered that she was so popular. In private, he confided to one of his friends that though he did not yet love her, she was lovable and warm-hearted, and he

---

* Sir Robert Fellowes (1941–   ), assistant private secretary to the Queen 1977–86; deputy private secretary 1986–90; private secretary since 1990. He married Lady Jane Spencer in 1978.

was sure he could fall in love with her. She also had some of the cardinal virtues that Mountbatten had been so insistent upon. Unlike some of the Prince's previous girlfriends, she had no 'past', no lovers to 'kiss and tell' or for the tabloid press to expose. Nor had she been in love before; the Prince could expect, therefore, if Mountbatten's primitive psychology was correct, that as her first love, he would also be her last. She was also young enough to be moulded to the role of wife and mother according to the special needs of the institution. The Prince did not apply these calculations in the clinical way that Mountbatten had identified them, but clung to them as beacons of apparent clarity in the state of emotional confusion to which the pressure to reach a decision had reduced him.

By the autumn, when it was common knowledge that Diana Spencer had been a guest at Balmoral and Sandringham, the pressures on the Prince began to seem like a tidal wave sweeping him towards an inevitable destiny. The tabloid media was more insistent than in any previous 'sighting'. Knowing that her social background was suitable, admiring her youth and beauty, and unable to discover any scandal in her closet, the press had concluded that in 'Lady Di', the Prince had at last found the ideal consort to adorn his life and to bear his children. Reporters and photographers camped out on the steps of the flat at Coleherne Court in Chelsea which she shared with three friends, staked out the kindergarten where she worked, and trailed her car whenever she left home to go to the shops or the cinema. Whenever they could close in on her, she was bludgeoned with questions to which she responded with a disarming but coquettish smile that said very little but quite enough, at least for the tabloid speculators.

In November, a report in the *Sunday Mirror* to the effect that Diana Spencer had secretly joined the Prince on the royal train at a siding in Wiltshire goaded Michael Shea, the Queen's press secretary, to take the rare step of demanding a retraction, insisting that the story was 'a total fabrication'. Early in December, her mother, Frances Shand Kydd, wrote to *The Times* appealing to the editors of Fleet Street to stop harassing her daughter. 'Is it fair,' she complained, 'to ask any human being regardless of circumstances, to be treated this way?'[20] Her plea inspired sixty Members of Parliament to draft a motion deploring the intrusion into Diana Spencer's private life, but their intervention had no discernible effect on the media. It was evident to the Prince that this melodrama could not be allowed to continue indefinitely.

More persuasive than the media were his official advisers, his family and his friends, who almost without exception offered their eager approval. When he pressed them for advice, they could find no grounds for dissent. Characteristically (in relation to such intimate matters) the Queen refrained from tendering her opinion but Queen Elizabeth the Queen Mother, who was a significant influence, counselled strongly in favour of marriage, as did her lady-in-waiting, Ruth Fermoy, who was Diana Spencer's grandmother.* If any of his close friends had residual doubts, only two of them tried actively to dissuade him from the course along which he was being propelled: Penny Romsey and Nicholas Soames.

Penny Romsey, the wife of Mountbatten's grandson, Norton, swiftly realised that the Prince had very little in common with Diana Spencer, except apparently a shared enthusiasm for the outdoors. Sensing the absence of intensity in his feelings for Diana Spencer, she was also alarmed at her attitude towards him. To Penny Romsey it seemed that the nineteen-year-old had fallen in love with an idea rather than an individual. In one conversation with her, Diana Spencer had used the phrase 'If I am lucky enough to be the Princess of Wales', rather as if she were auditioning for a central role in a costume drama, not lacking in sincerity but quite unaware of the enormity of the real undertaking that she seemed to contemplate so light-heartedly. It also seemed to her that while Diana Spencer echoed the animosity towards the intrusion of the cameras that the Prince felt so fiercely, she nonetheless managed invariably to pose for them to her best advantage. Frustrated that no-one else seemed to notice what was to her transparent, Penny Romsey raised her doubts with the Prince some weeks before the engagement. Her husband went further and with less tact. Riding through the park at Broadlands (which he had inherited from his grandfather), Norton Romsey argued his wife's case strenuously, but succeeded merely in provoking the Prince to an outburst of indignation.

During this period, an intervention from the Duke of Edinburgh had a powerful if not a decisive impact. In what he presumably hoped would

---

* A little before her death in 1993, Ruth Fermoy told the author that she had been against the marriage but had thought it wrong to share her doubts. Not then knowing the Prince very well, she concluded, 'If I'd said to him, "You're making a very great mistake," he probably wouldn't have paid the slightest attention because he was being driven.' (Conversation with Ruth Fermoy.)

be interpreted as a piece of sound fatherly advice, the Duke counselled his son that he could not delay a decision for much longer; that to do so would cause lasting damage to Diana Spencer's reputation, which was in any case in danger of being compromised by her presence with him at Balmoral. The Prince was left in no doubt that his father believed that he had only two honourable options: either to offer his hand in marriage, thereby pleasing both his family and the country – which might otherwise become impatient at his procrastination; or to end the relationship immediately. Whichever choice he decided to make, he should not delay.

In the absence of any other significant discussion with his parents about the prospect of marriage to Diana Spencer, the Prince interpreted his father's attitude as an ultimatum. Detecting in the Duke's advice an insinuation that he had callously exploited an innocent girl and that, by his hesitation, he was threatening to dishonour the family, he felt ill used but impotent. Soon afterwards at a dinner party attended by the Duke's private secretary, Rupert Neville, Nicholas Soames was overheard by the other guests berating the courtier for the part played by the Duke in imposing such a terrible mismatch on his son.

In what he confessed was a 'confused and anxious state of mind', the Prince tried to reconcile himself to the inevitable, confiding to another of his friends, 'It is just a matter of taking an unusual plunge into some rather unknown circumstances that inevitably disturbs me but I expect it will be the right thing in the end . . .' Without referring directly to his father's words but clearly mindful of the rebuke contained in them, he added, 'It all seems so ridiculous because I do very much want to do the right thing for this Country and for my family – but I'm terrified sometimes of making a promise and then perhaps living to regret it.'[21] Making every allowance for last-minute nerves, it was hardly the most auspicious frame of mind in which to offer his hand in marriage.

He proposed to Diana Spencer early in February after his return from a skiing trip to Klosters, where he had stayed as usual with the Palmer-Tomkinsons, whose support helped to steel his nerve for the future to which he was now committed. When he asked formally for her hand, the Princess is reported by her friends to have broken into a fit of giggles.[22] However, she assented. The Prince would remember his surprise and pleasure that his offer had been accepted with such alacrity.

If his betrothal to Diana Spencer was hardly the love match for which his friends had hoped, that she had perhaps wanted, and which the nation certainly assumed, he was determined that their marriage should succeed. Now that he had made what he referred to in 'franglais' as '*la grande plonge*', any unease that he still retained was kept to himself. His loyalty to his fiancée was to be absolute, a resolve which was reflected in his most intimate conversations and his correspondence with his closest friends. 'I do believe I am very lucky that someone as special as Diana seems to love me so much,' he wrote to two of them. 'I am already discovering how nice it is to have someone round to share things with . . . Other people's happiness and enthusiasm at the whole thing is also a most "encouraging" element and it makes me so proud that so many people have such admiration and affection for Diana.'[23]

The evening before the announcement of the engagement, Diana Spencer left her flat in Coleherne Court to stay at Clarence House. A few days later, she moved into Buckingham Palace, where a set of rooms had been prepared for her. From what she told her friends, it is clear that she felt bewildered and lost. To her, the Palace seemed remote and inhospitable, and whatever efforts they might have made, the courtiers seemed stuffy and unapproachable. For the first time, the enormity of the decision began to sink in. She felt trapped and frightened.

Her spirits sank further when the Prince left for an official visit to Australia and New Zealand, a long-planned and, as he referred to it, 'much-regretted'[24] expedition. After almost five weeks in the Antipodes, he flew directly from Australia to Venezuela, where he honoured a commitment to discuss the establishment of a new United World College. From Caracas he flew on to Washington and thence to Williamsburg, where in his speech to William and Mary College he referred to the marriage of his forebears, William and Mary, in 1677, entertaining his audience by telling them that when her father, the Duke of York, informed her two weeks before the wedding that she was to marry a man twelve years older, Mary had collapsed in tears. 'There is also a twelve-year gap between myself and my fiancée, but there, ladies and gentlemen,' he declared to an enraptured audience, 'the similarity comes to an abrupt halt.'[25]

At home, the wedding had become a national preoccupation. No minutiae were too trivial for the tabloids. 'Royal memories are made of . . . Charles and Di mugs, Charles and Di plates, bookmarks, beach balls, bottle openers and bags,' the *Daily Mirror* reported,[26] identifying some of the 971 items of 'commemorabilia' which had already been launched onto the market in advance of the celebration, including commemorative stamps and coins. On 13 June, *The Times* gave notice of a great concert and firework display to be held in Hyde Park on the eve of the wedding in the presence of the royal family, who would arrive 'down an avenue of torchbearers with escorts carrying torches'. Once in Hyde Park, the Prince of Wales was to light 'the first of a national network of beacons and bonfires, many on the same sites as those in the sixteenth century that gave warning of the approach of the Spanish Armada.' A 'firework palace' was to be constructed with hundreds of special effects and, before an expected audience of 500,000 people, there was to be a re-creation of the first performance of Handel's *Music for the Royal Fireworks*.[27] Even the news that the leader of the Greater London Council, Ken Livingstone, was to forgo the public holiday which had been declared for the day of the wedding by spending it at his desk failed to dampen the mood of excited anticipation which had seized the great majority of the population.

During the weeks between the engagement and the wedding, as the Prince continued a full round of public engagements, foreign tours and private consultations, his fiancée felt immured within the alien confines of a gilded prison. She was often alone, although her sister, Jane, was at hand to offer her support and advice. It has since been reported that during this period she became bulimic for the first time, starving herself so severely that her waist measurement contracted from twenty-nine to twenty-three inches, although the weight loss was not easily detectable until the final weeks before the wedding. According to her former flatmate Carolyn Bartholomew it was the transition to Buckingham Palace which caused the onset of the disorder: 'She went to live at Buckingham Palace and then the tears started. The little thing got so thin. I was worried about her. She wasn't happy, she was suddenly plunged into all this pressure and it was a nightmare for her.'[28]

The Prince was not prepared for this transformation and was perplexed by it. Although he had been supportive when her sister Sarah was suffering from anorexia, he did not pretend to any knowledge of the pathology of eating disorders. At this stage, it did not even cross his mind that his fiancée might be similarly, or more seriously, afflicted. Having known only the 'jolly' girl who had enlivened Balmoral six months earlier, he had been baffled to discover her sudden shifts in mood – 'her other side', as he referred to it.[29] In the early summer of 1981, he ascribed her changeable behaviour simply to the tremendous pressure of her new life. Experiencing for the first time the full glare of media attention, she once or twice showed signs of strain. At a charity gala at Goldsmiths Hall in London, she met Princess Grace of Monaco and spoke of her anxieties. 'Don't worry,' Princess Grace is said to have replied. 'It will get a lot worse!'[30] At a polo match in July, she was reported by the *Daily Telegraph* to have been 'flustered and tearful when spectators pressed too close', and the Prince commented that 'it was hardly surprising' that the strain of being under such intense scrutiny 'told eventually'.[31]

While the Prince was away in Australia and New Zealand, Diana Spencer's rite of passage into public life was guided by the Prince's private secretary, Edward Adeane, his assistant private secretary, Francis Cornish,* the secretary of the Prince's office, Michael Colborne, and Oliver Everett,† who had served as the Prince's assistant private secretary between 1978 and 1980 but had been recalled specifically to help Diana Spencer as her unofficial private secretary.

At first, all four of them felt a powerful sympathy for her predicament as a very young woman trying to come to terms with a role for which she had no training or preparation. She had a desk in Colborne's office and, as the wedding approached, was frequently there. As they talked, it became clear that his employer's fiancée was exceptionally interested in the Prince's previous relationships and, in particular, his friendship with Mrs Parker Bowles. Francis Cornish was put under similar pressure. To both of them she would say, in effect, 'I asked Charles if he was still in love with Camilla Parker Bowles and he didn't give me a clear answer. What am I to do?' If they evaded the question on principle, they most certainly had no answer.

The Prince had himself raised the subject of his relationship with

---

* Francis Cornish (1942–   ), assistant private secretary to Prince of Wales 1980–83; High Commissioner, Brunei 1983–86; Counsellor in Washington 1986–90; press secretary to the Foreign Secretary, Douglas Hurd 1990–93; British Trade Commissioner, Hong Kong, since 1993.

† Oliver Everett: assistant private secretary to Prince of Wales 1978–80; private secretary to Princess of Wales 1981–83; librarian, Windsor Castle, and assistant Keeper of the Queen's Archives since 1985.

Camilla Parker Bowles with his fiancée, explaining to her that she had indeed been one of his most intimate friends but that now that he was engaged to be married there was, and there would be, no other woman in his life. Without going into what he presumed to be unnecessary detail, he assumed that this would be enough to convince his fiancée that he meant what he had said. Indeed, from the moment of his engagement in February, he saw Camilla Parker Bowles on only one occasion and that was more than four months later to say farewell.

His feelings for Camilla Parker Bowles had not changed, but they had both accepted that their intimacy could no longer be maintained. Anxious not to seem dismissive, the Prince consulted one of his friends about the most graceful way to mark his gratitude for her understanding and support. Some days later, he asked Michael Colborne to arrange the purchase of a bracelet with the letters GF stamped on it. As Colborne knew very well, GF stood for Girl Friday, the Prince's nickname for Mrs Parker Bowles, whose role in his life was thus neatly commemorated.

In July, the bracelet was duly delivered to Colborne's office, where it joined a pile of cards and presents, a small sample of the scores of thousands which had begun to pour into Buckingham Palace in the weeks leading up to the wedding for Colborne to wrap. Somehow Diana Spencer discovered the bracelet and evidently concluded the worst.

Later, she confronted Prince Charles. He explained the bracelet. She was not mollified. There was a heated discussion in which the Prince insisted that, as an act of courtesy, he felt obliged to give Camilla Parker Bowles the bracelet in person. A few days later, true to that word, he gave her the present and said goodbye for what both of them intended to be the last time.

CHAPTER
SIXTEEN

O n the eve of their wedding, after the fireworks in Hyde Park, the Prince stood at a window of the Palace with one of his closest friends, one of the Queen's ladies-in-waiting. They looked down towards the Mall where already the sense of tomorrow was at hand: the flags and the barricades, the people strolling in the late night air; the huddle of family encampments on the pavement and under the trees. Around the Victoria Monument they saw policemen removing their helmets to join in the impromptu singing and dancing which continued into the early hours. According to his companion, he was in contemplative mood, not at all elated but aware that a momentous day was upon him, clear about his duty and filled with concern for his bride at the test she was to face.[1]*

It had been billed 'The Wedding of the Year' and those expectations were not disappointed. The Prince had been closely involved in the final preparations. In particular, he had gone through the guest list to ensure that his own friends and dependants (including two housemaids

---

* Twelve years later, it was reported that the Prince had spent his wedding eve in Buckingham Palace with Camilla Parker Bowles. In support of his allegation, James Whitaker of the *Daily Mirror* cited a conversation with the Prince's valet, Stephen Barry. Unhappily, by the time of publication (1993) Barry had been dead for nine years. He was therefore never able to rebut the charge against either his employer or his own integrity.

from Windsor and Buckingham Palace) were invited – at the expense, if necessary, of the traditional list of the Great and the Good compiled by the Palace. Against one preliminary list of prospective guests, which included 21 sovereigns, 20 heads of state, and 26 governors-general, he noted against the figure of 281 members of the diplomatic corps, 'ridiculous'.[2] In a later note, he asked rhetorically, '1. How is it that I have only 4 people from the societies with which I am connected? Surely there should be many more? Please check. 2. All sorts of people have got onto the list of "friends" who are not . . . Please could I have a copy of the complete list of guests to check what is going on?'[3]

There was an eccentric letter from Spike Milligan* apologising for the publicity caused by an interview he had given. In it, he described the pressure he had been under from the anti-blood sports groups with which he was associated to turn down his invitation to the wedding as a formal protest against the Prince's enthusiasm for fox-hunting. In the end, however, he had resolved this dilemma and was thus able to confirm, 'It's okay for you to go ahead with the wedding, I am coming, and this is with the total agreement of the anti-blood sports people, also my Mother is very pleased – is yours?'[4] For a time, the delicate task of seating more than 2,700 guests was further complicated by the animosities that divided the bride's family and which led several of her relatives to threaten a boycott of the wedding if Barbara Cartland, the mother of Diana's stepmother, Raine Spencer, were to attend. Edward Adeane suggested wanly that the eighty-year-old novelist might be prevailed upon to stay away. Before anyone dared to canvass that notion with her directly, the threat from the relatives mercifully evaporated.

With the help of the director of the Royal College of Music, Sir David Willcocks, the Prince chose much of the music, including 'Christ Has Made the Sure Foundations', which he found so beautiful that he was moved to warn publicly that he would probably 'spend half the time in tears'. At his invitation, Kiri Te Kanawa was to sing 'Let The Bright Seraphim' from Handel's *Samson*, while his bride chose 'I Vow to Thee My Country'. In a television interview two days before the wedding, the Prince said, 'I can't wait for the whole thing. I want everybody to come out having had a marvellous musical and emotional experience.'[5]

---

* One of the Goons, of whom the Prince was an enthusiastic fan, and with whom he was in frequent and self-consciously eccentric correspondence.

The wedding was transmitted to a congregation of three-quarters of a billion people – by loudspeakers to the million or so who lined the route from Buckingham Palace to Ludgate Hill to cheer the royal passage and by satellite to the rest of the world. The service was punctuated by cheers from the crowds and when both bride and groom fluffed the lines of the marriage vows there were sighs of sympathy. As they left St Paul's, the throngs of people cheered and waved in adulation, and shouted, 'We love you.' The bride, 'whiter, thinner, more beautiful than on her engagement day',[6] smiled shyly and captured every heart.

Echoing the international response to 'a grand but homey occasion. A family affair laid on for love', *Time* cited the distinguished writer Rebecca West, who had said, 'The Royal scene is simply a presentation of ourselves behaving well; if anybody is being honoured it is the human race', and quoted, with approval, from the address of the Archbishop of Canterbury, Robert Runcie, who had said, 'All couples on the wedding day are "royal couples".'[7]

In fact, the Archbishop went a good deal further, saying, 'This is the stuff of which fairy tales are made; the Prince and Princess on their wedding day . . .' before reminding his congregation in St Paul's Cathedral that, according to Christian precepts, the wedding day is not:

> the place of arrival but the place where the adventure begins . . . As husband and wife live out their vows, loving and cherishing one another. Sharing life's splendours and miseries, achievements and set-backs, they will be transformed in the process . . . Those who are married live happily ever after the wedding day if they persevere in the real adventure which is the royal task of creating each other and cre-ating a more loving world . . .[8]

If his theme lacked divine inspiration, it fitted the mood by being both solemn and soap operatic, fulfilling Walter Bagehot's familiar aphorism that, 'A princely marriage is the brilliant edition of a universal fact, and, as such, it rivets mankind . . . A royal family sweetens politics by the sea-sonable addition of nice and pretty events. It introduces irrelevant facts into the business of government, but they are facts which speak to "men's bosoms" and employ their thoughts.'[9] In tune with the romantic illusions of an otherwise utilitarian age, the Archbishop failed even to mention the constitutional reverberations of a royal marriage, and no-one seemed to notice or care.

Aside from Ken Livingstone, the desk-bound leader of the Greater London Council, the only public figure who had appeared to appreciate the formal aspects of the wedding was the Revd Ian Paisley, the leader of Northern Ireland's Protestant Loyalists, and his was a peculiar perspective. Outraged that a representative of the Pope in the person of Cardinal Hume, the Catholic Archbishop of Westminster, should have been invited to officiate at the ceremony, he wrote to the Lord Chamberlain to decline the sovereign's invitation to the wedding. 'The whole structure of the State Church', he wrote, had been 'undermined and repudiated' by the Cardinal, whose presence in St Paul's Cathedral therefore 'strikes not only at the heart of the Revolution Settlement but at the Protestant Reformed Church of England and at the Queen herself as its civil Head'.[10] From a different perspective, the eleven members of Clay Cross Parish Council voted unanimously to celebrate the wedding with a Republican Day. In response, 3,000 local people (a third of the town's population) dispatched a message of congratulations to the royal couple, while almost all the rest bedecked their streets so lavishly with bunting, streamers and Union Jacks that Clay Cross appeared to be the most royalist enclave in the realm.

Neither Ian Paisley nor the Clay Cross councillors inhibited the mood of universal celebration. In hard times, the wedding seemed to provide just that reminder of past glories and future possibilities which the nation needed, a day of rejoicing that suggested, in the words of an American onlooker, 'nothing less than a national renewal'.[11] Confirming this hunch, the polls revealed that the popularity of the monarchy was as high as in the years of the jubilee and of the coronation. Before leaving for their honeymoon, the couple stood on the balcony of Buckingham Palace to acknowledge the roars of approval from below. Responsive to the outpouring of popular affection, the Prince overcame his diffidence (and his sense of decorum) to kiss his bride on the lips in full televisual close-up. Thus trapped in perpetuity on celluloid, the image confirmed the impression that in this marriage the fairy tale would come true and that the handsome Prince and his beautiful bride would indeed live happily ever after.

The bridegroom was deeply touched by the popular embrace. 'I shall never, ever forget Wednesday,' he wrote to one of his friends a few days later:

What an unbelievable day it was – that went far too quickly. I couldn't somehow savour all I wanted to savour and I was <u>totally</u> overwhelmed and overcome by the way in which the <u>whole</u> country seemed to have been a favourite guest at the wedding, right down to the way everyone cheered when we said 'I will' etc., and then threw confetti at us when we drove to Waterloo. It was one of the most moving experiences I've ever known . . . a revelation to find the real heart and soul of the nation being exposed for a moment in good, old-fashioned, innocent enjoyment . . .[12]

After staying at Broadlands for two nights, the couple joined the royal yacht at Gibraltar on 1 August for the start of a Mediterranean honeymoon. The decision to embark at Gibraltar gave pleasure to the inhabitants of the colony but it caused a predictable if unavoidable diplomatic incident with Spain. The King and Queen of Spain had both accepted an invitation to the wedding without knowing the Prince and Princess of Wales intended to start their honeymoon from the disputed territory. A little over a fortnight before the wedding, the Foreign Office belatedly realised the delicacy of the situation. The Spanish people were unlikely to relish the television images of Prince Charles and his bride being escorted to the royal yacht by cheering crowds of Gibraltarians so soon after watching their own King Juan Carlos and Queen Sofia at the celebrations in London; the juxtaposition was bound to inflame nationalist sentiment which might itself rebound on the Spanish monarchy. The Foreign Office was also aware that the Lisbon Agreement, which had been signed only a year earlier, and under which the frontier separating Spain from Gibraltar was to be opened, could be jeopardised.

As soon as the Spanish authorities were alerted to the predicament facing their King and Queen, they suggested that the British royal couple might like to embark on the royal yacht from Cadiz instead of Gibraltar, a proposal which they presumably hoped would give both governments a way out of their mutual embarrassment. However, it was by now too late for the British to change the existing arrangements without seeming to boycott Gibraltar – which, from the perspective of the Foreign Secretary Lord Carrington, was unthinkable.

With no other escape route open to them, it was announced on 21 June that the King and Queen of Spain had cancelled their plans to attend the wedding. The decision was widely praised in the Spanish media, which duly interpreted the embarkation from Gibraltar as a reaffirmation of British sovereignty over the Rock, and judged that the 'arrogance' of the British over the issue had strewn the path towards a solution of the Gibraltar conflict with even more obstacles.[13] A royal honeymoon was not like others.

On their arrival in Gibraltar (according to the Flag Officer of the royal yacht in a message to the First Sea Lord) the royal honeymooners were given 'a tumultuous and almost hysterical welcome by the people of Gibraltar in a display which combined their loyalty to the Crown with their affection for the Prince and Princess of Wales'. The Flag Officer noted that the Gibraltarians did not lose this opportunity to demonstrate to the Spanish where their loyalties lay, adding, 'The flotilla that put to sea to escort *Britannia* out of harbour presented a memorable sight and the incessant sounding of sirens and hooters for once completely drowned the Royal Marine Band.'[14]

The royal yacht sailed down the coast of Italy and then nosed through the Greek islands, stopping at carefully selected anchorages along the way. There was a barbecue at a secluded beach on Ithaca; in a remote bay on Crete, there was windsurfing, and in the late afternoon the Prince did a watercolour of the Venetian fortress on the top of the cliffs above them.

A royal honeymoon could never be entirely private, and in the royal yacht, even with all the discretion of a devoted crew, it was not easy for a complement of more than 200 officers and men to replicate the atmosphere of post-nuptial intimacy that a honeymoon couple might have desired. The very efficiency of a highly trained crew militates against informality, except of a peculiarly nautical kind. In the royal yacht, even an intimate dinner by candlelight was hardly a private affair, accompanied as it was by the camaraderie of senior officers at the table and a band of Royal Marines playing a romantic medley in the background.

As a naval officer, the Prince was entirely at home, appreciative, or at least tolerant, of that peculiar naval banter which makes life at sea endurable. He played a game of deck-hockey and caused much ribaldry among the officers by trying to fly a large and elaborate kite which took off with such force that no-one could restrain it from departing in the general direction of Turkey. When he was not sailing or bathing, he sat in the sun reading from a selection of books provided for him by van der Post, including his own study of Carl Jung, *Jung and the Story of Our*

Time. Otherwise, he sat in the Duke of Edinburgh's cabin where he wrote copious letters of gratitude to those who had helped make such a success of the wedding. 'All I can say is that marriage is very jolly and it's also extremely nice being together in *Britannia*,' the Prince wrote on the second day of their cruise, adding indulgently, 'Diana dashes about chatting up all the sailors and the cooks in the galley etc. while I remain hermit-like on the verandah deck, sunk with pure joy into one of Laurens van der Post's books . . .'[15]

His bride was less at ease, although no member of the crew would have known; her charm and grace were quite perfectly modulated to the environment, and the ship's company was indulgent and enchanted. In private, however, the Prince was perplexed by her sudden shifts of mood, which he ascribed to the transient pressures of adapting to her new and exacting role as his consort. Assuming that the tension would soon subside, he dismissed them from his mind.

From the Greek islands *Britannia* made for the Suez Canal, where President Sadat cut short a visit to Austria to attend a dinner held by the Prince and Princess in his honour. After fifteen days on the royal yacht, the royal couple flew from Cairo to Lossiemouth and drove on to Balmoral where they stayed throughout September. For the Prince it was a blissful interlude at his favourite home, complete with his books, his fishing rod, and his friends. He assumed that the Princess would share his happiness but, as she confessed to his closest friends (as well as to her own), she was quite unable to surrender herself to his good humour. So far from being the focus of her husband's attention, he seemed to go out of his way to avoid the moments of intimacy with her that she craved. Instead – so it appeared to her – he seemed either to prefer his own company or to have others about him as well as her. Her insecurity about his feelings for her were fed by the canker of jealousy. According to her friends, the Princess was convinced that her husband was still deceiving her with Camilla Parker Bowles. According to his friends, with whom the Prince had agonised before ending the relationship, the Princess had already reached the point of obsession. Unable to accept his word and dismissive of his protestations, she more than once exploded into a tirade of anger from which he retreated in bewilderment and despondency. Despite her quip at a photo-call beside the River Dee that she could 'thoroughly recommend' married life, their partnership was already far from easy.

*

In the autumn, on their first official engagement together, the Prince presented his wife to the people of Wales on a triumphal tour through the principality on the royal train. The Princess looked glorious and displayed a deft touch with the crowds, who pressed against the barricades for a glimpse of her, holding out their hands and calling her name as if for a blessing. She stooped to talk gently with children, touched the blind, and embraced the elderly, dazzling the cameras with a demure but seductive smile that found its way onto every front page. Once back on the train, she yielded to the strain of such overwhelming attention, suddenly drained of energy. Between engagements, she sometimes broke down in tears, protesting to her husband that she could not face yet another crowd. To add to the stress, she had started to suffer frequent waves of nausea, the presumed cause of which was confirmed on the second day when a telephone call to London certified that she was pregnant. The Prince was solicitous and protective. As they were drawn in different directions by the crowd, he instructed her lady-in-waiting, 'Stay close to her . . . she needs your support.' Despite the best efforts of everyone around her, the malaise did not lift. 'From then on,' according to a member of her staff who was with her on the train, 'she felt ghastly.'[16]

Throughout the autumn and into the following year, the Princess seemed listless and out of sorts. When she went out in public, the crowds were adulatory but she seemed to be at a loss. She spent long hours with the Prince's friends and advisers, talking about the plight in which she found herself: the loss of freedom, the absence of a role, the boredom, the emptiness in her life, the heartlessness of her husband. They listened and did their best to offer comfort and reassurance, telling her that it was bound to seem strange at the beginning and that to be pregnant as well was bound to complicate her feelings. The Princess seemed grateful for their solicitude and wrote effusive letters to thank them for their support. One or two of these friends took it upon themselves to instruct the Princess in the ways of the court and what they saw as her duties in the unique circumstances of a royal marriage. They explained that her future role as consort to the heir to the throne would be more complicated than she might have realised, and that her husband would not be at her side as often as either of them might have wished. They also told her that his constitutional position meant that she would always be expected to walk somewhat in his shadow; that the distinction between the private person and the public role was, in the heir to the throne, less easy to define than she might have hoped but that she would surely learn to adjust. When they spoke in these terms, the Princess was, according to their accounts (which are confirmed by her correspondence with them), warm in gratitude and apparently eager to heed their advice. Her officials, however, shied away from any such encounter, preferring to assume that she would discover her proper place in her husband's life once the initial trauma of the transition from infant school helper to Princess had subsided.

According to one of her staff, who was witness to her isolation and loneliness, none of them approached the Princess's predicament with imagination: 'I don't think they had really thought about her role . . . and I'm sure she hadn't.'[17] After his marriage, the pattern of the Prince's public life had changed hardly at all; when he left Balmoral for Buckingham Palace, he returned to a full diary of official engagements which took him all over Britain. The Princess evidently felt excluded and bewildered. Although she spent time overseeing the decorations at Kensington Palace (which was to become their new home), shopping, or visiting her friends, she was unable to find other ways of fulfilment. Although her officials planned a diary for her, they were unable to tailor it to her interests because they were unable to establish where her own inclinations lay. It was suggested that she might take on some patronages, 'something in Wales, something with children', as one of them remembered,[18] but beyond that there was very little for her to do except brood.

Relations between the Princess and the senior members of the staff she now shared with her husband were not easy. Edward Adeane, his private secretary, was a member of the Palace establishment, steeped in the traditions of a courtier. According to his colleagues, Adeane found it hard enough to cope with the Prince who, by comparison with him, had an ill-disciplined mind and was prone to place an alarmingly high degree of trust in the vagaries of his own intuition. Irritated by the Prince's evident determination to ignore or circumvent his solid advice, he was protective but sometimes patronising. According to one member of the staff, Adeane had 'a conviction that Prince Charles was extraordinarily easy to lead by the nose'.[19] While the rest of the staff detected a trickle of 'close to the wind' entrepreneurs wanting to exploit the Prince for their own corporate or financial purposes, Adeane saw a constant stream of undesirables whom he tried in vain to keep at bay.[20]

Nor did Adeane appreciate the character of the Prince's commitment to the Prince's Trust. Along with others in the Palace 'old guard', he gave the impression to colleagues on the Prince's staff that the mere thought of the heir apparent spending his time at a summer camp filled with teenagers on probation appalled him. Nor was he much taken with the professionals who ran the course: 'If I hear the word "caring" again,' he was once heard to say, 'I am going to be sick.'[21]

His frustrations with the Prince were compounded by the difficulty of simultaneously establishing more than a superficial rapport with a very young woman whose lack of education and knowledge he found hard to accommodate. The Princess responded to what she and others regarded as his 'stuffy' manner with coquetry, teasing him about his cigars and ostentatiously picking up the butts which he had discarded as if to rebuke him for a bad habit. On more than one occasion early in the marriage, the Prince had to intervene to soothe his private secretary's feelings.[22]

In her confusion and uncertainty, the Princess was unpredictable and contradictory. Sometimes she shrank from the prospect of a public engagement, shying away from the thought of journalists and photographers and the awesome adulation of the public. Yet she scoured every tabloid newspaper for photographs of herself almost, so it seemed to those about her, as if hoping to discover her identity there. Her own staff were loyal though often put severely to the test by her volatile behaviour.

More disconcerting was the way the Princess had of so mesmerising individuals on her staff that they would find themselves drawn into her confidence and subjugated to the force of her personality, only to be expelled for no reason that they could fathom and to the point, it seemed to them, that so far as she was concerned they had virtually ceased to exist. The first of several victims of this arbitrary behaviour was Oliver Everett, the former assistant private secretary to the Prince who had been summoned back from his post as Head of Chancery at the British embassy in Madrid to work for the Princess as her first private secretary. A mild-mannered diplomat, trained in the ways of the Foreign Office, he was courteous to a fault yet he suddenly became a 'non-person' – not called to meetings, his memos and phone calls unanswered, his very presence in a room or corridor ignored. The Princess was never seen to be offensive to him, but nor did she explain what had caused her displeasure. The isolation lasted for months, a festering wound that his colleagues noticed but about which he maintained a loyal silence. Like others he was disposed to attribute her behaviour to the insecurity of her position, to the pressures of Palace life, and to the forgivable exercise of her new prerogative, a trial of patience to be endured with sympathy not rancour.

During bouts of unhappiness, the Princess would sit hunched on a chair, her head on her knees, quite inconsolable. When it proved impossible to cajole her from this state, those around her concluded yet again that the stress of her new life was more difficult for her to overcome than they had expected. Yet if there were already troughs of despair in the marriage, there were also periods of relative harmony. The Prince and Princess spent their first Christmas together at Windsor with the rest of the royal family. They followed the familiar rituals of a traditional Christmas, from children's stockings to the exchange of presents, from carols at Matins to turkey at luncheon. It was a large family in a great castle with many servants but they still played family games and laughed and quarrelled and teased one another. On Boxing Day, the Prince wrote a thank-you letter to a friend, reporting, 'We've had such a lovely Christmas – the two of us. It has been extraordinarily happy and cosy being able to share it together . . . Next year will, I feel sure, be even nicer with a small one to join in as well.'[23]

Early in January, however, this moment of marital calm was shattered by an episode at Sandringham which was later widely reported as the first of a series of 'messages of complete desperation'[24] from the Princess, when she apparently threw herself down a staircase from the second floor in an attempt to do herself harm. Mercifully, she was unhurt. According to those friends of the Princess who must have heard about the incident later, the Prince had behaved with what they regarded as indifference towards his wife. Others, who witnessed more than one such drama, interpreted them with sympathy for both the Prince and the Princess. They knew that the Princess was deeply unhappy, but they also knew that the Prince had become accustomed to spending much time at her side, haplessly trying to soothe her back to cheerfulness. When she entered these black phases, however, he was, like others, unable to reach her even though she continued to demand his presence and his attention, sometimes to the exclusion of all else in his life. Unable to help, he occasionally became so exasperated that he was indeed driven to ignore her demands in what, under the circumstances, might well have seemed to the Princess, in her unfathomable unhappiness, to be a neglectful fashion. Those of their friends who had sympathy for them both did not rush to judgement but did their limited best to help, knowing that to attribute blame in such a predicament would do nothing to solve what they regarded as an awful plight for them both.

By the spring of 1982, the royal couple were frequently at Highgrove, the Gloucestershire estate which the Duchy of Cornwall had acquired on the Prince's behalf in 1980 and which thus became his first 'home of his own'. For six years until then, he had had the use of Chevening House in Kent, the former home of the Earls of Stanhope, which had been bequeathed to the nation in 1967, but he had only been there on a handful of occasions. Long anxious to have his own home, Chevening, which was administered by a Trust, was not quite what he had in mind. He gave vent to his feelings in a note to his private secretary:

> I know there are advantages – particularly financial ones – in the Chevening set up, but I regret to say I am rapidly coming to the conclusion that they are the only advantages. I want you to know that I am seriously thinking of asking Tony Gray* to start looking for something decent and attractive to the West of London – ie in Gloucs. or Wilts or Somerset. It would be so much more fun if the Duchy would purchase a nice house with a small farm, having sold somewhere less useful in Cornwall, for instance, where I could learn some practical farming for a start – as well as being my own master.[25]

Within a few weeks, the hunt was on for what his private secretary referred to as 'another Gatcombe',[26] the name of the country estate in Gloucestershire which the Queen had bought for Princess Anne after her marriage to Captain Mark Phillips. The Prince's proposition was not without complications. A decision to divert up to £1 million (the presumed cost of an appropriate estate), turning high-yielding investments into a low-yielding agricultural property, would inevitably reduce the Duchy's net surplus. Given the political sensitivity of the royal finances, it would be impossible to go ahead without the approval of the Treasury

---

* Anthony Gray (1917–92), Secretary and Keeper of Records, Duchy of Cornwall 1972–81. Previously Gray had spent twenty years as treasurer of Christ Church, Oxford.

and the support of the royal household's financial advisers. It would have to be 'sold' to them as a valid purchase within the terms of the Duchy's remit. Yet the wealth of the Duchy was the Prince's only source of finance, his only means of becoming 'his own master'. By 1979, a scheme had duly been devised which allowed the search to start for a house in the Cotswolds, convenient for London and comfortably within the loosely defined boundaries of the Duchy.

In June 1980, the Prince wrote to the Prime Minister, Margaret Thatcher, to sever formally his connections with Chevening. Explaining that he thought it would be wrong to have use of such a 'beautiful and valuable property' when he would have very little opportunity to stay there, he mentioned that he hoped in future to spend more time visiting his properties in the Duchy, which would mean that he would have much less chance to be in Kent.

A few weeks later, it was announced that contracts had been exchanged for Highgrove House in the hamlet of Doughton, just outside Tetbury in Gloucestershire. By comparison with other estates in the area, Highgrove was very far from ostentatious. Its neo-classical façade, imposing but modestly so, lacked any embellishment, the grey stonework accentuating a simple, even plain, demeanour. Behind the house there was a set of traditional farm buildings, including a stable block which had been perfectly preserved. The grounds, which ran to the south and west of the house, were flat and lacking in identifiable character, suggesting, in the words of Charles Clover, Highgrove's historian, that the previous owner, Maurice Macmillan (son of the former Prime Minister Sir Harold Macmillan), had been 'indifferently fond of gardening'.[27] In front of the south elevation there was an ancient cedar tree that lent the house an atmosphere of calm and gentleness, softening its otherwise slightly forbidding aspect. Parkland stretched away to the east, beyond which the spire of Tetbury parish church rose delicately above the trees. There was a home farm of a little over 340 acres, large enough to run commercially if not at great profit. Inside, Highgrove had the potential to meet the Prince's needs: it was large enough, with four reception rooms and six principal bedrooms, to entertain and to have friends to stay, but small enough to be a private home. The faded but friendly elegance of the entire estate was suited to the Prince's taste and imagination, and – at a price of some £750,000 – to the Duchy's purse.

In the course of the next twelve months, the Prince was often at

Highgrove, camping in the house while planning the creation of a new garden that he wanted to be, as he later explained, 'the outward expression of my inner self'. He approached the Marchioness of Salisbury, whose talent for combining formality with romance within the same garden he had already admired at the Salisbury family seat at Cranborne Manor in Dorset. With his vision and her inspiration, the contours of the Highgrove garden were beginning to emerge: the paths, the hedges, the trees, the fruits and the vegetables. It was an enterprise so rich in imagination and character and so demanding of energy and finance that Sir Roy Strong, the former director of the Victoria and Albert Museum, was later to describe it as the most important garden to be made in the decade of the eighties. He detected two themes: 'a return to formality in design and a growing delight in wild nature'.[28]

In the summer of 1981, with the garden already starting to take shape, the Prince made plans for a swimming pool and a tennis court, ordered two estate cottages to be renovated, approved the drainage of some fields near Westonbirt, and arranged for two Jersey cows to be borrowed from the Queen's herd at the Windsor home farm, to provide milk for the house. Whenever he was there he schemed, he planned and he dreamt, walking in the grounds and across the fields, at ease. The Princess, who had first visited Highgrove nine months earlier, took charge of the interior of the house, supervising the decorations which, at the suggestion of her mother, had been put in the hands of the designer Dudley Poplak. For the staff on the estate, her frequent presence confirmed the impression that Highgrove was to play an important part in the heir apparent's family life. It was an appealing prospect.

For the Prince, Highgrove offered an antidote to the official round, the balm of privacy, but the Princess seemed less enamoured of rural life than she had been and was often at a loss. The days of serenity for which the Prince had hoped were infrequent; instead, the atmosphere was often turbulent. The violent swings in the Princess's mood did not abate and there were a number of incidents which their staff and the police could not fail to notice. In one of these, she drove off into the night alone, without telling anyone where she was heading, if indeed she knew, clearly in great distress.

The Prince sought to protect his wife from the consequences of what he believed to be her temporarily aberrant behaviour. Knowing that he could rely on the discretion of their staff, he implored his friends to try to understand her difficulties. He asked all those who knew of her unhappiness and its disturbing manifestations to keep silent about what they had witnessed or heard, and they heeded his injunction.

Sympathetic observers, who included the Prince's friends, found it hard to over-emphasise the pressures on the Princess. The love affair between her and the British people which began at her marriage had not cooled; whenever she appeared in public, even if it was to go shopping or have lunch with her friends, photographers and reporters were always at hand to record the event for their insatiable readers. Her ambivalence towards this adulation was understandable. Suddenly, and without preparation, she had been elevated to the status of a superstar. It was exhilarating but perplexing. She was flattered by the obeisance but it was alarming as well – confirming the sense of unreality which assailed her and draining away what little sense of her own identity she possessed.

The competition for an 'exclusive' photograph, taken without her knowledge, was unrelenting. In February 1982, less than four months before the birth of Prince William, the 'rat pack', as the royal press corps was called with a mixture of admiration and contempt by their colleagues, flew to the Bahamas. Their aim was to secure a photograph of the Princess in the bikini that it was feverishly assumed she would wear in the privacy of one of the secluded beaches on the island of Eleuthera, where, at the Prince's suggestion, he and the Princess had arranged to stay with Norton and Penny Romsey.

It took some effort but the voyeurs eventually achieved their objective, and the pregnant mother duly graced the front pages of the *Sun* and the *Daily Star*. Loftier rivals condemned the intrusion, while the *Daily Mirror* (which had not yet surrendered an enviable reputation) denounced the venture as 'squalid in conception, furtive in execution and grubby in publication'.[29]* The following day, the *Sun* claimed that it was 'deeply sorry' if the Prince and Princess had been distressed, reprinting the offending photograph alongside its apology to ensure that no-one should be in doubt about what had caused the offence. The Press Council

---

* A little over a decade later, however, the *Daily Mirror* was to publish photographs of the Princess of Wales 'working out' in a London gym taken with a camera concealed in the roof.

bestirred itself to condemn 'the gross intrusion' into the privacy of the Princess of Wales but to little effect. In the breach of that taboo, yet another veil around the monarchy was torn away.

Nonetheless, the Eleutheran holiday, the Princess's first experience of the Bahamas, was a success, albeit a modest one. They sunbathed, swam, water-skied and windsurfed. In the evening, the couples took it in turn to cook supper, and it was agreed that the culinary talent of the royal couple outmatched that of the Romseys. Afterwards, the Prince wrote to the Brabournes describing the ten days at their house as a 'second honeymoon' which had allowed the Princess to 'forget about her pregnancy for a few days and totally relax . . .'[30] Even so, signs of distress and incompatibility were only just below the surface. It was evident to the Romseys that the Princess was easily bored by her husband's conversation and resentful of his unquenchable urge to read and to paint.

As her pregnancy advanced, a sense of despair lurked about the Princess. Her bouts of misery lasted longer and her outlook seemed bleaker than ever. The Prince confided his anxiety only to a tiny circle of his most trusted friends, one or two of whom urged him to be tougher with what they interpreted as her self-pity. They said that she needed to 'pull herself together', and that would not happen if he indulged her bouts of gloom with tender words. His invariable response was to insist that he was to blame, that if it were not for him she would not be in such a state of misery, that what he had always feared might happen had happened. It was too much to expect anyone to be the wife of the heir to the throne: the demands were too great, the pressures too daunting, the loss of freedom too stifling.

The Princess also seemed extraordinarily self-absorbed, to the extent that events beyond her own life appeared to pass her by entirely. Even the Falklands campaign – which preoccupied her husband in his role as heir to the throne, as Colonel-in-Chief of two regiments fighting in the South Atlantic, and as the brother of Prince Andrew who was there as a helicopter pilot – failed to arouse her curiosity or to distract her from her own concerns. Some of those who bore witness to her disconcerting detachment were also perplexed by the fact that she seemed to resent the interest being shown in the Falklands rather than in her.

Their friends grew increasingly concerned by the degree to which the Princess became demanding of her husband's attention. Unable to explain this attitude, they started to imagine that in some obscure way she sought to possess him, but only in order to be able to reject him. These intermittent speculations were almost too awful to contemplate, however; although they feared for her health, they preferred to suppose that a combination of her new status and her pregnancy had temporarily disorientated her. They believed with a passion of loyalty to the monarchy that all would soon be well. As one of them explained, 'There was this extraordinary surge of joy at the time of their wedding . . . this feeling of a safe future for our country . . . this wonderful feeling of them uniting us as one country, one people and this being because of one person marrying the heir to the throne.'[31] The thought that all might not be for the best was too dreadful even to think about.

On 21 June 1982, the Princess of Wales gave birth to a son in St Mary's Hospital, Paddington. A bulletin was quick to announce that the birth had taken place at 9.03 p.m. and that the baby weighed 7lb 1½oz. Crowds had gathered outside the hospital to await the birth and afterwards, when the Prince emerged, they sang 'For He's a Jolly Good Fellow'. Reporters asked if they had chosen a name for him, which they had not. The next day, the Prince wrote to his friends the van Cutsems, 'I got back here just before midnight – utterly elated but quite shattered. I can't tell you how excited and proud I am. He really does look surprisingly appetising and has sausage fingers just like mine.'[32]

A few days later, when they were both back at Highgrove, he wrote to his godmother, Patricia Brabourne, describing his delight in fatherhood:

> The arrival of our small son has been an astonishing experience and one that has meant more to me than I could ever have imagined. As so often happens in this life, you have to experience something before you are in a true position to understand or appreciate the full meaning of the whole thing. I am so thankful I was beside Diana's bedside the whole time because by the end of the day I really felt as though I'd shared deeply in the process of birth and as a result was rewarded by seeing a small creature which belonged to us even though he seemed to belong to everyone else as well! I have never seen such scenes as there were outside the hospital when I left that night – everyone had gone berserk with excitement . . . Since then we've been overwhelmed by people's reactions and thoroughly humbled. It really is

quite extraordinary . . . I am so pleased that you like the idea of Louis being one of William's names. Oh! How I wish your papa could have lived to see him, but he probably knows anyway . . .[33]

By then, he and the Princess had decided that their first-born should be called William Arthur Philip Louis. For a while, their happiness was unalloyed.

CHAPTER
SEVENTEEN

I have often thought that one of the less attractive traits of various professional bodies and institutions is the deeply engrained suspicion and outright hostility which can exist towards anything unorthodox or unconventional. I suppose it is inevitable that something which is different should arouse strong feelings on the part of the majority whose conventional wisdom is being challenged or, in a more social sense, whose way of life and customs are being insulted by something rather alien. I suppose, too, that human nature is such that we are frequently prevented from seeing that what is today's unorthodoxy is probably going to be tomorrow's convention. Perhaps we just have to accept that it is God's will that the unorthodox individual is doomed to years of frustration, ridicule and failure in order to act out his role in the scheme of things, until his day arrives and mankind is ready to receive his message, which he probably finds hard to explain himself, but which he knows comes from a far deeper source than conscious thought.[1]

Those were not private reflections but public words addressed by the Prince of Wales as president of the British Medical Association on the 150th anniversary of its foundation in December 1982. Using his speech to attack some of the fundamental tenets of a hitherto impregnable profession. The theme had its source in the Prince's own immersion in the unconventional values of oriental culture, the writings of Jung, and the mystical revelations about the natural world he shared with Laurens van der Post. But as was often to happen, the particular inspiration came under the pressure of a deadline. On this occasion, he was at Highgrove in his study wondering precisely what to say at such an august gathering. He wandered across to his bookshelf and picked up a book about the sixteenth-century healer Paracelsus. He read a few pages, and suddenly a host of ideas and emotions took shape and found their expression in what the medical profession came to regard as a seminal outburst. No other hand was involved, neither adviser nor specialist – but only, as the Prince would say, 'my intuition'.[2]

The Prince told his audience that the principles upon which Paracelsus had based his treatment 400 years earlier 'have a message for our time: a time in which science has tended to become estranged from Nature'. In particular, he noted, paraphrasing Paracelsus who had been reviled in his own time, the doctor:

> should be intimate with Nature. He must have the intuition which is necessary to understand the patient, his body, his disease. He must have the 'feel' and the 'touch' which makes it possible for him to be in sympathetic communication with the patient's spirits . . . the *good* doctor's therapeutic success largely depends on his ability to inspire the patient with confidence and to mobilise his will to health . . .[3]

In essence, the Prince was arguing for 'holism'. Closely aligned to the psychology of Jung and to various reinterpretations of the structure of the natural world, explored by scientists like James Lovelock, who formulated the Gaia hypothesis,* the concept of 'holism' (a term which brought a curl to the lips of scientific materialists) invoked the principles of harmony, balance and the interconnectedness of natural phenomena, combining them with the search for inner awareness. Though he did not yet use the term 'holism' himself, the Prince did not shrink from urging

---

* Named after the Greek goddess Gaia, the Earth Mother, the Gaia hypothesis describes the planet as if it were one unitary living system. The conventional view is that plants and animals evolve on, but are distinct from, an inanimate planet. Lovelock maintained that the Earth, its rocks, oceans and atmosphere, and all living things are part of one great organism, evolving over the vast span of geological time.

that 'healing' should be reincorporated into the practice of medicine. He reminded his profoundly sceptical audience that 'through the centuries, healing has been practised by folk-healers who are guided by traditional wisdom that sees illness as a disorder of the whole person, involving not only the patient's body, but his mind, his self-image, his dependence on the physical and social environment, as well as his relation to the cosmos'. In a final flourish, while being careful to declare that he was 'a powerful supporter of modern methods in medicine', he bemoaned the nation's 'frightening' dependence on drugs (then costing the National Health Service more than £2 billion a year) as a 'universal panacea' and declared that 'the whole imposing edifice of modern medicine, for all its breath-taking successes, is, like the celebrated Tower of Pisa, slightly off balance'.[4]

The vivid imagery and the radical thrust of his words sent a shudder through the medical establishment, both the practitioners and their sym-biotic partners in the drugs industry. It was not the first significant speech the Prince had made, but it was by far the most opinionated and, strik-ing at the heart of a conventional culture, by far the most controversial. As he had suspected, it brought down on his head a form of praetorian wrath not so very different from that which Paracelsus had once endured. Nor was the royal evangelist at all certain about when or if, 'his day' would arrive.

The Prince's apostasy was as inspiring to the practitioners of 'alterna-tive' or 'complementary' medicine as it was outrageous to conventional opinion. His intervention sparked off an acrimonious debate in which the only common ground between the two sides was that the Prince's devastating intervention had suddenly changed the ground rules for their internecine combat. It would no longer be so easy for the medical estab-lishment to dismiss 'alternative' practitioners as a 'fringe' of quacks and eccentrics. However reluctantly, they were obliged to participate in the debate which the Prince had instigated, though they did not suppose for a moment that it would lead to a process through which, by the end of the decade, the virtues of 'complementary' medicine were so widely acknowledged as to make the original furore seem quite antediluvian.

In June that year, the Prince fanned the flames of the debate by returning to the theme of his speech in a written message as the out-going president of the BMA. In July, he heaped fuel on the fire by accepting an invitation to open the Bristol Cancer Help Centre, which had been running for three years, offering alternative therapies including yoga and meditation for its patients, many of whom were terminally ill and beyond hope of recovery by conventional means. Orthodox specialists were aghast at his decision to sponsor what one of them, a prominent Bristol surgeon, Dr Elizabeth Whipp, described as a set-up which was 'full of bogus notions'.[5]

Besieged by opposing forces, the Prince decided to intervene again, but not so publicly. With the help of Lord Kindersley,* he arranged a private dinner at Kensington Palace in the autumn of 1983 for leading figures from the opposing sides. Among the guests were a chiropractor, a herbalist and the presidents of all the leading medical colleges, including the president of the Royal Society of Medicine, Sir James Watt, who was to play a key part in changing the climate of orthodox opinion. The scene was set for an almighty collision of attitudes. Instead, the protagonists retreated from one another, the representatives of orthodox medicine being particularly muted, either too embarrassed or too polite to challenge their opponents in front of the Prince. According to Lord Kindersley, the Prince gradually drew them into conversation, breaking the ice between them with humour and charm. 'It was', he remembered, 'a brilliant start to what became an unstoppable movement.'[6] The Prince began by briefly restating his own position and then went on to suggest that the provision of health care had become too impersonal and remote, that patients were 'whisked off to hospital' for treatment without the personal consultation for which most individuals longed. He proposed that the medical profession should re-examine its methods, procedures and attitudes without prejudice and in a spirit of humility. He then went round the table asking everyone for a contribution. Only one of the orthodox practitioners spoke openly against 'alternative' medicine; the others, whatever their true feelings, were restrained and conciliatory. According to Sir James Watt, the Prince was so 'gracious and understanding' that his case for a serious examination of the issues at the highest level became irresistible. When the Prince asked about the next step, there was a brief silence until Watt spontaneously decided to offer the resources of the Royal Society of Medicine to explore the issue further, an offer which the Prince at once accepted.

---

* Lord Kindersley (1929–   ), businessman; chairman of Commonwealth Development Corporation 1980–89; chairman of Siam Selective Growth Fund since 1990. Prince Charles was a board member of the CDC from 1979 to 1987.

When Watt informed the officers of the RSM of his offer, they were incredulous at what seemed to them an entirely inappropriate gesture, a view which they were confident would be shared by the great majority of their 18,000 members once their opinions had been canvassed. Despite Watt's plea that it was in the distinguished tradition of the Society to take up controversial causes, they did not hesitate to warn that his proposal threatened to bring their august institution into disrepute. According to Watt, his trump card – without which he would have lost the argument – was the Prince of Wales. Reminded forcibly of his concern, the officers finally backed down and eventually agreed, though with great reluctance, that the RSM should host eight colloquia to explore the possibilities of collaboration with 'alternative' therapists.

In parallel, the British Medical Association also felt driven by their president's valedictory message to set up an internal working party to examine the role and practice of 'alternative' therapies. However, by inviting submissions from all manner of fringe therapists, the working party alienated the mainstream practitioners of complementary medicine – the qualified osteopaths, chiropractors, naturopaths, herbalists, homoeopaths and acupuncturists – who, for the most part, chose to boycott an inquiry which they suspected had only been set up to confirm the orthodox prejudices of the 'trade union' which it represented.

The colloquia organised by the RSM, which began in 1984, not only boasted more distinguished participants, but were much more thorough in approach. Under the chairmanship of Sir James Watt, they were conducted *in camera* to protect the participants from the glare of the media. With the Prince of Wales in attendance at three of the sessions to urge them on, the protagonists argued from first principles in search of common ground. The challenge was to overcome mutual suspicion, to explore the techniques adopted by alternative therapists, to establish a set of criteria to evaluate them, to identify shared concepts of treatment, to review the history of research into traditional therapies, and to pioneer standards of training and practice for complementary therapy that would meet the exacting demands of a sceptical establishment.

A glimpse of the obstacles in the way of finding a consensus emerged when a participant in one of the early colloquia took the Prince to task in the *Evening Standard*, under the headline 'With respect Your Highness, you've got it wrong'. Castigating an ancient philosophical approach that had 'remained unchallenged through the Dark Ages and is enjoying its own Renaissance in the year 1984', the Professor of Surgery at King's College Hospital School of Medicine, Michael Baum, was particularly scathing about 'fringe' practitioners who collected only corroborative data to justify their therapies. Their evidence, he complained, amounted usually to no more than 'anecdotal case reports' and formed part of an historical process which was littered with 'the tragic consequences of adopting therapeutic revolutions on the basis of a plausible hypothesis in advance of its scientific testing'. Although he exempted some of the alternative therapists at the colloquia from his strictures, he concluded that others were 'guilty of the most extreme intellectual arrogance, or more charitably, of confusing faith with fact'.[7] It was to be a long and rocky path, only somewhat smoothed by further dinners at Kensington Palace.*

Popular reaction to the Prince's part in the debate was far less sceptical than he had feared. 'It was unbelievable,' he told an interviewer some months later, 'I have never, ever had so many letters. I was riveted by this because while I was pretty sure I was going to stir up a hornet's nest – which I did I think – I also realised there was a great deal more interest in and awareness of this aspect than I'd imagined.' Concluding from this response that 'people often remain silent about what they really think . . . they are terrified of saying something in case "everyone" should think they are mad', he went on, 'I find I feel this about a lot of things.'[8]

The apparent vindication of his faith in intuition fired his self-confidence. Soon after his speech to the BMA, he sent a message of support to the organisers of the national organic food production conference at the Royal Agricultural College in Cirencester. Instead of accepting the anodyne draft prepared for him, he astonished his audience and horrified the agricultural establishment with a radical assault on conventional methods of farming:

For some years now, modern farming has made tremendous demands on the finite sources of energy which exist on earth. Maximum production has been the slogan to which we have all adhered. In the last few years there has been an increasing realisation that many modern

---

* Almost ten years later, this process bore fruit in the Osteopathy Bill of 1993. (See Appendix I, pages 567–75.)

production methods are not only wasteful but probably also unnecessary . . . I am convinced that any steps that can be taken to explore
methods of production which make better and more effective use of
renewable resources are extremely important. Even if it may be some
time before they are commercially acceptable, pioneer work is essential if our planet is to feed the teeming millions of people who live on
it by the twenty-first century.[9]

It was not the first time that he had entered the environmental debate.
In 1970, which had been designated European Conservation Year, he
had spoken as founding chairman of the Countryside in 1970
Committee for Wales of 'the horrifying effects of pollution in all its can-
cerous forms'.[10] He also established the Prince of Wales Awards for
projects designed to increase understanding of the urban or rural environment. In 1973, the year in which Fritz Schumacher published *Small
is Beautiful* – which soon became a bible for environmentalists – the
Prince met the author at Buckingham Palace, thereafter carrying many
of Schumacher's arguments into his own public statements. In 1980, he
established a Buckingham Palace 'bottle bank'. In the following year, he
wrote a full-page article in the *Observer*, lauding the objectives of the
Intermediate Technology Development Group, which had been set up
to provide practical forms of Third World development along the lines
advocated by Schumacher, who envisaged the growth of forms of technology compatible with the state of economic development in those
countries, and not simply imported from the West. But although all of
these initiatives were unfashionable, none of them overtly challenged
conventional opinion where it really hurt. The Prince's message to the
national organic food production conference in 1983 was different.

Like his speech to the BMA, his attack on modern production methods in agriculture posed a threat not only to established practice but to
powerful vested interests – in this case the agrochemical industry, whose
multi-billion-pound production of herbicides, pesticides and fertilisers
was dependent precisely on the systems of production which the Prince
had selected for rebuke. Likewise, it raised issues that seemed peripheral
to outsiders but which in reality identified core questions of public policy that went far beyond the small change of inter-party politics. In
both cases, the Prince's decision to take a stand had an immeasurable
impact – first on the debate between the specialists, and later on public

opinion, policy-makers and legislators. In both cases, more by chance than intent, he began not only to discover a purpose for himself but to redefine the role of the Prince of Wales, giving it a prominence in the constitutional hierarchy which surpassed that of any of his predecessors.

The significance of this was widely overlooked. The media responded for the most part precisely as the vested interests in medicine and agriculture would have wished. By turns indifferent, patronising and contemptuous, the tabloid press was more concerned with the failure of an identikit character called 'Action Man' to live up to the image which they had created for him than with the issues to which the Prince was hoping to direct their attention. Selecting key phrases like 'human spirit' and 'organic agriculture', the tabloids – often echoed by commentators in the broadsheets – began to reincarnate him in the image of a 'loony Prince'. *The Daily Mirror* imagined the future King sitting 'cross-legged on the throne wearing a kaftan and eating muesli'.[11] For the *Daily Mail*, the Prince was 'on the fringe',[12] while the *Daily Express* decided that he was 'lost in an identity crisis'.[13] When it was reported that he had used a Ouija board to make contact with Mountbatten, the Prince was driven to respond that not only had he never seen an Ouija board, but that he was 'fed up with getting letters saying, "Don't touch Ouija boards, they are bad for your health!"' The *Guardian* obligingly reported the Prince's complaint under the headline ' "Eccentric" Charles denies dabbling in occult'.[14] The television satire programme, *Spitting Image*, included a sketch in which its puppet caricature of the Prince attended a seance to make contact with the spirit of Mountbatten. When they made contact, the medium informed him that Mountbatten was playing a banjo. The puppet Prince protested, 'He didn't play a banjo,' to which the medium responded, 'He does now, luvvie. He learned it off Beethoven.' The puppet Prince persevered, 'Does he think I'm bonkers?' 'Oh! no,' the medium retorted. 'He says, "Trust Doris* . . . she's genuine . . . and she takes all credit cards." '[15]

Even if the Prince's words to the BMA that 'the unorthodox individual is doomed to years of frustration, ridicule and failure' had not originally been self-regarding, they had started to seem depressingly prescient. Though he expected to be misunderstood and criticised, he did

---

* A reference to the popular medium Doris Stokes.

not expect to be so carelessly mocked. With some naivety, he had presumed that merely because he was honestly striving for the truth and earnestly seeking a better way he would at least be respected for his valiance. Though he affected disdain, he was shocked and hurt; yet he was driven by so powerful a compulsion that he was quite unable to desist.

At a point when he might have been tempted to retreat from the battlefield, he chose instead to open up on yet another front. Forewarned about the ferocious reaction of established institutions under royal assault, he knew that a speech he had agreed to deliver at a banquet to celebrate the 150th anniversary of the Royal Institute of British Architects on 30 May 1984 would cause a rumpus, but he did not anticipate the fury his words would cause.

RIBA had thought at first to invite the Queen but, presuming that she would be too busy, plumped for the Prince. The highlight of the banquet in Hampton Court Palace was intended to be the presentation of a gold medal to the Indian architect Charles Correa for his contribution to the design of low-cost housing for deprived communities. The Prince accepted with alacrity and RIBA sent round the customary sheaf of briefing notes for him and his office to prepare an appropriate salutation both to the architect and to the Institute.

A few weeks earlier, a group of architects, including Michael Manser, the president of RIBA, had been invited round to Kensington Palace for an informal luncheon with a group of planners, architects and government officials to discuss ways of amending the Department of the Environment's building regulations to facilitate access for the disabled. The Prince had said very little about architecture itself, leaving the modernist contingent at the luncheon to presume either that he was not greatly interested in their specialist field or that his reticence signalled approval.

In fact, the Prince was not only interested but anguished. His instinctive traditionalism had long been offended by what he saw as the ugly and impersonal environment that post-war architecture had imposed on the urban landscape, and especially on the inner cities. His spontaneous reaction to tower blocks and deck-access housing estates was one of revulsion against a blight which defaced the inner cities and for which he was disposed to blame the planners rather than poverty. He had read, and been impressed by, the arguments in favour of 'community' architecture, which happened to dovetail ideologically with his vision of the rural village (a rapidly disappearing repository of communal life on a human scale). His interest in oriental culture had attracted him towards the harmonies of shape and size and colour created by Islamic and Hindu architecture and he had come to believe that the organic harmony of the 'built' environment was a vital aspect of the global harmony that was the framework for his own tentative but passionate cosmology. Although he discussed the speech with one or two private advisers, including the journalist Christopher Booker and the architectural historian Jules Lubbock, the threads were woven together at the last moment, under the pressure of a looming deadline. He did not complete his final draft until the early hours of the day itself, after which he instructed his staff to dispatch it to the editors of *The Times*, the *Guardian* and the *Observer*.

On the afternoon of 30 May, officials at RIBA were jolted out of their complacence about the royal contribution to their celebration by a telephone call from the *Guardian* to Patrick Harrison, the secretary of RIBA, warning him that the speech was to be 'difficult'. Harrison asked the *Guardian* to send round a copy. When he saw it, Manser was horrified: it was not so much difficult as a 'secret bombshell', as he would later describe it.[16] Harrison was deputed to ring the Palace, where a junior press officer disclaimed any knowledge of what the Prince was to say. Harrison protested that, 'It was the wrong speech at the wrong time.' And he demanded, 'Who leaked it to the *Guardian*?' According to RIBA, the Prince's office was conciliatory, and his private secretary promised to try to dissuade the Prince from his course. Later, Edward Adeane even rang Manser and apparently pledged to do what he could on the journey between Buckingham Palace and Hampton Court. Not for the first time, Adeane failed to measure his man; not for the first time, they had a fierce argument in which Adeane (according to the memory of his colleagues) sought to impress on the Prince that he was overstepping the mark; and not for the first time, he was overruled.

Manser and his colleagues waited queasily for their guest of honour to arrive. As he got out of the car, the Prince observed with apparent innocence, 'You've got a good turn-out of press here.' Manser led him to the platform and welcomed him to the celebration, still hoping that Adeane had prevailed upon the Prince at least to tone the speech down. His hopes were soon dashed. After congratulating Correa on 'his supreme skill' as an architect and his 'imaginative concern' for the poor of the Third World, the Prince moved swiftly to deliver his broadside:

> For far too long, it seems to me, some planners and architects have consistently ignored the feelings and wishes of the mass of ordinary people in this country. Perhaps, when you think about it, it is hardly surprising as architects tend to have been trained to design buildings from scratch – to tear down and rebuild. Except in Interior Design courses, students are not taught to rehabilitate, nor do they ever meet the ultimate users of buildings in their training – indeed, they can often go through their whole career without doing so. Consequently, a large number of us have developed a feeling that architects tend to design buildings for the approval of fellow architects and critics, not for the tenants.

Not content with that, the Prince went on to heap praise on the unfashionable and hitherto marginalised concept of community architecture. He spoke warmly of the 'gradual expansion of housing co-operatives' where 'the tenants are able to work with an architect of their own who listens to their comments and ideas and tries to design the kind of environment they want'. He continued:

> What I believe is important about community architecture is that it has 'shown' ordinary people that their views are worth having; that architects and planners do not necessarily have the monopoly of knowing what is best about taste, style and planning; that they need not be made to feel guilty or ignorant if their natural preference is for the more 'traditional designs' – for a small garden, for courtyards, arches and porches – and that there is a growing number of architects prepared to listen and to offer imaginative ideas.

Thus far, the rebuke had been forthright enough, but it was as nothing by comparison with the peroration that followed:

> It would be a tragedy if the character and skyline of our capital city were to be further ruined and St Paul's dwarfed by yet another giant glass stump, better suited to downtown Chicago than the City of London. It is hard to imagine that London before the last war must

have had one of the most beautiful skylines of any great city, if those who recall it are to be believed. Those who do say that the affinity between buildings and the earth, in spite of the city's immense size, was so close and organic that the houses looked almost as though they had grown out of the earth and had not been imposed upon it – grown, moreover, in such a way that as few trees as possible were thrust out of the way . . .

What, then, are we doing to our capital city now? What have we done to it since the bombing during the war? What are we shortly to do with one of its most favourite areas – Trafalgar Square? Instead of designing an extension to the elegant facade of the National Gallery which complements it and continues the concept of columns and domes, it looks as though we may be presented with a kind of vast municipal fire station, complete with the sort of tower that contains the siren. I would understand better this type of High Tech approach if you demolished the whole of Trafalgar Square and started again with a single architect responsible for the whole layout, but what is proposed is like a monstrous carbuncle on the face of a much loved and elegant friend . . . Goethe once said 'There is nothing more dreadful than imagination without taste.' In this 150th anniversary year, which provides an opportunity for a fresh look at the path ahead and in which you are probably regretting having asked me to take part, may I express the earnest hope that the next 150 years will see a new harmony between imagination and taste and in the relationship between the architects and the people of this country.[17]

The bombshell Manser feared had been detonated, and its impact was to reverberate not only around Hampton Court but throughout Britain. Apparently unaware of quite how much offence he had caused, the Prince handed Correa his gold medal – at which point the Indian architect, furious at the eclipse of his own moment, pointedly put his prepared speech away, mumbled a few sentences of gratitude and then said to the Prince, 'We have a lot to discuss over dinner.' They walked through to what had once been the Queen's bedchamber, where the architects Norman Foster, Sir Hugh Casson, Charles Correa and their spouses joined Michael Manser, his wife and the Prince of Wales at a candlelit table for dinner. According to one of the party, 'The Prince pitched in about architecture and defended himself quite well. He is quite good with words.'[18] It was an uncomfortable hour: like Correa, Norman Foster, one of the most eminent British modernists, was muted but fuming, while even the usually garrulous Sir Hugh Casson was uncharacteristically subdued. In an atmosphere suffused with repressed anger, the hosts longed only for the Prince to leave. Feeling that he had abused their hospitality, not to mention his role, their deepest outrage was reserved – revealingly – not for what he had said but for the fact that he had dared to speak at all: in the words of one of them, 'He was venturing into an area he so clearly knew nothing about.'[19]

As before in his remarks about alternative medicine and organic agriculture the Prince had advanced upon a citadel of the establishment, battered his way through its portals, and then set about its praetorian guard with unforgivable abandon. The counter-attack was swift and bitter. Although Manser, as president of RIBA, concealed his indignation, confining himself to the assertion that 'modern architecture [was] here to stay',[20] Peter Ahrends, the designer of the National Gallery extension, spoke for the entire modernist school when he declared, 'The Prince's remarks were offensive, reactionary and ill-considered. He seems to have a rather nostalgic view of buildings as if they grow out of the earth, a view of life no longer with us. He seems to be looking backwards rather than forward.'[21]

Ahrends had alighted, if only by chance, on the precise source of the Prince's onslaught, that same inspiration of intuition and feeling which had led him to promote organic agriculture and holistic medicine. In the case of 'organic' architecture, however, the censure of the professionals failed to unleash the ridicule which they might have hoped for. Even their acolytes in the broadsheet newspapers were, at this stage, unwilling to condemn the Prince openly for daring to trespass onto their privileged turf. Though his views were despised by the *avant-garde* in much the same terms used by the affronted Ahrends, even the guardians of the modernist shrine could not fail to recognise that on this occasion at least the Prince's apostasy had touched a popular nerve, that it had given public expression to a widespread if inarticulate sentiment which they could not entirely repudiate.

The Prince was not only unrepentant but ready to return to his theme again and again in a sharpening debate which would cast him as the David of traditionalism against the Goliaths of modernism. Though the Goliaths were not to be felled, there were some immediate casualties of the RIBA speech. A little over a year afterwards, Manser wrote to the Prince on his last day in office as RIBA president to say that 'after the initial shock, Hampton Court did us all good in a number of ways and I hope that your more recent contacts with our members . . . have given you a happier view of architects and the way they work'. But he went on to report that Peter Ahrends' career had been adversely affected by the Prince's pejorative comments about his plans for the extension to the National Gallery, and asked the Prince to find a moment to praise his other work. He concluded with the hope that the Prince's 'obvious interest and pleasure in architecture' would eventually extend 'to include some of the more recent designs which you presently find so alarming'.[22]

Given his own resentment at the RIBA speech, and his feeling that the modernist movement had been severely damaged by it and that his own business would suffer, Manser's valedictory letter was a conciliatory gesture. The Prince was unyielding. Expressing his distress that Peter Ahrends might have suffered, he commented, 'I can't believe this will be long-lived. I am not sure that I can really do very much to help, but I will explore the matter. Please assure him that such a development was furthest from my intentions when I spoke last year at Hampton Court.' Blaming the media for its 'extraordinary propensity to reduce everything to the level of absurdity', the Prince insisted that he could not imagine why 'this idea should have taken root that I am opposed to all recent designs of buildings'. He cited several contemporary buildings in London which he admired, including Sir Hugh Casson's Ismaili Centre opposite the Victoria and Albert Museum. His stricture on the media was characteristic but, on this occasion at least, either naive or disingenuous. Indeed, the final paragraph of the letter to Manser confirmed the impression that even if he could tolerate some contemporary architecture he was adamantly hostile to most of it. 'I am just against the impersonal nature of many of the designs which characterise the so-called "Modern Movement",' he wrote. 'I also feel that a lot of experiments – very often exciting ones – have been made with materials which have now been shown to be less than successful or aesthetically pleasing and this is another area which I confess I mind about. If that is "unleashing the forces of reaction" then I am afraid I am delighted to have done so . . .!'[23]

One of the guests at the RIBA dinner was an ambitious young pioneer of community architecture, a vice-president of RIBA called Rod

Hackney. When the Prince singled him out for praise in one passage of his speech, Hackney noticed that those standing around him moved imperceptibly away as if contaminated by his proximity. Afterwards, he was summoned to meet the Prince, who told him that he would like to visit an example of community architecture.

Later that year, Hackney showed the Prince round two housing co-operatives in Liverpool and, in February 1985, he took him to a 'self-help' rehabilitation scheme which he had developed in Macclesfield, where his practice was based. A few days later, in front of a startled array of business leaders from the Institute of Directors, the Prince spoke publicly of his reactions to the inner cities and his experiences in Macclesfield:

> The desperate plight of the inner-city areas is, I am sure, well known to you all, with the cycle of economic decline leading to physical deterioration and countless social problems. It is only when you visit these areas, as I do from time to time, that you begin to wonder how it is possible that people are able to live in such inhuman conditions . . . The hopelessness left in such communities is compounded by decay all around, the vandalism and the inability to control their own lives in any way beyond the basic requirements of day-to-day survival in a hostile environment.[24]

Though he himself was careful to ascribe no blame, it was inevitable that commentators would interpret this impassioned plea as a rebuke to every post-war government, not excluding the Thatcher administration, which, with the exception of a set of showy initiatives inspired by the former Environment Secretary Michael Heseltine, had been conspicuously irresolute in its approach to the regeneration of the inner cities. In these bleak circumstances, the Prince cited the architect Ludwig Mies van der Rohe, who had written in 1924 that architecture was 'the will of the epoch translated into space'. As quoted by the Prince, Mies believed that 'the individual is losing significance; his destiny is no longer what interests us. The decisive achievements in all fields are impersonal and for the most part unknown. They are part of the trend of our time towards anonymity.' Alarmed by that presentiment, the Prince urged 'it is high time we once again respected flights of the spirit; high time we concentrated our collective efforts on unleashing the vast, transforming and regenerative potential which lies within the individual as a member of the community'.[25]

If the emphasis was hardly Thatcherite in inspiration, it also lacked any element of socialist dogma. It was the Prince's authentic self, resolutely above the party battle, as he knew he had to be, but highly charged with political overtones that he hoped would challenge politicians of any party. Macclesfield was a case in point:

> I was electrified by the atmosphere I encountered in the communities I visited. I hadn't come across anything quite like it before . . . a very attractive village, containing the whole of the original slum street community, nestling like an oasis in the midst of a barren, urban desert. The residents of the houses I visited all told me that their new situation was like a dream come true, in some cases after waiting for *twenty-five years* to be rehoused. They were now responsible for the maintenance of their properties and that fact alone had virtually elim-inated the vandalism which was previously so rife in the area . . .[26]

Urging the government to adopt a more 'coherent' approach to the inner cities, for the public and private sectors to collude with rather than confront each other – for architects and planners to 'provide what people want and not what they think people should want', praising those individuals, companies and councils which shared at least some of his vision, the Prince urged those with power and influence to 'rediscover an awareness of the transforming value of the human individual, cocooned in the security of his own community, and enabled to take a personal pride in his own environment'.[27]

As often, the intensity of his passion carried the Prince through the occasional muddle in the structure of his argument; the meaning was clear even if the fine print was opaque. As with so many of his speeches, the immediate impact – the charge and counter-charge of headlines and of quotes taken out of context – was less significant than its reverbera-tions. By detonating his opinions in such a forum, he provoked politicians, officials, local authorities, financiers, businessmen, profes-sionals and architects to pause and think again, causing the rules of engagement to shift perceptibly. This residual authority, granted to him as heir apparent, gratified but perplexed the Prince. Borrowing the ancient metaphor of a stone tossed into a pool, he was disconcerted by the unpredictable manner in which the ripples he had intended could turn into tidal waves of public controversy.

Two days before his address to the Institute of Directors, the Prince had written to thank Rod Hackney for some background notes which he had used in preparing the speech. 'I am most indebted to you for your kindness in sending me those thoughts for my speech. They have been extremely useful and I am most touched that you should have taken such trouble,' he wrote. 'I am full of admiration for all your work.'[28] Hackney was quick to seize his opportunity. He escorted the Prince to other projects, and helped to organise a luncheon at Kensington Palace where the Prince presided over a gathering of industrialists and bankers – and where Hackney had a captive audience before which to propound his views about the critical links between the social and architectural regeneration of the inner cities. He was always at hand to deliver new contacts and to prepare further speeches.

It soon became known that Hackney was one of the Prince's closest 'advisers', an intimation that the Prince did not entirely appreciate. Some of Hackney's rivals concluded with envy that the brash northern architect was using the Prince to his own advantage, and that the Prince had been seduced by the down-to-earth demeanour adopted by Hackney. Although there is no doubt that Hackney's rapidly expanding business benefited from his association with the Prince, the charge was unfair. More serious was Hackney's apparent lack of discretion.

In October 1985, that indiscretion resulted in a siren of headlines on the front page of almost every newspaper in Britain and a party political fracas that severely embarrassed the heir to the throne. It began with a telephone call to Hackney from the Prince's office: would the architect join the Prince for an evening drink on the royal train in Somerset, where he was touring the Duchy? They were alone there for two and a half hours, discussing the social problems of the inner cities and the importance of community architecture. The Prince spoke openly of his deepening anxiety about the alienation of young people, which had preoccupied him since the establishment of the Prince's Trust eight years before, and they discussed the 'North–South' divide, which was then a sensitive public issue. Afterwards Hackney returned to Macclesfield and the Prince returned to London to make final preparations for an official visit to Australia.

As soon as he got home, Hackney received a telephone call from the

Manchester Evening News. According to Hackney, 'it was as if they had been on the train, they seemed to know exactly what we'd been talking about. I can't remember what they asked me. But I told them I'd seen Prince Charles on a train and said that Prince Charles had similar thoughts to me.'[29] He then expounded his ideas. It was a cardinal error, a flush of vainglory that he would live to regret. Under the banner headline 'Exclusive – Prince Charles: my fears for the future', the *Manchester Evening News* reporter, Peter Sharples, wrote that, 'The biggest fear of Prince Charles is that he will inherit the Throne of a divided Britain . . . The Prince is prepared to force his way through parliamentary red tape to ensure that his country is not split into factions of the "haves" and "have nots".' In a quotation attributed to Hackney, the Prince was said to be worried 'that when he becomes King there will be "no-go" areas in the inner cities, and that the minorities will be alienated from the rest of the country'.[30] The next day, national newspapers emblazoned the story across their front pages, inevitably interpreting the Prince's 'views' as a coded onslaught on the Conservative government. Hackney's protestations of innocence had no effect: he had spoken for the Prince, or had seemed to have done so. The damage was done.

By chance, the furore coincided with a debate on the inner cities in the House of Commons. The Shadow Home Secretary, Gerald Kaufman, who was not a man to miss a windfall, brandished one of the newspapers and quoted the views attributed to the Prince before denouncing the ruling party with characteristic hyperbole:

> Are this Government, some of their members well-meaning but ineffectual, others purblind and stiff-necked, determined to preside over this deterioration in the Queen's realm? Do the Government lack the will, or the compassion, or the patriotism, to insist upon including the whole of our society and all our people in the national commonwealth?[31]

The Prime Minister, who was in New York, was reported to be so angered by the reports of what the Prince was supposed to have said that she rang Buckingham Palace, where it is said she was told that the Prince had not at any stage or in any way sought to criticise the government. Certainly, the Prince's office was left in little doubt that Margaret Thatcher did not approve of the heir apparent's intervention.

The Prince was himself furious at the newspaper reports. In a letter to

Nicholas Soames, he wrote, 'I was particularly incensed because above all else I try to avoid anything obviously "political" and to talk of "inheriting a divided nation" etc. is so far from anything I would ever contemplate that I find the whole thing extremely aggravating. I spend my whole time trying not to polarise things and now someone has polarised me!'[32]

Clearly alarmed by the rumpus he had created, Hackney wrote at once to the Prince to express his regret and to explain his version of what had happened. The Prince wrote back from the aeroplane en route to Melbourne from London. In a measured rebuke, he offered a revealing clarification of the limits imposed on the Prince of Wales and, for that matter, on his advisers. His mood was less equable than the tone of his letter suggested:

London to Melbourne   October 26th 1985.

Dear Rod,

I was grateful for your letter the other day, although somewhat taken aback by the furore which suddenly crackled about my head and which you had rather unwittingly unleashed in an unguarded moment. I must confess that I was rather disturbed, to say the least, that I had been quoted here and there talking about 'divided nations' and 'haves and have-nots', not to mention references to inheriting things as King. It may be that you never mentioned such things, or they were put in your mouth by the way in which the questioner posed the question, but nevertheless they were overtly political phrases of a kind I would never, ever use because I know exactly what the political reactions are likely to be.

I know you like to talk to the press about your work in different parts of the country, and I was also most touched by the nice things you said about me, but it is very important not to talk to the press about our private conversations – unless we agree there is a reason to do so. Surely this is the normal situation between an architect and a client?

Although I know that you were acting under the best possible motives in all this, it is essential that I operate in this field of community architecture, inner city housing, deprivation etc. by steering my way very carefully through a political minefield. It isn't a help, therefore, to find myself being cheered by very high profile politicians whose words and actions so often arouse hostility and whose opinions polarise whole sections of the population. I am sure by now you have begun to understand all this and will realise the need for caution and discretion in the future. I am sure too that I can rely on your discretion concerning the forthcoming dinner you are arranging for me at Kensington Palace. From now on the press will be on the look out for anything like that and will blow it up out of all proportion – so beware!

As things turn out, I daresay some good will come out of all this controversy in the end, although I suppose they will now try and make something out of the community architecture film I contributed to the other day.

One other point – you must try and scotch the idea that you are somehow my architectural adviser. I don't know how this got about, but it is news to me. I <u>greatly</u> value your help, assistance and advice, but I also seek advice from other quarters and this impression that has gained credence is misleading. I can only say that I pray you win your battle with the powers-that-be in Macclesfield but please don't bring me into it!

I look forward to seeing you at our dinner and this comes with my best wishes, as always –

Charles.

The Prince was right to suppose that the media would latch on to his contribution to a London Weekend Television documentary, called *The Pride Factor*, for which he had been interviewed some days before the 'divided Britain' row broke out. Indeed, almost as he was writing to Hackney, the *Daily Mirror* published a leaked version of the interview which was swiftly picked up by every other newspaper. Though he said very little in it that he had not said already in his speech to RIBA, the context had changed dramatically. When he called for the 'unleashing' of the community spirit in architecture and the need to give the inhabitants of inner cities the means to help themselves create their own environment, it was interpreted as part of a concerted campaign for the British 'underclass' (though the term was not yet in vogue), motivated by compassion but underpinned by yet another implied rebuke to the government.

This impression was unwittingly confirmed when the director of the Royal Jubilee Trusts, Harold Haywood, set out to inform the nation that the Prince's concern for the inner cities was long-standing. 'From when we had the first disturbances in his wedding year, 1981, His Royal Highness has been very concerned to ask what we could do to co-operate with others to alleviate stress and help the young,' he said. Though the statement was itself bland enough, he illustrated the point by revealing that the Prince had been to see for himself the conditions in which the homeless lived in cardboard shelters under Waterloo Bridge, that he had visited a hostel for the homeless at King's Cross, and that he had spent time with the adolescents rescued from the streets by the charity Centrepoint. The media put two and two together and concluded, in the words of the *Guardian* under the headline 'Palace denies a symphony of leaks for the people's prince', that here was 'a Prince with a conscience unequalled since his great uncle, the future Edward VIII, said "something must be done" '.[33]

The cumulative effect of all the coverage was to suggest a stand-off between the Prince and the government, a potential rift which the *Daily Telegraph* moved swiftly to heal. Under the headline 'Prince and Politics', the leader writer rebuked Gerald Kaufman for 'hijacking' the Prince's concern about the inner cities 'for abusive political argument'. It asserted that, 'The Prince has shown the proper impartiality of a future monarch concerned for the peace and security of the realm.'[34] The *Telegraph* also endorsed his hostility towards modern architecture, insisting that drift and rootlessness in the inner cities was due more to the inhuman character of high-rise housing estates – which, the writer noted, represented in debased form the 'worker architecture' of those Weimar professors who had given birth to modernism – than to any shortage of government millions.

Likewise, the leading article in *The Times*, under the headline 'Something must be done', recalled with approval Edward VIII's youthful concern for the Welsh miners and reprimanded Kaufman for turning a prince's proper concern into a party political conflict. The editorial reflected the attitude of the paper's editor, Charles Douglas-Home, who had become a close friend of the Prince.* In private, Douglas-Home had

---

* The Prince and Douglas-Home were in frequent and affectionate correspondence even when Douglas-Home was confined to the Royal Free Hospital under

been strongly supportive of his stand; in public, his newspaper elaborated a constitutional argument in his favour:

> He is heir to the throne, not on it . . . He is not precluded from notic-
> ing large matters affecting the welfare of the nation, even if these
> matters attract party political controversy. In doing so, however, he has
> to be careful not to give the appearance of political partiality. He must
> not borrow party arguments. He must beware of party code-words.
> He must avoid personalities. But those limitations do not impose
> silence upon him or confine him to pious platitude. Our language is
> not so deformed and our politics are not so penetrating as to make it
> impossible for an important personage to say something important
> and influential about a large aspect of public life without sounding
> partisan.[35]

This *obiter dictum* was important. It was by now clear to all that the Prince was not to be diverted from using the authority of his position to speak out across a range of public issues – to an extent that none of his predecessors had even contemplated and in a public arena that was ever more in thrall to the power of mass communications. In this resolve, he had set a disconcerting precedent for which there were no explicit guidelines in the commentaries on Britain's unwritten constitution. Although his father, the Duke of Edinburgh, had established the fashion, and his speeches were sometimes provocative, they lacked the emotional candour that resonated through almost every speech made by his son. More to the point, the opinions of the Queen's consort were self-evidently of somewhat less moment than those of the heir apparent. As

---

treatment for the cancer which led to his premature death at the end of October 1985. Douglas-Home had borne his illness with humour and fortitude, writing on several occasions to the Prince making light of the pain he had to endure. After his death, the Prince grieved. 'I still cannot get over the thought that there I was talk-ing to Charlie for half an hour two weeks ago,' he wrote to a friend, 'but now he is somewhere else which defies imagination. The only way to cope is to view it as if he has gone on a long journey to the other side of the world and hope that one day, when that great journey has to be made by us, we shall meet in some unknown dimension. The thought of the suffering and agony he must have gone through, which always seems so remote when you're merely talking to someone, horrifies me.' (C, CL, 6 November 1985.)

the first to clarify the role and to identify the pitfalls, *The Times* provided a benchmark judgement which, through that process of intellectual osmosis by which the British establishment forms its collective opinion, was soon embraced as the received wisdom.

Despite the approbation bestowed on him by a range of serious commentators, the image of the Prince of Wales had become clouded and distorted in the popular mind. Why was someone apparently distressed by the state of the inner cities so preoccupied at the same time with 'fringe' medicine? If what mattered to him was 'inner peace', why was he so worried about the passing fashion for 'carbuncle' buildings? He was radical yet conservative, outspoken yet diffident, modest yet assertive: it was not hard to pile up such contradictory epithets to the point where to judge him from afar was like trying to make sense of the shards of colour and shape in a revolving kaleidoscope. Rather than contemplate that myriad, it was tempting to cling to one or other of the multiple caricatures that were so readily at hand. Those more in need of royal glamour than gravitas had, in any case, begun to focus their attention almost exclusively on the Princess of Wales.

CHAPTER
EIGHTEEN

———◆◄———

A
fter the birth of Prince William in June 1982, the Princess made few public appearances, a reticence which served only to intensify public adulation. When she did appear, she smiled demurely and displayed that particular quality of regal informality which had charmed and captivated so many hearts. Yet it was impossible not to detect that she had lost a great deal of weight. In fact, she was lean to the point of angularity. This evidence led to a spate of newspaper gossip to the effect that the stress of royal life was taking a heavy toll.* In her private office, it was common knowledge that she was eating little and that she was in a volatile state of mind. Presuming that she was suffering from post-natal depression, her staff made allowances for her erratic and arbitrary behaviour and did their best to adapt to her waywardness. Only a very close circle around the Prince and Princess were aware of how acute her distress could be. One or two of them already knew about her disconcerting propensity to consume large quantities of junk food (ice cream, biscuits and popcorn). In addition, they had become accustomed

---

* One such article was written by the ubiquitous James Whitaker. In a sympathetic portrait of the Princess, written ten years later, he explained himself by citing a conversation with her press officer, the late Vic Chapman, who, according to Whitaker, told him that the Princess was 'obsessed that everything and everyone around her should be perfect. She feels that so much is expected of her, she should be able to command the same'. (*Diana v Charles*, [Signet, 1993, p. 137].)

to another manifestation of her unhappiness: her ineradicable suspicion that her husband was persistently unfaithful. As apparently reported by her friends to the journalist Andrew Morton,[1] she was quite certain that the Prince had either failed to end his relationship with Camilla Parker Bowles or cynically recommenced the affair soon after their wedding; certainly she was unable to acknowledge what their friends, and especially those who were close to Camilla Parker Bowles, knew to be the truth, that the relationship had ceased entirely as the Prince had relayed to her before they were married. Notwithstanding his declarations of loyalty, the Princess's suspicion continued to grow to the point where it became a canker between them, destructive of every effort on both their parts to draw closer together.

Consumed by this false belief, the Princess seemed unable to rid herself of a further suspicion, that the Prince and his friends were conspiring to deceive her, that they were in some unfathomable way against her, and she left no one in any doubt about her feelings. Under these pressures, the Prince was not always solicitous. Burdened by the workload of his own official life, lacking the emotional support at home to which, in his romantic fashion, he had for so long aspired, and drained by the persistence of his wife's reproaches, he did sometimes rebuff her. Yet when she was dejected or in tears, he tried to console her and he rarely offered any rebuke for what his friends judged to be her waywardness. If his ministrations were inadequate and – given his public duties – intermittent, they lacked neither sincerity nor compassion, as the Princess herself confided to their mutual friends both verbally and in her correspondence.

Later, it was to be widely reported that during this period the Princess was driven to make several 'suicide bids', which were interpreted as 'cries for help' by those friends of the Princess who apparently disclosed them to Morton. When she 'threw herself against a glass display cabinet' or 'slashed at her wrists with a razor blade' or 'cut herself on the serrated edge of a lemon slicer' or 'cut her chest and thighs' with a penknife, her friends – as interpreted by their interlocutor – reported that her husband had 'scorned her' in the belief that 'she was faking her problems'. They had evidently been led to believe this alarming behaviour had in significant measure been caused by her husband's alleged indifference towards her, and specifically by his presumed infidelity with Camilla Parker Bowles.[2] Such incidents did indeed occur, and they were intensely distressing to those who witnessed them. Mercifully, however, the cuts were always less serious than they at first appeared; they drew blood but a sticking plaster invariably sufficed to stem the bleeding.

Those few who knew precisely what had happened were left as shocked and uncomprehending as they knew the Prince to be. However, they also observed his attempts to console his wife even when, as often happened, she rejected his efforts. However incompetent he may have been (and he laid no claim to any special understanding of such behaviour), it was clear to his friends in whom he confided his bewilderment that he felt tenderness and pity for his wife when she was stricken by these apparently inexplicable moods. Anxious to prevent any whisper of her distress from reaching the outside world, it was only when he had finally convinced himself that she was in need of specialist care that, in the autumn of 1982, he arranged for her to see a psychiatrist.

In trying to help her, it may be presumed that the psychiatrist asked about her family background. He was told about the Princess's 'broken' home; that her mother Frances had left her husband to marry another man when Diana was six years old; that Ruth Fermoy, Diana's maternal grandmother, had urged the Divorce Court to give custody to her son-in-law rather than her own daughter; that her father, doting but disconsolate, had later married Raine, the daughter of the romantic novelist Barbara Cartland; that the rift between the Spencer children and their stepmother had been unbridgeable; and that these traumas had blighted her entire upbringing.

The Prince remained exceptionally anxious. Able to confide only in his closest friends, he was often forlorn as, in his efforts to support the Princess, he looked for signs of progress. 'The trouble is one day I think some steps are being made uphill only to find that we've slid back one and a half steps the following day,' he wrote to one of their friends. 'Things were looking hopeful today and the "learning curve" was encouraging, but this afternoon a heavy feeling descended. I do hope this week will help a bit . . .'[3] It was not for lack of effort on the part of either of them that she was able to escape only intermittently from a pattern of behaviour that steadily wore away the insubstantial foundations on which their marriage had been constructed.

The following March, the Prince and Princess flew to Australia for their first official tour together. As they were to be away for six weeks they decided to take Prince William with them, a decision which prompted much public debate as it was alleged (falsely) that the Princess had defied her mother-in-law's wishes by insisting on taking her small child with her. They established a base at a sheep station called Woomargama in New South Wales. 'I still can't get over our luck in finding such an ideal place,' the Prince wrote to his friends, the van Cutsems, '. . . we were extremely happy there whenever we were allowed to escape. The great joy was that we were totally alone together . . .'[4]

Those moments were infrequent. The official schedule imposed a gruelling round of flights from one state capital to another for a succession of walkabouts, meetings, receptions and banquets. For the Prince, who had by now endured more than fifty official visits abroad, the tour was a repetition of familiar routine, a duty more than a pleasure. For the Princess, who was on her first official visit, the experience was daunting and overwhelming but magical. The adulation of the crowds, which in Brisbane for example exceeded a quarter of a million people, was beyond the experience of either of them. Though the public was warm towards the Prince, it was besotted with the Princess. The newspapers estimated that altogether no fewer than a million Australians turned out to welcome them and to express their adoration for 'Lady Di'.

The Prince did not relish the experience. When he could, he took refuge in music and literature, including Turgenev's *First Love* and *Fire at Sea* and Jung's *Psychological Reflections*, all of which, he wrote, 'help to preserve my sanity and my faith when all is chaos, crowds, cameras, politicians, cynicism, sarcasm and intense scrutiny outside'.[5]

He worried incessantly about the Princess. 'I do feel desperate for Diana,' he wrote to one of their friends. 'There is no twitch she can make without these ghastly, and I'm quite convinced mindless people photographing it . . . What has got into them all? Can't they see further than the end of their noses and to what it is doing to her? How can anyone, let alone a twenty one year old, be expected to come out of all this obsessed and crazed attention unscathed?'[6]

The Princess veered between elation and exhaustion, sometimes terrified by the surge of collective emotion she had aroused by her mere presence, sometimes delighting in her power to woo so many people at once. She relied heavily on her husband's reassuring presence, describing in a letter to one of their friends how he had pulled her out of her shell and taught her how to cope with the pressure; how he had rescued her when she had felt bewildered and swamped; and how she felt reassured by his presence beside her, especially when they were driving through the crowds in an open car when she could discreetly cling on to him for comfort. She heaped praise on him for all that he had taught her, wondering at his skill with people and that he could always find an apt phrase to brighten someone's day. In the warmth of the Australian welcome, she was able to report that the black moods which had assailed her in London had been banished, and that she now felt ashamed about what she referred to as the selfishness of her previous behaviour. The tendency of the crowd to scream 'Lady Di' had sometimes left the Prince unsure and unwanted, she wrote, but each supported the other; she was finding it easier every day to think only of Charles and the job.[7]

The Prince was indeed upstaged and outshone by his wife, a partial eclipse that was not a rewarding experience. Although he had never hungered for the spotlight, it was disconcerting to have it beamed away from him and onto his wife, who was there – both in his own mind and according to protocol – as his consort. Later, with the candour that endeared him to his friends, he would admit to harbouring resentment, yet also to being torn between pride in her performance and dismay – on her behalf – at the excess of idolatry. His wife, he wrote to the van Cutsems, 'has really won all kinds of hearts on this mammoth odyssey. It really has been a terrible baptism of fire for her . . .'[8] And to another friend he wrote, 'She has been marvellous and helps keep me going when I feel a bit gloomy,' although he remained preoccupied by the indignity of the 'circus' in which he and the Princess were obliged to perform:

> The terrifying part, as always in this kind of thing, is that they construct the pedestal; they put you on top of it, they expect you to balance on the beastly thing without ever losing your footing, and because they have engineered the pedestal along come the demolition experts amongst them who are of the breed that enjoy breaking things down. And it is all done for a sort of vicarious entertainment . . . Maybe the wedding, because it was so well done and because it made such a wonderful, almost Hollywood-style, film, has distorted people's view of things? Whatever the case it frightens me and I know for a fact that it petrifies Diana.[9]

After a month in Australia, they went on to New Zealand for a further two weeks, both tired. 'Six weeks is really much too long to keep up one's enthusiasm for the same thing every single day and after three weeks I usually find myself running out of the required steam for all these intensely public things,' he wrote.[10] Although, by way of contrast to Woomargama, they were 'imprisoned' in Government House where they were surrounded by buildings and policemen, they were at least alone with their son, on whom both doted. Some weeks earlier, the Prince had written to Lady Susan Hussey 'I must tell you that your godson couldn't be in better form. He looks horribly well and is expanding visibly and with frightening rapidity. Today he actually crawled for the first time. We laughed and laughed with sheer, hysterical pleasure and now we can't stop him crawling about everywhere. They pick up the idea very quickly, don't they, when they've managed the first move.'[11] In Government House, his son made further advances. 'William now crawls over it at high speed knocking everything off the tables and causing unbelievable destruction,' he wrote to the van Cutsems. 'He will be walking before long and is the greatest possible fun. You <u>may</u> have seen some photographs of him recently when he performed like a true professional in front of the cameras and did everything that could be expected of him. It really is encouraging to be able to provide people with some <u>nice</u> jolly news for a change!'[12]

The weather in New Zealand was damp and dispiriting. At the Anzac memorial service* at the Cenotaph in Auckland it rained relentlessly and the wind was so fierce that the plastic reeds which decorated the arena were blown across the parade ground at high speed. The Prince, whose sense of the absurd rarely deserted him, was distracted from the proper solemnity of the occasion as he watched the reeds run amok:

> Several of them passed between the legs of the service chiefs, going like the clappers, and thudded into the legs of the old Gallipoli veterans sitting around the perimeter! All of this was going on while the poor Archbishop of Canterbury was trying to make himself heard above the wail of the wind across the microphone! The whole thing became rather hysterical and surrealistic, and I had great difficulty keeping a straight face.[13]

---

* To commemorate 25 April 1915, the day that 70,000 Allied troops landed on Turkey's Gallipoli peninsula. Anzac Day is celebrated in New Zealand and Australia, which between them lost about 10,000 men in the seven-month campaign.

They returned to London in triumph and then, a few weeks later, achieved a repeat performance in Canada. The crowds were not so large but they also worshipped at the shrine: the Princess moved through them as graceful and fragile as a madonna, regal but innocent, and the Canadians lost their collective heart to the icon in their presence. In Britain, the commentators were weak at the knees. The Speaker of the House of Commons, George Thomas, was but the most distinguished to gush at such a conquest by the Princess and her husband: 'Not only the Royal Family have gained by their success but the whole nation and the Commonwealth have received a blessing beyond measure . . . In the rapidly changing world that we have I believe that the Prince and Princess of Wales and their son will give us the continuity that assures us stability.'[14]

While she was pregnant with Prince Harry and for six months after his birth, the Princess made no further official visits abroad, preferring to stay at home with her very small children. For much of the time they lived within the shell of a normal marriage, though they still lacked the intimacy and mutual understanding without which the relationship could not grow. As they shared no common interests there was little to talk about except the mundane arrangements that are necessary when two people share the same roof. The Princess had dispensed with the services of her psychiatrist, saying that she was better. However, her swings of mood continued, and there were periods of distress that were exhausting to both of them. At these times, the Princess still appeared to believe not only that the Prince's friends were conspiring against her, but that their very presence in her life was corroding their marriage. She clearly believed that a number of his oldest friends and advisers, including distinguished figures in public life, were, as she put it, 'oilers', sycophants whose influence on his judgement was malign. One by one, friends who in some cases he had known since childhood found themselves suddenly expelled. From a mixture of embarrassment and loyalty to his wife, the Prince evidently could not bring himself to explain his action to them, with the result that they discovered what was happening only when the phone calls stopped, the letters ceased to flow and the invitations to Highgrove and Balmoral failed to arrive.

Among others, the Brabournes, the Romseys, the Palmer-Tomkinsons and Nicholas Soames experienced an ostracism which was not only perplexing but hurt them more deeply than they would at the time admit. In the absence of any ready explanation, they guessed at the cause but never thought to embarrass the Prince by pressing the issue, imagining correctly that his pain was no less than theirs. Apparently in the hope of securing his wife's peace of mind, the Prince was even known to have surrendered his labrador, Harvey, at the Princess's insistence, but for no reason that anyone could fathom. It was to no avail: though they both still tried and though there were interludes of happiness, neither of them was able to reach across the gulf that separated them.

By 1984, the Prince was locked into a routine of official duties abroad that varied in place but not purpose. As the representative of the sovereign, as the Colonel-in-Chief of seven British regiments, and as the patron or president of a burgeoning list of charities, his task was to promote their various activities in all parts of the world.

In February, he represented the Queen at the Independence celebrations in the former British protectorate of Brunei, where he had been warned that 'anything was likely to happen'. 'I decided in advance to take everything as it came and to keep an open mind about the whole operation,' he noted.[15] At the airport, he was greeted by the Sultan's father, Sir Omar Ali Saifuddin, who was seventy years old and in poor health:

> He travelled in an immense Rolls Royce with semi-redundant air-conditioning and, as I subsequently found out, a series of knobs and buttons on the armrest, one of which I pressed only to find myself being squashed up against the roof of the car by an hydraulic seat-lifting device. I then couldn't get the seat to go back to its original position . . .

That evening, he called on the Sultan at his new palace: 'It is rumoured to have cost something in the region of £300,000,000 and has over 1000 rooms . . . I am not surprised that it cost that astronomic sum . . .' After walking through a series of long halls of immense grandeur, he was ushered into a vast octagonal room, empty except for the Sultan, his father, and his three brothers. The Prince sat on a burgundy sofa, perched between the Sultan and his father:

As always on these occasions I heard myself twittering away, repro-
ducing the most nonsensical rubbish while small gentlemen in white
uniforms crawled about on their knees in front of us, pouring out cups
of tea and offering plates of sticky cakes . . . Somehow I survived without saying something totally preposterous and then I thought I ought
to leave and let the Sultan get on with whatever he had to do.
Everyone rose to their feet with an audible sigh of relief and we moved
to another room where I was to present the Sultan with his British
general's sword, epaulettes and sash and also my present, consisting of
a polo cup (which I was told he wanted).

That night, he slept in the Sultan's own villa: 'I sank into bed,
exhausted with jet-lag and the humidity, and to my amazement found
that the modern style four poster bed had a mirror in its canopy! When
I later woke up at 0300, unable to sleep any more, I gave myself an awful
fright upon turning on the light in order to read.'[16]
The following day at the football stadium to watch the celebrations,
the Prince found himself talking with President Marcos of the Philippines
and President Zia of Pakistan:

who seemed to be exchanging notes on the problems they were facing with various subversives! President Suharto of Indonesia came and
shook hands . . . General Prem of Thailand appeared and I wished I
had been more alert and plucked up courage to ask him about the
abominable behaviour of the Thai pirates who rape, plunder and kill
the boatloads of Vietnamese refugees as they set to sea . . . I was told
by the C.O. of the Gurkha battalion stationed in Brunei that the condition in which these wretched people drift up onto the shores of
Brunei is more harrowing and sickening than anything he has seen
elsewhere. The doctor who went in to examine one boatload had to
go out and be sick . . .

The next day, he was required to watch a military parade and was
pleased to see the array of British weaponry on display. Then there was
a steam-past by the navy followed by a fly-past by the air force, all of
which was co-ordinated by a brigadier on secondment from the British
Army. In the evening, he had dinner at the High Commission, where he
enjoyed talking to the British ministers – Richard Luce, Minister of

State at the Foreign Office, and Lord Trefgarne, a junior Defence Minister – and teasing the Foreign Office official accompanying them. It had been a routine state visit, a duty to accomplish, official relations to foster, and very little to nourish the spirit. Nonetheless, he warmed to his hosts: 'I left with an impression of a very friendly and polite people who basically quite like the British, but who are so flushed with the joys of oil that reality seems sometimes to be a long way off.'[17]

The following month, he flew to East Africa to tour Tanzania, Zambia, Zimbabwe and Botswana. In Tanzania, in his role as a director of the Commonwealth Development Corporation, he endured the usual round of pleasantries, including a reception where, he noted wrily for the benefit of his friends, 'perspiring groups of ex-patriates and local people were drawn in labelled "kraals", for all intents and purposes looking like despairing cattle in the yard of an abattoir'. At the dinner at State House, President Nyerere educated him in the objectives of African socialism. Tanzania was at this time arguing over the terms of an International Monetary Fund loan which was only available in return for a package of deflationary measures which, Nyerere insisted, would provoke riots in the streets. The Prince suspected that Tanzania's recovery would be slow, but he was attracted to Nyerere: 'He is a good man with a strong Christian conscience, who lives what he believes, but who also expects everyone else to be able to do the same. He has not yet admitted that human nature requires a degree of pragmatism and compromise in order to avoid total stagnation . . .' He was not entirely persuaded by the President's socialism, however; he had been told about the black market, the corruption and the dire shortage of commodities. He had also picked up the gossip that the President had long been promising to make way for a younger man: 'He intends to retire next year, remain for two years as president of the party and then remove himself to his village. I wonder . . .?!'[18]*

In Zambia, he was met by a large crowd and a guard of honour, 'which performed extremely efficiently but rather ruined things, I thought, by goose-stepping past the dais during the March Past'. At State House, he was greeted by President Kaunda, a ceremony which

---

* Dr Julius Nyerere retired as President in November 1984, but remained a power-ful influence as chairman of the Revolutionary Party of Tanzania (CCM). He had become Prime Minister in 1961, the year Tanzania gained independence, and was elected the country's first President in December 1962.

was momentarily disrupted when, as the Prince noted, 'I put my foot in the mouth of a large lion which was pretending to be a carpet in the Hall.' He visited a sugar cane estate and was duly impressed by a scheme designed to sustain smallholders alongside the sugar mill which was operated by Tate and Lyle. That night, he spent over an hour in private conversation with President Kaunda, who explained his attempts to open up a dialogue with South Africa. If South Africa did not 'unbend', Kaunda foresaw an 'explosion' within three years. They talked also about the structure of village communities and the President was delighted to discover that the two of them shared a common interest in complementary medicine and the role of the 'traditional' doctor in tribal societies. Before the speeches, Kaunda led the entire dining room 'in a wonderfully harmonious party song' which prompted the Prince to muse whether state banquets at Buckingham Palace should be similarly enlivened. The next morning, the Prince said goodbye to the President and once more fell over the lion skin on his way out. He visited a copper mine, and walked so close to the Victoria Falls that he was drenched by 'the smoke that thunders', as the local people had described the spray to Dr Livingstone.

The next day, he arrived in Harare, where he was intrigued to visit an Agricultural Research Station that was applying the principles of 'appropriate' technology advanced by Fritz Schumacher and which the Prince had enthusiastically endorsed. He was especially entranced by 'some magnificent lavatories known as the Blair Privy' which were in experimental use:

They work on the principle of a pit with a concrete top and a hole in the middle and a plastic chimney pipe about 7 or 8 feet high (all built into a grass hut). The great problem with the traditional privies has been the frightful smell from the pit and the flies, which spread all sorts of nasty diseases. This privy works on the basis of the wind blowing across the top of the chimney and causing an updraught in the pit which takes the smells up the pipe. When the flies come in they are attracted by the light at the top of the pipe and get trapped by some gauze. Eventually they expire and drop back in the pit![19]

On another day, they visited an archaeological site, a twelfth-century settlement and a traditional shrine. While the Prince and his party were there, they were drenched by a tropical storm. A few days before the Prince's arrival, the witch doctors had asked the government if they could gather in their black robes in the 'holy of holies' in the centre of the ruins, there to make magic to bring the rains in order to relieve the severe drought by which Zimbabwe, like other parts of East Africa, was severely afflicted. The Prince had been told that the government had forbidden these rites out of fear that if they were to succeed, its authority would be undermined. 'So you can imagine my satisfaction,' the Prince noted, 'when, on reaching the self-same "holy of holies" the heavens opened and we all got wet.'

The Prince had looked forward to the presidential dinner. He had met Robert Mugabe at the Independence celebrations in 1980 and hoped for further good conversation. He was disappointed, therefore, when Mugabe was uncommunicative. As on many other similar occasions, the Prince did not take offence, treating what might have been regarded as churlish by others as a phenomenon of presidential anthropology. Instead, he spoke to Mrs Mugabe, who suffered from a painful kidney disease and whom he thought was 'unbelievably brave, amusing and vivacious'. With her he enjoyed a long conversation that was filled with 'endless laughter'.[20]

From Zimbabwe he flew to Gaborone, the capital of Botswana, for another round of pump-priming duty. Among the letters he sent out from the High Commission was one to Nicholas Soames in which he described in admiration the part played by British firms in the countries he had visited: 'I have met masses of consultants and engineers and it reminds me of just how much business is won by British firms overseas in the midst of fierce competition. Not nearly enough people realise how much goes on outside the UK . . .' But he also reflected gloomily on the state of Africa:

Is all this development really progress? Why is it they all want to become carbon copies of western industrialised societies with all the consequent disadvantages of crime, pollution, overcrowding, unemployment, squalid little houses in interminable lines? I know the removal of physical drudgery and the availability of health care etc. are powerful and understandable incentives, but the horror of it all is to witness that loss of human dignity and individuality which inevitably accompanies the change and to see the disintegration of traditional societies with their strong sense of community and their equally powerful sense of family.[21]

Although he genuflected in the direction of social advance, there was a note of privileged nostalgia in judgements like this which failed to acknowledge that even 'squalid little houses' might seem like palaces to those who lived in hovels surrounded by the stench of poverty. As his friends pointed out, but more often to each other than to him directly, the anguished outbursts of this kind in which the Prince was often apt to indulge might have had greater resonance if he had taken the time to think through the predicament that he had so trenchantly identified. Yet at least his eyes were open and his conscience was active as he worried away at problems that were quite beyond his power to resolve, but for which he was never able to shuffle off a lurking sense of responsibility. If he condemned the folly of mankind too freely and if he complained too often that no one would heed his warnings, at least he did not pass by on the other side – as he was perfectly entitled to do.

In August, he was in Papua New Guinea to open the new parliament building in Port Moresby on behalf of the Queen. It had been a twenty-three-hour flight and as a result he felt as though 'someone had kicked an entire sandpit into my eyes and had then tied a series of lead weights onto each limb'. Soon after his arrival, he was taken to Government House. He was relieved to discover that the Prime Minister had become rather more pragmatic than he had seemed at the Independence cele-brations nine years earlier, when he had been surrounded by 'all sorts of hairy Australian left-wing intellectuals and crypto-economists' who were all vying for his attention in their efforts to conduct 'various post-colonial ideological experiments on the country'.[22]

At a state dinner attended by the Commonwealth regional heads of government, including Bob Hawke of Australia and David Lange from New Zealand, the Prince once found himself 'twittering on', attempt-ing to make sensible conversation:

I saw the Kiwis, the Aussies and the Brits all doing the same while the others merely sat and contemplated the infinite by looking straight through the person sitting opposite them. Who has got it right? It is on these occasions that the real difference between eastern and west-ern cultures is observed. I sometimes wonder whether the people who sit throughout 2½ to 3 hours of dinner without uttering scarcely a word are in fact picking up a kind of thought transference from their neighbours by remaining silent? Slowly but surely I am beginning to indulge in little periods of silence – until the noise of clattering knives and forks becomes unbearable and the urge to say something provocative and outrageous becomes irresistible![23]

He duly opened the new parliament building, which he liked because it combined the best of traditional Papuan design with 'a suitably contemporary feel'. This was followed by much local dancing, some of which was deliciously suggestive. Dining for Britain yet again the following evening, his spirits were restored by the arrival of a troop of almost naked dancers who gyrated between the tables of bemedalled and dinner-jacketed grandees. After the Prince had made a speech the dancers started again, 'much to the disgust of some of the wives', the Prince observed, 'who had already had a series of naked flapping bosoms whizz past their faces on the first occasion'.[24]

Over the next three days, he criss-crossed Papua New Guinea, making speeches, seeing development projects, meeting regional leaders and receiving exotic gifts. On the last day, he flew to Manus Island, two hundred miles from Papua New Guinea. He was taken ceremoniously ashore in an outrigger canoe sitting cross-legged on a table:

I was then greeted by a bare-bosomed lady MP whom I met looking very smart in Parliament House a few days before, and conducted by her and several other bare-chested maidens to a pavilion where I was to be girded with dog's teeth necklaces and a dog's teeth head band. I was then given a very heavy bunch of betel nuts and had a spear thrust into my hand, followed by a small adse. That done, I had to wave the spear in the air and shout 'Woro, woro, woro, oi peopl bilong Manus mi hamamas tru!'. That apparently made me a local chief or Lapan.[25]

There were other foreign trips: to France for the commemoration of the role played by the US 6th Airborne Division in the Allied landings of 1944; to Monaco to attend a gala in aid of the United World Colleges; and to the Netherlands as Colonel-in-Chief of the Parachute Regiment for the 40th Anniversary of the Battle of Arnhem. In the spring of 1985, he visited the Parachute Regiment in Norway and the Welsh Guards in Germany, then later in the year set off on an official visit to Italy.

He had been there only once before – and then for just two days in Trieste the previous autumn, to visit the United World College at Duino – but had long been in love with the idea of Italy. His grandmother, Queen Elizabeth, had spent childhood holidays on the Mediterranean coast and as a young woman had travelled extensively through the cultural hinterland. She had described to him the magic of the great Italian cities, of Renaissance architecture, paintings and sculpture. His parents, whose teenage years had been overshadowed by war, had never discovered the delights of Italy and as a child the Prince had never wanted to abandon the family retreats at Sandringham and Balmoral. Now, at the age of thirty-six, he approached the chance to immerse himself in his grandmother's vision with rare excitement.

The media, especially the Italian media, were obsessed with the Princess. Following the birth of Prince Harry in September the previous year, this was her third official tour with her husband. The Italian press was agog to see what she would wear and the British media exulted that the aura of the British Princess should have such magnetic power; no detail of her clothes or demeanour was too slight to be ignored by the tabloid media of either country. The daily entries in the Prince's diary suggest that the character of the nation that welcomed the royal couple in Sardinia on their arrival from London on 19 April had little in common with the frenzied obsessions attributed to it by the media of both countries:

> It was lunchtime and a glorious day and there seemed to be a substantial crowd on the tarmac. Here and there were scattered the resplendent, be-feathered figures of the *carabinieri* in full dress; the press caged in the special pen and a guard of honour stretched along the length of an immense red carpet. The aircraft taxied to a halt and there ensued a wonderful comic interlude as the man driving the aircraft steps had several attempts lining up his recalcitrant staircase with the aircraft's door . . . After inspecting the Guard of Honour (an extraordinarily painless affair in Italy); and having plunged into a wonderfully joyful and welcoming crowd, which warmed the cockles of the heart, we were whisked off to a lunch at a place called Porto Rotondo, further down the coast. All along the route, we passed

groups of smiling, clapping Sardinians who invariably pointed at us and cried out 'Eccoli!' . . .

Wonderful and special though Italian food is, the trouble is you never know when it is coming to an end! The courses arrive thick and fast and in this case we were eating spaghetti, which I thought rather unfair when you are trying to be polite and on your best behaviour.[26]

Later in the afternoon, they were driven to the royal yacht *Britannia*, which was to take them up the coast to La Spezia. In the naval base there, he admired the armaments on an Italian naval frigate, but was very much more impressed by the galley: 'Each man had his own small bottle of red wine for lunch and the food being prepared was of excellent quality, with piles of fresh vegetables heaped on the galley tables. It is just as well that the Italian Navy hardly ever leaves the Med.!'[27] From La Spezia they drove to Pisa and then flew immediately to Milan. He was so looking forward to going to the opera at La Scala that – for once – he did not complain at the failure of the *prefettura* to provide hot water for a bath, interpreting the failure of the geyser as one of the native charms of Italy.

Horrified to discover that the RAF had dropped a bomb on the Opera House in 1943, he was fascinated by the boxes that line the auditorium from floor to ceiling and bemused by the enthusiasm of the audience when he and the Princess took their places:

I had been told that both national anthems would be played when we moved into the box, but nothing happened and still we were standing acknowledging the prolonged applause from the audience. We might have stood there for ages more unless I had slowly realised there was no conductor on the rostrum, so we sat down hurriedly, much to the relief of the long-suffering audience.[28]

The performance of Puccini's *Turandot* – 'a huge orchestra with endless gongs and drums etc. and spectacular scenery and sets' – was of a grandeur that he contrasted favourably with Covent Garden, 'with its shrunken grant and somewhat improvised arrangements'. It was, he wrote, 'an evening I shall never forget'.[29]

His romance with Italy was stimulated even more by seeing Leonardo's *Last Supper* in the Church of Santa Maria delle Grazie, where he noticed that the heads of the disciples resembled one or two of the drawings in the Leonardo collection at Windsor Castle. It was Florence, however, which fired his undying passion. The Prince and Princess stayed with Sir Harold Acton* in his fifteenth-century villa, La Pietra, which commanded a magnificent view over the city. The old historian greeted them at the front door, 'a taller figure than I had expected, with a slight stoop, a somewhat shuffling gait and an irrepressible twinkle in his eye which betrayed a great sense of mischief and a wonderfully dry humour'.

The following day, he woke early:

The day dawned clear and blue and as I lay in bed I could see those magical hills of Tuscany, about which I had heard so much, looking like a pale watercolour through my open window . . . I was already in a state of excitement at the thought of seeing Florence for the first time and after breakfast I read Sir Harold's introduction to a huge book on Florence which had been sent to us.[30]

Their first visit of the day was to the Church of St Minias, which has an exterior in marble of white and green. Beautiful though that was, the interior was even more impressive: 'I could <u>physically</u> feel my spirit being lifted (if that isn't a contradiction in terms) as I entered the Church,' he wrote, 'and when we were shown a small side chapel of such perfection it is hard to describe, decorated with the most exquisite Luca della Robbia terracottas in blue and white, I actually felt moved to tears.'[31]

He hurried to absorb all that he could see in the space of four days. In between, he climbed up to the top of the tower at La Pietra to sketch and paint until he was summoned prematurely for one of the many receptions and dinners which punctuated the tour. On 24 April, after visiting Santa Croce and the Duomo, he wrote, 'I find that my head and my heart are reeling from the sheer concentration of unadulterated beauty, whether it be architectural, sculptural, artistic or horticultural, in this astonishing city.' The intensity of his own response led him to conclude that none of the great artists by whom he had been so moved could have achieved such perfection without being driven by a 'dramatic

---

* Sir Harold Acton (1904–94), writer, aesthete, critic and historian who listed 'barbarians' as one of his recreations in *Who's Who*.

religious inspiration'.[32] He poured his soul into his diary, writing with intoxication about the colour of the houses, the intimacy of the streets, and the profusion of purple wisteria cascading over high walls, describing every detail as if the memory of it would disappear unless he had captured it in those pages.

From Florence the royal party went to Rome, where the Prince had to call on the President of the Senate, Signor Cossiga. The President was not happy. Apparently, the BBC had referred to him in a news bulletin as the 'head of the Sardinian Mafia'. The Prince was entertained to watch the British ambassador 'using every ounce of his diplomatic skill to try and smooth things over – "You must remember, Signor Presidente, that in Britain we use the term 'mafia' in a very wide sense, like the 'Whitehall mafia' for example." It was pure "Yes, Minister".'[33]

After the Senate, he went to the Chamber of Deputies, and then, with the Princess, he called on Signor Craxi, the Prime Minister:

He was definitely not what the Italians call 'simpatico' but then I daresay you need other attributes if you are going to succeed in holding together a coalition of five parties and remain as P.M. for two years . . . What has intrigued me in Italy has been the number of ministers and politicians who have implied that they can't stand the political system in their country – or rather the electoral, proportional system – which produces what the Finance Minister describes as an impossible system.*

From the Prime Minister's villa the Prince went to visit the headquarters of the Food and Agricultural Organisation of the United Nations. He was not impressed. 'I must admit', he noted:

that I find these organisations rather hard to take. I know this one does some splendid work in the technical assistance field, but out of the

---

* In 1993, swamped by a wave of scandals involving the highest echelons of government which led to the most severe political crisis in Italy's post-war history, the deputies voted to discard proportional representation in favour of a 'first past the post' electoral system. Whether that will prove less 'impossible' than proportional representation remains to be seen. In July 1994, Signor Craxi was sentenced, *in absentia*, to eight and a half years' imprisonment for fraud.

9,500 employees, 3,500 are in the Rome H.Q. Is it <u>really</u> necessary to have so many people shuffling paper about when some of them could be better employed out 'in the field' perhaps? Out of a budget of £400 million the vast majority is used up in admin. costs. In order to carry out projects in the field they have to seek sponsorship from other U.N. agencies and outside bodies. The 'jobs for the boys' aspect is the one that aggravates me . . .[34]

There were more official luncheons and dinners, visits to the Forum and the Pantheon, and a wreath-laying ceremony in the allied cemetery at Anzio, where a piper from the Gordon Highlanders played 'a most moving lament' as the Prince and Princess walked along the rows of headstones 'with their tragic and heart-rending inscriptions'.[35]

On 29 April, the royal couple were driven to the Vatican for an audience with the Pope: 'As we were swept through archway after archway and courtyard after courtyard it was only too obvious that everything was designed to make the visitor feel smaller and smaller and less and less significant as he approached the ultimate presence.' Once inside the Vatican, the Prince and Princess waited for a few minutes in an ante-chamber, where the Prince was obliged to conduct a stilted conversation with a French cardinal who either could not, or would not, speak in English. Then they were conducted along vast corridors and through great reception rooms, dramatically decorated by huge frescos depicting every kind of biblical and mythological catastrophe, until they finally reached the presence of His Holiness. The Pope greeted them both warmly: 'He took us into an enormous high-ceilinged room which had a desk at one end, behind which he sat, and two chairs in front of it on which we placed ourselves.' After reminiscing about his early life in Poland, the Pope went on to speak of his mistrust of 'liberation theology' – an antipathy which the Prince shared with the Pontiff. The Prince noted in his diary:

We then talked about unity between the different branches of the Christian faith, especially the Anglican, and I raised the problem of the 1896 bull which effectively declared the Anglican orders null and void. He said he thought that was past history. He also said he thought the Anglican Church was in fact closer to the Catholics than the Orthodox at the present time.[36]

The Princess asked the Pope about the stomach wound he had received in an assassination attempt two years before. The question elicited a moment of unexpected bathos. 'While asking him', the Prince noted:

> she patted her tummy to indicate where he had been shot, but he didn't seem to understand what she was saying and replied with a beatific smile that she was the creator of life and seemed to bless her tummy – presumably, Diana surmised, because he mistook her as saying she was pregnant! I can only imagine it was something to do with the immaculate spaghetti we had been having . . .![37]

After an audience of some forty minutes, the Prince asked the Pope to bless them – 'which he did very briefly by making the sign of the cross over us'.

Earlier in their forty-minute audience, the Prince broached a delicate matter which had embarrassed relations between the Vatican and the Palace: 'I apologised to him for the confusion over our possible attendance at his private chapel the following morning and said how much I admired the spiritual leadership he so clearly provided in such a difficult and uncertain world.'[38]

The Prince could have had no idea that at that very moment the wires had started to hum between the Vatican and London with a sensational story that was to provoke banner headlines the following day in every British newspaper: 'Prince's Mass Cancelled'[39]; 'The Queen banned Prince Charles and Princess Diana from attending a secret mass with the Pope . . .'[40]; 'The Prince of Wales is said to be highly indignant that he cannot join the Pope at Mass'.[41]

Despite strenuous efforts by the Palace to conceal the facts which lay behind these headlines, a source inside the Vatican had leaked just enough of a complicated truth to cause mayhem. The background to the subsequent furore sheds light not only on the Prince's own attitude towards the Christian religion, but also on relations between the Catholic Church and the Church of England, and more especially between both of them and the Palace.

With Robert Runcie as Archbishop of Canterbury, the apostles of ecumenicism had enjoyed a high noon of optimism in the early years of the eighties. In the spring of 1982, the Pope visited Britain on a pastoral visit which had not only inspired most Christians but had also thrilled secular opinion. The high point of a spectacularly successful tour was a service at Canterbury Cathedral, where the Pope and the Archbishop of Canterbury knelt together in prayer in an historic act of reconciliation. Many in the congregation and watching on television were moved to tears. The Prince, as heir apparent and prospective Supreme Governor of the Church of England, sat in the place usually occupied by the sovereign and was later photographed in conversation with the Pope before a brief private audience with him in the Deanery. The 'Celebration of Faith', as the service had been ecumenically entitled, was a resounding triumph not only of Christian goodwill but of public relations as well.

The Prince's presence at the celebration had been the subject of much heart-searching within the Palace. Some months earlier, in November 1981, the Archbishop of Canterbury had written to the Prince and Princess of Wales inviting them to attend the service. The Prince at once instructed his private secretary to put the date in his diary, adding, 'I hope this won't cause you apoplexy . . .'[42] Adeane communicated the Prince's intention to the Queen's private secretary, Sir Philip Moore, who in due course reported back to Adeane that the Queen, in her role as the Supreme Governor of the Church of England, had consented to her son's presence at Canterbury so long as he attended as a lay member of the congregation and not as a participant.[43] The way was cleared for a formal invitation from the Archbishop, who wrote of 'the great personal encouragement' that the Prince's presence would give him personally and how much it would delight 'your many loyal admirers in Canterbury'.[44]

Lambeth Palace had embraced the papal visit with greater enthusiasm than Downing Street, which was more sensitive to Protestant feeling beyond the Church of England. To distinguish between the Pope's 'pastoral' visit and the full obsequies accorded a state visit, it had been decided that the route to be taken by the Pope on his way to an audience with the Queen should be via Birdcage Walk rather than The Mall, the traditional route for such formal occasions – though no-one beyond the charmed circle of Whitehall appeared even to notice the intended message. It made precious little difference: as a senior courtier at the Palace had predicted, the use of the glass-bubble 'popemobile' and the presence of a vast crowd – far larger than for any mere state visit – turned the Pope's journeys to and from Buckingham Palace into 'triumphal progresses'[45] which rivalled even those of the Supreme Governor herself.

The delicacy of the moment was complicated by the war in the South Atlantic between Britain and Argentina over the disputed group of islands which Margaret Thatcher's electorate called the Falklands and the Pope's vast flock in Latin America knew as the Malvinas. Even three weeks before his scheduled arrival His Holiness had not finally decided whether to step on British soil, while the Prime Minister was still uncertain whether to lend her presence to the service in Canterbury. In the event, Margaret Thatcher stayed away, citing her responsibilities in the War Cabinet. To forestall adverse speculation, the announcement from the Palace, four days before the service, that the Prince of Wales would be in the congregation at Canterbury included the phrase, 'the Government are aware that his Royal Highness is to attend the service and welcome the fact'.[46]

The news provoked a predictable outcry from the evangelical wing of the Protestant Church. 'We cannot now, in conscience, refrain from conveying to your Royal Highness an expression of the pain and regret we have experienced on learning of your intention to attend divine service in which the Roman Pontiff will participate,' the Moderator of the Free Church of Scotland wrote in reprimand. 'We fear that the false and blasphemous claims of the Papacy may be given more credence by your Royal Highness' attendance at this service.'[47] Harbouring a long-standing disdain for the artifice, as he saw it, of the conflict between the Anglican Church and the papacy, the Prince was unmoved. He believed with intensity that by symbolic gestures of the kind proposed he could play a small part in helping to bridge a destructive gulf.

By 1985, relations between the Vatican and Lambeth Palace were warmer than ever. In this climate, the Prince wanted to use his visit to Italy to make a further gesture of reconciliation towards Rome. Accordingly, Adeane was dispatched to Lambeth Palace and to the Home Office (the government department responsible for advising Buckingham Palace on the constitutional implications of inter-faith relations) to take soundings. They discussed a range of options. The Archbishop favoured 'a special service' in St Peter's to celebrate what would have been the first formal act of reconciliation between the papacy and the royal family since the excommunication of Henry VIII. However, it was agreed that for the Prince to 'participate' in a Roman Catholic service might be taken to imply his acceptance of the authority of Rome, while merely to 'attend' such a service might seem patronising to the Vatican, which, as Adeane reported the consensus of the meeting, 'would still cause an awful flap at home'.[48]

Instead, it was agreed that the Prince and Princess should attend the Pope's domestic eucharist in his private chapel. As the Prince would not partake of communion, there would be no breach of his constitutional position as Supreme Governor-designate; only 'the extreme minority' who rejected the Pope's spiritual and ecclesiastical position could dissent. Likewise, recognising the force of the Home Office reservations about his own original preference, the Archbishop declared that by attending a private mass in the Vatican, the Prince would be far more effective than 'any number of theoretical statements by ecclesiastics' in moving the Pope more firmly in favour of ecumenicism. Moreover, by thus confronting His Holiness 'with Anglican piety and commitment at the highest level', the Prince would cause scandal in Britain only to 'a few on the lunatic fringe'.[49] Crucially, the Moderator of the General Assembly of the Church of Scotland also gave his personal blessing to the project.

The proposal was duly conveyed to the Vatican, where it was favourably received. Soon afterwards it received the Pope's blessing and the detailed planning for the private mass was put in hand. As part of this process the decision was taken early in April to impose a news 'blackout' on the occasion, which would be lifted only retrospectively. A press statement was even prepared for after the service which was designed to emphasise that the royal couple had attended the papal mass 'without receiving communion'.[50]

In the absence of any better explanation for this elaborate curtain of secrecy, it may be presumed that the intention had been to forestall a public fracas with 'the lunatic fringe'. A letter to the Prince from the Secretary of the Religion and Morals Committee of the Free Presbyterian Church of Scotland condemning his planned audience with the Pope (which had been announced before the proposal for the private mass had been finalised) gives some idea of the wrath which lurked in some evangelical breasts:

We would respectfully remind Your Royal Highness that the Pope of Rome was identified by our Reformers, and is still identified as 'the man of sin' revealed in scripture (11 Thessalonians, chapter 2, verses 3 and 4), and history has confirmed that his emissaries have been responsible for the bloodshed of many in the name of Christianity, of which he remains unrepentant, at least publicly . . . We affirm that, in our opinion, it is quite unnecessary for Your Royal Highness to visit the Pope of Rome who seeks to deprive us of the liberty of the Gospel . . . we must advise Your Royal Highness against such a proposed visit, against which, if our plea is ineffectual, we most vehemently protest.[51]

At this juncture, only two weeks before the celebration of the secret mass which had by now been fixed for the early morning of 30 April (the day after the royal audience with the Pope), the entire plan was suddenly scuppered, to the acute embarrassment of all involved. As this débâcle was reported in *The Times*' Diary on 16 April, 'A request by Prince Charles to attend a papal mass in the Vatican has been refused after a top level decision taken in the past 24 hours, involving Buckingham Palace, Church leaders and the diplomatic corps.' The unnamed source for this carefully placed snippet was the Queen's press office, which had contrived this pre-emptive strike to limit the damage that a less economical version of the truth would have been bound to cause. Guided by the Palace, *The Times*' columnist wrote, 'Besides the fear of protests from protestant loyalists, I am told objections were raised at the weekend within the hierarchy of the Church of Scotland, although the Moderator, the Right Revd John Paterson, is understood to have given the prince his personal blessing. I am told the agreement of the Archbishop of Canterbury was also given.'[52]

In the weekend press, there had been some exceptionally hazy speculation about the royal couple sharing in an act of worship with the Pope. It is quite possible, therefore, that at this stage some members of the Church of Scotland did indeed voice objections to the support given by their Moderator for the Prince's initiative. However, even if these doubts had reached the ears of the Palace, they could not have been decisive in the cancellation of the mass. As Paterson himself later insisted, the Church of Scotland neither objected nor applied pressure on the Palace. The first he had learnt of the alleged opposition of his Church was in *The Times*' report which the Palace had instigated.

What Buckingham Palace had failed to tell *The Times*' diarist was that, until the very last moment, the Queen's private secretary, Sir Philip Moore, had himself not been aware of the private mass. Thus in a serious breach of protocol, the issue had not been raised with the Queen. As a result, with only a fortnight to go, the Supreme Governor of the Church of England had been given no opportunity fully to consider the constitutional implications of her son's attendance at the Pope's mass. It may be presumed that the Queen was less than pleased at this oversight. In any case, in the days before *The Times* reported the Palace version of why the mass had been cancelled, the Queen had a long meeting with her son. Whether or not the Prince was 'indignant' with his mother, as the press subsequently reported, is a matter of conjecture. The outcome is not. On 15 April, a message was relayed from the Prince's office to the Holy See: the Prince would not after all attend the mass on which he had set his heart so many months before.

Apparently unaware of his colleague's exchanges with *The Times*, the Prince's private secretary, Edward Adeane, hoped at first to conceal the fact that a papal mass had even been considered. Accordingly, he agreed with Sir William Heseltine that the Palace press office would merely respond to inquiries by saying that 'a number of ideas were considered for the Vatican programme but that the programme that has emerged will involve only an audience with the Pope . . .'[53] As *The Times*' rivals failed to pursue the story, it seemed for a while that the ruse would work. It was wrecked by the 'sources' at the Vatican who told any journalist who cared to listen that, but for a last-minute cancellation, the Prince would have taken part in an historic act of reconciliation with the Church of Rome. According to these 'sources', the Queen's decisive opinion that a mass would be 'inopportune' had been relayed to the British ambassador to the Holy See, Sir Mark Heath. He was reported to have been 'surprised and embarrassed by the news'[54] – as well he might have been, given his intimate involvement in the detailed preparations for the event.

In public, various courtiers and officials did their self-contradictory best to limit the damage. None of them was any more effective than the hapless Victor Chapman, the Prince's press secretary. Assiduously contradicting the Vatican 'sources', he insisted that the mass had only been cancelled because it had been impossible to fit it into the schedule. 'It was', he declared, 'a logistical rather than an ecumenical decision.'[55] No-one believed him.

The controversy provoked by the cancellation of the mass was sustained and predictable. Prominent Catholics mourned a missed opportunity, Revd Ian Paisley thundered that any 'communion' between the throne and the See of Rome would be a defiance of the law, and the

Archbishop of York, Dr John Habgood, soothingly contradicted him.

A measure of the Prince's own feelings about the cancellation may be gleaned from his response to a letter which arrived some weeks later from the Moderator of the Free Presbyterian Church of Scotland, the Revd John MacLeod. Informing the Prince that 'the Westminster Confession of Faith, Chapter 29, Section 2, says the mass "is most abominably injurious to Christ's one, only sacrifice . . ."', and that 'reconciliation to the see of Rome could jeopardise Your Royal Highness' right to succession', MacLeod vouchsaved on behalf of his Synod that the Prince was being 'ill-advised in spiritual matters by some who have departed from the true teaching of the inspired, infallible and inerrant way of God . . .'[56]

The Prince was moved to draft a reply to this diatribe in forthright language. Reminding MacLeod that the proposed service had only been countenanced after close consultation with the Archbishop of Canterbury, the Moderator of the General Assembly of the Church of Scotland and the Home Office, he wrote, 'I would like to ask by what divine grace you have decided you have the monopoly of truth in this matter?' Castigating 'bigotry and prejudice in all its forms', he informed MacLeod that these failings were 'the main cause of so much human suffering and misery'.[57] The letter was not dispatched. A note on the typed draft from a member of his staff instructed, 'On no account is this letter to be sent.' Instead, the Prince was prevailed upon to allow his private secretary to respond on his behalf in a noncommittal reply rather less calculated to fan the flames of religious intolerance.

For the final leg of the Italian tour, the Prince was joined by the portrait painter, John Ward. Together they filled every spare moment between official visits and sight-seeing tours, sketching the landscape from the verandah deck of the royal yacht. 'As a result,' the Prince noted, 'I have been picking up some very useful hints and new techniques, the best of which is the value of a piece of white chalk. It has revolutionised the whole exercise for me! The only trouble is that while I am rubbing out my second drawing effort of a particular subject John is already painting another picture altogether, having finished the subject I am doing long before!'[58]

On 4 May, they sailed into Venice for the final weekend of their tour. Both the Prince and Princess were up early:

There was something uniquely exciting about entering the lagoon from the sea, in a ship, with all those remarkably familiar landmarks beginning to come into view and then to slip past as we continued up the harbour. We glided past the Doge's Palace and St Mark's Square, with the previous night's high tide sitting in glistening puddles here and there; past the entrance to the Grand Canal and the great white, domed shape of the Salute Cathedral on one side of it and on up the main canal until we could turn round in a wider area. All down the waterfront there were lots of little shops and restaurants with chefs, waiters, butchers and cleaning ladies standing outside them and waving dishcloths and towels etc . . .[59]

Britannia eventually berthed close to St Mark's Cathedral and the royal couple began a final round of cultural tourism. Unable to share the intensity of her husband's experience, the Princess disguised her ennui with a dazzling performance that, for the Italian public and the tourists who thronged their route, confirmed her status as a sublime presence amongst them. Her elegance and her beauty, the innocence of her poise and the modesty of her smile, were surpassing in their effect on men and women alike. For many millions of people, she was an apparition, real yet intangible, nearly available but almost ethereal: her mere presence was enough to intoxicate the surrounding atmosphere.

As he had been in Australia, the Prince was acutely sensitive to this response, aware that while there was warmth for him the adulation was for his wife. He could not resist a twinge of resentment that was sharpened by his own gnawing insecurity. Yet, in Italy, he was himself so enthralled by the glories about him that he was for once able to banish the sense of inferiority that so often debilitated him. 'I long to return to wander unmolested amongst the buildings and to see the pictures,' he noted at the end of his diary as *Britannia* left Venice with him, the Princess and their two children, who had joined them for a private holiday, but he concluded, 'It was still memorable.'[60]

CHAPTER
NINETEEN

———◆—◆———

I n a conscious exploitation of his unique ability to summon almost
anyone from almost anywhere, the Prince had been led to investigate
a broadening spectrum of public issues. In the process, he was struck
by the rigidity of the Establishment, and became increasingly frustrated
by the lack of communication and the rivalry that he came across in relations between competing groups in government, the civil service, local
authorities, industry, commerce and the voluntary sector. Issuing invitations to luncheon or dinner at Kensington Palace or Highgrove – which
few individuals were able to resist – he presided over a growing number
of informal meetings and seminars, trying to nudge his guests towards a
resolution of the conflicts that divided them.

His appetite for such endeavour was usually inspired by a sudden shaft
of intuition, though a passing encounter with a persuasive supplicant
sometimes sufficed. In either case he was exceptionally demanding of his
staff, bombarding them with notes and instructions and insisting on
immediate responses. Long-suffering though most of them were, one or
two complained to each other that the Prince's enthusiasms too often
bore the imprint of the last conversation he had held or the latest article
to have caught his eye. They respected his concern and his compassion
but were uncomfortable with his tendency to reach instant conclusions
on the basis of insufficient thought. There is no doubt that he did leap
to judgement but, as other officials observed, his intuition did not often
let him down. He approached new ideas like a swimmer diving among

rocks: sometimes he discovered a pearl and sometimes he banged himself on the head.

In these circumstances, the impression of order and precision conveyed by the Prince's entourage on public occasions concealed a disarray in his private office that he found hard to comprehend and impossible to rectify. Under intense pressure to meet the Prince's ever-shifting needs, a team of four officials supported by a dozen secretaries and typists found themselves reacting haphazardly to the flow of princely enthusiasms. No-one thought to complain openly but disorder was rife. Letters, which arrived each week in their hundreds, piled up, unsorted and unanswered. With only the crudest system for categorising such a weight of correspondence, it was difficult to distinguish the urgent from the important or the insignificant from the crackpot. Classified documents sent across from the Foreign Office were frequently left in the office unread for days.

One of the Prince's assistant private secretaries, David Roycroft, on secondment from the Foreign Office, tried to impose some discipline on the office by establishing a rudimentary filing system and ensuring that the 'bags' sent up to the Prince each day were at least colour-coded according to priority (though this by no means guaranteed that the Prince read his papers in the desired order). By these and other basic means, Roycroft managed to superimpose a vestigial discipline on the office, an achievement for which his successors were abidingly grateful.

Edward Adeane, his private secretary, belonged to the old school of Palace courtiers, honourable and cautious. Though he and the Prince felt mutual respect and affection, Adeane had always found it hard to reconcile himself to the Prince's unconventional enthusiasms and outspoken contributions to public debate and he did not hesitate to say so. Apparently failing to understand the roots of the Prince's convictions and profoundly suspicious of any appeal to intuition over reason, he grew more and more unhappy at his failure to corral the heir apparent within the confines of his narrower vision.

His colleagues also observed that he was ill at ease with the Princess, and sometimes impatient with what he saw as her shortcomings. Her failure to live up to his exacting standards was compounded by what he interpreted as arbitrary dictats. Late in 1984, she sent Adeane a note to the effect that the Prince would no longer be available for meetings early in the morning because he would be upstairs in the nursery after breakfast to be with William. Although Adeane liked the efficiency with which the Princess dealt with her paperwork (which he contrasted favourably with the Prince's more spasmodic approach), Adeane did not disguise from his colleagues his disapproval of this decision.

Early in 1985, after a long succession of disagreements that grew ever sharper with the Prince, Adeane finally tendered his resignation. With a dignity that concealed the chagrin he must have felt at such an untimely end to his career, he departed without any display of resentment, keeping his counsel about a relationship which had foundered on an irreconcilable clash of perspective and personalities.

Michael Colborne, the stalwart of the Prince's office, had already left a few months earlier. More than most of his colleagues, Colborne was aware of the stress and disruption in the Prince's life caused by his wife's erratic behaviour. On several occasions Colborne had been present during one of her bouts of despair; he had watched her tears flow; and on one occasion in Scotland he had spent much of the day alone with her, listening to the clock tick away the hours while she sat with her head bowed in silence, apparently insensible to his presence.

To his yeomanly eye, her general demeanour seemed like something out of a nightmare, beyond all reason and out of control. He also saw the extent to which these episodes drained the Prince of energy and morale. Equally, as a devoted lieutenant, he did not think to protest at the sudden storms of princely temper which occasionally broke about his head, and he bore these tirades with equanimity; but he had begun to lose his appetite for the job, feeling himself trapped between the Prince and Princess – and the experience had taken the sparkle out of his life.

Colborne's discomfort was compounded by another factor that rankled with him. As secretary to the Prince's office, Colborne had been responsible for handling the Prince's personal finances, rather in the manner of a ship's purser. However, he was not a member of the household and his lowly status in the royal hierarchy – which he attributed to the ossified class structure at the Palace – made him unacceptable for the new post of comptroller, which was to be established to regulate the carefree accounting arrangements that the royal couple had inherited from the Prince's bachelor years. He tendered his resignation in the spring of 1984 but was prevailed upon to postpone his departure by the strenuous efforts of, among others, the Queen's former private secretary, Sir Martin Charteris, who well understood how important he had become to the Prince. Colborne finally left at the end of the year; at his final meeting with the Prince both men were close to tears.

The departure of both Adeane and Colborne would have opened the way for a new order in the administration of the Prince's life but for the fact that his staff was quite inadequate to absorb his rapidly growing workload. In 1984, in an attempt to meet the Princess's desire that he should spend more time with her and their children, the Prince briefly pruned his official diary. In 1985, however, he filled the year with more than 240 public engagements; by 1986, the figure had risen to 312; and in 1987 it would rise to 340.* The preparations for these engagements were exhaustive: all required a 'recce' by the private secretary or one of his three assistants; detailed negotiations with the relevant hosts; travel arrangements booked with the royal train or the Queen's Flight; the appropriate security measures agreed between the Prince's personal protection team and the local constabulary; and a comprehensive brief for 'the boss', as they had come to call him. To sustain a treasured reputation for meticulousness in every aspect of the royal passage was taxing enough with such a schedule; to accommodate the Prince's myriad informal and private commitments as well tested his lieutenants to the limit – and sometimes beyond.

After Adeane's departure, Roycroft was temporarily elevated to the status of acting private secretary but, although he was an effective bureaucrat – 'titanically efficient', in the words of one colleague[1] – he lacked a close rapport with the Prince, and at the end of his secondment he returned to the Foreign Office. Yet the Prince was reluctant to have an 'insider' foisted on him by the Palace, and he seized on a suggestion by Sir Charles Villiers, the chairman of the County Bank, that he should find a private secretary with experience in the world of business and finance. Easier to propose than to accomplish, the search took more than six months. It was partly a problem of remuneration – Palace salaries were no match for those of the city – but that was not all. Rumours of the underlying tension between the Prince and the Princess, combined

---

* These figures were compiled by Mr T.C.M. O'Donovan, on the basis of the Court Circular and published in an annual letter to *The Times*. Although they were accurate, they were also misleading: for instance, as listed in the Court Circular, one 'official visit' incorporating a single meeting lasting an hour was not distinguishable from another incorporating ten meetings and lasting an entire day.

with the reputation for internal disarray that their office had acquired, made it less easy to recruit a successor than the Prince may have hoped. By the summer, news of this had leaked into the gossip columns, where Sir Michael Palliser,* who had just left his post as Permanent Under-Secretary at the Foreign Office, was reported to have complained that they had virtually run out of suitable candidates.

Within the royal household, the role of private secretary to the heir apparent – with the prospect of becoming in due course private secretary to the King – was considered to be a plum job. It was a jolt to the self-esteem of the court that such a position did not seem to have quite the same cachet for those outside the charmed circle. It was with relief therefore that the 'headhunter' hired by the Prince eventually alighted on Sir John Riddell,† a baronet and merchant banker who was renowned for his wit, elegance and charm. Well aware that he had been far from first choice, Riddell would later acknowledge 'without exaggeration but with a certain amount of false modesty' that by the time he had been discovered, 'they were pretty desperate'.[2]

Riddell was not a skilled organiser and he was easily bored by administration, but, as he soon showed, his antennae were sensitive to the niceties of court life. As an outsider, he was almost unknown to the Palace establishment, who later told him that they had been fearful he would turn up sporting a beard and wearing sandals and that they were greatly relieved to discover that his suits were pin-striped. However, he was altogether more effervescent than his predecessor and he had none of Adeane's premature stuffiness; in his company, the seriousness of the royal purpose was not in doubt but it was, at least by comparison, lightly borne. He was not above reminding the Prince that, 'If we manage to get the letters out without making too many mistakes, if we manage to get the diaries fixed up and we manage to get you transported from one place to another, we've already achieved quite a lot for twenty-one rather harassed amateurs.'[3] He only half believed those words. Over the next five years, he was to orchestrate the Prince's life through a period of

---

* Sir Michael Palliser (1922–   ), entered diplomatic service 1947; private secretary to Prime Minister 1966; ambassador to European Communities 1971, 1973–75; Permanent Under-Secretary, Foreign Office, 1975–82.

† Sir John Riddell (1934–   ), private secretary 1985–90 and treasurer 1986–90 to Prince and Princess of Wales; extra equerry to Prince of Wales since 1990.

intense public activity and private upheaval with notable tact and good humour.

The new private secretary cultivated his relationship with the Prince with care. To a far greater extent than his predecessor, he was able to convey the impression that he genuinely respected the Prince's expanding portfolio of 'inner city' commitments – which by the end of 1985 embraced not only the Prince's Trust (which was soon to spawn the Prince's Youth Business Trust) but Business in the Community as well. Although Riddell was to differ sharply with the Prince on several occasions, he never left the impression that he thought those ventures were in any way unbecoming commitments for an heir to the throne. Nor did he share the smart view that the Prince was unduly impressionable, believing, on the contrary, that he was 'far more sceptical' than his critics would allow. He also detected that the Prince had a 'very remarkable mind', although he was not in the conventional sense an intellectual. More than some of his peers, Riddell sensed that the Prince was driven by an inner conviction, which he did not always share but still respected. Though his boss's concentration span could be frustratingly inconsistent, he was, as Riddell soon appreciated, 'perfectly capable of working all night; when his interest and his gut was involved he was a very concentrated figure.'[4]

Riddell's appointment coincided with a flowering of the Prince's public life. He had settled on the causes that were most important to him and he set about promoting them with unprecedented vigour. If he had previously been dabbling his toe in the waters, testing the temperature, he now dived in and began to thrash his way along a course from which he was not easily diverted. In every cause, the manner of his involvement took a similar – if unconscious – pattern. In public there were the speeches, and in private the seminars, the receptions, the lobbying, the letter-writing and the fundraising.

In the decade from its official inception in 1976, the Prince's Trust had grown into a national organisation involving more than fifty regional committees and over 1,000 committed volunteers. In 1976, the Trust had only been able to raise £7,471, which came principally from a City of London Livery Company and the Prince's own endeavours. A decade later, the trustees were dispersing more than £300,000 a year, much of which came from royal film premieres and rock concerts, which helped to raise more than £900,000 in 1986 alone. Over the decade, tens of thousands of young people between the ages of fourteen and twenty-five who qualified as 'socially, economically or environmentally disadvantaged or physically handicapped' had been awarded small grants (not exceeding £300) to help them pursue a particular enthusiasm of benefit to the community or to their own future. In the process, many alienated individuals had been infused with a measure of self-confidence and hope.[5]

Explaining its success to the Prime Minister, the Prince stressed the importance of making grants 'as quickly as possible and with the minimum of red tape . . . to encourage self-help.'[6] Against the advice of his more cautious supporters, the Prince remained adamant that the Trust should take risks, insisting, 'Occasionally things will go wrong. Occasionally someone runs off with the money. Well, that is just one of those things. But they won't all do that. And having taken the risks you find that we'll get enormously beneficial results.'[7] Later, when the once-reviled Prince's Trust began to receive co-funding from the government, he wrote to the Secretary of State for Education, Kenneth Baker, to welcome his support. However, he warned the minister not to be too cautious in the selection of 'young leaders' to run the government's Inner City Scheme which was designed to work closely with the Prince's Trust. 'I feel very strongly that it is important to turn "poachers into gamekeepers", as it were, and that one should not worry about the past records of such people,' he wrote.[8]

Every year, the Trust ran a week-long course at Caister, organised to help upwards of 500 unemployed young people, most of whom came from the most deprived parts of Britain. Some of them had been in trouble with the police, some were on probation, most of them were demoralised and alienated. The purpose of the camp was to stimulate their self-esteem, to discover latent talent, to provide a modicum of training in the basic skills needed to apply successfully for a job, and to create a communal atmosphere in which they could have something of a holiday as well. Caister was a success from the start. Helped by star musicians like Phil Collins (who was to come year after year to teach and to entertain), even a week made a remarkable difference to what the Prince was wont to describe as 'the most difficult characters'. And they were appreciative:

Dear Prince Charles,

I take great Pleasure writing to you on behalf of the group representing Greater Manchester on the Prince's Trust holiday for the
unemployed at Caister on Sea 1987.
    I find it very difficult to put into words on Paper what a Great week
we had. It was a week of work and fun. I found the work very interesting and the fun was just as good.
    I Personally think it was a holiday that should never be forgotten,
and in my mind I will never forget it.
    Thank you very much for making it Possible for us to have such a
Smashing week, the atmosphere I experienced in itself was an experience to me, it was so warm and friendly, it was like being in another
world for a week. It would be lovely if it could be like that always.
Thank you from the bottom of my heart . . .[9]

The Prince replied, 'Nothing could give me more pleasure than to
know that it was a success as far as you were concerned and, as you say,
I do wish it was possible for the atmosphere you described to be a permanent feature of our life!'[10]
    It was in the spirit of risk that the Prince's Youth Business Trust
(PYBT) was established in 1986. The idea for the PYBT had sprung
from a conversation he had had four years earlier with George Pratt, the
chairman of the Prince's Trust, on the day that the official level of unemployment reached three million. Although concerned by these figures,
the government was convinced that the impact of market forces on the
competitive potential of the economy should not be distorted by public
spending programmes of dubious provenance. The Prince was also
doubtful about the value of public investment in the inner cities, but he
was dismayed by the apparent lack of compassion and imagination displayed by some Whitehall officials. 'We can do something,' he told Pratt,
who countered, 'But we are too small to have any effect.' 'Maybe,' Pratt
recalls the Prince as saying, 'but we have to set an example. Please give
me your thoughts by tomorrow morning.'[11]
    Soon afterwards, a project called the Youth Business Initiative was set
up as an arm of the Prince's Trust designed specifically to disperse modest loans and grants to embryo entrepreneurs, a somewhat different
'clientele' from the Trust's other beneficiaries. Although the target was

still the unemployed, ex-offenders, the ethnic minorities and the disabled, the candidates for support had to demonstrate that, even though the banks were not prepared to risk funding them, they had the flair and acumen to set up and run a successful small business. In 1986, the Youth Business Initiative was detached from the Prince's Trust and relaunched with its own identity as the PYBT, in an attempt to give it a distinctive identity. It had a faltering start, but in 1987 the Prince could draft a confident letter to Margaret Thatcher soon after her re-election as Prime Minister explaining why he had established the new trust: 'I felt very strongly that there was a great deal of hidden and wasted talent in the less prosperous parts of the U.K. and also that it was important to encourage the formation of new enterprises which could, in due course, become some of the major companies of the future.'[12]

In addition to providing 'seed corn' finance (loans of up to £5,000 and grants to a maximum of £3,000), the PYBT offered specialist advice to those who passed muster at an interview with one of the thirty-eight regional boards that were established across the country. The regional boards were managed by men and women seconded from private industry who gave free financial advice and support to each new business. In the latter half of the eighties, it was to expand rapidly, until by the end of the decade more than 10,000 enterprises had been established, involving more than 15,000 young people, 66 per cent of which were still operating after three years in business.

It was in this fertile soil that Stephen O'Brien,* the chief executive of an innovative charitable enterprise called Business in the Community (BITC), planted the thought of yet another initiative. A meeting was arranged with the Prince at which O'Brien spoke with eloquence about the urgent need to break through the barriers of class and race which separated the leaders of British industry from the leaders of the black community. Knowing a little about the Prince's own long-standing fears for the inner cities, he was nonetheless impressed by the Prince's response. 'I was very surprised how much he already knew about the issue. He was very knowledgeable. At the end of the conversation he said simply , "I'd like to help." I said, "If you are ready to take the risk, I'll organise an event." '[13]

---

* Stephen O'Brien (1936–), chief executive of BITC 1983–92 and executive vice-chairman since 1992; Trustee of Prince's Youth Business Trust since 1987; chairman and co-founder of Project Fullemploy 1973–91.

he wedding day, Buckingham Palace, July 1981

he nation celebrates

The honeymoon: about to board the royal yacht, Gibraltar (*left*) and at Balmoral (*below*)

The birth of Prince William, 21 June 1982

The family on tour in Auckland, New Zealand, March 1983

The Prince and Princess on tour in Sydney, Australia, 1983

At Ayers Rock, on the same tour

The Prince and Princess meet Pope John Paul II, Vatican City, April 1985

With Ronald and Nancy Reagan, the White House, Washington, November 1985

The private secretaries: Squadron Leader David Checketts (*top left*), the Hon. Edward Adeane (*top right*), Sir John Riddell (*bottom left*), Lt. Commander Richard Aylard (*bottom right*)

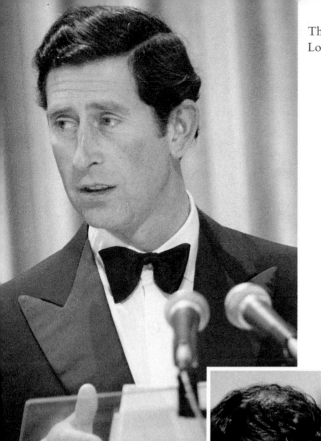

The Mansion House speech,
London, December 1987

Polo at Windsor Great Park:
the prize-giving

The Prince and Princess after a polo match in India, April 1992

At the National Cemetery in Seoul, November 1992

A few months later in the discreet ambience of a comfortable hotel in Windsor, some of the country's most powerful industrialists sat down to dinner with some of the most radical and frustrated black leaders in Britain. By every account it was an extraordinary occasion. The agenda for the twenty-four-hour seminar had been written by the black leaders, who had decided who should speak and in what order. One or two of the Prince's advisers had taken O'Brien to task for exposing him to such an explosive prospect but, with the Prince presiding, the event surpassed the expectations of all the protagonists. At the end of a fierce but good-natured dialogue, the Prince urged them to build on what they had established. Soon afterwards, he became BITC's first and, to date, only president.

According to O'Brien, the arrival of the Prince transformed BITC's prospects. In November 1985, only a month after the controversy provoked by Rod Hackney's indiscretions, the Prince flew to Edinburgh with his new private secretary to make his first speech in his new role. He was to appeal for greater investment of energy and finance by the private sector into local communities, coupled with a declaration in favour of the 'enterprise culture', a phrase which was borrowed from America but which already had a place in the Thatcherite lexicon of political virtues (and was later even to be embraced by the other main political parties). 'The problem', he had written (doubtless with the experience of the PYBT in his mind), 'is how to change people's attitudes so they realise that they can make a contribution themselves towards job creation and enterprise.' As usual, the Prince put the finishing touches to the notes that his private secretary had prepared for him. Riddell failed to scrutinise this additional handiwork and he was therefore as taken aback as the audience to hear the heir to the throne declare, 'What really worries me is that we are going to end up as a fourth rate country. I do not want to see that and I am sure none of you do.'[14] The phrase not only startled his private secretary but, as Riddell at once recognised it would, ricocheted to a much wider audience. 'Fourth rate Britain alert' was the headline in the Sun, and almost every other newspaper made the same point.

The Prince was usually ambivalent about the impact of his speeches. Always prone to detect a hostile impulse in the media, he was inclined to believe that they wrenched his words out of context merely to fuel a controversy of their own devising. Sometimes he had a legitimate complaint; more often, as in this example, he was himself the agent of the headlines. By pushing his case to what others thought to be the bounds of his constitutional position, and by selecting phrases that would inevitably attract attention, he was bound to generate not only conflict but criticism; the expression of strong opinions became contentious simply because he had given voice to them. Slow to adjust to this reality and with a naivety that led him persistently to underestimate the potential effect of his words, he frequently carped about the coverage he attracted. Surprised by the prominence of the headlines he provoked, and torn between delight and anxiety at the impact he made, he was generally not easy to please. In this case, however, his pleasure was unalloyed: by warning against a 'fourth rate Britain' he had drawn attention to his own deep anxiety and to the role of BITC in one 'sound-bite' phrase.

Realising the potential of BITC to harness financial and professional resources to the talent which he was convinced was buried in the inner cities and waiting for resurrection, he immersed himself in the challenge of his new presidency. Between 1986 and 1992, he was to undertake more than 200 public engagements on the organisation's behalf. Throughout this period, he bombarded industrialists, financiers and ministers with letters promoting a new scheme or urging greater effort. A sense of his anxiety at Britain's relative decline emerged clearly in much of this correspondence. In 1986, encouraged by O'Brien, he conceived a passion for 'import substitution' as a means of combating unemployment, and was infuriated by the reluctance of industrialists to take a 'Buy British' campaign seriously. As so often when he was fired by frustration, he did not pause to find out if such an aim was either possible or desirable in a modern world economy. His intuition simply told him that he was right.

'This is what I find so unbearably exasperating about the attitude in this country,' he wrote to O'Brien about the inadequacy of British marketing. 'There seems to be a degree of complacency which is little short of incredible. Having just returned from Texas and several visits to High tec companies etc., I find that I want to speak out about all the opportunities we seem to lose in every direction. The trouble is to find the right occasion on which to speak . . .'[15]

A few days later, after a visit to Merseyside, the clearing banks were in his sights, particularly their failure to fund enterprising small businesses. He wrote to one of his business contacts, citing the example of two companies, a furniture manufacturer and a light engineering works, neither of which could meet firm export orders from the United States because 'apparently there is much reluctance in banking circles to lend money in the Liverpool area'.[16]

On a trip to Boston the Prince was taken to see the old mill town of Lowell. He was inspired by the 'partnership' working there to revive the heart of the community and, on his return to London, proposed that BITC should initiate a similar venture in Britain. According to O'Brien, the executive board of BITC endorsed the idea at once. Two days later, the Prince was on the phone: 'Have you thought of a place to adopt? What about one of the old mill towns in the north like Burnley or Halifax?'[17]

BITC settled on Halifax as a test-bed for a new form of partnership between business and the community which was soon to be regarded as a model of good practice in the effort to regenerate the environment and housing, and to promote employment. A memorandum (in longhand) from the Prince to his assistant private secretary illustrates the character of his involvement in what was soon known as the Halifax partnership:

1. I am anxious that there should be an input from a good community architect. I strongly recommend he should get in touch with John Thompson, who is the architect involved with the Duchy tenants co-op. scheme . . .

2. The point about the community architect is that he/she is badly needed to coordinate the whole project, to encourage the participants, work with local authorities etc. and above all, ensure that the design of houses is decent. I am worried they will otherwise just build hideous little boxes . . .

3. I am not entirely convinced that it is a good idea to concentrate this scheme entirely on the unemployed. I would have thought a mixture of people was a better idea. I don't believe, for instance, that the self-help scheme I saw in Macclesfield 2 years ago was exclusively involved with unemployed people. The important thing is to try and recreate, or rejuvenate, communities as a whole . . .

4. I re-emphasise this question of design. If it is at all possible people should be able to express their own feelings about the design of

their houses, the layout of the scheme, gardens, front doors and windows. A community architect understands all this and knows how to work with people who have never had any experience of this sort of thing. They have to convince the local politicians to let them coordinate such projects and to be flexible about the inter-pretation of building regulations etc.

Please make sure I am kept fully informed about progress. C.[18]

Later, he wrote to the Prime Minister to promote the scheme:

I felt that we had much to learn in this field from the United States and as a result we decided, as a pilot project, to concentrate on one town in the north of England and to encourage a partnership approach towards regenerating the local economy, rehabilitating old buildings, restoring confidence . . .[19]

By championing the idea of a partnership so vigorously, the Prince – through BITC – became the catalyst for a fundamental shift in govern-ment thinking. The process might have occurred in any case; but it is unlikely that it would otherwise have acquired the rapid momentum which made BITC the pioneer of an approach that later became an established feature of government policy. By 1989, BITC had estab-lished nineteen partnerships led by Business Leadership Teams. The success of these encouraged the government to set up the first Training and Enterprise Councils (TECs), which were to a large degree modelled on BITC's partnership schemes. In public at least, ministers were reluc-tant to credit BITC with the original idea for the TECs, but in private it was conceded that the Prince's own involvement had played a signifi-cant part in establishing what, in the nineties, came to occupy an important place in the fabric of Britain's economic and social life.

According to Stephen O'Brien, the director of BITC, it was at the Prince's instigation that BITC launched the first of more than sixty inner-city 'compacts' between local schools and local employers. Once again, the idea originated in Boston, where, accompanied by O'Brien, he had in 1986 attended a seminar called 'Futures for Youth', of which BITC was a co-sponsor. There he discovered the Boston compact. In a run-down neighbourhood, employers, schools, parents and children had made a formal 'deal': any child who agreed to meet a set of social and academic targets would be rewarded by being allowed to leapfrog to the top of the queue for jobs in those companies involved in the scheme. The purpose was to improve the school system, integrate local businesses into training and education, and to offer hope to some of the most deprived children in the city. Back in England, the Prince urged BITC to adopt the idea, suggesting that similar schemes could be run by the schools themselves. He made it his business to lobby industry and the government, proselytising for the cause at dinner parties set up for the purpose at Kensington Palace. The Employment Secretary, Norman Fowler, who followed the Prince to see the Boston compact, was equally enthused. Before long, BITC's compacts had been turned into government-sponsored 'education and business partnerships'.

The Prince's indefatigable energy appealed to O'Brien, who wrote delightedly to him soon after the end of his first presidential year: 'I wanted you to know just how much your Presidency has meant to Business in the Community . . . The development has been enormous . . .' Citing a rapid growth in membership, a surge in funds, a renewed sense of motivation and co-operation which, he wrote, 'has come about directly as a result of your injunction to everyone in this area to "work together"', he concluded:

> Your visits to depressed areas have lifted spirits and made a real difference. Your visits to Skelmersdale, Brixton, Deptford and Handsworth live in our minds in this connection. The comment by the Chief Constable in Birmingham that your visit in the summer contributed substantially to easing tension was, I am sure, absolutely accurate. We repeatedly hear comments from the black community to the effect that 'at least the Prince of Wales cares about us'.[20]*

---

* In September 1985, an outbreak of communal violence in Handsworth left two people dead and caused damage estimated at £16 million. Nine months later, in the following June, the Chief Constable of the West Midlands Police, Geoffrey Dear, warned that the tension in the inner cities was 'running dangerously high'. The Prince's visit to Handsworth coincided with the first anniversary of the 1985 riots. The Chief Constable reported that his presence had helped to ease the tension 'quite dramatically'. (*Birmingham Post,* 26 September 1986.)

The Prince responded enthusiastically, endorsing O'Brien's proposal that for the next Annual General Meeting the members of the BITC board should be invited to a 'field day' in Hackney and Tower Hamlets. 'I think it would be a very good idea,' he wrote. 'This is just what is needed – less sitting round a table and more persuasion "on the ground"!' The Prince's urge to persuade decision-makers to come face to face with the problems and challenges facing BITC led directly to the establishment of his 'Seeing is Believing' campaign. The idea (and the slogan) was his own and centred on the belief that business leaders and politicians would only be seized with a sense of urgency about the needs of the inner cities if they were to see at first hand the character of deprivation and the potential of young people to restore pride and hope to battered communities. On frequent occasions, he led forays into what was for many of his guests an uncharted world of decline and despair. By the end of the eighties, 'Seeing is Believing' had already galvanised several hundred business leaders into direct support for a range of BITC projects by providing training and work in some of the most run-down areas of the country. It was clear that the Prince did not intend merely to be a figurehead: in his letter to O'Brien, he wrote, 'I can't tell you what a difference it makes to me to have someone like you who actually takes up some of my suggestions and puts them into practice.'[21]

In addition to his involvement with the Prince's Trust, PYBT and BITC, the Prince was still chairman of the Royal Jubilee Trusts, the management of which finally merged with the Prince's Trust in 1988 after what had been a sustained battle by the Prince against the old guard in Buckingham Palace – even down to the form in which the logo of his own trust should be incorporated into the new letterhead for all three of them. Not content with these ventures, he was also the driving force behind yet another organisation, the Prince of Wales' Community Venture, which was set up in 1985. 'The aim of this venture,' the Prince informed the Prime Minister later:

> was to try and find a way by which young people from all walks of life – those from state schools and private schools – could be brought together for a short period in their lives in order to live and work as a team, making a contribution to their communities in various ways. The important element of this project is that it involves several voluntary organisations agreeing to co-operate, together with the active

participation of the Fire Service, the Ambulance Service and the Police, to whom the young people are attached . . .[22]

This was the nearest the Prince was able to get to his vision of a nation disciplined by the experience of compulsory community service in the spirit of Kurt Hahn and Gordonstoun. In a draft of his letter to Margaret Thatcher, but excluded from the final version, he wrote:

My original hope was that eventually this project might become so successful that H.M.G. would notice it and see the value in some sort of community service for all young people . . . It may be wishful thinking![23]

It was. Although various ministers and shadow ministers would in private express some sympathy for a 'community' substitute for 'national' service, the concept of compulsion had long ago been discarded and was impossible to resuscitate. As a surrogate initiative, Community Venture provided a year-long programme of 'service and training'. The first pilot scheme was established in Sunderland and others followed in Llanelli, Blackburn, Bradford and Strathclyde. Although the scheme survived for six years, the Prince's ambition outran the available finance. By 1991, when the scheme was finally phased out, only 1,000 young people had participated.

This setback did not deter him. Although he sensed that it was a lost cause, he continued to argue the case for compulsory community service. A succession of government ministers and Whitehall officials grew familiar with his obdurate opinions on the matter, which were generally prefaced with a self-deprecatory, 'I'm sorry, I just happen to believe, for what it's worth, that . . .' When Tom Shebbeare, a Eurocrat who had been shortlisted for the post of director of the Prince's Trust, went for his final interview, he was surprised by the passion with which the Prince argued the case. 'Don't you agree?' the Prince asked finally. Shebbeare did not agree and, screwing up his courage, said so in forthright terms. Convinced that he had thereby talked himself out of a job that he very much wanted, Shebbeare did not restrain himself in the discussion that ensued. He failed to change the Prince's mind, but he got the job. Thereafter, not a little of his time was devoted to ensuring that his patron did not use any public platform associated with the Prince's Trust to deliver himself of what Shebbeare regarded as these sincere but anachronistic opinions.

The Prince's Trust Volunteers programme, which in 1990 replaced Community Venture, was based on the principles to which the Prince was committed but carefully calibrated to meet Shebbeare's sense of what would be acceptable in the last decade of the twentieth century. By 1993, the throughput of young people (including those in work as well as the unemployed) attending a sixty-day intensive programme had reached 4,500 and was projected to expand rapidly towards 25,000.*

By the end of the eighties, the Prince had become ambitious to take BITC's message to other countries. Enthused by the thought of inspiring the world's most powerful multinational companies to share his perspective, he and his team decided to hold an international forum in the American town of Charleston, South Carolina. They invited more than a hundred senior executives from the United States, Britain, Europe, Japan and Australia for a two-day meeting at which they talked freely about the responsibilities of international industry to the environment and to the community. Led by the Prince, they wandered through the old streets of Charleston to recapture the romantic essence of a traditional community and to admire the local architecture. Then they broke up into small groups for intense debate about the issues raised by the Prince through BITC in Britain. The event was a success. Within a few months, under the ambitious direction of a BITC executive, Robert Davies, what soon became know as the Business Leaders Forum (BLF) was in operation. Over the next few years, Davies was to organise seventeen similar international meetings, timed where possible to coincide

---

* By 1994 after much lobbying of ministers, spearheaded personally by the Prince, the government committed itself to providing matching funds for the scheme. A Whitehall working party involving twelve departments was set to find ways in which government employees might participate in the scheme. The Labour Party's Commission on Social Justice also adopted key aspects of the programme; its proposals for 'Citizens Service' bear a very close resemblance to the objectives and character of the Prince's Trust Volunteers programme. Although the Prince had not lost his enthusiasm for compulsory community service, he had the satisfaction of knowing that the principles of voluntary service which he had originated through the Prince's Trust had seeped into the thinking of Britain's two main political parties.

with the Prince's official tours abroad, involving more than 4,000 business leaders in North America, Latin America, Europe and Asia.

Under the umbrella of the Prince's charities, critics of the BLF would
complain that Davies' skills at promotion and presentation were not
matched by a clear focus or a coherent set of objectives and that the BLF
lacked adequate means of evaluating its achievements. They also wondered if it would ever be much more than a glossy talking shop for a
jet-setting business elite. With the opening up of Eastern Europe, however, the BLF was to form partnerships with more than ninety businesses
working in Russia, Poland, the Czech Republic and Slovakia, setting up
a range of training and environmental projects, forming a task force to
help regenerate the cultural life of St Petersburg, and transforming the
Red Army Barracks outside Budapest into a series of units for small businesses. If the BLF was prone to indulge itself in rather too many
self-promoting fanfares, it was starting to show that in practice, as well as
rhetoric, the Prince's message about the role of business in the community could reach an international audience to real effect.

None of these initiatives was calculated to steal thunder for the Prince;
they fell too easily into the category of 'worthy but dull'. It was also an
unwieldy portfolio in a complex area. Though his trusts were helping to
shape for the better the grim contours of the urban environment, 'Prince
Serves His People' was hardly the stuff of a tabloid headline. When
things went wrong, it was different. A case in point was another project
which had his blessing, Inner City Aid, set up to tackle urban deprivation by helping people improve their housing. In October 1987, under
the headline 'Fury as blunder wrecks Charles' charity', the *Daily Mail*
informed its readers that:

> A blunder at Kensington Palace which crippled Prince Charles' plans
> to raise millions of pounds for deprived inner-cities was condemned as
> 'stupid' yesterday. The ambitious Inner City Aid project was set up last
> November to fund community self-help projects. But because of an
> apparent administrative mix-up, it was launched on the same day as a
> competing campaign also backed by Charles – The Prince's Youth
> Business Trust. Now instead of raising £10 million, the inner city
> charity has had only £33,000 . . .[24]

Other newspapers carried the same message. In *The Times*, Lord Scarman, one of Inner City Aid's trustees, was quoted as conceding that 'a great mistake has been made', but he insisted that the charity still had an important role to play. 'It is essential that we now define our role more carefully. It was difficult in the early days because a general sense of enthusiasm tended to get in the way of sensible planning.'[25] A year later, Inner City Aid collapsed in acrimony. As Lord Scarman had hinted, the reason for the fiasco was more complex than a 'blunder' at Kensington Palace. The episode is revealing about the Prince of Wales, his advisers, and his network of overlapping trusts.

The idea for Inner City Aid had come from the architect Rod Hackney, who persuaded the Prince to become its patron. As its chairman, Hackney launched the scheme for a conference devoted to community architecture. Sceptical developers and hostile architects saw the launch as the climax of two successful campaigns, both of which had been orchestrated by Hackney: the first to promote his own reputation as a community architect, the second to ensure his election as president of the Royal Institute of British Architects the following year. After the Prince had opened the conference, Hackney made an appeal for funds. 'This is about regenerating Britain's inner cities,' he declared; benefactors, from whom he hoped to receive £10 million, would be investing 'in the renaissance of the United Kingdom from the inner cities outwards'.[26]

Fanfared with such dizzy rhetoric, the launch of Inner City Aid inevitably overshadowed that of the PYBT, to which the Prince went later in the day. Not surprisingly, Hackney was in buoyant mood when he wrote to congratulate the Prince 'on the marvellous reaction to the launch' at what had been a 'healing and friendly' conference.[27] The Prince, still smarting from what Riddell described later with his usual candour as 'a cock-up', was less sanguine.

Within ten days, Charles Knevitt, the architecture correspondent on *The Times*, who had been appointed as director of Inner City Aid, was summoned to see Riddell and told that he should stop all fundraising. He was left in no doubt that the PYBT had been horrified to discover that Hackney had set a target of £10 million, a sum which would undercut the PYBT's own fundraising appeal to which the Prince had given his name. Knevitt was bemused: if he were not permitted to raise funds, then Inner City Aid would be stillborn. Hackney seemed undeterred.

In February, the Prince summoned Hackney to Kensington Palace, where he had to face the disgruntled trustees of the PYBT. There was a fierce argument, at the end of which the Prince instructed Hackney to postpone any fundraising for two years. Inner City Aid, which lacked clear objectives let alone a strategy to achieve them, was to give the PYBT, which already enjoyed the prospect of matching funds from government, a free run. In the meantime, Inner City Aid should identify a precise role for itself and a suitable project for development.

Hackney did not readily accede. Aware that the Prince would be reluctant to end his patronage of Inner City Aid, he used this licence to keep the project alive. In the summer of 1987, he approached Bob Geldof, who had become a legendary figure after the international success of his Band Aid concerts for Ethiopia. Hackney apparently persuaded Geldof to put his talent at the service of Inner City Aid – or at least he persuaded him to accompany him to Kensington Palace to see the Prince, where Riddell the city banker and Geldof the unkempt rock star looked askance at each other. When one of the Prince's dogs started to chew his bootlaces, Geldof kicked the animal away. He also failed to delete the expletives from his discourse and the private secretary was aghast.

The meeting achieved nothing. Geldof emerged angry, Hackney dismayed, both complaining that the Prince had prevaricated and, in Geldof's case, that his time had been wasted. Knevitt felt likewise. For months, he had argued that Inner City Aid would only succeed if it severed its connection with the Prince, a view which not only irritated its royal patron but alienated Hackney, who had told Knevitt bluntly, 'No patronage, no Inner City Aid.' In September Knevitt resigned in what he described as despair and Hackney regarded as rancour.

The Prince had long come to repent his rather casual support for Inner City Aid. Hackney had never disguised his vision of Inner City Aid as – in the words of his new director, the Canon of Westminster, Revd Sebastian Charles – the 'crusading arm of the Prince's inner cities initiatives'.[28] From the point of view of the Prince's advisers, however, to think in terms of a 'crusade' was to sail dangerously close to a shifting political wind. Their unease had been heightened by the return of a Conservative government in the June 1987 election. As she swept up the stairs at Conservative Party Headquarters in Smith Square on the night of her victory, Margaret Thatcher had declared that 'Today is a day of history,' but added: 'We haven't a lot of time to sit around. Back to work,' indicating that her first priority was to tackle the problems of the inner cities.[29]* Unless Hackney's wings were clipped, he risked exposing the Prince to the charge of interfering in party politics as an anti-Thatcherite combatant.

Hackney used the first anniversary of the ill-fated launch to declare that Inner City Aid was soon to be born again. Never able to understate a case, he told a press conference, 'For the sake of the country, this venture will not be allowed to fail . . . The other charity, which does a fine job, has had the chance to raise money. Now perhaps it should be our turn.'[30] This outburst exposed for the first time the tensions which had been simmering for months. Not only did the headlines embarrass the Prince, but Hackney had now openly challenged the two-year moratorium which his patron had imposed. At a succession of acrimonious meetings, the Prince's advisers made strenuous but fruitless efforts to persuade Hackney that Inner City Aid should be folded into the embrace of Business in the Community, where its crusading zeal could be securely pinioned. Despite the pressure, both Hackney and Sebastian Charles failed to succumb to either blandishments or threats.

The Prince's advisers grew increasingly apprehensive. An internal strategy document from Inner City Aid had identified as a policy objective the need 'to articulate and present deprivation in the inner city communities in a manner which provokes public reaction . . . This populist approach implies raising the emotions and conscience of the Nation to a level where the inevitable consequence is widescale action.'[31] The messianic naivety of this strategy also alarmed the Prince.

Originally, he had seen Hackney as a kindred spirit; after this episode, however, Hackney was gradually eased out of the charmed circle. The Prince's advisers, including O'Brien and Shebbeare, found it impossible to make headway with the impulsive architect. At a meeting in June with Riddell, Shebbeare and Jim Gardner, the chairman of the Prince's Trust, the Prince was persuaded to tell Hackney that he could no longer remain as patron of Inner City Aid 'in its present form', although he 'might be prepared to do so if it were to develop into an advisory group'.[32]

The meeting duly took place a few weeks later. It was an uncomfortable

---

* Sceptical observers immediately presumed that the Prime Minister's remark was directed at the need to conquer the last bastions of socialism before the next election but the more compassionate interpretation held sway.

session at which the Prince, who found it painful to face such encounters, was less forthright than he had intended to be. His private secretary
followed up with a letter which was somewhat more explicit, pointing
out that the Prince's patronage of Inner City Aid was a 'temporary'
commitment, and that the time had come to 'run down' the trust and to
continue its activities 'in the form of an advisory group . . .'[33]

Hackney failed to take the hint, insisting that the Prince had not
resigned as patron and that Inner City Aid still had much work to do.
This led to a bizarre exchange of correspondence between the Prince's
advisers, one of whom noted that Hackney 'is resolutely resisting
attempts to shove him back in the bottle',[34] while another concluded,
'We should press for a meeting very soon at which we must be absolutely
clear that HRH has withdrawn his patronage and will only be patron of
an advisory body . . . We should never under-estimate Rod's ability to
bounce back.'[35]

Not only did Hackney bounce back, but he did so again and again.
Despite the best endeavours of the Prince's aides and advisers, Inner City
Aid survived into the nineties, if only as a shell, with the name of its royal
patron still blazoned on the letterhead – a symbol of the Prince's inability to reject entirely an erstwhile ally.

After Mrs Thatcher's election night commitment to the inner cities, the
Prince decided to seize the opening she had provided. At his next meeting with her, the Prince urged the Prime Minister to go into the inner
cities herself and meet those who were, in BITC jargon, 'community
entrepreneurs', local leaders who by their energy and talent were leading
others in the regeneration of their communities. He followed up by
proposing a luncheon at Kensington Palace to meet some of the 'characters' involved in such enterprises. 'I honestly believe that if you meet
them,' he wrote to her afterwards, 'they would tell you what the real
problems are and what is required to meet the potential that exists.'[36]

After some initial prevarication, he was rebuffed. The Prince persisted,
lobbying senior ministers to establish better co-ordination between ministerial departments, business and local communities. A year after the
election, he tackled the Prime Minister again and as a result she agreed
to host a luncheon at Number Ten to meet the inner-city 'enablers' by
whom the Prince had been so impressed. In proposing his own guest list,
the Prince minuted:

the important thing is for the PM to meet the real people at grass roots level who have struggled to get their housing co-ops, or whatever, off the ground. Inevitably, by the nature of their situation, they will probably not be conservative voters and will have 'radical' views. But then so does the PM! If she is going to have an impact on the situation in these inner urban areas etc., then she must hear at first hand from such people what it is like and what their problems are. I only hope she won't allow herself to be put off by people who may tell her that she shouldn't be seeing 'left wing' characters . . .'[37]

Soon afterwards, however, the invitation was withdrawn on the grounds that the news of the luncheon was bound to 'leak' and be exploited by the press, which would use it to highlight the widely reported antipathy between her and the Prince. The government's political opponents (the Prince's office was informed by Number Ten) would be sure to make capital out of the occasion, which would be damaging to all involved.

The Prince was not so easily diverted. At their next meeting, he persuaded Mrs Thatcher to attend a reception organised by BITC, which was described by one of his officials as 'neutral ground'. Soon afterwards, it was finally confirmed that with 'a suitable guest list' the occasion might also serve to meet the Prince's desire that the Prime Minister should – at last – have that first-hand contact with the community entrepreneurs which she had hitherto rejected.

The meeting was a success. Afterwards, Stephen O'Brien wrote enthusiastically to the Prince:

The atmosphere was extremely light . . . She said that she had learned a great deal, was enormously impressed by the scope and scale of activity and felt that leaders, like those in the room, were the starting point for local regeneration . . . I think much will flow from this and everyone present was deeply grateful to you . . .[38]

The Prince replied:

'Hooray' is all I can say – and I do hope this first encounter will bear fruit ultimately. Please keep me in touch with what transpires . . . I have written a note to the Prime Minister to thank her for seeing these characters and to say how important it is to encourage them.'[39]

It is not at all clear that the Prime Minister appreciated the Prince's obduracy. When she was introduced to one of his staff, she told him in effect, 'I really think that after all we've done, we could expect a bit more support from you,' after which she turned and walked away.[40] Nevertheless, she was later moved to request a list of inner-city 'enablers' whom she might meet on a visit to Liverpool that was planned for early in 1989.

Subsequently, the Prime Minister agreed to host the long-postponed luncheon. 'If you are going to do this you must not make political points, you must not ruin the whole thing by getting at her and scoring points,' the Prince advised the community entrepreneurs invited to Number Ten at his behest. At a three-hour meeting in the Cabinet Room, the Prime Minister listened politely to a litany of proposals for action and investment.

'Absolutely nothing happened' was the Prince's gloomy verdict on the outcome of his efforts. However, his perseverance with Margaret Thatcher, which few other individuals could have essayed, was not quite as unproductive as the Prince allowed himself to believe: a number of inner-city programmes were expanded and BITC secured matching funds from the government for a series of community-based projects organised around its entrepreneurs scheme.*

The Prince persisted with a range of parallel initiatives at BITC's behest, which by the end of the decade was growing towards a member-ship of over 400 companies, 75 per cent of which belonged to the 'top 100', to become the most influential organisation linking business to the community. According to O'Brien, the Prince was crucial to this process. Certainly his energy was unflagging, although his frustration was intense. After one of a succession of dinners at Kensington Palace and Highgrove, when he brought together business leaders with leading members of those working to rebuild their own communities, he wrote of the assorted bankers and investment managers, 'Oh! they were all very polite. They would eat my dinner and drink my wine. But I never got anywhere, and that is what I find so frustrating about this country: institutionalised short-termism which was, is, and will be, the death of us.'[41]

---

* This project is underway. If it is successful, BITC hopes to persuade the Treasury to offer tax breaks to businesses investing in such ventures which would then form the social equivalent of the business expansion scheme.

After another frustrating meeting at which one or two avowedly Thatcherite members of BITC had failed to respond with adequate enthusiasm to one of his proposals, he noted:

Somehow I must gather round me a powerful group of business leaders who really do understand what needs to be done to ensure that this country is able to play a worthwhile part in due course within the new European (and world) scene which is developing so fast. How do we go about finding these like-minded people – and fast? We have no time to lose . . .[42]

After the resignation of Mrs Thatcher, he wrote to congratulate her on her receipt of the Order of Merit. In the first part of his handwritten letter, he wrote of her remarkable contribution to world politics and especially of her 'extraordinary determination and courage' to which he attributed in large measure the fundamental changes in the Soviet Union and Eastern Europe. 'That's an astonishing and famous achievement,' he wrote, 'for which your name will go down in history as one of this country's most remarkable Prime Ministers.'

With that tribute paid, he did not refrain from reminding her that they had not invariably seen eye to eye. In particular, he reiterated his frustration at the reluctance of the government under her leadership to pay adequate attention to the notion of 'partnership'. Writing with passion, he insisted that the future lay in 'a genuine partnership between the different sectors that make up the life of our nation . . .'[43]

On the same day, the Prince also wrote to the new Prime Minister, to offer his congratulations on his election as leader of the Conservative Party. 'I can only wish you well as you take on this incredibly challenging task at a particularly difficult moment,' he wrote, before plunging once more into a statement of his unshakeable faith in the vital importance of partnerships between government, industry and the community for the regeneration of Britain. Clearly hoping to enlist the new Prime Minister in this cause, the Prince urged with some passion that 'the role of the state' should be one of 'strategic co-ordinator'. He concluded that he very much hoped to have a chance to discuss these matters in due course.[44]

CHAPTER
TWENTY

———— •◄ ————

On 11 November 1985, the American news magazine *Time* displayed a photograph of the Prince and Princess of Wales on its front cover, their heads inclined towards each other, their foreheads lightly touching, both smiling. 'Here They Come!' was the simple headline. Inside, the magazine's most accomplished reporters devoted no fewer than ten pages to the 'most glamorous couple' in the world. With that air of detachment required of American news magazines, the writers combined lofty editorial opinions with tabloid gossip, but could not conceal the adulatory excitement which had infected America at the imminent arrival of the royal couple directly from a further barnstorming tour of Australia.

The Prince shared none of their excitement. In Australia, the Princess had once again pulled vast crowds and charmed the media with the beauty of her smile and her radiant aura. So infatuated was the throng at every walkabout that as they got out of the car to 'work' the crowd, an involuntary moan of disappointment would rise from that part of the crowd which turned out to be nearest to the Prince and furthest from the Princess. Even as they drove through the streets, the Prince could hear the cries of disappointment, 'Oh no, she's on the wrong side.' It sapped his confidence and, momentarily at least, made him long to escape.

His distress, for which he rebuked himself even as he gave expression to it, was compounded by the placards and cartoons which exaggerated the mild protuberance of his ears which had caused him such agony as a child. Thirty years on, as he smiled his way through the clicking cameras and the faceless crowds, he could not resist a spasm of anguish as he confronted 'the fatuous remarks and insults [that] are made to me; rude things shouted out, gestures made, plastic masks waved about, woundingly unnecessary things written in the papers about me etc.'[1]

Aside from the walkabouts, the predictability of his seventh Australian tour was dispiriting. 'The protocol departments which arranged these things', he wrote to Nicholas Soames:

> always pull out the same file every time there is a tour in the offing and you might as well do everything blindfold! Not only that but the actual protocol here is so stultifying and rigid. They do stupid things like putting coloured sticky tape in a line along a carpet at a reception and make everyone stand behind the line while we walk along between rows of nervous drinkless people. They treat the tape line as if it was a 24,000 volt cable! The trouble with this kind of formality here is that it rubs many Australians up the wrong way and makes them extra 'anti' or determined to mock the whole thing.[2]

He derived some comfort from the presence of Riddell, experiencing his first royal tour: 'His approach to everything is thoroughly refreshing and he has a delightfully positive attitude . . . He must be amazed by all the intricacies and absurdities of Royal touring.'[3]

The Prince and Princess arrived in Washington to the decorous cheers of 4,000 invited guests at Andrews Airforce Base. 'After weeks of feverish anticipation and frenzied publicity, the world's most glamorous and relentlessly observed couple arrived in the capital of what was once their Kingdom's richest possession,' the *Time* correspondent wrote.[4] *Time* echoed the tone of the usually sober *New York Times*, whose headline read, 'The British have landed and Washington is taken'.[5] The Prince did not feel like a conquering hero. He noted in his diary:

> We arrived feeling <u>very</u> jet-lagged indeed. There were a lot of people on the tarmac to meet us – all extremely friendly as Americans so often are. Great batteries of photographers and TV people rose up like the Philharmonia Chorus mounted on white-painted scaffolds and made a noise like a giant sneezing as all the apertures went off in unison . . .[6]

At the White House, the royal couple faced a 'Hallé Chorus' of photographers as they were greeted by the Reagans. 'The President', the Prince noted, 'was looking wonderfully "Saturday morning-like" in a tartan blazer and once again, I was made to feel over-dressed in my very smart pinstripe suit!' Afterwards, they had a 'very enjoyable' forty-five-minute conversation at which the President discussed his forthcoming summit with President Gorbachev in Geneva:

The President said he wanted to offer to share the SDI [Strategic Defense Initiative] technology so that they would both be safe from nuclear missile attack – especially from someone else in another country who might develop such weapons. He said he had no illusions about converting Mr G., but they might at least get to know each other a bit better.[7]*

That night, there was a gala White House dinner, 'a swanky soiree for only 79 guests, certainly the hottest ticket in town', purred the *Time* correspondent.[8] Nancy Reagan had chosen the guest list herself after much consultation with the British embassy and Kensington Palace: 'We formed a receiving line almost immediately in order to shake the hand of all the guests. All sorts of people were there, from Clint Eastwood, John Travolta and Neil Diamond to Jacques Cousteau.'† The Prince sat between Nancy Reagan and the opera singer Beverley Sills.

Peter Ustinov was at the same table and kept telling hysterical stories in funny accents! Unfortunately I was not at my best that night and was suffering very badly from jet-lagged exhaustion. My brain refused to operate and I felt as though I had no batteries at all. Conversation

---

* The summit, which took place on 19 November, played a significant role in accelerating détente. Afterwards, President Reagan said, 'I cannot claim we had a meeting of minds . . . but we understand each other better.' At an unprecedented press conference lasting ninety-five minutes, Mr Gorbachev said, 'The world has become a safer place . . .'
† Others included the ballet dancer Mikhail Baryshnikov, the artist David Hockney, and Helen Frankenthaler, Jerry Zipkin and Betsy Bloomingdale, whom the American media described as 'Nancy's cat pack'.

would not come to me and I felt thoroughly useless, which was a great bore on an occasion like that![9]

At the end of dinner, the President rose to make a toast, referring graciously to 'Princess David' before correcting himself to make a short but engaging speech; 'Then I had to reply – not feeling up to it at all! I mumbled and fumbled my way through, talking unutterable nonsense and finally sat down in relief, only to find I had forgotten to drink a toast to the President! I got up again!' After dinner, the opera singer Leontyne Price sang a selection of arias and then there was dancing. 'Travolta asked Diana to dance,' her husband noted. 'He whisked her about the floor and everyone left them on their own until I joined in eventually with a very good American ballerina, whose name I forget. Sadly there were no lovely actresses or singers. I had been rather hoping that Diana Ross would be there . . .'[10]

The following day, they flew to Palm Springs for a gala charity dinner organised by Armand Hammer, the chairman of Occidental Petroleum. Hammer was in his eighties, a controversial businessman who enjoyed close links with the Kremlin and whose philanthropic gestures were as well publicised as they were extravagant. The presence of the royal couple at the Palm Springs gala had its origins in a telephone conversation between Hammer and the Prince eight months earlier.

The Prince had never been ashamed to exploit his unique ability to open other people's purse strings in aid of his charities. Tapping the vast range of high-level contacts at his disposal, he was particularly successful with the American 'super-rich' who were so flattered by his mere presence amongst them that they readily succumbed. Hammer was no exception. In February, one of Hammer's senior executives at the Washington office of Occidental Petroleum spoke to the British ambassador, Sir Oliver Wright, suggesting that the Prince and Princess might attend a charity gala dinner to coincide with their visit. He proposed that the proceeds should be dispersed in the proportions of 50 per cent to the United World College of the American West (of which Hammer was founder and chief executive under the presidency); 25 per cent to the Mary Rose Trust (of which the Prince was an active patron); and 25 per cent to another charity chosen by the Prince himself.

The embassy's first concern was to avoid offending the Reagans, explaining that the White House expected their first public engagement in the United States to be dinner with the President and Mrs Reagan, and that there was a danger that their hosts would be 'miffed' at being upstaged by Los Angeles and Dr Hammer.

On 1 March, Hammer rang the Prince himself offering to raise $1 million in return for the presence of the Prince and Princess of Wales 'at some ball in Los Angeles', as the Prince put it at the time. The Prince was in a dilemma. He was not at all anxious to attend a ball in Los Angeles, but one of his charities, Operation Raleigh,* was in dire financial straits; Hammer was the best available source of funds. The Prince agreed to meet the aged tycoon at Kensington Palace.

The new terms of trade proposed by Hammer were artful and manipulative: they did not find favour with Riddell, who was astonished by the crudeness of the proposal. As he told the Prince, he 'did not find the approach that if Their Royal Highnesses were to visit Los Angeles Dr Hammer would then underwrite the cost for all the fuel for Operation Raleigh as an attractive one.'[11] He nudged the Prince to confirm that, on careful consideration, he would not be able to attend the Hammer gala. However, the courtier failed to reckon either with the Prince's ability to drive a bargain or with the inveterate snobbishness and vanity of the old man, expressed in his passion to secure the royal couple as his guests on a worldwide stage.

At the meeting with the Prince, Hammer made yet another – and even more seductive – suggestion: the gala would not be in Los Angeles but at Palm Beach in Florida, and instead of funding a range of charities or providing fuel oil for Operation Raleigh, all the money would be allocated to the International Office of the United World Colleges, of which the Prince was president. As a result, he wrote after the meeting, the UWC would be blessed by an annual income large enough 'to allow you to step out of the burdensome obligation of UWC Presidency at a time of your choice'. If the Prince were to agree, he and the Princess would have the use of Hammer's private jet to take them to Palm Beach at the end of the Washington visit. The Prince could rest assured that Hammer 'would underwrite all the expenses' and guarantee the 'one million dollars net'.[12]

---

* A four-year round-the-world expedition launched in 1984 following the success of Operation Drake, aimed at providing young people from all backgrounds and nationalities with a personal challenge. The Prince was patron of Operation Drake, and then of Operation Raleigh, from 1979 to 1989.

Put in those terms, the offer was irresistible. If Hammer's promise were fulfilled, the Prince thought, the UWC would be so well funded as to allow him to step down gracefully from the presidency, leaving an organisation 'set up for life'.[13]

David Roycroft's response to this proposal reflected the sensitivities involved in any royal fundraising venture. After pointing out that the running costs of the UWC were in fact $200,000 a year, and that Hammer's promised $1 million would generate little more than £80,000 a year, he advised the Prince that Hammer should be told 'as tactfully as possible' that he should not labour under the illusion that his gesture would relieve the Prince from his fundraising obligations for the UWC.[14]

However, the principal concern of the Prince's office was that the presentation of the event should be so engineered as to avoid 'any suggestion' that the Prince and Princess were 'being "bought" for the evening', and that the guests should not feel they were 'being charged because of' the royal presence.[15] Quite how the organisers were to achieve this legerdemain was not made clear, particularly as the cover charge for attending the gala was to be $5,000 a head, and without the royal presence the event would not even have taken place. As it happened, the invitations to the gala were issued in the name of the board of the United World College of the American West to honour Hammer for his contribution to the UWC movement. It was not thought necessary to point out that the chief executive of the board thus honouring the ancient philanthropist in the presence of the Prince and Princess of Wales was none other than Hammer himself.

However, this omission was not overlooked in Palm Beach, where Hammer was widely regarded as less of a philanthropist than a fellow-traveller of the Soviet Union. Among several correspondents alerted to the issue by a flurry of hostile newspaper articles, a Palm Beach resident wrote to Riddell:

> We would like His Royal Highness to know that many loyal Americans would be offended if they looked upon a scenario in which one saw the Heir to the British Throne in any way to be in the pocket of a man they regard as a friend and ally of the Soviet Union and who seems to betray the best interests of the United States, and therefore, of Britain.

We hope that His Royal Highness will avoid being presented as a friend and confidant of such a man . . . As old Palm Beach residents it seems to us particularly unfortunate that this visit is to take place under such controversial auspices . . .[16]

The reportage and commentary were crude but effective. Joseph Kamp, billed as 'the dean of American anti-communists', wrote of Hammer as 'a Soviet-sympathising slicker of dubious character and integrity . . . [who] has used guile, gold and gall to rope in a lot of good, well-meaning people, including British Royalty, to help him organise a testimonial to himself'.[17] By the end of September, such sentiments had come to enjoy such widespread support in Palm Beach that when the Information Counsellor from the British embassy in Washington flew in for a 'recce' he discovered that the mayor, supported by a majority of city councillors, had refused to grant the necessary licence for the event to take place. With local hostility towards Hammer sharpened by the failure of senior employees at Occidental Petroleum (who had been drafted in to organise the gala on his behalf) to issue a single invitation to any resident of Palm Beach, the British official had to engage all his diplomatic skill to persuade the mayor to change his mind.

The controversy was eventually massaged into the background, though it had so irritated the Prince that, drafting his speech for the gala at the last moment, he used the occasion to make a trenchant defence of the UWC movement, venting some of his annoyance at those critics who had tended to dismiss it as an anachronistic concept dreamt up by authoritarian romantics anxious to create a like-minded international elite:

I find that I become increasingly fed up with hearing absolute non-sense talked about the United World Colleges. I keep hearing disparaging descriptions of it – that it's a pet project of my great-uncle. I also get tired of hearing United World Colleges being rather dismissed as an elitist educational experiment. And to cap it all there have been snide comments over the months about the actual business of fundraising . . .[18]

He then launched into each point. Mountbatten had lived through two world wars, he had witnessed misery and poverty and he had believed that by bringing young people together at an impressionable age the UWC movement could play a part in eliminating those vicissitudes. As to the charge of 'elitism', over the last twenty-one years the UWC had taken 6,000 students selected entirely on merit, from more than fifty countries.

Afterwards, delighted with the response of the audience to what he had said, he asked Joan Collins to dance with him. 'She was very amusing and with an unbelievable cleavage (all raised up and presented as if on a tray!)', he wrote in a letter on the flight back to London, 'so eye wander was a problem!'[19] In the same letter, he wrote of the 'angry' speech that he had made: 'As a result of getting irritated and hitting back the audience was electrified and I came to the conclusion that I must use the same technique again!'[20]

After Palm Springs, Hammer came gradually to bask in a reputation as one of the Prince's 'gurus'. In reality, the relationship continued as it had started, being more worldly than spiritual: a transaction between an old man with funds in search of prestige and a young man with prestige in search of funds. The correspondence between them until Hammer's death conveys well this unstated understanding. 'Once again you have been unbelievably generous . . .' the Prince grew accustomed to writing to the old man. 'Your wonderful contribution will enable this scheme to get off the ground . . .'[21] There was little more to it than that. If it pleased Hammer to be considered an intimate of the Prince, it was a highly productive myth that the Prince was far too canny to dispel.

The attitude of the American media to the Prince and Princess of Wales veered between worship and incredulity. As critics of royal vaudeville, reporters laboured to affect a detachment which their readers did not share; as commentators on a soap opera, they mocked the prurience of the British tabloids but could not resist repeating that speculative tittle-tattle for the edification of their own readers. In this state of journalistic schizophrenia, *Time* summarised the plot: 'The House of Windsor, imperturbable on the outside, has become a seething "Palace Dallas" on the inside. The Princess, once known as Shy Di, has become "Dynasty Di", and Prince Charles, once dubbed Action Man for his intrepid sky- and skin-diving, has become a hermetic, mystical crank.'[22] In a lengthy anatomy of the state of the royal marriage, *Time*, like its rivals in the American 'quality' media, drew heavily on frequently recycled anecdotes which had already appeared in the British press and, most sensationally, from a long article in *Vanity Fair* by its editor Tina Brown, who reported, under the headline 'The Mouse That Roared', that 'the heir to the throne is, it seems, pussy-whipped from here to eternity'.[23] The article had more in the same vein, much of it repetitive of others in content, though cleverly revamped in the British author's inimitable Americanese.

Seven months earlier, under the headline 'Mouse or Man?', the journalist Andrew Morton, billed by the *Daily Star* as 'the man who really knows the Royals', had asked rhetorically, 'Is the future King an ideal husband or the Prince of Wets?' Recalling his *Spitting Image* caricature as 'the dithering wimp who is the despair of his mother and the daily doormat for his diamond-hard wife', Morton adduced that although at Kensington Palace 'the roost is ruled by Diana', the Prince had 'iron in his soul'. Answering the question posed in the *Daily Star's* headline, he concluded, 'This is a Mouse that Roars.'[24]

Tina Brown's account of 'The Mouse That Roared' echoed some of Morton's themes, concurred with his assessment that the Prince was 'absolutely besotted' with his children, but, unlike Morton, implied that the relationship between the royal couple was unravelling; that while the Princess spent long hours dancing alone to her Walkman, or shopping compulsively for clothes, the Prince chose to seclude himself with gurus, mediums, and mystics – except when he was fulfilling his self-imposed duties as a 'house-husband'. The writer concluded that the Prince had discovered 'the flower children's concern with brown rice and spiritualism'.[25]

Refusing to be deterred by the ridicule, the Prince returned to his spiritual theme on more than one occasion. Opening an art festival during his tour of Canada in May 1986, he spoke of the importance of drama and music and of the impressive range of the performing talent that had mustered in the town of Prince George for the festival. In that context, he concluded:

I rather feel that deep in the soul of mankind there is a reflection as on the surface of a mirror, of a mirror-calm lake, of the beauty and harmony of the universe . . . So much depends, I think, on how each one of us is introduced to and made aware of that reflection within us. So I believe we have a duty to our children to try and develop this awareness, for it seems to me that it is only through the development of an inner peace in the individual and through the outer manifestation of that reflection that we can ever hope to attain the time of peace in this world for which we yearn.[26]

This 'mystical chat', as the *Daily Star* referred to his speech, was too much for many commentators. In the *Daily Express* Jean Rook, the self-proclaimed 'First Lady of Fleet Street', lived up to that sobriquet with a spiteful rebuke:

If he must reflect on 'the soul of mankind' as 'seen in a mirror' he should do it when he's shaving. And not fell a clump of Canadian lumberjacks with a mystical speech which invited them to query if his timbers are warped . . . He should stop rushing prematurely towards Mystical Man and Pressurised Parent and examine the mirror for nothing more than the secret of covering his bald spot.[27]

The absence of any attempt at understanding or sympathy was not so much cruel as crass, a reflection of a coarsening age in which the fashion was to repudiate all save the material achievements of the competitive instinct, and to admire the values of a theoretical construct which was soon to be popularly defined as 'Essex Man'. Essex Man was in fashion; the Prince was not.

The Prince attacked the issue again. At the 350th Anniversary of Harvard University, he said, 'Never has it been more important to recognise the imbalance that has seeped into our lives and deprived us of a sense of meaning because the emphasis has been too one-sided and has concentrated on the development of the intellect to the detriment of the spirit.'[28] The contrast between the response to that speech in the American and British press was instructive. The *Washington Post* praised his performance under the headline 'Harvard's Prince Charming'. Quoting extensively from the speech, the paper noted the wit, eloquence, candour and earnestness of a speech which 'showed that he understood his audience [16,000 Harvard alumni] perfectly'.[29] The British media hardly mentioned what he had said. The tabloids ignored it altogether: the silent 'Up Yours' of Essex Man.

Indifferent to his public role, the tabloids became ever more attentive to what they imagined to be his private life. Any sign that could be interpreted as evidence of marital disharmony was marked and noted, embellished and magnified: a glance here or a frown there was enough to establish a prospective certainty. They had appeared to have a row at a polo match; the Princess had complained in public that her husband disapproved of her taste in books; the editor of Burke's Peerage was granted spurious authority by the Sun, which under the headline 'Are Charles and Di Moving Apart?' reported him as saying that 'the Prince and Princess had come to a very special and civilised arrangement to allow the Princess much more time to herself'.[30] The accumulation and repetition of detail – the Prince's irritation when the Princess behaved less than decorously on the ski slopes, and when she giggled at the sight of him in an oversized hard-hat at a factory – provided a ready explanation for their lack of intimacy in public, a distance between them which in a kinder age might have been interpreted as a proper royal reserve.

By 1987, the speculation had reached a crescendo. The lead came from Andrew Morton in the Star, an assiduous member of the 'rat pack' although one of the least prone to viciousness. 'Separate breakfasts, separate timetables, separate friends,' he wrote. 'These days the Prince and Princess of Wales are leading active, interesting, but totally independent lives.'[31] In the royal soap opera, this theme became central to the script: the Prince and Princess had ceased to exist for the tabloids except in terms of their marriage. Their public duties were reported only to illuminate the presumed distance between them. As the more glamorous of the two, the Princess attracted far more attention. When she visited a Dr Barnardo's home or held the hand of an Aids patient, she did an inestimable public service, but the often explicit message in the tabloids was that while she could reach ordinary people, the Prince was closeted with eccentrics or trapped in a 'fogeyish' timewarp. When he visited a hospice or went on his regular walkabouts in the inner cities, the news was either too stale to print or too boring to mention. For the tabloids, the handouts from the Palace press office detailing the Princess's haute couture as if she were a mannequin made flesh, delicious but untouchable, were of much greater interest. It was doubtless in the interests of accuracy that such a handout should explain, 'Her Royal Highness is wearing a red lightweight wool suit with a long double-breasted jacket, narrow skirt and a red and white spotted blouse,'[32] but the effect was to elevate the wardrobe of the Prince's consort to a status that seemed to rival the point of the occasion at which her husband was presiding.

This tabloid distortion not only irritated the Prince but undermined his self-confidence and his sense of purpose. He complained to his friends, who were close enough to see, beneath the surface of self-pity, the anguish of a dutiful individual who had allowed himself to believe that the benighted perspective of the tabloids was not only damaging his own reputation but the standing of the monarchy as well. They knew that he was unable to turn to his parents to discuss the misery either of his private life or of his public persona. Their response to his charitable endeavours was incurious, while he was rarely left in doubt that they did not entirely welcome his contributions to controversial debate. The emotional gulf between the Prince and his parents was hard to bridge, while communication between them was normally limited to the exchange of social pleasantries and the formal business of the family enterprise. In his family, only his grandmother seemed able to give him the understanding and support for which he had always turned to her.

In this isolation, the handful of close friends whom he was still able to see were his only other source of comfort, and they knew it. They saw him on the retreat, eclipsed by the Princess, resentful of the public adulation of her, and wounded by the media's contempt for him. They listened, cajoled and encouraged, and they rarely remonstrated with him for the outbursts of anger and petulance which, with them, and only with them, he could freely indulge. They knew his weaknesses – his sudden tempers and his tendency to self-pity, self-righteousness and self-centredness – but they loved his strengths the more. If they appeased him more than was his due, it was in the knowledge that his wounds were too raw to endure further aggravation from them.

The real pain, far deeper than any caused by the tabloids, was that he could no longer see any way of arresting the disintegration of his marriage. He was horrified by the implications for the royal family and for the monarchy. 'That is the total agony about the situation,' he wrote, 'and I don't see how much longer one can go on trying to sweep it under the carpet and pretend nothing is wrong . . .'[33]

After five years, their marriage was indeed at a low ebb. Except for their children, the gulf of interests between them had not narrowed but widened. He had sacrificed some of his closest friends to ameliorate what he thought to be her feelings of insecurity. He had spent more time at home than was consistent with his sense of public duty. By the account of one member of their domestic staff, he had 'turned himself inside out'[34] for the Princess – and yet it was all to no avail. She remained desperately unhappy, insisting on his total attention, and apparently unable to respond to his attempts to make good the damage that their mutual isolation had inflicted.

The Prince had assumed that the rages which had consumed the Princess in the first years of their marriage would abate, that she would gradually settle into the role, accommodating herself to a place at his side as his consort and the mother of his children. Instead, there appeared to be a terrible conflict inside her that would suddenly erupt in anger or grief. As her public prestige soared, she grew correspondingly anguished in private. She complained that she could not bear to be the world 'mega-star' that she had become, yet she still scoured the newspapers for photographs of herself with an eagerness unalloyed by familiarity. Not for the first time, it seemed to their friends that she was searching for her own identity in the image of a princess that smiled back at her from every front page.

Whatever clinical or psychiatric label was appropriate to the Princess's distress, its effect on her marriage to the Prince could hardly be in doubt. Her extreme swings of mood from depression to rage; her overwhelming feelings of boredom, loneliness and emptiness, futility and abandonment; her lack of self-image or, as she expressed it to friends, her feeling that she did not know who she really was; the intense emotional pain that she must have endured in those years: all were bound to place a terrible strain on a marriage which was already subject to external pressures that no other relationship in the land had to experience.

The Prince did not react to the manifestations of his wife's predicament with indifference or hostility but rather with dismay, guilt, a sense of failure, frustration and the shared incomprehension of everyone around her. There was no specific incident that precipitated the end of the Prince's effort to hold his marriage together; it collapsed gradually. As their life with each other became increasingly unbearable, he confided in his friends that he felt powerless and beleaguered: 'It's agony to know that someone is hating it all so much . . . It is like being trapped in a rather desperate cul-de-sac with no apparent means of exit . . . It seems so unfair on her . . .'[35] In these circumstances, it was inevitable that instead of drawing closer together they would grow further apart until the gulf between them became unbridgeable.

The crumbling of their marriage was for both of them a private agony which was soon to be played out in public. With the benefit of hindsight it would become tempting to judge that, as they shared no interests or tastes and as their outlook was shaped by quite different experiences and expectations, they should never have entered wedlock. Certainly they had been driven by competing priorities: he, by the need to give substance to a role that he had created for himself, and which had become an overriding duty; she, by an urge both to fulfil the role of a princess without adequately understanding it and to play the part of the idealised bride, cooking suppers and darning socks for her husband (as, in her desolation, she often confided). In 1981, neither of them had understood enough about themselves or each other to be confident of climbing the foothills of such a public marriage; both needed the support from the other that neither was competent to provide.

Given the pressures to which they were both subjected by the demands of public life, theirs would have been an exceptionally testing partnership even if they had been able to stumble towards true companionship. However, the Princess's persistent and intense distress combined with his bafflement and exhaustion to make that modest ambition, which they both shared, impossible to realise. Thus, by 1986, their marriage had begun slowly to disintegrate in what were, for both of them, the most excruciating circumstances. That handful of their friends who knew and understood felt only compassion and pity for their shared predicament.

In May that year, they were in Canada for an official visit to Expo '86. The Prince was gloomy and the Princess on edge; she hardly ate at all and struck her entourage as being 'very, very thin'. When she fainted in public, the Prince seemed less than solicitous, and afterwards she complained that he had thought she had done it for effect. The truth was that he had started to withdraw the support which for so long had drained his reserves of sympathy and compassion. It was on this tour that the tabloid press heaped ridicule on him for referring to 'the soul of mankind' and to 'the beauty and harmony' of the universe that lay deep therein like the reflection in 'a mirror-calm lake'. In that speech he had added: 'But so often the beauty and harmony is obscured and ruffled by unaccountable storms'.[36] He was, as usual, speaking from the heart.

Although the Prince and Princess managed to preserve a show of public unity, the unhappiness of their marriage continued to fester, to the extent that within the outer forms of marriage they had started to live separate lives; even together, they were apart. As the Prince wrote in November 1986:

> Frequently I feel nowadays that I'm in a kind of cage, pacing up and down in it and longing to be free. How awful incompatibility is, and how dreadfully destructive it can be for the players in this extraordinary drama. It has all the ingredients of a Greek tragedy . . . I fear I'm going to need a bit of help every now and then for which I feel rather ashamed. All I want to do is to help other people . . .[37]

He began to turn once again to his friends, bringing back into his life those whom he had expelled at his wife's behest, including the Brabournes, the Romseys, the Palmer-Tomkinsons and Nicholas Soames. As he would explain much later, 'When marriages break down, awful and miserable as that is . . . it is your friends who are most important and helpful and understanding and encouraging. Otherwise you would go stark, staring mad.'[38]

Among those to whom he turned was Camilla Parker Bowles, with whom he began to re-establish the intimacy of their earlier friendship. Following his engagement to the Princess in February 1981, the Prince had made virtually no contact with Camilla Parker Bowles for over five years. Apart from the one occasion before the wedding, when he gave her the 'farewell' bracelet, he saw her only fleetingly at occasional social gatherings. Aside from a few telephone conversations during the four months of his engagement and only one after his marriage (when he rang to report that the Princess was pregnant with William), they had not talked to each other at all: like his other close friends she had been wholly excluded from his life. Until he reached the point of desperation, when, as he would later confine himself to saying in public, his marriage had 'irretrievably broken down',[39] he had been loyal to his wife and faithful to his marriage vows. Now, in the search for support, he once again began to talk to her on the telephone and they started to see each other at Highgrove; she usually came with either her husband or some of the Prince's other close friends, and the opportunities to be alone with each other for any length of time were infrequent. That they loved each other was not in any doubt: in Camilla Parker Bowles, the Prince found the warmth, the understanding and the steadiness for which he had always longed and had never been able to find with any other person.

Their relationship – about which the tabloids soon began to speculate with such incontinence – was later to be portrayed merely as a tawdry affair: for the Prince, however, it was a vital source of strength to a man who had been saddened beyond words by a failure for which he invariably blamed himself. 'I never thought it would end up like this,' he wrote. '. . . How <u>could</u> I have got it all so wrong?'[40]

The Princess was no less a victim, trapped in a marriage drained of life by the absence of love. In this predicament, she also came to rely more and more heavily for emotional support on her own close circle of friends, which included her former flatmates and others whom she had met in the intervening years. Among these were her protection officer Barry Mannakee, Catharine Soames, Kate Menzies, Philip Dunne, a merchant banker, and David Waterhouse, a major in the army. The latter was a frequent visitor to Kensington Palace, arriving accompanied by his dog to spend long hours with the Princess. A little later, another army officer, James Hewitt, joined her circle of friends. He gave riding lessons to the Princess, and sometimes her children, at a barracks near Windsor and on several occasions invited her to his family cottage in Devon. Later, he saw fit to publicise his friendship with the Princess in a tabloid newspaper and subsequently claimed to have had an affair with her. For a while, a London car salesman, James Gilbey, also spent much time in her company.

Although these close friendships provoked much tabloid speculation and photographers spent long hours trying to snatch pictures of these friends, the Prince of Wales was incurious about them. He had no urge to interfere in her private life. As he wrote in one letter, 'I don't want to spy on her or interfere in her life in any way.'[41] For his own sake and for that of his children he wanted their relationship at least to be amicable so that they could share their public duties for the benefit of the nation while finding a *modus vivendi* in their private life together. It was not to be.

By 1987, the pattern of the marriage for the next five years had been established. That autumn, the Prince remained in Scotland for some three weeks after the Princess had returned to London at the end of the school holidays. He had been joined by some of his old friends, but even they could not cajole him out of his bleak mood. He had long ceased to read any tabloid newspaper, but he knew what they were writing about him: that he had stayed in Balmoral to avoid the Princess, that he was a cold father who ignored his children, and that he ought to put his family above all else. In one article, he was told, there had been an insinuation to the effect that he was indulging in an affair with Sarah Keswick, a friend who had been a visitor to Balmoral during the stalking season for many years.* In another, based on photographs snatched by a 'paparazzi' but wrongly identified, it was implied that he had 'rekindled' a similar relationship with Dale Tryon, the wife of Lord Tryon. 'The fact that she wasn't within six hundred miles of the place [Birkhall]', he complained privately, 'didn't seem to matter.'[42]

He wrote despairingly that these innuendos had:

> unleashed a positive hurricane of self-righteous, pontificating, censorious claptrap in the newspapers . . . and has led to car loads of beastly photographers etc., careering about Balmoral and following me up the track to Loch Muick† etc. etc. I have told myself I am damned if I'm going to let all this stuff intimidate me. If I read one word I would have agonised about it for hours.[43]

Back in London, he sank into deeper gloom. He had been miserable to leave his grandmother in Birkhall, where he had felt insulated from the worst of the onslaught, and Kensington Palace was under siege by photographers. 'Diana is followed everywhere by freelancers on motorbikes,' he wrote despairingly. 'Her life is made more miserable than usual.'[44] In Scotland, 'amongst the hills, rivers, trees and animals that I love so much', he had at least felt himself among people who understood him. Yet the Princess persistently rebuked him for staying so long in his Scottish retreat while she and the boys were in London. Her anger filled him with guilt. In vain, he tried to explain that he craved the peace there that she loathed. Trapped in a relationship which had never penetrated beyond the everyday superficialities of their shared existence, neither of them could reach each other to explore the way ahead. The Prince wrote, 'I am beginning to experience that kind of confusion and rundown of confidence which makes me feel temporarily miserable . . . I can't see a light at the end of a rather appalling tunnel at the moment.'[45]

---

* Lady Sarah Keswick, married to Sir Chippendale Keswick, the chairman of Hambros.
† One of his favourite haunts, as it had been for Queen Victoria. It stands on part of the estate which is accessible to the public and is much used by hikers.

PART IV

A private citizen may feel his interest repugnant to his duty; but it must be from a deficiency of sense or courage that an absolute monarch can separate his happiness from his glory, or his glory from the public welfare.

Edward Gibbon, *The History of the Decline and Fall of the Roman Empire*, XLVIII

CHAPTER
TWENTY-ONE

In September 1987, Margaret Thatcher flew to Scotland for the annual prime ministerial weekend at Balmoral. One afternoon, she went for a stroll alone with the Prince in Rose Garden. She went straight to the heart of an issue which was troubling her, though she expressed her anxieties with the restraint that she seemed to reserve exclusively for members of the royal family.

Ten months earlier, the Prince and Princess had made an official tour of the Gulf States, accompanied by a Foreign Office official called Stephen Day, the head of the Middle East department. He and the Prince established an immediate rapport and over the course of a ten-day tour they discussed ways in which the Prince could put his status to more effective use in a region where the desert rulers have long presumed a special affinity with the British royal family. They agreed that it would be in British interests for the Prince to establish a more effective and methodical framework for maintaining links with that region, and indeed with the Middle East more generally, than that provided by the ritual audiences in air-conditioned palaces.

The idea found favour in the Foreign Office and was advanced to the stage where it was agreed to set up a special unit in St James's Palace, to be run initially by Day himself. At this point, the Foreign Office remembered that the Prime Minister should be informed. Mrs Thatcher was not amused; in the words of one Foreign Office official, 'The sound of breaking furniture could be heard all round Whitehall.'[1] To Mrs Thatcher it seemed as though the Prince was in the throes of setting up a Foreign

Office in miniature, which would formulate policy and conduct relations with the Gulf quite independently of the proper machinery of government. Although this was not at all what the Prince or the Foreign Office had in mind, Mrs Thatcher was implacable and the idea was dropped.

· In the Rose Garden, the Prince explained to her that, in effect, she had got the wrong end of the stick. The discussion broadened to take in the problems of administering his increasingly complex public life, and sympathetic to his needs, she offered to find him a senior administrator to help put his affairs in order. The Prince, who knew that his office was in a muddle, agreed with alacrity.

The man chosen for the task was David Wright, the former private secretary to cabinet secretary Robert Armstrong, and at the time head of personnel services at the Foreign Office. After a vigorous discussion about public spending at his interview with the Prince, Wright felt that he must have spoilt his chances of being appointed; but the Prince enjoyed the forcefulness of their argument and and appointed him to the post of deputy private secretary in March 1988. Wright, the most gifted official yet to join his team, was greeted by the same administrative confusion that had long characterised the Prince's office – a morass of unsorted paperwork (from cabinet minutes to fan mail for the Princess), no clear division of responsibilities, and too many 'dizzy Sloane Rangers' who were too busy being dizzy to focus on anything else. His boss, John Riddell, had brought an agile mind and languid humour to the job, but administration had never been his forte, and when Wright suggested the office was in a 'hopeless state' and offered to put it right, Riddell was delighted.

Wright set to work, devising a system for grading correspondence, and taking personal charge of the paperwork sent up to the Prince, sifting and selecting material with the precision that any cabinet minister would demand but the Prince had never before enjoyed. He succeeded in instituting something in the nature of an office routine, but the underlying problems remained. At the twice-yearly planning meetings, which were intended to finalise the Prince's official diary for the coming six months – confirming a list which by now numbered more than 400 engagements over the whole year, selected from at least 2,500 significant invitations – the approach taken was ad hoc and inchoate, with each member of the team pressing for 'their' invitations to find favour. The whole process was dreaded by the Prince and his staff alike, and exemplified how badly the office needed a well-focused strategy to exploit the Prince's interests and enthusiasms.

The issue came to the fore with the arrival of another new recruit, Guy Salter. His background was in industrial marketing, and his manner was so brash and self-confident that both Riddell and Wright had doubts about his suitability for the appointment. However, he was supported by Stephen O'Brien of BITC, on whose judgement the Prince had come to rely, and was duly appointed to the role of assistant private secretary for industry and commerce. Salter soon identified the 'diary mentality' as being to blame for corralling the Prince into an arbitrary succession of public engagements. 'This is crazy,' Wright remembers Salter saying when he saw how the diary was planned. 'We need to think what we are doing. What is this man doing? Why is he doing it and how should he be allocating his time?' Salter realised that the quality, impact and pattern – if any – of the Prince's public life was currently dictated entirely by the nature of the invitations he received. What was needed was a 'proactive' stance, an overall strategy which allowed them to decide how best to make use of the Prince's time. In a succession of papers and memos which did little to endear him to his senior colleagues but drew an admiring response from the Prince, Salter placed his forthright criticisms of the current regime on record. There was 'a lack of specialisation and co-ordination' in a system which tended to encourage only rivalry between 'petty baronies'; the private secretaries were overworked, and too often engaged on trivial matters; worst of all, the present system did not 'encourage or reward creative thinking, initiative or the pursuit of excellence', but fostered a 'head below the parapet attitude', a 'clean (rather than an outstanding) record being the most important objective'.[2]

Salter further advised the Prince to cease trying to be even-handed with the organisations that had mushroomed in his name, but to 'concentrate on the emerging issues'; in this way, he continued, 'YRH can "stay ahead of the game"'. To facilitate this approach, Salter suggested that each planning meeting should concentrate on a number of themes, which he divided into two categories, 'quality of life' and 'mainstream'. Among the former, he listed work in support of community architecture schemes, promoting the idea of community service, and encouraging practical schemes for improving the environment; in the latter category came BITC-related activities, and action to promote a more enterprising approach to exploiting opportunities for trade with overseas markets.

Salter's list was cleverly compiled to reflect both the Prince's long-standing commitments and his ability to make an impact. Yet his sense of the possible was optimistic: to expect such a small team of aides to deliver the proposed strategy and a communications programme to 'get the message across' was an ambition too far. Moreover, the Prince had other messages to convey as well; Salter's series of documents identified a deep-seated problem, but his proposed strategy offered far too narrow a concept of the Prince's role to serve as an effective 'mission statement'. Even though he was delighted by the clarity of Salter's presentation, the Prince was quite incapable of tailoring his role to such a precise set of objectives, either by disposition or by his inherited sense of public duty. Despite the best efforts of his staff to sharpen the Prince's profile – and in this respect Salter was a pathfinder – the task was doomed to failure. The Prince was a man for all seasons and for none, a man for his time but not of his time. This paradox was part of his identity as well as his charm. Any attempt to hone his image or to straitjacket his role to the vagaries of a shifting market would be to chase a will-o'-the-wisp, undesirable in principle and impossible in practice.

In the following twelve months, the Prince did focus on some of the themes identified by Salter, and to good effect. However, he also gave his support to a campaign to save the National Fruit Collection at Brogdale in Kent; he launched the publication of his *Vision of Britain*, the book which accompanied his television assault of the same name on the 'carbuncle' culture which he believed had mesmerised British architects; at the Thomas Cranmer Schools Prize awards, he made an impassioned plea in defence of the Book of Common Prayer against the 'crassness' of the Alternative Service Book; he was deeply engaged in a struggle to develop his own 'model' village on the outskirts of Dorchester; he became embroiled in a debilitating squabble over the preservation of King Henry VIII's warship, the *Mary Rose*; he gave an hour-long lecture at the Botanical Gardens, Kew, pleading for the rainforests; he addressed the students of Budapest University on the evils of communism; he made a second television film called *The Earth in Balance*, in which he warned against the accelerating depradation inflicted on the planet by human greed and folly; he made preparations for an international seminar on board the royal yacht which helped to lay the groundwork for the Earth Summit in Rio de Janeiro; and he made official visits to Indonesia, Hong Kong, Nigeria, Cameroon, Hungary and Spain.

In the same twelve months, he had private meetings with ten government ministers – John Major, John Gummer, David Mellor, Lynda Chalker, Chris Patten, John Wakeham, Michael Heseltine, Sir George Young, Ian Lang and David Hunt – and with three shadow ministers, John Smith, the leader of the Labour Party, Tony Blair and Gordon Brown. He wrote more than 1,000 personal letters, ranging from missives to cabinet ministers – about government policy in relation to (among other matters) the disabled, South Africa, the Gulf and Romania – to appeals for funds for a Centre for Islamic Studies at the University of Wales, his Architectural Summer School in Italy, and a schizophrenia 'help-line' set up by a charity called SANE. He wrote letters of condolence and of gratitude: he wrote to every one of the contributors to a ninetieth birthday concert that he had arranged for his grandmother, Queen Elizabeth, and he responded to those who had sent him gifts – which in this period included a novel by Catherine Cookson, a watercolour, a jar of mushrooms and another of truffles. He also went fox-hunting in the Midlands, skiing in Klosters, shooting at Sandringham, stalking at Balmoral, painting in Italy, and polo-playing (for much of June and July) at Windsor, Cowdray and Cirencester.

The despairing courtier and the wondering sceptic might both have been forgiven for concluding that, with such an array of commitments, any attempt to give his programme 'increased purpose, shape and direction' would be suborned by the Prince himself, torpedoing their best intentions with his own fervent eclecticism. 'The trouble is,' the Prince himself confessed with engaging candour, 'I always feel that unless I rush about doing things and trying to help furiously I will not (and the monarchy will not) be seen to be relevant and I will be considered a mere playboy!'[3]

Against the evidence, there were still those who tended to the traditional view that the Prince was a dilettante. This criticism missed the point; the Prince's shortcomings were different in character. Ignorant of office organisation, he had little sense of how hard it was for his staff to meet all the demands he made of them. He expected his senior officials to be available at all hours to respond to an idea which had suddenly stimulated him, and as a result critics complained that he had 'a butterfly mind', ignoring the fact that his enthusiasms were usually connected, if loosely, to one or another of his long-standing commitments. When challenged he could be intemperate and when frustrated he was known to throw his papers about the room. He was nigglingly critical and somewhat parsimonious with praise.

The Prince was not an easy master; and yet the thoughtlessness he sometimes displayed was in sharp contrast to the care with which he nurtured personal friendships, and the compassion he revealed when any of those among his staff found themselves in personal misfortune. He not only sent flowers or bottles of whisky, but wrote copious letters; he angled for jobs when former aides fell on hard times, and sometimes provided them himself; most of all, he found time to listen and comfort. When one of his trusted advisers, the secretary to the Duchy, John Higgs, was terminally ill with cancer, the Prince wrote:

> John is still determined that no-one should know and thinks that no-one does. He is without doubt the bravest man imaginable but I do wish he could have talked to someone. He won't talk to anyone and it must be agony for him mentally. I really don't know what to do. I am devoted to John . . . I really can't bear the thought of losing him.[4]*

His letters of condolence, to staff and tenants, were not just matters of form but touched by genuine feeling. When he wrote to friends in similar circumstances, his sympathy welled over. In September 1987, when his own personal life was in disarray, he wrote to Nicholas Soames after the funeral of his father, Lord Soames:

> I have minded <u>so</u> much for you and thought so much of you during these last few days while you had to watch your father gradually slip away before your eyes. I kept thinking that it might have been my father and I can imagine all the thoughts and feelings that you were probably experiencing, both before and after he died. Relationships with fathers can be such complex ones – I remember we often talked about our own relationships with our own respective fathers and how they've not been easy always. But that difficulty pales into insignificance when faced with the fact that a very important figure in one's life is no longer going to be there but is embarking on a mysterious

---

* When Higgs was close to death, the Prince, who had personally intervened to secure a knighthood for him, went to his bedside to confer the honour and subsequently erected a memorial to him at Highgrove.

journey into a new and more glorious dimension.

So often, I suppose one must long to have got on better or to have been able to talk freely about the things that matter deeply, but one was too inhibited to discuss. I pray you had a chance to talk to your father about those sort of things before he journeyed on.

I could hardly bear saying goodbye to you outside the church. You were being <u>unbelievably</u> brave and I knew what a struggle you were having. I can only pray that when you got back to the Mill you went for a long walk up the river and had a damn good cry. Somehow rivers help to assuage one's grief and sorrow and the current symbolises the transient nature of our lives on this visible Earth.

I still pray for you all and will say special prayers for you all . . . I long to see you on the 16th October when I hope these beloved hills up here will help in some way to heal the aching chasm in your life . . .[5]

It was the Prince's sensitivity and honesty along with his enthusiasm, his humour and the absence in him of any malice, which inspired the intense loyalty and affection of his staff. They were frustrated by his pre-varication and his occasional ill humour, and wished, in the words of one of them, that he did not rely so much on the mere *hors d'oeuvres* of knowledge; yet they were, with very few exceptions, devoted to the man and admiring of his commitment, however imprecisely it seemed to be directed.

In March 1987, Laurens van der Post finally achieved the objective for which he had striven a decade earlier: to show the Prince the intangible wonder of the Kalahari Desert. The Prince flew into Francistown in Botswana after a five-day official visit to Swaziland, Malawi and Kenya, and was joined by van der Post for the flight up to Orapa on the edge of the Kalahari, where they transferred to a helicopter which took them on a fifty-minute flight into the desert. Van der Post was disappointed that instead of the three weeks during which, he had hoped, they could explore deep into the interior, the Prince had only four days. However, it was better than nothing. The small party travelled by Land Rover, ate around the camp fire and slept under canvas, far from journalists and tourists. By day, the Prince sat in the sun, when the temperature was 120 degrees in the shade, sketching and painting. In the evening, they watched the sun fall off the edge of the landscape and they listened to the sounds of the desert. Between camps they drove across the barrenness, through vast river beds and endless tracts of scrub and rock. There was grandeur and beauty in the wilderness, but not enough time, it seems, for the mystical truths for which van der Post was prophet to reveal themselves.

On the third day, they came upon a herd of zebra, perhaps 20,000 animals scattered from flat horizon to flat horizon. Van der Post spoke in his quiet insistent voice, telling the Prince that this was Africa in the beginning. For van der Post it was a sacred, blessed moment, and his own feeling for it was expressed with such power that others in the party remember that the Prince was moved to tears. He sat there for over two hours, looking at the vision of earthly eternity and then sketching amongst the zebra, who browsed about them, indifferent to the human apparitions in their midst.

That night they slept in the Makarikari, 'the great bareness', on the edge of a route favoured by lions in their trek for water. Although they had been advised to sleep under the protection of canvas and the High Commissioner's Office in Gaborone had warned them not to speak outside their tents at night to avoid attracting the lions to their encampment, van der Post insisted that they lie out under the stars as he had done when he was a young explorer. It was a haunting spot in any case; the silence under the stars enhanced the sense of mystery.

In his diary for the four days, written as usual on the aircraft back to London, the Prince was unaccountably prosaic. 'On first contact,' he wrote:

the desert is pretty harsh and unforgiving and I wondered what on earth I had let myself in for! But after 4 days, which was similar to an S.A.S. selection test, it began to grow on you! So did the dirt, dust, and hair and I have never been so filthy before. I hardly ate anything and only felt like liquid. It was just the place to be during Lent, but the sunsets were out of this world. It was worth going for these alone and there was something very special about lying under the stars on the last night in the bush.[6]

That was all. If he had been moved by the experience, he had – uncharacteristically – concealed his feelings. Perhaps he was too tired to express them adequately on paper, perhaps he wished to keep them to himself, or perhaps they were not there – at least to the degree van der Post had originally hoped.

The following year, the Prince was in Africa again on another safari, not with van der Post, but as the guest of Geoffrey Kent, the owner of the travel company Abercrombie and Kent, and his wife, Jorie. The Prince had flown to join them in Tanzania from Australia via Thailand, where he had been on official tours with the Princess. As usual, he had been ambivalent about the visit to Australia where he was a guest at the 1988 bicentennial celebrations. Eighteen months earlier, he had been approached by the Governor-General, Sir Ninian Stephen, who mooted the idea that the Prince might like to succeed him in that post for the bicentennial year. The Prince was not averse to the notion but he responded cautiously, saying that he would accept the offer (over which, by tradition, an outgoing Governor-General has some influence) only if he could be reassured that the proposal had unanimous political support in Australia. Although he was not surprised to learn that Bob Hawke, the Prime Minister, was not in favour, he nonetheless felt rejected. 'What are you supposed to do,' he complained much later, 'when you are prepared to do something to help and you are told you are not wanted.'[7]

The bicentennial fuelled the debate between monarchists and republicans. The Prince, who was privately agnostic on the issue, was nonetheless irritated by what he saw as the predictably hostile commentaries in parts of the media, which he was prone to attribute to the inferiority complexes of the writers concerned in relation to the old colonial power. He was particularly irked by the journalist John Pilger who, in the Prince's words, had 'been stirring it up' about the possible involvement of the CIA and MI5 in the removal of the Prime Minister, Gough Whitlam, in November 1975 by the then Governor-General, Sir John Kerr, an allegation which Hawke told him was 'arrant rubbish'. Nor did he care for a series of articles written in the *Sunday Times* by Malcolm Turnbull, an Australian barrister, and 'the chap . . . who gave poor old Robert Armstrong a hard time over *Spycatcher*.'* Turnbull's account of Australian attitudes confirmed for the Prince that a growing

---

* As cabinet secretary, Robert Armstrong was the British government's chief witness in the 'Spycatcher case' which Britain took to the Australian courts to prevent publication of the memoirs of the former MI5 officer, Peter Wright. After cross-examination by Malcolm Turnbull, Armstrong apologised to the court for giving misleading evidence, confessing that he had been 'economical with the truth', a phrase which at once entered the lexicon of British politics.

number of his fellow citizens were at best lukewarm towards the monarchy. 'I must say I'm in two minds nowadays about how to approach Australia – let alone Canada or New Zealand', he wrote to Nicholas Soames, 'because I am fond of Australia, like the Australians, and would like to do more to help the various enterprises there . . .'[8]

The temperature was well over 100 degrees. During a speech in Adelaide, 'half the audience was carried off on stretchers' while he was speaking. They were 'mostly ancient circular ladies who appeared totally to have expired. As the number of stretcher cases increased rapidly before my eyes and the chairs rapidly emptied I could hardly contain a rise in hysteria! . . . I do hope they have recovered since . . .'[9]

It was a relief to join up with the Kents in Tanzania, where they drove into the Serengeti with his friends, Charlie and Patty Palmer-Tomkinson and Major Ronald Ferguson, the Prince's polo manager and the father of Sarah Ferguson, who had married Prince Andrew in July 1986. If the trip with van der Post had been an austerity package, this was the luxury tour. Abercrombie and Kent specialise in pampering the rich in wild places, and Kent's safari camp was like a sumptuous version of a regimental mess. His guests dined at tables and ate food that might have been plucked from a five-star hotel. They were served by waiters and maids to the same level of expertise, living in comfortable tents complete with their own showers and 'thunderbox' lavatories. The incongruity of such an establishment, the juxtaposition of such opulence and the wildlife of the Serengeti, was carefully calculated to provide a *frisson* of delight for the jaded palates of the American super-rich. It evidently delighted the Prince.

Kent had timed the safari so that they could witness the mass migration of the wildebeest through the Serengeti Plain. Between times the Prince painted or sat in the sun listening to Mozart. Afterwards, he wrote effusively from Highgrove:

> Now that I am back here again it all seems like a wonderful dream. I keep wondering whether it actually happened and how I could have been so happy in that unique environment . . . You made everything so easy and relaxed and thought of every single small detail that I felt unbelievably spoilt . . . I am left with evocative images of mentally retarded wildebeest jamming the Serengeti plains; of lions with appalling bad breath; of cooperative cheetahs, semi-recumbent rhinos,

mud-spattered elephants and parties of camera-bedecked tourists taking photos of me rather than the site at which ancient man was discovered![10]

Though he could only befriend those with whom he had shared a genuine affinity, and though some of his very closest friends were of modest means, it was by no means a handicap to the growing friendship between the Prince and Geoffrey Kent that the latter not only admired the heir to the throne but was honoured to put at his disposal one of the best polo ponies in the world. Kent was a British subject but he and his American wife lived in the USA, where he had captained his own Abercrombie and Kent team to win the US Open in 1978. When the Prince went to Palm Springs a year later at the end of an official trip to Canada, Major Ferguson approached Kent to ask him to provide some ponies so that the Prince could play a chukka while he was there. Kent at once assented. The match took place on a boiling afternoon and the Prince, who had practised for much of the morning and then spent an hour sunbathing, played to the edge of his endurance. At the prize-giving afterwards, Kent noticed that he was looking faint, so moved close to him on the podium. 'I'm feeling very strange,' the Prince muttered. Kent grabbed him and helped him down from the dais. He was taken back to the house, where he collapsed, to be diagnosed as suffering from dehydration, a painful and disconcerting experience.

In 1986, Ferguson approached Kent again, suggesting that he might like to bring his ponies to England for the season to play with the Prince in a reconstituted Windsor Park team. It was a summons not to be refused, and in the spring of 1987 the Kents arrived in England with forty polo ponies, their grooms and equipment, to set up house near Windsor at Wentworth. In June and July, they played three or four times a week with the Prince, eventually reaching the finals of the British Open in which they were defeated. Although the Prince's horsemanship was no more than adequate, his co-ordination was good and he played fearlessly. As a 'four goal' member of the team (the best are 'ten goal' players), he was almost competent enough to play as a professional, and he became a regular member of Kent's team.

A month after the Serengeti safari, the Prince and the Princess flew to Klosters for a skiing holiday. It was their third trip together to the

Prince's favourite haunt. On the second day of the holiday, 10 March 1988, the Princess, who had a severe cold, stayed in the chalet. There had been heavy snowfalls earlier in the week but the weather had cleared enough for the steeper runs to be reopened. In the morning, the Prince, accompanied by the Duchess of York, the Palmer-Tomkinsons, Major Hugh Lindsay (a former equerry to the Queen) and a Swiss policeman, Sergeant Cadruvi, skied on the Drostobel, one of the most demanding slopes at Klosters, before moving off to an even more testing run, the Gotschnawang, which had just been opened. During the morning, the Duchess had a heavy fall, ending up in a stream where she was soaked. Badly shaken, she was helped to the bottom of the run and thence, with icicles hanging from her hair, was taken to hospital for a medical examination to ensure that neither she nor the child in her womb had been damaged. She then joined the Princess at the chalet.

At lunch, the Prince's depleted party was joined by Bruno Sprecher, who, as one of the most experienced guides in the resort, had been hired to ski with the Duchess in the morning. With the Duchess confined to the chalet, the Prince's party invited him as a friend to join them for the afternoon. They decided to take the lift to the top station, the Gotschnagrat, and from there set off down the Haglamadd, an exceptionally testing unmarked descent which lay between the two runs they had skied in the morning.

They skied down to the entrance to a steep and narrow gully, the most difficult part of the run, hemmed in between a sheer rockface on one side and a precipice on the other. There they paused for breath. Suddenly they heard a great roar of noise. They looked up and saw gigantic slabs of snow, each the size of a large room, crashing down towards them. 'I've never forgotten the sound of it,' the Prince said later, 'the whole mountain apparently exploding outwards . . . vast blocks came crashing down past us . . .'[11]

Charlie Palmer-Tomkinson was in the lead. He paused for Sprecher to take over. The guide shouted, 'Jump!' The Prince obeyed instinctively and reached a ledge on the other side of the gully. He stood there with Sprecher, Palmer-Tomkinson and the Swiss policeman, and looked round. 'I've never seen anything so terrifying in my life, this maelstrom went past, vast clouds of snow and I thought to myself "My God!" I mean the horror . . .' he recalled.[12]

It was obvious that Patty Palmer-Tomkinson and Hugh Lindsay had been swept away by the avalanche. In fact they had both been hurled over the precipice, falling vertically 400 feet before hitting the slope again and tumbling a further 400 feet down the mountain, until they came to a halt, buried under the snow. Sprecher was the first down the slope and by the time the Prince had picked his way round the slope to join him, the guide had already located Patty Palmer-Tomkinson and was giving her mouth-to-mouth resuscitation. He had a spade and, together, he and the Prince managed to work her free. Sprecher then went off in search of Lindsay, discovering his body a few metres away but three feet under the snow, his skull fractured. Meanwhile, the Prince worked to bring Patty Palmer-Tomkinson back to consciousness, talking to her, murmuring that all would be well, that help would soon be at hand, that the helicopter was on the way. Her face was blue and she was cold and at first there was no reaction. He carried on talking. As she slipped in and out of consciousness she could hear him and tried to formulate words in response, but she was unable to speak. 'I was hanging on every word, it was like a lifeline. He was so calm, so conversational. "The helicopter is coming. You'll be all right." '13 The Prince, who had remembered that when Patricia Brabourne's life was in the balance after the bomb blast that killed her father, it was the sound of the doctors talking at her bedside which she believed had saved her, and he did not stop talking until his friend was lifted on to the helicopter for the flight to the hospital. On arrival, she was rushed into intensive care, critically ill. After the body of Lindsay had been recovered, the rest of the party followed down the mountain.

Back at the chalet, the horror of what had happened began to sink in: Hugh Lindsay, a young man and a good friend, was suddenly no longer with them; Patty Palmer-Tomkinson was on the critical list; and the heir to the throne was only with them by the grace of God, spared by no more than a couple of seconds.

In the confusion, Charlie Palmer-Tomkinson, greatly shocked, sat in a corner, repeating that they should return to the slopes the next morning, insisting 'that is what Hugh would have wanted'. The Prince, who managed to contain his emotion, became obsessed with the urgent need to protect Sprecher from being pilloried by the media for leading them to disaster and to explain what had happened before false rumours began to circulate. He resolved to address the press at once and say exactly what had happened. Philip Mackie, the Prince's press secretary, and Richard

Aylard* (who had recently joined his staff as assistant private secretary) tried to divert him, fearful that he would break down in the stress of the moment or lose his temper with the media. They argued that any statement should be issued by Buckingham Palace. Eventually, he was persuaded at least to put his statement on paper before meeting the press.

When the Prince had finished his draft statement, he seemed calmer and agreed that Mackie should read it out for the media at the airport, where the grim atmosphere was given a touch of bathos by his poor eyesight, his Glasgow accent, and the Prince's hurried handwriting. However, it was typed out by the Duchess of York on the flight to London and published the following day:

> In order to dispel some of the wild and unreasonable rumours which may have arisen as a result of the tragic accident in which I and my friends were involved, I would like to clarify a few points. Firstly I would like to emphasise that all the members of my party, including myself, were skiing off the piste at our own risk. We all accepted, and always have done, that the mountains have to be treated with the greatest respect and not treated lightly. There is a special dimension to skiing off the piste which is hard to describe to those who may not have experienced it or may not wish to. My friend, Major Hugh Lindsay, who so tragically died in this appalling accident, shared these feelings to the full, and also understood that there is inevitably a risk involved . . . Avalanches are a natural phenomenon of the mountains and when it comes to avoiding them no one is infallible . . . I would like to stress that Herr Sprecher behaved throughout in the most exemplary fashion and was instrumental in saving Mrs Palmer-Tomkinson's life. Not only is he a friend of mine, but by the way in which he operated, he did honour to the noble profession of which he is a member. We shall always be grateful to him.[14]

Before he left Klosters, the Prince went to see Patty Palmer-Tomkinson. She was still in intensive care, her breathing supported by a

---

* Commander Richard Aylard (1952–   ), equerry to Princess of Wales 1985–88; assistant private secretary and comptroller to Prince and Princess of Wales 1988–91; private secretary and treasurer to Prince of Wales since 1991.

ventilator. She had multiple fractures to her thighs, her knees, her lower legs and ankles, but her neck and her back had been spared serious injury. She would remain in hospital for many weeks to undergo major surgery, after which, it was presumed, she would be confined to a wheel-chair indefinitely. However, she was no longer on the danger list.

A week later, the Prince returned to Klosters to see how his friend was progressing. He had thought to escape into the high peaks with Charlie Palmer-Tomkinson for the silence and for reflection, but Mackie, a sharp-minded if prosaic Scotsman, had told them bluntly that to be seen wearing skis would be interpreted not as the act of communion they craved, but as evidence of callousness towards their dead comrade. His view prevailed.

To the lasting dismay of all those affected, the facts of the disaster were persistently to be distorted. In what appears to have been a conscious effort to damage the Prince, he was widely accused of leading his party down a 'closed' run despite warnings to stay clear, and thus to blame for causing the tragedy that followed.* The truth was otherwise: there were no warning signs and the run was not closed. The five-page official report by the Public Prosecutor of Graubunden confirmed the findings of the Federal Institute for Snow and Avalanche Research at Davos, that the group had 'disturbed the blanket of snow that triggered off the avalanche', and that on the day of the accident, the avalanche bulletin warned of 'a considerable local avalanche danger' in the region where they were skiing. Nonetheless, the Chief of the Parsenn service, respon-sible for the safety of the marked and controlled pistes at Klosters, had thought it safe, after blast tests, to open both the Drostobel and the lift to the top station. The prosecutor thought it possible that the continuation of blasting led the group to assess 'wrongly' the danger on the Haglamadd, which, however, had not been tested as it lies outside the area controlled by the Parsenn service.

Exonerating Sprecher from any liability, the report found that, as no single member of the party had an 'explicit leadership role', it was 'the

---

* On 18 March, the *Sun* headline read 'ACCUSED. Official: Charles DID cause the killer avalanche'. Among many others making similar points, James Whitaker, writing five years later in *Diana V Charles*, stated that 'after pushing his party to go down an off-piste run when there were clear signs warning them not to, Charles was forced to take responsibility for the tragedy that followed.' (p.154).

task of each single member to assess the dangers and carry the responsi-bility for himself'. The prosecutor also ruled out 'culpable negligence'. The party formed 'a group of experienced, risk-conscious skiers prac-tising the sport at its extreme demands', 'practically equally skilled skiers [who] had joined for descents on territory well known to them . . . [and who] made a personal decision to ski on the fatal slope thereby con-sciously accepting the inherent risk'. The case was closed and the state treasury ordered to bear the costs of the investigation.[15]

The decision by the Prince and the Palmer-Tomkinsons to return to Klosters in subsequent years was cruelly misinterpreted by some com-mentators, one of whom asserted that the Princess of Wales had been appalled by this evidence of her husband's 'insensitivity'.* In reality, the Prince and the Palmer-Tomkinsons found it impossible to expunge the memory of what had happened, and whenever they met the con-versation came back to Klosters. 'We all agreed that we could never go anywhere else,' Patty Palmer-Tomkinson was to recall with some emo-tion. 'We don't want to walk away from it . . . we don't want to forget it and it's very important that we go back every year and remember it . . . It's not <u>the</u> reason for going back, it is <u>one</u> of the reasons. It would have been like turning our back on <u>him</u> and leaving him there. We can't ski together, the three of us, without remembering Hugh . . .'[16]

Through the tragedy at Klosters, the Prince acquired a tabloid reputation as 'accident prone'. Commentators allowed themselves to wonder whether the heir to the throne should be allowed to indulge in 'high-risk' activities and suggested the time had perhaps arrived for the Prince to cut back on his more strenuous and dangerous sporting pastimes. The tabloid press, especially, delivered itself of numerous editorials on the subject, but *The Times* came to his rescue. In a leading article entitled 'Risk and the Crown', it stated, 'The human impulse for combat with nature is, in particular, something to be cherished. It should not be feared and reprehended . . .' Acknowledging that the sovereign, by virtue

---

* Whitaker wrote that 'Diana told Hugh's widow Sarah, who was pregnant when he died, that she would never set foot in Klosters again, yet Prince Charles was back there the following year, skiing away as if nothing had happened. Such insensitivity chilled her blood.' (op. cit., p. 155.)

of her constitutional duties, was under a special obligation to protect herself from unnecessary hazard, the leader writer argued that:

> these awesome duties have not yet descended upon the Prince. His are
> different. He represents the future and it is right that his example
> should be addressed largely towards the young. The example he sets
> them is one of bravery: physical prowess in healthy pursuits and intel-
> lectual enterprise in good causes. What is more, he is a relatively
> young man who must be allowed to live, not transformed into a
> museum piece . . .[17]

It is conceivable that this attitude reflected the attitude of the majority of men and women in Britain. Two years later, however, the
jeremiahs acquired further ammunition in the Prince's passion for polo.
In twenty years of playing the game he had suffered the usual mishaps,
acquiring the bumps and bruises that the sport inevitably inflicts, including a cut on his face which had required twelve stitches. But in 1990 he
came seriously to grief.

On 28 June, he was playing in a match at Cirencester. Galloping to cut
off an opponent in pursuit of the ball, his pony swerved to the right at
precisely the moment the Prince leant out to take a backhanded shot.
The Prince lost his balance and fell between the two ponies, one of
which half fell over him, kicking him on the right arm in the process. It
was at once obvious that the Prince was in severe pain. An ambulance
was summoned and, with Jorie Kent at his side, he was driven to the
Cirencester Memorial Hospital. In the ambulance, the muscles around
the fracture began to contract and his arm began to concertina.

Waiting in the emergency room, he was given morphine to ease the
pain. X-rays showed a double fracture of the arm above the elbow. With
the approval of the orthopaedic surgeon to the Queen, Sir Rodney
Sweetnam, the doctors elected to set the fracture without first pinning it.
He came out of hospital a few days later, still in pain. When he discussed
with his friends what the surgeons had done, one of them, Patty Palmer-
Tomkinson, suggested that he should consult Professor Peter Matter, the
Swiss surgeon who had operated on her legs to such effect that she was
out of a wheel chair and on crutches, for an informed second opinion.

Matter's immediate reaction was that a double fracture needed to be
pinned and should not be left to heal naturally. As soon as he saw the

x-rays, he confirmed this view. The Prince invited Matter to visit him at Highgrove, where he concluded that the way it had been strapped at Cirencester would hamper the healing process – about which he was, in any case, dubious. He re-strapped the arm, which then caused so much discomfort that the Prince summoned the Cirencester doctors to restore the original strapping. Throughout July and early August, the pain did not abate. Informally, since the Prince was not his patient, Matter insisted with growing conviction that it was imperative to operate. He warned that otherwise the Prince's arm would be so crippled that he would, for example, be unable to salute, which, he added mischievously, 'I think it is necessary for an English Prince to do from time to time.'[18] He explained in graphic language that the elbow was freezing up – that the point of fracture was in the process of replacing the joint so that, grotesquely, the Prince's right forearm would swing from a point half way between the elbow and the shoulder. To avoid this ghoulish prospect, he urged an early operation.

When this opinion was relayed to Sweetnam and his team, they persisted in their opinion that the arm would heal on its own. However, on 20 August, almost eight weeks after the accident, Sweetnam held a case conference at Balmoral where the Prince was in residence at which he and his team came to the reluctant conclusion that their approach had failed. The following day, two of Matter's former students, both eminent British surgeons, flew to Balmoral to give second opinion. Confirming Matter's diagnosis, they at once booked the Prince into the Queen's Medical Centre, Nottingham, and effectively replaced Sweetnam and his team. The operation took place on 2 September, and even before he had recovered from the anaesthetic his Australian physiotherapist, Sarah Key, began an intensive course of physiotherapy. The manipulation caused intense pain but six weeks later his right arm was strong enough for the Prince to use it to throw a log on the open fire in his grandmother's drawing room at Birkhall.

The episode provided a run of field days for some of the tabloids, which discovered that the Nottingham hospital had reopened a small wing for the royal party, which included his office staff and his detectives, who camped there while the Prince wrote memoranda and letters laboriously with his left hand. The 'rat pack' heard rumours that he had enjoyed a candle-lit dinner with Camilla Parker Bowles (he did have a candle-lit dinner but it was with the Kents and Emilie van Cutsem, although on a separate occasion Camilla Parker Bowles did visit him in the company of Penny Romsey); they reported that the Princess had 'confronted' Camilla Parker Bowles at the hospital (they did not see each other there); and they complained when he came out at his failure to look as cheerful as they would have liked. They also decided that he should give up polo. In their concern for the monarchy, they advised that for the heir to the throne to take such risks with life and limb was bordering on the foolhardy and the irresponsible; after all, he was almost forty-two years old. In this case, they had unlikely allies.

Some of the Queen's most senior courtiers had long disapproved of the extent to which the Prince had committed himself to polo, but for different reasons. They worried less about the physical risks of the game than about the damage it threatened to his image, especially when it seemed to consume so much of his summer. One or two of them, including William Heseltine, had not refrained from expressing their reservations to him directly if discreetly. Heseltine's successor, Sir Robert Fellowes, judged that the sport took up an inordinate amount of time and, however unfairly, left the Prince open to the 'playboy' image to which the heir to the throne was usually so sensitive. Even the Prince's own staff, juggling the competing demands on his time, inclined to the view that his commitment to a 'rich man's sport' occupied an excessive place in his life. With Britain gripped by a long recession, with the monarchy under critical scrutiny and, by 1992, with his private life the subject of sensational and bruising gossip, his closest advisers began to counsel openly that he should be seen to reduce the number of June and July afternoons that he spent on polo fields at Windsor and Cowdray Park. The Prince was unimpressed, protesting that as polo took the form of tournaments, he had to be available for all games or for none; that he enjoyed mixing business with pleasure (and that the charity matches in which he played raised many thousands of pounds for worthy causes); that he needed the excitement of an – admittedly – high-risk sport; and that it was a release from the growing tensions and miseries of his marriage. Without polo, he insisted, he would go 'stark, staring mad' – his favourite phrase when driven to defend himself against unpalatable advice. Any inference that he was shirking his duties goaded him to recite a litany of his workload. Reminding his friends and his staff of what they already knew, that there was rarely a day in his life in which he failed to hold meetings and write letters or memoranda, he judged the critics of his commitment to polo to be carping killjoys.

However, other factors were harder to resist. The 1991 season was the last in which Kent was able to bring his team over for the English summer, and in 1992, when he played in a team financed by the Greek shipping magnate Anthony Embericos, he missed the exuberance and zest that the Kents had brought to the season. Moreover, his long-standing back problem was getting steadily worse: a degenerative disc at the base of the spine, which had for some years made it uncomfortable for him to sit in one position for any sustained period, was aggravated by polo to the point where his doctors warned that unless he curtailed such violent activity his back might 'lock up', which would seriously incapacitate him. There had already been occasions on which he had been obliged to receive visitors while lying on his back, and by the end of the 1992 season he was moving, with extreme reluctance, to the conclusion that at the least he would have to give up 'high goal' polo and concentrate on a few charity tournaments at a lower level of play. The prospect filled him with gloom.

CHAPTER
TWENTY-TWO

—◆—

Towards the end of the eighties, the environment became a fashionable cause, formally embraced by prime ministers and presidents, while inter-governmental conferences and UN reports vied for public attention as the world discovered more about 'greenhouse gases' and the 'ozone layer'. Organisations like Greenpeace and Friends of the Earth, long repudiated as woolly-minded doom-mongers, became the soothsayers of the age while the Green Party, an anarchic and ramshackle political enterprise, alarmed conventional politicians by securing 15 per cent of the vote in the 1989 European Elections. The Prince was a beneficiary of this awakening: as one journalist reflected, following the transmission in May 1990 of his environmental film *The Earth in Balance*, 'The loony prince of tabloid fable begins to look like a man in harmony with public opinion, not to say at its cutting edge. We're all friends with plants now.'[1] It had taken a long time.

Twenty years before, in what had been dubbed 'European Conservation Year', the Prince had made his first public speech on the environment. He was twenty-one years old and chairman of the Countryside in 1970 Committee for Wales. Under the influence of his father, his principal concern was then for the preservation of natural habitats in the wild and the protection of the rural landscape, but he touched prophetically on 'the horrifying effects of pollution in all its forms', citing 'oil pollution at sea, chemical pollution discharged into rivers from factories and chemical plants, and air pollution'. In the speech, which he had drafted in his own hand, he continued:

> But to install filter plants at a factory, for example, is expensive; it increases the production overhead costs which in turn are going to be added to the price of the product. In the end it will be the general public, the consumers, who will have to pay. Are we prepared to accept these price increases to see our environment improved? . . . Are we also prepared to discipline ourselves to restrictions and regulations that we feel we ought to impose for our own good? We must be prepared to do so . . .[2]

In the same year, in a maiden speech at the Cambridge Union, he expressed scepticism about Concorde, asking his audience rhetorically, 'If it is going to pollute us with noise, if it is going to knock down churches, or shatter priceless windows when it tests its sonic boom – is that what we really want?'[3] The British Aircraft Corporation was driven to confirm that Concorde would not fly supersonically overland, and murmured, through a spokesman, 'Prince Charles must listen to both sides in the controversy.' The motion, 'This House believes that technological advance threatens the individuality of man and is becoming his master,' which might have been composed by the Prince, was carried by 214 votes to 184.

Later that year, in Australia, he was taken to task by the local mayor after he criticised the condition of the beach at St Kilda's outside Melbourne, reporting, after a swim, that the sea was 'like diluted sewage'. The mayor, councillor James Duggan, complained that pollution, 'has become the in-thing. It all follows the visit of the Prince of Wales. When that crank came here he didn't have the brains to tell us he was going to St Kilda's beach or we would have cleaned the place up . . . Australians didn't give pollution a thought until that crank came here.'[4]

In Britain as well as in Australia, the political dilemmas posed by the degradation of the environment were as yet no more than a matter for muted debate among specialists. Reflecting a spate of similar literature, the publication in 1972 of *Limits to Growth*, a doomsday analysis by the Club of Rome, argued that 'if the present growth trends in world population, industrialisation, pollution, food production and resource depletion continue unchanged, the limits to growth on this planet will be reached some time within the next 100 years'.[5] Though the impact of this prognosis was weakened by an overstatement of the case, the authors confirmed in more sophisticated terms the instincts to which the Prince had already given expression in the Cambridge Union. 'Technological optimism is the most common and most dangerous reaction of our findings,' they warned. 'Technology can relieve the symptoms of a problem without affecting the underlying causes. Faith in technology as the ultimate solution to all problems can thus divert us from the fundamental problem – the problem of growth in a finite system – and prevent us taking effective action to solve it.'[6]

The Prince was more influenced by another publication of the era, *Small is Beautiful*, a less vociferous but seminal study written by Fritz Schumacher, in which the author placed his political and economic analysis of the global predicament in a spiritual dimension. Arguing the case for small-scale production, for 'technology with a human face', he wrote, 'Human scale thinking must have a spiritual content. If we are to move from partial, fragmented, compartmentalised living towards completeness and holistic living, we have to put back what our dominant industrialist-materialist-scientific world view leaves out. The omitted area is what we mean by spiritual.'[7] The Prince concurred so unequivocally with these sentiments that in 1980 he became patron of the Intermediate Technology Development Group which had been formed by the author fifteen years earlier to develop means of production specifically designed for the needs of what was still called the Third World.

For sharing these attitudes the Prince was mocked relentlessly, not only by the tabloid press but even in 'progressive' newspapers like the *Guardian*, which, in the year that he gave his support to the disciples of Schumacher, dubbed him an 'Eco-King' and conjured up an image of 'the grounds of Buckingham Palace converted into allotments, with windmills creaking away in an attempt to provide electric power'.[8] When the Prince inaugurated a bottle bank in the trade yard at the Palace a few weeks later, it was described by the *Guardian*, which perhaps found it difficult to reconcile its generally sensitive attitude towards the environment with its scepticism about the monarchy, as a 'strange machine'.[9]

By the mid-eighties, when the Prince was already patron of the Royal Society for Nature Conservation, the tabloid media decided that he was a 'loony' for talking to his plants. At the peak of the economic boom, when developers had never had it so good, Lord Northfield, head of a building consortium, was goaded into saying in public that the Prince had been hijacked by the 'Loony Green Brigade'[10] – in this case for having the temerity to suggest in a speech that developers should build on vacant land in the inner cities rather than pushing the planners to open more land in the Green Belt.

In 1987, the publication of the Brundtland Report, *Our Common Future*, shifted the environmental debate onto a more elevated and yet wider stage. Linking the twin themes of the environment and development, the report introduced into political discourse the concept of 'sustainability', a modification of the ideas explored by the Club of Rome and Schumacher fifteen years earlier adapted to meet the political imperatives of economic growth. Chris Patten, the influential Minister for Overseas Development,[*] seized on this theme, declaring as Conservative government policy ideas which would have been regarded as heresy in the early years of Thatcherism. 'What is needed is growth that can be sustained,' he said in a speech to an audience of specialists gathered at Cumberland Lodge, Windsor, to offer a critique of the role of the World Bank. 'Growth must be pursued within – and not despite – the limits of ecological resilience.'[11]

Emboldened by the shifting attitudes within government, the Prince went on the offensive at the opening of the North Sea Conference in London. Without identifying his target, he castigated the attitude adopted by the Secretary of State for the Environment, Nicholas Ridley,[†] who was in his audience. In a passage inserted into his speech at the last moment, the Prince said, 'Some argue that we do not have enough proof of danger to justify stricter controls on dumping or to warrant the extra expenditure involved.' He continued, 'If science has taught us anything, it is that the environment is full of uncertainty. It makes no sense to test it to destruction. While we wait for the doctor's diagnosis, the patient may easily die!'[12]

The Green movement was delighted, as, more significantly, were one or two senior civil servants within the Department of the Environment,

---

[*] Christopher Patten (1944–   ), Minister for Overseas Development 1986–89; Secretary of State for the Environment 1989–90; chairman of Conservative Party 1990–92; Governor of Hong Kong since 1992.

[†] Nicholas Ridley (1929–93), Secretary of State for Transport 1983–86; for Environment 1986–89; for Trade and Industry 1989–90.

who were deeply frustrated by Ridley's apparent indifference – to the extent that it was widely believed that Martin Holdgate,* a senior official in Ridley's department, had collaborated with the Prince's advisers in the preparation of the speech. The declaration by the Prince of this 'precautionary principle' not only broke new ground in the public debate but helped to shift opinion within the government. By tacitly rebuking Ridley, he gave powerful ammunition to those who were trying to nudge and bludgeon the Prime Minister towards a more sympathetic stance. In this period, the Prince and Patten had a number of private conversations at which each warmed to the other; the former was impressed by the latter's political intellect, while the latter was taken by the Prince's knowledge and commitment.

The following February, as patron of the European Year of the Environment, the Prince again urged the government to act with greater conviction. 'Why then are we so slow in this country to respond to what is, I think, a growing public feeling?' he complained. 'Why has environmental regulation of one kind or another taken so long to come about here when you find that in West Germany, for instance, or the United States, they have had many more regulations and controls for a long[er] time than we have?' He went on to attack directly the Central Electricity Generating Board for 'doing too little too late' to combat 'acid rain'; he told industrialists that in such matters 'they were out of step with the ordinary bloke on the street'; and, in a reference to ozone depletion, he told his audience that, 'I, as I become older and more autocratic, have banned the use of aerosols in my household.'[13]

It was a 'scattergun' speech but it peppered enough vested interests to guarantee the headlines on the following morning. With the exception of one or two tabloids which chose to focus on his self-confessed 'autocracy' at Kensington Palace, the significant aspect of this speech, as with all those that he delivered in the latter half of the eighties, was that the media began to take what he said seriously: he had touched a public nerve and they knew it. For example, and despite the protests of the manufacturers, aerosols fell rapidly out of fashion.

---

* Sir Martin Holdgate (1931–   ), Chief Scientist and Dep. Sec., Department of the Environment 1979–85; Dep. Sec., Environment Protection and Chief Scientist, DoE, and Chief Scientific Adviser, Department of Transport, 1985–88; Director-General, International Union for Conservation of Nature since 1988.

Were there any lingering doubts about the shift in public opinion, they were dispelled at the Conservative Party Conference in October 1988. To the astonishment of environmentalists, the Prime Minister informed her audience, in words which seemed to have been crafted by Patten, 'No generation has a freehold on the earth. All we have is a life tenancy with a full repairing lease.'

Although Patten and Sir Crispin Tickell, Britain's permanent representative to the United Nations,* had both helped to persuade the Prime Minister of the political and scientific merits of the 'precautionary principle' and of the argument for 'sustainability', there is no doubt that the lead taken by the Prince in championing an informal coalition of environmental groups had played a significant part in shaping a public opinion to which she had felt obliged to respond. He had intervened directly in the political debate, challenging government and industry, and – for the first time – he had emerged unscathed. Thatcher's rhetoric promised more than her government was willing to deliver, but the environment now had a permanent if uncomfortable place at the lower end of the political top table.

By this time, the Prince had started to form around him a core of environmental advisers, which he described in a letter to a friend as 'a small team of knowledgeable people who can help me put as much pressure on international agencies, governments, and so on, via speeches, lunches and dinners, as possible. Whether anyone will listen to me is another question but I feel I must try to make my own contribution towards stirring people's consciences . . .'[14] The early members of this group included Richard Sandbrook (executive director of the International Institute for Environment and Development), Jonathon Porritt (then director of Friends of the Earth) and Janet Barber (head of conservation at the World Wildlife Fund UK, later renamed Worldwide Fund for Nature), and they were to become increasingly influential. With them he explored and tested issues and ideas, endlessly wrestling with the conflicts between economic growth, the needs of the community and the protection of the environment. Others who also offered

---

* Sir Crispin Tickell (1930–   ), permanent secretary ODA 1984–87; permanent representative to UN 1987–90; warden of Green College, Oxford, since 1990; chairman of International Institute for Environment and Development since 1990 and of Earthwatch (Europe) since 1990.

advice included Paul Ekins, an academic environmental economist, Tim O'Riordan (Professor of Environmental Sciences at the University of East Anglia) and Tom Burke (later to become Patten's adviser at the Department of the Environment). The Prince's new aide, Richard Aylard, who had graduated as a zoologist before entering the Royal Navy, and who was himself a committed environmentalist, played a growing role in co-ordinating this expertise, collating the relevant evidence and preparing preliminary drafts of what the Prince might say in public.

Some ministers found the Prince's speeches infuriating, and one or two of them muttered that he had overstepped his constitutional bounds. Yet not one of them had the temerity to voice this resentment in public. 'I like to think that I haven't strayed into party politics,' the Prince was to say later:

I look at each situation as I think it is. I don't come armed with a lot of baggage . . .I understand the parameters in which I can operate but at the same time I'm quite prepared to push it here and there because I happen to be one of those people who feel very strongly and deeply about things . . . I don't see why politicians and others should think they have the monopoly of wisdom . . .[15]

Convention demanded that his speeches were sent to the relevant minister for comment. Often, they suggested minor alterations or requested that a passage be omitted, but, in general, he found their advice helpful. Usually he complied, although on occasion he refused. When the final draft of a speech he had written about the threat to the ozone layer was sent to the Department of the Environment, he received word that the Secretary of State was not entirely happy. 'I have just heard that Nicholas Ridley has seen the speech and wants to cut out two pieces. I'm afraid I'm not going to!'[16] In his address to the heads of delegations at the 'Saving the Ozone Layer' World Conference in the spring of 1989, he made a direct and passionate exhortation to the world's political leaders:

Until we have managed to discover somewhere else in some other galaxy which has a comparable set of atmospheric conditions it makes absolutely no sense to me at any rate to mess about unnecessarily with the fragile and delicate chemical compositions which perpetuate life on this globe as it hurtles mysteriously and harmoniously through space. It certainly makes no sense to destroy the ozone layer . . . We certainly can't pretend that we aren't aware of the potential long-term dangers to the intricate balance of Nature. Since the Industrial Revolution, human beings have been upsetting that balance, persistently choosing the short-term options and to hell with the long-term repercussions. It seems to me that countless numbers of people are looking to their leaders and representatives to take bold decisions *now* – decisions which our descendants, yet unborn, will thank us for – and not to put off those critical decisions that will ultimately cause our grandchildren to curse us.

Then, in a passage which bore the footprints of his specialist advisers, he acknowledged the lead taken by the British government with a commitment to cut the use of CFC gases, but, citing compelling new evidence about the rate of ozone depletion, he insisted 'there is surely an *overwhelming* scientific case to change the treaty from a reduction to complete elimination'.[17] To call for the total elimination of CFC gases from the world's industrial inventory was to throw down the gauntlet to the government, and he knew it. So did the press; the speech attracted large headlines and was extensively quoted.

At a European Environment Conference in the spring of 1988, he had taken a more spiritual approach:

It would seem that there is still a prejudiced misconception in certain circles that people concerned with the environment, and what happens to this Earth, are bearded, be-sandalled, shaven-headed mystics who retreat every now and then to the Hebrides or the Kalahari Desert to examine their navels and commune with the natives!* But this is simply not true. There is a great groundswell of genuine concern about these issues of our day and age . . .There is a growing realisation that we are not separate from Nature; a subconscious feeling that we need to restore a feeling of harmony with Nature and a

---

* In 1987, the Prince had spent a few days staying with a Hebridean crofter, following his foray into the Kalahari with Laurens van der Post earlier that year. Both had been the occasion of ribaldry in some quarters of the media.

proper sense of respect and awe for the great mystery of the natural order of the Universe . . . We are beginning to realise that whatever we do to Nature – whether it is on the grandest scale or just in our own gardens – is ultimately something that we are doing to our own deepest selves.[18]

Three years earlier, the tabloid media had smirked at such sentiments. Now, when he said, 'Many people are now aware of the problems and dangers of the possibly catastrophic climatic changes through air pollution; of the mass extinction of species threatened by the loss of tropical forests and other essential habitats,' they reported his words without a single sneer. Likewise with his rhetorical declaration that, 'When we read that over the next sixty years, if we go on as we are doing, something like a third of all the forms of life at present living on this planet may be extinct, can we feel anything but a kind of cosmic horror?'[19] Of course, as he well knew, the Prince was not alone responsible for this shift in attitude, but by playing such a prominent part in the campaign, he had given great impetus to it.

In May 1990, the *Sunday Mirror*, which had been more sympathetic than most of its tabloid rivals, observed:

Prince Charles could be forgiven for adopting an air of quiet self-satisfaction these days. For the years of sneers and cheap jokes are over. The causes and enthusiasms that earned him taunts like the Potty Prince have suddenly become everyone's concern. Now it's his bandwagon everyone wants to jump on. He's the champion of the Green Revolution. A man admired for his foresight.[20]

There remained some dissent. In October 1990, the *Observer* was moved to an oddly boorish and patronising leading article. 'It is not uncommon for a middle-aged man with an unsatisfactory home life to conceive a mission to set the world to rights,' this erstwhile bastion of enlightened liberalism opined. 'Nevertheless Prince Charles ought to resist the urge if he wants the Royal family to survive . . . Yet Prince Charles is now deeply embroiled in one of the major political issues of our day – the great, and some may think, rather boring question of the environment.'[21]

At that shallow level, the *Observer* was right: the peak of environmental concern coincided with the onset of a recession which was to diminish the impact of the argument as the public began to worry about the rise in unemployment. Although the Prince had long been concerned with this, the environmental crisis was for him of paramount importance. Even as the 'chattering classes' turned away, he redoubled his efforts in the run-up to the Earth Summit in 1991, borne along by the inner conviction that he had no need to follow fashion; that if he were right, the fashion would once again follow him; and that if he were not, it was only his credibility which would suffer. He felt no self-satisfaction, but for once there was little self-doubt either, as many thousands of people hurried to demand action from their governments in all parts of the world. 'I told them that years ago but they wouldn't listen . . .' was his characteristic reaction when he was informed that an industrialist or a politician or a civil servant had praised one of his initiatives, or that an idea of his had been adopted. Pessimistic by nature, he had by now convinced himself that the world was on a downward course, that he could not reverse the trend but that his duty was to ally himself with those who thought as he did, and to persevere.

The *Observer's* comments were stimulated by his film for BBC television, *The Earth in Balance*, in which he gave open expression to his feelings for the natural world and his anxieties about the degradation of the planet. It was a direct and heartfelt personal statement which earned ritual scorn from most of the metropolitan television critics, but it was a popular success. His correspondence, which was overwhelmingly sympathetic, included a supportive letter from the Duke of Edinburgh in which his father only protested mildly at his son's failure to reach any conclusion at the end of the film. The Prince wrote back reporting that his conclusions were far too gloomy to offer on television – that (as he reported subsequently in a letter to Jonathon Porritt), 'conventional growth was unsustainable and that some kind of ecological or environmental catastrophe was required before there was any likelihood of a serious reaction to the problems'.[22]

The Prince's innate pessimism was reinforced by his impatience at the lethargy and complacency of governments, including that of Her Majesty. In August 1988, he asked the Foreign Office about British policy towards the regime of President Ceausescu of Romania, and in particular the dictator's policy of 'systematisation', a projected blitzkrieg on the environment involving the destruction of some 8,000 villages and their replacement by 'agro-industrial' centres. For more than a decade, British relations with the man whom the Prince described as 'that monster and tyrant' had been constructed on the harsh realities of the Cold War. Ostracised by the Soviet Union, Ceausescu was regarded by NATO as 'our enemy's enemy', while his ramshackle 'socialist' economy was a modest source of easy export pickings for British industry. Once alerted to the unfolding horror in Romania, the Prince formed the view that the government's attitude was dilatory and pusillanimous.

Over the next four months, he pressed gently for a stronger stand. In January 1989, his deputy private secretary, David Wright, felt able to advise him that, 'There is wide understanding in the Foreign Office and on the part of our Ambassador at Bucharest of YRH's strong feelings on this subject. I hope these may have contributed to the forceful statements by Sir Geoffrey Howe.'[23] At a meeting in Vienna of the Conference on Security and Cooperation in Europe, the Foreign Secretary had spoken of the 'lamentable performance' of one participant (without identifying Romania directly) in failing to observe the Helsinki accords, and in a radio interview from Vienna he described systematisation as 'totally incompatible with what we are trying to do'.[24] The Prince was not greatly impressed by this diplomatic *démarche*. In February 1989, he wrote personally to Howe saying that the policy of systematisation was 'inhuman and diabolical':

> The point of this letter is really to say that I do believe the situation in Romania should be an urgent priority for the European nations to address. After all, for what did so many of our courageous countrymen die during the last war? Was it merely to see one system of tyranny and misery exchanged for another? Somehow, we in Western Europe seem so complacent about these matters . . . I do so hope it might be possible for there to be greater public awareness of what is going on . . . The press is full of Gorbachev and glasnost but they seem to ignore those other parts of Eastern Europe where abominable tyranny still reigns. Are there no Members of Parliament exercised about the situation? Why doesn't the Foreign Affairs Committee report on it?[25]

Howe wrote soothingly in reply, agreeing with the Prince that it was 'extraordinary that such a cruel and anachronistic regime' should still survive, but asserting that the government had been at the forefront of the campaign against the abuse of human rights in Europe. At a recent gathering of EC foreign ministers, when his Dutch colleague said that the twelve could no longer remain silent about the situation in Romania, he had not only agreed entirely but also proposed that the foreign ministers' political committee should study appropriate ways in which to react.

This was not quite what the Prince meant by an 'urgent priority'. On 30 March, he wrote again, this time suggesting, in his capacity as Great Master of the Order of the Bath, that Ceausescu's GCB* should be withdrawn, protesting, 'I see his membership as an affront to such an order of chivalry . . . I very much hope that you will not be put off by those who will at once say that precedent will be made by such a move . . .!'[26]

Four weeks later, on 27 April, the Prince decided to go public. In a speech at the Building A Better Britain Exhibition, he became the first significant figure in western Europe unequivocally to condemn the Romanian tyranny. 'President Ceausescu has embarked on the wholesale destruction of his country's cultural and human heritage . . .' he declared. 'The object is to reshape the nation's identity, to create a new type of person, utterly subordinate to its dreams . . .'[27]

Afterwards, the Prince wrote to Jessica Douglas-Home, the widow of his friend Charlie, about the strain involved in making such speeches:

> I find I have a terrible knotted feeling in the pit of my tummy as the courage is plucked up from somewhere deep inside . . . Having made the speech I then usually have dreadful second thoughts and feel I shouldn't have done it and it would be so much easier to lead a quieter life! But there's something, somewhere, telling one that I can't do that and that I wouldn't be true to myself if I did stay quiet instead of taking the risk and accepting the challenge . . . Anyway I hope what I said helps to stir up the debate and raise some people's awareness. I also hope you receive this before some frightful undercover agent stabs me in the left buttock with a poisoned umbrella![28]

---

* Knight Grand Cross, the highest class of members of the Order of the Bath, awarded to Ceausescu during his state visit to Britain in 1978. Non-British recommendations are made by the Foreign Secretary.

In fact, the BBC World Service and Radio Liberty gave prominent coverage to the Prince's damaging attack and it was widely covered in the British press. *The Times*, for instance, carried his remarks verbatim under a cartoon by Peter Brooks portraying Ceausescu as Count Dracula. Coming from such a source, the Prince's message both strengthened the spine of other European leaders and, smuggled into Romania, gave renewed hope to the swelling ranks of dissidents.

The British Foreign Secretary, however, kept his counsel. In reply to Labour backbencher Paul Flynn, who urged the government to strip Ceausescu of his knighthood, Howe answered in exactly the terms which the Prince had foreseen in his letter: 'Although there have been occasions in wartime when our enemies in recent conflicts have had their awards taken away, there is no precedent for depriving the holder of an honorary award in peacetime. It is not judged right to depart from the rule in this case.'[29] It was not until the dying days of the Ceausescu regime, eight months later, that the government was belatedly shamed into heeding the Prince's request. However, when the dictator was over-thrown and executed on 24 December 1989, he was no longer a Grand Companion of the Order of the Bath.

The Prince not only wrote letters to ministers; he lured them to Kensington Palace or Highgrove with the inducement of a *tête-à-tête* over lunch. Even the busiest ministers did not refuse such an offer. In pursuit of his environmental objectives, the Prince invited Peter Morrison,* the Minister of State at the Department of Energy, to Highgrove in the summer of 1989, where they had what in diplomatic terms is known as 'a frank exchange of views'. Although the Prince's public manner was diffident and self-deprecating, he could be excep-tionally forceful in private, surprising his guests with his vehemence, often banging the table with the palm of his hand to reinforce an argu-ment. He was prone to start such conversations innocently: 'Now I know you'll say I am wrong, but what I would like to know is why . . .' There would then follow not a question but a statement. In those matters

---

* Peter Morrison (1944–   ), parliamentary Under-Secretary of State 1981–83; Minister of State, Department of Employment 1983–85, DTI 1985–86, Department of Energy 1987–90; parliamentary private secretary to Prime Minister 1990.

where he laid little claim to detailed knowledge he was open to persuasion, although he was always inclined to suspect that he had been fobbed off – and did not hesitate to say so. Morrison was not over-endowed with tact and perhaps because he and the Prince had known one another for many years, he did not restrain himself. In the matter of dispute between them – whether the government should intervene by bringing in energy conservation legislation – the Prince knew his subject and had very strong opinions.

Afterwards, the minister wrote to thank his host for lunch but could not refrain from commenting, 'I wish that the answers to the questions were quite as easy as Your Royal Highness would like them to be . . . You see, everyone without exception wants more energy efficiency, unless they are an idiot [*sic*], but the trick is to teach them how to put theory into practice.' Morrison's tone was irritating enough, but when the minister chose the example of straw-burning he compounded the offence:

> We can both afford not to but some hard-pressed farmers, who are in every way good conservationists and real countrymen, have no option – and like it or not, that is the truth. There are hundreds of other examples and the solution is ultimately having the wealth to be able to afford the necessary cost. Hence I hope your Royal Highness will remember just that.[30]

The Prince wrote a vigorous riposte:

> Dear Peter,
>
> I am afraid your letter has made it impossible for me to avoid writing a reply! Your argument about hard-pressed farmers having no option but to burn straw is a remarkable one. They do have an option – they could incorporate [it] into the soil or, if an alternative market was created to utilise it, it could be turned into an energy source. But I can see that we are going to have to disagree on this one. What I do feel, however, is that governments surely have some responsibility for looking ahead and for deciding that a coordinating role needs to be played when we are confronted by a growing problem such as the environmental issues of which we have been made aware. Surely, when other

countries in Europe and countries such as Japan and the U.S.A. are taking these issues seriously and their governments are coordinating the response we ought to be considering doing the same sort of thing? . . .

You say that the solution is ultimately having more wealth to be able to afford the necessary costs. But how, then, do you achieve the wealth to afford those costs if by creating that wealth you are compounding the damage that is being done – especially if you assess these costs simply by using the economic theory which has succeeded in bringing us face to face with an environmental crisis in the first place? Wealth creation is all very well, but wouldn't it also be sensible to take into account real and ethical costs of conventional and renewable sources of energy? . . .

All best wishes,
As ever,
Charles.[31]

Some weeks later the minister replied, saying that the Prince's letter had prompted him 'to some constructive work and thought'. Presumably guided by his officials he altered his tone and shifted ground: 'I hope we can agree that retaining the environment as a free good, which has happened in the past, is palpably mistaken and morally wrong. However that is easier to say than it is to work out who pays the cost . . .' As for strawburning, 'We have an R and D programme here aimed at improving technology so as to make straw more competitive with other fuels . . . But, in any case I am advised by my experts that to burn straw is more beneficial than leaving it to rot in the field . . .' The minister concluded by inviting the Prince to open a forthcoming conference on energy efficiency: 'I can assure you that neither I nor the Department will try in any way at all to put any words into your mouth . . .'[32]

If the Prince regarded the phrasing of Morrison's invitation as maladroit he refrained from saying so directly but replied drily, 'I am grateful for your assurance not to try and put any words into my mouth, otherwise I might be tempted to quote from Tony Paterson's recent Bow Group Paper "The Green Conservative". Writing on page 56 about Energy Efficiency, I see he says:

"There is probably no more inadequate area of policy in the whole spectrum of the Government's policies on any topic!"[33]

In a further exchange about straw-burning, the minister retreated from his original position, assuring the Prince that he, like his colleagues at Agriculture and Environment, was 'taking very seriously the recommendations of the Royal Commission on Environmental Pollution', and that were the government:

> to decide to follow their advice, then, of course, there would be a considerable surge of commercial interest in this new 'captive' market . . . However there remains the problem of the stubble. It can, of course, be ploughed in, but its decay will release some methane, thus contributing to the greenhouse effect. Either way it all goes to show that, like there is no free lunch, whatever we do has an environmental cost.[34]

The Prince was unimpressed. Later that year, the reason for Morrison's volte-face became clear when the government announced a ban on straw-burning, for which, among others, the Prince had argued so strenuously.[*]

The Prince kept up the pressure on the Department by reproaching the new Secretary of State, John Wakeham,[†] for the government's grudging response to the Commons Energy Select Committee report on the 'greenhouse effect', and asking what proposals were in hand for developing renewable sources of energy as alternatives to coal. Wakeham had recently commissioned a report on that very subject, but when a copy landed on the Prince's desk he was quick to spot an appendix indicating clearly that Great Britain lagged far behind other countries in expenditure on research and development in this field. Taxed on this point,

---

[*] In 1990, Morrison was summoned from the Department of Energy to the more congenial surroundings of 10 Downing Street, where, as Margaret Thatcher's parliamentary private secretary, he helped to organise the leadership campaign which ended with her resignation as Prime Minister later that year.

[†] John Wakeham (1932–), Secretary of State for Energy 1989–92; Minister responsible for co-ordinating development of presentation of government policies 1990–92; Lord Privy Seal and Leader of House of Lords 1992–94.

Wakeham informed the Prince that the figures were misleading since they ignored British Coal's own R & D spending, which was financed indirectly by government grants. However, he failed to provide a revised table showing by how much this funding would have reduced the vast gap in expenditure which the original table had identified. This omission was not overlooked by the Prince. 'Why publish such a misleading table then,' he scrawled in the margin.

Ministers thus bombarded by the heir to the throne, and more particularly their civil servants who had to draft a defence, might have been forgiven for wondering who might rid them of their turbulent Prince. For his part, he believed that as a Privy Councillor, a member of the House of Lords and, more especially, as heir to the throne, he had a right to warn, protest and advise.* For their part, ministers felt obliged to furnish a considered response in terms that were respectful of his unique position and sensitive to his concerns, even when there was a profound gulf of attitude between them. Over the course of the eighties, the Prince had become ever more convinced that government had a direct 'enabling' role, not only by financing R & D in the public and private sectors but by creating an effective regulatory framework that would compel both sectors to satisfy the most exacting environmental standards. To this extent, his approach put him at odds with the prevailing ideological assumptions of the government. The Prince was under no illusion about this, nor did it inhibit him, and, although one or two ministers ground their teeth in irritation, most not only accepted his prerogative but seemed to welcome his use of it. Many of those who had half expected him to be woolly-minded and utopian came away from meetings at Highgrove or Kensington Palace impressed by his grasp of the issues and the cogency of his arguments. Disposed, in any case, to honour his peculiar status as heir to the throne, they found themselves drawn to his seriousness of purpose, his modesty and his humour. Despite their frequent differences, ministers usually emerged from their encounters with him encouraged, even on the rare occasions when they were gently chastised. Obliged to hear him out, they went away reassured that even though he had entered the fray he was, in a deeper sense, also above it.

---

* The Prince's interpretation of the constitution in this respect is open to question.

The attitude of most senior ministers towards the Prince emerged in an exchange of letters with Michael Heseltine at the end of 1991. 'I heard the other day', the Prince wrote, 'that I was becoming a menace to the Tory Party because I was subjecting ministers to a letter-writing campaign on a whole range of subjects . . . !'[35]

Heseltine, whose own approach was close to the Prince's on many issues, replied:

> The accounts which I too read of your 'menacing' activities grow the more inaccurate as the frequency of their appearance increases. I was relieved to hear from Nicholas Soames that your disdain and disbelief have all the hallmarks of a seasoned politician. I hope in saying that you will not regard it as the unkindest cut of all![36]

On occasion, his competing enthusiasms collided with one another to embarrassing effect. In a speech to a European Community Conference on the Urban Environment in Madrid, the Prince spoke of the destructive impact of motor vehicles, clogging streets, polluting the atmosphere, and rapidly becoming a 'monster of our own making'. A few days later, it was reported that his Bentley had been driven half-way across Europe to be available for his official visit to Czechoslovakia. The conjunction was unfortunate and, to the media, irresistible: as they were swift to observe, the only detectably green feature of the ten-miles-to-the-gallon limousine was its colour.* The incident, trivial in itself, was a sharp reminder that in an age of impressions, the image is usually king.

The Prince was on safer ground when preaching the virtues of waste management. In the Madrid speech, he had invoked the theme of 'sustainability', citing the unfashionable example of waste disposal:

> Surely we have to get away from the idea of waste disposal with all its connotations of 'out of sight, out of mind' and work towards a concept of waste *management* in which our refuse can be properly regarded as an alternative source of raw materials. Recycling of domestic refuse

---

* The Prince had agreed to use a Bentley in Prague (at the request of the company) instead of a Mercedes or BMW, in support of 'UK plc'. Unfortunately, his office was told at the last moment that it had proved impossible to prepare a vehicle in Germany in time; thus the decision to take his own Bentley.

ought surely to be a high priority . . . But we also need to look at recycling such potentially beneficial materials as sewage sludge. Believe it or not this is a subject which has long fascinated and aggravated me![37]

At Highgrove, he was already in the throes of installing an organic sewage system based on the use of a reed bed to absorb the waste and a pond through which the purified water is circulated before seeping away into the river. In obeisance to his belief in 'Seeing is Believing', few of his guests were allowed to escape without a conducted tour of his 'sewage garden'. With some justice, the Prince could claim that at Highgrove he was putting his principles into practice; by the turn of the decade, the entire estate was in the process of conversion into an organic holding. As he was to write later, 'the "experts" were very nice' in his presence when in 1985 he said he wanted to farm part of his land on an organic basis, 'but what they were saying about this latest demonstration of insanity once they were out of earshot can only be surmised!'[38] By 1990, when it became clear that the home farm had every prospect of running at a profit, those attitudes – which were precisely as he had imagined – began marginally to alter. For the Prince, organic farming was 'a means by which we can discover the rashly abandoned, but nevertheless entirely relevant, traditional principles which for thousands of years have helped to preserve the health and fertility of the soil for each successive generation'.[39] His farm manager, David Wilson, not only shared that belief but had the talent and commitment to realise the Prince's vision. Without the use of chemicals and pesticides, Highgrove was soon established as one of the best organic holdings in the country, a demonstration to the agricultural community that it was possible to run an efficient holding and to enhance the environment at the same time.

In his enthusiasm, he tried to persuade his tenants in the Duchy to follow his lead, but with a marked lack of success. Unlike the Prince they lacked the resources or the passion to change their familiar ways. 'I have put my heart and soul into Highgrove,' he wrote:

All the things I have tried to do in this small corner of Gloucester have been the physical expression of a personal philosophy. When I was younger I recall the nascent stirrings of such a philosophy; I felt a strong attachment to the soil of those places I loved best – Balmoral, in

Scotland, and Sandringham, in Norfolk. As far as I was concerned, every tree, every hedgerow, every wet place, every mountain and river had a special, almost sacred, character of its own.[40]

Those feelings had not diminished. Although his father had the responsibility for running both Sandringham and Balmoral, the staff on both estates knew how strongly his son felt about the 'stewardship' of the land on which they worked. At Sandringham, which had been turned into a profitable family estate, the Prince winced when old barns made way for modern sheds constructed of steel and asbestos; and, though he understood the need to make a profit, he was instinctively uncomfortable with the commercial imperatives by which, as a result, the estate was managed. As the heir apparent to Sandringham he would in the future be free to modify the farming practices in tune with his own guiding principles. In the meantime, he was attentive to those aspects of estate management in which he could participate without risk of interfering with his father's stewardship.

He knew the tenants, the farm workers and their families, their names, their histories and their lives. He had become meticulous with Christmas cards and he did not forget to write in congratulation or condolence, and he was careful to set aside a number of 'estate days' each year on which he toured the land, talking to the staff and visiting their homes. As alien and quaint as this practice might have seemed in any other environment, the Prince's personal involvement in the land that he was to inherit was treasured by those who earned their livelihoods from it. Lacking condescension on the one hand or obsequiousness on the other, the relationship was touched by a common faith in 'values that hold good indefinitely; the personal involvement of a family with the people, families holding the land in trust for the future'.[41]

His greater love was for Balmoral, where, he has confided, 'I . . . desperately want to look after it and care for it and ensure that it can be handed on in the best state for the future.'[42] It became his dream to allow the natural regeneration of the Caledonian forest that was destroyed by the demand for timber in the early Industrial Revolution. When he went stalking day after day in the autumn, he had his sandwiches, his telescope, his rifle and his dogs, and he stayed out until nightfall regardless of the weather. To the chagrin of lesser spirits who felt obliged to join him, he was indifferent to snow and to rain, being quite content to lie in the wet undergrowth for an hour at time, slowly edging forward on his stomach, regardless of the streams which lay between him and his quarry. He came to prefer the hunt – 'grandmother's footsteps', he called it – to the denouement, pulling the trigger himself only once or twice a season and then only to demonstrate that his eye was still sharp and his hand steady. Though he did not relish the task, he became adept at 'bleeding' and cleaning the carcass, before dragging it towards a waiting pony to be carried down the hill, to be chilled and sold on the market as prime Scottish venison.

The Prince would say that he has a 'Tolstoyan feel' for the soil. In conversation with the estate staff he had certainly discovered that form of easy communication which betrays a shared instinct for the natural world and man's place in it; discussions that start nowhere in particular and meander with unhurried purpose from the shortage of salmon in the Dee, to the damage caused by the deer, to the prospect of fencing some of the glen to protect the trees, to memories of childhood and, inevitably, to the weather. It is the kind of conversation that is not circumscribed by time but drifts to a conclusion, unfinished but easy to continue a day or a week or a month later. In these surroundings, the Prince found himself elementally at home and at ease with himself.

Until the day when the stewardship of Sandringham and Balmoral would pass from the Duke of Edinburgh into his hands, the Prince was obliged to content himself with overseeing the Duchy. Unlike the two family estates, the Duchy is spread over a vast area in widely dispersed blocks of land; it is therefore amorphous in character and has been saved from being treated merely as a property company by the Prince's own instinct for stewardship. Under another owner, the Duchy might well have adopted a more ruthless policy of sale and acquisition, adapting to meet the shifting opportunities of the market.

The Prince only began to interest himself seriously in the Duchy in the early eighties, when John Higgs became its secretary. Under his guidance, the Duchy managed to be both financially aggressive and environmentally sensitive. Lacking the identity of a great estate like Chatsworth or Blenheim, the Duchy impinged very little on the life of the communities in which its farms were located, except when it took unpopular decisions. The initiatives begun by Higgs to increase revenue from a range of under-exploited assets met at best a grudging response from those who were in any case disposed to regard the Duchy merely as a milch cow for the scion of the royal household. The long-running conflict over the Duchy's decision to licence land on Dartmoor to the Ministry of Defence came to symbolise the uncomfortable relationship between its managers and the public. The income from the MOD lease was to rise sharply from £10,000 in the late seventies, until by the early nineties it made a substantial contribution to the Duchy's income. Although successive decisions to extend the deal, in defiance of the fierce opposition of amenity groups in the area, had more to do with the Prince's reluctance to deny the army a training area which he believed to be vital to the defence of Britain than with a useful financial return (which accounted for one twentieth of the estate's income by 1994), public scepticism did not abate.

It was not in the Prince's nature to seize control of the Duchy and bend it to his will; he was too busy, too romantic and too lacking in management experience to define a detailed strategy for future development. Yet although the Prince's Council, an advisory group of financiers and landowners, met only four times a year under his chairmanship, he was in frequent contact with his secretary by telephone, memoranda and meetings. He also set aside seven 'Duchy days' a year, which meant that by the end of the eighties he had visited nearly all the tenants on the estate and was familiar with their concerns and aspirations. In this process, he not only acquired a strong urge to reconcile financial and environmental imperatives, but he also began to feel that paternalistic sense of obligation which for him made the Duchy much more than a property company. Increasingly, therefore, the Duchy began to be fashioned in his image, not overtly but implicitly. A reproach from the Prince became tantamount to a veto, and his proposals became quasi-imperatives. Under his direction, the Duchy resisted the sale or amalgamation of small farms (which were for him one of the defining features of a healthy rural landscape); as a result, revenue which could have been invested in the stockmarket for greater return was foregone.* On Dartmoor, the Duchy began a long-term programme of stone-walling, pond clearance and opening footpaths. Throughout the estate,

---

* The tenanted farm, valued at £250,000, might be worth £500,000 freehold; an amalgamation of two tenanted farms worth £250,000 each would yield (say) £150,000 from the sale of one farmhouse and permit a rent increase on the total holding derived from the economies of scale enjoyed by the larger unit.

hundreds of thousands of trees were planted in new blocks, at the corners of fields or as shelter belts, and wildlife 'corridors' were developed; and more than ninety redundant farm buildings, which could have been sold as potential 'barn conversions', were turned into workshops to create local employment. The process was hardly contrived for dramatic effect and it would never rival the impact of the same kind of work undertaken on an estate of similar size but contained within a 'ring fence', but by the early nineties it was clear that the financial future of the Duchy was secure and that its stewardship had real meaning for its owner. It was not Sandringham or Balmoral, and he would never feel for the Duchy what he felt for those family estates, but from his seat at Highgrove, where he was virtually free to practise precisely what he preached, he could contemplate the development of the Duchy without shame and even with a modicum of pride.

CHAPTER
TWENTY-THREE

———◆◆———

On 2 August 1987, the *Sunday Times* ran an article under the headline 'Charles stirs new row over St Paul's design' which reported that the Prince had intervened in a controversial development scheme for the seven-acre site around St Paul's Cathedral, known as Paternoster Square. 'The architectural profession has been flinching at the prospect of another outburst along the lines of "monstrous carbuncle",' the newspaper reported. Among those who were flinching was Michael Manser, the former president of the Royal Institute of British Architects, who had been his woebegone host at Hampton Court for the ill-fated 150th anniversary of RIBA. 'Architects are getting fed up with the Prince's interference,' he said. 'The trouble is he has tremendous influence among people generally. What he says has an effect out of all proportion to the comment itself.'[1]

A few weeks earlier, Stuart Lipton, the developer of the Paternoster scheme, had invited the Prince to cast his eye over the plans submitted by the seven finalists in the competition which his firm had organised and which a number of prestigious architects – including Norman Foster, James Stirling and Richard Rogers – had been invited to enter. When the Prince saw the seven proposals, he was appalled and said so in unambiguous terms. After it was announced that the winner of the competition was Arup Associates, *The Times* reported that it was 'understood' that the Prince's views would be 'taken into account in the final designs'.[2]

As the architectural establishment had feared, the Prince was not

444

prepared to leave it at that. Four months later, in what became known as the Mansion House speech, he went much further than in his 'carbuncle' attack of two years earlier, and it was a more sophisticated assault as well. By this time, he had gathered about him a small group of advisers, all of whom were architectural traditionalists: they included Colin Amery, the architectural correspondent of the *Financial Times*; Christopher Martin, a BBC television producer who, in 1978, had made a documentary diatribe against modernism with Christopher Booker, called *City of Towers*; and Jules Lubbock, an architectural historian who had been the seminal influence in stimulating the Prince's original interest in community architecture.* These three, led by Lubbock, worked on shaping the themes of a speech that ricocheted around the architectural establishment.

Facing what he knew to be a hostile audience, and planting his standard shamelessly at the head of an army of 'countless people' who were 'appalled by what has happened to their capital city, but feel totally powerless to do anything about it', he summoned Winston Churchill as evidence for his prosecution:

> Why does St Paul's matter so much? Because it is our greatest national monument . . . On the terrible night of December 29, 1940, when the surroundings of the cathedral were devastated and an incendiary bomb lodged in the outer dome, it was Mr Churchill himself who had dispatched the message to the Guildhall: 'St Paul's must be saved at all costs.'

Recalling the dramatic photograph of the black dome standing out against the swirling smoke and the flames, he continued, 'Then it gave new meaning to the cathedral as a symbol of faith and a monument to Britain's resolve. *Now* it reminds us of the place St Paul's occupies at the very heart of our nation as the spiritual centre of the capital city.' Then he moved onto the offensive:

---

* Others who joined the architectural group included the writer Candida Lycett-Green; the architect Theo Crosby; the planning QC Jeremy Sullivan; Keith Critchlow, the head of the Islamic studies department at the Royal College of Art (who later joined the Prince's Institute of Architecture); and Brian Hanson, who acted as secretary to the group (and later became the director of the Prince of Wales's Institute of Architecture).

What, then, have we done to it since the bombing? In the space of a mere fifteen years, in the sixties and seventies, and in spite of all sorts of elaborate rules *supposedly* designed to protect that great view, your predecessors, as the planners, architects and developers of the City, wrecked the London skyline and desecrated the dome of St Paul's . . . You have, Ladies and Gentlemen, to give this much to the Luftwaffe: when it knocked down our buildings, it didn't replace them with anything more offensive than rubble. We did that . . .

Before his audience had recovered from a phrase which was to enter into the architectural lexicon as memorably as 'monstrous carbuncle', he moved on to denounce not the past but the present:

I believe I have been accused of setting myself up as a new un-democratic hurdle in the planning process, a process we are supposed to leave to the professional. But the professionals have been doing it their way, thanks to the planning legislation, for the last forty years. We poor mortals are forced to live in the shadow of their achievements. Everywhere I go, it is one of the things people complain about most and, if there is one message I would like to deliver this evening, it is that large numbers of us in this country are fed up with being talked down to and dictated to by the existing planning, architectural and development establishment . . .

. . . most of which, as he very well knew, was sitting in ashen silence a few feet away from him.

As for the competition for Paternoster Square, he had 'been deeply depressed that none of them had risen to the occasion'. He had been demoralised, too, by the brief, which, within the planning constraints, required the competitors to design as much office space as possible along with a 'bold concept for retailing'. The Prince did not restrain himself: 'A bold concept for retailing! What a challenge! I suppose Sir Christopher Wren was inspired by the same sort of brief. "Give us a bold concept for worship, Sir Christopher – and the most effective praying area within the planning constraints."' Moving from sarcasm to contempt, he wondered why it was that the competitors, 'all of them world-famous architects', had failed to question such a brief:

Surely here, if anywhere, was the time and place to sacrifice some profit, if need be, for generosity of vision, for elegance, for dignity; for buildings which would raise our spirits and our faith in commercial enterprise and prove that capitalism can have a human face, instead of that of a robot or word processor. On such a site, market forces, I would suggest, are not enough.

Not content with this indictment, the Prince at once launched into a root and branch denunciation of the planning system itself:

Should a private developer be allowed to set up a private competition for a site of such historic importance, about which the public have been kept in the dark – and still are – whose winner will eventually submit a single scheme to the City Planning Committee, which will have no option between accepting or rejecting it? If they reject it, the developer can then appeal to the Secretary of State. Suppose he calls for a public enquiry and then turns it down, another and yet another scheme can be produced and go through the same process until at last all the opponents of the scheme are worn down by the length of the proceeding and the hideous expense of it all . . . There must be something wrong with a system which involves public opinion at so late a stage that the only course open to the public is to obstruct the development through whatever means the planning system allows. If the planning system is to blame, if the rules are at fault, then why don't we change them?

In the absence of a fair and democratic system, he proposed that at least there should be a 'proper debate' about Paternoster Square: 'Let there be an informative exhibition showing the area as it was, the plans of Wren, Hawksmoor and Lutyens, as well as the present plans. Then people could judge for themselves . . .'

Advocating his own vision, he argued for a scheme designed on 'a human scale' with small shops and businesses at ground level and with the mediaeval street plan of pre-war Paternoster reconstructed, 'not out of mere nostalgia, but to give meaning to surviving fragments like Amen Court and the Chapter House, now left like dispossessed refugees in an arid desert of God-forsaken buildings'. He wanted to see a roofscape that would give the impression 'that St Paul's is floating above it like a great ship on the sea' and he imagined 'architects working with artists and craftsmen, showing that pleasure and delight are indeed returning to architecture after their long exile'.[3]

Immediately after the speech, a group of like-minded architectural journalists gathered for a drink at the house of one of their number, Dan Cruickshank, to assess the impact of the Prince's onslaught.* They were joined by John Simpson, a classical architect who had been in contact with the Prince before the speech. The Prince had suggested that Simpson might work on an alternative masterplan along the lines of the vision with which he had sought to inspire his shell-shocked Mansion House audience. The architect outlined his ideas to one of the journalists present, Mira Bar-Hillel, who was a voluble advocate of traditional architecture. She urged him to submit his plan to the authorities as an alternative application. He agreed in principle, but explained that the cost would be prohibitive.

The next day the journalist convinced her editor at the *Evening Standard* to take up the cudgels on Simpson's behalf by financing the cost of a formal planning application and using the paper to crusade for the Prince's vision, which they both knew would be a hugely popular cause with their readers. It was already clear that the Prince had caught the public mood, although they could not then have known that the Palace was to receive more than 2,000 letters, 'the vast majority' of which, the Prince wrote to the journalist Christopher Booker, were 'in fairly passionate agreement. They have come from such fascinating people – a whole cross-section of the population.'[4]

However, there was a problem. Lipton had sold the Paternoster site to another developer, Tony Clegg, who in turn had committed himself to honouring the results of his predecessor's competition. On paper, therefore, the prospects for any alternative plan were dim. Even with assiduous promotion, the Simpson 'alternative' had at best a modest chance of mounting an effective challenge to Arup Associates, which had not only won the competition but also had backing from a formidable array of the architectural establishment. Peter Foggo, a member of the Arup group,

---

* The headlines the next morning, 3 December 1987, give some flavour of their response: 'Charles Accuses Spoilers' (*Daily Express*), 'Charles Blitzes London' (*Daily Star*), and only marginally more sedate, 'Prince charges planners with rape of Britain' (*The Times*).

was reported to have sat 'white-faced and silent'[5] as the Prince finished his speech. 'What kind of defence can there be when you are being pilloried by the heir to the throne as worse than the Luftwaffe . . .?' the *Telegraph*'s architectural correspondent, Deyan Sudjic, wrote, reflecting the views of the modernist tendency to which he belonged:

> Here was the first public acknowledgement of what has become increasingly clear over the past year. Little by little, Britain's tortuous planning system, ostensibly a democratic process administered by skilled officials, and run by elected representatives, has sprouted a new unofficial, but vastly more powerful, tier which has neither of these attributes. It is called Prince Charles.[6]

The architectural establishment was baring its knuckles. Recollecting that the Prince had torpedoed the original plan for the National Gallery extension and Peter Palumbo's 'glass-stump' skyscraper at the Mansion House, Sudjic complained that the Prince had acquired such influence behind the scenes that hardly any new development of significance could be advanced unless it had been presented to him for his approval. In the absence of firm evidence, his eloquent tirade was hedged about with escape clause phrases like 'It seems that . . .'; nonetheless, he painted a colourful portrait of a reign of architectural terror which he described as 'the largest extension of the royal prerogative seen this century'.[7]

Although there is no evidence that the Prince sought to arrogate any such authority to himself, a growing number of commercial architects did indeed begin to offer 'classical' or 'traditional' designs to their clients, if only to spare themselves the misery of public humiliation at the hands of the Prince; and certainly in the case of Paternoster Square he worked assiduously in private as well as in public to secure Simpson's 'alternative'. Elated by the public response, the Prince was not to be deterred by his critics. 'Perhaps it is something to do with advancing age, or just increasing experience and knowledge,' he wrote to Christopher Booker, 'but I am certainly a <u>bit</u> less anxious about what other people think . . .'[8] If there was a touch of arrogance in his attitude, there was also insecurity. Entirely lacking in vainglory, he still veered between astonishment, alarm and despondency when his words hit the headlines. In the case of Paternoster Square, however, he was driven by an indignation so intense that he was determined to prevail.

Two weeks after the Mansion House speech, Simpson sent some out-line sketches for Paternoster Square to Kensington Palace. The Prince was enthusiastic: 'I hope the debate will continue, although I am not at all optimistic that Nicholas Ridley will see the point. I don't think he favours any controls over anything, and being a free-market kind of buccaneer, also seems to think that conservationists are a general menace!'[9]

In April, accompanied by a group of planning consultants, the archi-tect presented the Prince with his completed proposals. The Prince wrote afterwards saying that he had been 'enormously impressed' and concluded, 'We must now do our best to find someone prepared to finance the construction of a model and also a developer who has the necessary vision and imagination to adopt your masterplan.'[10] The finance for the model was soon found, and in June Lord St John-Stevas, the chairman of the Royal Fine Arts Commission, organised an exhibi-tion in the crypt of St Paul's at which Simpson's design was on show beside the 'official' scheme. As a result of the *Evening Standard*'s cam-paign, Simpson was already favoured to win the battle of public opinion; when Londoners saw the two masterplans for themselves, any doubts were laid to rest. When the Simpson plan was submitted to the City planners in the same month, his supporters were confident that the design would find favour – and they were right.

However, things were not so simple. As Britain slipped into the reces-sion, the property market began to slump. Paternoster Square was sold and resold from developer to developer. The Prince remained at Simpson's side. When the architect had a setback, the Prince would intervene to help. 'Thank you for your letter which has left me some-what demoralised,' he wrote to the architect in June 1989. 'However, it has also given me further ammunition to fire off at various people and with which to make myself even more unpopular! I will pursue some of your points in the relevant quarters and see what happens . . .'[11]

By October 1989, the site had changed hands again, with the new owners promising Simpson a pivotal role in a scheme which they said would be carried out according to 'traditional concepts of urban design'. It would be 'human in scale, defer to the cathedral, and use materials that are in harmony with the stone and brick'.[12] The words could have been written by the Prince of Wales.

In the same period, the Prince was developing his ideas about 'com-munity architecture'. In June 1988, he wrote to Nicholas Ridley, the

Secretary of State for the Environment, to try to persuade the government, through him, to restrain the free market in favour of the environment in the Green Belt, and more generally in towns and villages. Ridley had spent his tenure as Secretary of State trying to liberate developers and architects from the restraints imposed by his predecessors. The Prince was not optimistic:

> I also appreciate you don't much care for the sort of controls I believe are necessary to ensure that the demand for houses in the South East doesn't vanish under a welter of little boxes. I think it would be a tragedy for our descendants, simply because not enough care or thought were taken in the first place.[13]

Two weeks later, the minister replied to the effect that he agreed with much that the Prince had said, but that his prescription, as the Prince had suspected, was fewer rather than more planning controls. In a scathing and, to the Prince, depressing assessment of the quality of district planners, he mused:

> I sometimes wonder whether the standards would not be higher if we took away their powers of control. It is possible the developers would do better than the Planning Committees . . . I feel we need a renaissance of good and sensitive design. Government cannot do this, nor can local government. I hope your efforts will make a major contribution to re-awakening dormant talent.[14]

Ridley's final reference may have been no more than a general *bon voyage*, but it is more likely that he had in his mind a recent dinner party at which he and the Prince had discussed a range of environmental issues. It is likely that the Prince told Ridley about his forthcoming film, *A Vision of Britain*, in which, with the help of BBC producer Christopher Martin, he was to present some of the themes about architecture and the environment, community and development, and grace and harmony which he had first launched on an unsuspecting audience at the RIBA celebrations at Hampton Court in 1984. Transmitted in October 1988, *A Vision of Britain* was combative and heartfelt. The following day's headlines reflected the evident fact that once again he had touched a popular nerve, an instinct which was confirmed by the Prince's postbag:

99 per cent of the more than 5,000 letters he received congratulated him for expressing so forcefully feelings that they had long held. A year later, after the publication of the book of the film, the *Sunday Times*, reflecting much popular opinion, observed in its leading article:

> Britain has been enjoying a remarkable sight of late, an entire profession on the run before a single citizen. With a mastery of the media worthy of the most professional communicator, the Prince of Wales has done for architects what Mr Ralph Nader in the 1960s did for car manufacturers . . . he has confronted those most responsible for the appearance of built-up Britain, savaged their reputation and forced them on the defensive. [15]

Many of the modernists and post-modernists, the architectural establishment that the Prince regarded with distaste, complained gloomily that the Prince's architectural hegemony would leave Britain adrift in the nostalgic backwaters of lowest common denominator taste, inspired only by caution and pastiche. Though they exaggerated to make their case, they clearly resented the temerity of the Prince in challenging their certainties with his own. A dispassionate observer would reckon that the balance between the traditional and the *avant-garde* had tilted but marginally towards the former, but each was unforgiving of the other: thus Peter Palumbo (the developer who had proposed the Mansion House skyscraper which the Prince had torpedoed as a 'glass stump'), 'God bless the Prince of Wales and God save us from his architectural judgement'*; or Peter Ahrends (the 'carbuncle' architect), 'He has done nothing to further the debate on modern architecture . . . [the Prince's views] are out of step with the country as a whole'; or Richard Rogers (whose designs for Paternoster Square had failed to 'rise to the challenge'), 'Time and again the Prince has singled out individual architects for criticism; in so doing he is violating the principles of a constitutional monarchy.'

Whatever animosity the Prince aroused in the victims of his attack on the architectural establishment, it remained difficult for them to argue

---

* Palumbo had his revenge when he was given planning consent for a design by James Stirling, which the Prince had likened to 'an old 1930s wireless', to replace the old Mappin and Webb building in the City.

convincingly that he had misused his influence. However, when he turned the full blast of his outrage on the educational establishment, the Prince trespassed to the very edge of party political controversy. His distaste for modernism in the arts and in education, as much as in architecture, surfaced publicly in a fiery denunciation of the language of the New English Bible and the 'crassness' of the Alternative Service Book in a speech he had delivered as patron of the Thomas Cranmer Schools Prize at the end of 1989. Aiming his fire at the modish attitudes which he believed were the source of these misbegotten works, he extended his theme to embrace what he regarded as an insidious but dominant culture.

'The fear of being considered old-fashioned seems to me to be so all powerful that the more eternal values and principles which run like a thread through the whole tapestry of human existence are abandoned under the false assumption that they restrict progress,' he told his audience of students and teachers. Spicing his contempt with ridicule, he went on:

> Looking at the way English is used in our popular papers, our radio and television programmes, or even in our schools and our theatres . . . [I and others] wonder what it is about our country, and our society that our language has become so impoverished, so sloppy and so limited; that we have arrived at a wasteland of banality, cliché and casual obscenity. It leads me to wonder, for instance, how Hamlet would deliver his great 'To be or not to be' soliloquy in the language of today . . . What about this?
>
> > 'Well, frankly, the problem as I see it at this moment in time is whether I should lie down under all this hassle, or whether I should just say OK, I get the message, and do myself in. I mean, I'm in a no-win situation, and quite honestly I'm so stuffed up to here with the whole stupid mess that I can tell you I've just got a good mind to take the quick way out. That's the bottom line . . .'[16]

Although he was rebuked by an editorial in the *Independent* for sounding like 'a rather reactionary club bore' at risk of being seen as 'the curator of a national heritage centre, selling a safely sanitised version of the past',[17] and by the literary editor of *The Times*, Philip Howard, for talking 'unhistorical and reactionary rubbish' in referring to the 'dismal wasteland' of modern English,[18] he was otherwise widely applauded for his outspokenness.

It was not the first time that he had courted such controversy. A few months earlier, in off-the-cuff remarks to what he thought was a private gathering of business executives, he had complained, 'All the people I have in my office, they can't speak English properly, they can't write English properly. All the letters sent from my office I have to correct myself. And that is because English is taught so bloody badly.'[19] This injudicious outburst provoked a variety of responses: ribaldry about his syntax and his blasphemy, indignation from affronted teachers, and a delegation from his staff to his private secretary protesting at his calumny against them. Mortified at the distress he had caused in his own office, he was swift to express his regret and to confess that he had exaggerated to make his point. However, a survey conducted by the *Sunday Times*[20] and a readership poll conducted by the *Sunday Mirror*[21] suggested that his sentiments, however crudely expressed, enjoyed a deal of public support. The general response to his Thomas Cranmer speech overwhelmingly confirmed this impression. In its role as spokespaper for 'Middle England', the *Daily Telegraph* reflected a much wider sentiment when it editorialised, 'On architecture, there may sometimes be room to differ from the Prince. On the decline of the English language there is none . . . When we realise that what the Prince of Wales is attacking has persisted through ten years of *Conservative* government we get some idea of just how far the road back will be.'[22] It was here, in attacking the failures of an educational system over which the Conservatives had presided for more than a decade, that the Prince found himself in dangerous territory.

Sixteen months later, in the spring of 1991, he delivered the Shakespeare Birthday lecture in the Swan Theatre at Stratford-upon-Avon. Drawing from *Othello, Hamlet, Macbeth, The Tempest* and *The Merchant of Venice* to exemplify the human predicament so matchlessly revealed by 'the world's greatest playwright', he went even more vigorously on the attack against the educational establishment than he had ventured in his Thomas Cranmer speech. Drawing on contributions from a group of advisers which included by Dr Eric Anderson, his former teacher at Gordonstoun and now the headmaster of Eton, his critique was unsparing:

There are now several GCSE English literature courses which pre-scribe no Shakespeare at all. There is at least one A-level English literature syllabus on which Shakespeare is not compulsory. Thousands of intelligent children leaving school at sixteen have never seen a play of Shakespeare on film or the stage, and have never been asked to read a single word of any one of his plays . . .

As a practical man, with practical human concerns, Shakespeare doesn't ask to be canonised, but to live alongside and illuminate the modern realities of life. Look how school groups can respond to live experiences and experimentation! Six-year-old children can be enthralled by *Twelfth Night*, slightly older children become frenzied at the sword fights in *Hamlet*. And during school matinees children call out 'Don't do it!' when Romeo is on the point of committing suicide, not knowing that Juliet is still alive . . .

As we move towards a National Curriculum for our schools – sometimes known as an entitlement curriculum – I find myself won-dering why the students of our schools are not as entitled to Shakespeare as to other parts of the syllabus. Do those who disapprove of Shakespeare, arguing for some *extraordinary* reason that he is elitist, wish to prevent those not already familiar with his work from acquir-ing an understanding of it or of other great literature? The marginalising of Shakespeare seems to be symptomatic of a general flight from our great literary heritage . . .

Are we all so frightened and cowed by the shadowy 'experts' that we can no longer 'screw our courage to the sticking place' and defi-antly insist that they are talking unmitigated nonsense? You forget – I have been through all this before with the architects! I've heard it all over and over again, and it is high time that the bluff of the so-called 'experts' was called . . .

Offering a moment's obeisance to the many hard-pressed teachers who would 'willingly rise to the challenge of introducing their pupils to an experience which, while initially difficult, will be with them for the rest of their lives', he re-doubled his onslaught on the 'experts':

There are terrible dangers, it seems to me, in so following fashionable trends in education – trends towards the 'relevant', the exclusively contemporary, the immediately palatable – that we end up with an entire generation of culturally disinherited people. I, for one, don't want to see this happen in this country. Nor, I suspect, do countless parents up and down the nation, who probably feel utterly powerless in the face of yet another profession, this time the 'educationalists', which I believe has become increasingly out of touch with the true feelings of 'ordinary' people . . .

He then broadened the front of his attack, confronting not only the educational establishment but, directly, the failures of government policy as well:

Here in Britain, we seem to get it wrong almost before we have begun. In France, Italy and Belgium every child under five receives nursery education from the state. Here, less than half our children have that right . . . It is almost incredible that in Shakespeare's land one child in seven leaves primary school functionally illiterate . . . In most schools, children are deemed incapable of learning foreign languages before the age of eleven – yet by the age of fourteen half of them have given it up. As if that wasn't enough, present indications are that after the age of fourteen children will not be required by the National Curriculum to study any aesthetic subject . . . Perhaps most alarming of all, only a third of our 16–18 year olds are still in full-time education. In France, the figure is 66%, Japan 77%, the Netherlands 77%. 40% of our children leave full-time schooling with no significant educational qualifications at all . . .

Conceding that the concept of a National Curriculum seemed to enjoy cross-party support, he proffered that 'the prospects for getting things right may therefore be better than they have been for a long time', before insisting that the nation should:

resist the temptation to deny the cultural heritage of our country to so many young people simply because of expediency or because of a mistaken utilitarian approach . . . After all there is little point in becoming technically competent if at the same time we become culturally inept. In pleading for a restoration of sanity, I have to admit to a feeling of profound sadness that a very great deal of damage has already been done . . .[23]

The speech was at once denounced by the National Association for Teachers of English as 'nonsense' but the headline writers sensed that the public was with the Prince, sharing his sense of outrage and applauding his intervention. The government, in the person of the Education Secretary, Kenneth Clarke,* was less pleased. Bombarded by journalists for a reaction to what almost every commentator and editorial writer interpreted as a severe rebuke to his department, Clarke was forced onto the defensive, although as a consummate politician he was adroit enough to identify those passages from the Prince's critique which could have been interpreted – out of context – as offering royal support for the government. In private, Clarke expressed his irritation at the speech in the bluntest language, asserting that, on this occasion at least, the Prince had offended against constitutional propriety. As the Prince's own staff at once recognised, the cabinet minister had a right to be affronted. Embarrassingly for them, the convention by which the Prince invariably sent a draft of his speeches to any government minister likely to be affected by what he intended to say had, in this case, been inadequately honoured. As Clarke's office did not receive a copy of the speech until the very morning on which it was to be delivered, he had no time to read it, let alone to suggest any ameliorative alterations to it. This apparent discourtesy compounded the irritation of a busy minister who had been caught out by the controversy and he did not hesitate to make St James's Palace aware of his feelings.

A month later (following official visits to Brazil and Czechoslovakia, where, respectively, he made powerful and widely reported speeches about the environment and communism), the Prince wrote to apologise, explaining that he had not completed the speech until the early hours of Sunday morning:

> My office got in touch with yours first thing on the Monday morning to try to ensure that you had a copy of my speech without further delay, so that you did not find yourself wholly unprepared for the door-stepping inquisition of the media! I am sorry if, in the event, logistics prevented you seeing the text before I read it out.

---

* Secretary of State for Health 1988–90; Education 1990–92; Home Secretary 1992–93; Chancellor of the Exchequer since 1993.

However, he was unrepentant about the content:

> The speech was very much a personal statement about Shakespeare
> and the deeper values that underlie a study of our great literary her-
> itage. I tried my best to minimise anything which could be construed
> as 'party political' and I consulted very widely indeed. I have certainly
> been encouraged by the positive letters I have received from all sides –
> Labour and Conservative, teachers and university lecturers, pundits
> and 'experts', academics and members of the public. The last thing I
> wanted to do was to make your life any more difficult than it already
> is, but at the same time I believe there are profound values at stake
> which I feel it is my duty to emphasise.[24]

The speech had indeed been endorsed as he described. Congratulations poured into St James's Palace, including letters from luminaries
like the novelist P.D. James,* who wrote, 'The speech was tremendously
impressive, beautifully written and argued with the persuasive force of
conviction and enthusiasm, qualities which are only too rare in public
speaking';[25] and the Warden of Wadham College, Oxford, Sir Claus
Moser,† who enthused, 'I should like to say how moved and thrilled we
were by what Your Royal Highness said about Shakespeare, about
English, and about education in general. As you will have seen your brilliant lecture has had a most galvanising effect, and everyone I have
spoken to in the educational world is enormously grateful for your
forceful remarks. I have no doubt that they will have an immense impact
on our educational future.'[26]

Moser judged correctly. Almost certainly as a result of the Prince's
speech, Moser secured the private funds needed to establish his own
National Commission on Education, which was to challenge many of
the precepts of the educational establishment and the Department of
Education's policies which flowed from them. More broadly, the tortu-
ous debate about the National Curriculum (which, at government level,

---

* Baroness James of Holland Park, governor of the BBC since 1988.
† Moser knew the Prince through their association at the Royal Opera House,
  Covent Garden, where the former had been chairman (1974–87) and the latter
  was the patron.

was inherited from Clarke in 1992 by John Patten,* who openly endorsed the Prince's views) was directly influenced by what he had said in the Stratford-upon-Avon speech. The final version of the National Curriculum reflected a popular opinion which he had articulated to greater effect than even he had perhaps expected; Shakespeare was, after all, to be taught in all schools to all children. If, as Clarke supposed, the Prince had indeed trespassed across a constitutional dividing line, he had done so to remarkable effect and emerged from the experience virtually unscathed.

The Prince did not leave the matter there. In December 1991, he invited a group of senior educationalists, including Eric Anderson and Brian Griffiths,† the chairman of the newly established School Examinations and Assessment Council, to lunch at Kensington Palace. There, they discussed the impact of his speech and an idea, originally proposed by Anderson, for the establishment of a summer school at which English teachers and actors could work together to discover ways of attracting schoolchildren to the plays of Shakespeare. Griffiths was an enthusiastic contributor to the discussion. 'Like everyone else at the lunch,' he wrote to the Prince afterwards, 'I would very much like to encourage Your Royal Highness to continue speaking out in this field. The idea of the Prince's seminars for teachers – as summer schools – is, I believe, an excellent one. Morale in the teaching profession is at the moment very low and this is just the kind of initiative which will help to restore confidence.'[27]

A few days later, the Prince wrote to the headmaster of Eton, 'This is just to say that I have had some very encouraging letters from the majority of guests at our Education lunch before Xmas, and many of them were extremely positive about the Summer School idea . . . Taking this all into account, I can't help feeling we should pursue your Summer School idea with vigour! Perhaps we could discuss how to proceed with this and you could give some serious thought to the concept . . .'[28] A little over eighteen months later, the Prince of Wales Shakespeare School welcomed its first thirty-five English and drama teachers, who had been

---

* Education Secretary from 1992 to July 1994, when he was sacked by the Prime Minister, John Major, in a government reshuffle.

† Baron Griffiths of Fforestfach, head of Prime Minister's Policy Unit 1985–90, chairman of Centre for Policy Studies since 1991.

selected from several hundred applicants for a twelve-day course organised by the Royal Shakespeare Company at Stratford. As president of the RSC, the Prince had helped to raise £50,000 to sponsor the course, which was overseen by the RSC's artistic director Adrian Noble. So successful was the first summer school that the RSC was eager to organise a successor in 1994, so long as the finance could be raised.

In October 1993, at his own instigation and financed from his own pocket, the Prince organised a 'William Shakespeare' evening in the Ballroom at Buckingham Palace. At his (handwritten) invitation to each of them, some of the RSC's most distinguished stars, including Derek Jacobi, Judi Dench, Dorothy Tutin, Robert Stephens and John Gielgud, performed extracts from the plays before an audience of the 'great and the good' from the theatre, the professions, government and business. Introducing a 'spectacular event', the Prince said:

> We have succeeded in keeping Shakespeare on the school curriculum – but now, surely, we must ensure that it remains a living rather than a 'dead' subject . . . This year saw the first Prince of Wales Shakespeare School, which the RSC mounted with great panache . . . I am pleased to say that the teachers gave our school very high marks. Their enthusiasm was tremendous – and I hope that we can continue the venture in future years.[29]

The occasion was quite different in tone and style from the starchy formalities normally associated with Buckingham Palace. According to many of those present, the Prince, who seemed to know everyone by name, brought an élan to the evening redolent of the age of Prince Albert. After the performance, the Prince's guests sat down to dinner. He had arranged for senior executives of Allied-Lyons to join him at his table; a few days later, the company confirmed that it would enter a £3.5 million sponsorship of the RSC, not excluding the Prince of Wales Shakespeare School, which thus re-opened in August 1994, on a secure financial footing for the indefinite future.

Though the Prince affected not to mind what was said about him, the scorn and the homilies, particularly the homilies, got under his skin. He was especially stung by those of his critics in the architectural establishment who had, in so many words, told him 'to put up or shut up'. If he was such a visionary, was their message, why did he not practise what he preached? His wealth derived from a huge estate in the Duchy of Cornwall, where land was always available for development: why, then, did he not put his money where his mouth was? Richard Rogers was particularly scathing: 'Sadly, in recent years our Royal family have had a poor record as patrons of the arts and sciences,' he commented with silky venom. 'As yet there is little to suggest that the Prince is an exception in this respect. As a man with strong views about architecture, a high public profile and enormous private wealth, he has an extraordinary opportunity to commission buildings for his large estates. But he has yet to produce a noteworthy construction . . .'[30]

Fortuitously, the Duchy of Cornwall was in the throes of preparing a development plan for a site on the south-western outskirts of Dorchester, where it had owned land for over 600 years. In the early eighties, the Duchy had sold Fordington Fields with planning permission for a conventional development; in 1985 the West Dorset planners were considering further development around the edge of the town and they approached the Duchy again. The agents Drivers Jonas, the Duchy's planning consultants, were instructed by David Landale, the Secretary of the Duchy, to draw up a masterplan for what promised to be a lucrative development. The site chosen was a triangular block of 350 acres to the west of the town, adjoining a modest housing estate, bordered on the other two sides by a ring road, and with a view across to the Iron Age settlement at Maiden Castle. Drivers Jonas drew up outline plans for a conventional housing estate of between 2,000 and 3,000 dwellings, not dissimilar to the successful scheme which they had sold at Fordington Fields.

Early in 1988, at what the bureaucrats in the Duchy had assumed would be a routine meeting, the Drivers Jonas masterplan was presented to the Prince for approval. He looked at the plans carefully, but clearly felt that the proposed scheme was inappropriate in scale, out of character with its surroundings, and at odds with his beliefs about urban development in rural England. Instead he would have his own scheme devised according to his own principles. In September, Landale was urged by the Prince to give the distinguished classical designer, Leon Krier, 'a blank sheet' as masterplanner for Poundbury (as the site was to be named); Drivers Jonas would be retained by the Duchy to keep a watching brief on the Prince's selection. Early in 1989, after spending many hours at the site, Krier unveiled his masterplan for the site. The Prince was excited by it, although even he was somewhat overawed by the scale of Krier's conception. In a letter to the developer Stephen Mattick, the Prince wrote of:

> my, very probably, over-ambitious dreams for Dorchester and else-where. My problem is that I become carried away by enthusiasm to try and improve things and also feel very strongly that the only way to progress is by setting examples and then hoping others will eventually follow . . . At present Leon Krier is in charge of a masterplan. We then have a rather complicated and terrifying consultation/participation weekend at Dorchester in 2 weeks time (another attempt at staving off the worst forms of criticism, while at the same time trying to enlist the help and active support of the local people). After that we shall see what happens.[31]

The principle behind the 'weekend consultation' was to marry two strands of the Prince's vision, adding community participation to the classical ideals represented in Krier's masterplan. The idea for such a weekend was discussed at what one of those present described as 'a very difficult meeting' at the Prince's new offices at St James's Palace. For over an hour, the Duchy officials argued strenuously against the very idea of such a consultation process; one of the Prince's planning advisers, John Thompson – a renowned community architect who, at the Prince's instigation, had become closely involved with various BITC projects – was equally vociferous in its favour. The bureaucrats insisted that the notion of 'community' involvement was ill suited to Poundbury and would merely produce a 'wish-list' of impossible demands which neither the planners nor the developers would be able to satisfy, and that hostile local councillors would use the Prince's name to sharpen their own axes. For the first and last time, Krier found himself on the same side as the Duchy, making it clear, with what his critics judged to be 'teutonic' doggedness, that the genius of his masterplan was not to be tampered with by the good burghers of Dorset. However, supported strongly by the Prince, Thompson won the day.

Thus in the middle of June 1989, more than 1,000 people turned up for the Planning Weekend which took place around a large marquee erected on the proposed site. The audience was evidently flattered and impressed by Krier's exegesis, which was delivered with all the biblical authority of Moses at the foot of the Mount. He told them about four model villages comprising 3,000 homes for 8,000 people, with shops, offices, schools and recreational facilities all in self-contained communities that would later be graced with elegant civic spaces, squares and public monuments. They inspected the model of the first phase, which was to comprise 650 dwellings, and they liked what they saw – though, as the Duchy had predicted, they thought that Poundbury would benefit from the inclusion of a theatre and a concert hall. Mercifully, the warring factions involved in the project managed to conceal their divisions and came away from the weekend glad to have emerged more or less unscathed.

In his letter to Stephen Mattick, the Prince had written with a certain insouciance about the cost of the project. 'Obviously,' he wrote, even though he had not explored the issue in any detail:

> the crucial question hanging over everything is the economics of the scheme. Many people, especially cynical old developers and accountants are worried – but I am not surprised. I want to explore every conceivable means – novel, revolutionary or old-fashioned – to succeed with my aim. And that is to show that a rediscovery and restoration of traditional values and principles with regard to urban design and layout is possible and desirable, and that it coincides with a largely unconscious desire on the part of so many 'ordinary' people . . .[32]

The more closely the 'cynical old developers and accountants' examined the Krier masterplan, the more worried they became. On the basis of Krier's drawings, Drivers Jonas estimated that, in its entirety, the Krier masterplan was destined to cost the Duchy some tens of millions, which, in the words of one of its officials, 'would have bankrupted us. Simple as that.'[33] Krier's supporters, while acknowledging that he had displayed a sublime indifference to the labyrinthine niceties of British planning legislation, scoffed at the figures produced by Drivers Jonas. Nonetheless, phase one of the masterplan was soon scaled down from 650 to 250 houses, while the later phases were quietly buried from view. At this stage, the scale of these projected losses was not brought to the attention of the Prince, though he was already aware of how difficult it would be to reconcile Krier's aspiration with the Duchy's sense of reality.

The Duchy's attorney, Robert Carnwath QC, touched delicately on the issue, writing to the Prince in admiration of Krier's genius but pointing out that:

the major challenge now is to move from his general perspective to a first phase which will be able to secure detailed planning permission, and which will also be economically feasible from the Duchy's (and the Treasury's) point of view . . . From what I have seen there is a great deal of detailed work to be done by the team to achieve this . . .[34]

The Prince replied:

It has already been quite a battle to proceed this far and to enable Leon to get to this stage . . . so I dread to think of all the future hurdles and obstacles. Whatever happens the Treasury and others will <u>believe</u> that various aspects of this project will not be economically feasible and somehow I will have to find a way of overcoming this negative vision. These things need an act of faith – and long term vision, neither of which come easily to treasury officials, or for that matter, organisations like the Duchy! My battles have only just begun . . .[35]

The Duchy bureaucrats agonised about how to convey to the Prince that Krier's masterplan needed drastic revision. What he regarded as their 'negative vision' was for them necessary prudence. Under the 1982 Management Act, the Duchy had been given more discretion over the deployment of capital than under the 1863 Act (which embodied the reforms undertaken by Prince Albert) that it replaced, but it was still answerable to the Treasury. Caught between this obligation to the Exchequer and their duty to the Prince, the Duchy officials gave Drivers Jonas the task of telling the Prince that, as it stood, Krier's proposal would never meet the approval of the Treasury.

In these circumstances, the relationship between Krier and the Duchy, which had been born in mutual suspicion, began to deteriorate sharply. Krier regarded the Duchy as myopic; the Duchy detected a flaw in his genius, that he was unable to transform a brilliant concept into a detailed development plan. Uncertain how to proceed, the Duchy hired a consultant, Sarah Oborn, in the hope that she would be able to persuade him to reconcile his vision with the realities of modern housing. She swiftly discovered that in the grandeur of his design, Krier had ignored the fact that a modest four-bedroomed house could be constructed with a floor area of 1,200 sq. ft., and not 6,000 sq. ft. as his masterplan envisaged. Krier accepted many of the modifications imposed by the financial logic of a succession of 'viability' studies prepared by Oborn, but by the middle of 1990 it was evident to Duchy officials that the Krier plan was still financially ruinous. There was a bitter dispute between Kevin Knott, the Duchy's deputy secretary, and Krier, who were barely on speaking terms in any case. Krier accused the Duchy of frustrating the Prince's dream and of using the Treasury to obstruct the project; Knott, in vain, tried to convince Krier that the Duchy could not proceed unless the project was demonstrably viable. Not for the first time, Krier threatened to resign.

With the project almost at the point of collapse, the Prince accepted a proposal that a group of consultant architects should be appointed to the team to try once more to convert Krier's vision into a detailed planning application. In January 1991 at Sandringham, a revised scheme was put on the table for the Prince and his advisers to scrutinise. Accusing the Duchy of thwarting his plans, Krier once again threatened to resign. Others at the meeting, which included Colin Amery and Brian Hanson, took Krier's part. Threatened with the disintegration of an enterprise into which he had poured his soul, the Prince used all his influence to reconcile the warring parties. As a result, the project survived to stumble onwards.

In 1991, the Prince had sight of Krier's sketches for the scaled-down first phase of Poundbury. The project developer, Andrew Hamilton, who had been brought in at the Prince's insistence to co-ordinate the scheme, had reservations about some of the details, but he forwarded the sketches to Kensington Palace for the Prince to assess. For once, the masterplanner had failed. Although the Prince admired Krier's overall concept, his neo-classical designs seemed to him to be quite unsuited for Dorset, where he wanted the vernacular to prevail. He therefore noted regretfully, 'I am afraid that none of this sketch is what I am looking for at Poundbury.'[36]

The Prince was determined to shape Poundbury to his own strong but imprecisely articulated vision. To this end, the outside architects worked at the masterplan, urged on by the Prince who insisted that his vision for Poundbury could be reconciled with the financial constraints identified by his Duchy officials. By October, they were ready to submit a formal planning application for an eighteen-acre development to incorporate 244 houses and flats. According to Hamilton's prosaic but worldly-wise sales pitch, the units were 'aimed at providing value for money, varying from £55,000 to £140,000 for a four-bedroomed detached house'. If the scheme was not on the heroic scale that Krier had imagined, much of the basic concept had been preserved: the buildings were to be constructed to a semi-octagonal plan hugging the contours of the land, cars would be discreetly hidden, the streets would curve gently through the estate, and the houses and cottages would be in runs of five or six, differing in size and shape but uniformly vernacular in style. A strict building code would be imposed, demanding the use of traditional features and designs. If all went well, the first houses would be finished in 1993.

All did not go well. By bringing in outside architects to 'deliver' the masterplan, the Duchy had succeeded in sidelining Krier, who remained in overall direction of the project, but distanced from it. In July, without warning, he decided to pour out his pent-up frustration to the journalist Mira Bar-Hillel. Her article duly appeared in the *Sunday Telegraph* on 19 July, under the headline 'Poundbury planner takes Duchy to task; discord reigns as Prince's pipedream of architectural Utopia waits to get off the ground'. Although Krier was not quoted directly, he accused the Duchy, in the words of the writer, of adopting a 'negative attitude', saying that its officials 'never wanted to build the Poundbury that the Prince envisaged, and persistently undermined his role'. In particular, he cited the plans for a primary school, which had been revised without his knowledge and in defiance of the 'basic codes and principles' of his masterplan. Revealing that he had broken off all direct contact with Duchy officials two years earlier, he threatened that 'unless control of the project was restored to him' he would resign.[37]

That afternoon, the Prince wrote to Krier outlining with clarity the Treasury constraints by which the Duchy was hamstrung. He tried to reassure the prickly masterplanner that the plan for the school still conformed to the Poundbury code, but insisted that there were 'real difficulties when dealing with these local authorities over cost. . . . Anyway,' he continued, referring to the newspaper article:

this kind of publicity is not helpful. This recession is making everything impossible anyway. They are shutting down defence

establishments in Dorset,* which is having a critical effect on employment and housing demand etc. so it is very hard to push Poundbury
forward in these circumstances . . . So please be more patient and
come to talk to me first before talking to the press on these matters![38]

Krier was neither repentant nor mollified. Three weeks later, he wrote
to the Prince reiterating his complaints about the Duchy and his dissat-
isfaction with the design for the school. Insisting that events were now
beyond his control, he asked the Prince to release him from any relationship with the Duchy, 'out of loyalty to the masterplan and to you
personally'.[39] Apparently, faced with the formal resignation of someone
whose genius he venerated, the Prince was in despair:

> I need hardly say how demoralising your letter was as far as I am con-
> cerned. I am mortified that you feel you want to remove yourself from
> all further involvement with the Duchy over the Poundbury project –
> even though as I said in my previous letter, I do understand your
> sense of frustration and exasperation. I think in the circumstances that
> the best thing I can do is to be utterly frank with you. Personally I
> would be very upset if you resigned from the Committee which over-
> sees the Poundbury development and, in all truth I don't want to
> release you from any relationship with the Duchy. I say this because I
> think it would be an absolute tragedy for the future and for so many
> of the principles that I believe in and which you so eloquently and
> brilliantly espouse. I know how passionately you defend those princi-
> ples and the integrity of your principles, as encapsulated in your
> masterplan but, if I may say so, I would support you one hundred per
> cent in their defence if you were working for me in a private capacity
> on my own private property and if I had several billion pounds to
> spend on doing everything the way you and I would wish to see it
> done . . . I would be deeply saddened and, indeed, offended if you
> were to abandon me at this stage especially when we will need all your

---

* A consequence of the defence cuts under *Options For Change*. Published on 23 July
1991, *Options For Change* outlined the government's detailed plans to 'restructure'
Britain's armed forces following the end of the Cold War and the collapse of the
Warsaw Pact and under pressure from the Treasury, which presided over a growing budget deficit, projected to exceed £50 billion.

talents for the forthcoming phases and to help put as many of your principles as possible, and reasonable, into practice . . .[40]

Succumbing to the intensity of this plea, the masterplanner quietly forgot about his resignation.

Over the four years during which the Poundbury project had been in gestation, the Prince had experienced at first hand the bewildering complexities of attempting to break with the conventional attitudes towards design, planning and development. He had witnessed the animosities produced by a clash of attitudes, culture and perspective that had drained the morale of all involved. Had he been less single-minded and resourceful, the project would have strangled itself much earlier. As it was, he had persistently intervened to nurse and cajole, to charm and to remonstrate, to fight and to inspire. In consequence, by the end of 1992, the project had survived to the point where the first part of the first phase of the Prince's vision of a new ethic had been accepted by Krier, approved by the Duchy, sanctioned by the Treasury and authorised by the Council.

Any relief that he might have felt about Poundbury was overwhelmed by another dispute which combined the same seemingly incompatible ingredients as the Poundbury débâcle: a visionary but hypersensitive masterplanner, anxious planning officials, and a limited budget. In this case, the Prince found himself cast even more in the role of roving diplomatist, soothing, urging, prodding and provoking the protagonists in a desperate attempt to translate grand design into acceptable practice. This time, the project concerned the *Mary Rose*, a warship which had sunk in 1545 a mile and a half out from Portsmouth Harbour. From the moment he first heard of the project from Mountbatten in 1973, the romantic in the Prince had been captivated by the historical drama encapsulated in the wreck, and when she was finally raised to the surface in October 1982 he immediately became involved in a succession of conflicts involving funding for the restoration work and plans for a museum to house the vessel. The first set of plans for the latter, which was to form part of a £26 million redevelopment of the dock area, was described by an unnamed conservationist as 'a glorified Nissen hut with spikes on', and, as patron of the Mary Rose Trust, the Prince used his influence to secure a commission for the California-based architect Professor Christopher Alexander of Berkeley University to draw up an alternative.

These plans became the subject of an intractable wrangle between Alexander, officials of the Mary Rose Trust, planning officers at Portsmouth Council, and the Prince's office. In his attempts to resolve this impasse, the prince's sheaves of letters to Alexander echoed the tone he had simultaneously adopted with Krier over Poundbury. Like Krier before him, Alexander repeatedly threatened to resign, and then caused even deeper offence by taking his grievances to the press through the good offices of Mira Bar-Hillel. The Prince was mortified, and wrote to Alexander pleading with him as one of those 'who I thought were my friends and allies' to restrain himself from 'talking to the press'. Far from holding back after this plea, Alexander proceeded to submit a modified version of his design in opposition to the 'stopgap' plans which the Mary Rose Trust had by now commissioned, and for which they had finally secured planning permission from Portsmouth Council. Once more, Mira Bar-Hillel published the story. Angered by Alexander's obduracy, the Prince wrote to him:

> Why, oh why, do you persist in being deaf to what I ask you to do? To submit a separate planning application for your building is bound to be counter-productive in the present climate with the Trust. I have always said that if the Mary Rose Trust approved of your design and if the money could be raised to build it, I would dearly love to see your scaled down version erected in the dock over the Mary Rose . . . And now yet again you have apparently leapt into print in the newspapers with Mira Bar-Hillel. What exactly are you trying to do to me when I have begged you to be circumspect . . . You are making it impossible for me and I am deeply saddened by your behaviour.[41]

By late 1992, the Prince was deeply concerned that the rifts with Krier over Poundbury and Alexander over the *Mary Rose* would threaten a much bolder project through which he hoped both to answer his critics and to realise his architectural vision: the establishment of a national Institute of Architecture in his own name. In his anguished correspondence with Krier and Alexander, he implored them not to desert that cause because of their frustrations over the Duchy and the Mary Rose Trust. The Prince had taken the first tentative steps in this direction by running summer schools at the Villa Lante, a Renaissance masterpiece owned by the Italian government just outside Viterbo, in 1991 and the following year. These were so successful that he decided to press ahead with the establishment of a permanent institute, taking a lease on 14 and 15 Gloucester Gate in Regent's Park from the Crown estates, establishing an Academic Board, and overseeing the design of a foundation course. Later that year, with a thin layer of finance from the Prince's own charitable trust and the support of a few individual benefactors, the Prince of Wales's Institute of Architecture was launched publicly – to scepticism from the architectural establishment but approbation from the media.

In May 1992, reporting on progress to the Prince, his 'secretary in architecture', Brian Hanson, wrote that the Institute would be attacking at 'the very roots' of the established

> architectural mafia . . . It is essential, then, for our broad vision to remain unsullied, the independence of our actions unbreached, and essential also, Sir, that you continue to communicate directly to us your own hopes and ambitions for your Institute, and for architecture. We are here, after all, to carry through a vision which you articulated, and which has become associated in the public mind, throughout the world, with yourself.[42]

In reply, the Prince wrote:

> I hope you can keep in mind the overriding need for the Institute to act as a catalyst to bring together the professions associated with the built environment so that we can emphasise the need to rediscover a kinder, more appropriate approach . . . I want the Institute to teach its students reverence – reverence for the landscape and the soil; for the human spirit which is a reflection in some small measure of the Divine; and for the 'grammar' of architecture which, as in a language, enables an infinite variety of forms to be expressed within the context of harmonised sentences . . .[43]

In that short note, written in haste, he spontaneously wove together the complementary themes which had been with him, growing in clarity and definition, for most of his adult life: man's identity within the natural world; the correspondence of the natural world with the idea of

God; the expression of God within the human spirit; and the potential for architecture to give physical form to those sublime relationships. Saved from an embarrassing defection by either Krier or Alexander (although the latter became ever more embroiled in a worsening relationship with the Prince's office), the prospect of realising his aspiration for the Institute took a step forward when the first full-time students enrolled for the foundation course in the autumn of 1992.

Under normal circumstances the Prince might have been forgiven for indulging in a sigh of relief and a moment of self-congratulation. However, these were not normal circumstances. If his efforts to negotiate Poundbury, the *Mary Rose* and his Institute away from the rocks had been troubled, the experience was as nothing in comparison with the torture to which he was now to be subjected, following the publication of a book written by a tabloid 'royal-watcher' purporting to reveal the facts about his relationship with the Princess of Wales. *Diana: Her True Story*, as Andrew Morton's book was unblushingly entitled, was, for the Prince of Wales, a humiliation of almost unendurable proportions.

CHAPTER
TWENTY-FOUR

T he truth about the marriage of the Prince and Princess of Wales
was protected by a skein of silence woven by the press office at
Buckingham Palace to shut out the most prurient journalist.
When a tabloid article, careless as usual with the facts, skirted close to an
aspect of the truth, one loyal press secretary to the Queen after another,
from Michael Shea to Charles Anson, abiding by a long-standing policy,
issued courteous but firm 'no comments'. When journalists pressed for
'clarification' of a rumour or a supposition and claimed an array of
unnamed sources in its support, the Palace had nothing to say. Under
other circumstances the strategy might have worked; as it was, successive
press secretaries, well aware that the marriage was in trouble but unwilling to mislead, found themselves trapped by their own honourable
disingenuousness, not least because some of the sources available to the
royal-watchers were leaking a version of the facts, from 1987 onwards,
which bore more than a passing resemblance to reality. As a result, their
office was brought close to the edge of ridicule and its already fragile
credibility was undermined, if not entirely shattered.*

---

* In hindsight, many of those involved came to believe that it would have been sensible to have been more open about the deteriorating state of the marriage. At the
time, however, it was hard to find the right moment to issue a statement which
would have been both intrusive and damaging while serving only to fuel further
speculation. They believed that any such statement might well have precipitated a

Between 1987 and 1992, a growing number of reports appeared in the tabloid press which cast the Prince as the villain of the royal soap opera – a drama in which the banality of the script was illuminated only by shafts of cruelty. This form of persecution required the Prince to be seen as remote and unloving, not only towards the Princess but towards his children as well. To provide authenticity, a ready phalanx of popular psychologists, 'agony aunts' and columnists was always at hand to reprimand the errant father with reach-me-down homilies about the duties of parenthood.

The apotheosis of this genre of journalism was reached in June 1991, when Prince William was hit on the head by a fellow pupil with a golf club. The Princess was at lunch in London and the Prince was at Highgrove when the news was brought to them. As their son was taken from Ludgrove School to the Royal Berkshire Hospital, his parents converged there to be with him. Like the Princess, the Prince was horrified when his policeman broke the news to him. 'I knew it was something terrible. My heart went cold,' he said later. 'My policeman said that it was not too serious but I worried all the way to the hospital until I found him sitting up in bed chatting away. Then I knew he was going to be all right.'[1] Nonetheless, the golf club had left a small indentation at the point of impact in the child's skull and the doctors decided that he should be transferred to the Great Ormond Street Hospital for Sick Children, to be examined by a group of neurological specialists. After a brief consultation, the surgeons decided to operate. Explaining to both the Prince and the Princess that the procedure would be routine, they reassured the Prince that there was no point in both parents waiting in the ward for what was to be a straightforward operation involving negligible risk. Only then did the Prince decide to leave Great Ormond Street for the West End, where he was host to both the European Environment and Agriculture Commissioners and a party of officials from Brussels for a performance of *Tosca* at Covent Garden. Afterwards, confirming that the operation had been successful and that his son was comfortable and asleep in the hospital with the Princess at hand, he boarded the royal train and travelled overnight to Yorkshire for an official visit to the Dales

---

crisis in the increasingly difficult situation which they were dutifully attempting to conceal. In any case, by 1992, it would have been impossible to get either of the two parties to agree to such a statement.

with his European guests and British officials. The next day, he returned to London and went immediately to Great Ormond Street, where, as he had been promised, William had made a complete recovery.

The version of this episode which appeared in the tabloid press over the following days may be summarised in the *Sun* headline: 'What kind of dad are you?'. The theme had become a refrain, the gist of which was that the Prince was a neglectful parent, indifferent to the wellbeing of his children. A year later, a friend of the Princess was quoted by Morton as confirming that the Princess had shared this tabloid verdict: 'Had this been an isolated incident it would have been unbelievable. She wasn't surprised. It merely confirmed everything she thought about him . . .'[2] One of the Princess's intimates, James Gilbey, was more explicit: 'She thinks he is a bad father, a selfish father . . . he will never delay, cancel or change anything which he has sorted out for their benefit,'[3] he was quoted as saying. The words bore a marked similarity to those attributed with such damaging effect to unnamed sources or 'friends of the Princess' in the months before and after Prince William's accident.

The truth was somewhat more complicated, as their staff knew only too well. One of the most difficult tasks they faced was not only to dove-tail the competing demands of the Prince's public and domestic life, but to accommodate them to the Princess's own arrangements for their children. As the relationship between the parents deteriorated, it became an increasingly fruitless endeavour. On several occasions, Richard Aylard, the Prince's private secretary, cleared space in the Prince's otherwise inflexible diary for a private outing with his sons, only to discover that at the last moment the Princess had made other plans for them that could not apparently be unravelled.

Before long, the belief that the Prince was, at best, a poor father began to seep into an already poisoned public consciousness. Inaccurate reports allied to lazy commentary demonstrated the validity of the proposition that a falsehood repeated often enough gradually acquires the status of hallowed truth. The lies about his feelings for his children were a source of persistent torment to him. Yet he felt it was impossible for him to allow the truth to be known without humiliating himself and provoking a surge of 'tit-for-tat' articles in the tabloid press, which he believed would wreak even more havoc on his marriage and, in the process, open the institution into which he had been born to a form of ridicule that he feared might prove fatal.

His friends and his staff chafed under the vow of silence he imposed on them. Hoping the marriage could survive, they forbore to mention that the Prince was sometimes effectively denied access to his children by his wife: that, for example, Prince William's first visit to the principality, which was to Cardiff for a service in the cathedral on St David's Day, was arranged by the Princess without the Prince's knowledge and when he was already committed elsewhere, and that to be with them in Wales and save all of them embarrassment ('Where WAS the Prince of Wales?') he had to cancel his other engagements at the last moment.

In other lives, this humdrum evidence of a doomed marriage would have been a private matter; but as the tabloid press were inspired to rush to adverse judgement of the Prince on the basis of partial leaks and pernicious innuendo, his reputation was further undermined. It was in this environment that Aylard strove to find dates that fitted the diaries of both parents. In the Prince's files there is a memorandum from Aylard proposing possible 'windows' for an outing with the children and asking whether the Prince would like to discuss the possibilities with the Princess directly or whether he wanted the prospects to be explored by their staff. In what seems to be an allusion to the difficulty of accommodating his diary to that of the Princess, the Prince had scrawled in capital letters on the memo, 'I'LL TRY!'* (He did, but only to intermittent effect.)

The impression that the Prince was a distant father was sharpened by his attitude towards the media in general and to photographers in particular. Unlike the Princess, who had no qualms about demonstrating her love for their children in public, the Prince had an aversion to displays of affection except in private. 'I'm not very good at being a performing monkey,' he has explained and, in response to those who have concluded that his failure to be more effusive in public betokens a lack of warmth,

---

* In *Diana: Her True Story*, Morton cites a memo from Aylard that allegedly urged the Prince, in Morton's words, 'to be seen in public with his children more frequently so that at least he could be seen to be behaving as a responsible father'. According to Morton, Aylard ended this plea by writing in capital letters, 'TRY!' (op. cit., p.123). Not only does no such memorandum exist, but it is inconceivable that any private secretary in the household would ever have been so impertinent as to address a member of the royal family in such terms. The memo with the Prince's 'I'LL TRY' scrawled on it was a confidential document which only the Prince and his private secretary would normally have seen.

he has retorted, 'I would have thought that was a fairly facile kind of judgement to make . . . I'm not prepared to perform whenever *they* want me to perform.'[4*] His reluctance even to be seen with his children in public was in marked contrast to the attitude of the Princess, who gave no sign of irritation when photographers chanced to arrive as if on cue for what were billed internally as private outings.

By this time, relations between the Prince and the Princess of Wales were conducted mostly through their respective private offices, which faced the task of accommodating the sometimes irreconcilable requirements of their principals. On more than one occasion, the Princess wished to be apart from her husband under circumstances bound to provoke adverse media criticism which could only make their predicament even worse. In 1991, one such problem emerged when, well in advance, the Prince indicated to his staff that he would like to ski with the children in the spring holidays. At first, the Princess seemed to demur, but her office managed to overcome the practical difficulties and persuaded her that the Prince's wish to be with their children was not easy to deny. On 28 March, therefore, the family arrived in the Austrian ski resort of Lech.

The next afternoon, 29 March, the news came through from London that the Princess's father, Earl Spencer, had died in hospital. Very distressed, the Princess decided to return at once to London, making it clear that she wished to travel alone. Their staff were sympathetic to her grief but could not ignore the fact that this would leave the very public impression that she could not bear to be with her husband during such a crisis. It was only after prolonged and intense discussion that the Princess relented and saved both of them a tabloid mauling.

Similarly, on the day of the funeral itself, the Princess made it clear that she wished to travel to the funeral without her husband. In deference to her wishes, their staff did not seek to change her mind but, aware yet again of the damaging speculation that would be provoked by

---

* In the summer of 1993, the Prince finally allowed the cameras to film him playing with his children on the edge of Loch Muick at Balmoral for the television documentary, *Charles: The Private Man, The Public Role*. He agreed to this with great reluctance and only because he was persuaded by his friends that the absence of such pictures would serve to confirm the false impression that his reticence had created.

such a public sign of disaffection, they reinstated a meeting in London which the Prince had cancelled because of the funeral and arranged for a helicopter to take him to Northamptonshire in time for the service. He was thus spared the indignity of arriving at the same destination at the same time but in a separate car, but he did not entirely escape tabloid censure when it was widely commented that his failure to be at his wife's side on the way to the funeral was further evidence of his coldness towards her.

During this period, their staff continued to hope – despite the growing evidence to the contrary – that by shielding the Prince and Princess from hostile scrutiny, they might yet help to stave off the disaster of an irrevocable public breakdown of the marriage. Not one of them, however, was prepared for what became known as 'the Morton book'.

On 7 June 1992, the first extract from Morton's *Diana: Her True Story* appeared in the *Sunday Times*, shocking the British people and horrifying Buckingham Palace. Even though speculation about the state of the royal marriage had become a national pastime, for many people it was chilling to discover that the 'fairy-tale' marriage in which they had been encouraged to believe was a charade. Even worse, it was, for once, not possible to dismiss the book as ill-informed gossip, the usual currency of royal journalism. Morton's account was not drawn from disaffected butlers, footmen or maids; in this case the sources were close friends of the Princess. Their portrayal of the royal marriage, as reported by Morton, was unsparing of the Prince. He was depicted as a faithless husband, whose cruelty and indifference had driven his wife into a state of near-suicidal despair. The author purported only to have reported faithfully what he believed to be the Princess's own version of reality; and, as conveyed by her friends, there was enough anecdotal detail to make that claim credible. As the horror of this betrayal reverberated through Buckingham Palace, one question came to the fore: had the Princess authorised her friends to disclose the intimacies with which she had entrusted them, or were they, for whatever reason, betraying her confidences to them?

The question had also perplexed the editor of the *Sunday Times*, Andrew Neil. Some weeks before publication, Morton's publisher approached Neil and summarised the revelations contained in *Diana: Her True Story*. Neil's first instinct was to dismiss the book as yet another exercise in tabloid sensationalism. However, as the *Mail on Sunday* had already bid more than £200,000 for the serial rights, he rang his proprietor, Rupert Murdoch, in Los Angeles, who told him, 'It's up to you.' Some days later, Morton himself came into the office to discuss another matter. Neil, with characteristic bluntness, said that he didn't believe the stories about bulimia and suicide bids. According to Neil, Morton said, 'I swear to you that this is all fully documented and it is documented by far more than you'll see in the book itself.'[5]

Neil decided to reconsider. 'The clincher for us,' he has explained, 'was that there are six or seven people widely quoted in the book and Morton got statements from them saying that they had read what was attributed to them in the book and they stood by what they had said.'[6] Neil's judgement was reinforced by his colleague Andrew Knight,* who was a friend of one of the named sources; this source had given further corroboration that the book was authentic, confiding in Knight that she had indeed talked to Morton, and had done so at the instigation of the Princess, who had told her to hide nothing because she wanted to 'end the fairy tale'.[7] Apparently, the Princess had also made it clear that she hoped to see the book published as fully and widely as possible. Neil checked once more with his proprietor, who told him 'You'll be hung out to dry by the Establishment. They'll have a real go at you. But I'll back you whatever decision you make.'

During the negotiations between the *Sunday Times* and Morton's agent, Andrew Knight had further telephone calls with his contact, and was left in no doubt that she was speaking for the Princess. On one occasion, Knight queried a view that she had attributed to the Princess. She promised to check. Within five minutes she rang back to confirm what she had said. There was little doubt within the *Sunday Times* that, directly or indirectly, the Princess of Wales had authorised the publication of Morton's book. That judgement clinched the deal.

Murdoch's republican instincts have often been cited to explain the attitude towards the monarchy sometimes adopted by his newspapers, although his infrequent public statements about the monarchy are somewhat contradictory. In a television interview with Mary Goldring in 1989, he said that although he had been a republican as a student in Britain, he had since tempered his attitudes, telling his interlocutor that

---

* Andrew Knight (1939–), executive chairman, News International plc, 1990–94; chairman, Times Newspapers Holdings, 1990–94.

the royal family symbolised 'a lot of permanence here, a lot of things that are very good in this country . . . So I think one can believe in it, respect it, but also be a responsible critic.'[8] Four years later, in an interview with the *Courier Mail* in Brisbane, he was less positive about the institution, commenting, 'My feeling always was that it did harm in Britain. They're not bad people but it led to delusions that Britain was greater than it was and more powerful and therefore more competitive.' When his interviewer asked, 'The monarchy is a contradiction in terms of a flexible society?', Murdoch replied, 'Yes.'[9] At least one of his senior executives, who has discussed the issue with him, became convinced that he is a committed republican but believes it unwise to trumpet the fact in Britain. In this case, it may be presumed that Murdoch's attitude was governed less by ideology than by commercial instinct.

In the run-up to the serialisation, the chairman of the Press Complaints Commission,* Lord McGregor, came under intense pressure from politicians and members of the public, urging him to condemn the press speculation about the collapse of the marriage of the Prince and Princess of Wales, which had become increasingly obtrusive as rival newspapers ran 'spoilers' against the *Sunday Times*.

On Monday 8 June, the day after the first revelations in the *Sunday Times*, the PCC responded to this pressure by preparing a press statement denouncing this 'odious exhibition of journalists dabbling their fingers in the stuff of other people's souls in a manner which adds nothing to legitimate public interest in the situation of the heir to the throne'.[10] In the presence of three members of the Commission, McGregor rang Sir Robert Fellowes to read him the statement. However, he added that he had heard rumours from senior editors that the damaging leaks about the state of the royal marriage had emanated either directly or indirectly from the Princess of Wales herself. Before releasing the statement, he needed an assurance from Fellowes (who was, disconcertingly, the Princess's brother-in-law as well as the Queen's private secretary) that these rumours were false. Fellowes gave this assurance in good faith and the statement was duly published.

---

* The PCC was established in January 1991 following recommendations by the Calcutt Committee. It replaced the Press Council as the industry's self-regulating but independent body. All editors and publishers in Britain have declared their commitment to the PCC's Code of Practice.

The following day Andrew Knight wrote a pained letter to McGregor, assuring him that the *Sunday Times* had serialised the Morton book also in good faith. McGregor was unconvinced. On 10 June, in a telephone conversation, Knight explained his reasons for believing that the Princess had collaborated in the publication of the book. McGregor was incredulous, and the more so when Knight went on to tell him that later in the day the Princess was going to call on her former flatmate Carolyn Bartholomew (who was one of the principal contributors to the book) with the apparent purpose of corroborating her friend's damning indictment of the Prince and the Palace; not only that, but that a photographer on another Murdoch paper, the *Sun*, and possibly others, had been tipped off as to where and when the meeting would take place. 'Read the tabloids tomorrow,' Knight admonished the chairman of the PCC, 'then you'll believe me!'

The next morning, with newspapers filled with pictures of the Princess embracing Carolyn Bartholomew, Knight's prediction was amply fulfilled. McGregor was furious, both with the Palace press office, which had unwittingly misled the media, and especially with Fellowes, whom he held personally responsible for his part in bringing the PCC into ridicule. He rang two of his colleagues in the House of Lords, Lord Wakeham, the Leader of the Lords, and Lord Mackay, the Lord Chancellor, urging that the government should intervene directly with the Palace to stem the downward spiral of relations with the media. Wakeham rang Fellowes, who was with the Queen on an official visit to Paris. By this time, the Queen's private secretary had been driven to the conclusion that his sister-in-law must have been involved in the Morton book. Deeply embarrassed, he telephoned McGregor to apologise profusely and, as McGregor recalled the moment, 'to say that his assurance had been given in good faith'.[11] McGregor accepted this apology, believing correctly that Fellowes had acted with honour and had indeed been misled. It may be presumed that Fellowes had confronted his sister-in-law with the allegations and that she had vehemently denied them.*

---

* Fellowes was mortified by this episode. As further evidence accumulated, he realised that the Princess, his sister-in-law, had misled him about her involvement in the book. As a man of integrity, he felt that he had no other course but to offer his resignation to the Queen. The offer was refused. Later, in 1993, he also offered his apologies to the Prince of Wales.

The damage done to the Prince's reputation by the publication of the Morton book could scarcely have been greater. It was compounded by a number of reports to the effect that, for some months, friends of the Prince had been emulating the friends of the Princess by leaking damaging stories about her. However, as his friends knew, it was a fundamental rule of their relationship with the Prince that they should never speak to the press about him or on his behalf without his assent.* One or two may have breached that injunction but, apart from the evidence of one speculative conversation between McGregor and Lord Rothermere (the proprietor of the *Daily Mail*), which the latter subsequently repudiated, the PCC had never been offered any information to suggest that the Prince or his friends had at any time sought to use the media against the Princess. The converse, both before and after the publication of the Morton book, did not apply.

However, the rumours were given greater currency by an article which appeared in the *Sunday Times* after the serialisation of *Diana: Her True Story* under the headline 'The Case for Charles'.[12] Claiming to have spoken to some of his closest confidants, including Patricia Brabourne, King Constantine of Greece, and Norton and Penny Romsey, the writer purported to give 'the other side' of the story. As senior Murdoch executives have since confessed, the claim was misleading.

The basis for the article was a private conversation at Lord's cricket ground between Andrew Knight and Norton Romsey, the Prince's cousin, who did indeed pour out his anger and dismay about the treatment of the Prince by the media. Afterwards, Knight returned to his office and passed on the gist of his conversation, insisting, however, that the *Sunday Times* could run a story if, and only if, Romsey, and any other friends of the Prince which the reporting team might be able to contact, were prepared to talk. Several of his friends, desperate to put the record straight, had in fact contacted Richard Aylard effectively asking for permission to speak out. Aylard was adamant: no-one should say a

---

* In 1990, the journalist Penny Junor was given access to the Prince's and Princess's staff and some of their friends. Her book, *Charles and Diana, Portrait of a Marriage* (Headline, 1991), was a sensitive account of a working partnership which judged that the marriage was, in those terms, 'actually very healthy' – a conclusion which, pre-Morton, did not seem so far from the truth as it would do with the benefit of hindsight.

word about the marriage or about the Princess; to do so would only make a terrible situation even worse. The private secretary had good reason for his judgement.

By the eve of the serialisation of the Morton book, Buckingham Palace had more than an inkling of what the *Sunday Times* was going to print. After consultation with the Queen's assistant private secretary, Robin Janvrin, Aylard came to the conclusion that the Palace could no longer stay silent as the reputation of the heir to the throne was torn to pieces by the media. With the reluctant consent of the Prince he drafted a statement to the effect that in many respects the book was inaccurate and distorted to the point of fabrication. It stated that both the Prince and the Princess regretted the publication, which would damage their family life and make it more difficult to carry out their joint and separate public duties. The statement was never released. When the Princess's private secretary, Patrick Jephson,* and Philip Mackie read the draft to the Princess, she refused to authorise it, telling them bluntly that the book was not inaccurate and that she would not put her name to a document which claimed that it was. For Buckingham Palace this refusal was persuasive, if not conclusive, evidence of her collusion either directly or indirectly with Morton. In these circumstances it was imperative to prevent the Prince's friends making an appalling situation even worse by retaliating in the heat of the moment, as some of them were tempted to do. As one of his more restrained friends noted at the time, 'He wants all of us to say NOTHING and nothing is what we'll all say.'[13]

Thus when a reporter from the *Sunday Times* rang the friends, all of them refused to comment. As one senior executive later intimated, 'My impression was that they were all under instructions not to talk.'[14] Neil confirmed this, saying, 'We did have terrible problems because we were led to believe that Charles had put the word out that he did not want his friends to reply because it would be seen almost like retaliation.'[15] Despite this wall of silence, the *Sunday Times* did not refrain from publishing the article, which, to Knight's lasting embarrassment, was based entirely on his exchange of confidences with Norton Romsey at a cricket match. Inevitably, the article had a corrosive effect, endorsing the false belief that the Prince and Princess were engaged in a public slanging match,

---

* Patrick Jephson, formerly the Princess's equerry, became her private secretary in 1991.

courtesy of their most intimate friends, and that in the matter of media manipulation there was nothing to choose between them. This conclusion was reinforced by one further breach of the Prince's injunction to his friends to stay silent. On 6 July, the *Today* newspaper published a four-page article by Penny Junor, headlined 'Charles: His True Story'. According to the newspaper, Junor 'was contacted by his circle and asked to write her article'.[16] Although the article was in every way as sympathetic as the headline implied, the Prince was infuriated by it, and also with Norton Romsey, whose intemperate devotion inevitably made him the prime suspect. On the Prince's behalf, Aylard once more instructed his friends to keep their counsel.

Until the publication of *Diana: Her True Story*, the Prince had insisted to himself and to his friends that the marriage could survive. Even in 1992, he talked of his hope that the Princess might learn to become his friend, and that in any case, both for the sake of their children and for the sake of the monarchy, they could live separate lives under the same roof and perform their public duties together. Indeed, though he was appalled by the Morton book, he still clung to the thought that the Princess might be innocent of involvement in such malice. Quite unaware of the circumstances in which the serialisation had occurred and of the dramas at the PCC, he still wanted to believe that it was not her but her friends who were at fault. It was only when Robert Fellowes apologised for misleading the PCC, and afterwards, in some embarassment, confirmed that he had been misled himself, that the Prince was forced to acknowledge the truth.

Thus far, the foundering of the Prince's marriage had not been a matter for family discussion. When the family was together at Balmoral or Sandringham, they had witnessed symptoms of the Princess's distress, but, not wishing to interfere, they had become accustomed to averting their gaze. For the Prince's part, the prospect of discussing such problems with his parents was almost inconceivable. Yet, incapable as they were of reaching out to each other, all three understood only too well the overriding rule of royal life: the show goes on. The Morton book shattered that presumption.*

---

* The '*annus horribilis*', as the Queen was to describe 1992, seemed to have reached its apotheosis with *Diana: Her True Story*, but the scandals did not abate. In August, the *Sun* published the 'Squidgy tapes', the purported transcript of an indiscreet

After the publication of the first instalment of the Morton book, a handful of the Prince's closest friends, including the Romseys and the van Cutsems, felt compelled to tell both the Queen and Prince Philip how stoical they thought their son had been through the long trauma of his marriage. Perhaps nudged by this intervention but certainly shocked by the media blitzkrieg surrounding the publication of the book, both the Queen and the Duke, who had been at pains not to take sides, rallied to the Prince; in particular, the Duke wrote a long and sympathetic letter to him in which he praised what he saw as his son's saint-like fortitude. It was in this atmosphere that the Queen and the Prince discussed for the first time whether he should seek a separation from the Princess.

Soon afterwards, the Prime Minister made sure that he was fully briefed about a situation which clearly had the potential to become a constitutional issue about which he might be required to address the House of Commons. In more than one meeting with those closely involved in the crisis, he was acquainted with the scale of the problem and the prospects for the marriage. At one of those meetings, he asked what the chances were of avoiding a separation. He was told 'less than fifty-fifty'.[17]

Soon afterwards, the Prince took the first tentative steps towards a formal separation by authorising an approach to the prominent lawyer Lord Goodman* to establish the legal alternatives open to him. Some days after the preliminary meeting, the Prince himself saw Goodman. He was not yet convinced that such a drastic step was inevitable but, as the Princess was talking openly about a separation, he and his advisers needed to understand what that possibility might entail.

The glare of the media made the Prince and Princess's predicament

---

* Arnold Goodman (1913–   ), senior partner, Goodman Derrick and Co., Solicitors. He came to prominence in the early sixties as a mentor to the Prime Minister, Harold Wilson. For more than a quarter of a century he exercised a discreet but powerful influence within the British establishment.

---

conversation recorded illegally by an electronic eavesdropper, in which the Princess of Wales allegedly spoke despairingly of her life and disparagingly of the royal family to her friend James Gilbey. In the same month, the Duchess of York left Balmoral prematurely after photographs appeared in the *Daily Mirror* which showed her sunbathing topless in the south of France, attended by a toe-sucking admirer.

even more difficult to bear. In February, they had gone to India for a six-day official visit to discover that (well before the publication of the Morton book) the British royal-watchers had eyes only for the state of their marriage. Twelve years before, the Prince had visited the Taj Mahal and had been moved to say that one day he would return with his bride. In the event, the official schedule was so crowded that the Princess went alone while the Prince stayed to make two speeches and to launch a new charity.

Nevertheless, the Prince was optimistic about the tour: 'I have always felt that people on the whole either love India or hate it. I actually love it – partly because I rather like the Indians themselves, but also because certain aspects of the culture and philosophy appeal to the feelings I experience about life in general.' On the day that the Princess left for the Taj Mahal, the Prince prepared to make a speech at the Indo-British Industrialists' Forum,* still in good spirits. Even a mishap entertained him. 'I arrived at the I.B.I.F. gathering to give my speech,' he noted:

> having asked in advance if I could pop into the loo before going into the hall. I shook hands with the organisers outside the building and then was led to a door – also on the outside – which I thought would be the required convenience. To my horror, I stepped straight onto the platform of a hall containing 700 expectant people. My face fell a mile and I tried initially to back out of the door, but was carried through and onto the platform by an unstoppable tidal wave of policemen, secretaries and officials! I then had to deliver my address hopping from one foot to another![18]

Meanwhile, at the Taj Mahal, the Princess was besieged by photographers as she posed alone in front of the great tomb, built by the seventeenth-century Mogul Emperor, Shah Jahan, in memory of his wife who had died in childbirth. For the British newspapers, most of which had already determined that this was a 'tale of two tours with Charles and Diana going their own ways',[19] the photo opportunity at the Taj Mahal provided an ironic if unintended symbol: poised before one of

---

* The IBIF was established in 1986 by the Confederation of British Industry and the Confederation of Engineering Industries in India (now called the Confederation of Indian Industry).

the world's great monuments to love, the image both suggested an unbearable isolation and administered a fearsome rebuke to a loveless and errant husband. For most British reporters, who stuck dutifully to the script of the soap opera, this was almost the only significant event of the entire royal visit to India. One journalist was overheard to say, as she scribbled in her notebook, 'She's seen the world's greatest monument to love. Now perhaps she's ready to work again at the failed marriage which has broken a nation's heart.'[20]

Two days after the Taj Mahal there was a polo match. The Prince arrived at the ground in Jaipur to be impressed by the officers of the 61st Cavalry, immaculately dressed in blue blazers and Hermès scarves 'tied round their throats as a cravat'. The regimental grooms in puttees, jodhpurs and stiffened turbans, 'all of them looking exactly like a Raffles painting and as if Time had somehow stood still', made him feel underdressed. In front of a crowd of 30,000, the Prince wrote in his diary that he 'managed to score a pretty spectacular, and very lucky, goal from 60 yards out on the boundary . . . No-one could have been more surprised than me – or the spectators.'[21]

Afterwards, as a member of the victorious team, he went up to receive his trophy from the Princess, who had been persuaded, against her will, to attend the match and to present the prizes. Beforehand, she had been agitated about the forthcoming photocall, debating at length with her aides whether or not she would be expected to kiss her husband in front of the crowd and the cameras that were already poised for what in the fevered imagination of the tabloid press had become a critical moment. The Prince evidently had little idea what was at stake as he leant forward to brush his wife's cheek with his lips but, as the shutters clicked, the Princess moved her head almost imperceptibly to the side, leaving his kiss to die in the air. It was an indelible image. It mattered not that the Prince (and the Princess) had been about their public duties with tireless humour and charm, that their visit had helped to promote a £1.5 billion arms deal, that they had been greeted with warmth wherever they went, and that they had even smiled and joked with one another; all that counted was the Taj Mahal and the 'Kiss that wasn't': 'proof positive' that the marriage was indeed on the rocks.

If India had been bad enough, the Prince had every reason to believe that, eight months later, their official visit to Korea would be even worse. In August, while the royal family was still trying to reconcile itself to the repercussions of the Morton book, the Princess unexpectedly announced that she was not prepared to go to Seoul. As the Prince's staff contemplated the nightmarish task of explaining to the Korean authorities that the Princess would not after all be accompanying her husband on the first royal visit to their country, Peter Westmacott, the deputy private secretary to the royal couple, was obliged to do the Korean 'recce' as if he were organising a joint visit – which, from his conversations with the Princess, he was convinced would not in fact take place. At Balmoral, the Prince tried to persuade the Princess to change her mind. Even the Queen intervened to advise her daughter-in-law that she ought to go (a discussion which, billed as a 'showdown', became yet another leak to reach the press). The Princess did not yield. Finally, the Prince told her bluntly that she would have to come up with an explanation of her own for staying behind. At this, the Princess finally relented, saying meekly that as the Queen had asked her to go she would after all accompany him.

The tour started badly and did not improve. In India, the royal reporters had been in hot pursuit; in Korea, they were moving in for the kill. Yet again, in terms of trade deals and governmental ties, the visit was an unequivocal success. On this occasion, however, both the Prince and the Princess were aware that their lovelessness was the only story in Britain. For both of them, therefore, the visit was a dreadful experience. When they paid their respects at the military war memorial in the national cemetery, the royal couple stood solemnly in silence, an image which was used to confirm the tabloid contention that the marriage was a sham and that the royal couple had come to loathe one another's presence.

In these circumstances, it was not surprising that the Princess was under great stress. It was made worse by telephone calls from London from her friends telling her about the tabloid coverage of the trip and about newspaper reports that the Duke of Edinburgh had been writing to admonish her, whereas he had in fact started a correspondence with her which, judging from her own comments later, had been as helpful and constructive as he had intended. There had been many occasions in the past when the Princess had been in a state of anxiety before or after one of her invariably polished public performances, but in Korea she was often distraught, and, in her anguish, she was unable, or unwilling, to hide her sorrow from the public. Not surprisingly, on more than one occasion, the photographers caught the loneliness and misery on both their faces.

At the end of every tour there was by tradition a farewell 'prize-giving', when the Prince and Princess gave a small memento to each of their accompanying team. On the last morning in Seoul, the Princess was in a state of desperation, overcome by nausea and tears. According to one of their aides, who had a fondness for both of them, the Prince 'was marvellous. He did all the talking, all the smiling, covered up for her. He was very protective, very professional.'[22] By this time more than one of her aides had come to the conclusion that the Princess could no longer endure her marriage and wanted to break free, whatever the consequences.

The royal couple flew from Korea to Hong Kong, where the Prince disembarked for a three-day visit to the colony while the Princess returned to London. On 8 November, he flew back to RAF Lyneham in a mood of deepening gloom. On the aircraft, he wrote to one of his closest friends describing his despair that the Princess could not be 'a friend' to him and how he had been battling with himself against succumbing to the temptation to cancel his engagements. 'The strain is immense,' he wrote, 'and yet I want to do my duty in the way I've been trained.' Momentarily, he found it difficult to contemplate the future, yet he also knew that he had no real choice but to persevere: 'I feel so unsuited to the ghastly business of human intrigue and general nastiness . . . I don't know what will happen from now on but I dread it.'[23]

Back in England, the Prince made preparations for one of his annual weekend parties at Sandringham. It had become the custom for the royal couple to invite some sixteen of their friends to stay for three days of relaxation, shooting and walking. The weekend had been timed to coincide with an *exeat* from Ludgrove, so that Prince William and Prince Harry, from whom the royal couple had tried to hide the crisis in their marriage, could be with them as well. In what was an otherwise grim period, the Prince looked forward to welcoming his friends into what he hoped would offer at least the semblance of a happy family occasion.

It was to his astonishment, therefore, that less than a week beforehand he discovered that the Princess had decided to stay away from Sandringham and that she intended to take their children to stay with the Queen at Windsor Castle instead. Dismayed by this news, the Prince had a long conversation with his mother, after which the Princess came under strong pressure to reconsider her refusal to join him at Sandringham. However, she was adamant: if she could not stay at Windsor, she would go to Highgrove instead. Moreover, she would take the children with her, despite the Prince's insistence that, even if she were to stay away, they at least should join him at Sandringham as originally planned.

During the next week, the Prince and Princess exchanged letters and phone calls in which the Prince tried to persuade his wife that he could not cancel the weekend house party; even if it were possible, he argued, it would in any case soon become public knowledge and the subject of yet more speculation in the press. Eventually, when it became clear that she was not going to relent, he snapped. Unable to see any future in a relationship conducted on these terms, he decided he had no choice but to ask his wife for a legal separation.* On 25 November, the royal couple met privately at Kensington Palace where the Princess accepted that his decision was the only option that now faced them. The following day, through her private secretary Patrick Jephson, the Princess provided the Prince's lawyers with the name of her solicitor, and the appropriate letters were exchanged. The Queen and the Prime Minister were consulted through their respective private secretaries and it was agreed that an announcement should be made nine days later.

On 9 December, the Prime Minister stood at the dispatch box in front of a crowded but silent House of Commons to read a prepared statement:

> It is announced from Buckingham Palace that, with regret, the Prince and Princess of Wales have decided to separate. Their Royal Highnesses have no plans to divorce and their constitutional positions are unaffected. This decision has been reached amicably and they will both continue to participate fully in the upbringing of their children.
>
> Their Royal Highnesses will continue to carry out full and separate programmes of public engagements and will, from time to time, attend family occasions and national events together.

---

* By grim coincidence, the weekend in question coincided with the fire that began to rage through Windsor Castle on Friday 20 November. Rather than cancelling the weekend gathering, the Prince hurried from Sandringham to Windsor as soon as he heard the news, returning in the early hours of Saturday morning to re-join his guests.

The Queen and the Duke of Edinburgh, though saddened, understand and sympathise with the difficulties that have led to this decision. Her Majesty and His Royal Highness particularly hope that the intrusions into the privacy of the Prince and Princess may now cease. They believe that a degree of privacy and understanding is essential if their Royal Highnesses are to provide a happy and secure upbringing for their children, while continuing to give a whole-hearted commitment to their public duties.

Afterwards, the Prime Minister provoked a gasp from the otherwise hushed rows of MPs around him when he said:

The House will wish to know that the decision to separate has no constitutional implications. The succession to the Throne is unaffected by it; the children of the Prince and Princess retain their position in the line of succession; and there is no reason why the Princess of Wales should not be crowned Queen in due course. The Prince of Wales's succession as head of the Church of England is also unaffected.

Although the Prime Minister's statement correctly interpreted the constitutional position, the image of the Prince and Princess arriving separately at Westminster Abbey for a coronation service at which both would be crowned respectively King and Queen struck many politicians and commentators as an unimaginable prospect.* Indeed, some commentators were quick to suggest that the Prince himself would be unlikely to inherit the Crown, let alone the role of Supreme Governor of the Church of England. What prompted this speculation, which was particularly feverish in the tabloid press, was not at all clear, except that many of them had rushed to the judgement that the Prince had 'caused' the breakdown of his marriage and was therefore unsuited

---

* By tradition, the Queen Consort is crowned and anointed after the King, although the precedent of Queen Caroline, who was barred entry from Westminster Abbey in 1821, is a reminder that the custom is not a constitutional obligation. Following their separation, it seemed unrealistic to suppose that the Princess would act as Queen Consort or, indeed, that she would wish to be anointed as his Queen at the new King's side.

to inherit either role. In fact, before making his statement to the
House, the Prime Minister had taken careful advice from the Lord
Chancellor, Lord Mackay, and the Archbishop of Canterbury, George
Carey.

Some months earlier, when it was already clear that the marriage was
in difficulties, the three men had discussed the constitutional implications
of both separation and divorce. In this discussion, the role of the
Established Church had not been merely to provide an ethical or
Christian perspective but to alert the Prime Minister and Buckingham
Palace to the likely repercussions within the Anglican communion.
Afterwards, for their benefit, the Archbishop summarised the attitude of
the Church of England towards both options. Essentially, Lambeth Palace
took the view that a formal separation within marriage would be likely to
win widespread understanding, as it would signal the importance of the
institution of marriage and the seriousness of the marriage vows made
before God. By putting that consideration above their emotions as individuals, the royal couple would be widely admired for their dedication to
serving the public interest. According to the Archbishop, there were two
important provisos: both parents would have to be seen to maintain close
bonds with their children; and extra-marital love affairs that might be
brought to public attention would need to be avoided. Assuming the conditions were met, then respect and gratitude, touched by sadness, would
be widely shared sentiments in the Anglican communion.

Two nights after the announcement of the separation, the Prince
dined with Nicholas Soames. Afterwards, he wrote, 'I know how incredibly lucky I am to have such wonderful friends . . . It is at times like this
that friends are most important and I'm so grateful to you for all your
loyal support and understanding . . . God knows what the future will
hold.'[24]*

---

* The publication a few weeks later of an alleged telephone conversation between
the Prince and Camilla Parker Bowles which apparently took place three years earlier (in December 1989) was a further source of pain and embarrassment. Many
people were shocked by the published transcript of what became known as the
'Camillagate' tape, while the tabloid media salivated over it with censorious prurience. Among the few columnists to retain a sense of decency and perspective was
the *Guardian* writer Sebastian Faulkes, who wrote that there were 'two things' to
say about the tape: 'First it is intensely private, full of the silly remarks, repetitions

and non-sequiturs that characterise the unguarded exchange of two people who are fond of each other. Second, while it would certainly constitute grounds for separation, there is nothing in it that would affect any reasonable person's view of Prince Charles's suitability for the throne.' (*Guardian*, 14 January 1993.)

he Prince windsurfing

aying polo at Cowdray Park

Knight Companion of
the Most Noble Order
of the Garter

A 'Duchy day'

With the Prime Minister Margaret
Thatcher at 10 Downing Street,
December 1986

With the Prime Minister John Major at
t James's Palace, March 1994

"COME ON, GIVE US A HAND."

Seeing is believing'

Paints, brushes and paper...

Klosters, Switzerland

Committee work, 1993

The Prince's Trusts 25th
Anniversary celebration at
Penygraig, Wales, 1994

The shooting incident in Sydney, Australia Day, January 1994

Inspecting the Queen's Lancashire Regiment at their final parade, Berlin, May 1994

The Prince with Prince William, Klosters, 1994

Fishing with Prince Harry, 1994

The Prince with his sons, 1994

CHAPTER
TWENTY-FIVE

————◂▸————

21 January 1993

For the past 15 years I have been entirely motivated by a desperate desire to put the 'Great' back into Great Britain. Everything I have tried to do – all the projects, speeches, schemes etc. – have been with this end in mind. And none of it has worked, as you can see too obviously! In order to put the 'Great' back I have always felt it was <u>vital</u> to bring people together, and I began to realise that the <u>one</u> advantage my position has over anyone else's is that I can act as a catalyst to help produce a better and more balanced response to various problems. I have no 'political' agenda – only a desire to see people achieve their potential; to be decently housed in a decent, civilised environment that respects the cultural and vernacular character of the nation; to see this country's real talents (especially inventiveness and engineering skills) put to best use in the <u>best</u> interests of the country and the world (at present they are being disgracefully wasted through lack of co-ordination and strategic thinking); to retain and value the infrastructure and cultural integrity of rural communities (where they still exist) because of the vital role they play in the very <u>framework</u> of the nation and the care and management of the countryside; to value and nurture the highest standards of military integrity and professionalism, as displayed by our armed forces, because of the role they play as an insurance scheme in case of disaster; and to value and retain our uniquely special broadcasting standards which are renowned through-out the world.

The final point is that I have always wanted to roll back some of the more ludicrous frontiers of the 60s in terms of education, architecture, art, music, and literature, not to mention agriculture!

Having read this through, no wonder they want to destroy me, or get rid of me . . .!

As a statement of the principles and intentions which guided his pub-lic life, this letter written to Tom Shebbeare, the director of the Prince's Trust, was forthright if a touch despondent. His decision to write in such terms had been stimulated by one of his regular meetings with Shebbeare and Julia Cleverdon, the chief executive of Business in the Community, both of whom had offered to do what they could to boost the morale of his supporters which had been dented by the media onslaught against him. Although the Prince had been touched by their concern, he was frustrated by the fact that they seemed to need a 'mission statement' from him when he believed that he had always made his objectives perfectly clear. However, by allowing himself to be goaded into reiterating his message for their benefit, he managed to reassure his two lieutenants (and his staff at St James's Palace) that their boss was still very much in business.

As always, the problem for his small and hard-pressed team was how to put his expansive vision into practice. In 1990, David Wright had reached the end of his secondment and taken his administrative muscle and experience back to a high-flying career in the Diplomatic Service. Riddell departed a few weeks later. Although his five-year contract with the Prince still had six months to run, with an option to renew, he had been tempted to return to the City, where his bank had offered him the job of deputy chairman; the Prince did not seek to stop him. Although Riddell had failed to grasp the administrative nettles which threatened to choke St James's, his departure was keenly felt. At his farewell party, Aylard summed up the feelings of the Prince's staff: 'I cannot count the number of times I have been into John's office with a disastrous problem to solve,' he said, 'to come out again with the problem still unsolved but feeling that the world was a much nicer place.'

Riddell's successor was in a different mould altogether. Major-General

Sir Christopher Airy* had just completed a stint as General Officer Commanding London District and Major General Commanding the Household Division. His close acquaintance with the royal household led Buckingham Palace to conlude he was a 'safe pair of hands'; and he was, in royal household terms, most certainly 'one of us'. The Prince, whose approach to all appointments was remarkably detached (until, at the final moment, and sometimes disastrously, he would allow his intuition full rein) asked Aylard, who had become his most trusted lieutenant, Jimmy Savile† and others to sound him out. Although Aylard expressed some doubts about the general's willingness to operate in the collegiate environment of St James's, a consensus emerged that Airy would provide the ballast that was needed in such a volatile atmosphere. Airy lasted a year.

It soon became clear that the Prince had underestimated how difficult it would be for an outsider to grasp the overlapping strands of responsibility that now passed through Airy's hands. A sense that he was a decent and honourable man who was out of his depth soon came to permeate the office. In a period of growing stress in the Prince's personal life and a burgeoning portfolio of public duties, morale at St James's sank rapidly. As some members of the staff, nominally under his direction, began to sideline his involvement, influential advisers from outside the office also voiced their misgivings. Before long, it was widely assumed that Airy's days were numbered. The Prince himself was driven reluctantly to the same conclusion: that in appointing an army officer to the post of private secretary to the Prince of Wales, he had misjudged. The mistake was, in truth, elemental. The Prince had thought that he needed someone to organise the administration of his office, to ensure the smooth flow of correspondence and the efficient operation of his hectic life; in fact, his range of activities had grown so rapidly that he was in need of a strategic co-ordinator, able to identify priorities and to build a team around the Prince accordingly. Airy was unable to satisfy this need. However, sensitive to the pain it would cause, the Prince shrank from the task of

---

* Sir Christopher Airy (1934–   ), General Officer Commanding London District and Major General Commanding the Household Division 1986–89; private secretary and treasurer to Prince and Princess of Wales 1990–91; extra equerry since 1991.
† Sir James (Jimmy) Savile (1926–   ), TV and radio personality, presenter of BBC television's *Jim'll Fix It* and a tireless fundraiser for charitable causes.

confronting Airy directly. His hand was forced, however, in the spring of 1991, when one of his other aides, Richard Aylard, warned him that the *Sunday Times* was about to run a 'Prince sacks Airy' story and advised that 'either we will have to deny it or make it fact very quickly'. That Friday, fortuitously, there was a meeting of the Prince of Wales Coordinating Committee which had been established under Airy's control to oversee the activities of the Prince's overlapping and often rivalrous charities. The most powerful members of the Committee were Stephen O'Brien and Allen Sheppard, the tough-minded chief executive of Grand Metropolitan. As soon as the meeting had finished, the Prince went for a walk in the garden while Sheppard took Airy to one side to inform him that that the time had come to write a letter of resignation. Reluctantly and sadly, he consented.

His successor was the assistant private secretary, Richard Aylard, the first choice of the Prince's advisers, who believed that he was certainly better suited than any other internal candidate. Although Aylard had not expected to be offered the post, his closeness to the Prince aroused envy among one or two of his colleagues, who later put it about that he had engineered his own preferment at their expense. Though Aylard was indeed more ambitious than his modest demeanour would suggest, there was no evidence for the accusation against him, although for many weeks the atmosphere at St James's was to be soured by this jealousy.

As a former grammar school boy, with a degree in Applied Zoology and Mathematics, Aylard came from an unusual background for so senior a member of the royal household. Although he had been a naval officer (serving in HMS *Invincible* during the Falklands War), Aylard lacked the social connections that traditionally eased the path to preferment in the household.* Yet in Aylard the Prince detected, if not a kindred spirit, at least someone who appreciated his purpose and, as an environmental specialist, understood his vision. To an unusual degree, Aylard combined reticence and intensity, his deference concealing a resolute and calculating intellect.

---

* By the time Aylard had been in the post for three years, the Prince's senior staff contained two public school boys, three grammar school and two comprehensive school pupils, which, in terms of social background, sharply delineated St James's from Buckingham Palace.

From the late eighties, Aylard had been responsible for co-ordinating the preparation of some of the Prince's most outspoken and influential speeches. When others raised their eyebrows on the discovery that the likes of Jonathon Porritt had the Prince's ear, Aylard affected an innocent concern about their anxieties, but ignored them. Porritt, supported by Aylard, became an increasingly influential figure at the Prince's environmental court; but it was Aylard who held the threads together and, with a finely tuned ear for the Prince's verbal mannerisms, wrote increasingly effective drafts for the Prince to work on.

By 1991, the momentum generated by the Prince's speeches on the environment had secured him an international reputation. In the run-up to the Rio summit which was planned for 1992, the Prince was determined to have his own input by bringing together key international figures in an attempt to achieve a degree of harmony between the conflicting attitudes of Europe, the United States and the developing nations, led by Brazil. He alighted on the idea of using the royal yacht as the base for a two-day international seminar at the end of an official tour of Brazil in April 1991. Among others, he invited Senator Albert Gore*; senior officials from the World Bank; chief executives from companies such as Shell and BP; the principal non-governmental organisations; European politicians, including the British ministers of Overseas Aid and the Environment; and, most important of all, the host of the prospective summit, President Fernando Collor of Brazil.†

Even for the Prince, it had not been easy to bring together such a group. At the last moment, the Brazilian President threatened to cut short his appearance on the royal yacht, pleading pressure of work. The Prince wrote to him as soon as he heard:

You may remember that the reason why I was so keen to arrange this seminar, following our first meeting just before your inauguration as President, was because I wanted to find a way of providing some moral support for you over the enormous challenges you were courageously

---

* Albert Gore (1948–   ); former senator for Tennessee; Vice-President of United States since 1992; author of *Earth in Balance*; led US Senate delegation to Earth Summit in Rio.

† In November 1992, President Collor resigned to avoid pending impeachment for corruption.

facing in terms of how to reconcile conservation requirements with development pressure. Responding to your apparent enthusiasm for this idea, a great deal of time and effort has been expended by a team of people in order to put this seminar together and to attract the most influential and effective participants. The Royal Yacht is sailing all the way out to Brazil especially for this seminar so as to provide what I hoped would be a reasonably neutral and relaxed setting for such a gathering . . .

I, personally, would be disappointed and disheartened by your absence because, apart from anything else, I think it would give the wrong signals to many people who are looking towards the importance of the 1992 United Nations Conference. If it is possible, even at the last moment, for you somehow to re-arrange your programme we would all be delighted.[1]

Written in longhand, it was a characteristic letter with a characteristic effect: the President yielded to the Prince.

According to some of those present, the *Britannia* seminar played a crucial role in preparing North and South for the accommodation in their positions which would be needed if the Rio summit were not to be a diplomatic fiasco. As the participants explored each other's attitudes, they moved towards a much closer understanding of the predicament facing them all. However, the Prince's satisfaction at this outcome had been diluted by concern for Airy. Before their departure for Brazil, Aylard had suggested that, as Westmacott was to handle the Brazil tour and he had organised the seminar, it would perhaps be sensible for the private secretary to remain in London as there would be very little for him to do. Airy had not been appreciative of this advice. During the seminar, it was painfully apparent that he had nonetheless been reduced to the role of a bystander, able only to engage in a kind of courteous small talk that did not quite measure up to the needs of the moment. It was this episode which finally convinced the Prince that, whatever his other qualities, Airy should be replaced by Aylard.

The rapid turnover of private secretaries dismayed some senior courtiers at Buckingham Palace who were already worried about the effectiveness of the Prince's office. For them, it confirmed the fears that St James's was failing to provide the stability and direction required by the growing range of his interests and enthusiasms. Among them there were those who felt that Aylard, far from curbing the Prince's zeal on issues like the environment and the unemployed, would positively encourage it. Equally, there were others who recognised that after six years on his staff Aylard at least had a track record. Knowing the faith that the Prince had in his new private secretary, this group was also hopeful that as a result of Aylard's promotion the Prince would become more closely involved in the major decisions affecting the royal family, from which the old guard at Buckingham Palace had tended to exclude him – and from which, as a result, he had somewhat excluded himself.

Like his boss, Aylard was a far more resilient character than some supposed. Knowing that it would take time to inject more trust into the edgy relationship between St James's and Buckingham Palace, he made it his first task to resurrect morale at St James's, not easy given the propensity of some of his team to suppose that he had schemed his way into the Prince's favour at their expense. At first, he was not very popular, particularly as he moved swiftly to restore control over the management of the office. Gradually, however, his colleagues (including some of the sceptics at Buckingham Palace) came to respect his dedication and his judgement. Knowing that he enjoyed the full confidence of the Prince, those who might have been inclined to work against him discovered that they could after all work with him.

Aylard set about the establishment of an administrative structure that, for the first time in the short history of the Prince's office (which had been a byword for genial disorder), would soon give St James's the beginnings of a reputation for efficiency and clarity of purpose. By allocating quasi-cabinet portfolios to the senior staff under his direction and allowing them direct access to the Prince accordingly, he fostered an atmosphere in which suspicion and anxiety yielded slowly to openness and enthusiasm. To outsiders, St James's could still seem impenetrable and dilatory, but by comparison with the past – and with Buckingham Palace – it was unstuffy, outgoing and progressive. The preponderance of graduates from grammar and comprehensive schools (including two women) appointed by the Prince to his household soon helped to foster at least the impression that the Prince's office at least was adapting to meet both his needs and the demands of the late twentieth century.

More than any of his predecessors (except perhaps Checketts in the early years), Aylard understood the Prince's psychology; rather than confronting him head on, he had discovered that it was more effective simply to point out the unseen pitfalls in any course of action which he felt inadvisable but to which the Prince had been drawn by one or other of his enthusiasms. Building on the Prince's own urge to construct his role around themes, which Guy Salter had tried to turn into a gameplan, Aylard began to put theory into practice. He also had a sharp eye for public relations and he shared the Prince's frustration with the failure of Buckingham Palace to 'get the message across'. Although he abhored the excesses of the tabloid press, the Prince had long grumbled about the the press office in the belief that a more positive approach was needed to confront a changing world from which, beyond Buckingham Palace, deference and awe had long since been expunged. In Aylard, he found an ally who was willing to go on the diplomatic offensive on his behalf and who believed that despite the tittle-tattle about his private life the Prince, as he put it, 'had a very good story to tell'.

In a long memorandum to the Queen's private secretary, written in the autumn of 1992, the Prince gave vent to some of his criticisms and, influenced by his senior advisers, proposed a number of remedies. Although the timing of the memorandum was prompted by the most debilitating aspects of the *annus horribilis*, it was remarkably free of the self-pity to which the Prince was prone in those dark days, and revealed instead a marked fortitude under fire. 'I know that this summer has been particularly difficult for everyone close to the Royal family,' he wrote:

> and that the Press Office have had to bear the brunt of a media onslaught without precedent in our lifetimes. I know, too, that the problems which have given rise to this thoroughly unpleasant state of affairs are entirely outside the control of the Press Office. But, however depressing the thought might be, I do think we must realise that certain sections of the media have now proved to their own satisfaction that sensationalised royal stories are one of the best ways of selling newspapers in a recession. There is every reason to suppose that they will continue to operate in a thoroughly unpleasant way. We all thought things were bad enough five years ago, but they are now far worse and I see no prospect of improvement in the foreseeable future . . .[2]

Against that background, he made a number of points about the relationship between the Palace and the media. While endorsing the 'blanket

policy' of the Palace press office of refusing to comment on press allegations about the private lives of the royal family, he went on to assert:

> I believe we need a relatively narrow definition of 'private lives' and
> that there are many cases where things which we would prefer to
> keep private must, nevertheless, be commented upon because they
> have been brought (whether we like it or not) into the public domain.
> Particularly where 'facts' are concerned the balance of advantage will
> often lie with correcting something rather than allowing it to pass
> unchallenged into the cuttings library, from whence it will be resur-
> rected periodically – gaining credence each time . . .[3]

Aside from questions relating to the private lives of the royal family, he
argued that the press office should adopt:

> a consistent line of responding in a positive, self-confident and profes-
> sional manner . . . A degree of cheerful self-confidence that there is a
> good story to be told and willingness to tell it (after checking the facts)
> is crucial. Any hint of defensiveness will only encourage a negative
> story . . . I do hope that every serious question or proposal for an arti-
> cle, film, etc, can be seen as an opportunity rather than a threat . . . I
> do hope we can make as much use as possible of television. As the
> medium which carries the greatest weight of authority with the pub-
> lic, it should be a real asset in countering tabloid excesses.[4]

In pressing his point, he urged a further break with precedent by
suggesting that royal press secretaries, and even private secretaries, should
allow their names to be attached to the statements emanating from
Buckingham Palace to differentiate their comments from the 'unnamed
sources' which gave a spurious authority to many articles in the tabloid
press; that a small group of sympathetic outsiders should be fully briefed
and authorised to speak on behalf of the royal family; and that the press
office itself should be far more accessible to 'responsible' journalists and
editors – on the grounds that 'forging working relationships based on
mutual respect will greatly assist in putting across, authoritatively and
with confidence and conviction, the many positive points about the
issues which members of the Royal family are tackling . . .'[5]
The Prince also proposed a far more robust response to factual

inaccuracies than Buckingham Palace had deemed appropriate. Where facts were distorted or wrongly reported, the Prince wanted the press office to deal with the case by (1) faxing an immediate correction to the offending editor, not for publication but sufficient to stop the newspaper 'selling' the story further*; or (2) sending a factual correction intended for publication; or (3) by briefing the Press Association†; or (4), as a last resort, demonstrating a readiness to sue for libel.

Buckingham Palace's response to the Prince's intervention was divided, but even those who were somewhat resentful of his strictures accepted the force of his argument and as a result a major review of the press office was put in hand, drawing staff from both Buckingham Palace and St James's. Fully aware of the need to restore the credibility of the press office, this group recommended a shift in policy in line with some of the Prince's recommendations. Though these were less radical than the Prince's office might have wished, they signalled a more forthright and open attitude towards the media which one or two of the senior staff at Buckingham Palace had long sought, and which, crucially, was endorsed by the Queen and Prince Philip.

If there was a certain edginess between the two households, this reflected a difference of perspective and approach: the one, long-established and slow to welcome change, the other less formal in character and, by comparison with Buckingham Palace, far less defensive in outlook. The tendency of each court to regard the other with a certain frustration was exacerbated by a feeling among some courtiers at Buckingham Palace that the Prince was overly active on the public stage (where, inevitably, he attracted rather more attention than the Queen in the performance of her duties) and an anxiety at St James's Palace that the senior household lacked the vision and drive needed if the monarchy were to adapt effectively in the decades ahead.

It was against this background that, in 1992, with the monarchy under

---

* As an example of this, the Prince enclosed an offending article from the *Daily Express* (which was by no means one of the worst culprits). The press office had decided against responding to its errors. The Prince had countermanded that decision and instructed that the inaccuracies should be carefully identified and forwarded to the editor. It was an illuminating example of his (and Aylard's) attitude towards both the press office and the media. (See Appendix II for details.)

† A British news agency with a reputation for factual accuracy.

intense scrutiny, senior figures in the household undertook a review of the royal family's responsibilities with the purpose of identifying the objectives of the monarchy over the next ten years and the most effective way of achieving them. The objectives were, of course, bound to be determined in large measure by the sovereign's obligation to carry out her responsibilities as head of state, whether in relation to the Prime Minister, the Church, the judiciary or the armed forces. Beyond that narrow constitutional role, more difficult to define but no less important, was the traditional need to act as a focus of national unity above party politics, but representing shared values and aspirations and providing a source of stability and continuity in changing times.

Like other members of his family, the Prince was keenly aware that it was easier to state objectives than to achieve them. He knew, as they did, that it was important to share in the nation's life, to symbolise its mood at times of rejoicing or grief, to travel throughout what was still quaintly called 'the realm', and to identify with those who were hard-pressed while recognising excellence and achievement as well. He knew the importance of heritage and tradition to the national psyche, but he also knew that to survive the monarchy had to adapt. As part of a sustained contribution to this internal debate, he repeated a suggestion which had long been in the minds of those at Buckingham Palace. 'Is not part of the problem with the media,' he asked rhetorically, 'that it is considered in the country at large that there are too many members of the family and too much public money being spent on them?' And he went on, 'Would it not be better to sit down and examine how many members of the family you actually need [in order to achieve the monarchy's objectives]?' To examine the issues more closely, he proposed that Buckingham Palace should 'bring in some thoughtful, wise and intelligent people from outside "the system" and discuss the question over a drink . . . They might come up with some useful ideas and thoughts.'[6]

These problems of role and presentation which came so sharply into focus in the royal family's *annus horribilis* of 1992 coincided with a growing debate in the media about the tax exemptions granted by Parliament to the sovereign and her family. The demoralising effect of the recession combined with the adverse publicity by which the royal family was afflicted provided fertile soil in which to germinate the seeds of public resentment. In 1991, the opinion polls suggested that up to 90 per cent of the Queen's subjects thought that she should pay tax. In 1992, the publication of a hostile but thoroughly researched book, *Royal Fortune: Tax, Money and Monarchy* by Philip Hall,[8] nourished an increasingly acrimonious debate. Late in November, the genial and usually astute Heritage Secretary, Peter Brooke, badly misjudged the public mood after the Windsor fire by announcing, as if it were a decision of little moment, that British tax-payers would finance the repairs to the castle's state apartments, at a cost then estimated to be in excess of £60 million.[*] Brooke's maladroit handling of the issue angered even loyal monarchists and demonstrated that, although the contract between Crown and People was not in imminent danger, the surge of popular resentment required a swift response. On 26 November, six days after the Windsor fire, the Prime Minister took the House of Commons by surprise with an announcement that the Queen and the Prince of Wales had volunteered to pay tax on their private incomes and that the Queen would reimburse the cost of Civil List annuities used to support five of Her Majesty's closest relatives,[†] so that they would no longer be supported by public funds but by the revenue from the Duchy of Lancaster instead.

It was an undignified episode that did little to enhance the reputation of the House of Windsor. The impression that the Queen had been bounced into surrendering her tax privileges simply to head off her disenchanted subjects embarrassed royalists and gave weight to the minority prejudice which held that the monarchy was an anachronism lacking in any genuine sensitivity for public opinion. A Gallup poll published early in 1993 found that four out of five respondents thought that 'too many members of the family lead an idle, jet-set kind of existence', while bookmakers were reported to have cut the odds against the abolition of the monarchy by the year 2000 from 100–1 down to 8–1 (caused in part,

---

[*] The cost was later revised down to £40 million, and, following a suggestion by the Lord Chamberlain, Lord Airlie, and the Queen's Director of Finance, Michael Peat – rapidly endorsed by the Prince – it was announced that the state apartments at Buckingham Palace would be opened to the public for eight weeks every summer and that the money raised from the entrance fee would be used to finance most of the repairs.

[†] The Princess Royal, the Duke of York, Prince Edward, Princess Margaret and Princess Alice.

apparently, by two over-excited punters who wagered £4,000 at the higher odds).[8]

The details of the tax regime to which the Queen and the Prince of Wales had volunteered to submit themselves were announced on 11 February 1993. The sovereign was to pay income tax on her private fortune, though inheritance tax would not be levied on bequests from the sovereign to her successor. The Prince of Wales was to replace the arrangement by which he paid a quarter of the net revenue from the Duchy of Cornwall to the Treasury with an agreement to pay tax on the income that he drew from the Duchy after the deduction of legitimate expenses. The Duchy itself would remain exempt from all capital taxes.

So far as the Prince was concerned, the financial impact of these changes in the tax year 1993–94 was likely to be modest: the Duchy was projected to realise a surplus of over £4 million and, after deducting expenditure on his and the Princess's official duties (as agreed between Aylard, in the role of the Prince's treasurer, and the Inland Revenue), the heir to the throne was expected to be subject to a tax bill of about £1 million. Most of the deductions, amounting to perhaps £2 million, would relate to travel and staff costs. Including the Princess's staff, the Prince employs in his office a total of thirty-eight people, among them ten executives (private secretaries, assistant private secretaries and press secretaries), a management team of three (an accountant, an administrator and a personnel officer) and a team of secretaries, typists and telephonists. Elsewhere, he employs an additional thirty-six people full time, some of whom work at Kensington Palace for the Princess and others primarily at Highgrove. However, the core staff – two chefs, two butlers, two valets, two orderlies and two drivers – is mobile, available to travel with him abroad or to accompany him to Sandringham, Balmoral and elsewhere in Britain; usually one member of each pair is with the Prince while the other is preparing for the next visit, tidying up after the last or taking leave. Although the principle was straightforward, the detailed calculations needed to identify the cost of his official duties was likely to be complicated, especially when, in his case, the distinction between his public role and his private life was itself not clear-cut. However, it was projected that he would be left with a little over £1 million of disposable income, from which he and the Princess would have to care for their children and finance their private travel, staff costs, entertaining, holidays and clothes; it would also finance the Highgrove garden, two hunters, two retired polo ponies, and any other form of non-deductible expenditure either of them might incur. In 1994, the Prince was likely to be marginally better off as a result of the new tax regime than he had been when he made the 25 per cent voluntary payment. However, by electing to pay income tax, he had made himself subject to a tax structure which was susceptible to change; in this respect his position was now similar to that of other tax-payers.*

The announcement of the details by which the Queen and the Prince would pay tax was welcomed with relief by monarchists and grudgingly by commentators. Although even the sceptics accepted that the Queen's official residences, the Crown Jewels and the Royal Collection should be exempt from any form of tax, they were swift to point out that the royal family was not to be taxed for the private use of the royal yacht, the royal train or the Queen's Flight; they asked (in common with the leader of the Labour Party, John Smith) why the Queen's private wealth should be exempt from inheritance tax; and they commented unfavourably on what the *Independent* described as the royal family's 'lifestyle', which included 'expensive peregrinations between Buckingham Palace, Windsor Castle, Sandringham, and Balmoral'.[9] The feeling persisted that the reforms had been forced on Buckingham Palace to head off increasing public animosity which, if not appeased, could swiftly have become an anti-royalist crusade. The truth about the reforms was somewhat different.

For some years, the Prince had been aware that the issues of royal wealth, tax and the Civil List were matters of growing public concern,

---

* As the Prince is not allowed to use the Duchy's capital, he has had to build up his own source of private wealth. Over the years he has invested any Duchy income which he has not spent, amassing a personal fortune of some £2 million in the process (which represents the total wealth at his disposal). This capital is invested to make provision for his children and especially for Prince Harry, who cannot look forward to any other source of 'unearned' income.

As only the eldest son of the sovereign (and only then when he has reached his majority) is entitled to draw any income from the Duchy, even Prince William cannot be assured of inheriting his father's income. If Prince Charles were to die before the Queen, no-one would be entitled to the Duchy income until Prince William himself had succeeded and his eldest son had reached the age of eighteen.

and that the royal family would have to respond and adapt accordingly. Since the reign of Queen Victoria, the issue of royal taxation had been an intermittent source of political controversy. By the second half of the twentieth century, the underlying conflict between the state's need to preserve and finance a unique family dynasty and Parliament's urge to respond to the vagaries of public sentiment was exacerbated by the complexity of the financial arrangements that had evolved over the centuries (often in secret) and which very few people understood.

In the late eighties, the Prince floated the notion that the income from the Crown estates (which went directly to the Treasury) should revert to the sovereign in lieu of the Civil List payment from the Exchequer and the departmental expenditure on the official residences, the royal yacht, the royal train and the Queen's Flight. According to his back-of-an-envelope calculations, the yield from the Crown estates (which was then approximately £60 million) would more than match the total government expenditure on the monarchy. It would restore to the royal family a measure of control over their finances and, he thought, it would remove a contentious question from the political agenda.

Aside from the legal difficulties that arose out of the historical circumstances in which George III had surrendered his income from the Crown estates in exchange for payments from the Civil List, the attractions of the Prince's proposal were, prima facie, clear. According to one of those involved in the discussions that ensued:

> It would have been enormously effective in making the household independent and vigorous, and it would have been even better in terms of financial management. It would also have been good for the standing of the monarchy as an autonomous institution . . . If you are going to have a strong and vigorous monarchy, you need a strong and vigorous household and in financial terms this had been slowly withering away.[10]

By the end of the eighties, the household had felt itself to have been sucked financially and administratively so far into the Whitehall machine that the detachment and impartiality of the constitutional monarchy would, in the long run, be at serious risk of erosion. However, there was an overriding objection to the Prince's suggestion: it was almost inconceivable that Parliament would support such a radical reversal of two hundred years of history and thereby undermine the unstated but fundamental principle that the Monarchy exists only by the consent of the people. As an alternative, the Treasury proposed in 1990 that instead of an annual payment (which, each time, required the consent of Parliament) the Civil List should once again be funded on the ten-yearly basis agreed by Parliament in 1972. The Treasury also proposed that the administration and management of the royal palaces should pass to the household, to be funded by a grant-in-aid from the government.

Devised as a means of protecting what was widely referred to as 'the Queen's annual pay rise' from constant public debate, this outcome also restored a significant measure of autonomy to the household; yet it was far from clear to the Prince that it would solve the wider problem of reconciling the function of the monarchy with the growing public perception, as revealed in a succession of opinion polls, that the royal family was too large, lived on too lavish a scale and enjoyed too much wealth.

The household itself had long been aware of this dilemma. Although there was a divergence of views within Buckingham Palace about the urgency of the problem, it was widely recognised that the tax issue could not be indefinitely postponed. Late in 1991, a group of household and government officials was formed to work out a basis on which the Prince might pay tax under a voluntary arrangement on his accession. With the enthusiastic endorsement of the Prince, the royal household's director of finance, Michael Peat,* was the guiding hand within the Palace in devising the framework for a workable scheme with the Treasury and the Inland Revenue. The only issue which had caused them a serious difficulty was inheritance tax. Somehow they had to find a way of protecting the wealth – and thus, in their view, the independence – of the monarchy from decimation (following a succession of premature deaths, for example) while avoiding the political minefield of leaving the sovereign exempt altogether. In the end, they decided that to allow exemption on all bequests made from sovereign to sovereign would protect the royal estates from a probate sale while ensuring that bequests to other members

---

* Michael Peat (1949–   ), formerly a senior partner in the accountancy firm Peat Marwick McLintock. His great-grandfather had been auditor to King Edward VII. Peat had been auditor to the Privy Purse until, in 1990, he was appointed to the household as Director of Finance and Property Services.

of the family would be subject to tax in the normal way; a clause was also included to confirm that the sovereign would not abuse the arrangement by using it as a tax shelter, but would make use of the exemption only for its declared purpose of preserving the royal heritage.

At that stage, the Queen agreed that it might be appropriate to introduce these reforms sooner rather than later. Now endorsed not only by the heir to the throne but by the sovereign as well, the group merely had to put the finishing touches to the document. According to one senior courtier, 'The Prince was absolutely crucial in getting it off the ground. Once it was off the ground, everybody knew where we were likely to end up. It was a perfectly wonderful piece of diplomacy. Without the Prince it would not have happened.'[11]

By the autumn, it became clear that the proposed reforms would be in a form to announce publicly within six months; and, while no precise timetable was drawn up, the Prime Minister, John Major, was informed accordingly. By November, with the media becoming increasingly agitated about the issue, it was decided to make the announcement when Parliament returned after the Christmas recess in late January or early February 1993. Even then, barring accidents, the announcement would have stood every chance of being hailed as an enlightened response to a changing environment. As it was, fate intervened in the form of the Windsor fire, when, after an urgent meeting between representatives of the household and the government, the Queen's decision to pay tax was rushed out in an atmosphere which left many of her subjects commenting 'and about time too'.

When the details of the tax reforms were made public in February, the occasion was graced by the appearance on radio and television of Michael Peat, explaining the changes on behalf of the Queen and the Prince of Wales. Although it was hardly noticed at the time, Peat's emergence into the limelight was unprecedented: never before had a serving member of the royal household been authorised to speak on television and radio in this way. As Peat had been largely responsible for devising the reforms and had a suitably telegenic manner, the Prince let it be known that he thought the Finance Director was the obvious candidate for the task. For the media review group, it was a test case for the Prince's hypothesis that to 'get the message across' the Palace had to go on the offensive. Permission for such a break with precedent would have to come from the Queen herself, who was initially reluctant to agree; however, the Prince was able to convince her of the merits of his suggestion. After worrying away the hours until the BBC *Nine O'Clock News,* his staff were greatly relieved when Peat performed with such competence that very few viewers realised that they had been witness to a minor Palace revolution. It was a signal victory for the Prince's campaign in favour of more openness with the media.*

Although he had argued for change, the Prince was by no means radical about what critics conceived to be the 'trappings' of the monarchy. He was robust in defence of the Queen's Flight† and was himself quite ready to use its aircraft not only for business but for pleasure as well (so long as his programme incorporated the latter into the former). Likewise, he had no doubts about the value of the royal train‡ which he now used more frequently than any other member of the royal family. He enjoyed the isolation and the convenience with which it provided him. It allowed him, so he argued, to ensure that he could reach faraway destinations on time and it gave him precious hours in which to read documents, write letters and prepare speeches before retiring for the night to the accompaniment of Mozart, while he was trundled gently to the following day's official function.

If there seemed to be an element of special pleading in his case, his aides argued strenuously that the royal train and the Queen's Flight were crucial to the smooth operation of the Prince's crowded programme; that

---

* The following year, at the Prince's instigation, Richard Aylard set another precedent by becoming the first private secretary in the royal household to be interviewed on the record. He appeared on the BBC television programme *Newsnight* on 16 March 1994, answering questions about the media coverage of the Prince's private life.

† In 1993–94, the three BAE 146 Whisper jet aircraft and two Wessex helicopters of the Queen's Flight cost the Ministry of Defence £12.43 million to run. In June 1994, as part of the cost-cutting measures imposed by the Treasury, the Secretary of State for Defence, Malcolm Rifkind, announced that the Queen's Flight would move from RAF Benson to RAF Northolt to join the other RAF communications aircraft of No. 32 Squadron, and that the single unit would be known as 32 (The Royal) Squadron. He also announced that the Queen had volunteered for the MoD to be reimbursed for private use of the Queen's Flight. Private use has been restricted to the Queen, the Duke of Edinburgh, the Queen Mother and the Prince and Princess of Wales.

‡ At an annual running cost of £2.5 million in 1993.

it would be impossible without that resource to accomplish so many official visits; that to use British Rail or scheduled flights on a regular basis
would remove essential flexibility and threaten the meticulous timing by
which his visits were governed; that his use of public transport would be
intolerable for other passengers because of the security measures required
to protect him; and that, in his hectic schedule, both the royal train and
plane offered vital moments of rest and privacy, a chance to change his
clothes, and a brief reprieve from the public gaze while he prepared himself for the next engagement. These arguments were persuasive to those
who were sensitive to the peculiar strain imposed by the relentless round
of official visits to which the Prince committed himself – and he was
irritated and disheartened that these royal 'perks' were even a matter of
public debate. In addition to the practical case for them advanced by his
office, he considered that in return for the proper execution of his public duties he had a right to these privileges bestowed on the monarchy,
and he was impatient with those who, to him, seemed to carp and quib-
ble about their cost to the taxpayers.

The royal yacht was a different matter. The Prince had an abiding
affection for HMY *Britannia* and for the yachtsmen who crewed her, to
the extent that he knew the long-serving crew members by name and
never went aboard without visiting their quarters. As a romantic sailor,
he thrilled at the sight of her graceful lines and the immaculate condition
in which she was maintained. Although he relished the occasional days
when he could bask on the sun deck alone with his sketch book and his
sun lotion in the Caribbean, he was careful not to abuse that right of
access. Whenever the yacht was dispatched for one of his official visits, it
was invariably so that he could use it to host seminars or conferences, or
to entertain the rich and the powerful: 'I think it is incredibly effective
in terms of entertainment and creating the right atmosphere, making
people feel welcome . . . When they leave, hopefully they go away with
a warm afterglow.'[12] He worked hard at generating that sentiment, presiding over the dinner table with charm and courtesy, ensuring that by
the end of the evening he had spoken to every guest, skilfully conveying
the impression that their presence mattered to him as his did to them. 'It's
not as if we're all going off on junkets all the time on this yacht,' he complained when he heard of newspaper articles attacking the expenditure:
'It's not a sort of private yacht. It goes with the position. It is part of the
process of trying to represent Britain abroad.'[13]

When it became clear that for financial reasons the survival of the yacht was in jeopardy, he urged an effective marketing campaign to save her. In February 1993, he wrote to the yacht's commanding officer, Admiral Robert Woodard:

> It is clear from talking to them that the yachtsmen are worried about all the awful things that have been said about the Yacht recently* and are desperate to find ways of putting the record straight and making sure people know of the value of the Yacht especially abroad. I am sure you share their concern, so I can't help feeling we ought to consider doing two particular things – apart, that is, from arranging visits to the Yacht by 'opinion-formers', politicians etc. One is to allow more people to see the <u>inside</u> of the Yacht by, in effect, opening her to the public on certain occasions. I can't help feeling, horrible as such a thing is to contemplate, that this would help to dispel some of the more ludicrous myths (I hear the *Daily Mail* has had articles about 'marble bathrooms and gold taps' etc.)† . . . After all, if Sandringham and parts of Balmoral can be open to the public, why not HMY?
>   . . . I feel that time is of the essence in this area because I believe the aim should be to try and keep the Yacht in service until the year 2000 – and whatever happens next is in the lap of the Gods . . .[14]

The Prince's proposal was investigated but came to naught and, in any case, it was too late. In June, the residents of the Isle of Wight, who had asked, through the Junior Defence Minister Archie Hamilton, to be allowed to go aboard the yacht during Cowes Week (and by paying an entrance fee contribute to the cost of the yacht's upkeep), were told

---

* On 1 February 1993, the Armed Forces Minister, Archie Hamilton, informed the House of Commons that the future of the royal yacht was under review; that her reserve role as hospital ship had been abolished. A spate of critical articles, commenting on the £10 million annual cost to the Ministry of Defence of maintaining a ship that was used by the royal family for no more than six weeks a year, concluded that the yacht was a lavish royal indulgence that the taxpayer should no longer tolerate.

† For the record: the VIP bathrooms are in the 'Formica and chrome' style which was fashionable in the early fifties when *Britannia* was commissioned. The cabins are of modest size and decor; an owner of one of the modern 'gin palaces' that fill the posher kind of marina would look askance at their plainness and simplicity.

politely by Buckingham Palace that the proposal did not find favour. A spokesman commented that while allowing paying tourists on board was 'a most interesting suggestion', the primary purpose of the yacht was to provide 'a secure base for the Royal family to live on.'[15] That security was to be shortlived. In June 1994, after lengthy discussions within the Palace and with the government, it was announced than *Britannia* would be decommissioned in 1997, rather than undergo the £17 million refit required to keep her in operation for a further five years.

Although he was involved in these consultations, the Prince regretted the need for the decision, although he freely acknowledged his own bias. He believed the yacht to be an enduring monument to the genius of British craftsmanship and when the Royal Marines marched and counter-marched to British sea shanties under the stars in a foreign port, he took a nostalgic pride in their precision and their musicianship. He also believed, with good reason, that the impression of smartness, discipline and skill conveyed subliminally to their audience of Gulf oil magnates or New Jersey industrialists or Japanese technocrats a sense that Britain was far from clapped out; that the standards they witnessed on the royal yacht were emblematic of the quality of British workers and their products. His complaint against Whitehall was that too much power lay in the hands of accountants who could count the cost but failed to appreciate the value. 'We are classic geniuses at not valuing our assets,' he said of the royal yacht. 'There are so many things we do brilliantly, far better than anyone else. Let's use them for God's sake, instead of moaning about them all the time . . . But I'm biased because I know her, I've known her all my life.'[16]

CHAPTER
TWENTY-SIX

———◆———

The boy who had grown up with the sounds of marching bands and the sight of saluting sentries at his front door was, in his attitude towards the armed forces, unequivocally a traditionalist. As Colonel-in-Chief of six* regiments and the Army Air Corps, and Colonel of the Welsh Guards, he took an intense and personal interest in the training and morale of the soldiers under his titular command, and in the shifting policies of government towards the armed forces. He not only knew the ways in which the history of the royal family is inextricably linked to the nation's military history, and that the custom and ceremony of state reflects the role of kings and queens in that long saga, but he revered this tradition, woven as it was into his very identity. For generations, the royal family has been served by junior officers as aides and equerries, while the senior ranks of the royal household have always offered a haven for retired generals and redundant colonels.† Like many

---

* This was to drop to five in September 1994 after the Gordon Highlanders amalgamated with the Queen's Own Highlanders to form the Highlanders, of which the Duke of Edinburgh is Colonel-in-Chief. The Prince is Deputy Colonel-in-Chief.
† In *Elizabeth R: The Role of the Monarchy Today*, Anthony Jay has noted that in 1991–92, 'the Master of the Household was a Rear-Admiral, his Deputy was a Lieutenant-Colonel, the Comptroller of the Lord Chamberlain's Office and his assistant were also Lieutenant-Colonels, and so was the Crown Equerry, the Keeper of the Privy Purse was a Major, and the Marshal of the Diplomatic Corps was a Lieutenant-General'.' (Anthony Jay, *Elizabeth R* [BBC Books, 1992, p.168].)

of his family, the Prince had always been at ease in this company, which shared with him a culture in which notions of honour, duty and public service were the unstated imperatives that defined their caste. Its members were unquestioningly loyal and discreet.

As a Colonel-in-Chief, he attended regimental ceremonies, wrote letters of congratulation and commiseration, and made flying visits either in Britain or to Germany and Northern Ireland to see 'his' troops in training. Although these occasions were a routine part of his programme, he took them with the utmost seriousness, talking at length especially to junior officers and NCOs whom he was disposed to believe knew more than their superiors about the morale of the men under their command and the difficulties they faced. It was these private discussions that fuelled his concern at the timing and size of the cuts which began as Britain tried to redefine a role for the armed forces following the end of the Cold War. Thus in 1992 (when he was fighting to save the Poundbury project and advancing some of his more testing environmental initiatives) he did not hesitate to enter the lists on behalf of all his regiments in the bitter debate surrounding the publication of the government's *Options For Change*.* His interest was not confined to the complexity of grand strategy, however. In the same year, among other initiatives, he took up the cudgels on behalf of a paratrooper who had been mutilated in an IRA atrocity and he issued a stern rebuke at what he regarded as a slovenly turn-out at a regimental march-past.

As heir to the throne, he was the prospective head of the nation's armed forces, a responsibility that he shouldered with conviction. Despite his occasional air of otherworldliness, he was a meticulous student of military procedure and discipline, who liked order and neatness and believed in 'standards'; and as his correspondence of over a decade reveals, he was also held in high regard by the officers and men who owed allegiance to him. He was fiercely loyal, especially when any of his regiments came under civilian fire. In 1980, the Mayor of Bridgend made the error of writing to him to protest that the Welsh Guards had marched through the town without saluting the War Memorial. The Prince wrote back in high dudgeon, referring to the Mayor's 'extraordinary' complaint:

---

* See page 467.

I would draw your attention to the fact that there are quite definitely no regulations which require troops to pay compliments to war memorials . . . the implication that it was any disrespect by not doing so is, to say the least, extremely offensive to a regiment which lost over 1400 officers and men killed in action in two world wars, and on operations since 1945, and which does not forget, nor fail to honour, those who made the supreme sacrifice . . . The final thing I would like to say is that I strongly recommend you check your facts more carefully before you make unfair complaints about a regiment, which on the whole, takes enormous trouble to conduct their business in the most correct manner possible and which also takes great pride in its long and close connections with the principality. I also take great pride in my regiment and in its ties with Wales and I must admit I find it extremely difficult to understand your particular attitude in this whole business.[1]

In the same year, he wrote to the grandmother of an eighteen-year-old in the Junior Parachute Regiment at Aldershot, who was worried that he might be sent to Northern Ireland. 'I know he is in training to be a soldier,' she had written to him:

It is his duty to his Queen and Country to go wherever he is needed but why oh! why do they have to go so young to N. Ireland among those murderers . . . I want to stop him going, my son, his father, wants to stop him going but we also know we cannot interfere in his chosen career. This sacrifice, this pointless killing of such young men . . . what can be done? My heart is heavy . . . All I can do is write to you for perhaps some glimmer of hope for the future.[2]

By 1980, the Prince received at least a thousand letters a week, but they were sifted to ensure that he saw those to which it was likely he would want to respond personally. In this case, he replied:

I entirely appreciate your concern about your grandson serving in Northern Ireland. No one wants to see a member of their own family in danger, but one of the duties of being a soldier is to be prepared to face danger and very often to overcome it in the end. Your grandson seems to be a thoroughly dedicated and determined individual who wants to have the special pride of serving in the Parachute Regiment. Many recruits fail to make it, so the standards are high. This country needs people like your grandson. God forbid that we had a nation where no-one was prepared to face danger or take risks . . .[3]

In 1982, his frustration at being so far from his regiments during the critical weeks of the Falklands campaign was intense. Afterwards, in August 1982, the Chief of Defence Staff, Admiral of the Fleet Sir Terence Lewin,* wrote to thank the Prince for 'your support and concern for our people during and after the Falklands Campaign. That you should devote so much of your time to meeting returning units, and the manner in which you did it, has been an inspiration to us all, and enormously appreciated servicewide, not just by those concerned.'[4]

The Prince replied:

Having felt extremely guilty and frustrated that I could do nothing during the S. Atlantic operation, the least I could do was to try and show all the returning servicemen how much we appreciated their efforts. The response to the South Atlantic Fund† is quite overwhelming . . . I thought you might like to know that one or two ministers have told me how superb you were throughout the S. Atlantic crisis and how straight and sound your advice was.[5]

The following year, a chance meeting with a soldier who had been wounded in action provoked an angry memory. In a letter from Australia he wrote to a friend about the importance of what he used to refer to as the 'personal touch'. To illustrate the point he noted:

I have also had several letters, as Colonel-in-Chief of the Paras, from distressed relatives of dead soldiers who received their son's or husband's Falklands medals through the post in a jiffy bag and with a

---

* Lord Lewin (1920–   ), Chief of Defence Staff 1979–82. He was also Commander of *Britannia* 1957–58; Chief of Naval Staff and First Sea Lord 1977–79; Flag ADC to the Queen 1975–77; First and Principal ADC to the Queen 1977–79.

† The Prince was patron of the South Atlantic Fund, which gave support to those bereaved and wounded in the Falklands campaign. By March 1983, the Fund's total receipts stood at almost £15 million.

printed slip attached to it. You can imagine how dreadfully bitter they feel.[6]

This episode, among others, prompted him to write to a senior officer to remonstrate:

The aftermath of the South Atlantic campaign has highlighted for me the importance of the 'personal touch' and the business of remembering that each chap is an individual . . . That sort of thing clearly hurts people a good deal. In the case I have mentioned, the regimental system slipped up somewhere but the bigger the bureaucracy the more impersonal everything seems to become.[7]

The reminder of that crass behaviour provoked a further feeling of outrage about the bureaucratic way in which medals were awarded after the Falklands War. An official in the Ministry of Defence had told him that to qualify for a Victoria Cross (the supreme decoration for gallantry), the candidate had to have 'a 90% chance of being killed', and he wrote:

Can you imagine . . . sitting round a table and pontificating about that sort of criterion for an award of valour? . . . What about the S.A.S. officer who refused to evacuate his position when being attacked by a vastly superior Argentinian force; enabled his sergeant to escape and then stayed on, fighting, until he was overrun, single-handed? That is what I call courage beyond the call of duty but . . . there weren't the requisite number of people there to record the incident, save a whole host of the enemy . . .[8]

In badgering Defence Ministers on behalf of his regiments, the Prince was fulfilling no more than his interpretation of the duty of a Colonel-in-Chief, and throughout the eighties he was remorseless in the task. On his return from a visit to the Gulf in December 1990, where he not only met General Schwarzkopf but men and women from all three British services, he wrote to the Prime Minister to report on 'their indefatigable spirit, their unquenchable humour and their sheer professionalism'; but he also raised a number of factors which he thought had the potential to damage the morale of the British troops. In particular, he was troubled by one aspect of the 'very basic conditions' which the soldiers deployed tactically in the desert had to endure: the threatened withdrawal of a daily allowance to finance the purchase of bottled water to supplement their army provisions:

> It has to be said that the water provided by the Sappers, while pure, tastes filthy. Bearing in mind the difficult conditions in which they live and work, for months on end, and the uncertainties they face, it strikes me that it would have a particularly detrimental effect upon morale if soldiers were to be deprived of this allowance now.[9]

Following his own visit to the Gulf a fortnight later, the Prime Minister replied to the Prince on 19 January 1991, responding to every point which he had raised with care and precision. In the case of the water allowance, Major confirmed that it had originally been instituted because the available supplies of tap-water were of uncertain quality; that as the quality had improved so the allowance had been discontinued, but only for some personnel; and that most of the men at the front were still eligible for their daily allowance.

In his letter to the Prime Minister, the Prince also raised a further issue (which he added in longhand to his final draft) about the impact of *Options For Change* on the men serving in the Gulf.* Reflecting on the effect of the constant publicity about possible cuts, he worried (with many others) that it was 'hardly calculated to contribute to the maintenance of good morale in the Gulf'.' For a regimental soldier, expecting to fight in the desert, it was, he suggested, 'very unsettling not to know whether he will have a regiment to belong to or a job to return to when this crisis is over . . .'[10]

The Prime Minister responded to this concern by acknowledging that some anxiety was inevitable, but insisting that the government was trying to convey the message that redundancies would be kept as low as possible, and that all three forces would continue to have a significant role in Europe and beyond. He informed the Prince that discussions about the future of individual regiments would not start until after the end of

---

* On 26 July 1990, the Defence Secretary, Tom King, announced that under the *Options For Change* review agreed by the cabinet, the overall manpower of Britain's armed forces would be reduced by 18 per cent and that the Army would be cut by 25 per cent from 160,000 personnel to 120,000.

the Gulf operation. The Prince seized this opening to write back that in the light of the Falklands campaign and the Gulf War (which by now was in progress) it seemed important to him that 'we retain the most flexible possible force structure, able to respond to unexpected "out of area" operations'.[11]

In a speech at the Mansion House following the Gulf parade, the Prince raised a further concern, this time in public. After paying tribute to the 'unbounded, selfless sense of duty' displayed by Britain's armed forces against Iraq, he added, 'I hope that we will never underestimate the intangible value of the regimental system. It is a unique British feature which takes account of the vital human factor which can so often make the difference between success and failure . . .'[12] He was soon to learn of the bitterness in the tactical battle between the Army and the Ministry of Defence that developed over the regimental amalgamations and manpower cuts imposed by *Options For Change*. Immediately before the publication on 23 July 1991 of the White Paper which detailed the proposed restructuring of the armed forces in the wake of *Options For Change*, the Chief of General Staff, General Sir John Chapple, wrote to the Prince to inform him that four of his regiments were due for amalgamation. The decision to merge the Gordon Highlanders with the Queen's Own Highlanders and the Cheshire regiment with the Staffordshire regiment caused particular resentment among the officers and men affected, and as Colonel-in-Chief of the Gordons and the Cheshires, he was soon made aware of their anger. He wrote to a Scottish friend that he felt powerless to do anything about it:

> To me, it is a tragedy to do away with the best things; with something which in this case represents all that is good and true; that has the best traditions and highest standards and the greatest family feeling . . .[13]

To another friend, he wrote, 'I can't tell you how many letters I have had via all my regiments and from Generals of all kinds! I am now thoroughly depressed and have spent hours composing a rather ineffective letter to the Prime Minister . . .'[14]

In his 'ineffective' letter to the Prime Minister, the Prince reiterated his anxieties about the proposed reductions. Acknowledging that the changes in the Soviet Union and Eastern Europe necessitated a review of the role of Britain's armed forces, he expressed his concern about what seemed to him to be the precipitous haste with which the cuts had been introduced, questioning the wisdom of such a drastic course 'when the world inevitably remains in so uncertain a condition . . . The unexpected tends to occur with monotonous regularity.'[15]

In October, the Prince's unhappiness about *Options For Change* resurfaced when extracts from part of a letter which he had written in August to the Colonel of the Cheshire regiment, Brigadier Keith Prosser, were leaked to the *Sunday Times*. Under the front page headline 'Royal Family and Generals unite to fight army cuts', the Prince was reported to have expressed his 'astonishment', 'anger' and 'amazement' at the 'drastic reductions' imposed by *Options For Change*.[16]

His letter to Prosser was in fact altogether more measured than the report in the *Sunday Times* had suggested, and it was certainly no more forceful than a letter from the Chief of the General Staff – also leaked to the *Sunday Times* – in which General Sir John Chapple informed the Defence Secretary, Tom King,* that 'across the whole spectrum of ranks and regiments' the 'most strongly felt and most vehemently expressed view . . . is that the army will not have enough men or units to carry out its peacetime tasks and duties without greater overstretch or unacceptable penalty. I took a positive line about this . . .'[17]

The rumbles in the armed forces against *Options For Change*, and in particular about what came to be widely regarded as the inept handling of the process by Tom King, persisted. After the 1992 election, King was replaced by an altogether more gifted politician, Malcolm Rifkind,† who was to negotiate his way around the political abyss with greater cunning. In May, the Prince wrote to him reiterating his concern that Whitehall failed to understand the full implications of cutting the Army's manpower as sharply as his predecessor had envisaged:

> Talking to the C.O.'s of my regiments, I have been struck by their concern about the manpower levels they will be provided with in order to carry out their commitments. The problem, as I see it, is how to maintain people's morale and motivation if the demands made

---

* Tom King (1933–   ), Secretary of State for the Environment 1983; Employment 1983–85; Northern Ireland 1985–89; Defence 1989–92.

† Malcolm Rifkind (1946–   ), Secretary of State for Scotland 1986–89; Transport 1990–92; Defence since 1992.

upon them – and their families – become somewhat excessive and unrealistic . . .'[18]

In February 1993, after British forces were sent to Bosnia, the Prince was vindicated when Rifkind publicly referred to the 'significant' extra commitments on behalf of the United Nations in Bosnia, Cyprus, Cambodia and elsewhere in what was widely reported as the 'first retreat from the 1990 *Options For Change* review'.[19] In the face of a sharply critical Commons Defence Committee review warning that the army was seriously overstretched, the Defence Secretary reversed some of his predecessor's cuts, leaving the army with 5,000 more front-line troops and saving four historic regiments, including the Cheshires, from amalgamation.

By this time, the Prince had identified another threat of somewhat less strategic moment but, for him, intense significance, and which was closely tied to his belief in the regimental system. On 24 November 1992, the *Daily Telegraph* reported that 'Defence ministers are expected to decide soon, possibly as early as this week, whether to cut the number of Army bands by more than half and the number of musicians to fewer than 800. A decision is long overdue under the *Options For Change* review . . .'[20] Eight days earlier, the Prince had written to Rifkind to express his 'deep concern' about the proposals: 'I feel most strongly that any decision that may be taken to reduce or remove regimental bands would be a thoroughly shortsighted one and would fail to take into account the crucial role played by bands in the regimental framework of the British Army . . .'[21]

To make sure that Rifkind should be left in no doubt of the potential feeling of every Colonel-in-Chief in the land, the Prince took an uncharacteristic initiative, arranging for a copy of his letter to the Defence Secretary to be sent to the Queen, the Duke of Edinburgh, the Queen Mother, Princess Margaret, the Princess Royal, the Duke of York, the Princess of Wales, the Duke of Kent, the Duchess of Kent, the Duke of Gloucester, the Duchess of Gloucester and Princess Alice. In the hope that they would transform his single initiative into a royal collective enterprise, he urged his relatives to write to the Defence Secretary as well, suggesting that such a right royal intervention would not be entirely ignored.

The extent to which his lobbying effort was successful is uncertain. In March 1993, the Armed Forces Minister, Archie Hamilton, announced a 'reorganisation' of Army bands to ensure the 'right' numbers of bandsmen in proportion to the army's total size. Indicating that this would mean 'fewer but larger bands', which would improve the standard of music available to the Army, the Minister went out of his way to say that 'it has been considered highly desirable to ensure that a substantial link is retained between an infantry or cavalry regiment and an allocated band.' The minister's statement gave no figures but the message was clear: the regimental bands, like so many other traditions the Prince favoured, had no future in the 'cost-effective' world of which he was so suspicious.*

In relation to the historical perspective of the cost accountants, the Prince's attitude towards the armed forces was not only traditional but openly reactionary. The apparent clash within the one individual between the military concerns of the Colonel-in-Chief and the spiritual concerns of the environmentalist exposed only a superficial paradox: the pursuit of order and harmony and a commitment to the 'precautionary' principle were fundamental to both (as they were to his involvement in almost every venture to which he had given himself). If he had a nostalgia for forgotten hierarchies – in natural as well as human relationships – it was because he believed in preserving values that would endure through periods of rapid change to protect the advance of civilisation from what he saw as the false gods of progress.

To this extent he was attracted to the concept of the regiment as he was to the notion of the village community: in both, everyone knew their place, the customs were familiar and the mutual commitments of obligation and service were inescapable; the fact that deference also played a prominent part in both structures offended him not at all. Likewise, he rejoiced that the regimental system nurtured chivalry and honour and discipline, mores that were generally out of fashion elsewhere but which he thought were intrinsic to a healthy society. He also believed that the armed forces sponsored 'good manners' and the spirit of 'doing unto others what you would have them do unto you', which was one of the reasons why he hoped that Prince William would follow him into the armed forces. In all of this he indulged a romance with the idea of military life that the naval rating or the corporal might have

---

* The British Army had 1,991 musicians in 69 bands before the announcement; following the announcement, the numbers have fallen to 1,168 musicians in 30 bands.

found difficult to recognise; yet, limited though his perspective might have been, it was consistent with his overall vision.

The Prince was convinced that smartness of turn-out and precision in drill were not only important in themselves but emblematic of higher values. Sensitive to being thought pernickety, he did not refrain from making his opinions known. On one occasion he wrote to the Colonel Commandant of the Parachute Regiment:

> At the risk of being a dreadful bore, and frightful fusspot, I did just want to say that I thought it was decidedly odd to see quite a few members of the P.R.A.* marching past yesterday wearing 'T' shirts or scruffy anoraks.
>
> For what it is worth, I really do think that a little bit more trouble ought to be taken if these characters actually want to take part in the march-past. Is there any way of making this point to the P.R.A. branches, or perhaps there could be a few ties and jackets available to borrow if they come ill-equipped.
>
> Frankly I am amazed that an ex-Para soldier would even consider turning up so badly turned-out, and I would hope the next time I attend Airborne Forces Day a difference might be detected! Otherwise it was a very enjoyable occasion . . .[22]

As the prospective Head of the Armed Forces watched the progressive contraction of the Navy, the Army, and the Air Force,† he continued to fear that Britain would one day pay the price for what he regarded as a precipitate retreat. 'I'm afraid that I believe that we delude ourselves if we think that humanity is becoming ever more civilised, ever more sophisticated and ever more reasonable,' he argued in 1993:

> There will always be dangerous, evil people, and people who will seek to take advantage of others in a weaker condition . . . You only

---

* The Parachute Regiment Association, for ex-members of the Parachute Regiment and Airborne Forces.

† On 14 July 1994, the Defence Secretary, Malcolm Rifkind, announced a defence cost study called *Front Line First* which outlined savings of £750 million for the financial year 1996/97 by trimming the support infrastructure and headquarters of the three armed forces and the Ministry of Defence.

have to look at the way the world is now. It's becoming a far more dangerous place . . .

We've been through periods of reduction of our capacity and then there has been another requirement. And then, of course, all the people who've been loudest in their desire to see these forces reduced are the ones who complain loudest when we are unable to meet the threats or the challenges: the one certainty is that we have to face the unexpected. Look at the Gulf War. The Ministry of Defence sold all the desert clothing three or four years before the Gulf War because they said there will never be a requirement again for desert warfare. And they sold them to the Iraqis. They said there'd be no requirement for tank battles, tank warfare on a large scale. Look what happened![23]

In an attempt to reconcile his commitment to a powerful military 'insurance policy' with a billowing defence budget,* the Prince was tempted to argue for British troops to play a permanent role within the United Nations as a standing army, financed by the member states. 'I foresee that we will have to play a policeman's role all over the world. That involves disciplined manpower, professionally trained. We've built up a remarkable tradition and an expertise and we have a genius for improvisation.' After the end of the Cold War, one or two senior politicians had started to murmur in similar terms, and likewise some leading servicemen, but the Prince became the first public figure to suggest openly but tentatively that Britain might be 'paid' to provide its military services overseas. Knowing that to advocate openly a 'mercenary' role for the British armed forces was to court the charge that he was ready to see British soldiers die on foreign battlefields for alien causes, he countered that the Sultan of Brunei had already 'hired' a battalion of Gurkhas from the British army and that, in any case, to play a leading part in a permanent United Nations force was an entirely honourable prospect. 'It wouldn't be an entirely mercenary army,' he insisted, adding drily that 'in this age of the free market',[24] his proposal was not at all egregious.

As head of the armed forces, the Prince of Wales would inherit the Queen's role as a focus for their loyalty and unity. Although this was easy to exaggerate, there remained a sense in which the men and women who

---

* The defence budget in 1993–94 was £23.5 billion.

belong to the armed forces feel that they serve 'Queen and Country', defending the nation and not just the state. For a significant proportion of those who serve in the armed services, the sovereign still embodies those transcendent values which arouse that feeling of patriotism which distinguishes the armed services of one nation from those of another. The formal distinction between serving the Crown – 'taking the Queen's shilling' or accepting 'the Queen's commission' – rather than the government of the day may be a constitutional nicety but the sentiment that underpins this symbolic relationship is not insignificant, particularly in an age when politicians are held in low regard. The Prince has been so steeped in this culture and its values that as King he would be quite at ease in the role. The same could not so easily be said of the other great symbolic duty imposed on the sovereign: to be Supreme Governor of the Church of England and Defender of the Faith.

'I am one of those people who searches,' he has said. 'I'm interested in pursuing the path, if I can find it, through the thickets. There are other people who prefer to remain in a tidy concept which they've worked out, and who don't want to pursue other areas or paths.'[25] Although he was a regular communicant of the Church of England who would never end the day without kneeling in prayer before going to bed, and although he had long been aware of the dangers of straying too far beyond what he referred to as his 'own cultural and religious roots'[26] the Prince had never given up the religious quest which he had begun in the late seventies. He had not only explored Hinduism and Buddhism but remained unwilling to dismiss the idea of reincarnation. He had also decided that it was important to understand Islam and in the process he was drawn towards some of that great religion's guiding tenets; he identified strongly with those who saw in Islam, Judaism and Christianity a common belief in a monotheistic creation which was of greater significance than the doctrinal hostilities which over the centuries had pitted each faith against the other.

He was also dismayed by the schisms within the Christian communion. In particular, as he had demonstrated so forcibly in his attempt to attend mass in the Pontiff's private chapel during his official visit to Italy in 1985, he was contemptuous of doctrinal and liturgical disputes that divided the Roman from the Anglican Church. As a scion of the House of Tudor, his attitude towards King Henry VIII's repudiation of the authority of Pope Leo X, who had bestowed on him the title of Defender of the Faith in 1521,* was far from reverential:

> The title was given to him at a time when he had happened to please the Pope quite enormously. Whereupon he decided – because he wanted to get divorced† – that things were a bit different and that the Pope was a damned nuisance because he wouldn't grant him a divorce, which is one of the reasons why the Church of England developed. So the title remained rather because, I suspect, King Henry VIII liked it.[27]‡

As the Prince was well aware, the emergence of the Anglican Church was a more fraught and intricate process than his summary had allowed; yet it was in those terms that he chose to remember the establishment of the Church of England. Taken together, his belief in the contiguity of the monotheistic religions and his impatience with inter-denominational disputations had come to form the bedrock of his conviction that salvation springs less from religion than from faith:

> All the great prophets, all the great thinkers, all those who have achieved an awareness of the aspects of life which lie beneath the surface, all have showed the same understanding of the universe or the nature of God or of the purpose of our existence – and that is why I think it so important to understand the common threads which link us all in one great and important tapestry.[28]

His attitudes are not bounded by ecumenicism. Although he has long deplored the schisms within the Christian Church and has been scathing

---

* Following the publication by the British monarch of a book, *In Defence of the Seven Sacraments*, largely written by Sir Thomas More, which was an attack on Luther.
† In fact, Henry VIII had sought an annulment, which the Pope had denied him. He divorced none of his wives but secured annulments through the Church of England.
‡ The title Defender of the Faith was recognised as an official title of the English monarch in 1544. In 1534, the Act of Supremacy asserted that King Henry VIII was 'the only supreme head on earth of the Church of England'; the Act was repealed by Queen Mary, but Elizabeth I's Act of Supremacy of 1559 declared her to be 'the only supreme governor of this realm . . . as well in all spiritual or ecclesiastical things or causes as temporal'.

about the exclusive forms of evangelism represented by Protestant sects like the Free Presbyterians, his sympathy for the ecumenical movement fails to explain his statement that, 'I've always felt that the Catholic subjects of the sovereign are equally as important as the Anglican ones, as the Protestant ones. Likewise, I think that the Islamic subjects or the Hindu subjects or the Zoroastrian subjects of the sovereign are of equal and vital importance.'[29] In this case, he was not merely talking about the rights of non-Christian religions (and he would most certainly have wished to include Judaism in his list), but giving expression to his empathy with other faiths, and to the fact that at the very least he feels himself to have more in common with those who have faith (of whatever religion) than those who have none.

To this extent he finds himself at ease walking between and within all those religions in addition to being a practising Christian. It was in this context that in June 1994 he expressed strong sentiments in the television documentary *Charles: The Private Man, The Public Role* (that he had long espoused in private) about the relationship of the sovereign to the Church of England. In a direct reference to the title Defender of the Faith, he said:

> I personally would rather see it as Defender of Faith, not the Faith, because it [Defender of the Faith] means just one particular interpretation of the Faith, which I think is sometimes something that causes a deal of a problem. It has done for hundreds of years. People have fought each other to the death over these things, which seems to me a peculiar waste of people's energy, when we're all actually aiming for the same ultimate goal, I think. So I would much rather it was seen as defending faith itself which is so often under threat in our day where, you know, the whole concept of faith itself or anything beyond this existence, beyond life itself is considered almost old-fashioned and irrelevant.[30]

He had not only weighed his words carefully, but reiterated his meaning so that there could be no doubt of his perspective. To be Defender of the Faith was for him to be 'Defender of the Divine in existence, the pattern of the Divine which is, I think, in all of us but which, because we are human beings, can be expressed in so many different ways.'[31]

For the heir to the throne to express unease about inheriting the title of Defender of *the* Faith was bound to send a *frisson* through the Anglican establishment and through Westminster. Although leading Churchmen, including the Archbishop of Canterbury, had long suspected that he was not quite 'sound' in these matters, they were not to know that his departure from convention would be so unequivocal.

Before the transmission of the documentary, a rumour of what he intended to say had reached the *Sunday Times*, and his office felt obliged to forestall speculation that the Prince intended to use the interview to call for the disestablishment of the Church of England. In fact, he had long been clear about the distinction between his own attitude to faith on the one hand and the relationship of the Anglican Church to the Crown on the other. He believes that the latter is not a matter for the sovereign but for the Church of England itself to determine; nor, curiously, is it an issue in which he has himself taken a close interest. The present constitutional position is that were the Church to decide in favour of disestablishment, then the tripartite relationship between Crown, Church and state would be dismembered; the role of the sovereign as Defender of the Faith would cease to have constitutional significance, while the coronation, which in its present form gives sacred meaning and symbolic expression to the relationship between Church and Crown, would theoretically become redundant. Fortuitously, twelve days after the Prince's televised remarks, the Synod* voted by a substantial margin (273 to 110) against moves to weaken the links between the Church and state; the Church of England was therefore unlikely to give serious consideration to the issue again before the turn of the century at the earliest.†

---

* The governing body of the Church of England, drawn from the clergy and lay members of the Church.

† Disestablishment first emerged as an issue in the nineteenth century, when it was driven by Nonconformist pressure groups. The Irish Church was disestablished in 1869, the Welsh in 1920. In the second half of the twentieth century, the impulse has come from within the Church of England itself. Paradoxically, the other branches of the Christian Church and other 'mainstream' faiths in England, Judaism, Islam and Hinduism, seem to welcome the existence of the Established Church as a conduit for their moral and ethical concerns into the corridors of temporal authority at Westminster and Whitehall. It is conceivable that in future the Church of England could follow the Church of Scotland (which is also 'established') by opting for self-governance. In this case, Parliament would not have to

In these circumstances, the dilemma for the Church of England and for the Prince of Wales was how to reconcile the latter's spiritual conviction with his prospective role as the former's Supreme Governor. The Archbishop of Canterbury, George Carey, came from the evangelical wing of the Anglican Church and his public pronouncements have frequently reflected the bias of those origins.

Nine days before the Prince's comments about wishing to be 'Defender of the Divine', the Archbishop delivered an address at a conference in Canada entitled 'Essentials 1994'. In the course of a powerful theological affirmation of the primacy of the Christian vision – of the need 'to live within the gospel' and to 'develop our commitment to Mission' – he declared that the time had come to 'proclaim the uniqueness of Christ . . . One of the most disturbing trends in the Western Church', he argued:

> has been a tendency for some to loosen their grip on the singularity of Jesus Christ who is, of course, the centre of the Christian faith. We have been bullied into this by powerful theological voices which have suggested that Christianity must come to terms with its own 'parochiality'. It has no right to challenge Islam or any other religion. It is merely a Western face of God. It must therefore surrender its commitment to being accepted in every part of the world and be content to be one face and one voice among many. This view is to be firmly rejected . . .[32]

Had that speech been delivered after, rather than before, the Prince's remarks, these words would have been widely interpreted as a rebuke; the contrast in focus and emphasis between two of the most important members of the Established Church was self-evident.

After the publication of the Prince's interview, perhaps in an attempt to help the Supreme Governor 'apparent', the Archbishop allowed himself to be tempted into remarking on BBC Radio that the Prince had 'intended' to say that he wanted to be Defender of the *Christian* Faith, but that he 'didn't have the opportunity to express his fully-formed

---

approve its decisions and the sovereign would not be Supreme Governor, but the Church would remain 'established' and the sovereign would retain the duty to protect it.

views'.[33] According to the Archbishop, what the Prince had said 'was perfectly compatible with being Defender of *the* [author's italics] Faith. As heir, he has to be concerned with every citizen, regardless of creed and colour. I believe that that is what he intended to say.'[34] If the Archbishop had interpreted the Prince correctly, then the primate had neatly disposed of a quandary for the Established Church: a rearrangement of the furniture at the Coronation service to give prominence to leaders from other faiths would suffice to accommodate the Prince's sensibilities. The Coronation Oath – by which the new sovereign is enjoined by law to swear solemnly 'to maintain and preserve inviolably the settlement of the Church of England, and the doctrine, worship, discipline, and government thereof, as by law established in England"* – would not trouble the prospective 'Defender of the Divine' as profoundly as some observers had supposed. The importance to the Established Church of the Archbishop's gloss on the Prince's remarks was made explicit when the former went on: 'It's clear that if you tamper with the Coronation Oath we could be in real trouble because it would require primary legislation. What can be changed is the Coronation Service which can reflect the multicultural society in which we live.'†

The Archbishop's minimalist interpretation of what the Prince had said was not easy to reconcile with the Prince's words as broadcast or from the context in which he uttered them – or, indeed, from the extended expression of his views from which the broadcast interview (with his approval) was drawn. In a passage from part of the interview which was not broadcast, the Prince amplified his perspective thus:

---

* The Coronation Oath is based on the Coronation Oath Act (1688) and is obligatory under the Act of Settlement (1701) as modified by the Acts of Union with Scotland (1706).

† Sixteeen months earlier in February 1993, Carey had endorsed his fellow Primate, Dr Habgood, who had indicated that the Oath might have to be changed before the next coronation. 'The Coronation Oath is a difficult one,' he said, 'and whether that needs to be revised I think is a matter to be debated, because it does give a very privileged position to the Church of England, and it is some possible embarrassment.' At that time, the Archbishop of Canterbury said, 'The Archbishop of York was raising a question that must be addressed at some point in the future . . .' In the intervening months, they had both been warned about the constitutional ramifications implicit in such a revision and had backtracked accordingly.

I feel, you know, that certainly the great Middle Eastern religions – Judaism, Islam, Christianity, all stemming from the same geographical area – all have a great deal in common. And I think Christianity had a great deal more in common a long time ago than it does now – sadly in my opinion. And I think a lot of that is due to the great schism between the Orthodox Church and the Roman Church before the Reformation produced Protestantism. But I also think there are aspects of Hinduism and Buddhism, again further east, which are attached by very profound threads to Islam, Christianity and Judaism. And when you begin to look at what these religions are saying you find that so much of the wisdom that is represented within these religions coincides . . .[35]

Those sentiments led directly into the broadcast extract where the Prince referred to the 'great prophets' sharing 'the same understanding of the nature of God' and to the importance of understanding the 'common threads' in the 'great and important tapestry'. In those words, the Prince was not merely giving expression to his future multi-cultural responsibilities as the Archbishop had claimed, but was in addition reflecting on his own deeply held spiritual commitment. The singularity of his faith could not be so easily swept aside as the Primate appeared to have imagined.

However, the Prince was at pains to make it clear that he did not believe that his views necessitated any precipitate action. Thus, after consultation with his office, the Archbishop of York, Dr Habgood, informed the Synod on 10 July 1994 that the Prince had confirmed that his remarks should not have been seen as implying support either for disestablishment or 'for any other change to this country's constitutional arrangements'.[36] The Archbishop also welcomed the drift of the Prince's comments about the importance of faith in an increasingly secular society. However, the central issue – how to reconcile the meaning of a sacred oath with his own Christian outlook – was still to be resolved; the participation by the leaders of other faiths in his coronation would be an ecumenical gesture that the Prince favoured, but it seemed unlikely to meet the full challenge of the Prince's faith. The prospect of swearing an oath which was interpreted as asserting the supremacy of the Church of England over all other religious denominations remained as a spiritual dilemma of far more than incidental significance.

*

In one of the most influential of recent essays on the coronation, the theologian Professor Paul Bradshaw has asked rhetorically:

> Cannot the position of the established Church be affirmed without it sounding so exclusive of other churches and faiths? In any case, regardless of the specific wording of this part of the Oath, is there not something rather distasteful about the spectacle of the Archbishop of Canterbury exacting a commitment from the monarch to secure the interests of the Church before proceeding to anoint and crown him/her? No doubt in earlier times such a concession was the price which often had to be paid by sovereigns throughout Europe in order to procure the Church's cooperation in the act, but the oldest extant version of the English Oath (that made by King Edgar in 973) contained no such demands, merely the promise that 'The Church of God and the whole Christian people shall have true peace at all times.'[37]

The Coronation Oath has been adapted many times in the intervening years. Some advisers believe that even if primary legislation were required, it should not be beyond the wit of parliamentary draughtsmen to modify the Oath to meet the Prince's vision of his spiritual role as 'Defender of Faith' without causing the unwritten constitution to unravel. Others believe that it should be possible to include in the coronation a supplementary declaration affirming the Prince's belief in the divinity of other religions and, in the process, diluting the 'exclusive' character of the Oath to which Bradshaw refers and which so disturbs the Prince. This, or any similar modification that the Church might devise, would at least meet the spirit of King Edgar's original declaration of fealty.

As sovereign, the Prince would have to meet three other legal requirements apart from taking the Coronation Oath. He would have to declare himself to be a faithful Protestant (under the Accession Declaration Act [1910]); that he was in communion with the Church of England (under the Act of Settlement [1701]); and that he would 'maintain' the Church of England and the Church of Scotland (under the Act of Settlement [1701]). In themselves, none of these three would cause him any anxiety. It is only the Oath with its present meaning and inference that remains an obstacle for a Prince for whom it would not be in character to resile from the particular quality of his faith.

The Church of England, like the monarchy, and like the British constitution into which both are woven, has survived by adaptation. Precedent suggests that a way would be found to resolve the dilemma. However, this objective had not been realised by the summer of 1994; the dialogue between Buckingham Palace, St James's Palace and Lambeth Palace on the subject was far from over.

CHAPTER
TWENTY-SEVEN

On 7 December 1993, the Archdeacon of York, the Venerable George Austin, a minor cleric of Pickwickian demeanour and modest accomplishment, who was well known for his eagerness to animadvert on public issues, chose to inform the nation that the Prince was unfit to become King. 'Charles made solemn vows before God about his marriage, and it seems – if the rumours are true about Camilla – that he began to break them almost immediately,' he informed listeners to BBC Radio 4's *Today* programme. 'He has broken the trust on one thing, and broken vows to God on one thing. How can he then go into Westminster Abbey and take the Coronation vows?'[*] Even by his own standards, Austin had excelled himself: self-confessedly happy to rush to unforgiving judgement on the basis of rumour, he left Broadcasting House to bounce his way from studio to studio, and thence from headline to headline, not only intolerant and self-righteous but evidently hugely gratified by the stir which he had provoked.

In different circumstances, the reach-me-down verdict of the

---

[*] The ostensible reason for his appearance on the *Today* programme was a report in the *Sun*, which had already been denounced as a 'total fabrication' by Lambeth Palace, to the effect that the Archbishop of Canterbury had told other Church leaders that the Prince might have to 'consider his position' as prospective Defender of the Faith.

Archdeacon of York would have been treated as marginalia; as it was, his intervention followed close on the heels of an announcement by the Princess of Wales that she was intending to withdraw from the limelight. With royal 'stories' thus catapulted back into the headlines, the cleric's pontifications became the unlikely focus for a further bout of speculation about the Prince's future. At least two papers reported that the Queen favoured the Crown passing over the head of her son to Prince William. 'The Monarchy is self-evidently in crisis,' opined the *Evening Standard*, reflecting the general tone: 'The heir to the throne finds the legitimacy of his claim to the throne questioned by a leading churchman. His wife, the mother of a future monarch, announces she is going into purdah. There are those, of course, who dismiss all of this as just another media hare. That is nonsense . . .'[2]

As the storm raged, Buckingham Palace and St James's Palace refused to comment, in the belief that there was little they could say without fanning the flames. Exasperated by the failure of anyone to put the record straight, Nicholas Soames consulted Richard Aylard and then used his authority as a government minister to go on the offensive on the Prince's behalf, declaring forcefully, 'Being heir to the throne is not an ambition but a duty and one which will befall him on a sad moment later in his life. He will inherit the throne and that is the end of the matter.' For good measure, he added that the Archdeacon's 'hugely unrepresentative vapourings' had filled him with 'outrage and disgust'.[3] Soames's intervention restored a modicum of balance. Reporters rang their sources in Whitehall and in Westminster and discovered that the Prince commanded the confidence of senior figures in the political establishment, and that the Archbishop of Canterbury had no qualms about crowning him as King.[4]

It was the Princess's public request for 'time and space' which had – unwittingly – prepared the ground for the damage wrought by the Archdeacon. 'Over the next few months I will be seeking a more suitable way of combining a meaningful public role with, hopefully, a more private life,' she told the guests at a charity luncheon on 3 December 1993:

> I hope you can find it in your hearts to understand and give me the time and space that has been lacking in recent years . . . I could not stand here and make this sort of statement without acknowledging the heartfelt support I have been given by the public in general. Your

kindness and affection have carried me through some of the most difficult periods, and always your love and care have eased the journey.[5]

The speech aroused powerful feelings. Many were shocked at the
sudden loss from the public stage of so charismatic a figure and turned at
once on the media, speculating that she had been forced to the decision
by the persistent and intolerable intrusions of reporters and photographers from the tabloid press. (By way of illustration, a few weeks earlier
pictures of the Princess 'working out' in a gym, taken by subterfuge, had
been published in the *Daily Mirror*.) More insistently, however, the Prince
and the Palace were held responsible for driving her out into the cold by
spurning her as an individual and downgrading her role. ('Royal
Watchers Ask: Did Diana Go or Was She Pushed?' was the *Times* headline.[6]) Although a handful of sceptics wondered why someone so anxious
for seclusion should have chosen to stage such a melodramatic exit, the
overall impression was that the Princess had been a victim of a heartless
and hapless husband in league with his acolytes in the establishment.

In her statement at the charity luncheon, she had referred to the support given her throughout her ordeal by the Queen and the Duke of
Edinburgh, but she had refrained from mentioning the Prince, an omission which (perhaps inadvertently) had reinforced speculation that his
actions had somehow caused her decision. However, the record of events
which led up to her announcement suggests that neither the Prince nor
the Palace had been as recalcitrant as some of the leak-inspired speculation supposed.

The build-up to her departure began in the early autumn of 1993,
when the Princess began to drop hints that she was thinking seriously
about withdrawing from public life. For some weeks, it proved impossible to discover exactly why or how the Princess intended to do this,
although her intention was recognised to be more than a momentary
impulse. Following her separation from the Prince, she had felt free to
continue all her public engagements for her charities in Britain and
abroad, which excluded only those official tours on which the Foreign
Office and the Palace had agreed it would now be inappropriate for her
to represent the Queen. The Foreign Secretary, Douglas Hurd, had
made it clear to her personally that the government welcomed her role
as an informal ambassador and would be pleased to facilitate her travels
accordingly. There may have been those who were frustrated by this

compliance. The prevailing wisdom, with which the Prince concurred, was that with the exception of the constraint on official tours the Princess should determine her own pattern of life. When it became known that, of her own volition, she had it in mind to withdraw from public life, it was generally hoped that she would gradually cut back on her commitments by the simple device of accepting fewer and fewer engagements. However, it began to emerge that she was thinking of staging an altogether more dramatic exit.

On Wednesday 1 December, the Prince was at the headquarters of the Duchy of Cornwall in Buckingham Palace Road, where he was chairing a meeting of his Council, when he received word that the Queen wished to speak to him as soon as possible. It transpired that the Princess had already spoken to her mother-in-law to inform her that she was to make an announcement at a public gathering two days later. The Palace was dismayed at the notion and by the draft text of her speech. At the instigation of the Queen's private secretary, Robert Fellowes, the Princess's private secretary, Patrick Jephson, and the Queen's deputy press secretary, Geoffrey Crawford, had, between them, modified the draft but even so it was clear that the impact of what she intended to say would not only be damaging but would leave the Princess herself with very little room for manoeuvre. That afternoon, the Prince spoke to the Princess on the phone to try to find out more about her real purpose and whether she could find other, less resounding means to achieve it. He had no success. At an hour-long meeting the following morning, both the Queen and the Duke of Edinburgh urged her to reconsider her decision. Like the Prince on the previous afternoon, they said that they appreciated her need to withdraw but urged her not to use a public platform to do it. The Duke repeated the suggestion that if she wished to scale down her engagements she should do so gradually month by month, thus leaving herself with the option of working at whatever pitch of intensity she wished. However, the Princess was adamant: she owed it to her public to give them a full account of her decision and why she had made it. Her mind was made up.

Helped along by the egregious Archdeacon of York, the furore that followed the Princess's statement was of a magnitude that not even the most pessimistic loyalist had expected. With a fresh excuse to regurgitate all the allegations and innuendoes about his marriage, tabloid moralisers, who treated facts with disdain and saw comment as sacred, re-erected a familiar scaffold from which once again to hang the reputation of the heir to the throne. Although he was far tougher than a year earlier, the Prince was not immune. A year of sustained public duty had apparently been obliterated from the public mind.

The tabloid press appeared to be oblivious to any aspect of his life that could not be used to promote a damaging innuendo however grotesque. Among many examples of this genre, their coverage on 26 April 1993 was characteristic. On that day, *Today* ('Charles' picnic partner'), the *Daily Mirror* ('Charlie's Bonny Mystery Guest'), the *Daily Express* ('Charles's shy fly-fisher') and the *Sun* ('So Who's Your Angel, Charlie') ran 'paparazzi' photographs and stories about a 'mystery brunette' who was allegedly staying with the Prince at Balmoral. Under a photograph of the 'mystery beauty', the *Sun* wrote:

> This is the pretty brunette who has been keeping Prince Charles company on holiday. The mystery girl, in her early 30s, is staying with Charles at the Queen Mother's home Birkhall, near Balmoral. She arrived last Tuesday and has often been seen with the Prince, laughing and joking. The slim beauty joined Charles, 44, and other guests for a picnic lunch at the Queen Mum's fishing lodge. But she hid in trees when she spotted photographers trying to take her picture. On Saturday, Charles's pal slipped away from the party to fish on the River Dee. But she fled again when she saw newsmen. The slim, outdoor girl is a complete contrast to glamorous Princess Di, Charles's estranged wife. Yesterday she stayed away as the Prince drove three guests to Crathie Church in his silver Volvo.

On the same day, the Prince's private secretary responded by writing to all the newspapers concerned as follows, making it clear that his letter was 'for publication in full':

Dear Sir,

The 'mystery woman' in your latest story about the Prince of Wales is my secretary, as you would have discovered if you had bothered to check. She is here, because, contrary to the prevailing myth, HRH uses his time in Scotland to complete a great deal of paperwork, and last week prepared two major speeches. For her, a first attempt at salmon fishing was a reasonable way to spend a Saturday afternoon break. Being driven from the river by the incessant attentions of patrolling photographers was disappointing, but a good introduction to the ethics and methods of the tabloid press.

Yours faithfully,

Richard Aylard.

All of the offending papers printed extracts from Aylard's letter (although *Today* needed further pressure to elicit a correction). However, none of them reproduced the final sentence, while the *Sun's* editor wrote to Aylard:

Dear Sir,   26th April

I decide whether letters are published in full – not you.
   My advice to you in future is to show the same courtesy to those outside The Palace as undoubtedly you do inside.

Yours faithfully,

Kelvin MacKenzie.

On 27 April, as if to underline this arrogance and disdain, the *Sun* published a large cartoon depicting a young woman leaving Balmoral carrying her suitcases: a photographer is standing at the gate with a colleague who is holding a newspaper with the headline, 'Charles' New Mystery Woman'. The caption below the cartoon reads, 'I caught him on the phone to Camilla!'

It was against this background that the Prince finally achieved an objective which he had set himself fifteen years earlier by establishing his own press office at St James's, run in collaboration with, but quite independently of, Buckingham Palace. Journalists were quick to notice the difference: the new press team was not only competent but, at least by comparison with the past, welcoming and open; members of the Prince's staff, who had started to adopt jargon terms like 'pro-active', became far more easily available for background briefings; and, by the same token, the Prince's team made it clear that St James's was quite ready to go on the offensive against pervasive and malicious distortions. The Aylard riposte to the 'mystery beauty' stories was a harbinger of an attitude towards the media that promised to be much more robust than Buckingham Palace had been willing to countenance.

To those around the Prince, it sometimes seemed that his future subjects were not even given a chance by the media to assess his contribution to public life. In 1993, he had officiated at eighteen functions of state; attended fifty events on behalf of his charities, most of which were linked to the Prince's Trust; presided or made speeches at twelve environmental and sixteen architectural engagements; participated in eight occasions promoting healing and complementary medicine; attended twenty meetings involving the Duchy of Cornwall; visited Cambridge, Derby, Birmingham, Stoke-on-Trent, Yorkshire and Kent on six domestic 'Away Days' as well as making formal visits abroad to Mexico, Poland, Czechoslovakia, Turkey and four Gulf states; established the Prague Heritage Fund;* became the chairman of the Royal Collection Trust;* and had been present at thirty-five miscellaneous functions promoting a range of good causes.

Before his departure for the Gulf, the Prince made a speech in Oxford about relations between Islam and the West. The speech had been carefully planned to help prepare the way for his visit, as well as to give an opportunity to address a subject which had increasingly excited his curiosity and concern. Following the normal practice of the Prince's office for any speech with significant overseas content, the text was shown in advance to the Foreign Office, although the writing was done in St James's Palace and the theme was the Prince's own. As with the environment and architecture, he called together a group of experts to brief him on the historical background and the intricacies of the issues he intended to raise.

In the Sheldonian Theatre, before an audience of scholars, he went further than any international politician in expressing his 'despair and outrage at the unmentionable horrors being perpetrated in southern Iraq [by] Saddam Hussein and "his terrifying regime"'; and he asked, rhetorically, of Iraq's claim that the destruction of Marsh Arabs' habitat

---

* See Appendix I (pages 567–75).

was for agricultural purposes, 'How many more obscene lies do we have to be told before action is taken? Even at the eleventh hour it is still not too late to prevent a total cataclysm. I pray that this might at least be a cause in which Islam and the West could join forces for our common humanity.'[7]

Inevitably, this angry plea attracted the headlines in the West, but in the Arab world it was his remarks about the suffering of the Bosnian Muslims which had greater impact, and even more so his appeal to the West to overcome its 'unthinking prejudices' about Islam and its customs and laws. Making a set of clear distinctions between 'revivalist' Muslims and 'extremists' (whom he described as using the devotion of the former for political ends), he warned against the temptation to regard extremism as the hallmark of Islam. 'Extremism', he said, 'is no more the monopoly of Islam than it is the monopoly of other religions, including Christianity.' He also spoke warmly of the western world's debt to the culture of Islam, which, he reminded his audience:

> is part of our past and our present, in all fields of human endeavour. It has helped to create modern Europe. It is part of our inheritance, not a thing apart. More than this, Islam can teach us today a way of understanding and living in the world which Christianity itself is poorer for having lost. At the heart of Islam is its preservation of an integral view of the Universe. Islam – like Buddhism and Hinduism – refuses to separate man and nature, religion and science, mind and matter, and has preserved a metaphysical and unified view of ourselves and the world around us . . .'[8]

Not surprisingly, the response to this speech in the Islamic world was ecstatic. Newspapers across the Middle East reprinted the speech in full while commentators on radio and television dissected its meaning with enthusiastic conviction. The leaders of the four Gulf states he visited offered him their gratitude and praised him for his 'understanding and wisdom'. In an unprecedented gesture, the King of Saudi Arabia did not summon the Prince to his own palace but, instead, paid political homage to him by attending on him at the guest-house which had been set aside for the Prince and his party. The reports of his receptions dispatched from the Gulf to the Foreign Office by the British ambassadors to Saudi Arabia, Kuwait and Abu Dhabi reflected the feeling that the empathy in the Prince's speech had helped put Britain's relations with the Gulf onto a new plane of goodwill (a matter of no little importance in diplomatic and economic terms).

With the exception of the *Financial Times* (whose correspondent had accompanied the Prince on his tour), the British media gave scant coverage to this achievement. As with so many of his engagements, a trip by the Prince to the Gulf was deemed too insignificant to merit extended coverage, too routine, too repetitive, too banal. Even on those occasions when his engagements were given attention, they were frequently placed in a context which had been pre-ordained by newspaper editors as the Prince's attempt to 'rehabilitate' himself after his separation from the Princess, regardless of the fact that the density of his official programme had hardly varied for more than a decade.

Those public events, routinely listed day after day in the Court Circular, did not include the many hours he spent each week on the telephone or writing letters to promote the variety of causes to which he had put his name and given his commitment.* Nor had he ceased to chivvy and harass government ministers. During 1993, in separate meetings with the Environment Secretary, John Gummer, the Agriculture Minister, Gillian Shephard,† the Employment Secretary, David Hunt,‡ and the Trade Minister, Richard Needham, he pressed the causes of the environment, organic farming, the long-term unemployed, and the need for greater collaboration to exploit royal visits overseas. In the latter case, the Prince confided his frustration to a journalist from the *Financial Times* in an off-the-record briefing and then reiterated the point publicly, saying, 'I've tried in the past to bring all the different parties together from the Foreign Office, the British embassies, the Department of Trade and Industry, to work out how we can make a particularly British impact in any country that I visit . . . but it's very difficult to do it.'[9]

In the middle of October 1993, exercising for himself 'the right to be consulted, the right to encourage, the right to warn' ascribed by the Victorian commentator Walter Bagehot to the sovereign and extended

---

* Up-to-date details of the work of the many organisations with which the Prince is associated are given in Appendix I on pages 567–75.

† In July 1994, Shephard was replaced as Agriculture Minister by William Waldegrave. She took on the post of Minister of Education.

‡ In July 1994, Hunt was replaced as Employment Secretary by Michael Portillo. Hunt became Chancellor of the Duchy of Lancaster.

by informal convention to the Prince of Wales, he wrote to the Prime Minister, covering as usual a range of issues about which he had doubts and questions – 'a few of the points', as he would put it, 'I would like to raise with you when we next meet.' His tone was rarely combative and he was careful to avoid any expression which might be interpreted as a statement of political dogma, but in his self-deprecatory style – which his own staff labelled 'art-naive' – he commented, in this case, on the contentious debate in the media about the public services:

> It seems to me so incredibly sad to hear people nowadays denigrating those whose careers are in public service as people having 'jobs for life' or who are somehow 'wasting tax-payers money' . . .[10]

The Prime Minister replied, welcoming his letter and making it clear to the Prince that he agreed with him about the importance of public services to which the Prince had long been unambiguously committed.

The extent to which the Prince has had any impact on the evolution of policy is impossible to gauge, but within the political establishment it always became known when he 'had a view', and his opinions were by now regarded invariably as a matter of more than passing interest. For his part, the Prince had convinced himself that to refrain from involvement at this level and in this form would be a dereliction of duty that he could not countenance.

With this sense of duty persistently overlooked by an indifferent media, and in the wake of the bombardment he suffered at their hands at the end of 1993, he left for Australia at the start of his twenty-fifth anniversary year without great optimism. He had been ambivalent about the tour from the moment when it was first mooted twelve months earlier. He had no desire to become embroiled in the sharpening debate about the future of the monarchy in Australia (a matter on which he was, in any case, agnostic), but he knew that if he were to visit the country it would be impossible to remain above the fray. He could hardly stay silent about what was the central constitutional issue, but he was aware that any intervention he might make would be open to acrimonious misinterpretation by one side or the other. He had nothing to gain but much to lose.

However, given that the initial idea for the visit had come from Australia, it was difficult to refuse the formal invitation which followed without appearing faint-hearted or churlish – and if leaked to the media, such a refusal would certainly be so interpreted by the Australian public. After long discussions with his advisers, the Prince decided in principle that it would be wiser to accept than to reject the invitation which duly arrived from the Australian Prime Minister, Paul Keating, in June 1993, proposing dates in late February and early March 1994. In July, the Prince replied accepting the invitation but advising that he could only find an appropriate gap in his diary during early February as he was already committed to other engagements during the period proposed by Keating.

In August 1993, Richard Aylard flew to Sydney to take soundings about the visit, where it soon emerged that the premier of New South Wales hoped that the Prince would attend the celebration of Australia Day* on 26 January in Sydney. This also suited Aylard, who recognised that Sydney would provide the best possible platform for the Prince from which to deliver his keynote speech about the monarchy. At the federal capital in Canberra, the reaction from Keating's office to this suggestion was markedly cool. After a sharp but inconclusive negotiation involving the officials from New South Wales and the federal government, Aylard returned to London without settling the dates but with a draft programme which assumed the Prince's presence in Sydney on Australia Day.

Early in September, it emerged that there were doubts in Canberra about the advisability of the Prince attending Australia Day in Sydney (at what would be a huge celebration attracting many hundreds of thousands of people); the anxiety was apparently that his presence might provoke anti-monarchist demonstrations. The Prince's advisers (both official and unofficial) were adamant that the risk of a demonstration was slight, while some of them suspected that the real reason for Canberra's reluctance to welcome the Prince on Australia Day was the fear that it would provoke an upsurge of public feeling in favour of the monarchy. The Prince made it clear that he would prefer to face the risk of demonstrations than to miss the national celebrations of a country for which he had such affection.

A further attempt to dissuade the Prince took the form of the none too subtle advice that if he were to insist on attending, his presence

---

* Australia Day marks the anniversary of British settlement in the former colony on 26 January 1788.

might not only provoke demonstrations and counter-demonstrations, but would reflect poorly on the Prince and on the monarchy. This, too, was given short shrift by St James's. In the end, the issue was settled during Keating's visit to Balmoral on 18 September, when he made it clear he was looking forward to the Prince's visit on the dates originally proposed by the Prince's office: the Prime Minister had clearly come to the conclusion that there was more to be lost than gained from impeding the heir to the throne from attending Australia Day.*

The Prince arrived in Sydney exhausted. On the plane, he had worked on the draft of what was intended to be the centrepiece of his visit, a speech in which he had resolved to elaborate on the Queen's view (which she had imparted to Keating at Balmoral) that the future of the monarchy was for the people of Australia to decide and not for the monarchy to influence. The speech was to be delivered before an audience of 1,500 people at the end of Australia Day, and would be followed by a programme which had been devised around his own interests rather than a dusted-off package compiled on traditional lines. At the end of his first full day in Sydney, the eve of Australia Day, he walked across from Admiralty House, where he was staying, to the Prime Minister's residence next door for an evening drink.

He was much taken by the friendliness of the Keatings and their four 'very polite and well-mannered children'. Although Keating had a reputation for ruthlessness and was, as the Prince had already discovered, 'a great exponent of the "art" of the monologue', he was relieved to discover that they were 'kindred spirits as regards questions of urban design, architecture and aesthetics'.† They also found themselves in accord about the need at the very least to maintain the links between the Crown and Australia through the sovereign's role as head of the Commonwealth,

---

* After the transmission of the ITV documentary, *Charles: The Private Man, The Public Role*, in which the author referred briefly to this contretemps, a spokesman for the Australian Prime Minister denied all knowledge of this episode. In this case, it must be presumed that officials in Keating's private office were acting on their own initiative, without his authority.

† Later, the Prince and Keating met the Prime Minister's Task Force on Urban Design, the members of which cross-questioned the Prince about his own efforts in Britain. As a result of that meeting, the Prince offered to co-operate with them via his Urban Villages Group and his Institute of Architecture.

even if, as Keating intended, Australia were to become a republic. The Prince noted, 'I have always believed that if Australia did become a republic at some stage in the future it would not prejudice the friendly relationship between the Sovereign and many Australians.'[11]

On Australia Day itself, the Prince crossed the bay to Darling Harbour where, accompanied by the governor of New South Wales, the premier and the mayor, he sat on a dais in front of a vast crowd while they sang patriotic songs. He described what happened next in his diary of the tour which he wrote on the way back to London:

> At one dreaded point I had to stand up, and as I thought, present two prizes to the schoolchildren of the year and then 'say a few words'. I stood there, feeling rather stupid as the audience politely clapped and wondering why no-one was coming forward to receive their prize. No-one in sight, and still I stood there, cursing the organisers under my breath . . . when suddenly, a man leapt out of the crowd to the right and started running flat out towards the dais, firing a pistol as he ran. Initially I imagined that this must be part of the proceedings and then I thought it must be one of the prize winners who was particularly keen to receive his trophy! My ruminations were then abruptly terminated as I was barged across the stage by my policeman just as this demented man crashed in a charging heap on the floor, having tripped on the edge of the dais or caught himself on the invisible plastic lectern. While I was resisting efforts to remove me from the stage a very large number of policemen, premiers and officials of all sorts piled on top of the unfortunate Cambodian person who vanished under a struggling heap of bodies.[12]

In contrast to the Prince's laconic account, others who reported the moment were horrified. 'For a few seconds I thought I was witnessing the assassination of the Prince of Wales,' wrote one of the cooler journalists. 'It happened with terrifying speed – the whole incident lasted a bare 15 seconds . . . Prince Charles looked in my direction as the man ran directly between us. He had a bewildered look but showed no fear or panic.'[13] A guest sitting on the platform was quoted as saying, 'As it happened I thought "Oh! My God, it's Kennedy all over again." I put my hands to my face but couldn't even scream.'[14]

The assailant was David Kang, an Australian student of Cambodian extraction who wanted to draw attention to the plight of the 'boat people' in Australia, and the weapon in his hand was revealed to be a starting pistol.* Nonetheless, as the television images flashed around the world, viewers were struck by the *sangfroid* displayed by the Prince, who did not flinch or move until his personal protection officer, Colin Trimming, shoved him unceremoniously aside to get between him and his attacker. The Prince's reaction to the praise that was heaped on him was characteristic:

> When asked later how I managed, seemingly, to keep so 'cool', I recounted the story of when I was charged by an elephant in the Aberdare mountains in Kenya years ago. I remember the elephant crashing out of the bush, trumpeting wildly and with its ears spread out and trunk extended. I was so amazed by the suddenness of it all that I was rooted to the spot and unable to make my legs respond to any signals from the brain. Consequently I stood my ground and the elephant was so taken aback by my not running away that its charge was reversed and it slunk away into the bush again. Everybody came up and said how brave I'd been and how I never flinched etc.! The case of the galloping Cambodian was somewhat similar but the great thing was to appear unruffled after the incident.[15]

Later that evening, with many Australians still in some shock at the thought of what might have been, the Prince delivered the speech that had been intended to take the headlines the following day. 'It was not the ideal environment in which to speak,' he noted, 'as everyone was chatting away over glasses of champagne and most of them were hidden from my view as the vast concourse we were in (like an airport lounge) went round a corner.' Once he began to speak, however, his audience fell silent:

> It is perhaps not surprising that there are those who would wish to see such a rapidly changing world reflected by a change in Australia's

---

* On 25 February 1994, the Australian government dropped firearms and assault charges against the twenty-three-year-old Kang, but filed a new charge of using threatening behaviour. At that time, Kang was out on bail under psychiatric observation.

institutions. And perhaps they're right. By the very nature of things it is also not surprising that there are differing views: some people will doubtless prefer the stability of a system that has been reasonably well-tried and tested over the years while others will see real advantages in doing things differently. The point I want to make here, and for every-one to be perfectly clear about, is that this is something which only ¬you – the Australian people – can decide.[16]

Declaring that it was the sign of a mature and self-confident nation to debate these issues and to use the democratic process to re-examine the way Australia wanted to face the future, he added, 'Whatever course you finally decide upon, I can only say that I will always have an enormous affection for this country. I can't help it.'[17]

In the months leading up to the Prince's visit, the republican debate had been edged by rancour on both sides. The effect of his intervention may not have been to influence the outcome but it indubitably cooled the political temperature. The country remained evenly divided; likewise, the uncertainties about Keating's intentions – about the consti-tutional form of republic he favoured, the procedure for determining the issue, and his proposed timetable for ending the formal link with the monarchy – were not resolved, although by the summer of 1994, it was still widely assumed that Australia would eventually assert its own iden-tity in the form proposed by Keating. However, all passion at the prospect seemed to have evaporated. By carefully withdrawing the monarchy itself from any participation in the debate, while stressing his abiding affection for the country and its people, the Prince had managed to deprive the protagonists of political oxygen. It had been a carefully calculated speech which further enhanced his reputation not only in Australia but in Britain as well, where those close to him knew that he had spoken from the heart. When he talked of the issue being for the 'people' to decide, he expressed a deeper conviction about the broad principles of a constitutional monarchy than the context suggested. Though he did not trumpet the thought, the prospect of inheriting the throne of a nation in acrimonious dispute about the monarchy was dispiriting. He was very well aware that if a monarchy survives only by the consent of the people, it flourishes only with their goodwill.

CHAPTER
TWENTY-EIGHT

———◆———

A t the start of the nineties it became fashionable to suppose that 'a great debate' about the monarchy was afoot. Against the harsh backdrop of a deepening recession, this opinion gained momentum. A spate of books, pamphlets and articles, some malevolent, some hortative, argued with varying degrees of conviction that the House of Windsor was approaching the point of no return and that the days of the monarchy were therefore numbered. These iconoclasts drew inspiration from a variety of weathervane indicators that seemed to support their own animosities or predilections.

In particular, the grievances of the electorate were thought to be compelling evidence; the resentment of those whose material aspirations had been dashed against the rock of economic mismanagement was deep and infectious. The experience endured by the victims of the recession, who had lost jobs, homes and dreams, frightened those who suspected that they might be next and distressed those who had the sensitivity to empathise with their plight. The avidity of the eighties, when fortunes were made overnight by computer-gamblers and property sharks who dressed in formal suits and loud ties, began to seem tawdry. The low reputation of the politicians who had presided over the 'economic miracle' that never happened fell even further, and the institutions they represented as legislators (which had already been battered by the stridencies of Thatcherism) seemed, to the popular mind, alarmingly incompetent and irrelevant.

Trapped in the glare of this atavism, the monarchy seemed suddenly overblown and lavish; too grandiose for a Lilliputian generation. The frivolous behaviour and extravagant style of one or two of the minor royals irritated a large proportion of the public, who became increasingly susceptible to tabloid jeremiads about the cost to the public purse of the royal train, the royal flight, the royal yacht and the royal exemption from taxation – the 'trappings' of monarchy, as the critics described them. The failure of the marriages of three of the four children of the sovereign finally began to expose the illusion of half a century that the role of the monarchy could be defined in terms of the character of the current generation of royalty; but the re-emergence of the distinction between the two did little at first to alleviate the travails of either.

The populist critics of the House of Windsor were easy to differenti-ate from the radicals, who cared less about the cost of the monarchy and the shortcomings of the royal family than about what they regarded as an outmoded and redundant institution that had long hampered progress and self-realisation. Some of them appeared to believe that Britain's rel-ative decline since the Second World War could be in large measure ascribed to the imperial nostalgia and national self-delusion that, for them at least, the monarchy seemed to represent. Among those who wished to see the hereditary monarchy replaced by an elective presidency were constitutional reformers who believed that Britain's governing institutions were both ramshackle and anachronistic. In the search for a modernised democracy appropriate to Britain's place in the European Union, they sought a set of wide-ranging reforms, including the aboli-tion of the House of Lords in favour of an elected upper chamber and the introduction of proportional representation, all within the framework of a written constitution, a Freedom of Information Act and a Bill of Rights to guarantee the freedom of the individual from the depredations of an over-mighty state. For many, the existence of an overarching monarchy at the apex of an outmoded establishment was incompatible with their modernising vision. Only a presidency, duly elected by the people (either by universal suffrage or by Parliament), would adequately represent the aspirations and the values of every British citizen.

In the royal dog days of the *annus horribilis*, the proponents of consti-tutional reform basked in the unaccustomed glare of popular curiosity. Television programmes mounted special debates in which the intellectual cogency of the radicals vied for attention with the *aperçus* of gossip columnists and 'royal-watchers'. Even *The Times* allied itself with Charter 88, the most prominent group campaigning for reform, to sponsor a debate in May 1993 entitled 'The Monarchy, the Constitution and the People', at which protagonists from across the spectrum addressed the issue with some reason and much passion before a participating audience of 500 people. Yet, despite the gravitas of some of the argument, despite the hyberbole of much of it, and despite a host of apocalyptic soothsayers off-stage, the national debate fizzled and sputtered but failed to ignite. Those heretics who had dared to hope that they might kindle the spirit of republicanism across the nation discovered that the British people were generally unmoved. Those who cared to look at the opinion polls saw that in the year of the Prince's investiture, 16 per cent (according to a survey by NOP[1]) favoured the abolition of the monarchy; twenty-five years later, as the Prince celebrated that anniversary, the figure (according to Gallup) had fallen to 12 per cent.*

This popular disposition in favour of the monarchy is frustratingly familiar to the most serious advocates of the republican cause, who reserve their most scathing criticism for the shallow and patronising anti-monarchism which spices the gossip of the metropolitan intelligentsia. Those who affect to find the monarchy a vulgar distraction, and the royal family faintly ridiculous, irritate the genuine radicals by failing to appreciate the symbolic authority and residual power of the sovereign. Thoughtful republicans and thoughtful royalists are in this respect at one: that to abolish the monarchy would be to unravel the threads of a vast and intricate tapestry woven over centuries of political and social evolution; that to contemplate a reformation would be so daunting and so time-consuming that in a functioning democracy it could only be

---

* A representative sample of 1,000 adults was asked, 'Which of these three statements comes closest to your own view?' and responded thus: (1) The monarchy and the royal family should stay pretty much as they are now – 29 per cent; (2) the monarchy and the royal family should continue to exist but should become more democratic and approachable, rather like the monarchy and royal family in the Netherlands – 54 per cent; (3) the monarchy should be abolished and replaced by a non-executive president like the ones they have in some continental countries – 12 per cent. (Gallup, May 1994.) In a MORI poll in January 1994, 17 per cent of the sample favoured abolishing the monarchy, 1 per cent higher than NOP's 16 per cent in 1969.

accomplished with the overwhelming support of a radicalised electorate.

That support has been lacking. Though the Queen's subjects have grumbled at the cost of the monarchy, debated whether the Queen was too remote or not remote enough, discussed the competing attributes of each member of the royal family, and been shocked, saddened and in some cases titillated by their private miseries, very few of them have begun to contemplate an alternative constitutional structure. The appeal of the monarchy springs from a variety of sources. For some, it merely provides the least worst way of producing a head of state, better than a college of cardinals and preferable to the election of a superannuated politician. For them, the intricate uncertainties that surround the royal prerogative do not represent a failure of democracy but the triumph of pragmatism over ideology. They do not detect in the royal prerogative (the residual authority of the sovereign over the dissolution of Parliament or at the emergence of a hung Parliament) or in her right to a weekly audience with the Prime Minister, or, indeed, in the existence of the Privy Council, a conspiracy by the establishment to frustrate the freedoms of the subjects of the Crown. They recognise instead an evolution of power and responsibility which may be superficially ornate and self-regarding, but which, by comparison with other states, is remarkably free of corruption. They might argue (like Peter Hennessy, the professor of government at Birkbeck College, University of London) that the prerogative should be more 'transparent', but the knowledge that the entire panoply is answerable to Parliament and thence to the will of the people satisfies most British pragmatists that in this nation a constitutional monarchy provides the least inadequate form of democratic governance.

However, the strength of feeling in favour of the monarchy runs in a deeper current than such pragmatism. A sense of history and the pull of tradition, however vulgarised by false sentiment and metaphorical grease-paint, still draws millions of people to the monarchy; and closely linked to this is a widespread need for continuity and stability, the reassurance provided by the hereditary chain that links one generation with another, and which is symbolised by a monarchy that can trace its roots back to mediaeval England and beyond, a reminder that the past is not another country. For some, there is the delight in ceremony, in the pageantry of Trooping the Colour and State Openings of Parliament that, with processions and bands and uniforms, allows pride and nostalgia to be wrapped unashamedly around the Union Jack, when any subject of the

Crown may share an experience of tribal unity that transcends social class and political allegiance.

It is possible to dismiss the sentiments in favour of tradition, continuity and ceremony that unite millions of people under the Crown as jejune or enfeebled. This is not only patronising but misses the point that these millions are free-thinking citizens, and yet owe deference to the monarchy; that even when they are locked into political, economic or social conflict with each other, the monarchy contrives still to symbolise the values and the assumptions which ultimately unite them in one nation. It is because so many millions of people clearly owe this residual allegiance to a monarchy that is above the clash and chatter of party politics that – despite the alarums of the early nineties – for the foreseeable future the throne will surely be available for the Prince of Wales and his heirs to inherit.

It is not a prospect to which the Prince has paid close attention. For more than a quarter of a century, he has lived under the shadow of the peculiar fate to which the heir to an hereditary throne is in thrall: knowing that at any moment he might become King Charles III, or that it may never happen at all. He has solved what would otherwise be a quandary by ignoring it much of the time. Nor is he eager to discuss the prospect; even in private he is loath to explore the future of the monarchy in case he should be misinterpreted as offering criticism of the Queen or lest he should make any commitment now that may seem inappropriate later. Yet he knows that the monarchy has survived by adapting and he freely acknowledges that his sovereignty would be different from that of his mother:

> I find myself born into this particular position . . . All I do as Prince of Wales is to make the most of it as I see it. It hasn't been perhaps as other occupants of this position have seen it; I have groped my way to how I feel about it . . . Likewise, if at some stage in the distant future I was to succeed my mama then obviously I would do my best to fulfil that next role. But it's very difficult to speculate myself about how I would function in that role . . . Sometimes you daydream about the sort of things you might do . . . I think you could invest the position with something of your own personality and interest but obviously within the bounds of constitutional propriety . . .[2]

In the nadir of 1992, in the absence of any evidence (and in defiance of the truth), the media speculated variously that the Prince intended to surrender his prerogative and retire to Italy, or, alternatively, that he was frustrated by the Queen's refusal to abdicate in his favour. There was no truth in either speculation. Not once, even in moments of despair over his personal life and the media coverage of it, did he seriously contemplate the surrender of what he has always thought to be an inescapable duty; nor has he ever favoured abdication. Those with any understanding of the recent history of the monarchy know that the very word 'abdication' is anathema to the royal family: it not only reeks of crisis and failure, but it denies the fundamental assumption of an hereditary institution.

In the meantime, the Prince enjoys the freedom which he knows would be curtailed once he became sovereign, when his life would be circumscribed by constitutional precedent and convention. Although he does not push the parallel very far, he cites Shakespeare's *Henry IV, Part II*, in which a carefree and dilettante Prince Hal is transformed into Henry V and at once adopts a gravity of demeanour and outlook in character with the burden of authority suddenly placed on his shoulders. Prince Charles is far more aware of the prospective burdens of kingship than its pleasures. He quotes with feeling from Henry V's soliloquy before the Battle of Agincourt:

> Upon the king! Let us our lives, our souls,
> Our debts, our careful wives,
> Our children, and our sins, lay on the king!'
> We must bear all. O hard condition!
> Twin-born with greatness, subject to the breath
> Of every fool, whose sense no more can feel
> But his own wringing! What infinite heart's ease
> Must kings neglect that private men enjoy!
> And what have kings that privates have not too,
> Save ceremony, save general ceremony?[3]

The Prince is in earnest when he says:

People may say this is an old-fashioned concept but I feel very strongly that there is an enormous weight of expectation which can be very difficult to come to terms with. And it is even more difficult in this day and age. But I have always been brought up to feel that one had a particular duty to this country and to the people of this country, to mind about it, which I do intensely. And whether the monarchy is an absolute monarchy or a quasi-absolute monarchy as in those days, or the monarchy of today, that attitude is the same . . . The difficulty is most of the time not feeling that one is worthy of it, inevitably.[4]

More by intuition than calculation, the Prince has personally contrived a significant shift in the role of the monarchy. Though he is still nostalgically attracted to the mystique which once surrounded the institution, he is aware that the veil has been parted and that much of the magic has already escaped. Knowing that what has been lost of this cannot be recovered, he has in any case been drawn towards a remarkably utilitarian answer to a question that would never have been asked before the disappearance of deference but has since become commonplace: what is the use of a modern monarchy? His answer has taken the form of an intense and personal involvement in a range of major national and international issues that overlap one another to embrace the concerns of many millions of those who would one day, in formal terms, be his subjects.

He has been scoffed at for this. There are those who believe that he has arrogated to himself a status that he does not deserve; that with little learning and much condescension he has pontificated about too much for too long; and that he has usurped his proper role by delivering himself of anachronistic and often antediluvian opinions when he would better serve the nation by being seen a little and heard even less. This opinion has often been expressed with stentorian vigour, especially by those who have been stung by the lash of his polemic, but it has not proved very persuasive.

An alternative opinion is that, by the age of forty-five, his achievements have been not only remarkable but beneficial. He has made hundreds upon hundreds of speeches, scores of which have certainly reverberated more than he might have hoped or feared; he has also adopted, created, supported and galvanised a host of organisations established to advance those concerns. In areas profoundly affecting the fabric of the nation, he has not only helped to shape the debate but immersed himself in it. His sustained involvement in issues relating to the environment, architecture

and unemployment has played a part in the evolution of policy and practice at the national and at the local level. By reaching out not only towards
Middle England but to the disadvantaged and, particularly, to the ethnic
minorities, he has – without any effort at self-promotion – quietly participated in the life of all the nation. In so doing, he has, according to this
perspective, modestly articulated a practical and symbolic purpose for
the monarchy of tomorrow.

He has also been swifter than some courtiers (and, indeed, successive
governments) to adjust to the financial implications for the monarchy of
Britain's relative decline. He is irked by overblown headlines about the
royal family's wealth and the barely suppressed charge that the household
runs a gravy train for royal flunkies* but he is well aware that this kind of
criticism is unlikely to fall away. He was in the forefront of the internal
debate about taxation and he has expressed his doubts about whether in
the next generation the institution could really accommodate so many
'minor' royals on public duty. If public opinion shifts further in favour of
a scaled-down monarchy, it is not hard to imagine that, as sovereign, he
would be swift to respond; the thought of fewer palaces run by a much
smaller household may not be enticing to him, but the Prince is quite
capable of accommodating himself to that prospect if that is what the
nation were to want.

Following the Prince's separation from the Princess of Wales, some commentators wondered less about his 'fitness' to inherit the Crown than
about the constitutional implications for the heir to the throne of divorce
and of remarriage. Speculation about the Prince's (or the Princess's)
intentions in relation to both possibilities has been, and would be, no
more than conjecture, but the constitutional position merits clarification.
In statutory terms, nothing stands in the way of a divorcee inheriting the
Crown; but the constitution is as much a matter of convention as statute.

---

* On 7 September 1994, a report of the All-Party Public Accounts Committee disclosed that all but eight of the 285 apartments at five palaces (Buckingham Palace,
  St James's Palace, Windsor Castle, Kensington Palace and Clarence House) are
  occupied by officials or used as 'grace and favour' residences for former members
  of the household, who pay rents significantly below market value. The Committee
  urged that the household should account for the £20 million it receives from the
  Exchequer each year to the National Audit Office.

As Vernon Bogdanor* has observed, 'It is precisely because the conventions of the constitution depend ultimately upon the state of public feeling that it is so difficult to determine with certainty at any one time what they actually are. Many conventions, indeed, are unspoken rather than explicit.'[5]

The task of establishing public opinion in this context is not, however, a matter of consulting the runes or the opinion polls; it would fall to the Church of England, in the person of the Archbishop of Canterbury, in consultation with others, including the Prime Minister, to assess. They would be obliged to judge the degree to which the accession of a divorcee, and his enthronement at a coronation, would cause dissent or controversy, and whether either would be of such a scale as to threaten the role of the monarch as a force for national unity. As all Christians are enjoined to believe that 'Those whom God hath joined together let no man put asunder', any divorce would be likely to cause them pain and regret, and this is likely to be particularly true in the case of the prospective Supreme Governor of the Church (although two members of the royal family, Princess Margaret and the Princess Royal, have both divorced without causing more than a mild tremor in public opinion). However, as the Archbishop of York pointedly noted following the separation of the Prince and Princess of Wales, 'the monarch is Supreme Governor of the Church by virtue of being the Sovereign: there is no other legal requirement.'[6] Moreover, the Church has come to accept that where a marriage has irretrievably broken down, a divorce may well be in the best interests of the couple, and particularly of the children; the Archbishop of Canterbury, clearly responsive to public sentiment in a nation where almost fifty per cent of marriages now end in divorce, has publicly said as much.

In these circumstances, it may be presumed that the Archbishop would take the view that although a small minority of Christians would feel a divorced person to be inherently unfit to be monarch, a substantial majority would understand that even the most dedicated and conscientious individuals can find themselves trapped in a broken marriage; and that, even for the Supreme Governor of the Church, divorce

---

* Reader in government at Oxford University, and fellow of Brasenose College, Oxford. His book *The Monarchy and the Constitution* is due to be published by Oxford University Press in 1995.

may be the better of two evils. Given the Prince's manifest dedication to public duty and his commitment to his children, there is no evidence to suggest that the Archbishop of Canterbury (or any likely successor) would seek to inhibit the formal accession and coronation of the Prince of Wales as King of England.

Were the Prince to be divorced and of a mind to remarry, very similar criteria would apply, although the judgement would be even more delicate. Under the Act of Settlement (1701) the Prince is barred from marrying a Roman Catholic, and under the Royal Marriages Act (1772) he cannot marry without the permission of the sovereign. Assuming these conditions were to be satisfied, a senior member of the royal family would normally apply to the Archbishop of Canterbury for a marriage licence. However, it is only in exceptional circumstances that a priest in the Church of England will grant a marriage licence when the applicant's former spouse is still alive.* However sympathetic the Archbishop might be in pastoral terms, it would clearly seem invidious to grant a marriage licence to the heir to the throne when it is regularly denied to other members of the Church in similar circumstances. It is not inconceivable that attitudes towards this ruling will shift; otherwise, the Prince of Wales could follow his sister's example and marry in a Scottish church. Nor is there reason to suppose that the Archbishop of Canterbury would wish to withhold the offer of a service of blessing in an English church following such a consecration. Although this might arouse controversy in the Church, the attitude of Lambeth Palace towards the remarriage of the heir to the throne would once again be influenced, if not determined, by the prevailing state of public opinion. Perceptions and expectations both of the marriage vow and of the Prince are susceptible to change, but it cannot be fanciful to suppose that were the Prince and Princess to divorce, the overwhelming majority of the British public would wish both of them to find happiness within marriage to other partners. Were that to be so, there would be no constitutional inhibition against the heir apparent divorcing and remarrying either before or after his accession to the throne.

---

* The Convocation regulations of 1957, confirmed in subsequent debates of the General Synod, express the collective view of the Church that, despite the anguish which may be caused to any individual, this position protects the integrity of the marriage sacrament.

On 29 June, the Prince was the subject of an ITV television documentary, *Charles: The Private Man, The Public Role*,* in which he spoke with candour about himself, his marriage, his infidelity, his aspirations, his beliefs, his role as Prince of Wales and his attitude towards inheriting the Crown. More than fourteen million people (just under 70 per cent of those watching television at the time) saw the two-and-a-half-hour programme and discovered what for many of them was evidently a revelation: that the Prince was thoughtful, sensitive and intelligent, that he had a quick wit and a warm way with all manner of people, that he had a daunting range of commitments, that he was diligent, and that he was driven by a powerful sense of duty and destiny. Afterwards, instant polls conducted by radio and television programmes showed that, in overwhelming numbers, those who had seen the documentary emerged from the experience to regard him in a different and very much more positive light. The Prince's office received more than 6,000 letters of support (and less than fifty of criticism); the national press was deluged with letters in similar proportions; likewise the ITV network and the programme-makers. Momentarily at least, the intensity of this public response had a salutary effect on those tabloid newspapers, the scriptwriters of the royal soap opera, which had long traduced the Prince's character and mocked his purpose to such devastating effect. In more than one tabloid office, there were furious post-mortems as editors and royal-watchers tried to reconcile their carping and censorious coverage of the Prince with their readers' attitudes towards him. Two days after the transmission of the programme, the *Sun*, which had been among the cruellest offenders, trumpeted 'Charles rules OK', and in a characteristically egregious editorial solemnly declared, 'The Prince will be King. The people have spoken.'[7]

For a while it seemed that the media, responsive to its audience, would treat the heir to the throne with more respect and sympathy. However, the market pressures that have driven the tabloids towards titillation and sensationalism are no less insistent; and, while it is possible that future legislation will curb some of the excesses that cause the greatest distress, so that tabloid editors will be less inclined to instruct reporters and photographers to intrude into the private lives of their royal

---

* It may seem invidious for the author to write about a programme in which he was himself involved, but in this context the impact it made cannot easily be ignored.

quarry, it may be presumed that the lies, the half-truths, the innuendoes and the distortions, which have for so long poisoned the script, will persist. As most of the royal family recoil from seeking redress, and as the public cannot be entirely immune to the conjectural malice which frequently passes for journalism in some, if not all, of the tabloids, the reputation of the Prince cannot be secure.

He knows this, but is disinclined to trust transient opinion, however favourable or unfavourable it might be. In his role as Prince of Wales, he has charted a course and shows no signs of allowing himself to be diverted from it by fashion or favour. He welcomes the good opinion of others, but he has been battered enough never to expect it. He has not lost his essential insecurity or self-doubt, but he has discovered the resolve, an inner resource, which helps him to persist; in the process he has gained a greater air of certainty, even an arrogance, that is concealed behind a self-deprecating manner. Paradoxically, he is also modest about his role and pessimistic about his impact. He is able to say that he believes every human soul has good within it, yet in the same breath he says that the world is in a downward phase, that life on earth will get worse before it gets better.

This pessimistic streak means that he is rarely disappointed by setbacks; he may grumble about the folly of those in public life, but he never expects very much from them. When they ignore his arguments, as they frequently do, he is not unduly surprised and only a little resentful; when they listen and adapt, as they have done, he allows himself only the slightest *frisson* of pleasure. The virtue of his pessimism is also that he does not expect any of the organisations which he has established and which he leads to have more than a marginal impact; when they have achieved far more than that he is gratified, but if they achieve little or a scheme fails, his instinct is to find another route to the same objective. He has large ideas but likes to see them realised on a small scale and, for someone who is liberally endowed with romanticism, he is remarkably realistic about the prospect of persuading others to share his visions. 'Seeing is Believing' is the cliché that he has turned into a slogan and then into a policy to combat the scepticism and cynicism of prospective collaborators in all his ventures. His modest expectations allow him a perspective on success and failure which has been crucial in making sense of the indefinite future which as heir to the throne he has inherited.

That future now stretches before him and, at the age of forty-five, in his public life at least, he has little to prove. He has become a consummate performer on the round of royal duty; he embraces 'ordinary' people, those he meets in shopping arcades and factories, youth clubs and hospices, with a charm and humour by which they are visibly affected; he handles his official duties with aplomb; and when he represents the nation abroad, his ambassadorial talents combine a crusading ambition 'to put the Great back into Britain' with the tact required of a royal diplomat. Throughout, he endures the banal and the boring with stoicism; he even manages to fall asleep in public with the air of someone reflecting on higher matters.

Yet if there is little to prove, the Prince is evidently unaware of it. He retains an insistent need to define and to redefine the role which he has created for himself, to shape and to mould the themes which have given it meaning – as if, were he to pause, his self-creation would evaporate and the stage on which he has striven to perform would suddenly lack any floorboards. His aides would like him to slow down, to relax and to pace himself more gently in the years ahead: still to intervene in public and in private, still to stir controversy in the national debate, still to advance his charities, but to engage in all of it at a less hectic and demanding tempo. Their ambition would be for 'a decade of consolidation' in which the Prince is confirmed in the image which they believe he has at last acquired – kind, compassionate, honest, dutiful, thoughtful, engaged and devoted to the common good: the very model, indeed, of a modern monarch. However, it is not at all clear that the Prince will oblige. He is too mercurial, too driven, too frustrated, too easily excited by new ideas, too fundamentally committed to the causes for which he has so often put himself on the line, altogether too intuitively inspired, to succumb easily to the blandishments of even his most influential and devoted advisers.

Yet he may be somewhat tempted to retreat. His appetite for reflection and contemplation which forms so absolute if paradoxical a feature of his character remains; an awareness of mortality is not, in him, pushed to one side, rejected in the rush for achievement. In his lack of material ambition, from which he is protected by every physical comfort, there is what he refers to repeatedly, in Jungian terms, as the 'search' for the inner self, the need to discover the truths of the spirit and of the soul. Mocked for this by those who have not yet discovered that need (which has long been appreciated by the great thinkers, the great writers and the great poets, those who possess creative genius in abundance), he remains an apt and conscientious student of what is 'other', of what does not belong to 'the here and now'. He wants the time to study and to reflect, to 'find a way through the thickets'.[8]

He also has a hunger to be better informed, to read more widely and more deeply than his existing schedule allows. At the moment he dips in and out of a wide range of literature and specialist writing, retaining the gist of the message, using it for the generalisations that form the stock in trade of the public speech, and also to underpin the feeling and the intuition that coalesce to impel him from one pronouncement to another. He is aware of the limitations of his knowledge and that he is not by talent or nature a scholar; yet he remains, to an exceptional degree for his generation, curious about the world. He knows that he can only satisfy that urge for greater understanding with self-discipline and with time; it is much easier, for him as for others, to convince himself that the unforgiving minute must always be filled with deeds and action, those escape routes from the demands of study and learning, although his insecurity, which leads him still to fear the accusation that he is not 'pulling his weight' remains a potent force. Yet in the balance of his life he may be tempted towards more thought and less action.

Then there is his family, and especially his children. His relationship with his parents has never been easy: the gulf of misunderstanding that often exists between the generations has been sharpened by the intense pressures of public life, and the expression of mutual affection does not come easily to any of them. The Prince is eager to establish a lasting relationship with his two sons, and it is ironical but true that as a separated parent he now has more time with his children and to better effect than ever before. He is a private man and organises their time with him privately. At Highgrove or Birkhall (his grandmother's house on the Balmoral estate), he likes to be with them – not all the time, and no more than many fathers, but enough for their relationship to deepen in trust and affection. When he is with them there is almost no formality in the house; they come and go as they please, there is frequent horseplay, and when they are in bed he reads to them before the lights go out.* Like his father, he enjoys teaching them the ways of the countryside, including

---

* In August 1994, Prince Harry was through him discovering the delights of Rudyard Kipling's *Just So Stories*.

those activities which the animal rights lobby abhor; it would seem quite unnatural from his perspective not to teach them how to shoot and how to fish, or, indeed, to allow them to go hunting in due course – not from bloodlust but because it forms part of the historical pattern of life into which he was born and which has become an essential element in his life. He also wants them to share with him a love for music, painting and the theatre. Those who go regularly to see the Royal Shakespeare Company perform at Stratford-upon-Avon know that the Prince is frequently in the audience, and latterly that he has been with his children as well. He has arranged for them to go back stage and to meet the cast, and he sits with them and a group of friends in the theatre restaurant. Other members of the audience are generally scrupulous about respecting the family's privacy. Since he hopes to influence his children towards sharing a growing number of his own tastes, but because he knows these can't be imposed, he looks forward to having more time with them in their teenage years.

As others in a similar predicament have found, his separation from the Princess has brought a measure of relief from the tensions of a broken marriage. In 1994, he is, as his friends and his staff have noticed, a happier man, more relaxed, more confident and far less given to moments of despair. They have seen his sense of humour return, and with it a gaiety of spirit that for several years has too often been stifled by melancholy. He is frequently alone and sometimes he summons them for company, but he rarely seems lost in his solitude. When he is walking at Highgrove or Balmoral, or when he is listening to music or painting or fishing, he seems, to them, more at peace with himself than they have ever known him – as if he were at last discovering more of that harmony which has for so long been his spiritual lodestar.

In the old, at least among the best of them, we are attracted by wisdom and kindliness. This is true of those who have lived on a public stage as well as those who have not. The charlatans, the chatterers and the inconsequential have generally been weeded out, or have faded away, parched from lack of inner nourishment. Those of finer stuff have discovered that life without an awareness of death is existence without meaning, and they turn from material to spiritual preoccupations. They distinguish more carefully what is of enduring value from that which is of passing moment, and focus their minds and pace their days accordingly. For a man of his age, Prince Charles has some of these attributes to an unusual degree. Among his friends there are those who liken him to 'an old soul', not that he is old before his time, but that he shows prematurely that sensitivity of insight and perspective which is associated with wisdom. They exaggerate: he rages too much at the folly of the world to be wise. Yet, to an uncanny degree, he stands outside the age in which he lives, and when he speaks quietly and with gentleness of timeless virtues and the unchanging nature of mankind, it is only the very unwise who dismiss him as an anachronism. And he is kindly, not only to his friends, but to those in trouble and in his general demeanour. Though he can mock and tease and caricature, and though he cannot abide discourtesy (especially from those who have grown brash and insolent with power), he does not knowingly hurt the feelings of others or cause offence to those who lack his advantages of birth, education and wealth.

For that tenderness of nature he is forgiven flaws that otherwise might rankle: the tendency to self-pity, the moments of selfishness and petulance, the impatience, the irritability, and the occasional flare of a hot temper. Those who love him and those who work for him (and among the latter there are also the former) recognise that he has his share of faults, but they are witness to his humility and to his compassion. They know that in him the seeds of wisdom are better nurtured than in many of his contemporaries, most of whom are still too busy trampling over one another for survival to care overly about generations yet unborn. If there is always lingering about him an air of sadness, it springs in part from unbidden nostalgia and in part from a sense of the sorrows which he believes the human race is storing up for itself.

An interim biography is by definition incomplete, an unfinished portrait which ends, as it were, not with a full stop but a colon. In the case of the Prince of Wales, who is hardly in middle age, this truth is particularly glaring. Like the rest of his generation, he has lived through more than four decades of accelerating change; unlike any of them, however, he has been judged according to the constantly shifting attitudes and feelings engendered by that change. To make full sense of a complete life, future historians will have the advantage of perspective on the entire age through which the Prince will have lived, an understanding of what is yet unknown about the evolution of the monarchy, and a detachment from the vicissitudes of judgement that inevitably afflict the contemporary biographer.

For these reasons it is probably premature to draw unambiguous conclusions about the achievement and potential of the Prince of Wales. However, it is not perhaps too fanciful to suppose that future generations will judge that in the latter half of the twentieth century Britain was blessed to have as heir to the throne an individual of singular distinction and virtue.

APPENDIX I

———◆———

The following notes bring up to date (August 1994) the achievements of the various organisations and projects with which the Prince of Wales is associated:

THE PRINCE'S TRUST

The Prince's Trust has grown to the point where it reaches 12,000 individuals each year with a programme of grants and training delivered through a network of 1,400 volunteers. The turnover for 1994 is projected to exceed £10 million.

In 1990, the Prince launched the Prince's Trust Volunteers programme, the latest phase in his passion to encourage service to the community as a means of building individual talent and self-confidence (this first phase took shape with his Community Venture scheme set up almost a decade earlier). The PTV provides young people, in or out of work, with the chance to participate in an intensive sixty-day programme to discover the value of 'team building' and to work on a variety of community projects. With a total 'throughput' of 4,500 young people by 1993, the programme is projected to expand rapidly to involve 25,000 young people a year. After much lobbying by the Prince, the Employment Secretary established an inter-departmental group involving twelve government departments to examine ways in which the government might help to expand the Volunteers programme further and involve its own employees in it; if this develops as expected then the PTV programme will enter the bloodstream of public sector training.

Key aspects of the Volunteers scheme have also been adopted by the Labour Party's Commission on Social Justice, with the result that its proposals for 'Citizen's Service' bear a close resemblance to the objectives and character of the PTV. Although the Prince is still committed to the principle of compulsory community service, he has the satisfaction of knowing that, through the PTV, the principles of voluntary service have seeped into the thinking of the two main political parties in Britain.

THE PRINCE'S YOUTH BUSINESS TRUST

Between 1988 and 1993, the Prince's Youth Business Trust had helped more than 22,000 disadvantaged young people set up their own businesses. With the support of a volunteer network of 5,500 advisers, almost two thirds of these young entrepreneurs were still trading after three years, a number of them with a turnover in excess of £1 million. As the largest organisation of its kind in the world, the PYBT has become a model for similar initiatives in the United States, Canada and India. As a direct result of the Prince's personal interventions in 1993, the Employment Secretary sharply increased the government's commitment to the PYBT by committing £10 million in matching grants (an equal amount being raised from the private sector) to finance a three-year expansion scheme.

THE PRINCE OF WALES' COMMITTEE

After twenty years as chairman of the Prince of Wales' Committee, the Prince still takes overall responsibility for its operations. Since 1971, the Committee has provided £3.2 million in grant aid to 3,533 voluntary groups working on projects to improve the environment of Wales. It now funds some 350 projects each year, operating on a budget of £1.2

million and with a staff of fifteen project officers. The Committee was directly responsible for introducing Environmental Studies into the syllabuses of the Welsh Joint Education Committee examinations. In the summer of 1994, its 'School Landscape' project was to attract 600 children to work on fifteen sites in different parts of the principality.

BUSINESS IN THE COMMUNITY

Business in the Community, the originator of the notion of 'partnership' between business, government and the community, and the progenitor of TECs, has expanded to a membership of 450 companies, including 80 of 'the top 100'. With a staff of 140 (including 40 seconded from other companies), it has a turnover of £5 million, 8 regional offices and 5 campaign teams. Business in the Environment, launched by the Prince in 1989, is linked to some 2,900 companies and 50 environmental networks promoting good practice through environmental management publications for medium and small businesses. 'Opportunity 2000', a campaign to increase the participation of women in the workplace, is supported by more than 250 employers, who between them represent 25 per cent of the British workforce.

SCOTTISH BUSINESS IN THE COMMUNITY

By 1993, Scottish Business in the Community was responsible for 44 Enterprise Trusts, helping to establish almost 17,000 new businesses and creating more than 28,000 new jobs in the process. The total income of these Trusts in 1993 was £13.43 million.

THE BUSINESS LEADERS FORUM

By early 1994, the Business Leaders Forum, which was founded by the Prince in 1990, had held seventeen International Forum meetings, which have involved more than 4,000 business leaders in North America, Latin America, Europe and Asia. In Poland, the Czech Republic and Slovakia, the BLF has now established networks of over 90 business leaders to involve themselves in regeneration through education, training and environmental projects. In St Petersburg, a similar scheme is afoot to help regenerate the cultural and economic life of the city. In a separate initiative, more than 7,000 international hoteliers, responsible for more than two million rooms, have been mobilised to set new environmental targets for their industry worldwide. In the autumn of 1994, as president of the BLF, the Prince is due to launch a new project called 'Inter-City Action', linking community leaders in the United States and other western countries to their counterparts in the developing world to tackle jointly their shared problems of youth unemployment, ethnic minority conflicts, shortages of housing and skills, and environmental degradation.

THE PRINCE OF WALES'S INSTITUTE OF ARCHITECTURE

Towards the end of its second academic year, the Prince of Wales's Institute of Architecture had secured the necessary validations and accreditations to offer professional qualifications and postgraduate degrees. By the summer of 1994, some 150 students from a dozen countries, including those who attended the summer schools, had benefited from the courses offered by the Institute. The Institute has yet to raise the capital needed (£40 million) to secure its long-term future. The architectural magazine *Perspectives*, launched in January 1994, has yet to establish a clear identity or a significant readership but the Summer School, which has prospered in France and Italy from 1989 to 1993, is planning to collaborate with the Academy of Fine Arts in St Petersburg in 1995 in helping to renovate and reconstruct the city.

PATERNOSTER SQUARE

In 1993, six years after his 'Luftwaffe' speech at the Mansion House, the Prince was informed that the Secretary of State for the Environment had approved a planning application for Paternoster Square that incorporated the designs by John Simpson for which the Prince had argued so tenaciously. He wrote to the developers, Paternoster Associates, 'It is a great relief that after all these years of effort and planning there is a chance that this scheme may come to fruition. You can rest assured that I will continue to take a very close interest in the whole project and will no doubt drive you all mad in the process!'[1] Hit by the recession, building work has yet to begin but is expected to start in 1995.

POUNDBURY

At Poundbury, the construction of the first phase of 61 houses (35 for the Guinness Housing Trust, 26 for owner-occupiers) began in 1993. The first Guinness Trust tenants moved in during the summer of 1994; the first seven private houses were under offer. The entire section is expected to have been completed and sold by the end of 1995, by which time the developers, working to the Prince's guidelines, will be marketing much of the next section, which is planned to include more than a hundred houses and flats.

THE PITCHFORD GROUP

A different aspect of the same commitment to Britain's architectural heritage led to the formation in 1993 of what became known informally as the Pitchford Group. Disturbed by the decision of the Heritage Secretary David Mellor to veto a scheme devised by English Heritage and the National Heritage Memorial Fund to buy the Elizabethan mansion Pitchford Manor in Shropshire (which had been put on the market) for the nation, the Prince summoned to Sandringham the most powerful conservationists in Britain. In addition to Jocelyn Stevens, the chairman of English Heritage, and Lord Rothschild, the chairman of the National Heritage Memorial Fund, the group included Lord Shelburne, the chairman of the Historic Houses Association, Marcus Binney, the president of Save Britain's Heritage, and Sir Angus Stirling, the director-general of the National Trust. That meeting led to a private presentation for the Prime Minister, given on behalf of the Pitchford Group by Simon Jenkins (the former editor of *The Times* and a prominent conservationist himself), on the heritage issues at stake in the decay or disposal of private and public properties of national significance.

The Prime Minister was impressed. He has since instigated a change of policy with respect to the sale of government property of historic architectural importance. Especially relevant in the case of the Ministry of Defence, estate agents negotiating the sale of surplus buildings on the government's behalf are now required to accept the 'best' as opposed to the 'highest' bid from private developers, the intention being to protect the national heritage within the framework of a market economy. In addition, led personally by the Prince, the Pitchford Group has lobbied successfully to increase the level of support from the National Lottery for the historically important 'built environment'. As a result, Lottery funds will be available to support the revenue costs of Lottery-funded capital projects.

THE DUCHY OF CORNWALL

By the end of 1993, the Duchy of Cornwall's original scepticism about the virtues of organic agriculture had been somewhat allayed by the fact than the 1,050-acre Highgrove estate had moved into profit and become one of the largest and most admired organic holdings in the country. Also in 1993, after sustained lobbying by the organic movement (reinforced publicly and privately by the Prince of Wales), the Ministry of Agriculture agreed to introduce a five-year incentive scheme to compensate farmers for the transitional costs of converting from a conventional to an organic regime.

In 1992, the Prince formed a charitable company for 'Duchy Originals', organic biscuits made with oats bought mainly from the Highgrove estate. The Prince oversaw their packaging and labelling. This followed the Prince's urge to encourage the Duchy and its tenants to secure 'added value' by marketing their own produce, including cheese and ice cream. 'Even though the Duchy hasn't done anything like this before,' he wrote to the Duchy's secretary David Landale in 1987,

'I believe we could take advantage of the 1992 situation and also create more employment . . .'[2] Initially, the Duchy had severe doubts, but the Prince was insistent. In 1993, 'Duchy Originals' were for sale in more than 300 independent retail outlets, expanding to more than 600 by 1994. Sales were projected to double in 1994 and to double again in 1995. The first exports have been shipped to France, Germany and the USA and negotiations are underway with Ireland, Canada and Japan.

Further products are in preparation including soups and soft drinks. These, however, will not be organic, a decision which grieves those who believed that the Prince would focus on demonstrating that, with imagination and flair, organic growers can compete successfully in the conventional market place. However, the organic produce for these products is not available in bulk, and the financial imperative to build up a broad marketing base means that this aspect of the organic dream has had to be postponed.

COMPLEMENTARY MEDICINE

The Prince's sustained campaign on behalf of the practitioners of complementary medicine bore its first fruit in 1993, when the Osteopathy Act became law. In July 1994, the Chiropractors Act went on to the statute book as well. It is now hoped that a Homoeopathy Bill will be laid before the House in 1995 or 1996. The hostility of the orthodox practitioners, led by the British Medical Association, has already yielded to cautious support for complementary medicine. (In 1993, the BMA published a report which was far more favourable towards complementary medicine than its 1986 report had been. Its focus was on how different therapies can be regulated, and what qualifications their practitioners should have.) In another important move, as president of the Royal College of General Practitioners, the Prince has urged GPs to act as 'gatekeepers', passing their patients, where appropriate, to orthodox or complementary practitioners. During 1994, health authorities in various parts of the country started to put this principle into practice. The Prince's contribution to the acceptance of complementary medicine by the medical establishment is thought to have been crucial by enthusiasts and sceptics alike.

THE PRAGUE HERITAGE FUND

In 1993, the Prince responded personally to a plea from the Czech President, Vaclav Havel, by establishing the Prague Heritage Fund. Identifying three projects in the Czech capital, the Fund set itself the target of raising £700,000 (with the Czech government promising matching funds). The principal source of revenue was to come from a 'concert' weekend in Prague Castle. The Prince wrote (in longhand) to Sir Georg Solti, to performers like Murray Perahia and Dame Kiri Te Kanawa asking them to take part, and also to European heads of state and government to secure their patronage. Originally scheduled for June 1993, the event had to be postponed until 1994, when these performers and the Prague Symphony Orchestra formed the centrepiece of a sponsored weekend which included receptions, a conference (led by the Prince and Havel), fireworks, and Dvorak's *Choral Mass* in St Vitus Cathedral. The concert, which was televised by the BBC, was eventually shown in 30 countries, helping to raise more than £600,000, which added to £200,000 already raised by the Fund, exceeded the initial target by £100,000. By the summer of 1994, the restoration work was in preparation.

THE ROYAL COLLECTION TRUST

In 1993, the Queen appointed Prince Charles to be chairman of the Royal Collection Trust which was formed in the context of her changed tax status. As sovereign, the Queen owns the Royal Collection but effectively holds it in trust for the nation, raising revenue for its conservation from the entrance fees and shops at the Queen's Gallery, Windsor Castle and Holyrood House. Following the 1993 reforms, these receipts, which technically formed part of the Queen's personal income, would – inadvertently – have been subject to tax; as the Trust is now a registered charity, the income from these and similar sources (£10 million in 1993–94) became exempt from any taxation. The Collection possesses some 10,000 paintings, enamels and miniatures, 20,000 drawings, 30,000 watercolours, and 500,000 prints which, in crude size, makes it comparable to the combined collections of the Victoria and Albert Museum, the National Gallery and the Tate Gallery. It is the intention of the Trust (passionately endorsed by its chairman) to make the Royal Collection very much more accessible to the public in Britain and abroad.

APPENDIX II

⸻

On 18 October 1992, the *Daily Express* published an article about Prince Charles headlined 'Charles's rift with the Queen'. The following is an abridged copy of the article, plus a memorandum outlining its inaccuracies, which was given to the paper's editor by Richard Aylard, the Prince's private secretary, shortly afterwards.

CHARLES'S RIFT WITH THE QUEEN
by Elizabeth Grimsditch*

After the most shattering few months of her reign, the Queen is back at work. The summer break which she had hoped would heal so much, has ended. Traditionally, the royals repair to Balmoral to regroup, lick whatever wounds may have been inflicted during the past year and emerge refreshed, to do battle once again.

The Balmoral conferences, held at the start of September, are famous throughout royal circles. Only the family is invited, as, basically, the Queen and Prince Philip tell everyone else in the Firm what is expected of them . . .

. . . And now relations between Charles and the Queen are at an all time low. The Prince snubbed his mother at Balmoral. For most of

⸻

* 'Elizabeth Grimsditch' was a pseudonym for a former *News of the World* reporter.

August he was at Craigowan Lodge, about a mile away. Then he jetted off abroad, went fishing in north Scotland and when he came back
to Balmoral, mid-September, it was for a 24-hour stay. That was to see
King Hussein of Jordan . . .

. . . The King . . . stayed at Balmoral for two hours to talk to the
Prince. Afterwards, Charles then left to see his grandmother at Birkhall
House, 12 miles away. He disappeared a few days later, and came back
only after his mother had returned to London, and then again only to
see his grandmother, who had been unwell all summer . . .

. . . In recent years, Charles has rarely seen his mother privately. He
never calls on her at Windsor, and even when he plays polo there, he
leaves immediately for Highgrove . . .

. . . She has also criticised him for his lack of discipline. He is notorious for the way he reads the red despatch boxes which as heir to the
throne he is supposed to pore over as assiduously as his mother does . . .

. . . He was bitterly conscious that his mother's last Christmas message, when she said she would never abdicate, amounted to a public
vote of no confidence in him . . .

. . . Now, when the Queen needs her family around her, the big
chill between herself and Charles could not come at a worse time. She
has finally been forced to see that the European royals, with their
informal life style, are the monarchs of the future. It is up to Charles
to instigate changes, and he, as the Queen knows too well, can only do
that with Diana by his side.

Richard Aylard's response was as follows:

DAILY EXPRESS ARTICLE
The following points are relevant:

'The Balmoral conferences . . . are famous throughout royal circles.'

These conferences do not exist and are a persistent media myth, as
any real 'insider' knows.

'The Prince snubbed his mother at Balmoral. For most of August he was at Craigowan Lodge.'

The Prince of Wales did not spend even one night at Craigowan Lodge this summer! In August he spent a total of 15 nights at Balmoral, as a guest of The Queen. Once again, a media myth persists due to use of a cuttings library.

'Then he jetted off abroad, went fishing in north Scotland . . .'

In the first half of September HRH spent some time in London and at Highgrove, including taking Prince Harry to Ludgrove school for the first time and carrying out a number of pressing public engagements. He flew to France for 3 days, but did not go to the north of Scotland or fish.

'When he came back to Balmoral . . . it was for a 24 hour stay. That was to see King Hussein of Jordan' and 'The King . . . stayed at Balmoral for two hours to talk to the Prince.'

The Prince of Wales was at Balmoral for six consecutive nights at the time of The King of Jordan's visit on 17th September. The King was actually a guest of The Queen and The Duke of Edinburgh, though HRH was pleased to be present since he knows the King well.

'In recent years, Charles has rarely seen his mother privately.'

During the course of this year HRH has stayed with The Queen for the following periods:

- For almost a month at Sandringham from Christmas Eve to late January.
- Easter weekend at Windsor.
- During Ascot week at Windsor.
- During Holyrood week in Edinburgh.
- For much of August and September at Balmoral.

Are you seriously suggesting that The Queen and The Prince of Wales did not speak privately to each other during these periods?

'He is notorious for the way he reads . . . supposed to pore over as assiduously as his mother does.'

Leaving aside the possibility that this statement is libellous, I suggest you ask one or more Government Ministers, environmentalists or business leaders about the level to which HRH briefs himself on a vast range of subjects. It is certainly true that he often works into the early hours of the morning, but not for the reasons you suggest.

'. . . he was bitterly conscious that his mother's last Christmas message . . . amounted to a public vote of no confidence.'

This is utter nonsense based on an inaccurate statement in a recent book. HRH has always dismissed any suggestion that The Queen might abdicate, because he knows it will not happen and because he would not wish to inherit in such circumstances. HRH is more than content with his current role which gives him the freedom to continue his involvement in a range of subjects, with the intention of making a contribution in several areas of national life, while preparing himself for a future role in which he will be much more constrained.

'It is up to Charles to instigate changes.'
Is it?

(I have made no comment on matters relating to other members of the Royal Family, but no doubt similar errors proliferate in those sections of the text as well.)

Notes

———◆———

The following abbreviations have been used:

C   Prince Charles
RA   Royal Archives
MA   Mountbatten Archives
NJ   Prince of Wales's Naval Journals
FJ   Prince of Wales's Foreign Diaries
CL   Confidential letter
CC   Confidential conversation

PART I

Chapter One (pages 3–14)

1. *Hansard*, 16 November 1948, vol. 458, p. 213.
2. Ibid., p. 212.
3. *Manchester Guardian*, 16 November 1948.
4. *The Times*, 15 November 1948.
5. Dermot Morrah, *To Be A King* (Hutchinson, 1968), p. 8.
6. Princess Elizabeth to Mabel Lander, cited in Morrah, op. cit., p. 80.
7. *Hansard*, 16 November 1948, p. 228.
8. *Hansard*, 16 November 1948, p. 233.
9. Truman to US Congress, 12 March 1947, quoted in Eds. Michael Sissons and Philip French, *Age of Austerity* (Hodder and Stoughton, 1963), p. 105.
10. Cited in Eds. Sissons and French, op. cit., p. 218.
11. John Wheeler-Bennett, *King George VI* (1958), cited in Ziegler, *Crown and People* (Collins, 1978), p. 31.
12. Frances Donaldson, *Edward VIII* (Weidenfeld and Nicolson, 1974), p. 252.
13. Wheeler-Bennett, op. cit., p. 298, cited in Ziegler, op. cit., p. 39.
14. Ibid., p. 42.
15. Ibid., p. 467, cited in Ziegler, op. cit., p. 77.
16. Ibid., p. 247, cited in Ziegler, op. cit., p. 42.
17. Mass Observation, cited in Ziegler, op. cit., p. 81.
18. *The Times*, 15 November 1948.

19. George Bernard Shaw, *The Apple Cart* (Penguin, 1988), p. 77.
20. *Hansard*, 16 November 1948, vol. 458, p. 212.

Chapter Two (pages 15–29)
1. Morrah, op. cit., p. 14.
2. Jonathan Dimbleby, *Richard Dimbleby: A Biography* (Hodder and Stoughton, 1975), p. 239.
3. Mass Observation, cited in Ziegler, op. cit., p. 94.
4. Conversation with C.
5. *Sunday Pictorial*, 22 July 1951.
6. CC.
7. Morrah, op. cit., p. 33.
8. Morrah, op. cit., p. 36.
9. *Daily Telegraph*, 22 February 1954.
10. *Manchester Guardian*, 5 May 1954.
11. Palace to Kaye Webb, 3 December 1973, RA/POW/Articles etc. written by HRH.
12. *Hill House, The History of the Foundation and Growth of the School*, pamphlet, 1993.
13. *Manchester Guardian*, 9 January 1957.
14. *Manchester Guardian*, 10 January 1957.
15. Morrah, op. cit., p. 48.
16. Morrah, op. cit., p. 53.

Chapter Three (pages 30–44)
1. *Leaves from the Journal of our life in the Highlands*, cited in Michael Steed, *Queen Victoria's Scotland* (Cassell, 1992).
2. Ibid.
3. Conversation with C.
4. Queen Victoria, op. cit.
5. Foreword to Edward Peel, *Cheam School from 1645* (Thornhill Press, 1974).
6. *Evening Standard*, 16 August 1957.
7. Peel, op. cit.

8. Morrah, op. cit., p. 59.
9. Conversation with C.
10. Peel, op. cit.
11. *Manchester Guardian*, 3 September 1957.
12. Conversation with C.
13. Ibid.
14. Ibid.
15. C to Mountbatten, 20 November 1956, MA.
16. Douglas Liversidge, *Prince Charles, Monarch in the Making* (Granada), p. 38.
17. Morrah, op. cit., p. 66.
18. C to Mountbatten, 12 October 1957, MA.
19. Mountbatten to C, 9 November 1957, MA.
20. Interview with Tim Heald, *Radio Times, 25–31 July 1981.
21. Conversation with C.
22. *Manchester Guardian*, 28 July 1958.
23. *Daily Telegraph*, 28 July 1958.
24. *The Times*, 28 July 1958.
25. *Manchester Guardian*, 28 July 1958.
26. *Observer*, 10 August 1958.
27. *Daily Express*, 12 February 1962.
28. Conversation with C.
29. Morrah, op. cit., p. 82.
30. CC.
31. Undated, RA/POW Education.

Chapter Four (pages 45–56)
1. C to Mountbatten, 8 June 1958, MA.
2. Undated, RA/POW Education.
3. C to Mountbatten, January 1960, MA.
4. *The Times*, 12 January 1959.
5. CC.
6. CC.
7. CC.
8. CC.
9. Basil Boothroyd, *Philip, An Informal Biography* (Longman, 1971), p. 75.

10. Letter from Geoffrey Fisher, Archbishop of Canterbury, to King George VI, quoted in Boothroyd, op. cit.
11. Boothroyd, op. cit., p. 23.
12. C to Mountbatten, 25 December 1961, MA.
13. CC.

Chapter Five (pages 57–76)
1. *Evening Standard*, 21 March 1957.
2. *Evening News*, 2 November 1960.
3. Conversation with C.
4. *New York Times*, 21 March 1962.
5. Morrah, op. cit., p. 83.
6. Plato, *The Republic*, tr. H.D.P. Lee (Penguin, 1960), Part Seven, Book Five, Section 473, p. 233.
7. Adam, Arnold-Brown, *Unfolding Character, The Impact of Gordonstoun* (Routledge & Keegan Paul, 1962), p. 18.
8. Ibid, p. 18.
9. William Boyd, *School Ties* (Penguin, 1985), p. 11.
10. Ross Benson, *Charles, The Untold Story* (Gollancz, 1993), p. 53.
11. Boyd, op. cit. p. 14.
12. Benson, op. cit., p. 52.
13. Cited by Benson, op. cit., p. 53.
14. Article by Patrick Pelham-Jones (Redbook, USA), quoted in *Daily Sketch*, 19 March 1964.
15. Conversation with Boyd.
16. C, CL, 9 February 1963.
17. Ibid.
18. C, CL, 5 November 1963.
19. C, CL, 8 February 1964.
20. Ibid.
21. Conversation with Ruth Fermoy.
22. Arnold-Brown, op. cit., pp. 43–4.
23. Arnold-Brown, op. cit., p. 44.
24. Boyd, op. cit., pp. 21–3.
25. C, CL, 8 February 1964.
26. Conversation with C.
27. *Daily Mail*, 28 April 1962.
28. *Daily Mirror*, 18 June 1963.
29. *Daily Telegraph*, 20 June 1963.
30. Press statement by Colville, 19 June 1963.
31. Conversation with C.
32. Ibid.
33. Colville to *Time*, cited in Morrah, op. cit., p. 106.
34. C, CL, 8 February 1964.
35. C, CL, 19 November 1966.
36. Cited in Liversidge, op. cit., p. 41.
37. C, CL, 24 November 1965.
38. Conversation with Ruth Fermoy.
39. C, CL, 8 February 1964.
40. C to Susan Hussey, 19 July 1964.
41. Conversation with Eric Anderson.
42. C, CL, 24 November 1965.
43. Conversation with Anderson.
44. Ibid.
45. C, CL, 24 November 1965.
46. C, CL, 9 February 1963.
47. C, CL, 19 July 1964.
48. C, CL, 24 November 1965.

Chapter Six (pages 77–94)
1. Checketts to C, 2 December 1965, RA/POW. Education E1/1/1.
2. Morrah, op. cit., p. 114.
3. CC.
4. Checketts to C, 2 December 1965, RA/POW Education E1/1/1.
5. Murray Tyrrell, official secretary to Governor-General of Australia, to William Heseltine, assistant press secretary to the Queen, 11 December 1965, RA/POW Education E1/1/1.
6. Heseltine to Tyrrell, 21 December 1965, RA/POW Education E1/1/1.
7. Checketts to C, 2 December 1965, RA/POW Education E1/1/1.
8. Tyrrell to Richard Colville, press secretary to the Queen, 18 January 1966, RA/POW Education E1/1/1.

9. C to Mountbatten, 8 March 1966, MA.
10. C, CL, 7 February 1966.
11. Ibid.
12. C to Mountbatten, 8 March 1966, MA.
13. C, CL, 7 February 1966.
14. Ibid.
15. C to Mountbatten, 8 March 1966, MA.
16. C, CL, 1 May 1966.
17. C to Mountbatten, 8 March 1966, MA.
18. C to Patricia Brabourne, 7 March 1966.
19. Conversation with Checketts.
20. C, CL, 1 May 1966, MA.
21. Circular letter signed 'Jean', from Anglican Mission, Dogura, 14 May 1966, RA/POW Education E1/1/1.
22. Essay by C in *Visit to Papua New Guinea*, Geelong Church of England Grammar School pamphlet, May 1966, p. 16, RA/POW Education.
23. Morrah, op. cit., p. 132.
24. Essay by C in *Visit to Papua New Guinea*, op. cit.
25. Ibid.
26. Circular letter signed 'Jean', op. cit.
27. C, CL, 1 May 1966.
28. Checketts to Michael Adeane, private secretary to the Queen, 4 June 1966, RA/POW Education E1/1/1.
29. Message read to press by Checketts, August 1966, RA/POW Education E1/1/1.
30. C to Mountbatten, 16 February 1967, MA.
31. C to Mountbatten, 4 December 1966, MA.
32. Ibid.
33. Conversation with Waddell.
34. Ibid.
35. Ibid.
36. C, CL, 26 January 1967.
37. C, CL, undated, April 1967.
38. C, CL, 10 July 1967.
39. *The Times*, 5 October 1967.
40. C, CL, undated, April 1967.
41. Ibid.
42. C, CL, 10 July 1967.

PART II

Chapter Seven (pages 97–117)

1. Alan Bennett, *Forty Years On*, Act II, cited in Bernard Levin, *The Pendulum Years* (Jonathan Cape, 1970).
2. Mass Observation and NOP, cited in Ziegler, op. cit., p. 127.
3. Lord Altrincham, 'The Monarchy Today', *National and English Review*, August 1957.
4. Ibid.
5. Malcolm Muggeridge, 'No Bicycle for Queen Elizabeth', *Saturday Evening Post*, 19 October 1957, reprinted in Lord Altrincham and others, *Is the Monarchy Perfect?* (John Calder, 1958).
6. Ibid.
7. Morrah, op. cit., p. 139.
8. Mountbatten to C, 23 November 1966, MA.
9. C to Mountbatten, 4 December 1966, MA.
10. Robin Woods to Butler, 10 March 1967, RA/POW Education E1/3 1967.
11. Marrian to Checketts, 5 January 1967, RA/POW Education E1/3 1967.
12. Checketts to Woods, 21 February 1967, RA/POW Education E1/3 1967.
13. *Varsity*, 9 March 1968.

14. Memo William Heseltine to C, 7 September 1967, RA/POW Education E1/3 1967.
15. Note by C on memo Heseltine to C, op. cit.
16. Memo C to Checketts, 20 September 1967, RA/POW Education E1/3 1967.
17. Ann Leslie, 'The Making of A Modern Monarch', *Daily Mail*, 20 March 1974, p. 12.
18. Robin Woods to Denis Marrian, 10 January 1967, RA/POW Education E1/3 1967.
19. Leslie, op. cit.
20. Memo C to Checketts, 18 April 1974, RA/POW/EA/73/28.
21. Mollie Butler, *August and RAB: A Memoir* (Robin Clark, 1992), p. 110.
22. C, CL, 16 October 1968.
23. CC.
24. Conversation with James Buxton.
25. Conversation with Hywel Jones.
26. CC.
27. C to Hugh van Cutsem, 15 November 1967.
28. C to Hugh van Cutsem, 31 January 1969.
29. C to Hugh Van Cutsem, 4 November 1968.
30. C to Hugh Van Cutsem, 1 May 1968.
31. Conversation with Harry Williams.
32. Ibid.
33. Memo C to Checketts, undated, 1968, RA/POW Education E1/3 1968.
34. Memo C to Checketts, 1 July 1967, RA/POW Education E1/2.
35. C to Mountbatten, 25 December 1967, MA.
36. Ibid.
37. C to Patricia Brabourne, 25 December 1967.
38. C to Mountbatten, 25 December 1967, MA.
39. C, CL, 8 July 1968.
40. Mrs Joseph de Bono to Mountbatten, undated, July 1968, MA.
41. C to Mountbatten, undated, July 1968, MA.
42. C, CL, 8 July 1968.
43. C, CL, 14 October 1968.
44. Ibid.
45. Ibid.
46. Ibid.
47. Conversation with Christian Bailey.
48. C, CL, 14 October 1968.
49. 'Prince of Wales Forgets His Lines', *The Times*, 23 February 1970.

Chapter Eight (pages 118–37)
1. BBC Radio 4, 1 March 1969.
2. Permanent under-secretary at Welsh Office to Queen's private secretary, undated, RA/POW/E1/4.
3. Queen's private secretary to permanent under-secretary at Welsh Office, 10 February 1967, RA/POW/E1/4.
4. Cited in Levin, op. cit., p. 159.
5. *The Times*, 19 April 1969.
6. *Daily Telegraph*, 20 April 1969.
7. BBC Radio 4, 1 March 1969.
8. *Daily Sketch*, 13 March 1969.
9. Davies to C, 26 January 1969, RA/POW Education.
10. *Daily Mail*, 21 April 1969.
11. *Guardian*, 22 April 1969.
12. C to Buxton, 23 April 1969.
13. Ibid.
14. Ibid.
15. Conversation with C.
16. BBC/ITV interview, 26 June 1969.
17. Handwritten note on memo Checketts to Duke of Edinburgh, 26 June 1967, RA/POW Education E1/4 1967/8.
18. *Daily Sketch*, 13 March 1969.
19. C to Buxton, 23 April 1969.

20. BBC/ITV interview, 26 June 1969.
21. C to Buxton, 23 April 1969.
22. Conversation with C.
23. Conversation with Checketts.
24. Diary, 31 May 1969.
25. Ibid.
26. University College of Wales to Checketts, 11 April 1969, RA/POW Education E1/4 1969.
27. J.F. Burke to Checketts, 16 April 1969, RA/POW/Investiture.
28. Memo by University of Wales, undated, RA/POW Education E1/4 1969.
29. C, CL, 10 June 1969.
30. Conversation with Heseltine.
31. Memo by Heseltine, undated, RA/POW/Investiture.
32. Ibid.
33. *Daily Mirror*, 25 September 1968.
34. Thomas to Checketts, 24 October 1968, RA/POW/Welsh Investiture.
35. Memo by Owen Edwards, 17 September 1968, RA/POW/Welsh Investiture.
36. BBC Radio 4, 3 July 1968.
37. Ibid.
38. D. Parsons to Secombe, 5 August 1968, RA/POW/Welsh Investiture.
39. Secombe to Checketts, 28 August 1968, RA/POW/Welsh Investiture.
40. *The Times*, 12 June 1969.
41. Ibid.
42. Office for the Investiture of the Prince of Wales to Earl Marshal, 11 November 1968, RA/POW/Welsh Investiture.
43. Conversation with Snowdon.
44. Ibid.
45. Memo by South Wales Constabulary, undated, 1969, RA/POW/Investiture.
46. Diary, 1 July 1969.
47. Ibid.
48. Diary, 3 July 1969.
49. Ibid.
50. Diary, 4 July 1969.
51. Diary, 5 July 1969.
52. Mountbatten to C, 4 July 1969, MA.
53. C to Mountbatten, 11 July 1969, MA.

Chapter Nine (pages 138–54)
1. C, CL, 9 October 1969.
2. Ibid.
3. Draft of speech to honour Gandhi centenary, 21 November 1969.
4. C, CL, 9 October 1969.
5. Diary, 15 July 1969.
6. Ibid.
7. Ibid.
8. Diary, 22 July 1969.
9. Diary, 28 October 1969.
10. Diary, 11 February 1969.
11. Ibid.
12. C, CL, 13 March 1970.
13. Ibid.
14. Ibid.
15. Diary, 10–13 March 1970.
16. Diary, 13 March 1970.
17. Diary, 9 April 1970.
18. Ibid.
19. Ibid.
20. Ibid.
21. Diary, 11 April 1970.
22. Diary, 12 April 1970.
23. Diary, 13 April 1970.
24. John Pilcher to Checketts, 27 April 1970, RA/POW/EA/70/20–21.
25. Diary, 28 April 1970.
26. Diary, 30 May 1970.
27. Telegrams between C and Edward and Katherine Smith, 1 and 2 June 1970, RA/POW/Education E1/3 1969/70.
28. Quoted by Ann Leslie, *Daily Mail*, 20 March 1974.
29. Diary, 30 May 1970.
30. Checketts to Marrian, 29 July 1970, RA/POW Education E1/3 1969/70.

31. RA/POW Education E1/3 1970/1.
32. Diary, 15–20 June 1970.
33. Ibid.
34. Washington Embassy to Checketts, 12 June 1970, RA/POW/EA/70/50/8.
35. Diary, 18 July 1970.
36. Ibid.
37. C to Sir Alec Douglas-Home, 23 July 1970, RA/POW/EA/70/50/8.
38. Diary, 18 July 1970.
39. C to Douglas-Home, 23 July 1970, RA/POW/EA/70/50/8.
40. Edward Smith to C, 7 December 1970, RA/POW/EA 70/104.
41. Speech to The Pilgrims of Great Britain, 8 December 1970, RA/POW/EA/70/104.
42. Diary, 21 July 1970.
43. Diary, 8 October 1970.
44. Diary, 10 October 1970.
45. C, CL, 17 October 1970.
46. Ibid.
47. Diary, 11 November 1970.
48. Ibid.
49. Ibid.
50. Diary, 12 November 1970.
51. Ibid.

Chapter Ten (pages 155–75)
1. Mountbatten to C, 23 November 1966, MA.
2. Prince Philip to C, 26 November (no year given), RA/POW/RNS. R2/2 PART 1.
3. Conversation with C.
4. Memo C to Checketts, undated, RA/POW/Flight training 67/69.
5. Michael Adeane to Checketts, 15 March 1971, RA/POW/AdvdFT F4/3 II.
6. C, CL, 18 March 1971.
7. Ibid.

8. C to Mountbatten, 18 March 1971, MA.
9. Diary, 31 March 1971.
10. C to Hugh van Cutsem, 23 April 1971.
11. Diary, 20 July 1971.
12. Diary, 28 July 1971.
13. Conversation with C.
14. Ibid.
15. C, CL, 1 August 1971.
16. Ibid.
17. C, CL, undated, 1971.
18. C, CL, 23 April 1971.
19. Conversation with C.
20. CC.
21. Memo, Office of the Chief of Naval Staff and First Sea Lord, undated, RA/POW/Naval Service.
22. C to Mountbatten, 24 September 1971, MA.
23. Ibid.
24. CC.
25. Memo C to Checketts, 20 April 1971, RA/POW/Naval Service.
26. Memo C to Smith, 1 August 1971, RA/POW/RNS. R2/3.
27. C to Mountbatten, 1 December 1970, MA.
28. NJ, 5 November 1971.
29. Unsigned memo, undated, RA/POW/Naval Service.
30. Ibid.
31. NJ, 6 November 1971.
32. NJ, 7 November 1971.
33. NJ, 6 November 1971.
34. NJ, 8 November 1971.
35. NJ, 12 November 1971.
36. NJ, 23 November 1971.
37. C to Mountbatten, 18 November 1971, MA.
38. NJ, 28 November 1971.
39. Ibid.
40. NJ, 17–20 January 1972.
41. NJ, 24 January 1972.
42. NJ, 31 January 1972.

43. Ibid.
44. NJ, 9–13 February 1972.
45. Conversation with C.
46. NJ, 13 February 1972.
47. Ibid.
48. NJ, 4 February 1972.
49. Ibid.
50. Ibid.
51. Ibid.
52. NJ, 6–10 March 1972.
53. C to Mountbatten, 11 March 1972, MA.
54. NJ, 6–10 March 1972.
55. Ibid.
56. NJ, 10–13 April 1972.
57. Ibid.
58. NJ, 18 April 1972.
59. NJ, 2–17 May 1972.
60. NJ, 17 May 1972.
61. NJ, 15 June 1972.

Chapter Eleven (pages 176–98)
1. C to Mountbatten, 8 December 1971, MA.
2. C to Mountbatten, 17 July 1972, MA.
3. Mountbatten to C, 13 November 1972, MA.
4. Mountbatten to C, March 1971, MA.
5. C to Mountbatten, 3 April 1971, MA.
6. C, CL, 11/12 March 1970.
7. Diary, 3 October 1971.
8. Diary, 2 June 1972.
9. Diary, 3 June 1972.
10. Diary, 5 June 1972.
11. Philip Ziegler, *Mountbatten* (Fontana, 1990, 2nd edition), p. 675.
12. Ibid., p. 681.
13. Duchess of Windsor to Mountbatten, 9 December 1974, cited in Ziegler, *Mountbatten*, op. cit., p. 681.

14. C to Mountbatten, 11 August 1970, MA.
15. Mountbatten to C, 14 February 1974, MA.
16. C to Mountbatten, December 1972, MA.
17. Memo Captain B.H. Kent, HMS *Mercury*, 25 July 1972, RA/POW/RNS R2/2 PART 2.
18. Rear Admiral I.G. Raikes, Naval Secretary, to Captain J.W.D. Cook, *Minerva*, 17 November 1971, RA/POW/Naval Service.
19. Ibid.
20. CC.
21. Memo from HMS *Mercury*, 25 July 1972, RA/POW/RNS R2/2 PART 2.
22. Raikes to Cook, 17 November 1971, RA/POW/Naval Service.
23. Memo, undated, RA/POW/Naval Service.
24. Report to Douglas-Home, 23 February–19 August 1973, RA/POW/Naval Service.
25. Ibid.
26. Ibid.
27. Ibid.
28. Memo by J.G. Marnham, FCO, 6 October 1972, RA/POW/Naval Service.
29. Report to Douglas-Home, op. cit.
30. Memo from Martin Charteris, Queen's press secretary, to Geoffrey Collins, 12 March 1973, RA/POW/Naval Service.
31. Extract from letter from High Commissioner, Jamaica, 3 April 1973, RA/POW/RNS R2/1.
32. C to Hugh and Emilie van Cutsem, 2 April 1973.
33. Colin McLean, British Ambassador, Bogota, to FCO, 18 April 1973, RA/POW/Naval Service.
34. NJ, 3 April 1973.

35. McLean to FCO, op. cit.
36. Report to Douglas-Home, op. cit.
37. C to Mountbatten, 17 March 1973, MA.
38. C, CL, 27 April 1973.
39. C to Mountbatten, 25 April 1973, MA.
40. C to Brabournes, 22 April 1973.
41. C to Mountbatten, 25 April 1973, MA.
42. NJ, 23 April 1973.
43. NJ, 22 April 1973.
44. C, CL, 27 April 1973.
45. C, CL, 20 May 1973.
46. Ibid.
47. C, CL, 22 June 1973.
48. Memo Mountbatten to Lady Longford, cited in Ziegler, *Mountbatten*, op. cit., p. 681.
49. Mountbatten to C, 8 June 1973, MA.
50. C to Lord Chamberlain, undated, 1973.
51. NJ, 1 June 1973.
52. NJ, 24 June 1973.
53. NJ, 7 July 1973.
54. NJ, 8 July 1973.
55. Memo C to Checketts, 1 July 1973, RA/POW/EA/73/10/3 Independence Celebrations of Bahamas.
56. Ibid.
57. NJ, 9–11 July 1973.
58. NJ, 29 July 1973.
59. C to van Cutsems, 2 April 1973.
60. C, CL, 22 June 1973.
61. NJ, 16 August 1973.
62. NJ, 21 August 1973.
63. NJ, 22 August 1973.
64. NJ, 24–28 August 1973.
65. NJ, 31 August 1973.
66. Report by J. Garner, Captain HMS *Minerva*, undated, RA/POW/Naval Service.

Chapter Twelve (pages 199–224)

1. Memo by Naval Secretary, 21 June 1973, RA/POW/RNS R2/2 PART 2.
2. Ibid.
3. Memo Checketts to C, 25 June 1973, RA/POW/RNS R2/2 PART 2.
4. CC.
5. C to Mountbatten, 16 January 1974, MA.
6. NJ, 3 January 1974.
7. NJ, 21 January 1974.
8. C, CL, 28 February 1973.
9. C, CL, 27 April 1973.
10. C, CL, 22 June 1973.
11. Ibid.
12. Ibid.
13. C, CL, 28 February 1973.
14. NJ, 15 February 1974.
15. NJ, 25 March 1974.
16. NJ, 21 February 1974.
17. NJ, 5 March 1974.
18. Mountbatten to C, 14 February 1974, MA.
19. C to Mountbatten, undated, March 1974, MA.
20. C to van Cutsems, 10 June 1973.
21. NJ, 23 January 1974.
22. Mountbatten to C, 6 January 1973, MA.
23. C to Mountbatten, 18 January 1973, MA.
24. NJ, 7–13 March 1974.
25. NJ, 15 March 1974.
26. NJ, 14 March 1974.
27. Ibid.
28. NJ, 17 March 1974.
29. Ibid.
30. NJ, 19 March 1974.
31. NJ, 20 March 1974.
32. C, CL, undated.
33. NJ, 19–24 July 1974.
34. Ibid.
35. NJ, 28 July 1974.

36. Palace press office verbatim extracts, 'As Others See Us', undated, RA/POW/Naval Service.
37. Memo press secretary to the Queen to Checketts, 13 February 1974, RA/POW/RNS R2/1.
38. Memo Checketts to Queen's private secretary, 12 March 1974, RA/POW/RNS R2/1.
39. NJ, 26 April 1975.
40. NJ, 28 April 1975.
41. NJ, 5 June 1975.
42. NJ, 21 March 1975.
43. Ministry of Defence memo, 29 October 1971, RA/POW/RNS R2/2 PART 2.
44. CC.
45. NJ, 24 May 1975.
46. Checketts to Mountbatten, 19 November 1975, MA.
47. Mountbatten to Checketts, 4 December 1975, MA.
48. NJ, 9 February 1976.
49. Ibid.
50. C to Mountbatten, 20 February 1976, MA.
51. NJ, 18 February 1976.
52. NJ, 20 February 1976.
53. Conversation with C.
54. C to Mountbatten, 29 March 1976, MA.
55. Ibid.
56. Memo C to Checketts, 10 July 1976, RA/POW.
57. Conversation with C.
58. Ibid.
59. Memo C to Checketts, 10 July 1976, RA/POW.
60. NJ, 2–3 September 1976.
61. Conversation with Roy Clare.
62. Report by D.C.W. Elliott, 14 December 1976.
63. Ibid.
64. Conversation with Clare.

Chapter Thirteen (pages 225–45)
1. C, CL, 21 May 1975.
2. *International Herald Tribune*, 18 November 1978.
3. Conversation with Carrington.
4. Memo Checketts to Moore, 21 December 1977.
5. Ibid.
6. Ibid.
7. Memo, undated, RA/POW/EA/78/260.
8. *Daily Mail*, 24 February 1978.
9. Memo Moore to Allison, 28 February 1978.
10. Memo C to Oliver Everett, assistant private secretary, RA/POW/PS78 Policy.
11. Memo Everett to Moore, 15 November 1978.
12. Ziegler, *Crown and People*, op. cit., p. 181.
13. C to Betjeman, 13 May 1976, RA/POW/Royal Jubilee Trusts.
14. Note by C on memo Checketts to C, undated, May 1976, RA/POW/Royal Jubilee Trusts.
15. John Betjeman, 'To the Queen', RA/POW/Royal Jubilee Trusts.
16. Conversation with Pratt.
17. Charteris to Checketts, 26 June 1974, RA/POW/Royal Jubilee Trusts.
18. Checketts to Charteris, 1 July 1974, RA/POW/Royal Jubilee Trusts.
19. Draft document by Pratt, 7 February 1975, RA/POW/Youth.
20. Memo C to Checketts, 1 July 1975, RA/POW/Prince's Trust 1976.
21. Ibid.
22. Checketts to Major Sir Michael Hawkins, 6 October 1975, RA/POW/Prince's Trust 1976.
23. Hawkins to Checketts, 30 October 1975, RA/POW/Prince's Trust 1976.

24. Note by C on letter from Captain R.J. Sheepshanks, 29 January 1976, RA/POW/Prince's Trust 1976.
25. Memo by C, undate, 1976, RA/POW/Prince's Trust 76–77.
26. Duke of Edinburgh to Checketts, 11 June 1976, RA/POW/Queen's Silver Jubilee Appeal Trust.
27. Memo Checketts to Duke of Edinburgh, 16 June 1976.
28. Farrer to Checketts, 20 September 1976, RA/POW/Prince's Trust 1976.
29. Secombe to C, 21 October 1977, RA/POW.
30. Note by C on memo Checketts to C, 12 June 1978, RA/POW/Royal Jubilee Trusts.
31. Philip Hall, Royal Fortune: Tax, Money and the Monarchy (Bloomsbury, 1992), pp. 53–9.
32. Memo R.E. Griffith to C, undated, May 1969, RA/POW/EA/69/36.
33. Note by C on letter Andrew Neatrour to Checketts, 25 September 1978, RA/POW/Prince's Trust Gen. Corres. 1979.
34. Note by C on memo Mrs R. to C, 25 July 1974, RA/POW/EA/74/35.
35. Note by C on draft letter C to Alan Tillotson, undated, May 1978, RA/POW/Royal Jubilee Trusts.
36. CC.

Chapter Fourteen (pages 246–67)
1. Conversation with C.
2. Conversation with Crosfield.
3. C to Vice-Chancellor, University of Wales, 24 June 1983, RA/POW/83 PWT.T0024.
4. Conversation with van der Post.
5. The Lost World of the Kalahari (Penguin, 1958), p. 21.
6. The Heart of the Hunter (Penguin, 1961), p. 129.

7. Ibid.
8. Van der Post to C, undated, RA/POW/EA/76/Visit to Botswana.
9. Ibid.
10. FCO to Checketts, 9 December 1976, RA/POW/EA/76.
11. Ibid.
12. Anthony Storr, Jung (Fontana, 1973), p. 10.
13. Storr, op. cit., p. 36.
14. Van der Post to C, 8 July 1978.
15. Julian Johnson, The Path of the Masters (Radha Soami Satsang Beas, Punjab, India, first published 1939).
16. CC.
17. Mountbatten to C, 21 April 19079, MA.
18. Draft of confidential letter to C, undated.
19. Conversation with C.
20. Conversation with Miller.
21. CC.
22. Prince Philip to C, 30 May 1974, RA/POW.
23. Conversation with Patty Palmer-Tomkinson.
24. Speech at luncheon to Parliamentary Press Gallery at Houses of Parliament, RA/POW/EA/75/36.
25. CC.
26. C to Mountbatten, 3 August 1975, MA.
27. Mountbatten to C, undated, 1978, MA.
28. Mountbatten to C, 21 April 1979, MA.
29. Mountbatten to C, undated, 1979, MA.
30. C, CL, 15 April 1979.
31. Mountbatten to C, 21 April 1979, MA.
32. Ibid.
33. C, CL, 15 April 1979.
34. Ibid.

35. Ibid.
36. C to Mountbatten, 15 December 1977, MA.
37. C to Mountbatten, 6 August 1974, MA.
38. Mountbatten to C, 27 January 1979, MA.
39. Ibid.
40. Ibid.
41. Ibid.
42. C to Mountbatten, 27 November 1978, MA.
43. C to Mountbatten, 13 August 1979, MA.
44. Diary, 27 August 1979.

PART III

Chapter Fifteen (pages 271–87)

1. Memorandum, RA/POW/Prince's Trust/Gen. Corres/1979.
2. *New York Herald Tribune*, 23 July 1981.
3. *The Times*, 25 February 1981.
4. Ibid.
5. Ibid.
6. Ibid.
7. Ibid.
8. *Daily Telegraph*, 25 February 1981.
9. *The Times*, 25 February 1981.
10. BBC/ITV interview, 26 June 1969.
11. *Observer*, 9 June 1974.
12. *Evening Standard*, 7 January 1975.
13. Ibid.
14. Conversation with C.
15. C to Susan Hussey, 19 July 1964.
16. C, CL, 10 June 1972.
17. Interview with Douglas Keay, *Woman's Own*, February 1975.
18. CC.
19. Conversation with Patty Palmer-Tomkinson.
20. Andrew Morton, *Diana: Her True Story* (Michael O'Mara, 1992), p. 53.
21. C, CL, 28 January 1981.
22. Morton, op. cit., p. 56.
23. C, CL, 5 March 1981.
24. C, CL, 29 March 1981.
25. Speech to College of William and Mary, Williamsburg, Virginia, 2 May 1981.
26. *Daily Mirror*, 28 May 1981.
27. *The Times*, 13 June 1981.
28. Morton, op. cit., p. 59.
29. CC.
30. Morton, op. cit., p. 61.
31. *Daily Telegraph*, 27 July 1981.

Chapter Sixteen (pages 288–305)

1. CC.
2. Memo, 21 May 1981, RA/POW/Wedding.
3. Memo C to Adeane, undated, May 1981, RA/POW/Wedding.
4. Milligan to C, 14 July 1981, RA/POW/Personal.
5. Quoted in *The Times*, 29 July 1981.
6. *The Economist*, 1 August 1981.
7. *Time*, 10 August 1981.
8. Address by the Archbishop of Canterbury at the marriage of the Prince of Wales and the Lady Diana Spencer, 29 July 1981.
9. Walter Bagehot, *The English Constitution* (Fontana, 1993).
10. Paisley to Lord Chamberlain, 3 July 1981, RA/POW/Wedding.
11. *Time*, 10 August 1981.
12. C, CL, 3 August 1981.
13. R.E. Parsons, British Ambassador, to FCO, 22 July 1981, RA/POW/Honeymoon.
14. FORY to Admiral Sir Henry Leach, 31 August 1981, RA/POW/Honeymoon.

15. C, CL, 3 August 1981.
16. CC.
17. CC.
18. CC.
19. CC.
20. CC.
21. CC.
22. CC.
23. C, CL, 26 December 1981.
24. Morton, op. cit., p. 74.
25. C to Checketts, 24 April 1978, POW/Chevening/Personal.
26. Checketts to C , 18 September 1978, RA/POW/Duchy of Cornwall.
27. HRH Prince of Wales and Charles Clover, *Highgrove, Portrait of an Estate* (Chapmans, 1993), p. 59.
28. HRH Prince of Wales and Clover, op. cit., p. 79.
29. Quoted in Douglas Keay, *Royal Pursuit* (Severn House, 1983).
30. C to Brabournes, undated, March 1982.
31. CC.
32. C to van Cutsems, 22 June 1982.
33. C to Patricia Brabourne, 2 July 1982.

Chapter Seventeen (pages 306–28)

1. Speech to British Medical Association, 14 December 1982.
2. Conversation with C.
3. Speech to BMA, op. cit.
4. Ibid,
5. *Daily Mail*, 16 July 1983.
6. Conversation with Kindersley.
7. *Evening Standard*, 13 August 1984.
8. Interview with Anne de Courcy, *Evening Standard*, 16 July 1984.
9. Message to third national conference on organic food production at Royal Agricultural College, Cirencester, 8 January 1983.
10. 'Conversation and Society', paper by C, Countryside in 1970 Committee for Wales, RA/POW/articles etc.
11. *Daily Mirror*, October 1984.
12. *Daily Mail*, 3 February 1985.
13. *Daily Express*, 7 May 1986.
14. *Guardian*, 21 October 1985.
15. Extract from *Spitting Image*, quoted in the *Star*, 6 May 1986.
16. Conversation with Manser.
17. Speech to celebrate 150th Anniversary of Royal Institute of British Architects, 30 May 1984.
18. CC.
19. CC.
20. *The Times*, 1 June 1984.
21. Ibid.
22. Manser to C, 1 July 1985.
23. C to Manser, 7 August 1985.
24. Speech to Institute of Directors, 26 February 1985.
25. Ibid.
26. Ibid.
27. Ibid.
28. C to Hackney, 24 February 1985.
29. Conversation with Hackney.
30. *Manchester Evening News*, 23 October 1985.
31. *Hansard*, 23 October 1985.
32. C to Soames, 24 October 1994.
33. *Guardian*, 28 October 1985.
34. *Daily Telegraph*, 25 October 1985.
35. *The Times*, 25 October 1985.

Chapter Eighteen (pages 329–55)

1. Morton, op. cit., passim.
2. Ibid., p. 74 and passim.
3. C, CL, 10 October 1982.
4. C to van Cutsems, 26 April 1983.
5. C, CL, 4 April 1983.
6. Ibid.
7. Diana, CL, 1 April 1983.
8. C to van Cutsems, 26 April 1983.
9. C, CL, 4 April 1983.
10. C, CL, 26 April 1983.

11. C to Susan Hussey, undated, 1983.
12. C to van Cutsems, 26 April 1983.
13. C, CL, 26 April 1983.
14. *Mail on Sunday*, 24 July 1983.
15. FJ, undated, February 1984.
16. Ibid.
17. FJ, undated, March 1984.
18. Ibid.
19. C to Soames, 28 March 1984.
20. FJ, undated, March 1984.
21. Ibid.
22. FJ, undated, August 1984.
23. FJ, 19 April 1985.
24. Ibid.
25. FJ, 20 April 1985.
26. Ibid.
27. Ibid.
28. FJ, 21 April 1985.
29. Ibid.
30. FJ, 23 April 1985.
31. Ibid.
32. FJ, 24 April 1985.
33. FJ, 26 April 1985.
34. Ibid.
35. FJ, 28 April 1985.
36. FJ, 29 April 1985.
37. Ibid.
38. Ibid.
39. *Daily Telegraph*, 30 April 1985.
40. *Sun*, 30 April 1985.
41. *The Times*, 30 April 1985.
42. Memo C to Adeane, 26 November 1981, RA/POW/EA/82/138.
43. Moore to Adeane, 19 February 1982, RA/POW/EA/82/138.
44. Archbishop of Canterbury to C, 7 May 1982, RA/POW/EA/82/138.
45. CL, 30 March 1982, RA/POW/EA/82/138.
46. Michael Shea to Adeane, 25 May 1982, RA/POW/EA/82/138.
47. Donald Lamont to C, 27 May 1982, RA/POW/EA/82/138.
48. Undated memo by Adeane following meeting between Prince of Wales's office and the Home Office on 19 January 1985.
49. Archbishop of Canterbury to Adeane, 7 January 1985.
50. David Roycroft to William Heseltine, 4 April 1985.
51. Revd Donald Boyd, Secretary, Religion and Morals Committee, Free Presbyterian Church of Scotland, to Adeane, 29 March 1985.
52. *The Times*, 16 April 1985.
53. Telegram Roycroft to British Ambassador to Holy See, 15 April 1985, RA/POW/VA Italy 85.
54. *The Times*, 30 April 1985.
55. Ibid.
56. Macleod to C, 28 June 1985.
57. C to Macleod, 28 June 1985.
58. FJ, 2 May 1985.
59. FJ, 4 May 1985.
60. Ibid.

Chapter Nineteen (pages 356–80)

1. CC.
2. CC.
3. Conversation with Riddell.
4. Conversation with Riddell.
5. *The First Ten Years: The Prince's Trust* (The Prince's Trust, 1986).
6. C to Margaret Thatcher, 16 November 1987.
7. Conversation with C.
8. C to Kenneth Baker, 12 January 1989.
9. Paula Counter to C, 6 May 1987.
10. C to Counter, 28 May 1987.
11. Conversation with Pratt.
12. C to Thatcher, 16 November 1987.
13. Conversation with O'Brien.
14. Speech to ScotBITC AGM, 26 November 1985.
15. C to O'Brien, 27 February 1986.
16. C, CL, 4 March 1986.
17. Conversation with O'Brien.

18. Memo C to Rupert Fairfax, 29 September 1986, RA/POW/PW P00137.
19. C to Thatcher, 16 November 1987.
20. O'Brien to C, 10 February 1987.
21. Draft letter C to O'Brien (written on letter O'Brien to C, 10 February 1987).
22. C to Thatcher, 16 November 1987.
23. Draft of letter C to Thatcher, 16 November 1987.
24. *Daily Mail*, 5 October 1987.
25. *The Times*, 6 October 1987.
26. Quoted in *Sunday Times*, 4 October 1987.
27. Hackney to C, 1 December 1986.
28. Sebastian Charles to O'Brien, December 1987, RA/POW/86PW P00174.
29. *The Times*, 13 June 1987.
30. *Daily Mail*, 6 October 1987.
31. Inner City Aid Proposed Strategy Paper, undated.
32. Memo, 'Management of The Prince's Trust', following a meeting on 6 June 1988.
33. Riddell to Hackney, 4 July 1988.
34. CL to C, 1 September 1988.
35. Shebbeare to Riddell, 12 October 1988.
36. Conversation with C.
37. Memo, 9 September 1988.
38. O'Brien to C, 22 March 1989.
39. C to O'Brien, 6 April 1989.
40. CC.
41. Conversation with C.
42. Memo C to Salter, 2 January 1991.
43. C to Thatcher, 7 December 1990.
44. C to John Major, 7 December 1990.

Chapter Twenty (pages 381–97)
1. C, CL, 6 November 1985.
2. C to Soames, 7 November 1985.
3. Ibid.
4. *Time*, 16 November 1985.
5. *New York Times*, 10 November 1985.
6. FJ, 9–12 November 1985.
7. Ibid.
8. *Time*, 16 November 1985.
9. FJ, 9–12 November 1985.
10. Ibid.
11. File memo by Riddell, 22 March 1985, RA/POW/VA85 USA.
12. Hammer to C, 28 March 1985, RA/POW/VA85 USA.
13. Note by C on letter Hammer to C.
14. Memo Roycroft to C, 11 April 1985, RA/POW/VA85 USA.
15. Ibid.
16. Valerie Stuart to Riddell, 26 August 1985, RA/POW/VA85 USA.
17. *Spotlight*, 23 September 1985.
18. Speech to International Gala, Palm Beach, Florida, 12 November 1985.
19. C, CL, 13 November 1985.
20. Ibid.
21. C to Hammer, 28 October 1986.
22. *Time*, 11 November 1985.
23. *Vanity Fair*, September 1985.
24. *Daily Star*, 4 February 1985.
25. *Vanity Fair*, September 1985.
26. Speech at Prince George, British Columbia, 4 May 1986.
27. *Daily Express*, 7 May 1986.
28. Speech at Harvard University, 4 September 1986.
29. *Washington Post*, 4 September 1986.
30. *Sun*, 13 August 1986.
31. *Star*, 28 April 1987.
32. *Mail on Sunday*, 28 April 1985.
33. C, CL, 24 October 1987.
34. CC.
35. C, CL, 11 March 1986.
36. Speech at Prince George, British Columbia, 4 May 1986.
37. C, CL, 18 November 1986.
38. Conversation with C.
39. Conversation with C.
40. C, CL, 11 February 1987.
41. C, CL, 11 February 1987.

42. C, CL, 24 October 1987.
43. Ibid.
44. Ibid.
45. Ibid.

PART IV

Chapter Twenty-One (pages 401–20)
1. CC.
2. Memo Salter to C, 23 August 1989.
3. C, CL, 31 March 1987.
4. C, CL, 11 March 1986.
5. C to Soames, 27 September 1987.
6. FJ, 2 April 1987.
7. Conversation with C.
8. C to Soames, 4 February 1988.
9. Ibid.
10. C to Geoffrey and Jorie Kent, 13 February 1988.
11. Conversation with C.
12. Ibid.
13. Conversation with Patty Palmer-Tomkinson.
14. Statement by C, 12 March 1988.
15. Communication by Public Prosecutor Graubunden, 27 June 1988.
16. Conversation with Patty Palmer-Tomkinson.
17. *The Times*, 12 March 1988.
18. Conversation with Patty Palmer-Tomkinson.

Chapter Twenty-Two (pages 421–43)
1. *Sunday Correspondent*, 27 May 1990.
2. C, 'Conservation and Society', undated, RA/POW/articles etc written by HRH.
3. *Daily Telegraph*, 3 May 1970.
4. *Daily Mail*, 27 August 1970.
5. Cited in Frances Cairncross, *Costing the Earth* (Business Books, 1991), p. 14.
6. Cited in Jonathon Porritt and David Winner, *The Coming of the Greens* (Fontana, 1988), p. 256.
7. Cited in Walter and Dorothy Schwarz, *Breaking Through* (Green Books, 1987), p. 233.
8. *Guardian*, 1 May 1980.
9. *Guardian*, 11 June 1980.
10. *Daily Telegraph*, 31 October 1986.
11. Cited in *The Coming of the Greens*, op. cit., pp. 35–40.
12. Speech to North Sea Conference, 24 November 1987.
13. Speech at the Environment Awards to Industry, 23 February 1988.
14. C to Jorie Kent, 30 January 1989.
15. Conversation with C.
16. C to Porritt, 6 March 1989.
17. Speech to 'Saving the Ozone Layer' World Conference, 6 March 1989.
18. Speech at European Year of the Environment Eyecatcher Awards, 22 March 1988.
19. Ibid.
20. *Sunday Mirror*, 27 May 1990.
21. *Observer*, 28 October 1990.
22. C to Porritt, 5 June 1990.
23. Memo Wright to C, 26 January 1989.
24. BBC Radio 4, 17 January 1989.
25. C to Howe, 1 February 1989.
26. C to Howe, 30 March 1989.
27. Speech at 'Building A Better Britain' Exhibition, 27 April 1989.
28. C to Jessica Douglas-Home, 1 May 1989.
29. Cited in John Sweeney, *The Life and Evil Times of Nicolae Ceausescu* (Hutchinson, 1991).
30. Morrison to C, 15 August 1989.
31. C to Morrison, 28 August 1989.
32. Morrison to C, 23 October 1989.
33. C to Morrison, 24 October 1989.
34. Morrison to C, 31 October 1989.

35. C to Heseltine, 28 December 1991.
36. Heseltine to C, 26 January 1992.
37. Speech at European Community Conference on the Urban Environment in Madrid, 30 April 1991.
38. HRH Prince of Wales and Clover, op. cit., p. 29.
39. Ibid., p. 31.
40. Ibid., p. 10.
41. Conversation with C.
42. Ibid.

Chapter Twenty-Three (pages 444–71)
1. *Sunday Times*, 2 August 1987.
2. *The Times*, 5 August 1987.
3. Speech at Corporation of London Planning and Communication Committee's Annual Dinner, 1 December 1987.
4. C to Booker, 24 December 1987.
5. *Daily Telegraph*, 3 December 1987.
6. Ibid.
7. Ibid.
8. C to Booker, 24 December 1987.
9. C to Simpson, 21 January 1988.
10. C to Simpson, 8 April 1988.
11. C to Simpson, 8 June 1989.
12. Cited in *Evening Standard*, 31 October 1989.
13. C to Ridley, 20 June 1988.
14. Ridley to C, 29 June 1988.
15. *Sunday Times*, 10 September 1989.
16. Speech at presentation of the Thomas Cranmer Schools Prize, 19 December 1989.
17. *The Independent*, 21 December 1989.
18. *The Times*, 21 December 1989.
19. 29 June 1989.
20. *Sunday Times*, 2 July 1989.
21. *Sunday Mirror*, 2 July 1989.
22. *Daily Telegraph*, 30 June 1989.
23. Shakespeare Birthday Lecture, Swan Theatre, Stratford-upon-Avon, 22 April 1991.

24. C to Clarke, 24 May 1991.
25. Baroness James to C, 24 April 1991.
26. Sir Claus Moser to C, April 1991.
27. Griffiths to C, 2 January 1992.
28. C to Eric Anderson, 11 January 1992.
29. William Shakespeare Evening, 28 October 1993.
30. *The Times*, 3 July 1989.
31. C to Mattick, 3 June 1989.
32. Ibid.
33. CC.
34. Carnwath to C, 5 July 1989.
35. C to Carnwath, 31 July 1989.
36. Memo by C, 27 June 1991.
37. *Sunday Telegraph*, 19 July 1992.
38. C to Krier, 18 July 1992.
39. Krier to C, 13 August 1992.
40. C to Krier, 18 August 1992.
41. C to Alexander, 2 December 1992.
42. Memo Hanson to C, 25 May 1992.
43. Memo C to Hanson, 9 June 1992.

Chapter Twenty-Four (pages 472–92)
1. Conversation with C.
2. Morton, op. cit., p. 118.
3. Morton, op. cit., p. 123.
4. Conversation with C.
5. Conversation with Neil.
6. Ibid.
7. Conversation with Andrew Knight.
8. Channel Four, 15 October 1989.
9. *Courier Mail*, 16 October 1993.
10. Press release by Press Complaints Commission, 8 June 1992.
11. McGregor to Calcutt, 11 December 1992.
12. *Sunday Times*, 28 June 1992.
13. Private diary.
14. CC.
15. Conversation with Neil.
16. *Today*, 6 July 1992.
17. CC.
18. FJ, 10–15 February 1992.
19. *Sunday Times*, 16 February 1992.

20. *Daily Telegraph*, 13 February 1992.
21. FJ, 10–15 February 1992.
22. CC.
23. C, CL, 8 November 1992.
24. C to Soames, 11 December 1992.

Chapter Twenty-Five (pages 493–513)
1. C to Collor, undated, 1991.
2. Memo C to Fellowes, 23 October 1992.
3. Ibid.
4. Ibid.
5. Ibid.
6. Memo C to Aylard, 22 December 1992.
7. Philip Hall, *Royal Fortune: Tax, Money and the Monarchy* (Bloomsbury, 1992).
8. Cited in *Sunday Times*, 14 February 1993.
9. *The Independent*, 12 February 1993.
10. CC.
11. CC.
12. Conversation with C.
13. Ibid.
14. Memo C to Woodard, 22 February 1993.
15. *The Times*, 18 June 1993.
16. Conversation with C.

Chapter Twenty-Six (pages 514–34)
1. Draft letter C to Mayor Bridgend, 14 August 1980, RA/POW/T and T/1980.
2. Frances Day to C, 1 January 1980, RA/C. POW. T and T/1980.
3. Draft letter C to Frances Day, undated, RA/C. POW. T and T/1980.
4. Lewin to C, 5 August 1982.
5. Draft letter C to Lewin, undated, RA/POW/T and T's/1982.
6. C, CL, 4 April 1983.

7. C, CL, 27 April 1983.
8. C, CL, 4 April 1983.
9. C to Major, 28 December 1990.
10. Ibid.
11. C to Major, 25 January 1991.
12. Speech at Mansion House, 21 June 1991.
13. C to Marchioness of Aberdeen, 19 August 1991.
14. C to Brigadier J.F. Rickett, 19 August 1991.
15. C to Major, undated, September 1991.
16. *Sunday Times*, 13 October 1991.
17. Chapple to King, quoted in *Sunday Times*, 13 October 1991.
18. C to Rifkind, 6 May 1992.
19. *The Independent*, 4 February 1993.
20. *Daily Telegraph*, 24 November 1992.
21. C to Rifkind, 16 November 1992.
22. C to Lt. Gen. Sir Michael Gray, 5 July 1992.
23. Conversation with C.
24. *Charles: The Private Man, The Public Role*, ITV documentary, 29 June 1994.
25. Conversation with C.
26. Ibid.
27. Ibid.
28. Ibid.
29. Ibid.
30. Ibid.
31. Ibid.
32. 'Essential 1994' Conference, John Abbott College, Montreal, Canada, 20 June 1994.
33. *Sunday*, BBC Radio 4, 10 July 1994.
34. Ibid.
35. Conversation with C.
36. Quoted in *Daily Telegraph*, 11 July 1994.
37. Professor Paul Bradshaw, 'On Revising the Coronation Service', *Theology*, Vol. 96, No. 770, pp. 130–37.

Chapter Twenty-Seven (pages 535–49)

1. *Today*, BBC Radio 4, 7 December 1993.
2. *Evening Standard*, 8 December 1993.
3. *Daily Telegraph*, 8 December 1993.
4. Ibid.
5. Speech to Headway luncheon, 3 December 1993.
6. *The Times*, 4 December 1993.
7. Speech, 'Islam and the West', Sheldonian Theatre, Oxford, 27 October 1993.
8. Ibid.
9. *Charles: The Private Man, The Public Role*, ITV documentary, 29 June 1994.
10. C to John Major, 15 October 1993.
11. FJ, 23 January – 11 February 1994.
12. Ibid.
13. Robert Milliken, *The Independent*, 27 January 1994.
14. Teresa Powell, quoted in the *Sun*, 27 January 1994.
15. FJ, 23 January – 11 February 1994.
16. Australia Day speech, 26 January 1994.
17. Ibid.

Chapter Twenty-Eight (pages 550–66)

1. NOP, 9–14 July 1969, cited Philip Ziegler, *Crown and People*, op. cit., p.137.
2. Conversation with C.
3. *Henry V*, Act IV, Scene i.
4. Conversation with C.
5. Vernon Bogdanor, *Observer*, 13 December 1992.
6. Statement by Archbishop of York, 9 December 1992.
7. *Sun*, 1 July 1994.
8. *Charles: The Private Man, The Public Role*, ITV documentary, 29 June 1994.

BIBLIOGRAPHY

———— ◆ ————

Rather than demonstrating my diligence and wearying the reader by listing all the books and periodicals that I have consulted (and in the process drawing attention to some that I would not wish on anyone), I have selected only those from which I have derived particular pleasure or profit.

Among the 'royal' biographies, *Victoria R.I.* by Elizabeth Longford (Weidenfeld and Nicolson, 1988), *Edward VIII* by Frances Donaldson (Weidenfeld and Nicolson, 1974) and Philip Ziegler's *Mountbatten* (Collins, 1985) stand out. *Philip* by Basil Boothroyd (Longman, 1971) is a muddled but revealing portrait of the Duke of Edinburgh. The journalistic insights about the post-war period in *The Age of Austerity, 1945–1951*, (ed. Michael Sissons and Philip French; Hodder and Stoughton, 1963) are themselves illuminated by Peter Hennessy's *Never Again* (Jonathan Cape, 1992). *Crown and People* (Collins, 1978) by Philip Ziegler is a lively commentary on shifting attitudes towards the monarchy from the first half of this century until the late seventies. Anthony Sampson's evergreen *Anatomy of Britain* (revised as *The Changing Anatomy of Britain*; Hodder and Stoughton, 1982) reminds the reader that the British establishment may have lost some of its power but retains much of its arrogance.

On the constitution and the role of the monarchy, Anthony Jay's *Elizabeth R* (BBC Books, 1992) is lucid and readable. Lord Hailsham's *On the Constitution* (HarperCollins, 1992) manages to be both trenchant and reflective. More testing but no less stimulating are Tom Nairn's *The*

Enchanted Glass: Britain and Its Monarchy (Picador, 1990), which is (or ought to be) a republican's bible, and its polar opposite, Ferdinand Mount's *The British Constitution Now* (Heinemann, 1992). The title of Stephen Haseler's *The End of the House of Windsor* (I.B. Tauris, 1993) is cataclysmic (but then he is also the author of *The Death of British Democracy* and *The Tragedy of Labour*) but his scholarship is entertaining and his bias is refreshingly lacking in compromise. Phillip Hall is also a 'hostile' witness but his *Royal Fortune: Tax, Money and the Monarchy* (Bloomsbury, 1992) is required reading for those interested in the intricacies of this subject. Little of substance has been written about the relationship between the press and the monarchy but Michael Leapman's *Treacherous Estate* (Hodder and Stoughton, 1992) is sharp and wry.

William Boyd's introduction to *School Ties* (the 1985 Penguin publication of two of his screenplays, *Good and Bad at Games* and *Dutch Girls*) is a comic but chilling account of his own schooldays at Gordonstoun and is in sharp contrast to Adam Arnold-Brown's *Unfolding Character, The Impact of Gordonstoun (1948–67)* (Routledge & Keegan Paul, 1962) which is rhapsodical but often just as funny – if unintentionally so.

Among a forest of books about the environment (where Schumacher's *Small is Beautiful* still reigns supreme), Robin Page's *The Wildlife of the Royal Estate* (Hodder and Stoughton, 1984) and *Highgrove, Portrait of an Estate* by HRH The Prince of Wales and Charles Clover (Chapmans, 1993) are informed, original and beautifully produced. *Standing On Earth* (Golgonooza Press, 1991) is by the American philosopher, poet and farmer, Wendell Berry whose sense of the relationship between man and nature is both reasoned and spiritual. Laurens van der Post's mysticism is sometimes sanctimonious but *The Lost World of the Kalahari* (Penguin, 1962) and *Yet Being Something Other* (Penguin, 1984) have a rare intensity of vision (and the latter has a description of whaling which makes *Moby Dick* seem almost pedestrian). *The Greening of Medicine* (Gollancz, 1990) by Patrick Pietroni is concise, commonsensical and inspired by the author's faith in 'holism'. Anthony Storr's *Jung* (Fontana Modern Masters, 1979) guides the student into Jung's explanation of the human psyche so painlessly that his *Jung: Selected Writings* (Fontana, 1986) becomes irresistible.

Tom Wolfe's *From Bauhaus to Our House* (Pocket Books, 1981) is politically incorrect and, as the *New York Magazine* wrote, 'a search-

and-destroy mission against architectural pretensions'; it does not find favour with modernists.

To refresh the spirit you may seek *The Path of the Masters* (compiled by Julian Johnson and published by Radha Soami Satsang Beas, Punjab, India), which explores 'the Yoga of the Audible Lifestream' in which it is tempting to bathe. Alternatively, there is Ivan Turgenev's *First Love* (translated by Sir Isaiah Berlin with an introduction by V. S. Pritchett; Penguin Classics, 1978), in which innocence yields to knowledge and thence to torment and tragedy. Limpid and tender with truth, *First Love* was recommended to the Prince of Wales by the translator and should be read by anyone who believes that human beings are in control of their own destinies.

INDEX

Abercrombie and Kent, 409, 410
Aberdare Mountains, 251, 548
Aberystwyth, 120, 121, 129, 138, 146
Abse, Leo, 135
Abu Dhabi, 140, 542–3
Academy of Fine Arts, St Petersburg, 570
Acapulco, 200, 203
Accession Declaration Act (1910), 533
Act of Settlement (1701), 276, 531n., 533, 559
Act of Supremacy (1559), 527n.
Act of Union (1706), 531n.
Acton, Sir Harold, 345 and n.
Adeane, Edward, 253 and n., 286, 349, 360; and
    the Prince's wedding, 289; and the Prince's
    RIBA speech, 315; relations with the Prince
    and Princess, 296–7, 357–8; and the Prince's
    visit to the Vatican, 350, 353; resignation,
    358, 359
Adeane, Sir Michael, 226, 253n., 256
Adelaide, 410
Aden, 201 and n.
Admiralty, 162, 167, 175, 220
Africa, 249–51, 407–9, 410–11
Ahrends, Peter, 318, 319, 452
Airy, Major-General Sir Christopher, 494–6 and
    n., 498
Albert, Prince Consort, 31, 241, 242, 243, 460,
    464
Alexander, Christopher, 468–9, 470
Alexander, Prince of Yugoslavia, 64
Alexandra, Princess, 22, 74 and n.
Alice, Princess, Duchess of Gloucester, 504n.,
    522
All Malta Polo Club, 115–16

Allied-Lyons, 460
Allison, Ronald, 230
Alternative Service Book, 404, 453
Althorp Park, Northamptonshire, 279
Altrincham, Lord, 101–2 and n.
Amery, Colin, 445, 465
Amnesty International, 108
Anderson, Dr Eric, 74–5 and n., 454, 459
Anderson, Mabel, 15, 16, 19, 33, 34–5, 52–3, 63,
    64
Andrew, Prince see York, Prince Andrew, Duke
    of
Andrew, Prince and Princess of Greece, 50
Anglesey, 42
Anglican Church see Church of England
Angry Brigade, 166 and n.
Anne, Princess Royal: birth, 16; childhood, 21,
    23, 35n., 48, 52 and n., 53, 54; character,
    33–4; relationship with her father, 49; horse
    riding, 54–5; It's A Royal Knockout, 133n.;
    visits America, 148; marriage to Mark
    Phillips, 191–2, 193; attacked in the Mall,
    210 and n.; the Prince's affection for, 278;
    Gatcombe Park, 299; excluded from Civil
    List, 504n.; and reorganisation of Army
    bands, 522; divorce, 558; second marriage,
    559
Annenberg, Walter, 208–9 and n.
Anson, Charles, 472
Antigua, 189, 191
Anzacs, 334 and n.
Anzio, 347
ANZUK, 200–1 and n.
Architectural Summer School, Italy, 405

Arctic, 213–14
Ardrey, Robert, 106
Argentina, 350
Ark Royal, HMS, 170, 175
Armstrong, Robert, 231 and n., 402, 409
    and n.
Armstrong-Jones, Antony *see* Snowdon, Earl of
Army Air Corps, 514
Arnold-Brown, Adam, 67
Arup Associates, 444, 448–9
Ascot, 147, 196
Atlantic College, 79 and n.
Attlee, Clement, 4, 6, 8
Auckland, 334
Auden, W.H., 113
Austin, George, Archdeacon of York, 535–6, 538
Australia: the Prince at Timbertop, 76, 77–85,
    87–9; the Prince's official visits to, 114–15,
    142, 143, 261–2, 284, 286, 331–3, 409–10,
    422, 544–9; and Britain's membership of
    EEC, 152; leaves ANZUK, 200–1; the
    Prince's love of, 201, 549; proposals that the
    Prince become Governor-General, 226–7,
    409; the Prince and Princess tour, 381–2;
    republicanism, 544–9
Avon, Earl of *see* Eden, Sir Anthony
Aylard, Richard, 414n., 505, 536; and the skiing
    accident in Klosters, 413–14; and the
    Prince's speeches on the environment, 427;
    and the Prince's outings with his sons, 474,
    475 and n.; refuses to let the Prince's friends
    discuss his marriage, 481–2, 483; on John
    Riddell, 494; and appointment of Sir
    Christopher Airy, 495; takes charge of the
    Prince's private office, 496–7 and n.,
    498–500; interviewed on the record, 510n.;
    refutes story of 'mystery woman' at
    Balmoral, 539–40, 541; and the 1993 tour of
    Australia, 545; and the *Daily Express's*
    allegations about the Prince's relationship
    with the Queen, 576, 577–9

Bach, J.S., 92
Bagehot, Walter, 125 and n., 153, 290, 543–4
Bahamas, 194–6, 302–3
Bahrain, 151
Bailey, Christian, 116
Baker, Kenneth, 362
Baldwin, Stanley, 11
Balmoral, 35, 160, 405, 564; royal holidays at,
    31–3, 576; shooting parties, 46; the Prince's
    love of, 30–2, 89, 116, 138, 397, 440–1;
    Diana Spencer at, 280; the Prince's
    honeymoon at, 294; Duke of Edinburgh
    manages estate, 440, 441

Baltic Sea, 222
Bar-Hillel, Mira, 448, 466, 469
Barbados, 194
Barber, Janet, 426
Barry, Stephen, 288n.
Bartholomew, Carolyn, 285, 480
Baryshnikov, Mikhail, 383n.
Battenberg, Prince Louis of, 168 and n.
Baum, Michael, 311
BBC, 117, 130, 147, 247, 346, 510, 530, 535,
    574; Christmas broadcasts, 10; the Queen's
    coronation, 20; reverent attitude to royal
    family, 102; the Prince's first radio interview,
    118; the Prince's first television interview,
    122, 127–8; *Royal Family*, 132–3; *It's A Royal
    Knockout*, 133n.; the Prince's investiture, 134;
    proposed film about the Prince in the
    Kalahari Desert, 250; *The Earth in Balance*,
    430; World Service, 433; *A Vision of Britain*,
    451–2; *Newsnight*, 510n.
Beaufort, Duke of, 256
Beck, Anne, 37
Beck, Peter, 36–7, 38, 39–40, 41, 42
Belgium, 230, 456
Beloff, Dr John, 248n.
Bennett, Alan, 98
Benson, RAF, 510n.
Benson, Ross, 60n., 61
Bermuda, 200
Bernini, Gian Lorenzo, 25n.
Betjeman, John, 233–4
Bevin, Ernest, 8
Binney, Marcus, 571
Birkhall, 397, 418, 539, 563, 577
Birmingham, 369, 541
BITC *see* Business in the Community
Blackburn, 371
Blair, Tony, 405
Bloomingdale, Betsy, 383n.
Blum, Maître Suzanne, 181
Bogdanor, Vernon, 558 and n.
Bogota, 189 and n.
Bolshoi Ballet, 53
Bonifacio Straits, 168
Book of Common Prayer, 404
Booker, Christopher, 315, 445, 448, 449
Bosnia, 522, 542
Boston compact, 367, 368–9
Botanical Gardens, Kew, 404
Botswana, 251, 338, 340, 407
Bow Group, 435
Bowes-Lyon family, 249
Boyd, William, 60n., 61, 63
Boys Brigades, 135
BP, 497

Brabourne, Doreen (Dowager Lady Brabourne), 266

Brabourne, John (Lord Brabourne), 133 and n., 189, 190–1, 216, 260–1, 264–5, 335–6, 395

Brabourne, Patricia (Lady Brabourne), 115, 133n., 189, 190–1, 216, 260–1, 263, 265, 266, 304–5, 335–6, 395, 413, 481

Bradford, 273–4, 371

Bradshaw, Professor Paul, 533

Brazil, 457, 497–8

Bridgend, 515–16

Brisbane, 332

Bristol, 273

Bristol Cancer Help Centre, 308–9

Britannia (royal yacht), 23, 26n., 293, 344, 354–5, 404, 497–8, 506, 507, 511–13, 551

British Aircraft Corporation, 422

British Army, 337, 514–26

British Coal, 437

British Empire, 8, 98, 99

British Legion, 135

British Medical Association (BMA), 306–7, 308, 310, 313, 573

British Rail, 511

British Sub Aqua Club, 228

Broadlands, Hampshire, 45, 164–5, 176, 182, 183–4, 216, 263, 264, 282, 292

Brogdale, Kent, 404

Bronington, HMS, 217–24

Brooke, Peter, 504

Brooks, Peter, 433

Brown, Gordon, 405

Brown, Mrs, 247

Brown, Tina, 389

Brundtland Report, 424

Brunei, 336–8, 525

Buckingham Palace, 24–5, 27, 30, 156; the Queen moves into, 19; garden parties, 115; Diana Spencer moves into, 284; bottle bank, 423; 'grace and favour' apartments, 557n.; opening of state apartments to public, 504n.; presentation parties, 102; 'William Shakespeare' evening, 460; press office, 472, 480, 500–2, 540

Budapest, 373

Budapest University, 404

Buddhism, 253–4, 526, 532, 542

Buddhist Society, 108

Building A Better Britain Exhibition (1989), 432

Burke, Tom, 427

Burke's Peerage, 391

Business in the Community (BITC), 361, 364–70, 372, 376, 377–80 and n., 403, 462, 494, 569

Business in the Environment, 569

Business Leaders Forum (BLF), 372–3, 569–70

Butler, Lord, 104 and n., 105, 106, 107–8, 109, 111, 146

Butler, Mollie, 109

Buxton, James, 108, 111, 112

Cadiz, 292

Cadruvi, Sergeant, 412

Caernarvon Castle, 128, 133, 134

Cairngorms, 69

Cairo, 294

Caister, 362–3

Calcutt Committee, 479n.

Caledonian forest, 440

Callaghan, James, 227 and n., 229, 271, 272

Cambodia, 522

Cambridge, 541

Cambridge Union, 422, 423

Cambridge University, 103–14, 116–17, 121, 129, 138–9, 146–7, 225, 247

Cameroon, 404

Camp David, 148

Canada, 17, 148, 213–14, 216, 261–2, 335, 389–90, 394, 410, 573

Canterbury Cathedral, 349

Cardiff, 120, 130, 131, 475

Cardigan, 135

Cards on the Table (government pamphlet), 8

Carey, George, Archbishop of Canterbury, 491, 529, 530–1, 535n., 536, 558–9

Caribbean, 183, 185–9, 193–8, 511

Carmarthen, 135

Carnwath, Robert, 464

Caroline, Queen, 490n.

Carr, Robert, 166n.

Carrington, Lord, 227 and n., 292

Cartagena, 188

Cartland, Dame Barbara, 289, 331

Cassandra (*Daily Mirror* columnist), 128–9

Casson, Sir Hugh, 317–18, 319

Catherine of Aragon, 25

Catholic Church, 276, 291, 347–54, 526, 528, 532, 559

Cawston, Richard, 133

Cayman Islands, 196

Ceausescu, President, 430–3

Central Electricity Generating Board, 425

Centre for Islamic Studies, University of Wales, 405

Centrepoint, 326

Ceylon, 150

Chalker, Lynda, 405

Chamberlain, Neville, 152

Chapmen, Victor, 329n., 353

Chapple, General Sir John, 520, 521

Charity Commissioners, 238
Charles: The Private Man, The Public Role, 476n.,
   546n., 560
Charles, Prince of Wales:
   early life:
      birth, 3–5, 9n., 12–13; christening, 5;
      childhood, 6, 15–16; separation from his
      parents, 16, 19, 22–3; at his mother's
      coronation, 19–21; titles, 19, 42; discovers
      his difference from other children, 20–1;
      visits his parents in Malta, 23; illnesses, 28–9
      and n., 43, 63; relationship with Mabel
      Anderson, 34–5, 52–3; at Sandringham, 48;
      at Windsor, 55–6; cherry brandy incident,
      68–9; confirmation, 72
   education:
      taught by a governess, 22, 24–5; visits
      museums, 24; Hill House, 25–9; Cheam
      School, 35–42, 43–4; Gordonstoun, 57–76,
      89–4; stolen essays, 70–1; at Timbertop, 76,
      77–85, 87–9; GCEs, 76; 'A' levels, 83–4, 93;
      choice of university, 103–4; at Cambridge
      University, 104–14, 116–17, 138–9, 146–7;
      University College of Wales, 118–24, 127n.,
      129; degree, 146–7 and n.
   naval career:
      Lord Mountbatten encourages him to go
      into Navy, 155–6; attachment to Royal Air
      Force, 157–62, 167; first parachute jump,
      160–1; Royal Naval College, Dartmouth,
      162–4, 167, 184; difficulties with
      navigation, 163, 169, 174, 184, 185, 196,
      199; on HMS *Norfolk*, 164–9, 174–5;
      journal, 165 and n., 171, 175, 198, 200, 211,
      218; on submarines, 170–2; 'work-up',
      173–4; HMS *Minerva*'s Caribbean cruise,
      183, 185–9, 193–8; uncertainty about his
      career in Navy, 199–200; on HMS *Jupiter*,
      200–3, 206–7, 210–14; naval flying officer,
      214–16; command of HMS *Bronington*,
      217–24; decides to leave, 225
   marriage and children:
      need for a wife, 192, 205, 261–3, 279;
      courts Diana Spencer, 279–84; engagement,
      274–7, 283–7; wedding, 284–5, 288–92,
      333; and the Princess's volatile behaviour,
      285–6, 298–9, 301–2, 303–4, 330–1, 358;
      the Princess's jealousy of Camilla Parker
      Bowles, 286–7, 294, 330; honeymoon,
      292–4; the Princess's isolation and
      loneliness, 295–6, 303; the Princess's
      resentment of his interests, 303; the Princess
      attempts to control his life, 303–4, 335–6;
      birth of Prince William, 304–5; seeks
      psychiatric help for the Princess, 331;

      outshone publicly by the Princess, 333, 355,
      381; devotion to Prince William, 334;
      media speculation about marriage, 389,
      390–2, 396–7, 472–88; deteriorating
      relationship with the Princess, 392–5;
      marriage breaks down irretrievably, 394–5,
      472–89; *Diana: Her True Story*, 471, 477–84;
      media criticism of him as a father, 473–6;
      Prince William's golf club accident, 473–4;
      disagreements with the Princess about the
      children, 474–5; and Earl Spencer's death,
      476–7; refuses to let his friends speak to the
      press, 481–3; hopes that the marriage can
      survive, 483; considers separation, 484; legal
      separation, 489–91 and n., 564;
      constitutional implications of separation,
      divorce or remarriage, 490–1, 557–60; and
      the Princess's decision to withdraw from
      the limelight, 537, 538–9; relationship with
      his sons, 563–4
   public duties:
      created Prince of Wales, 42–3; Counsellor
      of State, 114; first foreign visit, 114–15;
      Knight of the Garter, 115; assassination
      threats, 120, 166, 208; investiture, 126,
      128–32, 133–5; tours Wales, 135–6;
      increases public duties, 139–40; introduced
      into House of Lords, 141–2 and n.;
      frustration at circumscribed existence, 143;
      Privy Council, 145–6; attention to detail,
      195; need to find a role in life, 225–31, 245;
      proposed as Governor-General of Australia,
      226–7, 409; proposed as ambassador to
      France, 227; proposes himself as 'Defender
      of Faith', 246, 528–34; redefines role as
      Prince of Wales, 313; visits the Vatican,
      347–54; and the Pope's visit to England,
      349; private office, 356–61, 402–4, 405–6,
      407, 454, 494–7, 498–500, 505; number of
      engagements, 359, 402, 404–5, 541;
      introduces Margaret Thatcher to inner-city
      'enablers', 377–80; meetings with ministers,
      405, 433–8, 543; guiding principles, 493–4;
      proposes changes to Buckingham Palace
      press office, 500–2; relations between the
      Queen's household and his own, 502;
      review of the royal family's responsibilities,
      503; travel arrangements, 510–11; tries to
      save royal yacht, 511–13; commitment to
      the armed forces, 514–26; and the Church
      of England, 526–34; the Archdeacon of
      York declares him unfit to be King, 535–6;
      speculation about succession, 536;
      establishes his own press office, 540–1;
      attacked in Sydney, 547–8;

Charles, Prince of Wales – *continued*
  public duties – *continued*
    and the future of the monarchy, 554–7;
    achievements, 556–7; public opinion of,
    560–1; *see also individual countries visited*
  finances:
    income from the Duchy of Cornwall,
    241–3, 300, 505, 506n.; taxation, 242,
    504–6; comptroller, 358; personal fortune,
    506n.; proposes reform of royal family's
    finances, 506–10
  projects and issues of concern:
    selecting organisations, 228; the Queen's
    Silver Jubilee, 232–4; Prince's Trust,
    235–41, 297, 361–3, 371–2; Royal Jubilee
    Trusts, 240, 274, 326, 370; and the Duchy
    of Cornwall, 241–3, 441–3; instigates
    debate on complementary medicine,
    306–11; support for organic farming,
    311–13, 439, 572–3; environmentalism, 312,
    421–30, 438–9, 497–8; RIBA speech,
    314–19; community architecture, 314–16,
    319–25, 367–8, 450–1; concern for the
    homeless, 326; informal meetings and
    seminars, 356–7; Prince's Youth Business
    Trust, 363–4, 373, 374–5; Business in the
    Community, 364–70, 372; Prince of Wales'
    Community Venture, 370–1, 372; Business
    Leaders Forum, 372–3; Prince's Trust
    Volunteers, 372; Inner City Aid, 373–7;
    United World Colleges, 385–6, 387–8;
    condemns Ceausescu's tyranny in Romania,
    430–3; 'estate days' at Sandringham and
    Balmoral, 440; and the Paternoster Square
    plan, 444–50; Mansion House speech,
    445–8; criticism of educational
    establishment, 453–9; Poundbury scheme,
    461–8; and the *Mary Rose*, 468–9; Institute
    of Architecture, 469–71; calls for removal of
    prejudice against Islam, 541–3; organisations
    listed, 567–75
  books, radio and television programmes:
    first radio interview, 118, 124–5, 127; first
    television interview, 122, 124–5, 127–8;
    media opinion of, 126–7; *The Old Man of
    Lochnagar*, 278; *The Pride Factor*, 325; *The
    Earth in Balance*, 404, 421, 430; *A Vision of
    Britain*, 404, 451–2; *Charles: The Private
    Man, The Public Role*, 476n., 528–9, 546n.,
    560
  character:
    self-deprecation, 21, 73, 139, 163, 169, 561;
    sensitivity, 21; lack of self-confidence, 29; as
    a young child, 33; insecurity at Cheam
    School, 37–8; politeness, 44 and n., 66;

    appearance, 65–6 and n., 110, 381–2;
    kindness, 66–7, 85, 406–7, 565; attitude to
    the media, 69–70, 213, 221–2, 365–6;
    spirituality, 71–2, 86–7, 113–14, 246–56,
    389–90, 470, 526, 562–3; mimicry, 84, 91;
    inability to feign his feelings, 122; influence
    of Lord Mountbatten, 137, 155, 176–7,
    181–2, 207, 265–7; sense of the absurd, 145;
    selfishness, 164, 260–1; impatience, 165,
    243–4, 565; commentaries on people and
    places visited, 185–6; homesickness, 189,
    196; reaction to Princess Anne's marriage,
    191–2; mild depression, 196; flirtations,
    202–4; paradoxes, 212, 328, 404, 405–6,
    523–4, 562; 'Action Man' image, 221–2,
    256, 313, 388; self-criticism, 222; assertion
    of conviction, 234; influence of Laurens van
    der Post, 249–53; media image of 'loony
    Prince', 313, 388; naivety, 366; isolation,
    392; tabloid reputation as 'accident prone',
    416–17; fractures arm, 417–18; back
    problem, 420; sensitivity to criticism,
    460–1; pessimism, 561; as an 'old soul', 565
  friendships:
    close relationship with Queen Mother, 17,
    52; relationship with his father, 21–2 and n.,
    35, 48–50, 52, 65n., 78, 156–7, 392, 406,
    563; admires Lord Mountbatten, 54;
    relationship with his mother, 55, 157, 177,
    392, 563; at Trinity College, 108–9, 111;
    visits Duke of Windsor, 178–9; first meets
    Camilla Shand, 182; wishes to marry
    Camilla, 182–4; and Amanda Knatchbull,
    190, 204–6, 263–5; learns of Camilla's
    marriage, 191; girlfriends, 258–60; press
    speculation about his girlfriends, 262–3; and
    Lord Mountbatten's assassination, 266–7,
    279; close relationship with Camilla Parker
    Bowles, 277–8; affection for his brothers
    and sister, 278; ends relationship with
    Camilla Parker Bowles, 287; the Princess
    persuades him to drop some of his friends,
    335–6; the Prince re-establishes close
    relationship with Camilla Parker Bowles,
    395–6; restores relations with expelled
    friends, 395; skiing tragedy in Klosters,
    412–16; 'Camillagate' tape, 491–2n.; *Daily
    Express* alleges rift with the Queen, 576–9
  private interests:
    love of art, 22, 24–5, 26 and n., 91, 93, 190,
    354; love of Balmoral, 30–2, 89, 116, 138,
    397, 440–1; love of the outdoors, 32, 45–6,
    78; shooting, 32, 45–6, 111–12, 440–1; fox
    hunting, 46, 54n., 256–7, 289; love of
    music, 53 and n., 73–4, 92; love of Italy, 53

and n., 343, 345–6; horse riding, 54–5;
   pottery, 64, 91; plays the cello, 73–4, 92;
   acting ability, 74–6, 116–17; polo, 115–16,
   194, 208, 257, 411, 417, 419–20, 486;
   flying, 157–8, 159–60; proposed visit to
   Kalahari Desert, 250–1; records his dreams,
   251–2; vegetarianism, 254; skiing, 257–8,
   411–12; and Chevening House, 299, 300;
   Highgrove House, 300–1; visits Kalahari
   Desert, 407–8; Tanzanian safari, 409,
   410–11
Charles I, King, 25, 129n.
Charles II, King, 274
Charles, Revd Sebastian, 375, 376
Charleston, South Carolina, 372
Charter 88, 552
Charteris, Sir Martin, 40 and n., 41, 229, 236–7,
   358–9
Chatham, 197
Cheam School, 35–42, 43–4, 50, 53, 58, 67, 73
Cheam School Chronicle, 43
Checketts, Squadron Leader David, 78n., 91,
   167, 253n., 262, 499; and the Prince's stay at
   Timbertop, 77–8, 79, 80, 81, 82, 84–5,
   87–8, 89; at Cambridge University, 105,
   106, 146–7; sets up radio interview, 118n.,
   127; and the investiture, 126; the Prince's
   letters to, 164, 195; and the Prince's naval
   career, 199, 213; and the Prince's planned
   balloon flight, 216–17; proposes the Prince
   as Governor-General of Australia, 226–7;
   and the Prince's need for a role in life,
   228–9; and the Prince's Trust, 239; and the
   Duchy of Cornwall, 241–3
Checketts, Leila, 84, 85
Checketts, Simon, 85
Cheshire regiment, 520, 521, 522
Chester, 237
Chevening House, Kent, 299, 300
Chew, Robert, 59–60, 61, 89, 90
China, 148
Chiropractors Act (1994), 573
Christianity, 526, 530, 532, 542
Church of England, 86; the Prince's christening,
   5; Prince Philip received into, 51; the
   Prince's confirmation, 71–2; and the Prince's
   beliefs, 246–7, 526–34; constraints on the
   Prince's choice of a wife, 276–7; relations
   with the Catholic Church, 347, 348–50; and
   the Prince's legal separation, 490–1; and the
   Prince as 'Defender of Faith', 528–34;
   disestablishment, 529 and n.; and the
   possibility of the Prince of Wales's divorce
   and remarriage, 558–9 and n.
Church of Scotland, 351, 352, 354, 529n., 533

Churchill, HMS, 171–2
Churchill, Lord Randolph, 36
Churchill, Sir Winston, 3–4, 6, 13, 19–20, 25,
   51, 97, 99, 152, 445
Chuter Ede, James, 192
CIA, 409
Cirencester, 405, 417
Cirencester Memorial Hospital, 417, 418
Civil List, 241n., 242, 504, 507–8
Clare, Lieutenant Roy, 217–18, 220, 222–3
Clarence House, 15, 284, 557n.
Clarke, Kenneth, 457–8 and n., 459
Classiebawn Castle, 266
Clay Cross Parish Council, 291
Clegg, Tony, 448
Cleverdon, Julia, 494
Clover, Charles, 300
Club of Rome, 422–3, 424
Coastguard Service, Gordonstoun, 68
Colborne, Michael, 244–5, 286, 287, 358
Cold War, 9, 431, 467n., 515, 525
Coldstream Guards, 274
Collins, Joan, 388
Collins, Phil, 362
Collor, Fernando, 497–8 and n.
Colombia, 188–9 and n., 202
Columbia Studios, 209
Colville, Sir Richard, 24 and n., 27, 40, 68–9,
   71, 124–5, 126
Commission for Racial Equality, 231
Commission on Social Justice (Labour Party),
   372n., 568
Commons Defence Committee, 522
Commons Energy Select Committee, 436
Commonwealth: 201, 229; the Queen's 1953
   tour, 22–3; South African problem, 150; and
   Britain's membership of EEC, 152
Commonwealth Development Corporation, 338
Community Service by Offenders, 234–5
complementary medicine, 306–11, 573
Concorde, 422
Confederation of British Industry (CBI), 229,
   485n.
Confederation of Indian Industry, 485n.
Connell, Brian, 122, 276
Conservative Association, Cambridge, 108, 110
Conservative Party, 271–2, 323, 375–6, 424, 438,
   454
Conservative Party Conference (1988), 426
Constantine II, King of Greece, 481
Cook, Captain J.D.W., 166, 174, 175
Cookson, Catherine, 405
Cooper, Rev., 194
Cornish, Francis, 286 and n.
Cornwall, 237

Cornwall, Duchy of, 228, 541, 572–3; history, 241–2; the Prince's income from, 241–3, 300, 505, 506n.; management of, 243, 441–3; purchase of Highgrove, 299–300; organic farming, 439; Poundbury scheme, 461–8; 'Duchy Originals', 572–3
Coronation Oath, 531 and n., 533–4, 535
Correa, Charles, 314, 315–16, 317
Cossiga, Signor, 346
Countryside in 1970 Committee for Wales, 312, 421
Courier Mail (Brisbane), 479
Court Circular, 125 and n., 359n., 543
Cousteau, Jacques, 383
Covent Garden, 53, 344, 473
Cowdray Park, 257, 405, 419
Cowes Week, 512
Craigowan Lodge, 577, 578
Cranborne Manor, Dorset, 301
Cranwell, 157–62, 167
Crawford, Geoffrey, 538
Craxi, Bettino, 346 and n.
Craxton, Antony, 134
Crete, 293
Cripps, Sir Stafford, 7
Critchlow, Keith, 445n.
Crosby, Theo, 445n.
Crosfield, Revd Philip, 71–2 and n., 247
Crosland, Anthony, 251 and n.
Crown estates, 507
Crown Jewels, 506
Cruickshank, Dan, 448
Cuba, 209
Cyprus, 211 and n., 522
Czech Republic, 373, 570, 574
Czechoslovakia, 438, 457, 541

Daily Express, 43, 212, 313, 390, 448n., 502n., 539, 576–9
Daily Mail, 26n., 68, 101n., 121, 128–9, 213, 230, 313, 373, 481, 512
Daily Mirror, 69, 212, 213, 284–5, 288n., 302 and n., 313, 325, 484n., 537, 539
Daily Star, 302, 389, 390, 391, 448n.
Daily Telegraph, 23, 42, 69, 117, 120, 275, 286, 326, 449, 454, 522
Dalton, Hugh, 7
Darling, Dr, 81–2
Dartmoor, 243, 442
Davies, Robert, 372–3
Davies, Yvonne, 121
Day, Stephen, 401
Day-Lewis, Sean, 117
De Gaulle, General, 98, 152
De Manio, Jack, 118n., 120, 127

Dear, Geoffrey, 369n.
Debrett's, 274
Dee, River, 32, 280, 294, 441, 539
Della Robbia, Luca, 345
Dempster, Nigel, 230
Dench, Judi, 460
Department of Education, 458
Department of Energy, 433–6
Department of the Environment, 314, 425, 427, 436
Department of Trade and Industry, 543
Derby, 541
Diamond, Neil, 383
Diana, Princess of Wales: the Prince courts, 279–84; engagement, 274–7, 283–7; wedding, 284–5, 288–92, 333; weight loss, 285–6, 329; volatile behaviour, 285–6, 297–9, 301–2, 303–4, 329–31, 358, 393; jealousy of Camilla Parker Bowles, 286–7, 294, 330; honeymoon, 292–4; ability to talk to the public, 295; isolation and loneliness, 295–6, 303; first pregnancy, 295, 303; relations with her staff, 297–8; alleged suicide attempts, 298, 330–1; at Highgrove, 301; photographed in a bikini while pregnant, 302–3; pressure from the media, 302–3; photographed in a London gym, 302n., 537; attempts to control the Prince's life, 303–4, 335–6; resentment of the Prince's interests, 303; self-absorption, 303; birth of Prince William, 304–5; in Australia, 331–3, 381; family background, 331; psychiatric help, 331, 335; media obsession with, 332, 343; outshines the Prince publicly, 333, 355, 381; persuades the Prince to drop some of his friends, 335–6; Italian tour, 343–8, 354–5; visits the Vatican, 347–8, 351; relations with the Prince's staff, 357–8; American tour, 381, 382, 384–6; media speculation about her marriage, 389, 390–2, 396–7, 472–88; clothes, 391; deteriorating relationship with the Prince, 392–5; marriage breaks down irretrievably, 394–5, 472–89; friends, 396; and the skiing tragedy at Klosters, 411–12, 416 and n.; Diana: Her True Story, 471, 477–84; Prince William's golf club accident, 473–4; disagreements with the Prince about the children, 474–5; and her father's death, 476–7; the Prince hopes that the marriage can survive, 483; 'Squidgy tapes', 483n.; considers separation, 484; Indian tour, 485–6; photographed at the Taj Mahal, 485–6; Korean visit, 486–8; legal separation, 489–91 and n., 564; financial arrangements, 505–6; decision to

withdraw from limelight, 536–9; possibility
of divorce, 559
Dicey, A.V., 125 and n.
Dimbleby, Richard, 18
Disraeli, Benjamin, 135
Dogura, 85–7 and n.
Dorchester, 404, 461–8
Dorset, 243
Douglas-Home, Sir Alec, 99, 149–50 and n
Douglas-Home, Charles, 326–7 and n.
Douglas-Home, Jessica, 432
Drivers Jonas, 461, 463, 464
Dryad, HMS, 176
Dryden Society, 116–17
Duggan, James, 422
Duino, 343
Dunne, Sir Laurence, 101n.
Dunne, Philip, 396
Dutschke, Rudi, 147n.
Dylan, Bob, 100

Eagle, HMS, 170, 175
Eagle (comic), 39 and n.
The Earth in Balance (television documentary),
404, 421, 430
Earth Summit, Rio de Janeiro (1991), 404, 430,
497–8
Eastwood, Clint, 383
Ebbw Vale, 135
Eden, Sir Anthony (Earl of Avon), 97, 152–3
Edgar, King, 533
Edinburgh, 365
Edinburgh, Prince Philip, Duke of: marriage, 12,
50–1; moves to Clarence House, 15; the
Prince's birth, 4; absence from home, 16;
relationship with the Prince, 21–2 and n.,
35, 48–50, 52, 65n., 78, 156–7, 392, 406,
563; 1953 Commonwealth tour, 22–3; and
the Prince's education, 22, 35, 36–7;
holidays at Balmoral, 32; and the Prince's
childhood, 33–4; education, 36, 59, 163; at
Sandringham, 48; early life, 50; and the
Church of England, 51; family name, 51,
192; titles, 51; treatment by courtiers, 51 and
n.; character, 52; as the Queen's consort, 52;
indifference to music, 53 and n.; sends the
Prince to Gordonstoun, 58–9, 65; and the
Prince's confirmation, 72; and the Prince at
Timbertop, 78, 79; and the Prince's further
education, 103, 104, 105; Royal Family, 133;
and the Prince's introduction into the House
of Lords, 141; and Lord Mountbatten, 155;
and the Prince's naval career, 156, 199;
inspects HMS Bronington, 218; and the
Prince's Trust, 239; encourages the Prince to
play polo, 257; and the Prince's girlfriends,
260; opposes Amanda Knatchbull's presence
on Indian visit, 264; encourages the Prince
to marry Diana Spencer, 282–3; speeches,
327; and The Earth in Balance, 430;
management of Sandringham and Balmoral
estates, 440, 441; and the foundering of the
Prince's marriage, 483–4, 487; and the
Princess's decision to withdraw from the
limelight, 538
Edinburgh University, 248n.
Edward, the Black Prince, 241, 242
Edward, Prince: childhood, 35n., 74, 76; Royal
Family, 133; It's A Royal Knockout, 133n.; the
Prince's affection for, 278; excluded from
Civil List, 504n.
Edward I, King, 131
Edward II, King, 129n.
Edward III, King, 241
Edward VII, King, 10, 46, 47, 103, 241, 277
Edward VIII, King see Windsor, Duke of
Edwards, Sir Ifan ab Owen, 129–30
Eisteddfod, 123–4 and n.
Ekins, Paul, 427
Eleuthera, 189–91, 204, 216, 260–1, 263, 264,
302–3
Elizabeth, the Queen Mother, 249, 522, 577;
devotion to the Prince, 17, 52, 392; at the
Queen's coronation, 19, 20; at Sandringham,
48; abdication crisis, 53; and Lord
Mountbatten, 54, 155; and the Prince's
education, 58; singing ability, 73; seventieth
birthday, 147; refuses reconciliation with
Duke of Windsor, 178; marriage, 277;
approves of Diana Spencer, 282; love of Italy,
343; 90th birthday, 405
Elizabeth I, Queen, 527n.
Elizabeth II, Queen: marriage, 12, 13, 50–1;
moves to Clarence House, 15; the Prince's
birth, 3–5, 6, 13; preparation for becoming
Queen, 16; and the Prince's childhood, 16,
19; and her father's death, 17–18; becomes
Queen, 19; coronation, 19–21, 246; 1953
Commonwealth tour, 22–3; and the Prince's
education, 22, 26–7, 35, 36–7, 44, 89 and n.;
holidays at Balmoral, 32–3; creates Charles
Prince of Wales, 42; birth of Prince Andrew,
43; at Sandringham, 47, 48; and the Prince's
relationship with his father, 49; family name,
51, 192–3; and her husband's public role, 52;
relationship with the Prince, 55, 157, 177,
392, 563; and the Church of England, 71–2;
and the Prince at Timbertop, 79, 82; Lord
Altrincham's criticisms, 101; and the Prince's
further education, 103, 104 and n., 108, 119;

Elizabeth II, Queen – *continued*
the Prince's investiture, 133, 134; *Royal Family*, 133; speeches, 140; State Opening of Parliament, 140; and the Prince's treatment in the Navy, 186–7; Silver Jubilee, 232–4; and the Prince's Trust, 239; opposes Amanda Knatchbull's presence on Indian visit, 264; approves of Diana Spencer, 282; and the Pope's visit to England, 349; and the Prince's visit to the Vatican, 352–3; *annus horribilis*, 483n., 500, 503, 551; and the foundering of the Prince's marriage, 483–4, 488–9; advises the Princess to go on Korean visit, 487; and the legal separation, 489–90; relations between the Prince's household and her own, 502; review of the royal family's responsibilities, 503; taxation, 503–5, 506, 508–10, 574; household drawn from armed forces, 514n.; speculation about succession, 536; and the Princess's decision to withdraw from the limelight, 538; and the future of the monarchy in Australia, 546; Royal Collection, 574; *Daily Express* alleges rift with the Prince, 576–9
Ellington, Duke, 113
Elliott, Commander, 223
Embericos, Anthony, 420
Empire and Commonwealth Games, 41
English Heritage, 571
Enlightenment, 248
Erpingham Camp (Orton), 117
Eton, 57, 58, 64, 459
European Commission, 230
European Community Conference on the Urban Environment (1991), 438
European Conservation Year (1970), 312, 421–2
European Economic Community (EEC), 98, 149, 152, 227, 432
European Environment Conference (1988), 428–9
European Union, 551
European Year of the Environment, 425
Evans, Gwynfor, 119
Evening News, 57
Evening Standard, 57, 310–11, 448, 450, 536
Everett, Oliver, 231, 286 and n., 297–8
Ewing, Winifred, 119
Expo '70, 143, 145
Expo '86, 394

Fabian Society, 108
Falklands campaign (1982), 303, 350, 517–18 and n., 520
Farrer, Matthew, 239
Faulkes, Sebastian, 491–2n.

Federal Institute for Snow and Avalanche Research, Davos, 415–16
Fellowes, Lady Jane, 280 and n., 285
Fellowes, Sir Robert, 280 and n., 419, 479, 480 and n., 483, 538
Ferguson, Major Ronald, 410, 411
Fermoy, Ruth (Lady Fermoy), 66–7 and n., 73, 282 and n., 331
Fiji, 150–2, 213
Financial Times, 445, 543
Finland, 139
Fisher, Geoffrey, Archbishop of Canterbury, 5, 20 and n.
Fishguard, 135
Florence, 345–6
Flynn, Paul, 433
Foggo, Peter, 448–9
Food and Agricultural Organisation, 346–7
Foot, Michael, 135
Fordington Fields, Dorchester, 461
Foreign Office, 357, 543; Britain's special relationship with USA, 149–50 and n.; and the Prince's naval career, 165, 166, 186; opposition to the Prince's proposed visit to the Kalahari, 250–1; and the Prince's honeymoon plans, 292; and the Prince's visit to the Gulf states, 401–2; Romanian policy, 430–1; and the Princess's role as an informal ambassador, 537; and the Prince's speeches, 541, 542–3
Forty Years On (Bennett), 98
Foster, Norman, 317–18, 444
Fowler, Norman, 369
Fox, HMS, 190
Fox, Uffa, 49
France, 98, 100, 152, 178, 227, 342, 456, 573, 578
Francistown, 407
Frankenthaler, Helen, 383n.
Free Church of Scotland, 69, 350
Free Presbyterian Church of Scotland, 351–2, 354, 528
Free Wales Army, 120, 130, 134
Freud, Sigmund, 113
Friends of the Earth, 421, 426
'Futures for Youth' seminar (1986), 368

Gabarone, 340
Gallagher, Willie, 9n.
Gallup polls, 504, 552
Gandhi, Indira, 154
Gandhi, Mahatma, 139
'Garden House Riot', Cambridge, 113 and n.
Gardiner, Lord, 141n.
Gardner, Ava, 209

Gardner, Jim, 376
Garnett, Thomas, 78
Garnier, Captain John, 187–8, 197
Gatcombe Park, Gloucestershire, 299
Geelong Church of England Grammar School, 78, 81, 83
Geldof, Bob, 375
Geltaidd Society, 121
General Elections (1970), 147–8
George III, King, 116, 240, 507
George V, King, 276; Christmas messages, 10; popularity, 10; shooting ability, 46; love of Sandringham, 47; rescues Prince Philip, 50; Silver Jubilee, 235
George VI, King, 8; popularity, 11; in Second World War, 11–12; ill-health, 16, 17; devotion to his grandchildren, 16–17; love of Sandringham, 47; and the Queen's family name, 51; abdication crisis, 53; university education, 103; marriage, 277; death, 17–19, 178
Germany, 98, 343, 425, 515, 573
Gibbon, Edward, 399
Gibraltar, 23, 164, 165 and n., 174–5, 292–3
Gielgud, John, 460
Gilbey, James, 396, 474, 484n.
Girl Guides, 135, 235
Gloucester, Duchess of, 257, 522
Gloucester, Prince Henry, Duke of, 48
Gloucester, Prince Richard, Duke of, 257, 522
Goethe, Johann Wolfgang von, 317
Goldring, Mary, 478
Goldsmiths Hall, London, 286
Goodman, Lord Arnold, 484 and n.
The Goons, 73, 92, 159, 182, 289n.
Gorbachev, Mikhail, 383 and n., 431
Gordon Highlanders, 347, 514n., 520
Gordonstoun, 50, 57–76, 81, 82–3, 86, 89–94, 235, 246–7, 371
Gore, Senator Albert, 497 and n.
GPO, 220
Grace, Princess of Monaco, 286
Grand Metropolitan, 496
Granville, Lady, 6
Gray-Fisher, Clinton, 46
Great Ormond Street Hospital, London, 43, 473–4
Greater London Council, 285, 291
Greece, 8, 211, 293
Greek Orthodox Church, 51
Green, Donald, 68, 69
Green movement, 424
Green Party, 421
Greenpeace, 421
Grey, Anthony, 299 and n.

Griffiths, Brian, 459 and n.
Grimsditch, Elizabeth, 576–7 and n.
Guardian, 121, 313, 315, 326, 423, 491–2n.; *see also Manchester Guardian*
Guinness, Sabrina, 258
Guinness Housing Trust, 571
Gulf States, 401–2, 405, 541, 542–3
Gulf War, 520, 525
Gummer, John, 405, 543
Gurkhas, 525

Habgood, Dr John, Archbishop of York, 354, 531n., 532, 558
Hackney, Rod, 319–20, 322–5, 365, 374–7
Haglamadd, 412, 415
Hahn, Dr Kurt, 59–60, 61, 67–8, 78, 89, 228n., 235, 371
Haile Selassie, Emperor of Ethiopia, 153
Halifax partnership, 367–8
Hall, Philip, *Royal Fortune*, 504
Hamilton, Andrew, 465, 466
Hamilton, Archie, 512 and n., 522–3
Hamilton, William, 212n., 274–5
Hammer, Armand, 384–7, 388
Hampton Court Palace, 314
Handel, George Frederic, 285, 289
Handsworth, 369n.
Hanoverians, 31
Hanson, Brian, 445n., 465, 470
Harare, 339
Harris, Kenneth, 276
Harrison, Patrick, 315
Harrow School, 57
Harry, Prince, 335, 578; birth, 343; the Prince and Princess disagree over access arrangements, 474–5, 488–9; financial provisions, 506n.; the Prince's relationship with, 563–4 and n.
Harvard University, 390
Havel, Vaclav, 574
Hawaii, 204, 208
Hawke, Bob, 341, 409
Hawkins, Major Sir Michael, 238
Haywood, Harold, 326
Heath, Edward, 115, 119 and n., 123, 147–8, 149, 152, 271, 272
Heath, Sir Mark, 353
Hebrides, 428 and n.
Hennessy, Peter, 553
Henry V, King, 18, 132
Henry V (Shakespeare), 74–5
Henry VIII, King, 25, 350, 404, 526–7 and n.
Henty, G.A., 39
Herbert, Ivor, 57
The Heretics, 108

Hermes, HMS, 214, 215–16
Hermione, HMS, 171, 172–3
Heseltine, Michael, 320, 405, 438
Heseltine, Sir William, 106–7 and n., 124–6,
   127–8, 133, 353, 419
Heston, Charlton, 209
Hewitt, James, 396
Hickling, Norfolk, 45
Higgs, John, 406 and n., 441
Highgrove, Gloucestershire, 299, 300–1, 356,
   379, 433, 439, 505, 563, 564, 572
Hill House (preparatory school), 25–9
Hill-Norton, Admiral Peter, 164n.
Hinduism, 253, 315, 526, 528, 529n., 532,
   542
Hirohito, Emperor of Japan, 143–4
Hitachi, Princess, 144
Hitler, Adolf, 152–3
Hockney, David, 383n.
Holdgate, Sir Martin, 425 and n.
Hollywood, 209–10
Holt, Harold, 114 and n.
Holyhead, 220
Holyrood House, 150, 574
Home Office, 350, 351, 354
Hong Kong, 142, 143, 404, 488
Honolulu, 200, 213
Hope, Bob, 209
House of Commons, 11, 323, 484, 489–90, 504,
   512n., 553
House of Lords, 141–2 and n., 480, 551
Household Cavalry, 18, 140, 181
Howard, Philip, 117, 453–4
Howe, Sir Geoffrey, 431–2, 433
Hugo, Victor, 39
Hume, Cardinal, 291
Hungary, 404
Hunt, David, 405, 543 and n.
Hurd, Douglas, 537
Hussein, King of Jordan, 577, 578
Hussein, Saddam, 541
Hussey, Marmaduke 'Dukie', 74n.
Hussey, Lady Susan, 74 and n., 334
Hyde Park, London, 285, 288

Independent, 453, 506
India, 150, 255, 263, 264, 485–6
Indo-British Industrialists' Forum, 485 and n.
Indonesia, 404
Inland Revenue, 242, 505, 508
Inner City Aid, 373–7
Inner City Scheme, 362
Institute of Architecture, 469–71, 546n., 570
Institute of Directors, 320, 322
'Inter-City Action', 570

Intermediate Technology Development Group,
   312, 423
International Monetary Fund, 338
IRA, 166, 266, 515
Iraq, 520, 525, 541–2
Ireland, 266–7, 573
Islam, 315, 526, 528, 529n., 530, 532, 541–2
Isle of Wight, 171, 512–13
Italy, 53, 293, 343–8, 405, 456, 469, 555
Ithaca, 293
It's A Royal Knockout, 133 and n.
ITV, 122, 560

Jacobi, Derek, 460
Jamaica, 187–8, 196
James, P.D., 458 and n.
Janvrin, Robin, 482
Japan, 142, 143–5, 456, 573
Java Sea, 212
Jay, Anthony, 514n.
Jenkins, Roy, 230 and n.
Jenkins, Simon, 572
Jephson, Patrick, 482 and n., 489, 538
Jesus Christ, 247, 530
John F. Kennedy, USS, 175
John Paul II, Pope, 347–9, 526
Johns, Squadron Leader Richard, 159 and n.
Johnson, Lyndon, 115 and n.
Jones, Hywel, 110–11
Juan Carlos, King of Spain, 292–3
Jubilee Trusts *see* Royal Jubilee Trusts
Judaism, 526, 528, 529n., 532
Jung, Carl, 113, 251–2, 293–4, 307, 332
Junior Red Cross, 235
Junor, Penny, 481n., 483
Jupiter, HMS, 200–3, 204, 206–7, 210–14
Justice, James Robertson, 49

Kalahari Desert, 249–51, 407–8, 428 and n.
Kamp, Joseph, 387
Kang, David, 547–8 and n.
Kaufman, Gerald, 323, 326
Kaunda, President, 338–9
Keating, Paul, 545, 546–7 and n., 549
Kennedy, John F., 209
Kennedy, Robert, 100
Kensington Palace, 296, 309, 311, 322, 356, 379,
   397, 425, 433, 505, 557n.
Kent, 541
Kent, Duchess of, 522
Kent, Duke of, 522
Kent, Geoffrey, 409, 410–11, 418, 420
Kent, Jorie, 409, 410, 411, 417, 418
Kenya, 251, 407, 548
Kerr, Lady Cecily, 258

Kerr, Sir John, 226, 409
Keswick, Lady Sarah, 397 and n.
Key, Sarah, 418
Kindersley, Lord, 309 and n.
King, Martin Luther, 112
King, Tom, 519n., 521 and n.
King George's Jubilee Trust, 233, 235–6, 238, 239, 240
Kipling, Rudyard, 563n.
Klosters, 257–8, 283, 405, 411–16
Knatchbull, Amanda, 190, 204–6, 261, 263–5, 266
Knatchbull, Nicholas, 266
Knatchbull, Norton see Romsey, Lord
Knatchbull, Timothy, 266
Knevitt, Charles, 374
Knight, Andrew, 478 and n., 480, 481, 482
Knights of the Garter, 25, 115
Knott, Kevin, 465
Koestler, Arthur, 248
Korea, 486–8
Krier, Leon, 461–8, 469, 470
Kuwait, 542
Kyoto, 145

La Scala, Milan, 344
La Spezia, 344
Labour Club, Cambridge, 108, 110
Labour Party, 6, 170, 272, 372n., 405, 506, 568
Lancaster, Duchy of, 504
Landale, David, 461, 572
Lang, Ian, 405
Lange, David, 341
Lascelles, Sir Alan, 51 and n.
The Last Baron (Munir), 43
League Against Cruel Sports, 69
Lech, 476
Lennon, John, 140
Leo X, Pope, 527
Leonardo da Vinci, 55–6, 344–5
Leslie, Ann, 109
Lewin, Sir Terence, 517 and n.
Lewis, Isle of, 68
Lightbody, Helen, 15, 19, 33–4
Lillydale, 84
Limits to Growth, 422–3
Lindsay, Major Hugh, 412–14, 416
Lindsay, Sarah, 416n.
Lipton, Stuart, 444, 448
Lisbon Agreement (1980), 292
Liverpool, 273, 320, 366–7, 379
Liverpool, Lord, 147
Livingston, Dr David, 339
Livingstone, Ken, 285, 291
Llanelli, 371

Lochnagar, 30 and n., 89, 160, 252
Locke, John, 146
London, Duchy of Cornwall property in, 243
London Weekend Television, 325
Longfellow, Henry Wadsworth, 49
Los Angeles, 142, 208, 385
Lossiemouth, 294
Lovelock, James, 307 and n.
Lowell, Massachusetts, 367
Lubbock, Jules, 315, 445
Luce, Richard, 337–8
Ludgrove School, 488, 578
Lycett-Green, Candida, 445n.

Macbeth (Shakespeare), 75–6
Macclesfield, 320, 321, 325, 367
Macdonald, Captain Roderick, 175
McGregor, Lord, 479–80, 481
McGregor, Stuart, 82
Mackay, Lord, 480, 491
MacKenzie, Kelvin, 540
Mackie, Philip, 413–14, 415, 482
Maclean, Lord, 193
Maclean, Sergeant John, 166
Macleod, Revd John, 354
Macmillan, Sir Harold, 98–9, 152, 153, 209, 300
Macmillan, Maurice, 300
McNee, Sir David, 273
Madame Tussaud's, 24
Maiden Castle, 461
Mail on Sunday, 477–8
Major, John, 380, 405, 484, 489–91, 504, 509, 518–21, 544, 572
Makarikari, 408
Makarios, Archbishop, 154
Malawi, 407
Malaysia, 200n., 201, 212
Malta, 16, 23, 81, 115–16, 179
Manchester Evening News, 323
Manchester Guardian, 4, 23, 26, 42; see also Guardian
Mandela, Nelson, 150n.
Manser, Michael, 314, 315, 317, 318, 319, 444
Mansion House, London, 449, 452
Manus Island, 342
Mappin and Webb Building, London, 452n.
Maracaibo, 189
Marcos, Ferdinand, 115, 337
Margaret, Princess: at Sandringham, 48; marriage, 55; house on Mustique, 196; excluded from Civil List, 504n.; and reorganisation of Army bands, 522; divorce, 558
Marina, Princess, Duchess of Kent, 48
Marlborough House, 15

Marrian, Dr Denis, 105, 106, 146–7
Marsh Arabs, 541–2
Martin, Christopher, 445, 451
Marxist Society, 108, 110
Mary, Queen, consort of George V, 3, 15, 179 and n.
Mary I, Queen, 527n.
Mary II, Queen, 284
Mary Rose, 404, 468–9, 471
Mary Rose Trust, 384, 468–9
Masefield, John, 13–14
Mass Observation, 12 and n., 17n., 233
Matter, Professor Peter, 417–18
Mattick, Stephen, 462, 463
Max, Prince of Baden, 59
Maxwell, Paul, 266
Mediterranean, 164, 174, 292
Melbourne, 422
Mellor, David, 405, 571
Menzies, Kate, 396
Menzies, Sir Robert, 78
Mercury, HMS, 184 and n.
Merseyside, 366–7
Metropolitan Police, 15, 69, 273
Mexico, 541
Mexico City, 88
MI5, 409
Michael, Prince of Kent, 22
Michelmore, Cliff, 122
Middle East, 401, 542
Midlands, 405
Mies van der Rohe, Ludwig, 320
Mikardo, Ian, 112 and n.
Milan, 344
Miller, Lieutenant-Colonel Sir John, 54 and n., 55, 256, 257
Milligan, Spike, 84, 289
Millward, Edward, 123
Minerva, HMS, 183, 185–9, 193–8, 202, 206, 279
Ministry of Agriculture, 436, 572
Ministry of Defence, 39, 166, 184, 187, 211, 215, 221, 442, 510n., 512n., 518, 520, 524n., 525, 572
Ministry of Food, 7
Mintoff, Dom, 179
Monaco, 342
'The Monarchy, the Constitution and the People' debate (1993), 552
Monserrat, 187
Montefiore, Hugh, 71–2, 113, 117
Moonshot Club, Deptford, 273
Moore, Sir Philip, 228, 229, 349, 352
More, Sir Thomas, 527n.
MORI, 552n.
Morning Star, 212n.

Morrah, Dermot (Arundel Herald of Arms), 5n., 16n., 19, 27 and n., 58, 78, 86, 89n., 103
Morrison, Peter, 433–6 and n.
Mortimer, John, 57
Morton, Andrew, 330, 389, 391, 474; *Diana: Her True Story*, 471, 475n., 477–84
Moser, Sir Claus, 458 and n.
Mountbatten, Lord: in Malta, 23; the Prince's birthday presents, 39 and n., 40–1 and n.; character, 53–4; the Prince admires, 54; comments on the Prince's ears, 66n.; president of United World Colleges, 79n., 228n., 262, 387–8; the Prince's letters to, 82, 83, 90, 91, 115, 116, 136–7, 159, 164–5, 169, 173, 181, 200, 204, 218, 219, 260, 262; and the Prince's further education, 103, 104–5; All Malta Polo Club, 115; congratulates the Prince on his investiture, 136–7; influence on the Prince, 137, 155, 176–7, 181–2, 207, 265–7; seventieth birthday, 147; encourages the Prince to go into Navy, 155–6; the Prince stays at Broadlands, 164–5; hopes for reconciliation between Duke of Windsor and royal family, 177–8; and the Duke of Windsor's death, 180, 181; the Prince visits in Eleuthera, 189, 191; and the royal family's name, 192–3 and n.; hopes the Prince will marry Amanda Knatchbull, 204–6, 263–5; and the Prince's planned balloon flight, 216–17; and the Prince's impatience, 244–5; and the Prince's spiritual interests, 254; warns the Prince of selfishness, 260–1; advises the Prince on the choice of a wife, 281; assassination, 266–7, 279; the Prince rumoured to be trying to make contact with, 313
Mugabe, Mrs, 340
Mugabe, Robert, 340
Muggeridge, Malcolm, 102
Muick, Loch, 30, 160, 397 and n., 476n.
Mullaghmore, 266
Munir, David, 37, 43
Murdoch, Rupert, 80n., 478–9
Mussolini, Benito, 152
Mustique, 196

Nabarro, Sir Gerald, 112 and n.
Nahayyan, Sheikh Zaid bin Sultan bin Zaid Al, 140
Nassau, 194–5
National and English Review, 101
National Association for Teachers of English, 457
National Audit Office, 557n.
National Commission on Education, 458
National Curriculum, 455–6, 458–9

National Fruit Collection, 404
National Gallery, London, 317, 318, 319, 449
National Health Service, 308
National Heritage Memorial Fund, 571
National Lottery, 572
National Society for the Abolition of Cruel
    Sports, 46
NATO, 162, 167, 168, 175, 211–12, 216, 431
Natural History Museum, 24
Nazis, 59
NEDO (National Economic Development
    Office), 229
Needham, Richard, 543
Neil, Andrew, 477–8, 482
Neilson McCarthy, 118n.
Netherlands, 342, 456, 552n.
Neville, Rupert, 283
New English Bible, 453
New South Wales, 545
New York, 142
New York Times, 7, 382
New Zealand, 410; official visits to, 142, 143,
    284, 286, 333–4; and Britain's membership
    of EEC, 152; HMS Jupiter visits, 200, 204
News Chronicle, 21n.
News of the World, 576n.
Newspaper Proprietors Association, 24
Newtown, 135
Nigeria, 404
Nixon, Richard, 148–9
Noble, Adrian, 460
Nonconformists, 529n.
NOP, 552 and n.
Norfolk, HMS, 164, 165–9, 171, 174–5, 184, 202,
    244
Norfolk, Duke of, 20 and n., 128, 132, 133, 141
North Sea, 222
North Sea Conference, London, 424
Northern Ireland, 173, 515, 516–17
Northfield, Lord, 424
Northolt, RAF, 510n.
Norway, 343
Nyerere, Dr Julius, 338 and n.

Oborn, Sarah, 464–5
O'Brien, Stephen, 364–5 and n., 366, 367, 368,
    370, 376, 378, 379, 403, 496
Observer, 312, 315, 429–30
Occidental Petroleum, 384, 387
Odhams Ltd, 39
O'Donovan, T.C.M., 359n.
Officer, Sergeant Paul, 166
Ogilvie, Angus, 74 and n.
The Old Man of Lochnagar, 252, 278
Operation Drake, 385n.

Operation Raleigh, 208n., 385 and n.
'Opportunity 2000', 569
Options For Change, 467n., 515, 519 and n.,
    520–1, 522
Order of the Bath, 432 and n., 433
Order of the Garter, 25, 115
O'Riordan, Tim, 427
Orkneys, 211–12
Orthodox Church, 532
Orton, Joe, 117
Osteopathy Act (1993), 311n., 573
Ottawa, 148
Our Common Future (Brundtland Report), 424
Outward Bound Trust, 235
Oxford, 541–2
Oxford and Cambridge Schools Examination
    Board, 93
Oxford University, 103–4
Oxley, Tom, 194

Paisley, Revd Ian, 291, 353
Palliser, Sir Michael, 360 and n.
Palm Beach, 385, 386–7
Palm Springs, 208, 261, 384, 411
Palmer-Tomkinson, Charlie, 257–8, 280, 283,
    335–6, 395, 410, 412, 413, 415, 416
Palmer-Tomkinson, Patty, 257, 258, 280, 283,
    335–6, 395, 410, 412–15, 416, 417
Palumbo, Peter, 449, 452 and n.
Panama, 200
Papua New Guinea, 85–7, 88, 341–2
Paracelsus, 307, 308
Parachute Regiment, 161, 342–3, 516–17, 524
    and n.
Paris, 152
Paris Match, 117
Park Chung-Hee, 115
Parker Bowles, Andrew, 191, 277
Parker Bowles, Camilla, 535, 540; the Prince first
    meets, 182; the Prince wishes to marry,
    182–4; marriage to Andrew Parker Bowles,
    191; relationship with the Prince, 277–8; the
    Princess's jealousy of, 286–7, 294, 330;
    relationship with the Prince ends, 287;
    alleged to have been with the Prince on his
    wedding eve, 288n.; the Prince re-establishes
    close relationship with, 395–6; visits the
    Prince in hospital, 418–19; 'Camillagate'
    tape, 491–2n.
Parliament, State Opening of, 114, 125, 140–1,
    553; see also House of Commons; House of
    Lords
Parliamentary Press Gallery, 259
Pater, Walter, 269
Paternoster Associates, 571

Paternoster Square, London, 444–50, 452, 570–1
Paterson, Right Revd John, 352
Paterson, Tony, 435–6
The Path of the Masters, 253, 254
Pathé, 128
Patten, Chris, 405, 424 and n., 426, 427
Patten, John, 459 and n.
Paul, St, 247
Pearson College, 262
Peat, Michael, 504n., 508 and n., 509–10
Peck, Gregory, 85
Peebles, Catherine (Mispy), 22, 24–5, 64 and n.
Pembrokeshire, 135
Perahia, Murray, 574
Persian Gulf, 401–2, 405, 518–20, 541, 542–3
Perspectives (architectural magazine), 570
Persse, Michael, 85
Peters, Sylvia, 20
Philip, Prince *see* Edinburgh, Prince Philip, Duke of
Phillips, Mark, 191–2 and n., 210 and n., 299
Pilger, John, 409
Pilgrims of Great Britain, 149
Pinta (Gordonstoun school ketch), 68
Pisa, 344
Pitchford Group, 571–2
Planetarium, 24
Plato, 59, 61
Plutarch, 28
Plymouth, 169
Podgorny, Nicolai V., 154
Poland, 373, 541, 570
Pollock, Admiral, Sir Michael, 199
Pompidou, Georges, 154
Pontypool, 135
Poplak, Dudley, 301
Porritt, Jonathon, 426, 430, 497
Port Moresby, 341
Portillo, Michael, 543n.
Portsmouth, 176, 468–9
Portsmouth, New Hampshire, 197
Poundbury, 461–8, 469, 471, 515, 571
Powell, Enoch, 112, 113
Prague Heritage Fund, 541, 574
Prague Symphony Orchestra, 574
Pratt, George, 234–5, 236, 237, 273, 363
Prem, General, 337
Press Association, 128, 502 and n.
Press Complaints Commission (PCC), 479–80 and n., 481, 483
Press Council, 302–3, 479n.
Price, Leontyne, 384
The Pride Factor (television documentary), 325
Prince of Wales Awards, 312
Prince of Wales' Committee, 568–9

Prince of Wales' Community Venture, 370–1, 372, 567
Prince of Wales Coordinating Committee, 496
Prince of Wales Environment Committee for Wales, 228
Prince of Wales Shakespeare School, 459–60
Prince's Council, 442
Prince's Trust, 228, 235–41, 244, 273–4, 297, 322, 361–3, 370, 371–2, 541, 567–8
Prince's Trust Volunteers, 372, 567–8
Prince's Youth Business Trust (PYBT), 361, 363–4, 365, 373, 374–5, 568
Privy Council, 145–6, 553
Prosser, Brigadier Keith, 521
Public Accounts Committee, 557n.
Puccini, Giacomo, 344

Queen's Flight, 157–8, 215, 359, 506, 507, 510–11 and n., 551
Queen's Gallery, 574
Queen's Medical Centre, Nottingham, 418
Queen's Own Highlanders, 514n., 520
Queen's Silver Jubilee Trust, 236, 239, 240

Radio Liberty, 433
Ramsey, Michael, Archbishop of Canterbury, 72, 103, 113, 117, 140–1 and n.
Rank, 128
Rapp, Lieutenant James, 218, 220
Reagan, Nancy, 208, 383, 384–5
Reagan, Ronald, 142, 208–9, 383 and n., 384–5
Recorder of London, 8
Red Cross, 15, 39
Rees, Merlyn, 119 and n.
Renaissance, 247, 343
Resolute Bay, 213–14
Retail Candy Stores Institute of America, 39
Rhodesia, 250–1
Riddell, John, 360–1 and n., 365, 374, 382, 385, 386, 402, 403, 494
Ridley, Nicholas, 424–5 and n., 427, 450–1
Rifkind, Malcolm, 510n., 521–2 and n., 524n.
Rio de Janeiro, 404, 497–8
Robinson, Dr John, 71–2
Robson, Dr Robert, 105
Rogers, Richard, 444, 452, 461
Romania, 405, 430–3
Rome, 346
Romsey, Lord (Norton Knatchbull), 60n., 64, 282, 302, 303, 335–6, 395, 481, 482, 483, 484
Romsey, Lady (Penny Knatchbull), 282, 302, 303, 335–6, 395, 419, 481, 484
Rook, Jean, 390
Ross, Diana, 384

Rosyth, 211, 217, 223
Rothermere, Lord, 481
Rothschild, Lord, 571
Rowse, A.L., 241n.
Royal Agricultural College, Cirencester, 311
Royal Air Force (RAF), 120, 157–62, 170 and
    n., 344, 524
Royal Anthropological Institute, 228
Royal Berkshire Hospital, 473
Royal Collection Trust, 506, 541, 574–5
Royal College of General Practitioners, 573
Royal Commission on Environmental Pollution,
    436
Royal Family (BBC film), 133
Royal Festival Hall, 53
Royal Horse Artillery, 131
Royal Institute of British Architects (RIBA),
    314–19, 325, 374, 444, 451
Royal Jubilee Trusts, 228, 240, 274, 326, 370
Royal Marines, 293, 513
Royal Marriages Act (1772), 276, 559
Royal Mews, 54, 232
Royal Naval College, Dartmouth, 50, 103, 157,
    162–4, 167, 184
Royal Navy: Prince Philip joins, 50;
    Mountbatten encourages the Prince to
    enter, 155–6; the Prince at Royal Naval
    College, Dartmouth, 162–4, 167, 184; the
    Prince on HMS Norfolk, 164–9, 174–5; the
    Prince becomes naval flying officer, 214–16;
    the Prince's command of HMS Bronington,
    217–24; the Prince leaves, 225; defence cuts,
    524
Royal Regiment of Wales, 130 and n.
Royal Shakespeare Company (RSC), 460, 564
Royal Society of Medicine (RSM), 309–10
Royal Society for Nature Conservation, 423
royal train, 510–11 and n., 551
Roycroft, David, 357, 359, 386
Runcie, Robert, Archbishop of Canterbury, 274,
    290–1, 348–9, 350–1, 352, 354
Russia, 373
Ryan, Loch, 219

Sadat, Anwar, 294
Saifuddin, Sir Omar Ali, 336–7
St George's Chapel, Windsor, 180
St Giles Cathedral, Edinburgh, 92
St James's Palace, 462, 494, 540, 557n.
St John-Stevas, Lord, 450
St Kilda's beach, Melbourne, 422

St Kitts, 193
St Mary's, Cambridge, 113
St Mary's Hospital, Paddington, 304
St Paul's Cathedral, London, 99, 290, 316–17,
    444–50
St Peter's, Rome, 350
St Petersburg, 373, 570
St Vincent, 196
Salem, 59
Salisbury, Marchioness of, 301
Salter, Guy, 403–4, 500
Salvation Army, 255
Samoa, 203–4
San Diego, 204, 207, 208
San Francisco, 200
San Juan, 200
Sandbrook, Richard, 426
Sandringham: shooting parties, 30, 46–8,
    111–12, 405, 488–9; Duke of Edinburgh
    manages estate, 440
SANE, 405
Santa Cruz, Lucia, 109, 182
Sardinia, 343
SAS, 518
Saudi Arabia, 542
Savile, Jimmy, 495 and n.
'Saving the Ozone Layer' World Conference
    (1989), 427–8
Scapa Flow, 211–12
Scarman, Lord, 374
Schumacher, Fritz, 339, 424; Small is Beautiful,
    263, 312, 423
Schwarzkopf, General, 518
Science Museum, 24
Scilly Isles, 243
Scotland, 150, 170, 218; see also Balmoral
Scotland Yard, 70
Scots Guards, 180
Scottish Business in the Community, 569
Scottish Nationalist Party, 119
Scouts, 135
Secombe, Harry, 84, 130, 240
Second World War, 11–12, 98, 551
Seoul, 487
Serengeti, 410–11
Seymour Baths, Marylebone Road, 27n.
Shadow V, 266
Shah Jahan, 485
Shakespeare, William, 38, 74–5, 95, 454–5, 458,
    459–60, 555
Shand, Camilla see Parker Bowles, Camilla
Shand Kydd, Frances, 274, 281, 331
Sharples, Peter, 323
Sharples, Sir Richard, 189
Shaw, George Bernard, 13

Shea, Michael, 281, 472
Shebbeare, Tom, 371–2, 376, 494
Sheffield, Davina, 258
Shelburne, Lord, 571
Sheldonian Theatre, Oxford, 541–2
Shell, 497
Shephard, Gillian, 543 and n.
Sheppard, Allen, 496
Sills, Beverley, 383
Simpson, John, 448, 449–50, 571
Simpson, Mrs see Windsor, Duchess of
Sinatra, Frank, 209
Singapore, 200
Slovakia, 373, 570
Smith, Edward, 164
Smith, John, 405, 506
Snowdon, Earl of, 55 and n., 128, 131–2
Soames, Catharine, 396
Soames, Christopher (Lord Soames), 153, 154, 178, 227, 406–7
Soames, Nicholas, 151n., 438; goes snorkelling with the Prince, 151–2; doubts about the Prince's marriage, 282, 283; the Prince's letters to, 324, 340–1, 382, 406–7, 410, 491; the Princess forces the Prince to give up friendship with, 335–6; the Prince re-establishes friendship with, 395; and the Archdeacon of York's comments, 536
Society for Anglo-Chinese Understanding, 108
Sofia, Queen of Spain, 292–3
Solti, Sir Georg, 574
South Africa, 150 and n., 339, 405
South Atlantic Fund, 517 and n.
South Wales Constabulary, 133
Soviet Union, 148, 170, 380, 520
Spain, 165 and n., 174–5, 292–3, 404
Special Branch, 166
Spencer, Earl, 274, 331, 476–7
Spencer, Raine, Countess, 274, 289, 331
Spencer, Lady Sarah, 258, 279, 285
Spitting Image, 313, 389
Sprecher, Bruno, 412–13, 414, 415
'Squidgy tapes', 483n.
Staffordshire regiment, 520
Stanhope, Earls of, 299
Stephen, Sir Ninian, 409
Stephens, Robert, 460
Der Stern, 70
Stevens, Jocelyn, 571
Stirling, Sir Angus, 571–2
Stirling, James, 444, 452n.
Stockwood, Mervyn, Bishop of Southwark, 71–2 and n., 113, 247
Stoke-on-Trent, 541
Stokes, Doris, 313 and n.

Stornoway, 68
Storr, Anthony, 252
Stranraer, 219
Stratford-upon-Avon, 564
Strathclyde, 371
Streisand, Barbra, 209–10
Strong, Sir Roy, 301
Stuart, House of, 31, 274
Studland Bay, 160
Sudjic, Deyan, 449
Suez Canal, 294
Suez crisis (1956), 97, 153
Suharto, President, 337
Sullivan, Jeremy, 445n.
Sun, 213, 302, 365, 391, 415n., 474, 480, 483n., 535n., 539, 540, 560
Sunday Citizen, 80n.
Sunday Mirror, 281, 429, 454
Sunday Pictorial, 21
Sunday Telegraph, 466
Sunday Times, 409, 444, 452, 454, 477–8, 479, 480, 481, 482, 496, 521, 529
Sunderland, 371
Suva, 200
Swan Theatre, Stratford-upon-Avon, 454
Swansea, 135
Swaziland, 407
Sweetnam, Sir Rodney, 417, 418
Switzerland, 81, 91
Sydney, 545, 546

Tabor, Arthur, 35–6
The Tailor and Cutter, 25n.
Taj Mahal, 485
Tanzania, 150, 338, 409, 410–11
Task Force on Urban Design, 546n.
Tate and Lyle, 339
Te Kanawa, Dame Kiri, 289, 574
Tennant, Colin, 196
Tennant, Captain Iain, 61
Terry-Thomas, 240
Tetbury, 300
Thailand, 409
Thatcher, Margaret, 227, 271, 272, 274, 300, 320, 323, 350, 364, 368, 371, 375–6 and n., 377–80, 401–2, 425, 426, 436n.
Thatcherism, 254, 271, 424, 550
Third World, 312, 316, 423
Thirkell, Angela, 9
Thomas, George, 118–19 and n., 129, 131, 335
Thomas Cranmer Schools Prize, 404, 453, 454
Thompson, John, 367, 462
Tickell, Sir Crispin, 426 and n.
Timbertop, 77–85, 87–9
Time magazine, 70–1, 290, 381, 382, 383, 388–9

The Times, 5, 12–13, 42, 46, 101, 117, 120, 130–1, 275–6, 281, 285, 315, 326–7, 328, 352, 353, 374, 416–17, 433, 444, 448n., 453–4, 537, 552
Today, 483, 539, 540
Today programme (BBC radio), 535
Tokyo, 143
Tonga, 200, 203
Toulon, 167–8, 169, 202
Townend, Beatrice Lord, 25, 27, 28
Townend, Colonel Henry, 25–6 and n., 27 and n., 28, 36
Training and Enterprise Councils (TECs), 368, 569
Travolta, John, 383, 384
Treasury: Suez crisis, 153; and the Duchy of Cornwall, 242, 299–300; and BITC's entrepreneurs scheme, 379n.; and the Poundbury scheme, 464, 465, 466, 468; *Options for Change*, 467n.; and taxation of the Prince's income, 505; income from Crown estates, 507; reform of Civil List, 508; and the Queen's Flight, 510n.
Trefgarne, Lord, 338
Trieste, 343
Trimming, Colin, 548
Trinity College, Cambridge, 104–14, 116–17, 138–9, 147
Trooping the Colour, 125, 180, 212, 553
Truman, Harry S., 8–9
Truman Doctrine, 8–9
Tryon, Dale, 397
Tryon, Lord, 397
TUC, 229
Turgenev, Ivan, 332
Turkey, 211, 541
Turnbull, Malcolm, 409–10 and n.
Tutin, Dorothy, 460

United Nations (UN), 150n., 346–7, 421, 426, 522, 525
United States of America, 367, 368, 497, 573; Truman Doctrine, 8–9; Cold War, 9; Britain's relationship with, 98; Vietnam war, 100; the Prince's first official visit to, 148–9; 'special relationship' with Britain, 149–50; Suez crisis, 153; Americans' fascination with the Prince, 207; the Prince and Princess tour, 381, 382–90; environmentalism, 425; 'Inter–City Action', 570
United World Colleges, 79n., 228 and n., 262, 284, 342, 343, 384, 385–6, 387–8
Universal Film Studios, 209
University College of Wales, Aberystwyth,

118–24, 127n., 129, 138, 146, 228, 248 and n., 405
Urban Villages Group, 546n.
Urdd National Eisteddfod, 123–4 and n.
US Navy, 148
Ustinov, Peter, 383

Valetta, 23, 116
van Cutsem, Emilie, 418, 484
van Cutsem, Hugh, 111–12, 159, 205, 484
van der Post, Laurens, 249–53, 263, 293–4, 307, 407–8, 410, 428n.
Van Dyck, Sir Anthony, 25
Van Thiem, President, 115
Vanity Fair, 389
Varley, Eric, 75
Vatican, 347–54
Venezuela, 189, 196, 202, 284
Venice, 354–5
Victoria, Queen, 25, 30–1, 35, 46, 47, 50, 181, 397n., 507
Victoria Falls, 339
Vietnam war, 100
Villa Lante, Viterbo, 469
Villiers, Charles, 359
A Vision of Britain (television documentary), 404, 451–2
Viterbo, 470
Voluntary Service Overseas, 235

Waddell, Robert, 60n., 64–5 and n., 66, 91–3
Wadua, 86
Wagner, Sir Anthony, 132
Wakeham, John (Lord Wakeham), 405, 436–7 and n., 480
Waldegrave, William, 543n.
Wales: Prince Charles created Prince of Wales, 42–3; nationalism, 118, 119–20, 122–4, 130, 133–4; the Prince attends University College of Wales, 118–24; the Prince's investiture, 128–32, 133–5; the Prince tours, 135–6; the Prince and Princess tour, 295; Prince William's first visit to, 475; The Prince of Wales' Committee, 568–9
Wallace, Anna, 258
Waller, June, 63 and n.
Wallis, Hal, 209
Ward, John, 354
Warsaw Pact, 170, 467n.
Washington, 284, 382–3
Washington Evening Star, 148
Washington Post, 390
Waterhouse, David, 396
Watt, Sir James, 309–10
Welf, Prince of Hanover, 64

Wellesley, Lady Jane, 258, 259
Welsh Guards, 343, 514, 515–16
Welsh History Society, 121
Welsh Joint Education Committee, 569
Welsh League of Youth, 129–30
Welsh Nationalist Party, 119–20, 123
Welsh Office, 122, 131
West, Rebecca, 290
West Indies, 202
West Norfolk Hunt, 46
Western Samoa, 200
Westmacott, Peter, 487, 498
Westminster, Palace of, 129n.
Westminster Abbey, 19–20, 279, 490 and n.
Westminster Hall, 18
Wheeler, Mark, 36, 37
Whipp, Dr Elizabeth, 309
Whitaker, James, 288n., 329n., 415n., 416n.
Whitby, Mr (Gordonstoun housemaster), 62 and n.
Whitlam, Gough, 226, 409
Willcocks, Sir David, 289
William, Prince, 334, 358, 523; birth, 304–5; in Australia, 331–2; the Prince's relationship with, 334, 563–4; golf club accident, 473–4; the Prince and Princess disagree over access arrangements, 474–5, 488–9; financial provisions, 506n.; speculation about succession, 536
William III, King, 284
William and Mary College, Williamsburg, 254–5, 284
Williams, Revd Harry, 105 and n., 113–14, 247
Williamson, Malcolm, 234
Wilson, Sir Charles, 103
Wilson, David, 439
Wilson, Harold, 99, 103, 104, 115, 139, 140, 147, 152, 271, 272, 484n.
Windermere Island, 216
Windmill Lodge, Gordonstoun, 61, 62, 90
Windsor, 24–5, 30, 147, 574; the Prince's childhood, 28n., 54, 55–6; the Prince's confirmation, 72; polo matches, 257, 405, 419; Christmas at, 298; fire, 489n., 504, 509; 'grace and favour' apartments, 557n.
Windsor, Duchess of, 11, 178, 179–80, 181

Windsor, Duke of (Edward VIII), 260, 261, 266; abdication crisis, 10–11, 53, 177, 277; university education, 103; investiture as Prince of Wales, 129; popularity, 136; hopes for reconciliation with royal family, 178; the Prince visits, 178–9; King George's Jubilee Trust, 235; income from the Duchy of Cornwall, 242; social conscience, 326; death, 179–81
Windsor, House of, 51, 192
Woodard, Admiral Robert, 512
Woods, Edward, 108, 111
Woods, Robert, 107
Woods, Robin, Dean of Windsor, 71 and n., 72, 86, 103, 104, 105–6
Woomargama, 332, 334
World Bank, 424, 497
Worsthorne, Peregrine, 58
Wren, Sir Christopher, 446
Wright, David, 402–3, 431, 494
Wright, Sir Oliver, 384
Wright, Peter, 409n.

Yeomen of the Guard, 18
Yeovilton, 214
YMCA, 235
York, Prince Andrew, Duke of: childhood, 35n., 43, 64 and n.; *Royal Family*, 133; *It's A Royal Knockout*, 133n.; family name, 193n.; the Prince's affection for, 278; Falklands campaign, 303; marriage, 410; excluded from Civil List, 504n.; and reorganisation of Army bands, 522
York, Sarah, Duchess of, 133n., 410, 412, 414, 484n.
Yorkshire, 541
Young, Sir George, 405
Youth Business Initiative, 363–4

Zambia, 150, 338–9
Zia, President, 337
Ziegler, Philip, 11, 12n., 181, 233
Zimbabwe, 338, 339–40
Zipkin, Jerry, 383n.
Zoroastrianism, 528